Teaching and Learning
Personality Assessment

The LEA Series in
Personality and Clinical Psychology
Irving B. Weiner, Editor

Exner (Ed.) • Issues and Methods in Rorschach Research

Gacono/Meloy • The Rorschach Assessment of Aggressive
and Psychopathic Personalities

Ganellen • Integrating the Rorschach and the MMPI–2
in Personality Assessment

Handler/Hilsenroth (Eds.) • Teaching and Learning Personality Assessment

Hy/Loevinger • Measuring Ego Development, Second Edition

Kelly • The Assessment of Object Relations Phenomena in Adolescents:
TAT and Rorschach Measures

McCallum/Piper (Eds.) • Psychological Mindedness:
A Contemporary Understanding

Meloy/Acklin/Gacono/Murray/Peterson (Eds.) • Contemporary Rorschach
Interpretation

Sarason/Pierce/Sarason • Cognitive Interference: Theories, Methods,
and Findings

Tedeschi/Park/Calhoun (Eds.) • Posttraumatic Growth: Positive Changes
in the Aftermath of Crisis

Van Hasselt/Hersen (Eds.) • Handbook of Psychological Treatment Protocols
for Children and Adolescents

Zilmer/Harrower/Ritzler/Archer • The Quest for the Nazi Personality:
A Psychological Investigation of Nazi War Criminals

Teaching and Learning Personality Assessment

Edited by

Leonard Handler
University of Tennessee

Mark J. Hilsenroth
University of Arkansas

 LAWRENCE ERLBAUM ASSOCIATES, PUBLISHERS
1998   Mahwah, New Jersey   London

Lawrence Erlbaum Associates, Inc., Publishers
10 Industrial Avenue
Mahwah, New Jersey 07430

Cover Design by Kathryn Houghtaling Lacey
Cover Photograph by Leonard Handler

Library of Congress Cataloging-in-Publication Data

Teaching and learning personality assessment / edited by Leonard
Handler, Mark J. Hilsenroth.
        p. cm.
    Includes bibliographical references and index.
    ISBN 0-8058-2332-8 (alk. paper)
    1. Personality assessment—Study and teaching (Graduate) I.
Handler, Leonard, 1936–   . II. Hilsenroth, Mark J.
    BF698.4.T43 .997
    155.2'8'0711—dc21   97–17942
                                                                  CIP

Books published by Lawrence Erlbaum Associates are printed on
acid-free paper, and their bindings are chosen for strength and dura-
bility.

Printed in the United States of America
10 9 8 7 6 5 4 3 2 1

To my wife, Barbara Hershey Handler,
and our children, Amy Elisabeth,
and Charles Andrew

and

Jussi, Marianna,
and Tuomas Valle

With love and honor

To my wife, Jessica Hilsenroth,
for her love, support,
and encouragement

*I learned much from my teachers,
more from my colleagues,
and most from my pupils.*

Judah Ha Nasi
The Talmud

*It is the supreme art of the teacher
to awaken joy in creative expression
and knowledge.*

Albert Einstein

Contents

Contributors   xi

Foreword   xix
John E. Exner, Jr.

Preface   xxv

Introduction   xxix

I. SETTING THE STAGE

1   The Importance of Teaching and Learning   3
Personality Assessment
Leonard Handler and Gregory J. Meyer

2   The Trouble With Learning Personality Assessment   31
J. Christopher Fowler

II. CONCEPTUAL MODELS FOR INTERPRETATION

3   The Experiential Basis of Psychological Testing   45
Howard D. Lerner

4   Helping Students Integrate Rorschach Structure   61
and Psychological Theory
Philip Erdberg

5   The Impossible Takes a Little Longer: The Role of Theory 69
in Teaching Psychological Assessment
Bruce L. Smith

6   Critical-Thinking Applications in Personality Assessment: 83
     Classrooms as Laboratories and Studios
     Charles A. Waehler and Harry J. Sivec

III. THE INTERPERSONAL DIMENSION

7   Training in Assessment: Internalization and Identity   107
     Paul M. Lerner

8   Interpersonal and Actuarial Dimensions of Projective Testing   119
     Joseph M. Masling

9   Assessing the Social Subject   137
     Herbert M. Potash

IV. TEACHING AND LEARNING SPECIFIC TEST INSTRUMENTS

10   Teaching the MMPI–2   149
     Roger L. Greene and Poupak Rouhbakhsh

11   Teaching Assessment with the Millon Clinical Multiaxial   165
     Inventory (MCMI–III)
     Roger D. Davis and Theodore Millon

12   Teaching and Learning the Personality Assessment   191
     Inventory (PAI)
     Leslie C. Morey

13   Teaching the Rorschach Comprehensive System   215
     Irving B. Weiner

14   Teaching That First Rorschach Course   235
     Virginia Brabender

15   Approaching the Thematic Apperception Test (TAT)   247
     Phebe Cramer

16   Teaching and Learning the Administration   267
     and Interpretation of Graphic Techniques
     Leonard Handler and Robert Riethmiller

17 Teaching and Learning the Interpretation   295
    of the Wechsler Intelligence Tests as Personality Instruments
    Leonard Handler

V. TEACHING AND LEARNING
SPECIALIZED ISSUES IN ASSESSMENT

18 Personality Assessment and the Cultural Self: 325
    Emic and Etic Contexts as Learning Resources
    Richard H. Dana

19 The Rorschach and the Life World: Exploratory Exercises   347
    Constance T. Fischer

20 Teaching Therapeutic Assessment in a Required   359
    Graduate Course
    Stephen E. Finn

21 A Logical Analysis of Rorschach Autisms   375
    Edwin E. Wagner

22 Using Metaphor to Understand Projective Test Data: 391
    A Training Heuristic
    Mark J. Hilsenroth

23 Teaching Dissemination of Personality Assessment Results   413
    in Graduate Programs
    Barry A. Ritzler

VI. TEACHING AND LEARNING ASSESSMENT COURSES

24 Teaching and Learning Issues in an Advanced Course   431
    in Personality Assessment
    Leonard Handler, J. Christopher Fowler, and Mark J. Hilsenroth

25 Teaching Child Assessment from a Developmental-   453
    Psychodynamic Perspective
    Sandra W. Russ

VII. ASSESSMENT IN INTERNSHIP EXPERIENCES

26 Teaching Assessment Skills in Internship Settings   471
    Robert Lovitt

27 Jumping Into Fire: Internship Training   485
    in Personality Assessment
    Mark A. Blais and Marla D. Eby

    Author Index   501
    Subject Index   513

Contributors

Leonard Handler, PhD, received his degree from Michigan State University. He is a professor, director of the Psychological Clinic, and associate director of the Clinical Training Program, Department of Psychology, University of Tennessee, Knoxville. He is also Adjunct Clinical Professor, Division of Psychiatry, University of Tennessee Medical School, Memphis. Dr. Handler is a fellow, Society for Personality Assessment, and a member-at-large, Board of Directors, Society for Personality Assessment. He is a member of the Editorial Board, *Journal of Personality Assessment*. Dr. Handler has been a consultant for Headstart, a local mental health center, and the Veteran's Administration. In addition, he established and ran a psychosocial consultation program for cancer patients, their families, and the medical staff, at the University of Tennessee Hospital, 1972–1979, and at Baptist Hospital, 1979–1980. He has published numerous chapters and articles on various assessment techniques and procedures, with special emphasis on bridging the gap between assessment and psychotherapy, in an attempt to make assessment more useful in the treatment process.

Mark J. Hilsenroth, PhD, received his doctorate in clinical psychology from the University of Tennessee and completed his clinical internship at The Cambridge Hospital, Harvard Medical School. He has served as the coordinator for the University of Tennessee Psychological Clinic and is currently an assistant professor in the Department of Psychology at the University of Arkansas. He is also a research consultant for the Austen Riggs Center, Stockbridge, Massachusetts and the Veterans Affairs Medical Center, Mountain Home, Tennessee. Dr. Hilsenroth is a 1992 recipient of the Samuel J. and Anne G. Beck Award for outstanding early career contribution to the field of personality assessment. He has numerous publications on issues regarding personality assessment, psychotherapy, psychodynamic theory, and the synthesis of these three topic areas.

Mark A. Blais received his Psy.D. in clinical psychology from Nova University in Florida. He completed his internship and postdoctoral training in adult clinical psychology at Massachusetts General Hospital (MGH). He is currently the Chief Psychologist on the MGH Inpatient Psychiatry Service and co-director of the MGH Psychological Assessment Consultation Service. He also serves as the coordinator of the Adult Track of the MGH Clinical Psychology Internship. His research interests and publications broadly cover the areas of personality and psychological assessment. He is assistant professor of psychology (Department of Psychiatry) at Harvard Medical School.

Virginia Brabender, PhD, ABPP (Clinical) is the Associate Dean and Director of the Institute for Graduate Clinical Psychology, a graduate training program in professional psychology, at Widener University in the School of Human Service Professions. Dr. Brabender is the Director of the doctoral program, director of the Group Psychotherapy Concentration, and teaches courses on the Rorschach, group psychotherapy, and differential diagnosis. Her scholarly contributions also include the publication of numerous articles on the aforementioned topics. She also has coauthored a book titled *Models of Inpatient Group Psychotherapy* published in 1993 by the American Psychological Association. Dr. Brabender is Secretary and Membership Chair of the Society for Personality Assessment. She is also editor of the *SPA Exchange.* She was the 1994 cowinner of the Walter G. Klopfer award for a paper describing her research on the Rorschach Inkblot Method and affective disorders.

Phebe Cramer received her B.A. from the University of California, Berkeley, in psychology, and her PhD from New York University, in clinical psychology. She is currently a professor of psychology at Williams College. She is the author of three books: *Word Association; The Development of Defense Mechanisms*; and *Storytelling, Narrative, and the Thematic Apperception Test,* and has published numerous articles in refereed journals on the use of the TAT in research and clinical studies. Dr. Cramer has served as an associate and consulting editor for the *Journal of Personality* (former), as well as a consulting editor for the *Journal of Personality Assessment,* and outside reviewer for many other journals. She is a licensed clinical psychologist with a private practice of psychotherapy, as well as 10 years in community mental health settings and college mental health.

Richard H. Dana, PhD, retired from the University of Arkansas in 1988 as University Professor Emeritus to become Principal Investigator, Minority Cultural Initiative Project, Research and Training Center, Regional Research Institute, Portland State University, and later, Research Professor (Honorary). He is author/editor of 10 books, 15 book chapters/monographs, and well over 100 articles. His book, *Multicultural Assessment Perspectives for Professional Psychology,* was published by Allyn & Bacon in 1993. *Understanding Cultural Identity in Intervention and Assessment* was published in 1997 by Sage. Currently, he is editor of the in-process *Handbook of Cross-Cultural/Multicultural Personality Assessment,* scheduled for 1998 publication by Lawrence Erlbaum Associates.

Roger D. Davis, PhD, is a postdoctoral fellow and director of the Research Network at the Institute for Advanced Studies in Personology and Psychopathology in Coral Gables, Florida. His recent publications include "The Five Factor Model for Personality Disorders: Apt or Misguided," in *Psychological Inquiry*; "The Importance of Theory to a Taxonomy of Personality Disorders," a chapter in W. J. Livesley (Ed.), *The DSM–IV Personality Disorders: Objective Assessment of Anxiety*; a chapter in B. Wolman (Ed.), *Handbook of Anxiety,* and a book, *Disorders of Personality: DSM–IV and Beyond.* He is also a recent coauthor of the revised MCMI–III and MACI, as well as the recently constructed MIPS for "normal" personality styles.

Marla D. Eby received her A.B. from Harvard University, a PhD in clinical psychology from Boston University, and completed her clinical internship at The Cambridge Hospital, Harvard Medical School. She is currently the chief psychologist on the adult psychiatric unit at The Cambridge Hospital. Dr. Eby has taught and supervised clinical psychology interns at The Cambridge Hospital in the practice of personality assessment for over 15 years. She has taught the advanced seminar in psychological assessment for over 10 years. She also holds an appointment as an instructor in the Department of Psychiatry (Psychology) at Harvard Medical School.

Philip Erdberg, PhD, is a diplomate in clinical psychology of the American Board of Professional Psychology. He is the author of several current chapters on the Rorschach. Dr. Erdberg maintains an independent clinical and consulting practice in San Francisco. He is a past president of the Society for Personality Assessment and the 1995 recipient of the Society's Distinguished Contribution Award.

Stephen E. Finn, PhD, is in private practice and is an adjunct assistant professor of psychology at the University of Texas at Austin. Dr. Finn is the author of *A Manual for Using the MMPI-2 as a Therapeutic Intervention*, published by the University of Minnesota Press, and of many articles and chapters on psychological assessment. He is a fellow of the Society of Personality Assessment and is chair of the Psychological Assessment Work Group of the American Psychological Association.

Constance T. Fischer, PhD, ABPP, is a professor in the psychology department of Duquesne University and conducts an independent clinical practice. Her publications are primarily in the areas of human science approaches to psychological assessment and to qualitative research. She first published on collaborative assessment in 1970 (*Journal of Counseling Psychology*). She authored *Individualizing Psychological Assessment*, and co-edited *Client Participation in Human Services: The Prometheus Principle* (with S. Brodsky) and *Duquesne Studies in Phenomenological Psychology* (Vol. II) (with A. Giorgi and E. Murray).

J. Christopher Fowler received his PhD in clinical psychology from the University of Tennessee and completed his clinical internship at The Cambridge Hospital, Harvard Medical School. He is currently a postdoctoral clinical fellow at the Austen Riggs Center, Stockbridge, Massachusetts, where he practices psychoanalytic psychotherapy. Dr. Fowler also conducts psychodynamically informed research on issues concerning psychotherapy and personality assessment through the Erik H. Erikson Institute of the Austen Riggs Center.

Roger L. Greene, PhD is Professor and Director of Clinical Training at Pacific Graduate School of Psychology, Palo Alto, California. Dr. Greene is representative-at-large (1993–1998) on the Board of Trustees of the Society for Personality Assessment. He has written numerous articles and several books on the MMPI/MMPI-2.

Howard D. Lerner, PhD, is a practicing psychologist and psychoanalyst in Ann Arbor, Michigan. He is an assistant clinical professor of Psychology in the Department of Psychiatry at the University of Michigan and a member of the faculty of the Michigan Psychoanalytic Institute. He holds advanced certifications and diplomate status in clinical psychology, forensic psychology, and personality assessment. His research interests include the borderline personality, eating disorders, and severe psychopathology.

Paul M. Lerner, Ed.D., is in the private practice of psychoanalysis, psychotherapy, and psychological testing in Camden, Maine and is an adjunct in the Department of Psychology at the University of Tennessee. A past president of the Society for Personality Assessment, he was the 1996 recipient of the Society's Bruno Klopfer Award for distinguished contributions to personality assessment. He has authored one book and coedited three others on the Rorschach. His most recent book, *Psychoanalytic Theory and the Rorschach*, received a distinguished award from the Menninger Foundation. He also has authored numerous articles on psychoanalytic theory, psychopathology, and the Rorschach.

Robert Lovitt, PhD, is associate professor of psychiatry at the University of Texas Southwestern Medical Center at Dallas. He coordinates psychological services at Parkland Memorial Hospital, which is the main teaching hospital for Southwestern Medical Center. Dr. Lovitt teaches residents, medical students, and psychology graduate students regarding the application of psychological tests in medical settings. He has presented at numerous conferences regarding supervision and training.

Joseph M. Masling, PhD, was a member of the psychology department at the State University of New York at Buffalo from 1965 to 1991, when he became Professor Emeritus. He served as chair of the department from 1969 to 1972 and prior to that as director of the training program in clinical psychology at Syracuse University from 1959 to 1964. He has conducted studies and written on interpersonal factors in psychological testing, has experimentally investigated both the psychoanalytic concepts of perception below the level of awareness and the oral and anal character types, and coedits with Robert Bornstein a series of books, *Empirical Studies of Psychoanalytic Theories*.

Gregory J. Meyer received his PhD in clinical psychology from Loyola University of Chicago in 1990. He completed his internship in the Department of Psychiatry at the University of Chicago Medical Center. For the next 4 years he was on the faculty in the Department of Psychiatry at the University of Chicago. During this time he was the director of the Psychological Assessment Service in the medical center and he also trained students from a variety of disciplines, including clinical psychology, psychiatry, and medicine. In 1994, he left the plains and congestion of Chicago to join the faculty in the Department of Psychology at the University of Alaska, Anchorage, where he is currently the clinical training coordinator for the graduate program in clinical psychology. His primary research interests are in personality and cognitive assessment. He is particularly interested in the integration of assessment methods and the development of research designs that more closely parallel the case-by-case formulations that are made during clinical practice.

Theodore Millon, PhD, D. Sc., is professor of psychology at the University of Miami, professor in psychiatry at Harvard Medical School, and dean of the Institute for Advanced Studies in Personology and Psychopathology. Founder and co-editor-in-chief of the *Journal of Personality Disorders* for the past 10 years, he is also past president of the International Society for the Study of Personality Disorders. Dr. Millon is the author of several self-report inventories (MCMI–III, MACI, MBHI), as well as the recently published *Millon Inventory of Personality Styles* (MIPS). His books include *Disorders of Personality: DSM–IV and Beyond*; *Toward a New Personology: An Evolutionary Model*; and a recent collection of his seminal papers entitled *Personality and Psychopathology: Building a Clinical Science*, each published by Wiley-Interscience.

Leslie C. Morey, PhD is professor of psychology at Vanderbilt University. He also has held faculty appointments at Harvard University, Yale University School of Medicine, and the University of Tulsa. He received his PhD in clinical psychology at the University of Florida and completed his clinical internship at the University of Texas Health Sciences Center at San Antonio. Dr. Morey is the author of the *Personality Assessment Inventory* and has published extensively on the assessment of personality and mental disorders.

Herbert M. Potash, PhD, is professor and Coordinator of Graduate Programs in Psychology at Fairleigh Dickinson University, Madison, New Jersey. His most recent book, *Pragmatic-Existential Psychotherapy With Personality Disorders*, draws on both his clinical practice and his teaching of existential psychology. His earlier book, *Inside Clinical Psychology: A Handbook for Graduate Students and Interns*, was designed to assist students through the training process. He is currently engaged in ongoing research to validate his revision of the Miale–Holsopple Sentence Completion Test.

Robert J. Riethmiller, M.A., received his B.A. from Villanova University, and his M.A. in clinical psychology from Fairleigh Dickinson University, Madison, New Jersey, with Herbert Potash. He is a clinical psychology doctoral student at the University of Tennessee, Knoxville. Mr. Riethmiller has done research with the Miale–Holsopple Sentence Completion Test, the Rorschach, and figure drawings. He is an ad hoc reviewer for the *Journal of Personality Assessment*.

Barry A. Ritzler, PhD, is professor of psychology at Long Island University and a faculty member of Rorschach Workshops, Incorporated, directed by John Exner, Jr. Dr. Ritzler, a graduate of the Wayne State University PhD Program in clinical psychology, served as president of the Society for Personality Assessment from 1995 to 1997. He has studied personality assessment under the tutelage of Sidney Blatt, Margaret Singer, and Dr. Exner. He has a private practice in North Haledon, New Jersey, and is a consultant in the New Jersey state prison system.

Poupak Rouhbakhsh is a doctoral candidate in clinical psychology at Pacific Graduate School of Psychology, Palo Alto, California. She received her B.A. degree in child development from San Jose State University and her M.S. degree in clinical psychology from Pacific Graduate School of Psychology. Her primary interests are psychological assessment, particularly assessment and treatment of substance abuse and anxiety disorders.

Sandra W. Russ, PhD, is professor of psychology at Case Western Reserve University and is currently chair of the Psychology Department. She has been on the faculty since 1975 and has also served as Director of Clinical Psychology Graduate Training. She has written in the areas of teaching psychological assessment, play therapy, and creativity. Her research area is children's play and creativity which was summarized in her recent book *Affect and Creativity: The Role of Affect and Play in the Creative Process* (1993). Dr. Russ also has served as treasurer and is president-elect for the Society for Personality Assessment and as president of the Section on Clinical Child Psychology for Division 12 of the APA.

Harry J. Sivec, PhD, is presently employed as a licensed clinical psychologist in the department of psychology at WCA Hospital in Jamestown, New York. He specializes in assessment services for children and adults in both inpatient and outpatient settings. Dr. Sivec also has authored several research articles pertaining to various aspects of assessment and he presently serves as an ad hoc reviewer for the *Journal of Personality Assessment*. His current research interests include personality assessment with chronic pain patients and hypnosis. He is an adjunct faculty member at Jamestown Community College.

Bruce L. Smith, PhD, is on the clinical faculty of the University of California, Berkeley, the University of California, San Francisco, and is adjunct professor at the California School of Professional Psychology, Alameda. He is in private practice of assessment and psychoanalytic psychotherapy. Dr. Smith is coeditor of *The Facilitating Environment: Clinical Applications of Winnicott's Theory*, and is the author of numerous articles on the Rorschach and on psychotherapy. He is currently president of the Society for Personality Assessment.

Charles A. Waehler, PhD, is an associate professor of counseling psychology at The University of Akron in Ohio. He teaches courses in projective techniques, psychodiagnostics, intelligence testing, and advanced practicum. Dr. Waehler practices with Cornerstone Comprehensive Psychological Services in Medina and Tallmadge, Ohio, and is co-coordinator of Mental Health Services for the Summit County American Red Cross. His research interests include counseling, development, personality assessment, measurement, and psychotherapy. He is also the author of *Bachelors: The Psychology of Men Who Haven't Married*.

Edwin E. Wagner, PhD, holds the ABPP in counseling psychology and is a fellow of the American Psychological Association and the Society for Personality Assessment. A professor emeritus of the University of Akron, he is currently a diagnostic consultant with the Alabama Pain Clinic. He is the author

of the Hand Test and has published extensively in the field of personality assessment.

Irving B. Weiner, PhD, ABPP, is clinical professor of psychiatry and behavioral medicine at the University of South Florida and is in the private practice of clinical and forensic psychology in Tampa. He is past president of the Society for Personality Assessment and a recipient of the Society for Personality Assessment Distinguished Contribution Award. He served as editor of the *Journal of Personality Assessment* from 1985 to 1993 and is currently editor of *Rorschachiana: Yearbook of the International Rorschach Society*. He has been teaching and supervising assessment for over 35 years, and his contributions to the assessment literature include *Psychodiagnosis in Schizophrenia; Rorschach Handbook of Clinical and Research Applications; Rorschach Assessment of Children and Adolescents*, and numerous book chapters and articles.

Foreword

John E. Exner, Jr.
Rorschach Workshops

This well-organized book offers valuable information for both instructors and students. Its suggestions and guidelines can be especially useful for instructors and supervisors who feel somewhat burdened by the requirement to teach personality assessment. When reading these carefully prepared chapters, it is impossible to avoid awareness of a persistent issue: that the *requirement* to learn the skills of personality assessment is often viewed by students as a fearsome burden or insurmountable task for which the purpose is not always clear. Some authors even imply that personality assessment is perceived by students as peripheral to their primary interest of reaping the personal and tangible rewards that are anticipated for those who develop therapeutic expertise. If this is true, it is somewhat disconcerting to note that much of the rich heritage of clinical psychology, which is also the heritage of personality assessment, appears to have been discarded, or at least disregarded, as the contemporary model of clinical psychology has evolved.

Interestingly, had this book been written at any time between the early 1930s and the mid-1960s, the title might more appropriately have been *Teaching and Learning Clinical Psychology*. This is because, during that period, what is now known as personality assessment formed the core of training in clinical psychology. This is not to suggest that training for treatment was neglected or de-emphasized, for that was not the case. Numerous courses in treatment methods, some required and some elective, could be found in any credible clinical program. However, major emphasis was afforded to the challenge of understanding a person as an individual and understanding the problems of a person in a context from which the most appropriate treatment could evolve.

The methods and skills that are now recognized as commonplace in personality assessment did not develop quickly in psychology. Interest in people and their individuality has existed for centuries; however, the issue of personality as a subject for psychological study is less than 100 years old and the procedure of using various methods to assess features of personality is much younger.

It is true that many historians prefer to date the practice of clinical psychology and psychological assessment in the United States to Lightner Witmer's creation of a psychology clinic at the University of Pennsylvania in 1896 for purposes of studying the academic prowess and difficulties of children. Witmer clearly was a pioneer in child guidance, or what is now referred to as educational or school psychology. However, historians might as easily have attributed the origin of personality assessment to one of Witmer's mentors, James McKeen Cattell.

Cattell's influence on American psychology and on its applications was very considerable. Cattell took his doctorate with Wundt in 1886 and the next year became a lecturer in psychology at the University of Pennsylvania. It was Cattell who coined the term *mental test* and he was the first American psychologist to promote mental testing as a way of studying individual differences. Cattell founded a laboratory at the University of Pennsylvania specifically for that kind of research. He left the University of Pennsylvania in 1892 to accept a professorship at Columbia University, leaving Witmer in control of his new laboratory at Penn. But neither Cattell nor Witmer were interested in personality assessment or in so-called clinical issues.

During that time and well into the 20th century, most attempts to use tests to understand people did not include much personality testing. Those calling themselves applied psychologists, or later using the label "clinical" psychologist, did considerable testing, but their efforts focused mainly on issues of intelligence, aptitude, achievement, and interest. In fact, the term *personality* was often used interchangeably with *psychopathology* until the early 1930s.

A movement called "the psychology of personality" gained interest only after 1920, yielding numerous but conflicting theories and plentiful but piecemeal research. Interestingly, the very issue that had prompted the development of assessment methods, that is, individual differences, frequently became an embarrassment for those attempting to devise or apply theories of personality and those seeking scientific explanations to account for the uniformity of behaviors or deviations from them. Nonetheless, psychologists as a group struggled to acknowledge the importance of personality evaluation as an aspect of applied psychology when this speciality began to blossom in the late 1920s and early 1930s. In fact, the role of applied psychology in the area of mental health was the subject of debate for several years prior to a report agreed to by the American Psychological Association in 1935.

During that era, the designation *clinical psychologist* began to be used routinely for those whose primary work involved the use of procedures, now known as personality assessment, with those having adjustment difficulties. In 1935, a committee of the clinical section of the American Psychological Association (there were no divisions then) obtained statements concerning the definition of clinical psychology from a number of prominent psychologists whose work was generally recognized as being clinical in nature. The committee formulated the following definition: "Clinical psychology is a form of applied psychology which aims to define the behavior capacities and behavior characteristics of an individual through methods of measurement, analysis, and observation; and which, on the basis of an integration of these findings with [other] data, provides suggestions and recommendations for the proper adjustment of that individual."

Essentially, the speciality of personality assessment was defined as being synonymous with clinical psychology. It is intriguing and somewhat amusing to note that there was some objection from both psychologists and people outside of the field to the use of the word *clinical*. The objections were based on the fact that the word clinical comes from the Greek and pertains to a bed. Those objections made it necessary for the committee to clarify that the word clinical was being used by extension for the study of the individual as an individual. The committee report went on to emphasize that a broad relationship exists between psychiatry and psychology and that each discipline would profit considerably by scientific cooperation with the other, noting that clinical psychology cannot avoid the inputs from medicine when considering the human problem, and the medical profession cannot avoid the knowledge and skills of the psychologist in conjunction with its immediate task of health and adjustment.

Clinical psychology evolved rapidly after the 1935 report, in spite of the fact that more than a few theorists and most of those interested in defending psychology as a science were continuously annoyed by the frankly realistic definition of personality offered by Gordon Allport in 1937, that is, the dynamic organization within the individual of those psychophysical forces that determine his or her unique adjustments to the environment. The definition is simple but highlights the monumental challenge facing those dedicated to personality assessment as a professional area of interest and specialization; namely, the uniqueness of the individual.

Although the uniqueness of the individual continued as a stumbling block for personality theorists and those in quest of nomothetically based rules that would accurately explain behaviors, clinical psychology (personality assessment) flourished. This was probably because many authors associated with the field, including several in this volume, have persistently emphasized the importance of going beyond simplistic test results and achieving an integration of the data in a manner that will be meaningful to the well being of the individual. Such an integration combines the ideographic and nomothetic approaches to the study of people. This more global or clinical approach does not simply judge a person against others or against a broad theoretical model. Essentially, it acknowledges that each individual is like many other people in some ways, like a few people in other ways, but also different from everyone else in unique ways.

It was the emphasis on this integrated approach that prompted the interest in understanding people as individuals to grow at an almost incredible pace from the late 1930s through the mid-1960s. Clearly, World War II facilitated this growth by provoking the huge expansion of clinical services provided by the military and the Veteran's Administration. It was during this era that the notion of the *clinical test battery approach* was advocated by many. This approach was probably best articulated by the Rapaport group at the Menninger Foundation during the mid-1940s, leading to the procedure that came to be called psychodiagnosis and that is now called personality assessment.

Psychodiagnosis typifies the integrated approach, going well beyond identification or selection of diagnostic labels. It is a multimethod procedure designed to study the person as a unique entity. Implicit in this process is the premise that information about the subject concerning assets, liabilities, conflicts, and so on, will contribute in some significant way to the therapeutic well being of the subject. In other words, the findings will contribute to a meaningful treatment plan.

In a broader sense, psychodiagnosis or personality assessment reflects a concern for the individual. It is a specialty based on the premise that no two people are exactly alike and is oriented to detect the assets and liabilities of the person and to weave together a picture of the individual who is different from everyone else. Its purpose is to ensure that those responsible for aiding the individual in problem times, or making decisions concerning the individual, are fully aware of the nature of the problem and the composite of features of the person they are committed to help or describe.

This premise boded well for personality assessment throughout the 1940s, 1950s, and well into the 1960s. During that time, clinical psychologists became well recognized and highly regarded for their expertise and their input concerning patients when issues of diagnosis and treatment planning were important. But things began to change during the 1960s. The once reasonably homogeneous specialty of clinical psychology began to fragment considerably. In part, this was due to differences among those vested in assessment about whether personality could be studied as a series of traits or whether it must be regarded as a unitary entity. Further fragmentation occurred with the onset of radical behaviorism, which brought with it the notion of the black box and the message that there is no such thing as personality, or if there is, it cannot be measured.

Also, beginning in the late 1960s and early 1970s, training programs in psychiatry began to de-emphasize the tactics of individual therapy and emphasize instead pharmacological methods as a basis for or adjunct to intervention. This opened the door for a marked increase in emphasis on training for therapy in most graduate programs in clinical psychology by the late 1960s or early 1970s that has contributed to the diversification of clinical psychology and the de-emphasis that seems to exist concerning issues of assessment today.

The new clinical psychology clearly focuses on treatments, and it has been a confusing and wondrous experience to note the remarkable accumulation of fads about treatment that have appeared during the past two decades. At times, it would appear that there is an overly permissive atmosphere in the therapeutic community about treatment methodology. It is often marked by curious ignorance, creative exuberance, and a free-for-all expansion that proceeds happily and without abatement.

Propositions about various psychiatric–psychological entities have created a cadre of specialists in various disorders and these specialists often suggest that their credentials provide an implicit promise of cure or at least a clear understanding of the problem. Unfortunately, personality assessment has played an almost negligible role in contributing to these propositions and research on these fad disorders struggles to reach even a mediocre level.

Stated simply, people who purport to specialize in the treatment of specific disorders usually have little interest in personality assessment because, by their logic, they already know what is wrong with a prospective patient and have the methodology readily available for treatment. This unreasonable logic neglects the individual as a unique entity but that does not seem to matter. Thus, it is not surprising to hear that contemporary personality assessment is sometimes perceived as a necessary evil by students eager to complete their graduate training and establish themselves quickly among the roles of "wannabe" therapists.

Quite possibly, this negative attitude, or at least lack of enthusiasm, is a result of their therapeutic training not emphasizing the results of assessment as they become relevant to the therapeutic endeavor. In effect, some students fail to perceive any practical usefulness for personality assessment.

This argument was often put forth during the 1970s and 1980s by those seeking to alter curricula in a way that would reduce or eliminate training requirements for personality assessment, noting that it is an overly time-consuming exercise that has limited usefulness. Some who supported that position also argued that personality assessment is overly time-consuming when applied, and naively assumed that the same information about a patient would be revealed as treatment progressed. They disregarded the fact that the procedures involved in competent personality assessment usually take no more than a few hours if done by a trained professional, but that fact appears to have little merit.

Many critics of personality assessment have also used the argument that personality assessment reports sound very similar, not really focusing on the individual, but rather offering a theory-based report about psychological features, conflicts, and the like that may be broadly applicable to the person who has been assessed, but that fail to highlight the person's individuality and typically ignore or de-emphasize assets. Some of these criticisms have validity.

Learning to do personality assessment is neither easy nor quick. It cannot be done in a single semester survey course, and a truly meaningful assessment usually cannot be completed in one or two hours. Competent assessment is not a quick fix, and it should not be. What person would submit himself or herself to major surgery without being sure that all possible tests had been completed and that a review of the results confirmed the need for an invasive procedure and identified the type of procedure required? Should people with adjustment difficulties expect any less, or is it really true that psychiatry and psychology have become so scientifically sophisticated that the presentation of any symptom(s) inarguably dictates the appropriate course of treatment?

Personality assessment has not reached its full potential, but it has achieved a reasonable level of sophistication that should not be degraded or simplified because some students find it to be burdensome, and especially if the welfare of the patient continues to be held in high regard.

Possibly a time has come when clinical psychology should, more formally than has been the case, re-evaluate the role of personality assessment in graduate training programs. Perhaps it should be an elective training track. Obviously, there are currently students who do not learn it well, graduates who do not use it, and others who will abuse it by their incompetence. If they could "opt out" of the requirement to learn assessment skills and, instead, be subjected to a course in how to use the results of an assessment intelligently, many might profit. Certainly, some instructors would, and it is likely that some patients might fare better than is now the case. For others interested in learning this skill, personality assessment can continue to be a respected and successful speciality well into the next century, especially if it is properly conceptualized and its broad methodology taught wisely and thoroughly.

Regardless of whether personality assessment is a required or an elective training track, its purpose always should be clearly defined, probably more so than is often the case. It will always be a methodology designed to know the person as an individual. It focuses on understanding the individual in that context and, as such, strives to understand the problem(s) of the person in the framework of origins and consequences.

It seems important to emphasize that those vested in personality assessment must be careful about the use of theories when formulating a picture of the individual. It is very easy to be overly influenced by theoretical sets. If one strives to push the person (findings) into a theoretical model, there is always the risk that the resulting picture will be less than accurate and, in some instances, can be distorted considerably. Theoretical models should be used wisely and cautiously to enhance an understanding of the situation. Theories offer hypotheses about people. In part, assessment methods put those hypotheses to the test to determine whether they may be viable when cast against the data framework from which the individual, the person being assessed, is reviewed. In some instances, theories provide a useful explanation, but in other instances they fail miserably and must be cast aside.

Finally, as is emphasized in several chapters of this volume, students of personality assessment should be taught to select assessment procedures and the context of the objectives for which the assessment is designed wisely. That is critically important. If the purpose of assessment is treatment planning, the procedures should obviously make sense in that context. If the purpose of assessment is for other reasons—forensic, occupational, placement, disposition—the procedures will also make sense when selected in the logic of the situation. Using the right tools at the right time attests to the integrity of the professional skilled in personality assessment, and reaffirms the hard-won wisdom that marks the rich history of the profession.

Preface

University of Tennessee
Mark J. Hilsenroth
University of Arkansas

More than anything else, students' feedback about their learning experience and teachers' often expressed need for direction and structure are the prime reasons for this book. It is designed to highlight for student and teacher alike those issues that many consider of prime importance—issues that have been neglected in students' views, such as their anxieties about assessment, and those that are particularly difficult for students to understand, or for teachers to address effectively

We have organized the book to deal with teaching–learning techniques, as well as with theoretical and ethical concerns. We selected our emphases, in part, by listening to students' and faculty members' frustrations and complaints about learning and teaching personality assessment, and their beliefs about what was important.

A major difficulty discussed by both students and teachers was the transformation of test data, observational data, and history data into clinical interpretations, and the integration of these data to help the student make the link between assessment and psychotherapy. In an attempt to facilitate learning and teaching in this area, material is included on the interpretive process, and the facilitative use of metaphor. The communication of findings to patients and to referral sources also was mentioned as a problem and we included material on this process. Several chapters deal completely or partially with the concerns and anxieties experienced, but often not expressed, by students in the learning process—anxieties that, if not attended to, impair and inhibit learning. Finally, because assessment in internship settings is a natural extension of university and practicum work, and because it poses such a significant problem for interns and supervisors, we have included two chapters on teaching and learning assessment in these settings.

We hope this book will be of value to those who teach assessment, and also to those who want to maximize their ability to learn assessment. The chapters are written from both the point of view of the teacher and that of the student; the chapters focus the teacher and the learner on the central issues of assessment. We have found that discussing these issues with students, as well as discussing the processes by which they are communicated, facilitates the students' abilities to learn assessment. Courses in assessment are better learning experiences and meet the mutual needs of learner and teacher if both are aware of their own needs, and the needs of the other.

Of great importance is the emphasis that students put on what they found was the most or least helpful in learning assessment: the teacher. The teacher wants to impart information he or she views as quite important; the teacher also wants the student to respect the information conveyed, and to learn to use it ethically and responsibly. Students want to learn in an atmosphere free of tension and worry. They are pleased to learn the material from one who is inspired and who values the material. They search for structure and clarity where there is often little of both, and for an atmosphere of support and facilitation. A logical, straightforward, step-wise approach is not always possible, as the chapters in this book often indicate, but if this is made clear at the outset, disappointment will not lead directly to frustration and anger. Thus, both student and teacher must join to facilitate the communication of complex concepts in a mutually satisfying manner.

A good teacher is also a good learner, and good learners teach their teachers a great deal. Therefore, we join the many students and teachers who have taught us to learn and to teach personality assessment, as their teachers and students have taught them. May the circle be unbroken.

ACKNOWLEDGMENTS

We would like to thank a number of people who have been quite helpful in the production of this book. Our publisher, Larry Erlbaum, ever enthusiastic and always reassuring, believed in our project from the day we described it to him, at a Society for Personality Assessment conference. Many of the Society members were equally supportive and helpful; we owe the Society and its members a special thanks for the warm and congenial attitude with which we and our ideas have been received.

Irv Weiner helped us with a number of important problems, and Herb Potash was quite helpful in suggesting an organizational framework, as well as in demonstrating an illuminating way to teach assessment. We are also grateful to John Exner for writing the Foreword. Paul Lerner provided encouragement and assistance in several important ways.

A number of other people have been very helpful in various phases of the development and production of the manuscript. Linda Duffey patiently typed draft after draft of several chapters. She was also very helpful with a number of important organizational details, and in collaborating on the design for the front cover. Barbara Handler spent many hours facilitating our computer editing work and preparing the indexes; without her assistance with these issues and problems, and her emotional support, this book would not yet have been completed. Susan Church helped with guidance and inspiration concerning writing skills.

Manuela Schulze helped us with references. Debbie Woodward assisted with some of the manuscript typing. We appreciate the assistance of all these people, who made our editing and writing so much easier.

We also want to thank the staff at LEA for their support and assistance, especially Larry Hayden, Book Production Editor, Sharon Levy, Promotion Director, and Susan Milmoe, Acquisitions Editor.

We want to thank all the assessment experts who wrote chapters for this book. Everyone was quite cooperative, both with initial drafts and with any necessary revisions. They made the usually onerous task of editing a book much easier than we expected it to be. We would also like to thank the many students in our assessment classes who have helped us learn about important teaching issues and attitudes. We are grateful for their patience and forbearance. Foremost, however, we would like to thank our teachers, who approached the task of teaching us assessment with patience and enthusiasm, facilitating our ability to continue the teaching–learning process with equal patience and enthusiasm.

Introduction

Minimal attention has been focused on teaching and learning personality assessment, especially compared to that focused on teaching and learning psychotherapy techniques. Although courses in personality assessment are routinely taught in most U.S. doctoral and master's programs in clinical and counseling psychology (Watkins, 1991), very little has been written about the communication of assessment techniques and concepts to students. Even less has been written about the communication of the processes involved in the production of relevant interpretive hypotheses and about training students to generate interpretations of personality dynamics and treatment issues. We demonstrate our interpretive approach by publishing case studies, but we do not describe in detail our approaches to assessment instruction.

Despite the fact that scientific interest in assessment has grown greatly in the past 10 or 15 years, and there are now several relatively new journals entirely devoted to assessment, unfortunately a journal much of which was devoted to issues of training students to do assessment, *The Journal of Training and Practice in Professional Psychology*, was published for only 7 years, from 1987 to 1993. The absence of material on teaching personality assessment is quite troublesome, because graduate programs devote so much time and effort to assessment training (Piotrowski & Zalewski, 1993), and because a number of studies have suggested that internship supervisors are often dissatisfied with the academic preparation of graduate students to undertake personality assessment (Brabender, 1992; Durand, Blanchard, & Mindell, 1988; Garfield & Kurtz, 1974; Shemberg & Keeley, 1974). Internship directors often feel that many graduate students are inadequately prepared in assessment. For example, Durand et al. (1988) reported that 60% of internship sites have required remedial instruction of their interns in projective assessment. Watkins (1991), in a comprehensive analysis of surveys concerning the teaching and practice of psychological assessment, indicated that assessment is a critical component of most graduate psychology programs. However, other data indicate that some academic psychologists believe assessment is of little value and importance (Brabender, 1992; Kinder, 1994; Piotrowski & Keller, 1984; Piotrowski & Zalewski, 1993; Retzlaff, 1992).

Kinder (1994) and Weiner (cited in Kinder, 1994) noted that at internship sites and in other real-world clinical settings assessment skills are valued quite highly. Kinder also emphasized that we should be aware of the increased importance of assessment in the marketplace and "adjust our curriculum accordingly ... to meet these ... demands for individuals who are well trained for delivery of psychological services" (p. 58). Unfortunately, aside from a large number of informative surveys (e. g., May & Scott, 1989; Piotrowski & Keller,

1984; Schneider, Watkins, & Gelso, 1988; Walfish, Kaufman, & Kinder, 1980), there is little in the literature to guide an instructor in the communication of the assessment process to graduate students. It seems that although many graduate faculty are actively engaged in teaching personality assessment, few have attempted to communicate their approach by writing about their courses. The exceptions are an article by Harrower (1977) about teaching the Rorschach, three articles about teaching assessment in general (Morgan, 1989; Russ, 1978; Stagner, 1984), and an article by Rader and Schill (1973) that describes the use of blind analysis by instructors in an effort to "break through the students' entrenched skepticism and resentful negativism" concerning the value of assessment (p. 213).

Therefore, several years ago, we decided to remedy the lack of information about teaching and learning assessment. In planning this book, we have tried to select topics revelant to the expressed needs of students and teachers. For example, we have included ample material about the Rorschach because students report that they have problems with both scoring and interpretation (Hilsenroth & Handler, 1995). We have also included chapters on several other projective tests (e. g., the Thematic Apperception Test [TAT], drawing tests), as well as a chapter that teaches the interpretation of the Wechsler tests as personality instruments.

Students and faculty emphasized the importance of learning and teaching self-report measures as well and therefore we have included chapters on teaching the Millon Clinical Multiaxial Inventory (MCMI–III), the Minnesota Multiphasic Personality Inventory–2 (MMPI–2), and the Personality Assessment Inventory (PAI).

Students expressed a need to learn more theory, and the application of theory to assessment. Several chapters deal with the use of an organizing theoretical framework in the assessment process. For some time, we have recognized the need to develop coursework in which participants can experience resolution of the problem of the link between test data and effective, meaningful interpretation. The effort is to shed some light on the processes involved in going from interpretation to a diagnosis and a treatment plan (Hilsenroth & Handler, 1995). Although the theory-focused chapters provide some assistance in helping students transform the mass of assessment data into a report that communicates assessment findings effectively to patients and to those who referred the patient for assessment, we also have included several chapters on varying approaches to the interpretation process, as well as a chapter on the dissemination of results.

Students reflected on the great impact teachers and classroom experiences have on them; positive experiences in learning assessment were experienced as very supportive and satisfying, whereas negative experiences were reported to discourage use and understanding of personality assessment tools and activities (Hilsenroth & Handler, 1995). Hence, we include material on the importance of mentorship in the teaching–learning process. Two chapters on assessment in internship settings go some way toward filling what is almost an information void. Two chapters on hospital-based assessment address a major part of the trainees' activities: Assessment in hospital settings is a focus for understanding the patient.

The book is divided into seven main sections. Part I sets the stage: The chapters discuss the importance of learning and teaching personality assessment and the experience of learning personality assessment from the student's point of view.

Part II reviews the use of theory in learning personality assessment; Part III addresses the importance of the interpersonal dimension, including mentorship, the complex relationship between assessor and patient, and the interpretation of personal reactions to the patient as important data.

Part IV deatils ways to teach a variety of assessment instruments, whereas Part V presents innovative ways to communicate to students the importance of certain special issues, such as the effects of cultural variables on assessment data, the use of metaphor in the interpretive process, the dissemination of assessment results, and the therapeutic use of assessment. Part VI describes an advanced course in assessment and a course devoted to child assessment; Part VII discusses the use of assessment in hospital-based internship settings.

REFERENCES

Brabender, V. (1992, March). *Graduate program training models.* Paper presented at the meeting of the Society for Personality Assessment, Washington, DC.

Durand, V., Blanchard, E., & Mindell, J. (1988). Training in projective testing: Survey of clinical training directors and internship directors. *Professional Psychology: Research and Practice, 19*(2), 236-238.

Garfield, S., & Kurtz, R. (1974). A survey of clinical psychologists characteristics, activities and orientations. *The Clinical Psychologist, 28,* 7–10.

Harrower, M. (1977). The Rorschach and self understanding: The instruction-insight method. *Journal of Personality Assessment, 41*(5), 451–460.

Hilsenroth, M., & Handler, L. (1995). A survey of graduate students' experiences, interests, and attitudes about learning the Rorschach. *Journal of Personality Assessment, 64*(2), 243–257.

Keller, J. (1983, March). *Psychological testing: Trends in master's level counseling training programs.* Paper presented at the annual meeting of the Southeastern Psychological Association, Atlanta, GA.

Kinder, B. (1994). Where the action is in personality assessment. *Journal of Personality Assessment, 62*(3), 585–588.

May, T., & Scott, K. (1989, August). *Assessment in counseling psychology: Do we practice what we teach?* Paper presented at the annual meeting of the American Psychological Association, New Orleans, LA.

Morgan, R. (1989). Reciprocal teaching of personality assessment strategies: A description of one program to enhance learning. *Journal of Social Behavior and Personality, 4*(4), 347–362.

Piotrowski, C., & Keller, J. (1984). Psychodiagnostic testing in APA- approved clinical psychology programs. *Professional Psychology: Research and Practice, 15,* 450–456.

Piotrowski, C., & Zalewski, C. (1993). Training in psychodiagnostic testing in APA-approved PsyD and PhD clinical psychology programs. *Journal of Personality Assessment, 61,* 374–405.

Rader, G., & Schill, T. (1973). Blind test interpretation to overcome student resistance to projective techniques courses. *Journal of Personality Assessment, 37*(3), 213–216.

Retzlaff, P. (1992). Professional training in psychological assessment: New teachers and new tests. *Journal of Training & Practice in Professional Psychology, 6,* 45–50.

Russ, S. (1978). Teaching personality assessment: Training issues and teaching approaches. *Journal of Personality Assessment, 42*(5), 452–456.

Schneider, L., Watkins, C., Jr., & Gelso, C. (1988). Counseling psychology from 1971 to 1986: Perspective on and appraisal of current training emphases. *Professional Psychology: Research and Practice, 19,* 584–588.

Shemberg, K., & Keeley, S. (1974). Training practices and satisfactions with preinternship preparation. *Professional Psychology, 5,* 98–105.

Stagner, B. (1984). Techniques for teaching projective assessment. *Teaching of Psychology, 11*(2), 103–105.

Walfish, S., Kaufman, K., & Kinder, B. (1980). Graduate training in clinical psychology: A view from the consumer. *Journal of Clinical Psychology, 36,* 1040–1045.

Watkins, C. (1991). What have surveys taught us about the teaching and practice of psychological assessment. *Journal of Personality Assessment, 50*(3), 426–437.

I

SETTING THE STAGE

The first part of this book, Setting the Stage, includes two chapters. The first chapter, "The Importance of Teaching and Learning Personality Assessment," by Leonard Handler and Gregory J. Meyer, discusses the importance of assessment as an ideographic, integrative task that requires students to assimilate and organize vast amounts of psychological information from various disciplines in psychology, and from courses that discuss clinical materials, as well as requiring integration of the test data themselves. The chapter emphasizes a series of other important reasons to learn assessment, reasons that focus on the clinical enterprise, as well as on research-related issues. The authors argue that teaching and learning personality assessment are quite important to the science and profession of psychology, especially because assessment "regularly traverses the scientist–practitioner bridge" linking our ideographic and nomothetic traditions.

The second chapter in this part, "The Trouble with Learning Personality Assessment," by J. Christopher Fowler, discusses, in an experiental manner, students' prevailing difficulties in mastering the assessment process. Fowler focuses on several troublesome issues that serve to make learning assessment quite difficult and emotionally taxing for students. We hope that reading this chapter will sensitize the teacher to the underlying reasons for the resistances demonstrated by many students and the anxieties that fuel such resistances. Perhaps students will find some solace in the fact that other students have developed similar anxieties. In addition, we hope that teachers who read Fowler's chapter will understand the need to facilitate students' development by attempting to reduce anxiety. Several of the chapters later in this book focus on approaches and techniques to do just that. Paul Lerner, for example, focuses on the mentorship bond and the chapters by Cramer, and Handler, Fowler, and Hilsenroth focus on more direct resolution of these resistances as they are played out in the classroom setting.

1

The Importance of Teaching and Learning Personality Assessment

Leonard Handler
Univerisity of Tennessee
Gregory J. Meyer
University of Alaska Anchorage

About midway into this chapter the reader will meet Maria, who lived in a shelter and was destitute because she couldn't hold a job. She had a ferocious temper and often would explode into violent rages, endangering herself and others. Through the use of personality assessment data, the therapist learned how the patient would treat him in the therapy sessions and what he had to do in the sessions to facilitate her treatment. As the reader will see, what the therapist learned through the assessment process was instrumental in guiding him to a successful outcome with the patient.

In a second example, explored later in this chapter, the therapist was not so fortunate, because although the assessment data could have pointed him in the right direction, he did not recall it, and the outcome was quite negative. After two frustrating and nonproductive sessions for both patient and therapist, the patient terminated her treatment.

These two case examples, as well as a number of other vignettes in this chapter, using a variety of assessment techniques (e.g., the Rorschach, Minnesota Multiphasic Personality Inventory [MMPI], Earliest Memories, the Wechsler Adult Intelligence Scale [WAIS]), present one argument among many that focuses on important reasons to learn and to teach personality assessment. We hope these examples illustrate that well-done assessments offer a quite unique window into the character structure and the subjective world of an individual. Assessment can offer an in-depth understanding of what many people have described as an "experience-near," three-dimensional view of the individual, explaining how he or she demonstrates the effects of his or her past and present life experiences through the vantage points of "self" and "other."

Overall, in this chapter we argue that the teaching and learning of personality assessment are quite important to the science and profession of psychology. Several avenues are taken to support this suggestion. At the outset, we articulate two visions of personality assessment: that of the *testing technician* and that of the *assessment clinician*. Our view is that personality assessment probably should *not* be taught to doctoral-level psychologists if the goal is to produce a testing technician. However, if the goal is to produce an assessment clinician, or an expert consultant skilled in understanding personality and in the use of particular tools for evaluation, there are a multitude of good reasons for teaching and learning assessment. As an arm of psychology, assessment regularly traverses the scientist–practitioner bridge, linking our nomothetic and ideographic traditions. Assessment is also the only arm of psychology that requires a practitioner to have expertise in all of the core areas of clinical psychology: psychopathology, child and adult development, treatment intervention, and psychometrics, to name a few. Further, the ability to perform knowledgeable and skilled assessment is what distinguishes clinical psychologists from all other mental health professionals, including psychiatrists, social workers, counselors of all stripes, and various paraprofessionals. Thus, assessment in general and personality assessment in particular should be a core feature of our professional identity. As we hope to make clear in this chapter, we believe it is imperative that psychology continues to train students in personality assessment in order to contribute unique skills to clinical practice and to advance theory and the scientific understanding of human nature (e.g., Westen, 1991b).

TWO VISIONS OF PERSONALITY ASSESSMENT

At the outset, we must clarify the important distinction between psychological testing and psychological assessment. They are hardly synonymous activities. Testing is a relatively straightforward process wherein a particular test is administered to obtain a specific score or two. Subsequently, a descriptive meaning can be applied to the score based on normative, nomothetic findings. For example, when conducting psychological testing, an IQ score of 100 indicates a person possesses average intelligence (Wechsler, 1981); a T-score of 67 on Scale 1 of the MMPI–2 indicates a self-centered, pessimistic, and cynical person who has multiple physical complaints that tend to be exaggerated (Butcher et al., 1989); and a score of 4 on the Weighted Sum of Cognitive Special Scores of the Rorschach indicates a person with average abilities to keep his or her thoughts and impressions organized in a logical fashion (Exner, 1993). Psychological testing is a relatively simple process that can be carried out by clinicians with relatively little training (depending on the test), by testing technicians, or even by computer.

Psychological assessment, however, is a quite different enterprise. The focus here is not on obtaining a single score, or even a series of test scores. Rather, the focus is on taking a variety of test-derived pieces of information, obtained from multiple methods of assessment, and placing these data in the context of historical information, referral information, and behavioral observations in order to generate a cohesive and comprehensive understanding of the person being evaluated. These activities are far from simple; they require a high degree of skill and sophistication to be implemented properly.

As an example of the distinction between assessment and testing, reconsider the IQ score of 100 mentioned earlier. Let us assume this Full Scale score is derived from a person with above-average factual knowledge (i.e., crystallized intelligence), with this person having an average IQ of say 115 on tests that tap these abilities. However, this person also has below average ability when it comes to solving novel problems and thinking flexibly (i.e., fluid intelligence), with an average IQ of 85 on tests that tap these kinds of abilities. Assume also that this patient is a vascular surgeon who suffered a head injury during a car accident several months ago and appears at your office complaining of an inability to return to work, poor concentration, and impaired memory. Furthermore, the patient has difficulty following directions to your office and appears distracted and forgetful during your interview. In contrast to the conclusions that would be drawn from a psychological testing approach to the data, an assessment would not simply indicate the Full Scale IQ score of 100 denotes a person with average intelligence. Rather, the assessment clinician would probably also use the data to conclude this physician has suffered an intellectual decline from higher premorbid levels. This conclusion would be further bolstered if: (a) the clinician had prior test data indicating superior intellectual capacities (e.g., Medical College Admission Test [MCAT] scores, premorbid test data, college grade point average, etc.), (b) the clinician was able to use psychological tests sensitive to malingering to rule out the possibility that this physician was presenting herself in an impaired fashion in order to obtain financial compensation for her accident, and (c) the clinician had data from other tests that ruled out the possibility that this patient had a serious impairment in ego functions (i.e., a coincidental, late-life onset of psychotic-like functioning). Although members from other mental health disciplines could obtain information from the patient's history and behavior in the office, only a psychologist could employ the tests necessary to document and quantify all of the facets of this case and integrate the data in a meaningful way.

To further emphasize the distinction between testing and assessment, consider these processes in a medical context. The medical counterpart to psychological testing is found when technicians or medical personnel obtain scores on such instruments as a blood pressure gauge or a thermometer, or data such as a blood chemistry panel, deep tendon reflexes, and so forth. However, the medical counterpart to a psychological assessment is when a physician takes the information from these various tests and places them in the context of a patient's symptomatic presentation and history in order to accurately understand the full scope of his or her condition.

THE GOALS AND PURPOSES
OF PERSONALITY ASSESSMENT

Testing data utilized in the assessment process assist the clinician in under-standing a patient's conscious experiences and self-representations, his or her overt behaviors, and his or her unconscious dynamics. At the most intensive level, these data can provide a beacon for both apprentice and experienced clinician to negotiate uncharted waters in the journey into the depths of a patient's psyche, or, if the reader will forgive a poetic lapse, perhaps into his or her very soul. A high-quality assessment allows us to see behind the mask of mundane social intercourse, deep into the minds and hearts of our patients. A skillful assessor can explore and describe with empathic attunement painful conflicts as well as the ebb and flow of dynamic, perhaps conflictual forces being cautiously contained. The good assessor also attends to the facilitating and creative aspects of personality, and the harmonious interplay of intrapsychic and external forces, as the individual copes with day-to-day life issues.

In addition to such an understanding, the goal of clinical personality assess-ment is to provide expert consultation to patients seeking help and to the therapists or other professionals who refer them for evaluation. To be of value to the patient receiving an assessment, the description that emerges must answer some questions the person has about him or herself. As Finn (1996b, Finn & Tonsager, in press) has so clearly articulated, all people have some questions, fears, or concerns about their personality characteristics. Although it may generate mixed emotions, the feedback from an assessment must provide a mirror for the patient that helps to answer some of these questions. In essence, it must help the patient understand himself or herself better. That is, the assessment must simultaneously serve to expand the person's awareness as well as empathically resonate with his or her current identity, pointing out unrecog-nized or unappreciated strengths along with qualities that contribute to the trouble or symptomatology that brought the person in for an evaluation (Finn & Tonsager, in press; see also Finn, chap. 20 of this volume; Fischer, 1994; Fischer, chap. 19 of this volume).

To be of value to the person who referred the patient for an evaluation, the description emerging from an assessment must also address some important clinical questions. As with the client, the assessment must provide the referral source with a mirror of information that can be used to check and refine perceptions and hunches. The descriptive image generated from the assessment will confirm some of the referral source's suspicions while negating others, ultimately providing insight into the complex person seeking treatment so that optimal decisions can be made about the kind of help that should be provided.

Obviously, given these goals and the important role that the assessment description will serve, psychologists who aspire to be expert consultants must be sure the mirror they hold up for clients and referral sources is as accurate as possible. If it is not, the best that can be hoped for is that consumers will simply reject the assessment feedback. At worst, however, the social forces at play in the assessment setting may cause patients or referring clinicians to draw false conclusions, embark on an ill-founded course of action, and/or experience themselves as stigmatized.

How then does a psychologist ensure assessment descriptions are as accurate as possible? Also, how does a psychologist inform while simultaneously recognizing the limitations of the mirror being offered? Further, how does psychological science assist with this process? To answer these questions, it is useful to first address the nature of the assessment process.

THE NATURE OF THE ASSESSMENT PROCESS

Many years ago personality assessment was considered to be the psychological equivalent of the X ray in medicine. This conceptualization offered entirely too little in many respects, and entirely too much in other respects. On the one hand, an X ray is a static picture, whereas an assessment is an ongoing process, alive with the dynamic interaction of patient and assessor. Many subtle factors affect and modify the interaction and the assessment results, such as the patient's and the assessor's age, gender, and racial and ethnic identity, as well as the patient's and the examiner's expectancies. The importance of the often subtle interpersonal transactions as a central variable in assessment becomes focal in this view (see Schafer, 1954; see also Masling, chap. 8 of this volume, and Potash, chap. 9 of this volume). Assessment is carried out within an interpersonal context, where the clinician can evaluate this interaction as an additional source of diagnostic information. As part of this interaction there is an emphasis on the experience of the patient in the assessment process, especially as it relates to his or her real-world experience. Data to assist the examiner in the illumination of this experience come from an analysis of the structure, sequence, and content in a successive series of test responses, as well as from an understanding of the meaning of the various assessment tasks to the patient (see Handler, chap. 17 of this volume, and Handler, Fowler, & Hilsenroth, chap. 24 of this volume). Thus, because a personality assessment is an interactive process rather than an impersonal and static picture, the assessment clinician in many ways has a richer database of information to draw on than does the radiologist.

On the other hand, the X-ray analogy is overly optimistic because psychological test data are not as clear-cut and delimited as X rays. X rays, although limited in their own way, have the capacity to consistently peer within a person to reveal internal structures not otherwise evident to observers. Initially, testing data (and projective testing data in particular) were envisioned as having similar powers. However, this was an overly idealistic hope. As indicated previously, personality assessment is an interactive process. In addition, it is a collaborative enterprise that is not done "to" people but rather must be done "with" people. As a result, the quality of the data obtained from testing depends in large part on the characteristics of the person being evaluated and the characteristics of the evaluator. For ill or for naught, people can intentionally or unintentionally do many things that interfere with the accuracy of test-derived information.

The net result is that personality tests often end up quantifying more of these interference factors, known as method variance, than the actual personality characteristics one ideally hopes to measure (see Campbell & Fiske, 1959; Meyer, 1996b, 1997).

The impact of method variance is a major problem when one is conducting psychological *testing* (or when one is conducting research using test data), because psychological testing employs test scores that are taken at face value, treating the scores derived from many different kinds of patients in an equivalent manner. Method variance is a bit less problematic for psychological *assessment* because the sophisticated clinician can take these interference factors into account in an ideographic fashion when interpreting the conglomerate of assessment data (e.g., Ganellen, 1994; McClelland, Koestner, & Weinberger, 1989; Meyer, 1997; Rapaport, Gill, & Schafer, 1968; Shedler, Mayman, & Manis, 1993). In fact, every major text written about the clinical interpretation of test data includes at least some instruction on how the clinician should take these factors into account (e.g., Archer, 1992; Exner, 1993; Greene, 1991; Millon, 1991; Morey, 1991).

SCIENTIFIC CONTRIBUTIONS
TO PERSONALITY ASSESSMENT

Unfortunately, the science of personality assessment is currently in a curious state. On the one hand, complex statistical methodologies such as factor analysis, multiple regression, and discriminant functions have contributed a remarkable amount to the technology of personality *testing*. These procedures have produced refined multidimensional tests like the Neuroticism-Extroversion-Openness Personality Inventory (NEO-PI–R; Costa & McCrae, 1992), the series of Millon Clinical Multiaxial Inventories (MCMI; Millon, 1991), or the Personality Assessment Inventory (PAI; Morey, 1991), and they have contributed to the development of refined scales that can be used for descriptive purposes, such as the Rorschach Schizophrenia Index, and the Hypervigilance Index, or the Harris and Lingoes subscales of the MMPI.

On the other hand, most personality research deals only with psychological testing, not with psychological assessment. Virtually all research investigations with purported relevance to personality assessment examine the nomothetic (i.e., across people) association between isolated test scores and criterion measures. In this approach, the data derived from one scale are treated out of context from the data derived from other scales or other sources of information. For example, in a nomothetic approach, researchers may investigate whether or not the average MMPI Depression score is higher in patients diagnosed with depression than in patients without a diagnosis of depression. Such a strategy is perfect for *scale* validation because it allows for an understanding of the strengths and limitations of a single scale, divorced from the array of other factors that impinge on any assessment.

However, such a strategy does very little for the assessment clinician, who is never concerned with just a single scale. For example, an assessment clinician would never want to make a diagnosis of depression based solely on a high score on the MMPI Depression scale. Rather, an assessment clinician works ideographically (i.e., focused on the uniqueness of the person) and tries to find a meaningful pattern of information within the data generated by many scales, drawn from several testing methods, along with observations of the patient and information drawn from his or her history. Although it is informative, the assessment clinician does not really want to know if the mean of the Depression scale is higher in patients with a depressive diagnosis than in those without such a diagnosis. Instead, for example, he or she wants to know things like the probability that a patient has a genuine depressive condition given the following information: (a) the MMPI Depression scale is unusually low, (b) the Rorschach Depression Index is elevated, (c) clinical observation with the Brief Psychiatric Rating Scale (BPRS) yields scores indicating emotional withdrawal, guilt feelings, and tearfulness— despite a denial of depressive mood, (d) the history is positive for the recent loss of a loved one and increased difficulty sleeping, and (e) the patient's sister reports that since childhood the patient consistently coped with problems by "looking on the bright side" and discounting emotional distress.

With the assessment data construed in this fashion, it would not be hard for the clinician to draw the conclusion—firmly based in the data—that this person is currently struggling with an underlying depressive condition (as evident on the Rorschach and portions of the BPRS) brought about by his recent loss (as evident from the history). However, his generally effective coping strategies (as evident from observer description) preclude conscious acknowledgment of this state (as evident from the MMPI and BPRS), most likely because full recognition of his underlying emotions would leave him in a state of precarious psychological balance. Note that in this instance the MMPI scale has valid utility despite the counterintuitive finding that it is *lower* than expected in a patient who has genuine depressive struggles. The score is low in this instance because it reflects the patient's efforts to adapt by consciously denying depression. Also note that the interpretive value and accuracy of a low score like this is completely lost when a nomothetic analysis is conducted on simple scale scores that do not take into account the full complexity of many clinical conditions.

Embedded in the preceding example is an important point for teaching and learning personality assessment: Different methods of assessment provide qualitatively different kinds of information. One fact that has been consistently supported in the research literature is that methods of assessment generally disagree with each other more than they agree, at least when nomothetic associations are examined across heterogeneous groups of people. In other words, when a group of patients fills out a self-report measure of depression, these scores are minimally correlated with scores of depression that are measured by the Rorschach or by observer ratings (e.g., Achenbach, McConaughy, & Howell, 1987; Archer & Krishnamurthy, 1993a, 1993b; Meyer, 1996b, 1997;

Perry, 1992; Zimmerman, 1994). Although there are certainly some exceptions to this general principle (Fowler, Hilsenroth, & Handler, 1996, 1997; Meyer, 1997), the basic independence between methods is a robust phenomenon. Although some may fear that these findings challenge the validity of all assessment methods, the relative independence of methods is not cause for concern. Rather, it is a phenomenon that demands understanding and recognition of the unique strengths (and limitations) possessed by each assessment method.

As Miller (1987) and others (e.g., Achenbach et al., 1987; McClelland et al., 1989; Meyer, 1996a) have articulated, unstructured interviews elicit information relevant to thematic life narratives; structured interviews and self-report instruments elicit information relevant to conscious self-schema; performance-based personality tests (i.e., Rorschach and Thematic Apperception Test [TAT]) elicit information relevant to implicit dynamics and underlying templates of perception and motivation; and observer ratings elicit perceptions of behavior that are bound by the parameters of particular observational settings. Students who are learning assessment should be taught to understand the distinctions among these methods and should be instructed in ways to exploit these distinctions in order to obtain qualitatively unique sorts of information from each method and more fully understand the complexity of the person seeking an evaluation (e.g., Finn, 1996a; Ganellen, 1994; Meyer, 1997; Shedler et al., 1993).

Unfortunately, there is very little good science to help the assessment clinician navigate the process of drawing inferences from cross-method assessment data. In fact, the disparities that arise from different assessment methods have caused considerable consternation and confusion among personality assessment researchers. Furthermore, it is very rare for researchers to examine the interplay of multiple assessment methods. Finally, and perhaps because the task is so daunting, most researchers appear uninformed about how personality test data drawn from multiple methods of assessment should be integrated into a research design in a clinically meaningful manner. Thus, at least for the foreseeable future, personality assessment will remain an art and clinicians engaged in personality assessment will have to rely on their clinical judgment to guide the process.

JUDGMENT AND INFERENCE IN THE PROCESS OF CLINICAL ASSESSMENT

As a caveat, however, those who are interested in teaching and learning personality assessment skills must be forewarned about the pitfalls and lapses in reasoning that accompany the judgment process. Also, it is important to recognize that the available literature, flawed though it may be, does not consistently support the value of clinical judgment in the assessment process. Each of these issues is discussed briefly, although other sources should be consulted for more detailed arguments and findings (e.g., Dawes, Faust, &

Meehl, 1989; Garb, 1984, 1989; Garb & Schramke, 1996; Holt, 1970, 1986; Kleinmuntz, 1990).

A considerable literature that documents common errors in human reasoning has developed within cognitive psychology. Clinicians are not immune to these problems. Although clinicians can and do make judgments that are more valid than lay persons', in general, clinicians conducting assessments can err in at least five common ways. First, clinicians may inadvertently elicit only that information that confirms their hypotheses and hunches, neglecting the questions or findings that would challenge their assumptions. Second, when making diagnostic judgments, clinicians may recall prototypical examples of diagnostic categories and make judgments about how similar or dissimilar their patient is to these prototypes rather than systematically evaluating their patient on specific diagnostic criteria. Third, some clinicians are prone to err by being overconfident in their judgments rather than appropriately tentative. Alternatively, some other clinicians may err by being underconfident in their judgments rather than appropriately decisive and conclusive. Fourth, once a result or an outcome is known (e.g., a patient did eventually attempt suicide), clinicians may err by using this outcome information to retrospectively and falsely conclude that they could have predicted the results in advance. This cognitive error is commonly made by all people, not just clinicians, and is known as the "hindsight bias." Fifth, clinicians may err by making judgments or predictions without considering the relative frequency of the events they are judging. For example, clinicians may judge a patient to be suicidal without recognizing that suicide attempts are (fortunately) rare events.

All of the preceding judgment pitfalls should be highlighted and studied in assessment classes in order to prevent or minimize their occurrence. In addition, these errors can be minimized by employing several corrective strategies. First, clinicians should not embark on an assessment unless they can systematically identify the characteristics of the clinical condition they wish to diagnose or describe. Subsequently, they must systematically link test indicators (and their absence) to these characteristics. Second, as clinicians develop test-derived impressions, they should systematically challenge them by considering test data that may temper or counter their hypotheses. Third, when appropriate, clinicians should take into account the base rates of events they are trying to predict (e.g., dropping out of treatment) and should employ empirically validated statistical predictions when possible (e.g., the Goldberg Index from the MMPI, the Schizophrenia Index from the Rorschach, etc.). Fourth, clinicians should anticipate making errors of judgment and should be open to corrective feedback from patients and referral sources. Fifth, assessment clinicians should actively solicit this corrective feedback (again from both patients and other clinicians) in order to maximize the accuracy of their test-derived impressions. The latter is particularly important in order to gain an understanding of the strengths, limitations, and peculiarities associated with various tests.

Although the empirical literature does not consistently support the utility of test-derived judgments, Holt (1970, 1986) has vigorously and eloquently defended the role of clinical reasoning in the assessment process. In addition, he has pointed out many limitations in the general literature on this topic (e.g., irrelevant judgment tasks using nonclinical criteria, use of artificial pieces of information rather than data that are typically used in clinical practice, etc). By and large, these limitations are as germane today as they were when Holt first raised these points almost 40 years ago. In addition, even when clinicians are asked to make determinations about reasonable clinical matters, there are many problems with the available literature. The most fundamental problem is the absence of "gold-standard" validation criteria that would allow us to describe with certainty the "truths" and "fictions" regarding a patient's personality. As noted earlier, the literature suggests that clinical judgments are often inaccurate. However, it is exactly these judgments (or the judgments of lay raters) that are often used as the criteria for "validating" the accuracy of inferences drawn from assessment data. It does not take much to see the flaw in this arrangement. If the criterion construct itself is invalid or defective—and it almost always is—then there is no way to determine whether assessment-derived judgments are more accurate or less accurate than the criterion. Currently, in the research literature, one could easily argue that assessment-derived inferences are actually more valid than the criterion judgments against which they are evaluated.

Garb (1984) has noted that this problem with the literature "is especially intractable" (p. 651). In many respects, in the face of such a core methodological problem, it is surprising that good scientists continue to place faith in the available data. Nonetheless, despite problems with some of the research literature, it is clear that clinicians make errors in judgment. Because clinical assessment requires judgment, students must be educated about these constraints and both sides of the issues regarding judgment validity must be discussed. In addition, the five strategies mentioned previously for minimizing judgment pitfalls should be actively reviewed when learning and subsequently practicing assessment.

LEARNING ASSESSMENT SKILLS

As we have indicated already, we believe that assessment can inform the therapist and the patient about personality problem areas, the presence or absence of conflictual issues, and the severity of a patient's disturbance, if any. In addition, assessment can identify a patient's areas of strength, abilities to cope with intrapsychic and external stress, and adaptive level of object relations (the thoughts and feelings one has about others, and the interactions one has in his or her relationships with others). Assessment data can also illuminate various aspects of cognitive and affective functioning. We can utilize assessment to help identify the process and the outcome of treatment, the types of treatment that are likely to be beneficial, and the potential problems a therapist and patient will have in their ongoing relationship. Assessment data may also be helpful in the choice of a therapist—an older or younger person, man, woman, and so on. Assessment data, in conjunction with a thorough history and observational information, can also be used for diagnosis (see Ritzler, chap. 23 this volume, for a somewhat different view). Finally, assessment data are quite useful in determining whether there has been any actual therapeutic change during and following treatment (e.g., Blatt, & Ford, 1994; Kadera, Lambert, & Andrews, 1996; Toman & Padawer, 1995; Weiner & Exner, 1991).

Naturally, it is difficult to achieve the level of understanding that is required for the skills just discussed. This is especially true for students because learning about the various tests and techniques, learning how to integrate a complex array of information, and learning how to report the data are so very time consuming. Given the additional interpersonal demands, it is also no wonder that students typically find communicating the data to the patient almost as difficult to learn as crafting the written reports. Understandably, they feel frustrated when they spend countless hours doing their first assessments, collecting, scoring, analyzing, and integrating the data. However, when they have produced a report that captures the uniqueness of the individual they have assessed, they become quite proud of their work. There is no doubt, though, that the time commitment for learning to do even a journeyman's job is rather daunting, and often quite frustrating.

Understandably, as well, most students find learning assessment emotionally taxing because it is the first time in their training that they are required to integrate so many diverse areas of knowledge and so many technical skills. It is perhaps just for this reason that learning assessment skills is an important task in graduate students' training and development. Until that time students master diverse subjects by taking a variety of clinical and nonclinical courses; integration is not typically stressed, either in conceptual material or in the consideration of individual functioning. It is one thing to integrate abstract concepts; it is quite another type of task to integrate knowledge about a person who is asking for clinical services. Thus, whereas clinical psychologists in some academic settings are decreasing assessment demands, other psychologists utilize assessment in their clinical training programs as a focal point to train students in clinical conceptualization. This is because the assessment task calls for students to organize their knowledge in many areas (e.g., life-stage development, psychometrics, interviewing, psychopathology, learning theory, cross-cultural psychology, ethics, etc.). In the assessment process, with a patient and a referring clinician requesting expert input, all this knowledge is brought to bear in a far more complex and compelling manner than can be effected in the typical doctoral preliminary examination.

Some faculty members do not recognize this function of assessment and they are quite critical of courses in this area, as well as of the techniques taught. Unaware of the function assessment serves in the real-life integration and application of psychological skills and information, some have voted either to limit the number of assessment courses in the graduate curriculum or to remove them completely from the curriculum. Not only does this rob the student of the opportunity to apply his or her psychological knowledge directly, but it produces clinical psychologists who are poorly trained for applied work (Hilsenroth & Handler, 1995). The implication for recent doctoral psychologists of this negative attitude among academic psychologists is that a self-fulfilling prophecy is established. That is, if the assessment process is viewed as irrelevant, unreliable, or invalid, students will be poorly taught to do assessments, particularly with projective methods. By diminishing knowledge and interest in assessment techniques, subsequent research becomes poorly conceived and poorly executed, with the complexity of the assessment process often reduced to the investigation of single variables, unguided by theory, using oversimplified methods and small numbers of subjects to study complex relationships. The resultant research could not hope to validate aspects of the assessment process effectively. Ultimately, with enough research like this, the clinical assessment process would sink into a morass of disrepute. In turn, academic psychologists could point to the resultant poor validity studies to bolster the claim that scientists should abandon assessment efforts. Fewer students would then be taught these procedures, fewer would be prepared to make sophisticated contributions, and the downward spiral would continue (Handler & Meyer, 1996; Riethmiller & Handler, in press a, in press b).

The remainder of this chapter is devoted to a more detailed discussion of the important reasons to learn assessment, all of which follow from the major point presented earlier, that assessment provides a focus for the student to understand a patient's world, both in applied settings and in research settings.

ASSESSMENT IDENTIFIES THE PATIENT'S STRENGTHS AND WEAKNESSES

The assessment process illuminates for the student the very wide range of strengths and weaknesses people do not readily show in ordinary situations, or in an intake interview. The traditional assessment procedure is typically quite stressful for the patient, thereby stimulating responses that are not usually seen in their initial psychotherapy sessions, even though they are often typical of their responses to stressful situations in their everyday world. In other words, students who conduct assessments get to experience firsthand a variety of psychopathological conditions, coping styles, and defensive maneuvers that they ordinarily do not experience in face-to-face psychotherapeutic conversations with patients.

For example, a 35-year-old man refused to continue with the Rorschach because its unstructured nature stimulated fear of losing reality contact. He stated, "I'm stretched like a rubber band. I have to come back to reality so my imagination doesn't run away with me. I have to check out my imagination—with some proof, some facts. Two and two is four." Still another patient, straining to achieve cognitive control over disturbing impulses, at one point in testing took a matchbook cover from his pocket and wrote down the number of the Bender-Gestalt designs he was unable to recall from memory to "take it home and do them over more times, so I can prove I can do it, and so I will always remember it." Another patient, who initially seemed quite normal in his approach to the examiner, defined a thermometer as "the temperature of a certain reading—a guidance insomuch as determining the fever of an individ-ual," illustrating his inability to think clearly and logically, and to express himself in a less strained and overly pedantic manner. Another patient, when asked "Why does land in the city cost more than land in the country?" replied, "Because people want to be populated," also illustrating his disturbed thought processes.

It is one thing, for example, to state abstractly that a patient's thinking may be loose. It is quite another thing to witness an otherwise intact looking 30-year-old college-educated man respond to the Comprehension WAIS item, "What does this saying mean: 'Strike while the iron is hot?'" with the following: "Strike is to hit. Hit my wife. I should say push, and then pull the cord of the iron. Strike in baseball—one strike against you. This means you have to hit and retaliate to make up that strike against you—or if you feel you have a series of problems—if they build up, you will strike." Not only does this response tell a story of this man's failure in maintaining clear thinking, but it also indicates his difficulty in containing angry, aggressive impulses. Primitive aggressive intrusions into logical secondary process thinking are obvious here, as are the signs of disturbed thinking. This psychotic patient, who had been inappropriately placed in classical psychoanalysis, in which the therapist used free association, understandably became significantly worse in this treatment program. His pretreatment response to the preceding WAIS item was "You should attack at the proper and logical time." Given the change in this response, which was also evident in other assessment data, the examiner recommended a significant change in the treatment approach, one with increased boundaries, more activity on the part of the therapist, less stimulation of primary process material, and a significantly more structured holding environment.

ASSESSMENT ILLUMINATES
THE EXPERIENTIAL PROCESS

Often, sequences seen in testing illuminate dynamic processes in the patient's life. An example of the interpretation of changes in a patient's experiential processing comes from a man who appeared quite disturbed when he was presented with Card II on the Rorschach. He made a peculiar inhaling sound, indicating discomfort, and he produced a response that was rather dysphoric and poorly defined by form, suggesting problems with emotional control: "a bloody wound." His next response was "a rocket, with red flames, blasting off." This response, although it is good form quality, nevertheless illuminates the patient's style in dealing with troubling emotions—to become angry and to quickly and aggressively leave the scene with a dramatic show of power and force. However, the next response, given more slowly, with some care and detail, described "two people, face to face, talking to each other—discussing." It is possible to picture a sequence of intrapsychic and interpersonal events in these responses. The patient's underlying dysphoric emotions seem to be close to the surface, and perhaps poorly controlled. When they break through, they cause him immediate but temporary disorganization in thinking and in the ability to manage his emotions. The patient soon recovers control, however, and there is the desired rapprochement, indicating that with time, rather quickly in fact, he is capable of a more positive connection with a significant other. After careful exploration several months into therapy, this explosive pattern followed by the desire for the reestablishment of a satisfying relationship was first unearthed and discussed as a response pattern in the patient's work and family settings.

Again and again we encounter responses that illuminate significant emotional problems, and patients' ability to cope with them. For example, it is one thing to believe that a certain man is angry, but it is quite another thing to hear that person's Rorschach, filled with extremely primitive hostile and sexual content, as you become aware that this person's mental life is filled with images of sexually attacking and cruelly killing people. On the other hand, there is the opposite experience of seeing a person become overwhelmed with affective stimuli on the Rorschach, only to then see that person deal effectively with those impulses in subsequent responses or in their pattern of scores on more structured tests. Often, this can allow the examiner to feel comfortable predicting that such a person can cope more effectively than he or she thinks they can. For example, one patient expressed significant doubt in the interview that she could cope effectively with her emotions. However, the examiner felt more certain that she could, based on her demonstrations of coping on the Rorschach and other projective tests. She proved the prediction correct and the hospitalization that was being considered was unnecessary. However, despite rather benign interviews, several of the other patients discussed previously demonstrated that protective hospitalization was necessary, both for themselves as well as for the protection of others. We know of no procedure other than assessment that offers such a window through which to view the wide range of human functioning, from adaptive and healthy to maladaptive, pathological, and possibly dangerous, with the attendant opportunity to facilitate those who seem to need such facilitation.

ASSESSMENT ILLUMINATES UNDERLYING CONDITIONS

Learning assessment often allows the student to recognize the difference between a patient's public presentation and possible underlying emotional problems. For example, a somewhat reserved 21-year-old male patient did not present any overt signs of a thought disorder or any gross pathology during the initial interview. His presenting complaint was that he was having problems with his relationships, and was finding it difficult to establish intimacy. His Rorschach was unremarkable until he came to Card IX. With no delay, he responded: "It looks like, um, the skull of a really decayed or decaying body with, like, the physical representation of some noxious fume or odor coming out of it. It looks like blood and other fluids are dripping down onto the bones of the upper torso and the eyes are glowing, kind of an orange-purplish glow." In the Inquiry he stated that the skull was hidden behind fumes that were seeping out of it and that the blood was dripping all over the body.

The patient's first response to Card X was not unusual ("an undersea garden"), but his next response was an even more direct expression of this young man's extreme disorganizing emotions that were of crisis proportions: "It looks like someone crying for help, all bruised and scarred, with blood running down their face." What a jarring experience it was for the student to witness the quiescent presentation of his interpersonal problem, juxtaposed with this desperate dysphoric response. The student abruptly changed her stance with this patient, providing him with much more rapid access to treatment than would have been the case otherwise.

In a second example we see an illustration of a brain-damaged patient's inability to deal with the demands of everyday work and interpersonal situations, as well as his desire to depend on others to satisfy his needs. In telling a story about the picture of a cat he drew, this 43-year-old man stated: "Herman, the cat. Not neat and clean; doesn't have a place to stay; the people who had him got tired of him and turned him loose. He's in the forest, trying to live and he's poor, hungry—needs food. He'll just have to live the best way he can, out there alone in the forest." Subsequently, the patient said of the male figure he drew, "He's run down, broke, lacks shoes. Somebody will give him money because he's happy and jolly."

ASSESSMENT FACILITATES TREATMENT PLANNING

Treatment planning has taken on a position of prominence in recent years, in part because such planning makes psychotherapy more efficient and cost effective, and in part because insurance companies have become quite unhappy "with open-ended forms of psychotherapy without clearly defined goals ...Today there are [many] treatment options whose potential value must be studied in great detail and depth. The search for the 'right' therapy for the 'right' patient continues" (Strupp, cited in Butcher, 1990, p. iii).

Not only is assessment useful for treatment planning for the individual patient, but it is also a vehicle for assisting patients to learn about themselves, and to facilitate communication between patient and therapist. It can enhance the likelihood of favorable treatment outcome (Strupp, cited in Butcher, 1990) and it may serve as a guide or reference point during the course of treatment (Applebaum, 1990; Mortimer & Smith, 1983).

Although evidence for the predictive utility of assessment is limited almost exclusively to *testing* data (i.e., single scores divorced from contextual factors), and although many attempts to predict outcome have proved unsuccessful, this is not true for all measures. For example, Klopfer and his associates (Klopfer,

Ainsworth, Klopfer, & Holt, 1954) constructed the Rorschach Prognostic Rating Scale (RPRS) to predict which patients would be successful in psychotherapy. This scale is composed of a number of variables, including the type and quality of human, animal, and inanimate movement, the use of color and shading within responses, and the form quality of perceptions. Meyer and Handler (1997) performed a meta-analysis on the existing literature that used the RPRS to predict subsequent outcome. They found the RPRS had a powerful ability to predict outcome. When data from the primary research studies were corrected to take into account all patients, all RPRS scores and all outcome scores, the estimated effect size was $r = .56$. The authors also demonstrated that the magnitude of this relationship was much larger than the predictive validity coefficients that have been found for a variety of other medical, psychological, or educational tests (e.g., the Dexamethasone Suppression Test, the Cardiac Stress Test, the Scholastic Achievement Test, etc.).

Other research has examined which types of patients will do best in particular forms of treatment or with particular kinds of therapists (e.g., Beutler et al., 1991). Another example of the utility of assessment for treatment planning comes from its application in the treatment of patients with asthma. Here, in a series of studies by Dirks and his colleagues, psychological assessment data have been instrumental in predicting length of hospitalization, rehospitalization rates, and subsequent medication dosages, among other criteria (e.g., Dirks & Kinsman, 1981).

Currently, there are a number of large-scale projects under way that are designed to determine the value of assessment measures for predicting psychotherapy, medical, and criminal outcomes. For example, Meyer, Handler, and Hilsenroth are conducting a meta-analysis (sponsored by the Society for Personality Assessment and Rorschach Workshops) of those studies in which selected assessment instruments have been used in this manner (Handler & Meyer, 1996). Other somewhat similar projects are under way in Finland (Lindfors, 1996) and in Sweden (Carlsson, Nygren, Clinton, & Bihlar, 1996).

ASSESSMENT IS THERAPEUTIC IN AND OF ITSELF AND IT ALSO FACILITATES THERAPY

Another important reason to learn assessment is that it can be therapeutic in and of itself when the patient is approached in a facilitative manner (e.g., Finn & Tonsager, 1992, in press; see also Finn, chap. 20 in this volume). Students conducting assessments learn to provide support, praise, and encouragement in a somewhat structured paradigm, which provides an easy entry to the psychotherapeutic process. In addition, although a course in interviewing helps the student learn how to say "hello" to a patient, so to speak, it is the assessment courses that help the student feel more comfortable in the constructive interaction with the patient. The interviewing task, as well as the job of obtaining responses to the various tests in the battery, help both patient and therapist adapt to each other, measure each other, and evaluate each other, just as the therapist and patient might do over a much longer period in psychotherapy.

An example of test data used to facilitate therapy can be found in a recent article about the diagnostic efficiency of the Early Memories Procedure. Fowler, Hilsenroth, and Handler (1995) described the case of Maria, referred to at the beginning of this chapter. Maria, a 38-year-old divorced Hispanic woman, was destitute and living in a shelter when she came to therapy. She entered therapy to gain some control over her ferocious temper, which frequently placed her life in danger because of her tendency to explode into violent and impulsive rages. Her hair-trigger temper, extreme sensitivity to coercion, and pervasive paranoia made it impossible for her to keep a job for more than a few weeks. In response to the transitional object query (i.e., what is your earliest memory of a favorite blanket or stuffed animal?), she produced the following early memory:

> I had a blue doll—a Chatty Cathy—and I would dress her up like myself. But the blue doll had a beautiful blue dress and blue eyes. I remember drawing the blue marks on her arms, and I remember my mother took her away, and I remember having a fit and telling her that she was my doll ... I remember saying to the doll when I would put her to bed, "Now close your eyes," and I would expect her to close her eyes. And when I would pick her up, I would expect them to open. But sometimes they would not work and I would ask myself, "Why?" I expected the doll to go through a lot of punishment—to share the punishment I got. She shared my punishment. I had a lot of emotional punishment. (p. 95)

The interpretation of this memory as it relates to transitional objects and to therapy implications is as follows: "Maria is capable of imaginative fantasy and of using something outside herself to soothe herself over the abuses in the world. She is also looking to the therapist to fill this role (the therapist has blue eyes). Unfortunately, she ruthlessly controls and abuses the soothing object and expects this sharing of misery to create a special bond" (Fowler et al., 1995, p. 95).

Fowler et al. (1995) expected that the therapist would be used as a transitional object and would be subjected to the same kind of attacks. In fact, these anticipated attacks quickly developed and persisted for the first 9 months of treatment. The authors continued:

> As Winnicott ... made clear, the therapist had to survive these attacks without retaliation, thus becoming for Maria a dependable and reliable object with whom she could identify. But more important, the memory gave the therapist some hope of instilling in Maria an ability to use him in a more healthy manner.
>
> Prior to analyzing this early memory, the therapist had little hope of finding a way into Maria's extremely paranoid character. In light of this early memory,

the therapist believed it was necessary to teach Maria how she might best use him by imagining what he would say as she got herself into a potentially violent argument with anyone. Naturally, this training could not take place until she had made a strong positive connection with the therapist and generally viewed him as a good object. By being taught to control her violent outbursts through reflecting on the therapist's advice, Maria made progress beyond expectation. Although her paranoia was still quite intact, she was able to gain psychological distance and develop a capacity for delaying violent impulses. As a result, she was not only able to maintain employment for a year, but she was also promoted to a supervisory position in the company. (pp. 95–96)

THE ROLE OF ASSESSMENT IN QUALITY CONTROL, COST REDUCTION, AND QUANTIFYING OUTCOME

Maruish (1994) asserted that psychological assessment "can play an important role in the delivery of mental health care in the future" (p. 10). He emphasized the role of assessment procedures to ensure continuous quality improvement through more adequate treatment planning and outcome assessment. He also focused on assessment as a vehicle through which "clinicians and third-party payors ... communicate with and among each other with a common language" (p. 11). It is expected that in the near future all types of service delivery practitioners will be required to demonstrate their effectiveness, not only in the area of psychotherapy, but in the treatment of related problems, such as drug and alcohol abuse (Maruish, 1994). In addition, those who purchase and contract for insurance coverage are beginning to seek "meaningful, measurable assurances of quality" (Maruish, 1994, p. 13) from those who supply these services. Such assessment information will also be necessary to impress legislators with the importance of providing financing for clinical services, training funds, and necessary research. Whether or not the impetus for accountability is coming from third-party payers or from patients themselves, outcome assessment measures have assumed a great deal of importance for practitioners who wish to provide "the highest level of performance and the best care for the patient" (Maruish, 1994, p. 14).

Newman (1991) described an example of how personality assessment data, initially used to determine progress or outcome, "can be related to variables such as treatment approach, costs, or reimbursement criteria, and thus can provide objective support for decisions regarding continuation of treatment, discharge, or referral to another type of treatment (e.g., from outpatient to inpatient treatment" (Maruish, 1994, p. 15).

A number of surveys or studies are available that indicate how the major assessment instruments for adults and children can be used for outcome assessment (e.g., Blatt & Ford, 1994; Kadera et al., 1996; Maruish, 1994; Toman & Padawer, 1995; Weiner & Exner, 1991). However, it should also be noted that the field has not yet developed an understanding of how unique methods of assessment can and should be used together to quantify the psychological changes that are occurring as a function of treatment. For example, since psychologists began doing psychotherapy research, it has been fairly common to find that self-ratings of psychotherapeutic change are not strongly correlated with therapist ratings of change, and that each of these are not strongly correlated with ratings of change made by independent observers or projective test data (e.g., Cartwright, Kirtner, & Fiske, 1963). Given the issues discussed earlier in this chapter, the reader should not find this surprising. However, these findings have direct implications for practicing in today's managed-care environment: In order to fully quantify change or outcome, a simple and brief self-report instrument will not be sufficient. Rather, multiple methods of assessment must be utilized to map changes accurately in overt symptoms, observable behavior, internal structure, relational templates, and underlying dynamics.

As an example of these distinctions, consider the following. Numerous studies have demonstrated a dose-response effect in psychotherapy, such that a greater proportion of patients improve with increasing numbers of psychotherapy sessions (e.g., Exner & Andronikof-Sanglade, 1992; Howard, Kopta, Krause, & Orlinsky, 1986; Kadera et al., 1996; Seligman, 1995; Weiner & Exner, 1991). However, research relying on self-report data (which are presumably more responsive to conscious symptomatic distress) indicates that about half of the patients in treatment will be improved after 12 to 14 sessions, and about 75% of the patients will be improved after about 26 sessions (Howard et al., 1986; Kadera et al., 1996). Furthermore, this effect is often nonspecific, with self-reported improvement occurring across the spectrum of problems (Exner & Andronikof-Sanglade, 1992; Seligman, 1995). However, *structural* personality change, at least as measured by the Rorschach, appears to occur much more slowly and also in a much more differentiated manner. For example, if one calculates improvement rates using the data presented by Weiner and Exner (1991) and Exner and Andronikof-Sanglade (1992), it can be seen that brief treatment (with a mean of 14 sessions) generates improvement rates of 50% or more in only a few areas of symptomatology (i.e., emotional distress, loneliness, careless processing, and emotional withdrawal). Additional areas of functioning show this extent of relief after about a year of treatment (e.g., general coping deficits, inaccurate perceptions, poor emotional control, poor self-regard, interpersonal passivity). However, it is only after long-term and intensive treatment that one observes salient structural change across the full range of functioning that is measured by the Rorschach (e.g., limited internal resources, inconsistent coping styles, limited awareness, disjointed thinking, poor understanding of others, overreliance on fantasy, intellectualization, lack of relatedness, etc.).

ASSESSMENT PROVIDES
PROFESSIONAL IDENTITY

As indicated earlier in this chapter, it is important to know assessment skills because they distinguish us from other disciplines. The psychiatrist is distinguished from other mental-health professionals because he or she can write prescriptions for drugs. Comparatively, psychologists are the only professionals who are typically trained in assessment. This provides us with a personal identity and with some level of separation and distinction in the crowded field of mental-health providers (e.g., psychologist, psychiatrist, social worker, marriage and family therapist, counselor, psychiatric nurse, mental-health specialist, etc.), a field that confuses many people. We are often called on by other mental-health professionals to provide assessment services, as well as by school personnel, physicians, attorneys, the court, government, and even by business and industry. Each time we submit a report to a professional or to an agency, or give expert testimony in court, we demonstrate our knowledge of assessment science, our practical application of this knowledge, and our unique perceptiveness in applying this knowledge in a meaningful manner.

ASSESSMENT REFLECTS PATIENTS'
RELATIONSHIP PROBLEMS

Assessment also helps us understand patients' real-world relationships and their real-world patterns of functioning. For example, it is easy to understand why a person has difficulty with intimate relationships when the subjects in his TAT stories do not interact, when they interact in an aggressive manner, or when his stories reflect a simplistic, unemotional conceptualization of people (Westen, 1991a). In similar fashion, his Rorschach may contain certain responses in which people either ignore each other or are engaged in hostile or unproductive interactions (Urist, 1977).

It becomes easy, for example, to see what function a man's wife has in their relationship when the angry responses in his individual Rorschach are not present in the couple's consensus Rorschach (where the couple take the test again, this time deciding on the answers together). The cost of this control to the man was also evident, as his many creative and imaginative responses were absent in the consensus record (Handler, 1997). In a similar consensus procedure, where the Rorschach was given simultaneously to all the members of a family, including a schizophrenic adult child, the mother enthusiastically encouraged the child's confabulated responses rather than endorsing her husband's more normal responses (Singer, 1977). Frequent observations of such destructive interactions in a series of studies were used to support a family systems theory explanation for the genesis of schizophrenia.

ASSESSMENT IS USED
IN WORK-RELATED SETTINGS

Even our understanding of the dynamic reasons behind someone's professional choice can be illuminated through the use of assessment techniques. For example, Church, Hilsenroth, and Handler (1996), studied the Rorschachs of poets/novelists, journalists, and technical writers. They found significant depressive content in the records of the poets/novelists (8 of the 10 fiction writers had significantly elevated scores on the Depression Index), but not in the records of the other groups. The journalists and fiction writers gave significantly more Deviant Responses than technical writers, who gave almost none, suggesting that the first two groups are more creative. The technical writers also gave fewer responses that were scored as blends and had lower Complexity Index scores, suggesting that the technical writer's world is more simple and straightforward than the worlds of other two groups. The creative writers embellished their responses in unusual ways, leading to a significantly higher proportion of unusual or creative responses (Xu%). Finally, the journalists scored significantly higher on the Egocentricity Index compared with the other two groups, suggesting a strong need for recognition. This finding, in concert with the finding of a significantly higher Holt Level 2 Libidinal Content score, indicating the expression of socially acceptable primary process, suggests that the journalists seek to express themselves in a somewhat sensationalistic manner, focusing on recognition. The creative writers are seeking, in their writing, to work out depressive affect, whereas the technical writers seem to be focusing on control through the simplification and clarification of their world.

There are many additional studies devoted to the investigation of vocational choice and/or preference using personality assessment instruments (e.g., Krakowski, 1984; Muhlenkamp & Parsons, 1972; Payne & Sabaroche, 1985; Rassenfosse, 1975; Rezler & Buckley, 1977). There is also a large literature in industrial-organizational psychology, in which assessment is used as an integral part of the study of individuals in various work settings, in the study of work-related dynamics, and in the selection and promotion of various workers. For meta-analytic reviews demonstrating the utility of personality tests as predictors in these settings, see Barrick and Mount (1991), Tett, Jackson, and Rothstein (1991), and Robertson and Kinder (1993). For an interesting study on the value of assessment rather than testing in this context, see Dicken and Black (1965).

ASSESSMENT PROVIDES A RAPID WINDOW
OF UNDERSTANDING

Although we have advocated for the assessment clinician to utilize multiple methods for obtaining information, at times it can even be helpful to employ a circumscribed approach to testing that relies on data from just one method. For example, including some testing in an initial psychotherapy interview can provide a relatively rapid way to identify levels of symptomatic difficulty (i.e., the self-report method) or to obtain an alternate view of the patient and his or her major problem areas. These procedures can help reduce errors in understanding the patient. Fowler et al. (1995) described just such an error in assessment for therapy, using the Early Memories Technique:

> Sheila, a 22-year-old divorced nursing student was seven months pregnant. Her presenting complaint was a reemergence of long-standing depressive symptoms and a fear of a psychotic break. Precipitating events included the sudden end of her relationship with her boyfriend (the father of her child) and the fear of having to rear a child by herself. In response to the question, "What is your earliest memory of being fed, feeding, or eating?" Sheila responded:

> At the ranch house ... I wouldn't eat ... It was Hamburger Helper, and I wouldn't eat it. And my dad took a fork of it and shoved it down my throat. I think he whipped me or kicked me after that. (p. 91)

Ultimately, Sheila produced three early memories of her father behaving in a physically abusive manner. Two of these memories, including the one just described, had particular clinical value because they involved dramatic physical punishment that occurred in the context of eating. The authors continued:

> The eating memories provided a very focused interpretation regarding her likely reaction to a supportive male therapist. These memories were interpreted as prototypical examples of Sheila's experience of any type of supportive, nurturant relationship with men. [Because of her experiences with her father] Sheila experiences nuturance and support from men as an invasive, cruel and abusive impingement; when a man acts to support her, she feels like he is literally trying to shove something down her throat. (p.92)

Relying on these memories, the therapist anticipated that Sheila would not do well with a male therapist, would experience support from the environment as harsh and controlling, and would drop out of treatment early. Unfortunately, she could not be assigned to a female therapist and a man was assigned by default. The authors stated:

> The course of treatment in this case was extremely brief. Sheila attended two sessions before disappearing; yet during that time, the transference to her therapist was established, the predicted conflict arose, and her predicted reaction to it all came to fruition. Sheila began her first session by informing her therapist that she had been admitted to the emergency room two days earlier for vaginal bleeding and dangerously low blood pressure, both warning signs of overexertion during her final trimester of pregnancy. With shocking indifference, she explained that she had ignored these dangerous symptoms

and instead went to work. Once there, she collapsed and was rushed to the emergency room.

Sheila's indifference to this imminent risk left the therapist with the distinct impression that this was, in fact, a passive suicide attempt. Taking into account the serious pressing nature of the situation, the therapist interpreted this to her. She reflexively denied it, but added that she suspected that this interpretation would be made. The therapist then began to cautiously broach the subject of her work load and other practical matters that needed serious and immediate attention. What ensued was a foray into a most exacerbating rejection of each interpretation and each attempt at ego support. The therapist, having forgotten the assessment report, helped create just the transference relationship that Sheila had described in her feeding/eating early memory. By the end of the session, any semblance of rapport seemed to have dissolved, and Sheila had become extremely suspicious of the therapist. The session ended in a stalemate.

The second session was less destructive because the therapist had returned to the projective data and found just what had been forgotten—that Sheila could not accept the therapist's support, experiencing it as something being shoved down her throat. Returning to the interaction of the previous week, the therapist noted Sheila's difficulty in hearing any support from him. She disagreed: "When you told me what to do, it makes me think that you think I'm stupid ... That's like my mother and father treat me!" In the end, the damage done to the rapport in the first session was too great to be repaired. Sheila canceled her next two appointments, then moved from her apartment, leaving no forwarding address or telephone number. (pp. 91–93)

This vignette illustrates the predictive value of a brief assessment in the context of a theoretically driven interpretation. Unfortunately, the therapist's handling of this interaction was not informed by the assessment data, and a poor outcome was the result. Without this critical information, the counter-transference and role responsiveness went unchecked. Thus the destructive conflict emerged immediately, and was the major cause of the failed therapy.

ASSESSMENT IS USED IN FORENSIC
AND MEDICAL SETTINGS

There are a variety of settings in which assessment is used to answer legal questions or medically related questions. For example, in cases that involve custody determination for minor children, both parents are often assessed to determine their emotional soundness as parents. These assessment results are often used by judges to determine which parent will be granted custody. In addition, assessment is often used to determine whether or not someone charged with a crime is competent to understand the charges brought against him or her, or to determine whether the person is competent to stand trial, or to determine if a person is malingering psychiatric deficits in order to avoid criminal responsibility. Assessment is also used by state and federal agencies to determine if a person is emotionally disabled, and therefore should receive some type of disability pension. Finally, attorneys sometimes request assessment evaluations to determine the emotional effects of various physical and/or mental traumas.

Concerning the use of assessment in medically related problems, assessments are sometimes requested by physicians or insurance company representatives to determine the emotional correlates of various physical disease processes, or to make a differential diagnosis between emotionally caused physical symptoms and those symptoms caused by medical disease. Recently, an approach to the treatment of "the whole person" has resulted in the birth of a more inclusive approach, now called *biopsychosocial*, in which personality assessment is one part of a total assessment of the person, so that treatment can target emotional factors along with physical problems. Another relatively new term, *psychoneuroimmunology*, refers to the complex relationship among various psychological and physical factors in the person's ability to be disease-free. Each of these orientations has spawned new psychological assessment instruments, in an attempt to measure the various personality components involved in the "whole-person" approaches.

In addition, the field of health psychology has become quite important recently, and assessment is used in a variety of health-related issues, such as smoking cessation, medication compliance, chronic pain treatment, recovery from surgery, and so on. This has resulted in the construction of many new asessment measures that are not traditionally taught in graduate courses in assessment. We expect that this trend will continue in the future. For example, Dana (1984) indicated that there is a need for measures of coping behaviors and measures of other emotional resources because of the recent emphasis on the importance of the amelioration of stress effects on people. He asserted that assessment for health psychology is a new national mandate. Dana also suggested the construction of such new measures as one's belief in their personal efficacy, as well as indicators of partial mediators between stress and one's reactions to stress. Therefore, it is important that students begin to search the literature and become familiar with those measures that relate to their treatment and/or research interests with patients.

ASSESSMENT DEVICES FACILITATE RESEARCH

Finally, we note that another important reason to learn personality assessment is for its applications in research. Clinical assessment techniques are often used to test a variety of theories or conceptual relationships. Those psychologists who are intimately familiar with these methods can choose among them to find the most appropriate way to quantify the variables that interest them. Thus, both in clinical application and in research sophistication, in assessment for the patient's treatment, or for agency- or court-based assessment, knowing personality assessment techniques, their application, and their associated reliability and validity allows the researcher to make better choices in the use of instruments to measure various constructs, to measure possible change, or to analyze complex relationships. In these and countless other situations, those who know assessment are at a distinct advantage, compared with those who do not.

REFERENCES

Achenbach, T. M., McConaughy, S. H., & Howell, C. T. (1987). Child/adolescent behavioral and emotional problems: Implications of cross-informant correlations for situational specificity. *Psychological Bulletin, 101*, 213–232.

Applebaum, S. (1990). The relationship between assessment and psychotherapy. *Journal of Personality Assessment, 54*, 79–80.

Archer, R. P. (1992). *MMPI–A: Assessing adolescent psychopathology.* Hillsdale, NJ: Lawrence Erlbaum Associates.

Archer, R. P., & Krishnamurthy, R. (1993a). Combining the Rorschach and the MMPI in the assessment of adolescents. *Journal of Personality Assessment 60,* 132–140.

Archer, R. P., & Krishnamurthy, R. (1993b). A review of MMPI and Rorschach interrelationships in adult samples. *Journal of Personality Assessment, 61,* 277–293.

Barrick, M. R., & Mount, M. K. (1991). The Big Five personality dimensions and job performance: A meta-analysis. *Personnel Psychology, 44,* 1–26.

Beutler, L. E., Engle, D., Mohr, D., Daldrup, R. J., Bergan, J., Meredith, K., & Merry, W. (1991). Predictors of differential response to cognitive, experiential, and self-directed psychotherapeutic procedures. *Journal of Consulting and Clinical Psychology, 59,* 333–340.

Blatt, S. J., & Ford, R. (1994). *Therapeutic change.* New York: Plenum.

Butcher, J. N. (1990). *The MMPI-2 in psychological treatment.* New York: Oxford University Press.

Butcher, J. N., Dahlstrom, W. G., Graham, J. R., Tellegen, A., & Kaemmer, B. (1989). *Manual for the restandardized Minnesota Multiphasic Personality Inventory: MMPI–2. An administrative and interpretive guide.* Minneapolis: University of Minnesota Press.

Campbell, D. T., & Fiske, D. W. (1959). Convergent and discriminant validation by the multitrait-multimethod matrix. *Psychological Bulletin, 56,* 81–105.

Carlsson, A., Nygren, M., Clinton, D., & Bihlar, B. (1996). The Stockholm comparative psychotherapy study (COMPASS): Project presentation and preliminary findings. *Rorschachiana: Yearbook of the International Rorschach Society, 21,* 30–46.

Cartwright, D. S., Kirtner, W. L., & Fiske, D. W. (1963). Method factors in changes associated with psychotherapy. *Journal of Abnormal and Social Psychology, 66,* 164–175.

Church, S., Hilsenroth, M., & Handler, L. (1996, July). *The role of primary process in creativity: A Rorschach analysis of fiction writers, journalists, and technical writers.* Paper presented at the XV International Rorschach Congress, Boston.

Costa, P. T., Jr., & McCrae, R. R. (1992). *Revised NEO Personality Inventory: Professional manual.* Odessa, FL: Psychological Assessment Resources.

Dana, R. (1984). Personality assessment: Practices and teaching for the next decade. *Journal of Personality Assessment, 48*(1), 46–57.

Dawes, R. M., Faust, D., & Meehl, P. E. (1989). Clinical versus actuarial judgment. *Science, 243,* 1668–1674.

Dicken, C. F., & Black, J. D. (1965). Predictive validity of psychometric evaluations of supervisors. *Journal of Applied Psychology, 49,* 34–47.

Dirks, J. F., & Kinsman, R. A. (1981). Clinical prediction of medical rehospitalization: Psychological assessment with the Battery of Asthma Illness Behavior. *Journal of Personality Assessment, 45,* 608–613.

Exner, J. E., Jr. (1993). *The Rorschach: A comprehensive system* (Vol. 1, 3rd ed.). New York: Wiley.

Exner, J. E., Jr., & Andronikof-Sanglade, A. (1992). Rorschach changes following brief and short-term therapy. *Journal of Personality Assessment, 59,* 59–71.

Finn, S. E. (1996a). Assessment feedback integrating MMPI–2 and Rorschach findings. *Journal of Personality Assessment, 67,* 543–557.

Finn, S. E. (1996b). *Manual for using the MMPI–2 as a therapeutic intervention.* Minneapolis: University of Minnesota Press.

Finn, S. E., & Tonsager, M. E. (1992). Therapeutic effects of providing MMPI–2 test feedback to college students awaiting psychotherapy. *Psychological Assessment, 3,* 278–287.

Finn, S. E., & Tonsager, M. E. (in press). *Therapeutic assessment: Using psychological testing to help clients change.*

Fischer, C. T. (1994). *Individualizing psychological assessment.* Hillsdale, NJ: Lawrence Erlbaum Associates.

Fowler, C., Hilsenroth, M., & Handler, L. (1995). Early memories: An exploration of theoretically derived queries and their clinical utility. *Bulletin of the Menninger Clinic, 59,* 79–98.

Fowler, C., Hilsenroth, M., & Handler, L, (1996). A multimethod approach to assessing dependency: The early memory dependency probe. *Journal of Personality Assessment, 67*(2), 399–413.

Fowler, C., Hilsenroth, M., & Handler, L. (1997). *Transitional relatedness, the transitional object memory probe, and psychodynamic psychotherapy.* Manuscript submitted for publication.

Ganellen, R. J. (1994). Attempting to conceal psychological disturbance: MMPI defensive response sets and the Rorschach. *Journal of Personality Assessment, 63,* 423–437.

Garb, H. N. (1984). The incremental validity of information used in personality assessment. *Clinical Psychology Review, 4,* 641–655.

Garb, H. N. (1989). Clinical judgment, clinical training, and professional experience. *Psychological Bulletin, 105,* 387–396.

Garb, H. N., & Schramke, C. J. (1996). Judgment research and neuropsychological assessment: A narrative review and meta-analyses. *Psychological Bulletin, 120,* 140–153.

Greene, R. L. (1991). *The MMPI–2/MMPI: An interpretive manual.* Boston: Allyn & Bacon.

Handler, L. (1997). He says, she says, they say: The Consensus Rorschach in martial therapy. In R. Meloy, M. Acklin, C. Gacono, J. Murray, & C. Peterson (Eds.), *Contemporary Rorschach interpretation.* Hillsdale, NJ: Lawrence Erlbaum Associates.

Handler, L., & Meyer, G. (1996). Put your money where your mouth is: Mary Cerney's Legacy. *SPA Exchange, 6,* 6-7.

Hilsenroth, M., & Handler, L. (1995). A survey of graduate students' experiences, interests, and attitudes about learning the Rorschach. *Journal of Personality Assessment, 64,* 243-257.

Holt, R. R. (1970). Yet another look at clinical and statistical prediction: Or, is clinical psychology worthwhile? *American Psychologist, 25,* 337–349.

Holt, R. R. (1986). Clinical and statistical prediction: A retrospective and would-be integrative perspective. *Journal of Personality Assessment, 50,* 376–386.

Howard, K. I., Kopta, S. M., Krause, M. S., & Orlinsky, D. E. (1986). The dose-effect relationship in psychotherapy. *American Psychologist, 41,* 159–164.

Kadera, S. W., Lambert, M. J., & Andrews, A. A. (1996). How much therapy is really enough? A session-by-session analysis of the psychotherapy dose-effect relationship. *Journal of Psychotherapy Practice and Research, 5,* 132–151.

Kleinmuntz, B. (1990). Why we still use our heads instead of formulas: Toward an integrative approach. *Psychological Bulletin, 107,* 296–310.

Klopfer, B., Ainsworth, M., Klopfer, W., & Holt, R. (1954). *Developments in the Rorschach technique, vol. 1: Technique and theory.* New York: World Book.

Krakowski, A. (1984). Stress and the practice of medicine: III. Physicians compared with lawyers. *Psychotherapy and Psychosomatics, 42,* 143–151.

Lindfors, O. (1996, July). *Rorschach evaluation of psychotherapy outcome: research plan of the Helsinki Psychotherapy Study.* Paper presented at the symposium, Research on the Predictive Value of Personality Assessment to Inform Psychotherapy, at the XV International Congress of Rorschach and Projective Methods, Boston.

Maruish, M. E. (1994). *The use of psychological testing for treatment planning and outcome assessment.* Hillsdale, NJ: Lawrence Erlbaum Associates.

McClelland, D. C., Koestner, R., & Weinberger, J. (1989). How do self-attributed and implicit motives differ? *Psychological Review, 96,* 690–702.

Meyer, G. J. (1996a). Construct validation of scales derived from the Rorschach method: A review of issues and introduction to the Rorschach Rating Scale. *Journal of Personality Assessment, 67,* 598–628.

Meyer, G. J. (1996b). The Rorschach and MMPI: Toward a more scientifically differentiated understanding of cross-method assessment. *Journal of Personality Assessment, 67,* 558–578.

Meyer, G. J. (1997). On the integration of personality assessment methods: The Rorschach and MMPI–2. *Journal of Personality Assessment, 68,* 297–330.

Meyer, G. J., & Handler, L. (1997). The ability of the Rorschach to predict subsequent outcome: A meta-analysis of the Rorschach Prognostic Rating Scale. *Journal of Personality Assessment, 69,* 1–38.

Miller, S. B. (1987). A comparison of methods of inquiry: Testing and interview contributions to the diagnostic process. *Bulletin of the Menninger Clinic, 51,* 505–518.

Millon, T. (1991). *Millon Clinical Multiaxial Inventory–III manual.* Minneapolis: National Computer Systems.

Morey, L. C. (1991). *Personality Assessment Inventory professional manual.* Odessa, FL: Psychological Assessment Resources.

Mortimer, R. L., & Smith, W. H. (1983). The use of the psychological test report in setting the focus of psychotherapy. *Journal of Personality Assessment, 47,* 134–138.

Muhlenkamp, A., & Parsons, J. (1972). An overview of recent research publications in a nursing research periodical. *Journal of Vocational Behavior, 2*(3), 261–273.

Newman, F. (1991, Summer). Using assessment data to relate patient progress to reimbursement criteria. *Assessment Applications*, 4–5.

Payne, M., & Sabaroche, H. (1985). Personality type and occupational preference: Testing Holland's theory in the Carribean. *Internatioinal Journal for the Advancement of Counselling*, 8(2),147–156.

Perry, J. C. (1992). Problems and considerations in the valid assessment of personality disorders. *American Journal of Psychiatry*, 149, 1645–1653.

Rapaport, D., Gill, M. M., & Schafer, R. (1968). *Diagnostic psychological testing* (Rev. Ed.). New York: International Universities Press.

Rassenfosse, M. (1975). Determinants of the choice of professions: Clinical and projective data on pharmacy students. *Bulletin de Psychologie Scolaire et d'Orientation*, 24(3), 133–155.

Rezler, A., & Buckley, J. (1977). A comparison of personality types among female student health professionals. *Journal of Medical Education*, 52(6), 475–477.

Riethmiller, R., & Handler, L. (in press a). Problematic methods and unwarranted conclusions in DAP research: Suggestions for improved procedures. *Journal of Personality Assessment*.

Riethmiller, R., & Handler, L. (in press b). The great figure drawing controversy: The interaction of research and clinical practice. *Journal of Personality Assessment*.

Robertson, I. T., & Kinder, A. (1993). Personality and job competencies: The criterion-related validity of some personality variables. *Journal of Occupational and Organizational Psychology*, 66, 225–244.

Schafer, R. (1954). *Psychoanalytic interpretation in Rorschach testing: Theory and application*. New York: Grune & Stratton.

Seligman, M. E. (1995). The effectiveness of psychotherapy: The *Consumer Reports* study. *American Psychologist*, 50, 965–974.

Shedler, J., Mayman, M., & Manis, M. (1993). The *illusion* of mental health. *American Psychologist*, 48, 1117–1131.

Singer, M. (1977). The Rorschach as a transition. In M. Rickers-Ovsiankina (Ed.), *Rorschach psychology* (pp. 455–488). Huntington, NY: Krieger.

Tett, R. P., Jackson, D. N., & Rothstein, M. (1991). Personality measures as predictors of job performance: A meta-analytic review. *Personnel Psychology*, 44, 703–742.

Toman, K., & Padawer, J. (1995, March). *Use of the Rorschach and MMPI–2 in the assessment of change during psychotherapy*. Paper presented at the midwinter meeting of the Society for Personality Assessment, Atlanta.

Urist, J. (1977). The Rorschach test and the assessment of object relations. *Journal of Personality Assessment*, 41, 3-9.

Wechsler, D. (1981). *WAIS-R manual: Wechsler Adult Intelligence Scale–Revised*. San Antonio, TX: Psychological Corporation.

Weiner, I. B., & Exner, J. E., Jr. (1991). Rorschach changes in long-term and short-term psychotherapy. *Journal of Personality Assessment*, 56, 453–465.

Westen, D. (1991a). Clinical assessment of object relations using the TAT. *Journal of Personality Assessment*, 56, 56-74.

Westen, D. (1991b). Social cognition and object relations. *Psychological Bulletin*, 109, 429–455.

Zimmerman, M. (1994). Diagnosing personality disorders: A review of issues and research methods. *Archives of General Psychiatry*, 51, 225–245.

2

The Trouble With Learning Personality Assessment

J. Christopher Fowler
The Erik H. Erikson Institute of the Austen Riggs Center

This chapter focuses on the largely unspoken, often minimized aspects of the student's difficulties in learning assessment skills that lie beyond the normal concerns of proper scoring and administration of tests. It has been my experience that learning personality assessment, is quite similar, in many ways, to the tasks of learning to be a psychotherapist. In both endeavors there are complex psychic and interpersonal processes, like projection and projective identification, that must be slowly disentangled from subjective experience so that the student can gain a sense of what conflicts belong to the patient and what belongs to the student as therapist or as psychological examiner. Furthermore, students' intrapsychic wishes, fears, and defenses against the task can further inhibit the full articulation of interpretive skills. These processes must be brought into conscious awareness for the student to gain confidence and clarity of thought as he or she moves through the assessment courses.

It is my contention that for students to use the formal aspects of testing, to use their intuitions, affective, and cognitive capacities to the fullest, personal defenses and resistances must be recognized, confronted, and worked through. Just as student therapists are encouraged to undergo psychotherapy in order to aid in their development as therapists, students may need help getting beyond personal biases and fears to be free to use their total psyche in the inference-making process. This process of working through resistances may be the most challenging aspect of learning and teaching assessment skills. Therefore, this chapter explores some of the conflicts in learning assessment—from a student's perspective.

THE CONTEXT

In our painfully introspective profession of clinical psychology, there has developed a tradition of self-analysis that has brought the objective observer much closer to the phenomena under investigation. From Freud's letter to his friend Wilhelm Fliess (1954), to Roy Schafer's (1967) in-depth exploration of countertransference in the psychological testing process, theory and practice have been enriched by this method. Unfortunately, the intensity of such introspection has been distorted and elevated to new and nagging heights of self-doubt with the shift to a postmodern scientific view. Psychologists and physicists alike doubt "objective" scientific practice and seem to struggle with deconstructionist theories that cast doubt on all of science (Capra, 1981). The fallout from such a shift seemed to be a growing sense of futility about actually knowing anything because every observable phenomenon suddenly seemed to be tainted by "intersubjective noise." The students I trained with were embedded in this evolving scientific culture so that we could no longer assume that the Rorschach was as objective as an X ray. Nor could we take comfort in the idea that we were "only trying to help." Even the comfort and security of being an "empathic healer" could not be taken for granted. Therefore, we were often faced with complex questions that precluded a relaxed entrance into the testing process: Are these the patient's conflicts, or are they mine? Am I helping these patients by understanding and naming their mental processes, or am I reducing their uniqueness to a label? Am I simply calling these patients dirty names so I can feel better about my own sanity? The broader context of the postmodern scientific influence was, for some students, the least pressing and tangible area of conflict; but it certainly was not the least significant factor in how students developed resistances to the task of personality assessment. Objectivity in psychology had, by then, been banished, among my peers, as an antiquated and naive notion. And so my colleagues and I faced the slippery slope of "intersubjectivity" as an obstacle to ever really knowing the "truth" about a patient from their projective data. This ideological position made it difficult to be confident in one's interpretations, and posed a serious dilemma regarding how to guard against the projection of the examiner's unconscious processes on the hapless patient. I believe this uncertainty made for greater anxiety, while also creating a defense against dealing with other anxieties about testing and becoming experts.

A second major influence on learning and the fear of learning was the fact that students began the advanced course in psychological assessment in the second year of training, which coincided with the assignment of our first clinical patients. Both events stirred great excitement and trepidation because we came face to face with the complex and disturbing interaction with people whose forceful personalities and psychotic disturbances often pushed us all closer to the edges of our defenses. The palpable human pain and suffering, extremes of love and hate, and blurred boundaries between patients and students were only a few of the horrors that touched student therapists. With this whirl of confusion

and fear, many students, including myself, welcomed the sanctuary that personality assessment seemed to offer. I figured that the silent pages of data were an
escape from the tensions I felt with patients.

And yet personality assessment proved to be anything but an escape. I came
to see that the process of learning to fully use projective tests to assess
personality structure, character defenses, and fantastical ideational content was
inherently anxiety provoking. The data themselves disturbed my sense of the
world. Percepts of mutilated part objects and bizarre combinations of human
and animal percepts provoked both curiosity and repulsion. I became even more
anxious when a patient produced a response similar to the one I had given to a
card. I was convinced I had some deep psychotic disturbance lurking beneath
the surface of my rational exterior. These are but a few recollections of what it
was like to delve into projective data for the first time. And yet, the persistent
impact of knowing that *we, the students, were ultimately responsible* for interpreting, naming, diagnosing, and then writing about the patient proved to be the
most threatening factor of all.

The fact that we were ultimately responsible for the interpretations of test data
made the task of learning personality assessment unique among my experiences in
graduate school. In my role as "student therapist" I was free to be confused, to be
swept up in the stream of intersubjectivity, and to ask questions of the patient. In
fact, this level of ignorance was often an explicit expectation of my work as a student
therapist. Supervisors repeatedly reassured me that my job was to "Learn how to
listen to the patient". As "student examiner," by contrast, I was in the white-knuck-
led position of being the expert, the one who knows. Unlike my psychotherapy
experience, I could not go back to the patient and ask him or her what he or she
meant. With this realization, the anticipated comfort of the silent pages of data
turned into a disquieting pressure to produce the "right" answers. For the first time
in my fledgling career I was expected to draw inferences from the raw data that lay
dormant on the page.

A third aspect of context was my place in a department of psychology. During
the first years of graduate studies, I found myself face to face with many aspects
of my personality. Simple interactions like lunch breaks and parties were highly
anxious events because we were all practicing our new skills with one another.
The idea of a "psychic nudist colony" often seemed an apt metaphor for my life
during the first years of graduate training. This element of paranoia naturally
found its way into the testing seminars. What would frequent interpretations
of sexual perversion or dysfunction communicate about the speaker? What
about sadism? What about narcissism? What dark secrets might we inadvertently reveal about ourselves? It is something of a miracle that any of us found
a way to speak in the assessment seminar.

CORE CONFLICTS IN ASSESSMENT

Context shifts over time, and not all graduate training programs have the same
atmosphere. So what might be said about common concerns and fears among

graduate students facing an assessment course? As I see it, students face four common areas of difficulty that require special attention. Each of these areas of difficulty stems from the student's acclimation to a new role and from personal wishes and fears that then interfere with learning through defensive withdrawal and intellectual resistances to the task: (a) the wish and fear of the expert voice, (b) balancing morbid vs. Pollyanish interpretations, (c) using oneself as an instrument of assessment, and (d) integration and communication.

As a student I learned that a careful exploration and confrontation of these fears, in the context of the assessment seminar, was the most productive way of grappling with my resistances and moving beyond them. My hope is that highlighting this experience will offer assessment instructors a perspective on the complexities and vicissitudes that students live through on their way to becoming competent psychological examiners.

THE WISH AND FEAR OF THE EXPERT VOICE

More clearly than at any other time in a student's early career, the advanced testing seminar is the opportunity for students to take up the role of an expert. When the time comes for a thorough inspection of the Rorschach, for example, students are faced with the opportunity to find their voice by making interpretations and inferences. I will focus solely on the problems of committing oneself to the inference or interpretation.

My colleagues and I were faced with the burden of speaking with authority and conviction about another human's pathology. Self-doubt, anxiety, fear, and misguided optimism are but a few defenses that cropped up during our personality assessment seminar. The fear of taking up the voice of an expert was rife with personal meanings, but fears common to most of my colleagues were constantly being expressed. One path of resistance was a staunch resistance to committing to anything beyond a superficial and vague Barnum statement. Initial interpretations, for example, often sounded like the following: "This person becomes anxious when under stress," or "This person gets overwhelmed by strong emotions." The problem with both statements is that they may be true for any human under normal life circumstances. But we all knew that. The problem was that we feared being wrong, and we feared being right. To make an incorrect interpretation was to leave oneself open to public humiliation, to belie unconscious wishes and interests, and (probably the least worrisome) to receive a negative evaluation from the instructor. To accurately assess the underlying conflict, core dynamic, or object relationship was far worse. It meant to brand the patient as sick, mentally ill, or depraved. This created great conflicts in the majority of students, leading many to condemn the entire testing process as repugnant and discriminatory. In the current "politically correct" culture, such a complaint can hardly go unanswered. To ignore or minimize the complaint would only add fuel to the fires of righteous indignation, but to agree with the condemnation would be equally disastrous. The instructor helped the students grapple with this problem by asking if it seemed justifiable to ignore a broken leg or a cancerous biopsy. When all agreed such a practice would be negligent, he then wondered what made this process so different than that of a pathologist. I am sure students had a variety of reactions to this, but my own was to take testing and assessment much more seriously and proudly than before. By comparing the work of psychodiagnostics with that of a medical pathologist, the instructor communicated one vital role we could play in assessment and treatment.

Freud taught us that resistances are overdetermined, and despite being bright, insightful students, we were no exception. The Barnum statements persisted and so the instructor employed the Socratic/dialectic method of questioning, drawing us into the process of elaborating on the original statement. For example, a student read aloud a response to Card IV of the Rorschach, "This is a monster ... little head, big arms with claws and beady eyes. It's looking down at you ... it's real tall and it's smiling." The Inquiry exposed a duplicity in the representation of this monster in that the patient attributes a "mean face" to the smiling monster. One student offered that this patient was afraid of people because the patient experiences others as malevolent. Although this interpretation may be accurate, it does little to bring to life this patient's experience. The instructor would use this interpretation as a point of departure by asking any student to elaborate further. He asked specific questions such as: How do you make sense out of the smiling yet mean face? Why claws instead of hands? What do you make of the perspective taking of "looking down on you"?

Students were thus pushed to take up the voice of the expert by the instructor's implicit communication that students did know how to think critically and analytically. Paradoxically, the instructor reminded us that these were hypotheses to entertain, to play with, and to discard if disconfirming evidence overwhelmed the original hypothesis. Thus, we were being placed in the role of an expert, we were expected to take up a voice, and we were supported in this venture. At the time, this dialectic "game" allowed some students the freedom to play at being an "expert" while maintaining their more secure role as students.

For some this was enough to dispel their fears, but for others it only heightened anxieties. Several students protested that the instructor and some seminar members were "overpathologizing" the patient. In response, the instructor supported their concern about pathologizing and pointed out that strengths need to be assessed with as much gusto as ego weakness. Then he added, "But when has denial of real disturbance ever helped anyone? These are people who come to the clinic for help with their disturbances, and we are not doing them any favors by pretending it's not present, are we?"

In addition to offering students room to play with responses, and directly confronting denial, the instructor had several programmatic features that helped students manage insecurities about interpretations. First, each fully elaborated interpretation was placed into categories such as object relations, affect, cognition, and defense. At the end of the seminar, the interpretations were assessed for cohesiveness and clarity. If some interpretations were far outside the range of expectable variance with the core of interpretations, an effort was made to integrate them. If integration was improbable, the interpretation was reviewed further and discarded when it was at indisputable odds with the gestalt of the profile.

Although the resistance against taking up the expert voice persisted for some, there were times when even the most secure students needed some intervention to help them accurately articulate their interpretations. And whereas many students found comfort in the seminar, their fears of the expert voice returned when it came time to commit these interpretations to paper. Before the problem of report writing was faced, we had plenty of other problems with which to contend.

BALANCING MORBID VERSUS POLLYANISH INTERPRETATIONS

Paradoxically, the fear of being an expert can be joined by the thrill of voyeurism and fantasies of omniscience. For some new students like myself, this mitigated (and sometimes obliterated) any fear of saying the wrong thing. Instead of constriction and uncertainty, I (and other overzealous students) moved quickly to develop statements about the psychological makeup of the patient. These statements gravitated toward the morbid and pathologizing rather than the Pollyanish. Myself and a few of my colleagues implicitly lived by the motto "cancer lurks deep in the sweetest bud." Thus, any time there was disconfirming evidence, it was either ignored or minimized in favor of the deepest level of disturbance. This problem was dealt with by the instructor and the seminar participants in a direct confrontation of the dubious interpretations. This repeated pressure from peers and instructor helped mitigate wild analysis of the data.

On the other end of the continuum were students who had great difficulty in allowing patients to be disturbed. These students held to a Pollyanish view of psychopathology, often refusing to acknowledge the most blatant forms of thought disorder. Their keen minds and intellectual defenses found ways of discovering strength and health in some of the most disturbed responses. I was often confused by the discrepancy between the morbid and Pollyanish interpretations, especially because we were all analyzing the same data.

The obvious problem with both approaches is that a dialectic between the search for strengths and weaknesses must be part of every examiner's repertoire. Thus, most students needed some help in managing these tensions. Surprisingly, the open debates in and out of the seminar were probably most helpful in teaching this dialectic process. By modeling the thought process of interpretation itself, the instructor helped highlight the need for assessing both the strengths and the weaknesses of each patient.

At times the various types of resistances against taking up the expert voice were coupled with anxieties and a Pollyanish attitude. Faced with such strong resistances, the instructor was pressed to work more directly with the students to resolve the conflicts. In such instances the instructor worked to identify the resistance and to speak with the students using their language, frequently joining their accurate perceptions of the difficulty. In one case a bright, skeptical student couched the dilemma in a medical metaphor. The instructor took up this challenge, acknowledged the doubt, then offered a partial solution. Hearing the desire for more definitive evidence, the instructor said, "I'm going to give you a prescription for your legitimate concerns ..." The instructor then offered a prescription of two chapters from Piotrowski, and a healthy dose of empirical research in projective assessment.

These efforts to work with students' resistances are reminiscent of interventions in psychotherapy. When the task is to recruit students to use not only their intellect, but also their intuitions, hunches, and emotional reactions in the inference making process, it is essential that their fears and resistances be addressed.

USING ONESELF AS AN INSTRUMENT OF ASSESSMENT

The use of one's "intuitions" affective experience, and countertransference reactions has been of interest to test theorists and assessment experts for some time (Berg, 1984; Lerner, 1991; Schafer, 1967; Schlesinger, 1973; Sugarman, 1981, 1991). Yet this integral aspect of personality assessment has been overlooked or devalued by those who wish to transform psychological assessment into a "pure science." Although the debate between ideographic and nomothetic approaches continues to be fought in the journals (Acklin, 1995; Aronow, Reznikoff, & Moreland, 1995; Ritzler, 1995), it appears that students of personality assessment are learning to utilize nomothetic and atheoretical approaches as well as interpreting content (Hilsenroth & Handler, 1995).

Regardless of theoretical orientations, it appears that psychological examiners use their understandings of psychological development, models of psychopathology, and personality theories to synthesize an understanding of psychological test data. This means that each examiner brings to the interpretive process an internal working model of personality theory that is likely to be an amalgam of experience, theory, and personal biases. This, in turn, implies that the examiner will draw on both implicit and explicit knowledge of the way people work. It also means that personal preferences for certain theories may dominate an examiner's thinking and thus skew the interpretations toward a particular theoretical framework.

This process is considered objectionable to some who wish psychological testing to be a "hard science," atheoretical, and objective. Such a wish further divorces personality assessment from its partner, clinical psychology and psychotherapy. A pragmatic approach to this issue has been resolved in clinical practice when psychoanalytically oriented clinicians consult psychoanalytically minded examiners to test their patients. Thus, it seems reasonable to assume that students in graduate psychology programs should be encouraged to hone their interpretive skills through their particular theoretical positions.

Such was the case in my graduate training program. We were taught to think of the projective protocol as a representation of the patient's psyche. We were encouraged to integrate our understanding of the patient into psychoanalytic theories that could best capture the core conflicts, object representations, and defenses of the patient. And we were encouraged to use analytic concepts to aid in the task of interpreting. The purpose of blending theory with projectives was ultimately to construct a unifying set of principles that pulled together desperate, often contradictory states within the patient. Although this was a complex and daunting task, it nevertheless allowed for more sophisticated and systematic integration of test findings that frequently clarified the gestalt of the dynamic personality structure. The greatest difficulty facing the students was the fact that most of us were just developing our theoretical perspectives. I, for example, often vacillated between Kernberg and Kohut, and between Winnicott and Klein when it came to a particular protocol. As a result, I sometimes had the sense that I was forcing patients into certain theoretical molds that were most dominant in my thinking at the time. This gave me reason to feel unsure of myself, and somewhat guilty for having finally "pigeon-holed" a patient.

The second major obstacle to overcome in using oneself as an instrument of assessment is doubt about one's affective perceptiveness. Our instructor encouraged the use of students' perspective taking, empathic attunement to the response, and the use of "losing distance with the response." He explained by using the concept of *regression in the service of the ego*. As a way of introducing the method, the instructor assigned journal articles to read, and we discussed vignettes from his clinical practice. He also demonstrated this experiential method of interpretation using TAT, Rorschach, and Human Figure Drawings. He then encouraged us to play with this process.

With few exceptions, I observed in myself and my colleagues a willingness to be open to a certain level of regression. There was, however, resistance to committing to deeper interpretations. It was my impression, after speaking with some students, that the major difficulty was in formulating a verbal statement that could represent the experience. The crucial process that needed nurturing was the sharpening of the products of the regression into meaningful, usable interpretations. With persistent demands for greater specificity and clarification, the interpretations eventually developed into complex, multilayered inferences that often found support in the structural analyses of determinants.

It is important to mention here that the use of "regression" is but one method for harnessing students' intuitive and associative strengths. The use of such techniques, however, raises the issue of objectivity and the contamination of interpretations with the examiner's personal dynamics. It is my belief that a conscious effort to use such methods, while checking and balancing these interpretations against empirically driven findings, is actually a safeguard against the inevitable inclusion of personal preferences and biases. It has been my experience that this level of honesty with oneself and one's technique can have the opposite effect that the purists frequently warn against.

INTEGRATION AND COMMUNICATION

Once the inference-generating process is complete, there is one final task—the crafting of a psychological test report. This task is, in some regards, made easier because the student is in a position of recognizing typical reactions and anxieties. Nevertheless, report writing introduces two novel and formidable challenges: the fear of final and irreversible commitment, and the difficulty of integrating communications in isolation.

No matter how confident and conflict-free I felt during the initial phases of testing, the writing phase brought forth a redoubling of the anxieties and defenses that had plagued me during the seminars. I think the major struggle was committing my interpretations to paper. Although I knew I could delete anything from the page, the finality of this act was intense. Statements made in the seminar were dynamic in that they were spoken, considered, sometimes written down, and then considered as hypotheses. The written report, by contrast, was a movement away from the educated guess to a declaration about the patient. I believe that declaring and committing the words to paper (both acts that cannot be withdrawn) made writing extremely difficult because the act forced students to take up the voice of the expert.

In addition to commitment, the problem of integrating a well-articulated view of the patient was perhaps the most difficult aspect of writing. My hypothesis is that writing is complicated because the instructor and seminar participants are not present and cannot provide the intellectual structure and organizing function to the writer. Perhaps as a result of the felt need for external organization, some instructors offer structured formats and content areas for test reports. In contrast, others have argued that any imposed formalized structure limits the writer and forces unnatural distinctions among cognition, affect, and the like. Although both approaches seem to offer valid and useful ways of going about the task, it is my contention that students need an external structure to help organize the inferences, as well as to help titrate anxieties. I am sure that an externally imposed structure may frustrate some students who feel capable of crafting a report alone. However, several fundamental qualities of a structured report may be helpful to students early on in their career.

First of all, students in advanced courses benefit from having an instructor present during interpretation and inference-generating sessions. The instructor serves an organizing function by providing a clear framework for moving from surface-level interpretations to integrating interpretations that combine affects, conflicts, object relationships, and transference paradigms. This capacity for integration has its foundation in an internalized working theory of how psychic phenomena are mutually interrelated and influential. Students, unless they are remarkably precocious, do not possess such a framework and thus benefit from the instructor's thinking aloud in the seminars. By contrast, the student left alone to write a report suddenly faces the task without the benefit of the organizing functions created by the instructor. It was a common experience to sit down at the keyboard and find myself much duller and more confused about the patient than when I was surrounded by my peers and the instructor. In retrospect, I believe my confusion was attributable to my loss of the group consensus, the flow of ideas, and the organizing function of the instructor.

Clearly, the report writing could not be done "en masse" and so I relied on the report format offered by our instructor to help organize my thinking until I had enough experience and understanding of theory to replace the formal structures with my newly internalized structure.

At first, I found the use of a report structure, such as Lerner's (1991) outline, quite helpful in getting me started. The framework of a relatively flexible outline allowed some personal choice in placing greater or lesser emphasis on key areas of psychic functioning: At the same time it provided structure through prompts to include major areas of psychic functioning. This outline, truth be known, often functioned as a bridge between the empty page of the report and the mass of data in my head.

Of course, the structure offered by specific formatted reports does have drawbacks. For example, I found myself struggling against the temptation to produce "cookie cutter" reports that simply inserted separate statements about a patient without integrating them into a complex personality structure. In this sense, the structured format was a tempting tool for avoiding the complexities of the human mind.

And yet this difficulty was short-lived. After a few years of report writing, I found my skills much sharper and my foundation in psychological theory better consolidated. With that, anxieties of commitment diminished. Consequently, my need for a structured format diminished as well. Thus, the use of a structured format may be quite helpful for students first learning to write test reports; but, as the student's skill and confidence improve, the student can choose to modify the format. Given the intense anxieties, the students' resistances, and the complexity of the task, it makes sense to offer students a modicum of support in their first solo projects.

CONCLUDING REMARKS

I hope this retrospective review of the difficulties in learning psychological assessment will help broaden understanding of the multitude of complexities facing students and instructors. The forces of resistance and defense work against the learning process in personality assessment by inhibiting the full use of the student's intellectual, intuitive, and personal capacities. Because learning personality assessment shares many features with the learning process involved in conducting psychotherapy, it makes sense to attend to the student's fears and resistances to learning much in the same way psychotherapy supervisors help student therapists wrestle with anxieties and personal resistances in treating patients. In this way, the instructor and assessment supervisor may wish to act as a consultant who develops a contractual agreement with the student to help with personal resistances and defenses. Thus, the student may benefit far more from this approach than from a traditional assessment course that only empha-sizes accurate administration, scoring, and interpretation of test data.

REFERENCES

Acklin, M. W. (1995). Avoiding Rorschach dichotomies: Integrating Rorschach interpretation. *Journal of Personality Assessment, 64*(2), 235-238.

Aronow, E., Reznikoff, M., & Moreland, K. L. (1995). Projective technique or psychometric test? *Journal of Personality Assessment, 64*(2), 213-228.

Berg, M. (1984). Expanding the parameters of psychological testing. *Bulletin of the Menninger Clinic, 48*(1), 10-24.

Capra, F. (1981). *The turning point: Science, society, and the rising culture.* New York: Bantam.

Freud, S. (1954). *The origins of psychoanalysis: Letters to Wilhelm Fliess. Drafts and Notes: 1887–1902.* New York: Basic Books.

Hilsenroth, M. J., & Handler, L. (1995). A survey of graduate students' experiences, interest and attitudes about learning the Rorschach. *Journal of Personality Assessment, 64*(2), 243-257.

Lerner, P. M. (1991) *Psychoanalytic theory and the Rorschach.* Hillsdale, NJ: The Analytic Press.

Ritzler, B. (1995). A response to Aronow, Reznikoff, and Moreland. *Journal of Personality Assessment, 64*(2), 229-234.

Schafer, R. (1967). *Projective testing and psychoanalysis.* New York: International Universities Press.

Schlesinger, H. J. (1973). Interaction of dynamic and reality factors in the diagnostic testing interview. *Bulletin of the Menninger Clinic, 37,* 497-517.

Sugarman, A. (1981). The diagnostic use of countertransference reactions in psychological testing. *Bulletin of the Menninger Clinic, 45*(6), 473-490.

Sugarman, A. (1991). Where's the beef? Putting personality back into personality assessment. *Journal of Personality Assessment, 56*(1), 130-144.

II

CONCEPTUAL MODELS FOR INTERPRETATION

In Part II, Conceptual Models for Interpretation, the focus is on the description of various conceptual models and information concerning the use of these theories to integrate data. Howard D. Lerner's chapter, "The Experiential Basis of Psychological Testing" discusses the use of a conceptual approach to psychological testing, in this case an experientially based psychoanalytic approach. In a quite moving and highly personal manner, Lerner discusses the experiences that were most important to him in learning personality assessment: his own psychoanalysis, excellent supervision, and the identification of certain ideals, attitudes, and personal qualities of his teachers.

Lerner discusses the relationship between theory and testing, emphasizing higher-order constructs such as defenses, object relations, various modes of object representation, and so on. He compares the experience-near psychoanalytic approach to test administration and interpretation to an approach that is based on a more psychometric emphasis on test administration and interpretation. He lists a number of recommendations for communicating important theoretical concepts to students.

Phillip Erdberg's, chapter, "Helping Students Integrate Rorschach Structure and Psychological Theory" involves the use of theory in the interpretation of Rorschach data in order to generate more extensive descriptions of psychological functioning. The chapter discusses the intermediate level of teaching, with special reference to the Rorschach and psychoanalytic theory.

Erdberg discusses the conflicts students face between an atheoretical-empirical stance and one that is based on a particular theory of personality. However, the issues discussed in this chapter are applicable to other assessment techniques as well.

Erdberg points out the distance between the theoretician and the empiricist. He believes that those who value structural approaches have not attempted to test theories, and those who value the theoretical approach have not devoted themselves to understanding empirical findings. Erdberg indicates that students seem to take one extreme position or the other. Instead, he searches for a meaningful integration of the two approaches. Erdberg demonstrates how the use of theory allows the clinician to predict and then test this prediction, searching for the predicted findings in test data, as well as in real-world behavior.

In the chapter titled "The Impossible Takes a Little Longer: The Role of Theory in Teaching Psychological Assessment," Bruce L. Smith, argues that learning assessment should be approached only within a comprehensive theory of personality. Smith emphasizes a person-centered rather than a test-centered approach, the former interpreting test data as communications, rather than as signs of various personality problems. Smith describes various aspects of psychoanalytic theory to help the reader integrate cognitive and personality issues, such as a person-centered approach to intelligence testing. The nature of the theory used, Smith tells us, greatly affects the way in which test data are understood. He points out that there are sound theoretical reasons for the inclusion of various scores in the Structural Summary. He adds that psychoanalytic theory permits a hierarchical approach to interpretation, allowing the assessor to understand how concepts and data are interpreted at different levels, also allowing the assessor to know "what is a consequence of what".

Charles A. Waehler and Harry J. Sivec, in a chapter titled "Critical Thinking Applications in Personality Assessment: Classrooms as Laboratories and Studios," describe techniques pioneered by educators to help instructors find innovative ways to teach critical-thinking skills (defined as the ability to process information systematically and creatively), as they apply to personality assessment. The techniques they discuss come from laboratory research as well as from artistic sources. The authors describe a number of concepts derived from the work of Vygotsky, as well as a number of additional strategies for the development of critical reasoning about personality assessment data. The result, the authors emphasize, is a reduction in common judgment errors, as well as the production of a more meaningful integration of the data.

3

The Experiential Basis of Psychological Testing

Howard D. Lerner
*Department of Psychiatry, University of Michigan
and Michigan Analytic Institute*

The rapid growth of computerized test scores and test reports has contributed to an undesirable trend in assessment today toward an approach to diagnosis and treatment based on third-party reimbursement policies, and magical views of treatment that create a delusion that complex, multifaceted human beings can be changed over the course of 10 sessions or less. Within this context, the role of the diagnostician–clinician has been relegated to a "white coat technician"; test interpretations are made by computer programs, and assessment approaches are not geared toward "assessing those difficulties ... and capacities of the person which are most directly relevant to the way that person can use a helping relationship" (Shectman & Harty, 1986, p. 281). Instead, they are geared toward a quantitative gathering of test scores on a spreadsheet, with a view toward generating a computer test report and then making way for the next patient. One consequence of this approach is that clinical decisions about patients are made with an insufficient assessment of their psychological status because of overly rigid, textbook test administrative practices, poor training, and inadequate supervision. Understanding the subject empathically—the purpose of assessment—has given way to a relentless quest for "reliable test scores," swiftness, and cost containment at the risk of losing sight of the subject as a whole person.

In a previous report based on a blind clinical analysis of two test–retest protocols drawn from the Austen Riggs Psychotherapy Outcome Project, H. Lerner (1988) demonstrated that although two patients gained from treatment as shown by changes in test performance, their changes were in opposite directions; for quantitative research purposes, they essentially canceled each other out. A flamboyant, disinhibited schizophrenic young man became more organized and contained, whereas a withdrawn adolescent girl loosened up considerably. Such research indicates only one of the perils of adhering too rigidly to a quantitative analysis of complex psychological material.

Psychological testing offers a unique window into the communication and interactional process. The testing situation itself has been conceptualized as a container for the subject's pathological contents, defensive processes, and interpersonal transactions. The test situation offers a context analogous to that of psychoanalytic therapy in terms of providing an array of experiences along structured and ambiguous dimensions within a defined framework. It invites and systematically investigates the expression of a wide range of conscious and unconscious material, which provides a unique medium for the emergence of transference and countertransference phenomena, the database of psychoanalytic psychotherapy.

As Freud once was overheard remarking about experimental psychologists and others who put so-called scientific purity above clinical understanding, "they're so busy polishing their glasses, they never look through them" (Martin Maxman, personal communication). The purpose of this chapter is to put on the glasses and to look carefully at how we understand, administer, and utilize psychological tests, and to pose questions about what constitutes test data and exactly what is the role of the examiner. First, an empirical versus a conceptual approach to psychological testing is reviewed. This is followed by an examination of the relationship between theory and assessment. Third, the groundwork for an experiential approach to assessment is outlined. Fourth, a psychoanalytic experiential approach to assessment is proposed and a clinical illustration offered. The chapter concludes with some recommendations for training, clinical practice, and report writing.

THE CONCEPTUAL APPROACH
TO PSYCHOLOGICAL TESTING

Although speaking from the purview of projective tests in general and the Rorschach in particular, P. Lerner (1991) called attention to two streams of thought that have contributed significantly to a renewal of interest in the Rorschach as a means of studying and understanding people. These streams of thoughts are also applicable to psychological testing in general. An empirical approach is exemplified by the work of Exner (1974), which emphasized standardized test administration, careful scoring, and a reliance on quantitative scores, normative data, and traditional psychometric values of reliability, validity, and a view of the examiner as a source of error variance. A conceptual approach, on the other hand, is exemplified in recent attempts to apply psychoanalytic theory to psychological test interpretation. The two approaches to psychological testing differ along a number of dimensions, including the significance given to quantification, the role and value accorded the person of the examiner, data that are accepted as viable sources of information about the subject, approaches to validity, and most important, the role accorded to a theory of personality that rests outside of the tests themselves.

THE RELATIONSHIP BETWEEN THEORY
AND TESTING

Within a conceptual approach, psychological tests are wedded to a theory of personality, a theory that is outside of and independent of the instruments themselves. The theory serves various functions, several of which were outlined by Sugarman (1985). First, a theory of personality provides an organizing function. It allows the examiner to comprehend and systematically organize phenomena that are exceedingly rich, highly complex, and often inconsistent. Second, the theory calls for and directs the integration of seemingly unrelated pieces of data. Third, a theory of personality can provide a guiding function. For the clinician, the theory serves to fill in data gaps in an informed way. Finally, a theory of personality facilitates clinical prediction. Here, Sugarman reminded us the prediction can be successful only insofar "as the behavior being questioned is mediated by the personality variables tapped by the testing" (p. 134).

The current trend within the conceptual approach, as P. Lerner and H. Lerner (1985) noted, "is to reduce the welter of isolated but overlapping variables and ratios based on traditional scoring categories into what Blatt and Berman (1984) term molar variables that integrate various ... scores in a way that is psychometrically reliable and that measures central dimensions of personality" (p. 529). According to Blatt and Berman(1984), the molar or composite variables (e.g., object representation, modes of object relations, boundary representations, defenses, etc.) are not replacements for traditional scoring categories or scores, but rather, are higher-order conceptual constructs that provide a systematic framework for organizing data.

Now in this light, it is important to realize that psychoanalysis has never been a static body of knowledge. It is not one closed, tightly knit, totally coherent theory of personality. Rather, it is a loose-fitting composite of several complementary, internally consistent submodels, each of which furnishes concepts and formulations for observing and understanding a crucial dimension of personality development and functioning. Submodels that have been identified include drive theory (Freud, 1915), structural theory (Freud, 1923), and more recently, object relations theory (see Blatt & H. Lerner, 1991), self psychology (Kohut, 1977), and developmental theory (Pine, 1985).

Apart from the functions provided by a theory of personality, P. Lerner (1991) noted that it is important to look at the nature of the integration of theory and testing. Each submodel includes an array of concepts that can be placed on a continuum, based on their relative closeness or nearness to the object's experience. In general, concepts emerging from drive theory and structural theory such as impulse, apparatuses of primary autonomy, and ego states, are couched in a language that is more abstract and impersonal than concepts based on object relations theory and self psychology. Winnicott's evocative concepts such as "false self" and "good enough mothering" and Kohut's descriptive notion of "self objects" illustrate the "experience-near" quality of concepts issuing from these more recent models.

An experience-near perspective on psychological testing is the result of recent developments within psychoanalytic theory. These recent developments are an integral part of an attempt to extend the experience-distant metapsychology, which utilizes concepts of structures, forces, and energies to describe the functioning of the mind—concepts based primarily on a model related to the natural sciences— to a more experience-near clinical theory (Klein, 1976). This clinical theory is primarily concerned with concepts of the self and others in a representational world (Jacobson, 1964; Sandler & Rosenblatt, 1962), seen as a central psychological process within a model based primarily on hermeneutics (Home, 1966; Steele, 1979), which emphasizes meaning and interpretation rather than forces and counterforces. Within contemporary psychoanalysis, there have been attempts to extend theory beyond an exclusive focus on ego structures, such as impulse-defense configurations and cognitive styles, to include a fuller consideration of the experiences of an individual in an interpersonal matrix, as expressed in representations of the self and others (Blatt & H. Lerner, 1991).

Blatt and H. Lerner (1991) observed that, in a number of disciplines, there has been increasing emphasis on the need to identify and understand principles of structural organization that define interrelationships and potential transformations of elements that determine variations of surface phenomena. Despite this emphasis on internal structure in many fields throughout the 20th century, a large segment of psychology and psychiatry still adhere to an exclusive interest in manifest behavior and overt symptomatology. Attempts in the human sciences to identify principles of structural organization that underlie manifest behavior have emphasized two dimensions fundamental to the human condition: (a) humans' capacity for complex symbolic activity, and (b) recognition of the importance of the complex interpersonal matrix within which we evolve and exist. These two factors are unique to the human condition and must be accounted for in any understanding of the structural principles that underlie manifest behavior. In terms of psychological testing there is a need to investigate how individuals with varying degrees and types of psychopathology symbolically represent people and their interactions on psychological tests and during the testing experience. The challenge for testing from this perspective is to conceptualize the individual's total experience, his or her ever shifting yet stable sense of self, and sense of the world of people and things, actual and illusory. Assessment must now include a fuller consideration of phenomenological, experiential, therapeutically relevant constructs such as self and object representation. By sense of self and others, reference is both to conscious awareness and to preconscious and unconscious experiencing.

In this vein, Mayman (1977) attempted to systematize what he termed the "complex multi-level theory" of psychoanalysis into three distinct yet coordinated sets of concepts or language. First, according to Mayman, there is the language used by the therapist or tester in transaction with the patient during the treatment or assessment hour, an everyday language more akin to poetry than to science. Reference here is to non-jargon-driven language that is conversational in nature and includes such examples as administering directions, asking for clarifications, and other general details of the interaction between subject and examiner. Outside the consultation room, the clinician utilizes a "middle-level language" of "empirical constructs" that help to formulate clinical generalizations about an individual. A middle-level language includes formulating responses in terms of constructs, such as self- and object representation, modes of defense, self-esteem, and content themes that seem salient to the individual. A third, more abstract language consists of "systematic" or "hypothetical constructs," a system of impersonal concepts using more objective, distant, third-person terms that constitute psychoanalytic metapsychology. Reference here is to constructs such as ego structures, unconscious forces, and sexual and aggressive drives. Mayman argued that these three levels of abstraction should not be confused with each other but rather need to be coordinated with constant reference back to the original primary database, the clinical material.

In attempting to achieve an experience-near conceptual understanding of experience couched in a middle-level language, the testing process becomes a vehicle for systematically transforming a personal language of self-definition and understanding into a comprehensible, and hopefully modifiable, personal past, and present subjective world. It is the subject's present inner world—his or her sense of self and others, based primarily on a child's atemporal, magical, and frightening representation of the world, a world of primitive substances, body parts, images, actions, and contacts— that is the matrix of experience, the core data of testing, and the prime material of the treatment relationship. These concrete, evocative representations of unconscious and conscious understanding are not transparent and simply waiting to be organized. A complex dialectical relationship exists between the subject's somatically based, sensation-dominated experiences, and the examiner's organizing concepts. As the following example illustrates, these representations are paradoxically both found and applied (Schafer, 1978):

A boyish-looking, blond-haired, freckled-face young woman, M, was admitted to a hospital unit after presenting to the emergency room with complaints of depression and suicidal ideation. She reported that her mood had become more dysphoric, she had frequent crying spells, and she had developed a number of symptoms of depression such as psychomotor retardation, decreased concentration, decreased appetite with a 15-pound weight loss, episodes of insomnia and hypersomnia, and persistent thoughts of suicide. The patient identified as the precipitant of her depression the abrupt expulsion from a boarding school she attended. The reasons given by M were her "rebellious behavior" and substance abuse. She experienced the expulsion as a tremendous loss.

M was the youngest of two siblings; she had a brother, 3 years older. Her father had a long history of alcohol abuse dating from M's birth. Due to her father's career in the Navy, a crumbling marriage, and numerous moves in her early years, M was separated from both parents and her brother for long periods of time. Her parents divorced when she was 5 years old, her mother subsequently remarried, and M and her brother moved to a different city. The summer she turned 8, M and her brother were sent to Japan for what was proposed to be a limited visit with the father. On her return, M was sent to live with a paternal uncle and aunt. She recalled her own sense of confusion as to why she could not return to her mother. In point of fact, M never returned to her mother and subsequent contact with her was sporadic to the point that she had only a yearly phone call on her birthday. There were frequent moves, following two of which she overdosed, at ages 11 and 14. There were brief hospitalizations with no followup. After one hospitalization she was enrolled in a co-ed boarding school. She recalled that as being the happiest time of her life. She described a supportive environment with many friends, popularity, and good academic achievement. As student council representative, she complained bitterly of the administration's treatment of students. Her frequent use of drugs led to a sudden expulsion from school. Several ill-fated attempts to regain admittance led to increased substance abuse, depression, and ultimately, rehospitalization.

M approached testing in a hyper-alert and cautious manner. Her initial protestation that test administration was exploitive lessened when an appeal was made to her intellectual curiosity and attentiveness was paid to her enormous struggle in life. This resulted in an exceedingly rich protocol. M achieved a Full Scale WAIS–R (Wechsler Adult Intelligence Scale–Revised) IQ of 125. M maintained a core sense of herself as damaged, exploited, and victimized. Rorschach images of a "bark chip or a moth trying to look like one, more like a flake"(Card IV), "an alligator coming out of the mud" (Card V), and "a skinned cat" (Card VI) were all understood as self-representations. The image of a "really tired wet moth" was particularly telling. "The wings were drooping … it looks bleak, like a foggy, wet day and it can't find some place to go." When profoundly depressed and helpless, she experienced a sense of self as nonexistent, hidden, and melted away. Of interest, Blatt and Ritzler (1974) report that the representation of translucency/transparency on the Rorschach is an attempt to construct three-dimensional space and volume that collapses and that this phenomenon is correlated with suicide. M's self-experience appeared rooted in intense oral aggression turned inward, masochistically. This was relieved, however, by appealing to that part of her that also generated images of a "tug boat" (Card VI), "flower" (Cards VIII and X), and a "flame from a lantern," that is, her doggedness, sexuality, and continuous ability to struggle.

Many individuals such as M put their worst foot forward. When met by technicianlike examiners armed with textbook test administration values, they experience well-intentioned efforts to be objective and to glean "clean" test records as indifference. This recapitulates earlier developmental experiences of indifference and promotes in the test situation transference-countertransference distractions, and often, an impasse. It is of particular importance that assessment focuses on the subject's experience and on identifying difficulties in the subject's mode of object relating and dynamically determined responses that each mode of relating are apt to evoke from others. A test report that is balanced and attempts to reflect the whole person can preserve the wide scope of empathy, support, and objectivity needed for effective clinical decision making and treatment.

A Psychoanalytic Experiential Approach to Assessment

An experiential approach to psychological assessment within a psychoanalytic framework involves a particular attitude toward the testing process and the nature of test data, a set of test rationales that are applied to tests as a whole as well as to scores, and a particular view of the nature of the interpretive process. If testing could be understood as an attempt to understand and reconstruct as much of an individual's internal experience as possible, in order to capture the totality of an individual's experience, one must first appreciate that the testing experience takes place within the context of a specific *test task* and a particular *test situation*. According to Mayman (1964), "In testing a patient for clinical purposes, we are not simply measuring; we observe a person in action, try to reconstruct how he went about dealing with the tasks we set for him, and then try to make clinical sense of this behavior" (p. 2). In order to capture "the totality of the patient's experience," one must appreciate the context of testing. P. Lerner (1991), more than anyone else, has examined the specific test task and test situation that comprise the context of assessment.

Test task refers to the specific directions offered by the examiner to the subject. The examiner who tests from this perspective must pay close attention to test directions and recognize that the patient's responses will reflect as well as be influenced by the subjective meaning he or she may ascribe to the directions. The test situation has enormous impact on the subjective meanings for the subject and has a powerful influence on test performance. Testing in a forensic context is qualitatively different than testing in a clinical or diagnostic setting. The adversarial context of judicial proceedings must be taken into account in doing forensic work. Within this particular context, the examiner, who is often appointed by the court or one of the adversaries in the judicial hearing, must expect the subject to be more defensive and must take into account that defensiveness as he or she administers tests and interprets the findings.

Of the multiple dimensions of the test situation, of major significance is the consideration that testing takes place within the context of an interpersonal relationship. From an experiential, psychoanalytic perspective, the testing enterprise cannot be fully understood without an awareness of its interpersonal implications. The interpersonal relationship, with its realistic and unrealistic aspects, is intrinsic to assessment and this relationship has a significant impact on the subject's test responses and can, as well, provide a wealth of information. Several concepts such as transference-countertransference (Schafer, 1954), self-object transference (Arnow & Cooper, 1988), and projective identification (P. Lerner, 1991) have been advanced to understand and conceptualize the testing relationship. From this perspective, although test scores are deemed important, it is recognized that other facets of the individual's experience are expressed on tests in ways that are not reflected solely by scores. These dimensions need to be considered.

When testing from this perspective the examiner should make as exact and complete a record as possible of all that transpires between the subject and examiner, including the subject's verbatim responses, the direction of the examiner's own comments and reactions, and the subject's spontaneous, self-evaluative, and emotional expressions (P. Lerner, 1991).

A study conducted by Brickman and H. Lerner (1991), in what may be considered a typical internship and/or practicum setting, illustrates the profound significance of monitoring the subject–examiner interaction. This was a naturalistic study of testing with clients at a community-based agency that evaluated, treated, and placed children and adolescents. Cases typically were referred from the courts and the Department of Social Services with a view toward placement in residential treatment centers, specialized foster care homes, and supervised living programs. Typical cases involved abuse, severe trauma, neglect, and delinquency; a history of family pathology, often including abandonments and multiple reconstitutions; a history of school problems and failures; and records of many previous placements, therapists, and testings. Referral questions frequently involved issues of special educational services, differential diagnoses, clinical requests for help by staff because the subjects were "impossible to work with," court-ordered testings, placement decisions, and questions regarding medication.

Almost 20% of the test protocols in the file could be deemed "invalid or unscorable" by virtue of containing either too few or incomplete responses due to the subjects' unresponsiveness within the context of little examiner–subject alliance. The test protocols were all administered by master's level or doctoral students under the supervision of a licensed psychologist. We observed that there were few examiner notes. It became clear that the formal scores on the WISC–R (Wechsler Intelligence Scale for Children–Revised) and the Rorschach were not the most valuable ways to approach the data in these cases. The outstanding features of these protocols involved the clinical interaction between subject and examiner as well as spontaneous self-referential and critical remarks such as, "This makes me feel stupid" or "This is dumb." Rich clinical material all but slipped through the cracks of textbook administration procedures. Spontaneous "tangential" comments were so vivid that, far from being a diversion from the task, they constituted the actual data.

For example, on the Rorschach, a 15-year-old girl's first response was, "A bat—I had this before—I don't like it, it's hard to tell what these things are." (CAN YOU SHOW WHERE ON THE CARD YOU SEE IT?) "Here are the wings." (WHAT MAKES IT LOOK LIKE A BAT?) "Shape and form. That's it." (PEOPLE OFTEN SEE MORE THAN ONE THING IN THESE CARDS.) "Not me. [laughs]." By Card III the sadomasochistic dance between subject and examiner reached a point that the subject's response to Inquiry was simply, "It just does—it just does because I want it to!"

In considering resistant subjects and meager protocols, the interaction between subject and examiner is crucial, and the need for the examiner to respond to the subject clinically is imperative. Following Card III one subject said, "I really hate these cards—why do we have to do these?" (IT'S JUST ONE OF THE TESTS I NEED TO GIVE YOU AS PART OF THIS WHOLE THING. CAN YOU TELL ME WHY YOU HATE DOING THIS SO MUCH?) "These tests make me look stupid … they just make me look dumb."

(REMEMBER, I TOLD YOU BEFORE THAT THERE ARE NO RIGHT OR WRONG ANSWERS ON THIS.) [Apparently not convinced, the subject said] "They just make me look dumb and I don't like them!" (OKAY—I KNOW YOU DON'T LIKE THESE BUT WE PROBABLY SHOULD FINISH THESE UP. THERE AREN'T THAT MANY MORE CARDS. WHY DON'T YOU JUST DO THE BEST YOU CAN ON THEM.) Following this interaction, responses such as "a creature," an "insect," a "jackass," a "small shell," and a "wish bone" appeared with minimal interaction, elaboration, or examiner notes.

The point to be made with this example is the importance of the underlying context. Scoring, of course, ought not to be abandoned, but neither should it be made the primary emphasis in all cases. The test situation should be approached not as a laboratory but rather as a clinical paradigm. Often subjects encountered during internships, practica, and postdoctoral fellowships have a history of being tested—and treated—as many as six or seven times, which clearly influences their present experience of the task. Examiners, therapists, and staff, potentially important figures in their lives, are seen as faceless, interchangeable beings who really do not care about them. In addition, these patients have felt incompetent in school as well as in other areas of their lives. All of these test-specific conflicts abide within the broader context of the subject's having been abused, neglected, and traumatized.

Utilizing psychological tests as a clinical paradigm enjoins us to use good clinical technique in administering our instruments. Subjects are frequently narcissistically vulnerable, easily threatened, and therefore swiftly lose distance. Our task is less to provide scores that yield diagnostic profiles and document deficiencies, than to find "treatment levers" and points of contact. This can start at the beginning of testing by clarifying the task. With additional clinical training and experience one can diverge from standardized procedures when necessary, so long as there is a clear rationale for doing so. It is important to keep in mind that "feeling stupid" and "being crazy" are important issues in the lives of many subjects. They have the background and data to support these perceptions. At the same time, however, these issues are potential points of emotional contact with such patients.

The conflicts in which many subjects consistently engage examiners are representations of internal conflicts that are being expressed in action, in behavioral terms rather than in words. They evoke not only powerful but also more subtle countertransference reactions in the examiner that if gone unrecognized, become insidious. Although the task of treatment is to assist the subject in acknowledging the internal conflict, one task for the examiner is to document and note during testing any countertransference impulses and fantasies. In this context, it is important to note that on the examiner's part, avoidance or resistance to writing the psychological test report can often involve subtle and not so subtle countertransference reactions not only to the subject but also to the agency and supervisor. It is also important to note a phenomenon that frequently goes unnoticed: that is, a "parallel process" between the examiner and the supervisor that reflects transference-countertransference reactions emanating from the test situation itself. Arlow (1963) was the first to clarify the parallel process that occurs in supervision. Utilizing clinical material, he demonstrated the ways in which the therapist identifies with the patient and unconsciously repeats this particular aspect of the material in the supervision. He wrote about some of the similarities between treatment and supervision and about the frequency of transient identifications, both in the therapist and in the supervisor. For example, a highly critical, defensive test subject, can evoke counter hypervigilance and defensiveness on the part of the examiner, who through this transient identification, in a parallel fashion, can reenact the experience in the supervision. The parallel process works both ways; that is, for example, a supervisor who is experienced by the tester as overly critical, judgmental, and severe, can lead the tester to either enact these qualities in the testing or experience the test subject in ways similar to the supervisor.

An examiner is seen through the frame of the tests that stand between him or her self and the subject, and that thus itself becomes an important source of data. It is crucial for examiners to attend to their own internal responses to the subject in a disciplined way in order to better understand the quality of these interactions. Using the full range of data available to the test administrator aside from the scores themselves, the clinical examiner can better become aware of the effects of himself or her self on the subject and can use this understanding for the evaluative process.

RECOMMENDATIONS FOR THE TEACHER AND THE STUDENT

1. In conceptualizing the assessment task, the examiner needs to see psychological tests as a way of gaining a better clinical understanding of the subject rather than as just a means of scoring responses and generating diagnoses. It is important to approach psychological testing with a degree of flexibility. There is no perception or cognition without fantasy. The relationship between test scores and their underlying meanings is similar to that between the manifest and latent content of a dream. We are interested in more than the reliable and accurate description of the dream. The distortions, slips, spontaneous remarks, and associations of the subject often are the relevant data that contain and reveal the meaning of the dream. This is to say, test responses and test scores should not be taken solely at face value.

2. The testing experience is a clinical paradigm, with the interaction itself a transference paradigm. Resistance to the task can be understood clinically as a transference manifestation and dealt with accordingly. Theory and sensitive clinical technique as it bears on test administration, scoring, interpretation, and report writing protects the examiner and the subject from impulsive anger or retaliatory indifference.

3. Beware of the context of testing. Subjects with meager or difficult-to-score responses often have a history of trauma and severe deprivation that they may reexperience or re-create nonverbally throughout their lives. Accordingly,

they may experience the testing itself as a further abuse. The examiner needs to be able to engage the subject around these issues, less to garner "clean" scores than to understand the subject and to find levers for useful therapeutic interventions. Noting spontaneous fantasies and impulses during test administration may shed clinical light on what at first glance may appear to be empty or mundane test responses. Subjects may also be encouraged in the test situation to reflect on what makes this particular task so aversive or distasteful.

4. It is difficult for both subjects and examiners to reflect on meager protocols within the context of adversarial interactions, intense affects, unspoken fantasies, and tensions. Often this results in a testing ambiance of indifference. Supervisors need to help students feel more comfortable in not being slaves to scoring systems or robotlike test administrators. Examiners may need to unlearn what they have learned in courses and textbooks in order to become more comfortable with—and aware of—their trained clinical instincts. Test scores do not necessarily give the most important information; trained intuition should be used to explore what is clinically rich.

5. An experiential approach to psychological testing is an attempt to better understand and focus not only on the subject's experience, but also the experience of the examiner. What is being encouraged is a psychological mindedness on the part of the examiner that extends beyond the testing itself to other areas of concern including supervision, report writing, and feelings about agencies and academic programs. Psychological mindedness calls on flexibility, open-mindedness, a disciplined intuitiveness, as well as an openness to one's feelings and thoughts. A psychologically minded focus on the examiner's experience is the best way to safeguard and look after the best interest of both the subject and the examiner.

6. Psychological test reports need to be helpful documents that can be referred to at points of treatment impasse and clinical decision making. A focus on the subject's experience, his or her strengths, and perceived weaknesses can be of invaluable assistance in preserving the high degree of empathy, support, and objectivity required for effective clinical work and decision making with subjects. The test report, rather than a literary critique of the subject, should ideally help the individual feel better understood and help make that unique individual more comprehensible to others.

IMPLICATIONS FOR TRAINING

This chapter raises a number of questions regarding training. How is theory in clinical technique, as it bears on assessment, taught? How do we engage patients? How do we learn to attend to countertransference reactions? How do we train intuition? Unlike other approaches to assessment and treatment, learning an experience-near psychoanalytic approach is not just a cognitive task. In keeping with the experiential thrust of this chapter, I consider the implications for training of this approach in terms of what has been helpful in my own training.

My real training in assessment began after I finished graduate school, during my internship. I received immensely valuable clinical experience as an intern, working at a children's community mental health center in New York City. The opportunity to work clinically and diagnostically with a wide, diverse range of children, adolescents, and families was truly important. As I remember, at that time I felt a real absence of an integrated professional identity. Realizing that I lacked a mentor as well as experiencing a certain confusion in my personal life, I entered twice-a-week psychotherapy. Although the treatment itself was not with an analyst, the safety, acceptance, warmth, and practical help of my therapist, as well as the fact that I "took the plunge," helped me to sort things out personally, to integrate, and to move on to a postdoctoral fellowship.

My postdoctoral experience was by far the most meaningful growth experience of my career. Being immersed in clinical and diagnostic work with hospitalized schizophrenic and borderline patients provided the opportunity to conduct research, to attend stimulating diagnostic seminars, and to receive supervision from such people as Alan Sugarman, Sidney Blatt, Wayne Downey, Theodore Lidz, and Ira Levine. What was most significant was the opportunity to conduct research and to integrate clinical work with the rigors of quantitative methods, statistics, and in terms of the Rorschach, the opportunity to analyze a large number of protocols. It is one thing to be exposed to norms based on large samples and something quite different to immerse oneself in reading hundreds of protocols generated by patients exhibiting a wide range of psychopathology.

I would like to comment on the role of certain supervisors and supervisory experiences that have been influential. Without a doubt, the influence of my older brother, Paul, has been the most profound. Beyond his vast clinical experience, incredible knowledge of the Rorschach, and uncanny capacity for interpretation, it has always been my experience that Paul understood me. His capacity to put himself in my position and the beneficial result to me has been a major source of identification and point of departure for understanding others. What I learned from Paul is the importance of experience, both in working with individuals clinically and diagnostically, and in utilizing our psychological concepts and theories. Alan Sugarman, a supervisor for 2 years, was a model of disciplined intuition and self-analytic capacities. He was able to clearly spell out the clinically grounded, disciplined inference process in evaluating protocols and formulating cases. Sidney Blatt is at once a brilliant scholar, a prolific researcher, and a respected colleague. He never made me feel stupid and could move with ideas in enormously fascinating and creative ways. I have identified with his exuberance and enthusiasm for ideas. On completion of the postdoctoral fellowship and on assuming a faculty position at the University of Michigan, I was able to pursue a goal of undergoing psychoanalysis. I knew there were issues that I needed to work out from my distant but paradoxically all too near past, as well as recurrent problems in relationships. It was extremely expensive, at times immensely difficult, and yet enormously beneficial in terms of my own personal happiness and growth. I also undertook psychoanalytic training and found the course work, supervised analytic experience, and intellectual stimulation enormously meaningful and integrative.

In taking a step back, it is clear that identification is the central vehicle of education in my career. In my postdoctoral and psychoanalytic training, the accumulated history, continuity, and body of knowledge that have been transmitted to me has been in the context of a psychological ambiance that conveyed to me the ideals, attitudes, and personal qualities of my teachers, which happens to be essential for our profession. These goals cannot be achieved by cognitive teaching and learning alone. In any discipline, there is more to training than the transmission of information. My motivation for analysis was less as a training requirement and vehicle for a psychoanalytic career than out of recognizing the need to come to terms with conflicts that had previously held me back from being as happy and fully functioning as I could be. In terms of supervision—especially in psychological testing—analysis has been enormously beneficial because it has permitted me to become more aware of my own feelings and contributions to interactions, for example, blind spots, specific areas of sensitivity, and areas of personal strengths and weaknesses. I am more aware of myself and I know what I do not know. More than anything else, my own personal analysis has better enabled me to empathize with the patient.

Whether it is the task of administering and interpreting a Rorschach protocol or a particular patient's interaction within the therapeutic setting, I have learned that the exploration of the meaning of behavior, motives, and creation of others requires self-exploration. This is to say that the study of the subject requires a preconscious and conscious dialogue with the self. This dialogue is not the same as the deliberate effort to be fair, to search for evidence that contradicts one's own ideas and beliefs, important and indeed necessary as our attempts to be objective and scientific are. This dialogue goes on in everyone practicing the art of interpretation. This is not the exclusive province of psychoanalysis. Good scholars have experienced the sense that some understanding of the text, a painting, a life, demands but eludes because of some internal obstacle; but then, after some interchange and struggle has occurred, the material becomes more accessible to understanding. Psychoanalysis is the best method I know to cultivate and to give eyes to this otherwise blind struggle.

In summary, what has been least helpful in my training has been my undergraduate and graduate education. With a few exceptions, it was a barren wasteland of good role models. My real training as a diagnostic clinician began as an intern and postdoctoral fellow. What I gained from supervision was identification with important individuals and a way of clinical thinking. My training experience, ranging from clinical and psychodiagnostic work to research and to those who supervised me, can all be conceptualized on a philosophical continuum with the phenomenology of personal experience at one extreme and so-called objective, scientific inquiry at the other extreme. I have been blessed with learning experiences and supervisors as role models all along this continuum, and although there will always be a tension within our discipline between phenomenology and science, that tension within me is the source of enthusiasm and creativity.

I would like to offer one final recommendation. Do not enter psychoanalysis and treatment for training purposes. The motivation should be out of personal suffering and pain. Treatment can only be beneficial if it is entered into for the right reasons. Supervision is most profitable with students who are interested and genuinely eager to learn. In turn, the need to supervise must be out of the right reasons as well, that is, to be generative as opposed to an approach in which students or supervisees are experienced as extensions of oneself. The worst supervision experiences are with those who are continually asking and need to know what to do. The attraction of a cookbook approach to testing as well as treatment is a major resistance and obstacle to learning. I have come to see as a major goal of supervision the facilitatation of students in their attempts to get in touch with their own unconscious understanding of their patients and test subjects, for it is out of this understanding that a disciplined intuition and respectful integration of phenomenology and science is born.

REFERENCES

Arlow, J. (1963). The supervisory situation. *Journal of the American Psychoanalytic Association, 11*, 576–594.

Arnow, D., & Cooper, S. (1988). Toward a Rorschach psychology of the self. In H. Lerner & P. Lerner (Eds.), *Primitive mental states and the Rorschach* (pp. 53–70). New York: International Universities Press.

Blatt, S., & Berman, W. (1984). A methodology for the use of the Rorschach in clinical research. *Journal of Personality Assessment, 48*(3), 226–239.

Blatt, S., & Lerner, H. (1991). Psychodynamic perspectives on personality theory. In M. Hersen, A. Kazdin, & A. Bellack (Eds.), *The clinical psychology handbook* (2nd. ed., pp. 147–169). New York: Pergamon.

Blatt, S., & Ritzler, B. (1974). Thought disorder and boundary disturbances in psychosis. *Journal of Consulting and Clinical Psychology, 42*, 370–381.

Brickman, A., & Lerner, H. (1991). Barren Rorschachs: A conceptual approach. *Journal of Personality Assessment, 59*(1), 176–184.

Exner, J. (1974). *The Rorschach: A comprehensive system* (Vol. 1). New York: Wiley.

Freud, S. (1915). Instincts and their vicissitudes. *Standard Edition, 14*, 117–140.

Freud, S. (1923). The ego and the id. *Standard Edition, 19*, 12–66.

Home, H. (1966). The concept of mind. *International Journal of Psychoanalysis, 47*, 43–49.

Jacobson, E. (1964). *The self and the object world.* New York: International Universities Press.

Klein, G. (1976). *Psychoanalytic theory.* New York: International Universities Press.

Kohut, H. (1977). *The restoration of the self.* New York: International Universities Press.

Lerner, H. (1988, October). *Human Experience and the Rorschach.* Paper presented at the Conference on Psychological Testing and the Psychotherapeutic Process, Stockbridge, MA.

Lerner, P. (1991). *Psychoanalytic theory and the Rorschach.* Hillsdale, NJ: The Analytic Press.

Lerner, P., & Lerner, H. (1985). Contributions of object relations theory towards a general psychoanalytic theory of thinking. *Psychoanalysis and Contemporary Thought, 9,* 469–513.

Mayman, M. (1964). Some general propositions implicit in the clinical application of psychological tests. Unpublished manuscript, Menninger Foundation, Topeka, KS.

Mayman, M. (1977). A multi-dimensional view of the Rorschach movement response. In M. Rickers-Ovsiankina (Ed.), *Rorschach psychology* (pp. 229–250). Huntington, NY: Krieger.

Pine, F. (1985). *Developmental theory and clinical process.* New Haven, CT: Yale University Press.

Sandler, J., & Rosenblatt, B. (1962). The concept of the representational world. In *Psychoanalytic study of the child.* (Vol. 17, pp. 128–145). New York: International Universities Press.

Schafer, R. (1954). *Psychoanalytic interpretation in Rorschach testing.* New York: Grune & Stratton.

Schafer, R. (1978). *Language and insight.* New Haven, CT: Yale University Press.

Shectman, F., & Harty, M. (1986). Treatment implications of object relationships as they unfold during the diagnostic interaction. In M. Kissen (Ed.), *Assessing object relations phenomena* (pp. 279–306) . Madison, CT: International Universities Press.

Steele, R. (1979). Psychoanalysis and hermeneutics. *International Review of Psychoanalysis, 6,* 389–412.

Sugarman, A. (1985). *The nature of clinical assessment.* Unpublished manuscript.

4

Helping Students Integrate Rorschach Structure and Psychological Theory

Philip Erdberg
Corte Madera, California

There is nothing so practical, said Kurt Lewin, as a good theory. To that collaborative sentiment I would add the following corollary: And there is nothing so supportive of a good theory as the empirical finding it would have predicted and that it helps explain. A science has reached a new level of maturity when it can host a dialogue between the theoretician and the empiricist. It is a dialogue that tests our theorizing even as it helps us understand our findings. Yet, at least within the area of Rorschach study, that kind of dialogue has been rare until recently. Those who value structural approaches have not typically tried to test theories, and those whose approaches are based on one or another personality theory have not devoted themselves to helping understand empirical findings. The two approaches now coexist more peacefully than in the past, but coexistence is not the same as the mutually enhancing dialogue I think is possible.

Students are quick to note the rift and take a position on one side or the other. For some, thrilled by their first encounter with the richly idiographic style of psychoanalytic theory, a structural Rorschach approach seems mechanistic and off target. For others, entranced by the prospect of bringing methodological rigor to personality assessment, the vehement certainty with which widely varying theoretical positions are held seems matched only by the fragile uncertainty of their empirical foundations. For nearly all, the idea that theoretical and empirical approaches could be anything but mutually exclusive is startling and suspect.

One thing I would like to accomplish in my work with students is to help them discover that such polarization, although historically understandable, is artificial. Structural and theoretical approaches *can* interact with each other to the substantial benefit of both. It would be wonderful if the defining characteristic of the next generation of Rorschachers became the knowledgeable comfort with which they handle this integration.

What I hope to do in this chapter is to provide some examples of how I demonstrate the possibility of conversation between theory and empiricism, using Rorschach content as an example. Let me begin by expressing as clearly as I can the basic premise that underlies the conversation.

For a dialogue to be useful, the two participants must maintain the autonomy that allows each to make a unique contribution. The empiricist must remain descriptive and atheoretical; the theorist must take a stand on the mechanisms that predict and account for findings. Maintaining this autonomy in our work with the Rorschach means that we must not confuse a data source, which is what the Rorschach is, with personality theory. The Rorschach works best when it tests personality theory with the data it provides about how people handle a moderately ambiguous perceptual-cognitive task. Personality theory works best when it postulates the underlying structures that motivate and organize people to think and feel and behave the way they do. Their responses to our 10 inkblots constitute one manifestation of those underlying structures.

I have chosen content as an example because it is a part of the Rorschach whose interpretation has often been linked solely with a theory-driven approach to the test. That makes it a good candidate for a demonstration of how theory and empiricism can interact.

I begin by thinking with my students about where content fits in the overall enterprise. The Rorschach is a multidimensional data source. It works by presenting a task whose solutions can be investigated empirically and interpreted through the lens of personality theory.

One of the kinds of data that this multidimensional data source yields is content. Actually, content is not the best term for what I think we are discussing. A better term would be *elaboration*, what Exner (1989) called "the unique translations or embellishments" (p. 527) that sometimes occur. When someone looks at Card III and produces a percept that elaborates "Two people, each trying to be his own person, but finding it terribly difficult in a world which so frequently rewards cookie-cutter sameness and brutally punishes the fledgling attempts that these people may soon become too frightened to make," students know that something is up. And they know that they do not want to lose the data in the elaboration the Rorschach just elicited. The question is how to recognize and deal with this rich response rather than merely scoring it.

It is at that point that it is useful to remind students that elaboration is one among the several kinds of data that the Rorschach yields. It has a box on the same line of the organizational chart as do structural data elements, such as location. Rapaport foreshadowed this even-handed view of where elaboration fits when he wrote, "one can learn more about the subject sometimes by looking at a response from the point of view of its perceptual organization, and at other times by looking at it from the point of view of the associative process that brought it forth" (Rapaport, Gill, & Schafer, 1968, p. 274). The Rorschach works by mobilizing a variety of psychological operations, one of which is elaboration.

A few years later, B. Klopfer (Klopfer, Ainsworth, Klopfer, & Holt, 1954) encouraged this same-organizational-line approach to structural and elaboration data when he described the Rorschach as "a relatively standardized situation in which behavior can be observed. The assumption is that, on the basis of this limited sample of behavior, it will be possible to predict other kinds of behavior on the part of the subject in other situations. ... As a projective technique, the Rorschach has the further characteristic of providing a relatively ambiguous stimulus situation which will enable the subject to optimally reveal his individuality of functioning" (p. 3). Klopfer depicted the Rorschach as a source that provides both structural and elaboration data.

The first point of agreement to reach with students is that elaboration is one among the several kinds of data the Rorschach yields. The next question to resolve is how it should be handled. That is the sort of question of which lively arguments are made. Ultimately, students reach the understanding that elaboration should be handled like any other sort of data. To the extent that we treat elaboration data differently, we rob these data of their value.

This becomes a good time to review with students the standards we typically set for data acquisition and analysis—standards that I suggest are just as appropriate for elaboration data as for any other part of the Rorschach yield. First, we insist on the potential for intercoder agreement. We want two or more raters to be able to concur about the nature of the phenomenon they have just observed. With elaboration data, theory often helped alert us to the possibility of the phenomenon in the first place. This is a good place to remind students that this is a conversation, that theory plays an important alerting role. But then we want to be sure we can identify the phenomenon reliably if it happens.

Kwawer's work provides a wonderful example. Kwawer (1979, 1980) noted that contemporary object relations theory has emphasized the importance of early difficulties in separation and individuation in the genesis of borderline-level psychopathology. For individuals whose organization is at the borderline level, the "achievement of selfhood by means of differentiation from a primary mothering figure" (Kwawer, 1980, p. 90) continues to be conflictual. The theory alerted Kwawer to the likelihood that these core conflicts would show up on the Rorschach. They might emerge in percepts that, in his words, "reflect the interpersonal themes of merger, fusion, separation, and individuation" (Kwawer, 1979, p. 20). On the basis of theory, he went on to suggest that these percepts would "offer clear evidence for boundary disturbance—typically of weak, permeable, or diffuse boundaries, together with powerful internal pressure in the direction of symbiotic relatedness" (Kwawer, 1979, p. 520).

It is important that students note what Kwawer did next. He created a system for categorizing these elaborated percepts. He gave them names and provided a manual with defining criteria and examples for each. His separation-division category is a good illustration. Kwawer (1980) defined it as involving responses that manifest "conflict and ambivalence about separation and reunion" (p. 94). I doubt that it would be reassuring for the people my students and I left in existential despair back on Card III. But it is comforting to know that observers would agree that their distress should be coded as separation-division.

It is comforting, I remind students, because it means that we have data to which we can then apply our second usual standard: that it be valid. By validity, we mean the demonstration that these reliably identified Rorschach phenomena relate to real-world behavior or to other measures of conceptually similar constructs. On the basis of Rorschach data, including elaboration data, we make statements about a person's likely behavior in the world or about his or her likely internal experiences and attitudes. Validity studies help us modulate the certainty with which we make these statements.

Students are wonderfully intuitive, marvelously creative people. They can perceive phenomena of ephemeral subtlety and hypothesize relationships with elegant complexity. I would not have it otherwise. But it is important for them to learn to insist on some feedback—and that is what validity studies provide. They relate Rorschach data, be it structure or elaboration, to real-world behavior, to externally determined membership in diagnostic categories, to findings on other instruments that assess similar constructs, to outcomes of different types of intervention. It can be particularly tempting to hypothesize about elaboration data. Validity studies help us ensure that the correlations we propose are not illusory.

Let me summarize where I am with my students at this point. I have suggested that elaboration is one of the several kinds of data the Rorschach produces. As an equal among equals, it should be subject to the usual demands we make of assessment data: that we be able to identify it reliably and relate it validly to real-world outcomes.

What I then do is present an extended example that provides a good illustration of how elaboration data can be handled within the model I have suggested. It comes from the work of Cooper, Perry, Arnow, and their colleagues (1988, 1991). But it could just as easily have come from P. and H. Lerner's (1988) work on defenses or Urist's (1977) research on the mutuality of autonomy.

Cooper et al. (1988) were interested in how defensive operations are manifested on the Rorschach. Their emphasis on defense mechanisms was driven by theory. Kernberg (1975) suggested that splitting and the related defenses of projective identification, denial, primitive idealization, devaluation, and omnipotence are the defining characteristics of borderline personality organization. As is often the case in personality theory, Kernberg's view was controversial. Another group of theorists—Robbins (1976) and Lichtenberg and Slap (1973)—questioned whether this level of specificity in relating particular defense mechanisms to personality organization was warranted.

In any event, Cooper et al. (1988) reasoned that if defensive operations are pervasive components of personality organization, they would show up in the individual's Rorschach. On the basis of some preliminary work with participants with borderline personality disorder, antisocial personality disorder, and bipolar affective disorder, they thought that their hunch was correct: that these defensive operations did manifest in their subjects' elaborations of Rorschach percepts.

It is important for students to follow closely what Cooper et al. (1988) did at this point in their work. They came up with a system and gave names—Devaluation and Omnipotence are examples—to 15 defenses that theory suggested should show up in Rorschach elaborations. Then they provided a manual with defining criteria and examples for coding these 15 types of Rorschach percepts.

The Cooper et al. (1988) Devaluation code is a good example. They began with a theoretical understanding, noting that devaluation is a defense used to fend off wishes for need fulfillment or to minimize the disappointment that occurs when needs are unmet. Then they went on to provide guidelines for coding Rorschach elaboration data as Devaluation.

Another interesting aspect of the Cooper et al. (1988) system is that it can incorporate data that develop in the context of the participant's interaction with the testing situation or the tester. We code Devaluation, for example, for comments that disparage the testing procedure, the test materials, or the examiner. They provide a wonderful example: "I can't believe this is the way you spend your time—how boring." Carl Gacono (personal communication, April 13, 1995) told the story of the day he and a colleague tested a psychopathic prisoner. In a lightning strike as they began the Rorschach, the man said "I hope you boys have a lot of paper because you're going to hear some remarkable answers." We can reliably, and somewhat irritably, code Devaluation and Omnipotence in that response. Then we have elaboration data to put in the mix when we do validity studies.

In their first publication about their system for handling this sort of elaboration data, Cooper et al. (1988) began by describing their intercoder agreement. It was important for them to demonstrate that multiple observers could concur in placing Rorschach elaborations in the various defense categories. They reported intraclass correlation coefficients for the 15 defense categories that ranged from .45 to .80. The median correlation coefficient was .62. They then grouped the 15 defense categories into three broad classes: neurotic, borderline, and psychotic. The intraclass correlations for these broader defense classes was .71 for the neurotic group, .81 for the borderline group, and .72 for the group of psychotic defenses. Although by no means perfect in their agreement, it would appear that raters could concur on the presence of these elaborations when they happen in Rorschach percepts.

Having established that these Rorschach elaborations could be identified with reasonable reliability, Cooper et al. (1988) next turned to a demonstration of the validity of their system of identifying elaboration data. They gave Rorschachs to patients whose diagnoses of borderline personality disorder, antisocial personality disorder, or bipolar disorder had been externally determined by clinicians according to DSM–III (Diagnostic and Statistical Manual of Mental Disorders, 3rd ed.) or Research Diagnostic Criteria guidelines. Their correlational findings between the defense categories and these various externally determined diagnostic variables suggested some interesting relationships. As an example, there were significant positive correlations between a diagnosis of borderline personality disorder and Rorschach elaboration data that could be coded as Devaluation, Projection, Splitting, Hypomanic Denial, and Pollyannish Denial.

Another kind of validity study relates Rorschach data—in this case, elaboration data—to future outcomes. Cooper, Perry, and O'Connell (1991) followed their subjects every 3–6 months for 3 years. They collected two interviewer-rated scales, the Hamilton Rating Scales for depression and anxiety, and one self-report measure, the Profile of Mood States, at each follow-up session. Their structured interviews allowed ratings on various specific areas of psychosocial operation as well as overall functioning.

Their correlations between Rorschach defense data when the participants entered the study and their subsequent levels of clinical symptoms on follow-up provide the sort of validity that is meaningful for students. As an example, Devaluation was positively related to Hamilton ratings for depression and anxiety. On the other hand, Hypomanic Denial, Intellectualization, and Polly-annish Denial were negatively correlated with these Hamilton ratings of depression and anxiety.

It is important to emphasize with students the special value of validity findings that relate Rorschach defense data with a real-world measure, such as interviewer ratings of impairment in work and interpersonal relationships. Cooper et al. (1991) showed that elaboration data coded as Projection or Devaluation predicted a higher proportion of time impaired in Work Satisfaction. Isolation and Pollyannish Denial predicted less time impaired in Work Satisfaction. Omnipotence and Pollyannish Denial were predictive of less impairment in relationships, Projection with more impairment.

At this point, my students and I try to summarize what Cooper, Perry, Arnow, and their colleagues accomplished. Using psychodynamic theory, which suggests that defensive operations are important components of psychological function, they hypothesized that the Rorschach would provide data demonstrating the presence of these operations. The hypothesis was that as people solve other problems in their lives, so will they solve the Rorschach. Initial evaluation suggested that this might be the case, so Cooper, Perry, Arnow, and their colleagues identified several categories of Rorschach percepts that seemed associated with defensive operations. Then they created a manual that allowed the reliable identification of these phenomena if they occurred. Their first study provided intercoder agreement data that suggested it was possible to make these categorizations reliably. They next moved to a demonstration of validity. These Rorschach elaboration findings could be concurrently and predictively related both to other test data and to real-world findings: externally determined membership in diagnostic categories, or presence of symptoms on follow-up. Although significant, many of the relationships did not account for large portions of the variance. It is important to think with students about the clinical implications of such findings.

Throughout, I remind students of the kind of Rorschach data Cooper, Perry, and Arnow were using. It was elaboration, very much the unique translations and embellishments of which Exner (1989) spoke.

These percepts, which at first blush would seem very idiographic, are data. Students can observe how thoughtful researchers used theory to inform their ability to observe them effectively without stripping them of their uniqueness. They can look over the researchers' shoulders as the researchers create categories to try and encompass them, and they can watch as the researchers check to see if they could agree on their placement in those categories. Then they can follow as the researchers relate Rorschach data to real-world phenomena, all the way from observable behavior to the self-report of mood states. Finally they can loop back and use the findings to test the theory.

In the process, students have had an introduction to the interplay of theory and empiricism. They have seen how each informs the other and that neither would have been as useful without the other. They have seen how theory drives research and how research supports theory.

A next step involves asking students to create more of the links themselves. There is a substantial amount of Rorschach data that was not generated from any theoretical standpoint but that can form useful linkages with theory. An understanding of these findings is enhanced by theory, even as the data help either confirm or contradict what the theory would have predicted.

I might, for example, ask students to understand Exner's (1993) coding for incongruous combinations such as "A person with the head of a bird" on Card III in the context of Festinger's (1957) concept of cognitive dissonance. I would hope that they would note that the Rorschach provides frequent challenges to a person's ability to reduce cognitive dissonance. As an example, the D9 areas on Card III do mostly look like people. But there is a dissonant element. The parts that would be the heads really do not much look like heads. Festinger would argue that people would work hard to reduce dissonance, and indeed that is usually the case for most people. Human percepts—without incongruous combinations—are very common for these blot areas. The areas mostly look like humans, and most people are able to ignore the dissonant elements. But Exner's data suggest that individuals with thought disorders may have more trouble handling cognitive dissonance. His findings indicate that schizophrenic individuals quantitatively have more than five times as many incongruous combinations and qualitatively have more bizarre incongruous combinations than do nonpatients. We can suggest that the inability to reduce cognitive dissonance is an important component of serious thought disorder.

As I teach, my goal is the easy movement between theory and data. If I can accomplish it, I feel I have gone a long way in helping students use the Rorschach in the most productive way possible.

REFERENCES

Cooper, S. H., Perry, J. C., & Arnow, D. (1988). An empirical approach to the study of defense mechanisms: I. Reliability and preliminary validity of the rorschach defense scales. *Journal of Personality Assessment, 52,* 187–203.

Cooper, S.H., Perry, J.C., & O'Connell, M. (1991). The Rorschach defense scales: II. Longitudinal perspectives. *Journal of Personality Assessment, 56,* 191–201.

Exner, J. E. (1989). Searching for projection in the Rorschach. *Journal of Personality Assessment, 53,* 520–536.

Exner, J. E. (1993). *The Rorschach: A comprehensive system: Vol. 1. Basic foundations* (3rd ed.). New York: Wiley.

Festinger, L. (1957). *A theory of cognitive dissonance.* Stanford, CA: Stanford University Press.

Kernberg, O. (1975). *Borderline conditions and pathological narcissism.* New York: Aronson.

Klopfer, B., Ainsworth, M. D., Klopfer, W. G., & Holt, R. R. (1954). *Developments in the Rorschach technique: Vol. I. Technique and theory.* Yonkers, NY: World Book.

Kwawer, J. (1979). Borderline phenomena, interpersonal relations, and the Rorschach test. *Bulletin of the Menninger Clinic, 38,* 445–466.

Kwawer, J. (1980). Primitive interpersonal modes, borderline phenomena and Rorschach content. In J. Kwawer, A. Sugarman, P. Lerner, & H. Lerner (Eds.), *Borderline phenomena and the Rorschach test* (pp. 89–109). New York: International Universities Press.

Lerner, P., & Lerner, H. (1980). Rorschach assessment of primitive defenses in borderline personality structure. In J. Kwawer, A. Sugarman, P. Lerner, & H. Lerner (Eds.), *Borderline phenomena and the Rorschach test* (pp. 257–274). New York: International Universities Press.

Lichtenberg, J., & Slap, J. (1973). Notes on the concept of splitting and the defense mechanism of the splitting of representations. *Journal of the American Psychoanalytic Association, 21,* 722–787.

Rapaport, D., Gill, M., & Schafer, R. (1968). *Diagnostic psychological testing* (rev. ed., R. Holt, Ed.). New York: International Universities Press. (Original work published 1946)

Robbins, M. (1976). Borderline personality organization: The need for a new theory. *Journal of the American Psychoanalytic Association, 24,* 831–853.

Urist, J. (1977). The Rorschach test and the assessment of object relations. *Journal of Personality Assessment, 41,* 3–9.

5

The Impossible Takes a Little Longer: The Role of Theory in Teaching Psychological Assessment

Bruce L. Smith
University of California, Berkeley
and California School of Professional Psychology, Alameda, California

> The difficult we do immediately; the impossible takes a little longer.
> —*Seabees motto*

Psychological testing is impossible to learn. As such, it is, therefore, impossible to teach. Nevertheless, we routinely attempt to transform students into competent psychodiagnosticians. Even more surprisingly, we often succeed. The reason that I characterize the teaching and learning of testing as "impossible" is the fact that in order to really understand how to administer and interpret psychological tests, one must have a good grasp of the interpretive process and the kinds of inferences that can be drawn from test protocols. To know that, however, one must first know how to administer and interpret the tests. Hence, where do we begin? It is my view that this conundrum can only be approached through a firm grounding in theory. In this chapter, it is my intention to argue for a theoretically based approach to testing and to outline the role of theory in various aspects of the testing and inference process.

To use the Rorschach as a single example, there are approximately 90 different scores in the Comprehensive System, plus several other suggested scoring categories. Just memorizing the symbols and definitions of these scores would be a Herculean task, but various complicated rules governing the combinations of these must also be learned (see Brabender, chap. 14 of this volume, and Weiner, chap. 13 of this volume). In order to make this task meaningful, it is necessary to understand the rationale for scoring and for interpreting the scores. To understand how to interpret the scores, however, one must first know how to score.

I argue that the learning of assessment should only be approached within the context of a comprehensive theory of personality. Schafer (1954) wrote over 40 years ago: "What [a psychological test] accomplishes depends on the thinking that guides its application. This guiding thought is psychological theory, whether explicit and systematized or implicit and unsystematized" (p. xi). Not only is it impossible to conduct a meaningful assessment of an individual in which observations are integrated into a comprehensive description of a person without a theory of personality with which to integrate one's observations, but it is equally impossible to teach assessment without a theoretical context within which to learn the conduct of the assessment. As becomes abundantly clear, for me that theory is psychoanalysis (Smith, 1990, 1991a, 1994).

In what follows, I discuss the role of theory in assessment in general and then address how this may be applied in the teaching of various aspects of the assessment process. Because it is my main interest, I focus especially on the teaching and learning of the Rorschach.

PSYCHOANALYTIC THEORY AND ASSESSMENT

Early approaches to assessment stressed the superficial description of personality, the sorting of patients into relatively static categories based on descriptions of observable behavior. Clinical psychology, itself, began with the assessment of intelligence, with an emphasis on categorization (Routh, 1996). I like to remind students that up until 1955, *moron, imbecile,* and *idiot* were technical terms describing levels of mental retardation. Even Rorschach's own early work (Rorschach, 1942) was primarily concerned with the categorization of patients (e.g., manic-depressives, schizophrenics, obsessive-compulsives, etc.).

It was primarily the work of the Rapaport group at the Menninger Foundation and later the Austen Riggs Center (Rapaport, 1952; Rapaport, Gill, & Schafer, 1968; Schafer, 1948, 1954) that first ushered in the application of psychoanalytic ego psychology to psychological assessment. Instead of testing to establish a "diagnosis," the Rapaport approach stressed the assessment of psychological functions—cognition, defenses, affects, impulses, object relations, and so on—in order to paint as complete a picture of the person as possible. As I have noted elsewhere (Smith, in press), this development paralleled the ascendancy of the psychosocial model of psychiatric diagnosis, a model in which attention turned from the assignment of labels based on clusters of symptoms to an attempt to understand the *meaning* of behavior patterns in terms of the adaptation of the individual to his or her environment and the social and intrapsychic factors that enable/impede that adaptation. Thus, any particular datum could have multiple meanings depending on the context in which it occurred.

To conduct an assessment that merely seeks to establish class membership (i.e., diagnosis) or predict specific behavior patterns, no complex theory of personality is necessary (although researchers presumably have at least an implicit theory when attempting to establish empirical relationships between test scores and outcome measures). When attempting to go beyond this, however, one must have a theoretical matrix with which to relate variables at different levels of inference.

In my classes in assessment, I stress that a competent personality assessment can be conducted only in the context of a comprehensive theory. Indeed, we spend considerable time discussing psychoanalytic object relations theory and its relevance for the diagnosis of psychopathology. In particular, the distinction between *personality* and *character* (Brodie & Siegel, 1992) is stressed. Personality here is conceived as the sum of an individual's characteristic behavior patterns—traits, if you will—whereas character refers to the underlying structure, that is, the pattern of intrapsychic processes that lead to the observable behavior patterns. As such, character cannot be observed directly; it can only be inferred. In my opinion, it is the task of the psychodiagnostician to assess the character of the subject in order to go beyond simple prediction and develop an understanding not only of his or her characteristic traits, but why he or she behaves in these ways. In this discussion, I stress the contributions of Shapiro (1965) and McWilliams (1994) who articulated the position that psychoanalytic diagnostic terms reflect a consistency across the domains of thinking, affect experience, defensive operations, and object relations.

In addition, I stress a *person-centered* versus a *test-centered* approach (see Handler & Meyer, chap. 1 of this volume). Thus, the task of the psychologist is essentially an integrative one. Data from a variety of sources—for example, interview, projective testing, objective testing, and so forth—are combined into a single description of the subject. Where inconsistencies exist in the data, these need to be resolved into a single description of a person that takes them into account. The context of the testing and the subject's current life circumstance must also be taken into account. This model of assessment precludes a sign-based approach in which specific scores or indexes are seen as invariant signs of a particular trait.

Another aspect of the person-centered approach is the treatment of psychological tests as communications rather than as analogous to medical tests. A medical test is generally seen as an objective measure of some discrete biological function (e.g., presence/absence of HIV or blood glucose level). Its measurement is generally independent of the patient–examiner relationship, patient motivation, and so on.[1] By contrast, psychological tests are mediated by the subject's personality, and are highly influenced by the nature of the relationship between patient and examiner, as well as relationships between referrer and examiner, patient and referrer, and so forth. Patients' responses are a product of their expectations, their anxieties about the testing situation and the relationship with the examiner, as well as the images of themselves they wish to present. It is best to conceive of psychological instruments foremost as an opportunity for the patient to communicate something about himself or herself. One of the

---

[1] There are, of course, instances in which individuals may attempt to "fake" medical tests—as for example with urine tests for the presence of drugs—or in which emotions may affect the values, such as with anxiety and blood pressure. In general, however, medical tests are more "objective" and independent of such factors.

questions that always must be asked is: Why might this person wish me (the examiner) to see him or her in this way?

THE ROLE OF THEORY IN OBJECTIVE
PERSONALITY TESTING

It might seem at first glance that psychoanalytic theory is least relevant to the learning of objective personality testing, for example, the use and interpretation of personality inventories such as the Minnesota Multiphasic Personality Inventory–2 (MMPI–2), the Millon Clinical Multiaxial Inventory–III (MCMI–III) or the California Psychological Inventory (CPI). These instruments have been designed to yield personality descriptions based on empirical relationships between scores and specific observable behaviors. Students frequently attempt to utilize a cookbook approach, looking up scores in a textbook or manual and assuming that the descriptors for a particular score or profile are more or less invariant. The difficulty, however, is that without an approach that takes into account the entire person and utilizes a theory of personality that can relate different observations to an understanding of the totality of the person–situation matrix, the use of these instruments is limited to specific predictions, many of which are of limited validity (see Greene & Roubakhsh, chap. 10 of this volume, and Davis & Millon, Chap. 11 of this volume). Research evidence shows, for example, that certain MMPI scores will have different meanings for different subpopulations (Greene, 1987; Hutton, Miner, Blades, & Langfeldt, 1994; Lucio, Reyes-Lagunes, & Scott, 1994). If these aspects of the person are not taken into account, the resulting interpretation is likely to be inaccurate or biased.

Personality inventories are designed to generate specific descriptors that are associated empirically with specific scales. They are not designed to generate a comprehensive, integrated personality description. That can only be done by the psychologist. Without a theory of personality, it is impossible to know how to interrelate different aspects of personality. All one is left with is a collection of specific behavioral predictions or descriptions that are more or less accurate.

It is very difficult to teach a person-centered approach to instruments such as the MMPI–2, especially as the computerized scoring and interpretive programs tend to atomize the person, presenting a list of attributes that may or may not appear to have anything to do with each other. My goal in working with beginning students is to get them to ask the question: What kind of person would produce a protocol with these characteristics? I do not mean this question in a simple diagnostic sense (e.g., an hysteric, an obsessive, etc.), but rather in a descriptive sense. In order to develop this viewpoint—of looking at the subject in his or her entirety and interpreting test results in that context—I utilize different assignments. In addition to the more common assignments of administering, scoring, and interpreting an MMPI–2, I give students a series of brief case descriptions and ask them to draw an MMPI–2 profile for each case, along with a written formulation and explanation of their profiles; that is, why they would expect the elevations they predicted. I have found that, by presenting the assignment in this manner, students are forced to consider the person as a whole and to derive their predictions from that consideration, rather than letting the test compartmentalize their observations.

PERSONALITY THEORY AND COGNITIVE ASSESSMENT

There is considerable controversy among psychologists about the appropriateness of using intellectual assessment instruments as personality tests. The Wechsler scales, for example, have been validated as tests of intellectual functioning and not as personality inventories or projective devices. Therefore, so the argument goes, it is inappropriate to derive descriptions of personality from them. The problem with this argument is that it assumes that cognition and personality are nonoverlapping domains of psychological functioning (see Handler, chap. 17 of this volume). In fact, of course, it is well known that many emotional disorders affect cognitive functioning. Likewise, characterological traits are reflected not only in emotional and interpersonal functioning, but in cognition as well. As Shapiro (1965) convincingly demonstrated over 30 years ago, neurotic styles are reflected in modes of cognition as well as in other realms of behavior. The difficulty, of course, lies in the interpretation of these modes from the data of intellectual assessment. Many texts, beginning with Rapaport et al.'s (1968) classic *Diagnostic Psychological Testing* of nearly 50 years ago, offer a series of guidelines for deriving diagnostic impressions from Wechsler profiles (e.g., Information lower than Comprehension = hysteria; Comprehension higher than Picture Arrangement = psychopathy, etc.). The problem with such guidelines is that without a sound theoretical rationale they are next to useless. Many novice psychodiagnosticians "know" that a relatively low Information score, especially coupled with a relatively higher Comprehension score, suggests an hysterical personality; few, however, know why this might be the case. What is it about the cognitive style of an hysteric that leads him or her to fail a greater than expected number of questions of general information? Without a theoretical framework, how does the beginning psychologist differentiate between the subject with hysterical trends and the one who fails Information for other reasons (poor early educational background, organic memory disorder, cultural differences, etc.)? Those who are not taught to think theoretically tend to fall back on a sign-based approach to intellectual testing in which specific scores are seen as signs of particular disorders. Such an approach is worse than limited: it is frequently misleading.

Because intellectual functioning is a product of so many different factors, a single score can reflect one—or several—of multiple factors. If one is aware, for example, that hysterics tend to think globally, impressionistically, and imprecisely, and that they tend to rely heavily on the defense of repression in coping with conflict-laden material, it makes sense that they would have difficulty with a test that required precision, specificity, and free and easy access to long-term memory. Qualitatively, one would expect the hysteric to have trouble with questions involving numbers because of the need for exactitude, perhaps even resisting the request for precision. (For example, one such patient told me that the distance from New York to Paris was "thousands and thousands and thousands of miles.") On the other hand, such patients might do relatively better identifying people (e.g., "Who was Martin Luther King?") because of their interpersonal sensitivity. Knowledge of the psychodynamics of character styles allows one to examine the protocol itself in order to understand the scatter. Without such knowledge, the tester is reduced to a blind adherence to a sign-based approach.

One contribution of psychoanalytic theory that is especially germane to understanding intellectual assessment is that of the conflict-free ego sphere. This construct refers to the capacity of the ego to mobilize energy or attention in the service of practical tasks. This capacity, so necessary for day-to-day functioning, is conceptualized by Rapaport as the ego's autonomy from the id (Rapaport, 1951). To the extent that a subject's conflicts, anxieties, or impulses impinge on his or her thought processes, they are likely to impair the performance. Thus, for example, a female subject who experiences mathematics as the domain of men, who is made anxious by such problems, and who has built a gender identity that includes an inability to solve equations is likely to do more poorly on the Arithmetic subtest on the WAIS–R than might be expected given her overall intellect. We can conceptualize this failure as an inability to maintain a conflict-free ego sphere in this specific area. As a consequence, her ability to attend to and concentrate on the problems as neutral stimuli is impeded. Without an understanding of these dynamics, it becomes difficult to interpret such findings.

RORSCHACH THEORY

As I have argued elsewhere (Smith, 1991b, 1994), it is impossible to interpret a Rorschach competently without a coherent personality theory guiding that interpretation. The test itself is atheoretical. As Weiner (1994) pointed out, the Rorschach is more properly a method of data collection than a test in and of itself. As such, it requires a theory in order to organize and make sense of the data collected. In originally developing the Comprehensive System, Exner (1974) attempted to develop a method for scoring and interpreting Rorschach protocols that was atheoretical and based solely on the empirical relationship between Rorschach scores and external criteria. The limitation of this approach, however, lies in the fact that it is impossible to go beyond the specific statements generated by the scores. For example, one might be able to state that an extratensive mingles feelings with thoughts during decision making, but *why* that occurs, or how it fits into a coherent description of that subject's personality cannot be determined from scores alone.

Even more important, without a theory, there is no systematic method of interpreting the nonquantitative data. Exner (1993) noted that projection frequently occurs in responses scored minus, in Human Movement responses, and in responses scored MOR (Morbid Content). He suggested, however, that these do not require much interpretation, because they are usually "obvious" (p. 53). I question how obvious such responses are, in fact. A response of a "threatening giant about to pounce" on Card IV may represent a self-representation, an object representation, a condensation of both, a defense against a self representation (of the self as small and vulnerable), and so on. If it is a self-representation, it could be a wished-for identity, a feared identity, and so forth. It could reflect a transference, and thus aggression toward the examiner (or fear of the examiner's aggression). In this case, it would be necessary to attempt to determine the interpersonal event(s) that triggered the aggressive transference. It can be seen, immediately, that a simple, seemingly unidimensional response may have multiple complex meanings. Without a theory of personality that contains propositions linking phenomena such as these to other phenomena, it is impossible to do more than speculate as to the meaning of the response to that particular subject at that particular time. In fact, as Schafer (1954) pointed out in the quotation cited earlier, all psychologists operate on the basis of a personality theory. The question is whether it is explicit and systematized or implicit and unsystematic. Even Exner, himself, seemed to realize this fact; in later iterations of the Comprehensive System he characterized it as a perceptual-cognitive approach to the Rorschach (Exner, 1993).

The nature of the personality theory used directly affects the way in which the Rorschach is understood. In Exner's perceptual-cognitive approach, for example, the Rorschach response process is considered as a problem-solving task in which the emphasis is on perception. By contrast, Leichtman (1996), working from a developmental psychoanalytic perspective, understood the response process chiefly as a task of *representation*. In this model, the subject represents his or her inner world through Rorschach responses. As Leichtman pointed out, if the task were truly one of perception, the only correct answer for each blot would be "inkblot." Instead, we ask the subject to *create* a response out of the blot, thereby melding his or her inner and outer worlds. In an earlier work (Smith, 1991a), I likened this process to the creation of transitional objects by young children. A bit of external reality is imbued with personal meaning in such a way that it is enlivened. The task facing the subject is the reconciliation of inner and outer realities in such a way that the dictates of neither are violated. In Winnicottian terms, this occurs in potential space (Winnicott, 1971). By adopting this model, we can conceive of various forms of psychopathology in terms of the failure to create meaning or maintain potential space. Thus, for example, in psychosis, the subject replaces external reality with inner reality. In terms of his or her Rorschach protocols, he or she may ignore the perceptual demands of the card and superimpose fantasy on it in an arbitrary manner. By contrast, a rigid obsessional patient may strictly adhere to the perceptual properties of the blot, but fail to enliven it by projecting anything of his or her inner life into it. The result is a series of responses that are banal, constricted, impoverished, but of good form.

In teaching the Rorschach, I always begin with a consideration of the theoretical underpinnings of the response process. If students can grasp the process by which a response develops and its relationship to the subject's psychic structure, the process of scoring a Rorschach protocol can become comprehensible. The various scores in a Structural Summary are not just randomly chosen attributes that happen to be related empirically to psychological variables. There are sound theoretical reasons why these scores have the psychological meanings that they do. Unless those meanings can be understood, the process of learning to score and interpret a Rorschach is reduced to a task of rote memorization. It has always been my belief that if students can develop a clear understanding of the theoretical principles of the Rorschach, the scoring will come. This is why although I teach the Comprehensive System, I first assign such psychoanalytic texts as Lerner's (1991) *Psychoanalytic Theory and the Rorschach*, Leichtman's (1996) *The Rorschach: A Developmental Approach*, or Schafer's (1954) classic *Psychoanalytic Interpretation in Rorschach Testing*. It should be noted that initially this approach causes rampant confusion, as students attempt to assimilate a system written in one language with a theoretical framework in another.

It is important to stress that the theoretical structure that is used will, to a large extent, determine the nature of the interpretations that are derived from the Rorschach. Psychoanalytic theory permits a hierarchical approach to Rorschach interpretation. An interpretive strategy based entirely on a so-called empirical approach offers a series of hypotheses with no way of knowing what is a consequence of what. Simply put, many of the hypotheses or behavioral predictions that are derived from the Comprehensive System, although accurate, may be epiphenomenal; that is, they are, in fact, consequences of other, more basic, processes. For example, an excessive number of space responses is usually taken to reflect oppositionalism or negativity. Why should this be so? By what psychological process are oppositional persons drawn to white space? A quick perusal of typical Rorschach protocols suggests that it is nothing as simple as a refusal to respond to the blot because that is what is expected (if this were the case, presumably space responses would be the majority in such cases). If, however, we consider the white space as a representation of either an inner void or a separation (as when it is perceived between two animate figures), we can understand the need to "fill" space with a response as a defense against either separation anxiety or a sense of emptiness. Such individuals may, indeed, be oppositional, but this does not reflect so much oppositionalism as a trait as it does defensiveness. If a Rorschach variable is interpreted as evidence for this or that trait, that is a characteristic pattern of behavior, it reveals relatively little about the subject. From an analytic point of view, the goal is to understand the variable in dynamic terms, as representing a product of unconscious conflict, defense, and reality orientation. To remain with the preceding example, rather than describe a borderline patient who gives a high number of space responses as a negativistic person, we might characterize him or her as someone who tends to act in an oppositional manner in order to avoid the experience of separation anxiety whenever the stability of his or her interpersonal relationships is threatened.

THE PSYCHOLOGICAL REPORT

The task of assessment is not to interpret tests; it is to prepare a report that integrates all of the data—clinical and psychometric—into a coherent portrait of the subject. Of course, there are times when the task is somewhat simpler, namely to answer a particular clinical question, but generally even these "simple" questions require a complete context for the question to be answered appropriately. This is typically the most difficult task of all for beginning psychologists to master, the integration of data from different sources into a single description of personality. Students faced with the daunting task of integrating often conflicting data into a single report frequently find themselves at a loss as to how to even begin. Many psychologists give up and instead fall back on the model of preparing a report that is test centered rather than person centered, one in which the data from different tests are not integrated; each test is treated independently with, perhaps, a brief summary paragraph at the end. This is an approach that I will not accept. In teaching the person-centered approach to assessment, I stress three principles in report writing: *integration* of the findings, *utility* of the conclusions for that particular patient, and *clarity* of the presentation.

By integration I refer to the fact that the findings of the assessment must be integrated into a single, coherent description of the person. It is more common than not to find inconsistencies between the different instruments, or even between the meanings of different data points from a single instrument. Novice psychologists must learn to ask the question: What kind of person might give an MMPI–2 that looks like this and a Rorschach like that? This is where a psychological theory that includes a concept of depth or levels is crucial. To cite an example from a set of protocols that I frequently use in teaching, a 40-year-old woman produced an MMPI–2 that had few elevations on the clinical scales except for moderate ones on Scales 3 and 4. Her WAIS–R protocol was unremarkable in that the IQ scores were precisely average, there was little intra- or inter-subtest scatter, and no peculiar responses or odd verbalizations. Yet, her Rorschach was quite formally disturbed, with a positive SCZI (Schizophrenia Index), numerous instances of poor reality testing and thought disorder, and several responses with disturbing morbid content. The task, clearly, is to integrate these seemingly inconsistent findings into a description of a single person. The 3-4 MMPI–2 profile, coupled with the pattern of scores on other clinical and supplemental scales, suggests that this patient is a chronically angry woman who tends to express her aggression passively. Because the patient is a college graduate, we may assume that the WAIS–R results underestimate her level of intellectual endowment, although perhaps not her current level of functioning. That the protocol is "clean" would seem to indicate that she is capable of at least adequate functioning in relatively neutral tasks, although perhaps at the cost of efficiency. To understand the disturbed Rorschach protocol, it is necessary to go beyond the formal scoring and analyze the sequence of responses. It turns out that instances of formal disturbance in the response process occur with human or humanlike responses and typically involve a fusion of sexual and aggressive imagery. Subsequent responses, however, are frequently of adequate form quality and without evidence of thought disturbance. A picture now emerges of a personality organized at the borderline level. When she is able to keep her conflicts over primitive sexual aggression out of awareness, she is capable of adequate functioning. This requires considerable effort, however, and at the cost of social isolation. When data from other sources (interview, TAT) are factored in, it becomes possible to formulate the case in terms of her identification with a maternal introject as victim, and her representation of men as sexual aggressors. Her passive–aggressive interpersonal stance reflects an identification with the aggressor, but in a helpless and indirect manner, suggestive of a sense of herself as weak and vulnerable. This raised the question of possible sexual abuse in her background, a question that could not be answered from the test data alone. It was opined that she would be vulnerable to brief, circumscribed psychotic decompensations that were likely to be triggered by interpersonal closeness—especially with a man—or by a perceived aggressive threat. It was further suggested that careful monitoring of the psychotherapeutic transference would be necessary in order to avoid precipitating a transference psychosis (her therapist was male).

It should be clear that this formulation requires a theory that relates underlying dynamic themes to surface behavior. In this example, the case was formulated in terms of object relations theory, a set of psychoanalytic principles that organize psychological structure in terms of the internalization of early object relations.

The second principle of report writing that needs to be stressed is that of utility. Patients are referred for psychological assessment in order to answer complex clinical questions, to resolve treatment impasses, to assist in treatment planning, and so forth. The report should be written in such a way that the specific questions are addressed. Furthermore, the psychologist should strive for conclusions that are tailored to the particular patient. Recommending psychotherapy or observing that a patient poses a suicidal risk are of limited utility. A more nuanced interpretation might be to recommend that the therapist focus primarily on the here-and-now transference, because of the patient's tendency to misapprehend interpersonal events, or that interpretive work will need to await a period of so-called "ego building," during which time the therapist aids the patient in analyzing problems in his or her daily life to help develop the ego structures necessary for more intensive work. Similarly, it would be more appropriate to note that a suicidal patient does not particularly brood about suicide, that he or she acts impulsively when threatened with separation, and that these suicidal crises are not associated with a worsening of her or his depression. In this instance, the therapist can look for signs of weakening impulse control, especially around impending separations (e.g., vacations, long weekends, etc.), and can interpret the separation anxiety more aggressively.

Not only should the conclusions and recommendations be more specific, they need to be developed in the context of the patient's particular circumstances. Blind analyses of testing protocols are entertaining, but the task of the real-world psychologist is to integrate all of the data available. Recommending a female therapist for a patient who is deeply involved in a treatment with a man (as was the case in the previous example) makes no sense. Rather, the psychologist needs to develop recommendations for the therapist's handling of the transference to him. Similarly, one must take into account the patient's real-life situation in interpreting the meaning of the psychological structure that is revealed by the assessment. Sadness, for example, has a very different meaning to a patient who just lost a loved one than it does for someone who has suffered no recent losses. This may seem obvious, but I am impressed by the frequency with which students will sometimes forget the fact that patients have lives that need to be taken into account when trying to understand their personalities.

Finally, I stress the importance of clarity in the presentation of the results of an assessment. Of course, good writing is always essential, but what is of equal importance is addressing the report to its audience. Too frequently, students write test reports that include myriad references to the data in ways that are incomprehensible to the uninitiated ("The Rorschach reveals that Mr. X is introversive, although the high Lambda suggests a more coarctated Erlebnistypus"). Often this is a camouflage for the fact that the student does not truly grasp the underlying constructs and has not, therefore, fully interpreted the data. Data from the assessment should be used as illustrations, not as conclusions in and of themselves.

A second potential problem lies in the nature of the language used. In the days when ego psychology ruled supreme, it was common to read test reports that were elegant documents written in the highly sophisticated language of metapsychology. One read about the "distribution of attentional cathexes," or "partially de-libidinized drive derivatives." What such formulations have to do with the treatment of the patient, however, is not so clear. One of the advantages of an object relations approach is that object relations theory is generally couched in experience-near terms. As a consequence, the treating therapist can more easily translate the conclusions from an assessment into practical intervention.

Finally, the test report needs to be tailored to the purpose of the testing. Most of the examples in this chapter have assumed a clinical assessment in which the report will go to a treating therapist. There are, of course, numerous other circumstances in which an assessment might be conducted. Assessment might be conducted in a forensic context. In this case, although a complete formulation might be undertaken, only those statements that are "on point" and are easily justified by the data are appropriate for the report itself. Furthermore, any technical language needs to be translated into plain English, given the lay audience. For example, an assessment might be conducted for school personnel. In this case, the information should be presented primarily in terms of how the personality factors affect school performance. The testing might be done at the behest of the subject him or herself. In this case, it is necessary to write in such a way that he or she can understand the conclusions and will not be offended by them. Test reports are not documents that exist in a vacuum; they are communications. As with all communications, their effectiveness requires consideration of the receiver.

CONCLUSION

For a number of reasons, students are typically highly ambivalent about psychological assessment at the outset of their careers. Most are made uncomfortable by the role of the assessor. Drawn to psychology by a wish to help, imbued with a sense of the importance of being empathic, they frequently rebel against the role demands of testing, its authoritarian, demanding, and even sadistic aspects. They resent what they see as "pathologizing" or "labeling" of patients. They are often skeptical of the value of the entire enterprise. Some frankly doubt the validity of psychological tests, seeing them as little more than modern-day phrenology. Others may come to a beginning assessment class with an over-idealized view of the power of assessment instruments, seeing them as infallible windows onto the soul (see Handler, Fowler, & Hilsenroth, chap. 24 of this volume). These fantasies can, in part, be understood as reactions to the voyeuristic impulses that are stimulated by the process of assessment. Testing holds out the promise of finding out something about another person that they might not know about themselves or even might not wish to be known.

In responding to these preconceptions, it is imperative to stress the collaborative aspects of psychological assessment. In most circumstances, testing involves working together to find out something about the patient that will be helpful to him or her. This is the essence of a person-centered approach, and it requires the same empathy that psychotherapy does. Furthermore, it requires that the entire context of the assessment be taken into consideration: the patient's class, gender, ethnicity, current situation, expectations about the testing, and so on.

It is also imperative to stress the necessity of a coherent, comprehensive theory of personality for conducting an assessment. With a firm theoretical grounding that explains the relationship between test results and their interpretations and provides a framework into which results can be integrated, the process of assessment can be demystified. Forty years ago, Roy Schafer observed that psychological tests cannot think; hopefully, with persistence psychologists can learn to do so.

REFERENCES

Brodie, S., & Siegel, M. (1992). *The evolution of character*. Madison, CT: International Universities Press.

Exner, J. (1974). *The Rorschach: A comprehensive system*. New York: Wiley Interscience.

Exner, J. E. (1993). *The Rorschach: A comprehensive system: Vol. 1. Basic foundations, third edition* (2nd ed.). New York: Wiley.

Greene, R. (1987). Ethnicity and MMPI performance: A review. *Journal of Consulting and Clinical Psychology, 55,* 497–512.

Hutton, H., Miner, M., Blades, J., & Langfeldt, V. (1994). Ethnic differences on the MMPI Over-Controlled Hostility Scale. *Journal of Personality Assessment, 58,* 260–268.

Leichtman, M. (1996). *The Rorschach: A developmental perspective.* Hillsdale, NJ: Lawrence Erlbaum Associates.

Lerner, P. (1991). *Psychoanalytic theory and the Rorschach.* Hillsdale, NJ: The Analytic Press.

Lucio, G., Reyes-Lagunes, I., & Scott, R. (1994). MMPI–2 for Mexico: Translation and adaptation. *Journal of Personality Assessment, 63,* 105–116.

McWilliams, N. (1994). *Psychoanalytic diagnosis: Understanding personality structure in the clinical process.* New York: Guilford.

Rapaport, D. (1951). The autonomy of the ego. *Bulletin of the Menninger Clinic, 15,* 113–123.

Rapaport, D. (1952). Projective techniques and the theory of thinking. *Journal of Projective Techniques, 16,* 269–275.

Rapaport, D., Gill, M., & Schafer, R. (1968). *Diagnostic psychological testing* (Rev. ed.). New York: International Universities Press.

Rorschach, H. (1942). *Psychodiagnostics.* New York: Grune & Stratton.

Routh, D. K. (1996). Lightner Witmer and the first 100 years of clinical psychology. *American Psychologist, 51,* 244–247.

Schafer, R. (1948). *The clinical application of psychological tests.* New York: International Universities Press.

Schafer, R. (1954). *Psychoanalytic interpretation in Rorschach testing.* New York: Grune & Stratton.

Shapiro, D. (1965). *Neurotic styles.* New York: Basic Books.

Smith, B. L. (1990). Potential space and the Rorschach: An application of object relations theory. *Journal of Personality Assessment, 55*(3&4), 756–767.

Smith, B. (1991a). Dissociation and the collapse of potential space. *Rorschachiana, 17,* 275–279.

Smith, B. (1991b). Theoretical matrix of interpretation. *Rorschachiana, 17,* 73–77.

Smith, B. L. (1994). Object relations theory and the integration of empirical and psychoanalytic approaches to Rorschach interpretation. *Rorschachiana, 19,* 61–77.

Smith, B. (in press). Psychological testing, psychodiagnosis, and psychotherapy. In J. Barron (Eds.), *Making diagnosis meaningful: New psychological perspectives.* Washington, DC: APA Books.

Weiner, I. (1994). The Rorschach inkblot method (RIM) is not a test: Implications for theory and practice. *Journal of Personality Assessment, 62,* 498–504.

Winnicott, D. (1971). *Playing and reality.* London: Tavistock Books.

6

Critical-Thinking Applications in Personality Assessment: Classrooms as Laboratories and Studios

Charles A. Waehler
University of Akron
Harry J. Sivec
WCA Hospital, Jamestown, New York

Wanted: Good Cookbooks or Good Chefs?

Teaching critical-thinking skills has been championed by educators in many disciplines (e.g., Flavell, 1979; Halpern, 1992; Kaplan & Kies, 1994; Meyers, 1986; Morran, Kurpius, C. J. Brack, & G. Brack, 1995). Critical thinking has been defined in different ways in these undertakings. As a result of these varying connotations (e.g., sometimes referring to the learning process, at other times to an educational outcome) the construct has become mystical and elusive. No matter how it is defined, however, psychologists agree that critical thinking is a prerequisite to the formulation of reliable and useful personality assessments.

We conceptualize critical thinking as the ability to process information systematically and creatively. Critical thinking combines a focus on both acquiring a knowledge base and working with information effectively. For instance, when a class exercise is to explain the analogy *MMPI : Rorschach :: Ford Taurus : Jeep Cherokee*, students are sometimes perplexed initially. To address the problem students employ a variety of thinking skills. For instance, they generate relevant facts (either by recall or new learning) and transform this information into appropriate categories. Students then compare each item within the larger categories and generate hypotheses about the interrelationship of the items. Finally, they analyze the relationships between and among analogy items employing a "goodness of fit" test to determine suitability within the entire analogy. Finally constructing explanations, students summarize the analogy in a succinct and cogent manner by observing similarities such as the popularity, conservative cost, and conventional applications of the MMPI and Ford Taurus, and contrast this with the multipurpose nature, adventuresome appeal, and high price of the Rorschach and Jeep Cherokee. We propose that the foundational and complex thinking skills necessitated in this activity are similar to those necessary for assessing personality.

Effective personality assessment certainly requires familiarity with domain-specific knowledge (e.g., that MMPI–2 scales are deemed clinically significant above 65). However, personality assessment additionally requires that students move beyond simple factual recitation to transform observations and knowledge into a meaningful synthesis. Classes dedicated to teaching personality assessment techniques, of necessity, must impart more than just information—students must also learn how to apply this material. Imagine a report composed of verbatim interpretations pasted together indiscriminately from test manuals and lecture notes. Although perhaps technically accurate in one sense, the practice of collecting and reporting bits of information is obviously inadequate for holistic understanding of people. Therefore, assessment instructors are challenged to help students employ critical-thinking skills to understand clients rather than simply to piece together ready-made interpretations from textbooks and printouts.

Personality assessment instructors must ask themselves: How do my teaching methods influence learning? Rephrased in the language of critical thinking: How do my teaching methods influence the acquisition and application of requisite knowledge and skills? We suspect that such a self-evaluation would result in identifying many constructive methods already in practice. However, Alfred North Whitehead (1929/1967) observed that instruction in many classes leads to "inert knowledge," referring to information learned via rote memorization. The danger inherent here is that knowledge learned in one domain may not generalize to other relevant situations. Nummedal and Halpern (1995) noted that "learning to think critically is not an inevitable outcome of instruction" (p. 4) so that teachers also need to impart how and when to use information.

Critical-thinking skills may be conceptualized as possessing both content and process dimensions. Content involves factual knowledge about interview questions, test scores, assessment activities, diagnostic criteria, and the general human condition that lends itself to memorization. The personality assessment process requires cognitive skills to transform the content into accurate, coherent, and useful clinical statements. These cognitive activities might best be labeled critical-thinking skills. We argue that focusing directly on these critical-thinking skills has the potential to improve both teaching effectiveness and subsequent student learning.

Teaching critical-thinking skills requires overcoming several obstacles. As often happens when experts attempt to teach skills to novices, instructors may rely on personal frameworks (rich in critical-thinking processes), but they are less adroit when it comes to conveying these implicit paradigms to their students. Also, students tend to be more sensitized to course content than to thinking processes. Some students devalue activities that do not leave them with a full page of notes to memorize for a test. Indeed, students can become defensive and frustrated when participating in classroom activities that challenge them to exercise thinking skills. Finally, textbooks often disproportionately emphasize content above skill acquisition and application. Sometimes these factors combine and consequently dilute cognitive skills training so that students may finish assessment courses having intermittent practice with requisite skills.

We do not want to imply that mastering higher-order thinking processes alone leads to successful evaluations. Domain-specific knowledge is indispensable to valid personality assessments. Even good chefs need good cookbooks. However, in our classes we reinforce the idea that time spent on processing information enhances what students learn. Although it is true that attention to thinking processes may limit the amount of time a teacher has to lecture on particular subjects, both theory (e.g., Halpern, 1992) and research (e.g., Bransford, Sherwood, Vye, & Rieser, 1986) support the notion that focusing on critical-thinking skills can enhance new learning. By directly highlighting critical-thinking skills, students can establish relevant contexts and reference guides for novel information. As we sometimes say to students, "you will not get all the information you need in this class, but you will know where to find it and how to use it." As students come to find that absolute answers are rare in assessment, they appreciate the process of asking more sophisticated questions as a valuable activity in its own right. Students also need to know that, although not all questions have unwavering answers, they can always work to ask better questions. Properly framed, critical-thinking exercises stimulate a desire for knowledge.

We borrow Vygotsky's (1978) concept of the zone of proximal development for understanding the desire for and acquisition of knowledge via an explicit focus on critical thinking. Vygotsky's zone of proximal development refers to "the distance between the actual developmental level as determined by independent problem solving and the level of potential development as determined through problem solving under adult guidance or in collaboration with more capable peers" (p. 86). This paradigm provided Vygotsky with a way to conceptualize the influence of instruction on the development of higher mental functioning. A fundamental aspect of this work is that "human learning presupposes a specific social nature and a process by which children [students] grow into the intellectual life of those around them" (p. 88).

Teachers keeping Vygotsky's concepts in mind are more likely to forsake unidimensional classroom lectures in favor of group dialogue in which they are both facilitator and participant. We promote critical-thinking skills in our classes by asking probing questions (which in turn lead to further questions) rather than supplying immediate answers. Certainly we furnish important new information when needed, but we recognize that the personal struggle toward solutions from one's own resources is an important part of the learning process. Once basic information has been reviewed, questions just beyond the students' current understanding will promote critical thinking. For instance, the general question "How would we investigate the referral question about this client's depressive potential?" is better than "What does the elevated MMPI scale 2 tell us?", or, "Is the Sum Shading elevated for this client?" which instead capitalize on students' desire for knowledge.

Vygotsky's notions have explanatory power with regard to developing critical-thinking skills. For example, Meyers (1986) stated that teaching critical thinking "involves intentionally creating an atmosphere of disequilibrium, so that students can change, rework, or reconstruct their thinking" (p. 14). According to Vygotsky (1978), the zone of proximal development is characterized by a sort of instability that "awakens internal developmental processes that are able to operate only when the child is interacting with people in his environment and in cooperation with his peers" (p. 90). Learning is construed as a fundamentally social process by which advanced developmental skills (e.g., critical thinking) are acquired and internalized by virtue of mentorship and collaboration. Working within and shaping a zone of proximal development for students, instructors are challenged to identify students' actual level of development and chart their potential development. Within this atmosphere of discovery students move beyond their immediate experience and develop new mental structures for critical thinking when their present ways of understanding are insufficient for the task at hand. Thus, learning involves disequilibrium—an awareness that some important piece is missing. Some students handle the disequilibrium inherent in learning better than others, and all students have their limits. Teaching thinking skills to students involves sensitively gauging the amount of disequilibrium that will be most helpful. Too many challenges can overload students, whereas too few can result in warm, comfortable classes where no learning takes place. We encourage instructors to assess students' level of understanding actively and continuously as part of the process of developing instructional approaches.

CRITICAL-THINKING SKILLS TERMINOLOGY

Another way to manage the potential discomfort that can accompany disequilibrium is to provide concrete reference points both to guide and to provide familiarity to students and teachers. Therefore, we offer critical-thinking terminology for focusing on skills involved in personality assessment. Borrowing the organizing framework Halonen (1995) offered for demystifying critical thinking, we suggest that specific critical-thinking skills essential for personality assessment include those listed in Table 6.1.

We recognize that an abstract list such as this can be unwieldy. However, we also recognize that most terms will be self-evident and those that are not can be altered or revamped depending on the focus and importance to a particular teacher. We use this particular terminology list in a variety of ways: usually as a procedural guide, checklist, or evaluation mechanism. For instance, using the three progressive levels of intellectual activity to examine students' grasp on a particular assessment area, we may pose a typical referral question such as "Evaluate for psychotic process."

TABLE 6.1
Critical-Thinking Skills Essential for Personality Assessment

Foundation Skills	Higher-Level Skills	Complex Skills
Defining variables	Applying concepts	Analyzing relationships
Describing behavior	Broadening perspectives	Communicating results
Identifying assumptions	Categorizing statements	Constructing explanations
Observing behavior	Challenging assumptions	Evaluating theories
Quantifying information	Comparing observations	Inferring generalizations
Recognizing concepts	Finding relationships	Predicting behavior
Selecting procedures	Forming mental representations	Synthesizing observations
	Generating hypotheses	Transforming information

Students are instructed to "begin at the beginning" with critical-thinking foundation skills and to lead the instructor through their thinking about the evaluation. Using foundation skills leads students first to consider test options (selecting procedures) and to provide a preliminary rationale for their choices (identifying assumptions, recognizing concepts). We entreat students to be as specific as possible when justifying their test selection, asking for the essential scores and variables likely to provide the most fruitful information (defining variables). They discuss what they will look for and expect (observing and describing behavior), and how the interview, testing, and chart review sequence may influence their observations (identifying assumptions).

Higher-level thinking skills are addressed next. With hand to chin in pensive reflection, we ask students if they would wager their graduate stipends on the adequacy of their test selection and approach for addressing this referral question (broadening perspectives). During this review, students spell out the contribution of scores and tests to their overall evaluation (applying concepts). As test data and observations are provided, students scan the protocol for relevant information and report scores they believe to be pertinent to the evaluation (classifying statements). We look for students' ability to identify scores likely to address the referral question (applying concepts). To enlarge the discussion, we ask questions such as: "What are the consistencies and inconsistencies in the data?" "Which variables are assigned greater weight in your assessment?" In these examples, the critical-thinking skills employed (e.g., finding relationships, comparing observations, and broadening perspectives) become a way to comprehend the process being undertaken. As students describe their understanding of the data, we encourage them to draw a simplified sketch or diagram of their line of reasoning (forming mental representations) leading to a diagnostic conjecture (generating hypotheses). Sometimes we pose questions that directly stimulate certain critical-thinking processes and at other times we ask students to frame their own queries using a critical-thinking vocabulary item.

Next, we encourage students to exercise complex-level skills. That is, we ask them to synthesize the test data and observations into statements about personality functioning. To do this, students attempt to move beyond a test-by-test or variable-by-variable approach that might be characteristic of higher-order thinking; they must now synthesize observations in order to construct explanations, make predictions, and communicate results. Complex skills are best addressed one at a time. For example, analyzing relationships between and among test data requires time and energy. This is where we are most active in asking questions in an effort to help students move beyond their present level of understanding: "How do you synthesize test data that appear at times inconsistent?"; "What information would help you most to clarify these data (e.g., another test) or to test the hypotheses generated by the present data?"; "In concluding that there is evidence of psychosis, can we specify the quality, severity, and the circumstances that would lead to psychotic-level symptoms (inferring generalization) and with what level of confidence?" Finally, we consider the audience as we work to communicate results effectively. Reviewing the critical-thinking skills terminology helps us be sure that we have highlighted important skills through every step of the process.

Our vocabulary list is by no means exhaustive. We offer the critical-thinking skills terminology as a way to assist teachers to identify personality assessment procedures in a process paralleling the time-honored tradition of promoting growth in psychotherapy by making covert processes overt. We encourage students to employ this list as a way to track their skill development and to identify strengths and weaknesses in different skill areas.

Using this terminology to focus on critical-thinking skills may enhance the acquisition and retention of useful information by providing contexts and reference points. Bransford et al. (1986) reported that acquiring domain-specific knowledge and learning cognitive strategies complement each other because "informing [learners] about uses of strategies and allowing them to practice and evaluate the effects, help students 'conditionalize' their knowledge" (p. 1084). That is, they help students learn the conditions that call for particular thinking skills and a certain knowledge base. In this way, students remember more information because they have a sense of its utility and applicability. As Greeno (1994) discussed, research demonstrates that the context in which knowledge develops influences the extent to which that awareness can be applied in other areas. He suggested that learning that occurs in rich contexts filled with attention to thinking processes facilitates application of the knowledge acquired. Assessment procedures that provide only information (information-exclusive programs) may not promote generalization beyond the specific knowledge base involved. In these ways, learning the requisite information bits needed for successful personality assessment is arguably best achieved when learned within a context that makes productive use of this knowledge and that overtly reviews how and when this knowledge is applied.

We hope that this organized terminology will help teachers and students identify, structure, and highlight critical-thinking skills promoted and practiced in personality assessment. We suggest introducing these critical-thinking skills at the onset of courses by listing them in the "course objective" section of a syllabus and reviewing them during the first class session. Because these skills are both goals and methods to accomplish other objectives, this initial examination should be supplemented with periodic review throughout the course. We begin some class sessions by reviewing the skills as they relate to answering a referral question. At other times we will end a particularly exasperating class discussion or case conference by examining the list to document the complex level of cognitive activity that was being practiced. The next part of this chapter outlines several pedagogical strategies designed to enhance critical-thinking skills and strengthen metacognitive abilities.

STRATEGIES FOR ENHANCING CRITICAL-THINKING SKILLS

In contrast to being purveyors of truth and wisdom through lectures, teachers who promote critical thinking often find themselves in the less familiar roles of referee, coach, and mentor. It is our belief that psychologists can benefit from observing other professionals' pedagogical efforts to promote critical-thinking skills. In this section we briefly propose strategies to reinforce or promote teaching critical thinking in personality assessment classes. We organize the following teaching strategies according to three elements McKeachie (1988) proposed to enhance thinking skills: (a) active, deliberate discussion among students, (b) explicit emphasis on problem-solving procedures and methods using varied examples, and (c) verbalization and role-modeling methods and strategies. The strategies we discuss are not exhaustive. We intend them as sparks to ignite pedagogical fires and as guides that serve to orient each instructor.

Student Collaborative Strategies

Students often help each other learn to administer psychological tests. In spite of the mastery achieved, other forms of student interaction in classrooms are often perceived as "filler" exercises or possibly as detracting from lecture time. Unfortunately, the merit of student collaborative efforts tends to be undervalued. In longitudinal studies of effective practices in undergraduate education, Astin (cited in Cooper, 1995) reported that student–student and student–faculty interactions were two variables that impact on cognitive and affective student outcomes. Revisiting the "zone of proximal development" concept, it is no surprise that positive outcomes were engendered by greater opportunities for interactions with both peers and instructors.

Active, deliberate interactions among students can promote critical thinking. Guided student interactions provide a natural forum for rehearsal and material review. Other benefits of group activities include increased time spent on task mastery, group support, and immediate feedback on errors and faulty strategies. Teachers may shy away from group activities out of fear that "slower" learners will somehow "spoil," or drag down, top-performing students. However, self-reflection reveals that our knowledge often solidifies by virtue of teaching others, so students at varying levels of ability may benefit from the interaction. In addition, a solid research base (e.g., Dansereau, 1988; Ross, Walter, Malenka, Reilly, & Moore-West, 1989; Webb, 1982) supports the contention that one's own knowledge and skills are enhanced by educating others.

At the next level, properly structured cooperative exercises encourage divergent thinking (Cooper, 1995). Students can be encouraged to share their own perspectives to enhance the class process. The tension created by different viewpoints "often motivates students to achieve a resolution. D. W. Johnson, R. T. Johnson, and Smith (1991) termed this process *epistemic curiosity*, as students seek out information to help them resolve the conflict" (cited in Cooper, 1995, p. 7).

Propelled by the desire to reconcile disparate viewpoints, students often achieve increased understanding of the material and its application. In this way, student interactions are an important part of the struggle to move from concrete to abstract thought. Confronting questions and conclusions of fellow students, often different from one's own, adds to the disequilibrium that helps to shake students from egocentric perceptions of the world. Two collaborative strategies to promote critical thinking include negotiation methods and situated simulation designs.

Negotiation Strategies.   The art of negotiation involves a discussion of two or more different perspectives. Such approaches have been supported as facilitating critical thinking (Bernstein, 1995). An optimal goal in negotiation is a synergistic solution that transcends any individual perspective (i.e., a win/win solution). In Buddhism this solution is referred to as the "middle" or higher way. In this sense, middle does not necessarily denote compromise, but rather "a higher meaning as in the apex of a triangle" (Covey, 1989, p. 273). For the purposes of this chapter, negotiation represents the acquisition of a novel perspective and new mental structures.

A practical example of such a strategy would involve giving a specific referral question about a particular client to students assembled into groups of two to three. The group task is to list, in order of importance, the test variables to examine in order to answer the referral question. This problem-solving exercise invites students to combine specific knowledge with reference to practical and theoretical considerations. The group context encourages students to draw on each other as resources to support the final solution. Interactions among students with differing preferences and viewpoints (e.g., behavioral vs. dynamic) may accentuate inclusion criteria discussion. If multiple groups are formed within the same class, additional negotiations can be conducted so that the learning involved in supporting and challenging decisions can be reinforced. Projects such as this could be construed as end-of-class activities, or as semester-long undertakings.

Another negotiation activity requires students to review a personality assessment research proposal. Each student/reviewer is challenged to critique the manuscript, suggest revisions for the proposal, and render an opinion about whether he or she would support such research. Students are then assembled into teams that include equal numbers of those favoring the proposal and those who do not support the proposal. The new assignment for each team ($N = 4-6$ students) is to synthesize the independent observations into one set of comments and to achieve group consensus regarding support for the proposal. The final team document should contain a composite, integrated list of concerns and recommended course(s) of action. The activity could stop here or have a final negotiation between the groups involved.

These negotiation strategies require students to use and demonstrate their knowledge. They also are forced to prioritize and justify their observations to peers, a process that promotes higher-order thinking, such as analyzing relationships, building theory, constructing explanations, and synthesizing observations. When divergent views are negotiated, the limitations of an individual perspective are broadened so that higher-order solutions become possible.

Situated Simulation Strategies. Active struggle with realistic problems helps students evaluate what they know and what they need to know. Meyers (1986) made the following observation about classroom activity:

> One might smile at the idea of a college course in basketball in which students spend all their time learning basketball terminology, diagraming plays, and watching videotapes of the Boston Celtics setting up plays. Then, for the final exam, students are expected to play a competent game of basketball and maintain a shooting average of 50 percent. Yet this is similar to what occurs when teachers spend the bulk of classroom time lecturing, presenting theory, and testing for recall of information and then expect students to demonstrate good critical skills in a final term paper or student project (p. 10).

Activities that simulate real-world situations motivate students to apply their analysis framework, allowing them to generate and test hypotheses while minimizing the untoward effects of well-intended, albeit, inaccurate personality evaluations. Students can apply what they know and ascertain what they need to know. Put another way, they can experience their own zone of proximal development. Derry, Levin, and Schauble (1995) employed situated simulations in their statistics courses to apply thinking skills successfully to real-world problems. These exercises can be adapted by personality assessment instructors. By contriving scenarios in which personality assessments are used, situated simulations can be designed to emphasize different critical-thinking skills. For example, a forensic case can be presented in which students are asked to report on test data in a courtroom setting. This means that each student will present conclusions derived from test data and participate in constructive review (direct examination) and justification (cross-examination) proceedings. To avoid a battle between right and wrong, the instructor can serve as an observer who reports on critical-thinking skills employed or needed. In our classes, we employ the critical-thinking skills terminology at this point to review students' thinking process. Together with the class we identify that a student appears to be doing an adequate job with foundation skills (e.g., observing behaviors or defining variables), but is lacking complex skills (e.g., synthesizing observations or communicating results). This scrutiny reveals ways in which participants' thought quality can be improved. In so doing, students internalize a process for evaluating their own work that can then be applied in other circumstances.

This type of simulation emphasizes two features: accountability and direct comparisons of divergent hypotheses. These factors have been suggested to combat judgment errors such as "confirmation bias" (see, e.g., Arkes, 1991).

Another scenario involves students in the role of consultant. We arrange mock feedback sessions in which the student presents feedback to various sources: adult patient, referring professional, school teacher, or law enforcement agent. By role playing these interactions, they practice many critical-thinking skills including synthesis, understanding, applying theory, understanding flexibly, and communicating their results with heuristic value (such as the use of metaphors). The role-playing participants and observers evaluate both the feedback content, process, and reasoning involved.

Metacognitive Awareness Strategies

Metacognition, which we consider separate but related to critical thinking, is promoted when people reflect on their thinking skills and strategies. "Cognitive strategies are invoked to *make* cognitive progress, metacognitive strategies to *monitor* it" (Flavell, 1979, p. 909). Metacognition is the ability to apply a strategy for producing what knowledge is needed, to be conscious of the steps and strategies employed during the act of problem solving, and to reflect on and evaluate that thinking. Baker and Brown (1980) considered that metacognition includes "knowledge about cognition and regulation of cognition" (p. 354). They stated that there are two, necessarily interwoven, clusters of activities in metacognition: "The first cluster is concerned with a person's knowledge about his or her own cognitive resources ... the second cluster consists of self-regulatory mechanisms used by an active learner during an ongoing attempt to solve problems" (p. 354).

Metacognition includes checking to see if critical-thinking skills were used fully in the learning cycle. Activities to invoke metacognition may seem more daunting or time-consuming than need be. For instance, Angelo (1995) suggested using a 1-minute paper that "asks students some variant of the following two questions: What was the most important thing you learned in today's class? What question related to this session remains uppermost in your mind?" (p. 6). Bondy (1984) suggested promoting a general awareness of metacognitive activity by having students keep a daily "learning log" to monitor their own learning, thereby shifting the focus from academic products to cognitive processes. To facilitate conscious monitoring of comprehension, Bondy also suggested providing instruction in self-questioning techniques, teaching students to summarize material, and teaching students to rate their comprehension. Additional strategies to promote metacognitive awareness include writing assignments, case studies, and problem-solving activities.

Writing Strategies. We are confident that writing maintains a central role in personality assessment courses and we applaud all assignments that include a writing component because they can so effectively promote important thinking skills while also simulating real-world activities. Wade (1995) stressed that writing: "tends to promote greater self-reflection and the taking of broader perspectives than does oral expression. ... Written assignments ensure the participation of every student—a basic requirement for active learning. ... Writing allows time for reflection and a careful consideration of reasons for taking a position or making an assertion" (p. 24). Applying a metacognitive strategy to our own work, we recognize that writing this chapter has required complex thinking skills, including constructing explanations, synthesizing observations, transforming information, and communicating results.

The literature regarding pedagogical activities to promote critical-thinking skills is replete with writing assignments. This may be because the attention given critical-thinking skills and writing across the curriculum came about during the same late 1970s, and early 1980s time frame. However, the relationship between the emphasis on these two activities is not simply chronological; they are also highly complementary and reinforcing of one another. Indeed, Stout (1992) stated, "More than any other learning activity, writing enables student thinking" (p. 57). Consistent with our previously stated intentions, Rico (1983) noted that writing activities help students "map their subconscious," providing a means of bringing latent ideas and feelings to the surface. MacKinnon-Slaney (1991) advocated writing as a way to induce thinking because it "provides a moment of clarification" (p. 93). Bensley and Haynes (1995) noted several commonalities shared by critical thinking and writing so that writing is highly useful for the training of critical thinking:

> Like writing, critical thinking involves purposeful, goal-directed thinking. Moreover, the processes involved in critical thinking may be similar to those involved in scientific and rational writing. For example, process like planning, organizing, goal setting, reading, and editing ... may be similar to those used in critical thinking. ... Writing and critical thinking also often serve complementary purposes. For example, they both can be used to refine thought. ... Externalization of thought through writing may reduce the load on working memory and be important for developing the metacognitive component of critical and scientific thinking. (p. 41)

For all these reasons, we encourage personality assessment teachers to consider class writing assignments beyond the standard term paper and/or assessment report. Simple, yet effective, creative writing assignments have been proposed by educators in a variety of scholastic domains that can be extended to personality assessment classes. Stout (1992), for instance, outlined three "micro-writing" assignments that are successful in her art appreciation classes. Each assignment has a maximum length of three pages so that the effort goes into mental processing quality, not quantity. In Stout's "Classification" exercise, students observe paintings and, based on traits that pieces have in common, generate their own categories of style to classify each painting. As additional paintings are added, students are invited to create new categories. Within a personality assessment class focused on Rorschach variables, we challenge students to generate and justify a classification scheme for such variables as M, W, S, Lambda, and Z. They often focus on the cognitive elements involved, and are therefore additionally challenged when we add the variables Afr, D, V, and WSUMC. We continue to add variables of interest, or ask them to generate their own variables that would be similar to or contrast with their schema. When students do not include some important personality variable (e.g., interpersonal functioning or affective experiences), we question how they might address these areas. We are less concerned with the actual classification system derived as we are with the accurate understanding of the variable and the complexity of thinking involved. Discussing this exercise can also aid in students' appreciating that, within a domain as complex as personality assessment, there are often cases in which more than one "right" answer applies.

To promote full consideration of different perspectives, interpretations, and theories, Stout (1992) used a writing exercise that examines multiple viewpoints. She asked students to write as if they were famous artists, critiquing the work of another artist. Alternatively, a student may write from the perspective of an artist collaborating with a colleague of a different genre. Such activities could be easily translated into personality assessment classes so that hypothetical discussions between different theorists could be constructed. For example, we have students discuss a Rorschach protocol as if they were B. F. Skinner collaborating with Carl Jung (or, alternatively, we have them take on the role and perspective of various faculty members). By encouraging students to explore diverse viewpoints, this writing assignment can promote cognitive flexibility by promoting the recognition that there often exist multiple reasonable perspectives on almost everything human.

Within these shorter writing assignments, students can be encouraged to write what Stout (1992) referred to as a "meta-note," which relates to the thinking involved in solving the problem at hand. To write the meta-note, students reflect on how they derived solutions which promotes a self-conscious concern with their own thinking. (For example, our thinking at this point in this manuscript includes "recognizing and applying concepts," and we would label it as such.) In early written reports, marginal meta-notes using the critical-thinking terminology provided in this chapter may assist teachers and students alike in reviewing the thought processes underlying the student's personality assessment.

Case Study and Problem Solving Strategies. It would probably be rare to encounter advanced personality assessment classes that do not make use of case studies. However, it remains useful to review how critical-thinking activities are promoted by case studies and ways to make improvements. McDade (1995) noted that the case study/discussion method advances critical thinking because it actively involves students in their own learning processes. Case studies are enhanced when teachers prepare for them by considering "an outline of questions to facilitate the discussion and lead students through the thought process of analysis and application" (p. 10) rather than preparing an outline of statements as for a lecture.

Case study methods may be enhanced by designating some students to be responsible for observing and documenting the thinking processes being undertaken during class discussion. Similar to the meta-note suggested previously for the writing assignments, students assigned to reflect on classroom thought process will gain practice in this metacognitive skill and will assist other class members in gaining this higher-order awareness.

McBurney (1995) distinguished the case study method from the problem-solving method, seeing the latter as requiring students to find their own solution to the problem presented, whereas the case study method analyzes particular cases to identify facts and principles. Most teachers probably use case studies as stimuli for students to think about and generate personalized answers to referral questions, so that problem solving (as opposed to reviewing and evaluating the decisions made by others) is required. However, case studies in which solutions are provided promote different thinking skills than exercises that require original thought. Therefore, case studies that provide ready-made solutions (e.g., evaluating an MMPI profile) may lead well into more challenging problem-solving methods (e.g., assessing a client's potential for suicide using the MMPI).

Verbalizing/Role Modeling and Representing Strategies

We adopt an inclusive perspective for McKeachie's (1988) third suggestion to promote critical-thinking skills by verbalization and role modeling, so that any effort at making observable representations out of abstract concepts may promote higher-order thought processes. Verbally and visually depicting their ideas can become ways students recognize, analyze, and improve their thinking skills.

Visualization Strategies. Visualization approaches have been employed by numerous disciplines to enhance performance. Representing thoughts and ideas via visual representations often makes concepts more accessible to students while promoting advanced concept formation (Dansereau, Dees, & Simpson, 1994). Halpern (1992) suggested that teachers use, and encourage students to use, "concept mapping" for activities in which schematic descriptions can supplement primarily verbal information. She suggested that having a visual model for a process or idea reduces the load on working memory and activates nonverbal reasoning and processing abilities. An example of a concept map is Fig. 6.1, which presents a visual illustration of the material for this chapter. If space permitted it would be instructive to show the several iterations through which this figure evolved, and the thought processes invoked, in arriving at this representation of our central ideas and their interrelatedness. Such an exercise would also illustrate the evolving nature of concept maps, as well as the important notion that more than one representation may be acceptable. We

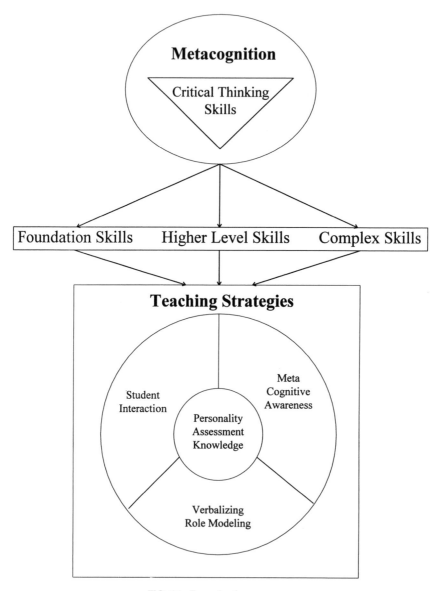

FIG. 6.1. Example of a concept map.

suggest using Fig. 6. 1 in conjunction with our vocabulary list when formulating instructional approaches.

More germane to teaching personality assessment, Exner (1993) used a basic form of concept mapping to introduce interpretations of Rorschach variables that are clustered into what he called the cognitive triad (p. 449):

INPUT ⎯⎯⎯⎯⎯→ TRANSLATION ⎯⎯⎯⎯⎯→ CONCEPTUALIZATION

(PROCESSING)   (MEDIATION)   (IDEATION)

More sophisticated and detailed visual depictions can be used, depending on the needs of the instructor and the complexity of the concept under considera-tion. Concept maps are effective tools because they are "based on cognitive theories of how people acquire and use information. They place emphasis on the relationships among topics rather than isolated'bits' of information and de-emphasize memorizing labels and lists" (Halpern, 1992, p. 5).

Similar to concept mapping, Stout (1992) described her assignment "Clus-tering" as "a non-linear brainstorming process that allows the writer to pull ideas and information out of the subconscious, to find out what is there, and to map the landscape of that hidden realm" (p. 63). Her students are encouraged to eschew the standard outline approach to written papers and instead represent abbreviated ideas and themes in visual/spatial relation to one another before attacking a writing assignment. Concept maps and clustering can be useful tools as preludes to writing assessment reports because "they offer a nonlinear alternative to outlines, and can be used to predict where errors occur—faulty groupings, wrong information, and skimpy structures" (Halpern, 1992, p. 5). Concept maps allow students both to "see" what they know, and to diagram structure and relationships for that knowledge.

Students also profit from methods that directly invoke visual images. For example, analogies and metaphors often stimulate concrete representations of abstract verbal concepts. More generally, relating course content to daily life events encourages visualization and, because it personalizes the meaning for that individual, it may increase recollection of that material.

It has long been a psychoanalytic tradition to attend to private thoughts stimulated in interactions with patients. In theory, this practice is thought to enhance the intuitive perceptions of others. Watts (1980) argued that training programs need to help students develop refined intuitive skills. Citing research, Watts reported that "only fantasy related training methods facilitated perform-ance on tests of intuitive perceptual abilities" (p. 105). In line with this position, an instructor teaching the Rorschach might entreat students to visualize a patient's M (human movement) response and imagine this M response in a variety of interpersonal situations (e.g., peer group, confrontation, with task demands; see Potash, chap. 9 of this volume). Similarly, when discussing an MMPI profile, students can be encouraged to fit the test data to movie characters. The actual visualization task employed will vary depending on the intended function; specific tasks are less important than recognizing the value in using visual modes to represent information in another contextual manner.

Role Modeling and the Classroom Culture.   In addition to the cognitive ele-ments that promote critical thinking, Halonen (1995) and others (e.g., Woods, 1987) have suggested that attitudes and emotions will influence critical-think-ing skills development. Attitudes thought to promote these skills include:

intellectual curiosity, skepticism, tentativeness, tolerance of ambiguity, appreciation of individual differences, openmindedness, persistence, tenaciousness, objectivity, and possessing a high regard for ethical practices. What we suggest is that teachers set the tone and model acceptable activity within the classroom and that they must be ever aware of the climate created. In this regard, the instructor is at the helm of the ship and can help navigate a course that is most favorable to engendering critical-thinking opportunities (see Handler, Fowler & Hilsenroth, chap. 24 of this volume).

A classroom culture that encourages critical thinking will offer opportunities to reflect on those skills. Kaplan and Kies (1994) suggested that the types of questions asked will develop the academic culture of the classroom. Acknowledging that "open-ended, divergent questions require more analytic thinking than do closed, convergent, yes/no, factual questions" (p. 26), Kaplan and Kies outlined six question levels, each promoting more sophisticated thinking: questions regarding knowledge, comprehension, application, analysis, synthesis, and evaluation. We suggest considering these question levels and how they promote learning *during class*. Such attention to the process can help students understand their thinking level and monitor their development. As students incorporate this thinking, and mimic the teacher's efforts to engage in more sophisticated reasoning, the self-questioning in which they will engage will mirror the metacognitive activity that King (1991) described as effective in promoting reading and lecture comprehension.

Meyers (1986) also suggested some keys to which teachers can attend to establish a classroom culture to promote critical thinking. These activities include: beginning each class with a problem or controversy; using silence to encourage reflection; arranging classroom space to encourage interaction; wherever possible, extending class time; and creating a hospitable environment. With regard to silence in the classroom, it has been observed that the average grade school teacher waits one second before responding to questions. This activity probably discourages active consideration of material by all members of the class and also implies that there is more value in getting something right versus thinking about it. Although addressing advanced graduate students is not directly comparable, teachers are encouraged to use more "wait-time" before responding to questions posed during class. Such an undertaking can lead to silences, which sometimes can seem uncomfortable, but it also provides ripe opportunities for all class members to consider the question carefully.

An additional teacher activity that promotes factual recitation and may shift reward to an external source is praising a student's statement. However, praising, which is appropriate when single, correct answers are desired, can inadvertently shut off diversity of expression when the full consideration of varying perspectives is a goal. An alternative to praise is active acceptance and elaboration, in which the teacher reflects, paraphrases, and clarifies a student's observation. Instead of saying "good, that is the correct answer," teachers can paraphrase and reflect the student's statement, thereby ensuring clarification, while also asking the class to modify the statement. This active acceptance tactic promotes exploration, thinking and self-criticism. Teachers practicing active responses (e.g., "You are saying that because the client has no inanimate movement in his Rorschach responses, he is not experiencing anxiety at this time?") promote higher order thinking and avoid being trapped in dichotomous, right or wrong, evaluations. Active responses can help students identify their own erroneous statements (e.g., "So, are you saying that an IQ of 115 puts him in the Superior range?"), or advance their own accurate thoughts (e.g., "So, what does it mean that his IQ score of 115 puts him in the High Average range?") so that they increase self-efficacy in these areas.

Talk-Aloud Strategies.   Fundamental to critical thinking is making covert thought processes available for observation and evaluation. Several authors (e.g., Nist & Kirby, 1986; Whimbey & Lochhead, 1984) advocate the use of "thinking aloud" strategies to improve thinking. These approaches ask students to verbalize their thinking as they attempt to solve problems or address issues. For the purposes of personality assessment, this approach can be applied in individual supervision or as part of a classroom exercise. Important to note, the process of thinking aloud is best facilitated when the instructor takes the lead.

When novices in any field attack a problem, they develop a hypothesis and follow a lead until it results in a dead end. Then they backtrack and start over with another approach. Novices also typically have difficulty prioritizing issues and sorting out variables; they act as if all considerations have equal importance. The experts, on the other hand, quickly identify central variables, eliminate noncrucial considerations, and, drawing on their vast previous experience of related problems, formulate an analysis (Hunt, 1982). Student–teacher dialogues that involve talk-aloud strategies help bridge the gap between novices and experts.

CRITICAL THINKING AND CLINICAL
DECISION MAKING

We believe that critical-thinking skills taught in personality assessment classes may help redress the long-disputed effectiveness of psychologists as diagnosticians (Dawes, 1994; Holt, 1970; Meehl, 1954). Suboptimal decision strategies along with human bias have been identified as problems in this literature. One of the most common impediments to sound clinical judgment has been referred to as "confirmation bias" (Arkes, 1981; Faust, 1986). This refers to a strategy for decision making in which a selective search for information leads to unwarranted support for a hypothesis (Arkes, 1991). In this regard, overlooking potentially disconfirming evidence is particularly problematic. Returning to an earlier example, students asked to evaluate for psychotic process sometimes zero in on only one or two variables that verify their search for evidence of psychosis on the Rorschach (e.g., "I've identified several Rorschach Special Scores that are often associated with schizophrenia"). However, in the process, students sometimes overlook or do not know what to make of other potentially disconfirming evidence (e.g., we might ask, "How do you explain the X+% and F+% within normal limits and several M responses with good form quality?"). More generally, psychologists who seek to confirm positive instances of a particular diagnostic hypothesis (e.g., this patient is schizophrenic), and do not sufficiently look for or attend to disconfirming evidence, are more likely to commit this type of error. Confirmation bias has been identified when assessors erroneously associate a particular test sign with specific pathological conditions (L. Chapman & J. Chapman, 1967). Emphasizing critical-thinking skills may have the potential to combat this naturally occurring tendency and to promote the examination of alternative explanations for similar test patterns (Spengler & Strohmer, 1994).

Additionally, Arkes (1991), in his discussion of "association-based errors," proposed implementing specific strategies that cue debiasing behavior. Improved decision making through tactics such as "considering the opposite" (Lord, Lepper, & Preston, 1984) parallel critical-thinking skills such as divergent thinking and testing alternative hypotheses. Revisiting the earlier example (assess for psychotic process), we encourage students also to "consider the opposite" and attempt to identify confirmation of intact reality testing. Students are then primed to search and consider disconfirming evidence. The next step would involve asking students to generate a variety of alternative hypotheses to explain the test data.

In these ways, critical-thinking strategies serve to enhance awareness of decision-making processes and thereby to improve them. Although focusing on critical-thinking skills will not provide students with immunity from common judgment errors, intentionally reviewing and highlighting thinking processes represents an approach that directly addresses some of the critical decision-making errors.

SUMMARY

To return to our original question—Wanted: good cookbooks or good chefs?—we conclude with an emphatic: Yes! We want both good cookbooks and good chefs. Meehl (1956), who originally posed a variation of this question, challenged psychologists to improve the quality of interpretive materials in order to enhance the reliability and validity of statements about personality. In many respects, psychology has responded to this challenge by producing a wealth of clinical and research data. However, in teaching the thousands of independent information bits necessary for personality assessment, we must not overlook the fact that the process requires critical-thinking skills to observe, reason, analyze, synthesize, infer, integrate, evaluate, translate, and communicate relevant findings. In this respect, we argue that teachers and students benefit from attending to the thinking skills necessary to formulate valid personality assessments. Pedagogy born from the genre of critical-thinking approaches provides a way to review and promote these important skills. We have tried to overcome the sometimes intangible and mystifying nature of critical thinking by providing an organized framework with orienting principles for understanding and employing critical thinking in classrooms.

Our cookbook has reviewed ingredients (i.e., working terminology) and broad recipes (i.e., teaching strategies) that may make critical thinking more palatable to the reader. We hope to excite instructors about possibilities and directions to spice up teachers' approaches rather than provide rigid guidelines. Therefore, the strategies are left open to novel variations on the part of each instructor to fit the needs of different students and disparate courses. In this way, we encourage teachers and learners to sample liberally from our presentation and season to taste.

Bon appétit!

REFERENCES

Angelo, T. A. (1995). Classroom assessment for critical thinking. Special Issue: Psychologists teach critical thinking. *Teaching of Psychology, 22*, 6–7.

Arkes, H. E. (1981). Impediments to accurate clinical judgment and possible ways to minimize their impact. *Journal of Consulting and Clinical Psychology, 49*, 323–330.

Arkes, H. E. (1991). Costs and benefits of judgment errors: Implications for debiasing. *Psychological Bulletin, 110*, 486–498.

Baker, L., & Brown, A. (1980). Metacognitive skills of reading. In D. Pearson (Ed.), *Handbook of reading research* (pp. 353–394). New York: Longman.

Bensley, A. D., & Haynes, C. (1995). The acquisition of general purpose strategic knowledge for argumentation. Special Issue: Psychologists teach critical thinking. *Teaching of Psychology, 22*, 64–65.

Bernstein, D. A. (1995). A negotiation model for teaching critical thinking. *Teaching of Psychology, 22*, 22–24.

Bondy, E. (1984). Thinking about thinking: Encouraging children's use of metacognitive processes. *Childhood Education, 60*, 234–238.

Bransford, J., Sherwood, R., Vye, N., & Rieser, J. (1986). Teaching thinking and problem solving: Research foundations. Special Issue: Psychological science and education. *American Psychologist, 41*, 1078–1089.

Chapman, L., & Chapman, J. (1967). Genesis of popular but erroneous psychodiagnostic observations. *Journal of Abnormal Psychology, 72*, 193–204.

Cooper, J. L. (1995). Cooperative learning and critical thinking. *Teaching of Psychology, 22*, 6–7.

Covey, S. R. (1989). *The 7 habits of highly effective people*. New York: Simon & Schuster.

Dansereau, D. F. (1988). Cooperative learning strategies. In C. E. Weinstein, E. T. Goetz, & P. E. Alexander (Eds.), *Learning and study strategies: Issues in assessment, instruction, and evaluation* (pp. 103–120). New York: Academic Press.

Dansereau, D. F., Dees, S. M., & Simpson, D. D. (1994). Cognitive modularity: Implications for counseling and the representation of personal issues. *Journal of Counseling Psychology, 41*, 513–523.

Dawes, R. M. (1994). *House of cards: Psychology and psychotherapy built on myth*. New York: The Free Press.

Derry, S., Levin, J. R., & Schauble, L. (1995). Stimulating statistical thinking through situated simulations. *Teaching of Psychology, 22*, 51–57.

Exner, J. E. (1993). *The Rorschach: A comprehensive system: Vol. 1. Basic foundations* (3rd ed.). New York: Wiley.

Faust, D. (1986). Research on human judgement and its application to clinical practice. *Professional Psychology: Research and Practice, 17*, 420–430.

Flavell, J. (1979). Metacognition and cognitive monitoring. *American Psychologist, 34*, 906–916.

Greeno, J. G. (1994). Some further observations of the environmental/model metaphor. *Journal for Research in Mathematics Education, 25*, 94–99.

Halonen, J. S. (1995). Demystifying critical thinking. *Teaching of Psychology, 22*, 75–81.

Halpern, D. F. (1992). A cognitive approach to improving thinking skills in sciences and mathematics. In D. F. Halpern (Ed.), *Enhancing thinking skills in the sciences and mathematics* (pp. 1–14). Hillsdale NJ: Lawrence Erlbaum Associates.

Holt, R. R. (1970). Yet another look at clinical and statistical prediction: Or, is clinical psychology worthwhile? *American Psychologist, 25*, 337–349.

Hunt, M. (1982). *The universe within: A new science explores the human mind.* New York: Simon & Schuster.

Kaplan, E. J., & Kies, D. A. (1994). Strategies to increase critical thinking in the undergraduate classroom. *College Student Journal, 28*, 24–31.

King, A. (1991). Improving lecture comprehension: Effects of a metacognitive strategy. *Applied Cognitive Psychology, 5*, 331–346.

Lord, C. G., Lepper, M. R., & Preston, E. (1984). Considering the opposite: A corrective strategy for social judgment. *Journal of Personality and Social Psychology, 47*, 1231–1243.

MacKinnon–Slaney, F. (1991). Discovery writing in introductory college student personnel graduate courses. *Journal of College Student Development, 32*, 92–94.

McBurney, D. H. (1995). The problem method of teaching research methods. Special Issue: Psychologists teach critical thinking. *Teaching of Psychology, 22*, 36–38.

McDade, S. A. (1995). Case study pedagogy to advance critical thinking. Special issue: Psychologists teach critical thinking. *Teaching of Psychology, 22*, 9–10.

McKeachie, W. (1988). Teaching thinking. *Update, 2*, 1.

Meehl, P. E. (1954). *Clinical versus statistical prediction.* Minneapolis: University of Minnesota Press.

Meehl, P. E. (1956). Wanted—A good cookbook. *American Psychologist, 11*, 263–272.

Meyers, C. (1986). *Teaching students to think critically.* San Francisco: Jossey-Bass.

Morran, D. K., Kurpius, D. J., Brack, C. J., & Brack, G. (1995). A cognitive-skills model for counselor training and supervision. *Journal of counseling and development, 73*, 384– 389.

Nist, S. L., & Kirby, K. (1986). Teaching comprehension and study strategies through modeling and thinking aloud. *Reading Research & Instruction, 25*, 254–264.

Nummedal, S. G., & Halpern, D. F. (1995). Introduction: Making the case for "psychologists teaching critical thinking." *Teaching of Psychology, 22*, 4–5.

Rico, G. (1983). *Writing the natural way.* Los Angeles: J. P. Tarcher.

Ross, J. M., Walter, J. M., Malenka, D. J., Reilly, B., & Moore-West, M. (1989). A new approach to preparing students for academic medicine. *Medical Education, 23*, 265–269.

Spengler, P. M., & Strohmer, D. C. (1994). Clinical judgmental biases: The moderating roles of counselor cognitive complexity and counselor client preferences. *Journal of Counseling Psychology, 41,* 8–17.

Stout, C. J. (1992). Critical thinking and micro-writing in art appreciation. *Visual Arts Research, 18,* 57–71.

Vygotsky, L. S. (1978). *Mind in society: The development of higher psychological processes* (M. Cole, V. John-Steiner, S. Scribner, & E. Souberman, Eds.). Cambridge, MA: Harvard University Press.

Wade, C. (1995). Using writing to develop and assess critical thinking. Special Issue: Psychologists teach critical thinking. *Teaching of Psychology, 22,* 24–28.

Watts, F. N. (1980). Clinical judgment and clinical training. *British Journal of Medical Psychology, 53,* 95–108.

Webb, N. M. (1982). Student interaction and learning in small groups. *Review of Educational Research, 52,* 421–445.

Whimbey, A., & Lochhead, J. (1984). *Beyond problem solving and comprehension: An exploration of quantitative reasoning.* Philadelphia: Franklin Institute Press.

Whitehead, A. N. (1967). *The aims of education.* New York: The Free Press. (Original work published in 1929.)

Woods, D. R. (1987). How might I teach problem solving. In J. E.Stice (Ed.), *Developing critical thinking and problem solving abilities* (pp. 55–71). San Francisco: Jossey-Bass.

III

THE INTERPERSONAL DIMENSION

This part includes three somewhat different chapters, all of which, however, emphasize one or another aspect of the interpersonal dimension that is important in learning personality assessment.

"Training in Assessment: Internalization and Identity," by Paul M. Lerner has little to do directly with test and technique interpretation. However, Lerner goes directly to the heart of the matter of learning assessment; he highlights the importance of the relationship between the teacher and the student in learning assessment. The focus here is on mentorship in transmitting and internalizing important values that are at the core of the patient–clinician dyad. Lerner explains that these issues are rarely considered in teaching assessment. He focuses on the personhood of the teacher and the place of clinical-humanistic values in the teaching process. This very sensitive and touching chapter illustrates quite well the mentorship quality described by Howard Lerner in Part II.

Joseph M. Masling's chapter, "Interpersonal and Actuarial Dimensions of Projective Testing," illuminates the emotional demands placed on the patient and the examiner, and the effects of these influences on the test data—the interpersonal aspects of the assessment process. He describes a teaching method to sensitize students to the role of the "test taker," teaching them to recognize indications of healthy personality integration. Masling also reviews a great deal of research concerning various examiner effects, including the effects of the examiner's needs and personality style on the resultant test data, and on the written report. He describes studies in which even unintentional reinforcement takes place because the examiner's expectancies somehow are subtly communicated to the patient, thereby affecting the test results. In addition, he discusses the communication to students of the "actuarial versus clinical prediction" issue, being quite fair to both sides.

"Assessing the Social Subject," by Herbert M. Potash, describes a method of sensitizing students to the effects that patients' dynamics have on others. He develops the notion that the emotional reactions a patient elicits in others is of central importance because these reactions determine the degree to which they either succeed or fail in the interpersonal world. The emphasis of this chapter is on how to communicate to students methods of assessing the subject as a social being, by focusing on the reactions he or she elicits in the examiner, as representative of the reactions they are likely to elicit in most people.

7

Training in Assessment: Internalization and Identity

Paul M. Lerner
Camden, Maine, and University of Tennessee, Knoxville

Kevin Arnold, a 13-year-old ninth grader, with his teacher's help, raised his math grade from a D to a C. Pleased with his own accomplishment but needing something more, he approaches his teacher, Mr. Collins, after class seeking recognition and praise. To his dismay, however, Mr. Collins instead points out that a C grade indicates average work and says he believes Kevin can do better.

Beyond seeing this potential in Kevin, Mr. Collins also offers him the opportunity to fulfill it, suggesting that they do more work together outside class. Somewhat reluctantly, Kevin accepts the offer. To his surprise, as they meet frequently over the next several weeks, his interest in math deepens. So does his relationship with Mr. Collins. Kevin eventually realizes it is not the subject that has captivated him so much as the teacher himself—his passion and commitment.

Several days before the all-important midterm exam, Mr. Collins abruptly, and without explanation, informs Kevin that he no longer will be available for extra help. Upset by the apparent rejection and fearful of the impending exam, Kevin pleads with him, finally screaming in desperation, "I thought you were my friend!" Seemingly unmoved, Mr. Collins responds, "I am not your friend, Mr. Arnold, I am your teacher."

Bitterly disappointed, Kevin intentionally fails the exam and mocks it by writing on his answer sheet snide comments such as "so what," "who cares," and "factor this." But over the ensuing weekend his anger diminishes and is replaced by increasingly painful feelings of guilt. This leads him, on the following Monday, to seek out Mr. Collins to apologize. Unable to find Mr. Collins, he is finally taken aside by the principal, who hesitantly tells him that Mr. Collins passed away over the weekend.

When you are 13 years old life feels like a series of unrelated events. Kevin still had his family, his friends, and his future. He has his own private agony too.

The exams, in several days, are handed back, but something odd has occurred. Kevin's exam is not there. Instead, there is a blank exam with Kevin's name on it and a note, written by Mr. Collins before he died, indicating that Kevin's exam was misplaced and that he should retake it. Kevin is given a second opportunity.

As he takes the exam, Kevin's thoughts turn to Mr. Collins and their relationship: how Mr. Collins had treated him like a man and how he had reacted as a boy; how he had let Mr. Collins down, and now he would not. Almost feeling his teacher's presence in the classroom, Kevin realizes that whereas he had thought he needed Mr. Collins for the answers and the praise, now he is on his own. As he hands in the completed exam, he confidently tells the replacement teacher, "You don't have to grade it—I know it's an A." And finally, as he leaves the room, Kevin looks back over his shoulder at Mr. Collins' desk. Imagining Mr. Collins sitting there, he whispers, just loud enough for each of them to hear, "Good job, Mr. Collins." Good job indeed.

The vignette involving Kevin Arnold and his math teacher is taken from the television program "The Wonder Years." Although the story pertains to teaching and the teacher–student relationship in a broad sense, it nonetheless has important implications for training in psychological assessment. In what follows I discuss learning as a form of internalization, implications of internalization for clinical training, the matter of professional identity and the role of a humanistic-clinical attitude as part of it, and the emergence of object relations theory in psychoanalysis.

ON INTERNALIZATION

Beginning with Freud, the concept of internalization has occupied a prominent position in the psychoanalytic literature. Based on different strands in Freud's writings, it has been discussed from various vantage points including the importance of inadequate or distorted internalizations in psychopathology, the place of internalization in the treatment process, the function of internalizing mechanisms as defenses, and the role of internalization in growth and development. It is this latter perspective—internalization as a vehicle for growth and development—that is emphasized here.

In his 1923 article "The Ego and The Id," Freud used the term *introjection* to account for the process by which external experiences are transformed and re-created on the terrain of inner experience. In his discussion of superego development he explained how the guiding, restraining, and punishing functions originally imposed on children by their parents in time become part of the child and are experienced not as other-regulators, but as self-regulators.

Authors subsequent to Freud replaced the term introjection with *internalization* and viewed introjection as one type of internalization. Representative of this refinement is Kernberg (1976), who distinguished between introjection and identification but saw both as subordinate aspects of internalization. For Kernberg, unlike introjection, identification implies a firm separation between self- and object representations and presupposes an actual relationship in which the individual experiences himself or herself as the subject interacting with another person.

For psychoanalysts, the internalizing process—the transforming of outer experiences to inner experience—occurs in the context of an object relationship. Prompting the process is the affective relatedness (i.e., love, hate, respect, fear, etc.) between the participants. Included in the internalization is not just the personhood of the other and the nature of the relationship, but also roles, functions, and attitudes. For instance, with internalization, the individual is progressively able to do for himself or herself what others previously had done for him or her. Or, as Cohen and Sherwood (1991) pointed out, when a child internalizes his or her mother he or she also internalizes the sense of being (or of not being) seen, defined, and validated.

Because internalization involves transforming functions, attitudes, and an entire array of external events, it is, as Loewald (1962) reminded us, structure building. This is to say, psychic structures, including cognitive ones, are based on and modified by internalized object relations.

This view of internalization as a mediating process for growth, development, and learning is highly consistent with Piaget's theory of cognitive development (H. Lerner & P. Lerner, 1986). Both emphasize the progressive internalization and structuring of external environmental experiences and both focus on the continuous growth, reorganization, and revision of existing internal structures. The time period that psychoanalysis pinpoints as the beginnings of emotional object constancy and consolidation of individuality coincides exactly, in Piaget's theory, with the interiorization of learning skills (Mahler, Pine, & Bergman, 1975). Then too, at stake in both models is the increasing autonomy from the external environment.

In addition to important similarities between the concept of internalization and Piaget's theory of cognitive development, there are significant differences between these two theoretical approaches. Piaget and virtually all learning theorists accord little if any attention to the relationship between the subject and the object (i.e., parent–child, teacher–student, etc.). By contrast, psychoanalysis places the relationship at the center of the internalizing process. Vicissitudes of the relationship such as the affective quality of relatedness, the object's capacity to hold and to contain, the object's consistency and continuity, and the fit between self and other all assume critical importance.

Involved in internalization, in counterdistinction to Piaget and other theories of learning, is the notion of loss. Whereas some take Freud's model of mourning as a metaphor for understanding internalization, others regard loss or threatened loss of an object as a necessary precondition for internalization.

References to the intimate connection between loss, or what Frankiel (1994) referred to as "shifts in relation to the object," and internalization appear in several of Freud's writings. For instance, in "Mourning and Melancholia" he described the melancholic's identification with the abandoning object this way: "Thus the shadow of the object fell upon the ego and the latter could henceforth be judged by a special agency, as though it were an object, the forsaken object. In this way an object-loss was transformed into an ego-loss and the conflict between the ego and the loved person into a cleavage between the critical activity of the ego and the ego as altered by identification" (Freud, 1917, p. 249). Later, in 1923, in "The Ego and The Id," he wrote, "The character of the ego is a precipitate of abandoned object cathexes and contains the history of those object choice" (p. 23).

Authors since Freud have both echoed and built upon his initial insights. Schwaber (1971), for example, suggested that the loss might not be of an object but rather of an earlier mode of relating to the object. Loewald (1962) noted that whereas early formative relationships are transformed into psychic structures, these structures, in turn, influence later relationships, and J. Bloom-Feshbach and S. Bloom-Feshbach (1987) pointed out that separation or other instances of loss not only spur internalization, but also foster representation, and that this process continues through life.

The example depicting the experience of Kevin Arnold and his relationship with Mr. Collins not only illustrates the internalizing process, but also breathes life into a more abstract, theoretical concept. Kevin's change in behavior, his learning of math, and his ability to achieve at a higher level, were not prompted simply by a growing interest in math. Kevin's interest in math did deepen. However, it was occasioned and stewarded by his evolving relationship with Mr. Collins. Initially, Kevin sought Mr. Collins' praise and approval, his love if you will. Yet, what Kevin received back and thrived from was not the praise, but his teacher's time, emotional availability, passion, and commitment to his students.

Like a good-enough parent, Mr. Collins knew Kevin well. He gave Kevin not what he asked for but what he needed. Mr. Collins tended their relationship. He defined boundaries (i.e., "I am not your friend, I am your teacher"), provided real opportunities, and saw Kevin as he was and as he could be. Although the relationship served as the foundation for Kevin's changing, the changes themselves were precipitated by the loss of Mr. Collins—first the rejection and then the abandonment. Following the loss Kevin identified with Mr. Collins and internalized Mr. Collins' attitude toward him and the functions he had provided. Underlying Kevin's external behavioral change was a more fundamental internal change. Kevin's self-representation shifted from that of an average student to one of an outstanding student. He was now able, based on his own accomplishments, to supply for himself the love he sensed he needed from others.

Internalization as a model of and explanation for growth and learning has significant implications when applied to clinical training. First, it reminds us that meaningful learning takes place in an interpersonal context. As teachers and supervisors, beyond issues of course content and dispensing information, we need to attend to our relationships with our students and supervisees.

Second, students identify with and internalize far more than our knowledge and our skills. They internalize our entire being; they embrace our values, our ideals, our passions, and our attitudes, including our attitude toward them (see H. Lerner, chap. 3 of this volume). This means that as one prepares to teach a fresh group of students or begins to work with a new supervisee, one asks oneself, what is it I want students to take in from me and take away from our encounters?

Internalization, and hence learning, presupposes a clear distinction between self and other concerning personhood and clarity concerning respective roles, functions, responsibilities, and goals. A mutually shared goal involves the student's eventual sense of greater autonomy. Progressively, knowledge and skills originating in the teacher become a part of and accessible to the student. Eventually, students are increasingly able to do for themselves those functions they originally looked to their supervisors to perform.

With internalization, significant changes are internal rather than external in nature. Therefore, successful training is judged not simply in terms of external criteria, such as amassing funds of information or functioning more competently, but also in terms of internal criteria, such as shifts in sense of self, progression toward a professional identity, and greater awareness and sensitivity in experiencing and relating to another.

VALUES AND IDEALS

In the previous section I suggested that one goal of training in assessment involves assisting a student in his or her movement toward a sense of "professional identity." The term *identity* is elusive; it is something one feels or senses, and therefore, is not readily definable. Nonetheless, philosophers, psychologists, and writers wrote about it long before it was popularized. William James (1920), for instance, in a letter to his wife, wrote, "A man's character is discernible in the mental or moral attitude in which, when it came upon him, he felt himself most deeply and intensely active and alive. At such moments there is a voice inside which speaks and says: 'This is the real me!'"" (p. 199).

And, in an address to the Society of B'nai B'rith in Vienna, Freud (1926) commented:

> What bound me to Jewry was (I am ashamed to admit) neither faith nor national pride, for I have always been an unbeliever and was brought up without any religion though not without a respect for what are called the "ethical" standards of human civilization. Whenever I felt an inclination to national enthusiasm I strove to suppress it as being harmful and wrong, alarmed by the warning examples of the people among whom we Jews lived. But plenty of other things remained over to make the attraction of Jewry and Jews irresistible—many obscure emotional forces, which were the more powerful the less they could be expressed in words, as well as a clear consciousness of inner identity, the safe privacy of a common mental construction. Beyond this there was a perception that it was to be my Jewish nature alone I owed two characteristics that had become indispensable to me in the difficult course of my life. Because I was a Jew I found myself free from many prejudices which restricted others in the use of their intellect; and as a Jew I was prepared to join the Opposition; and to do without agreement with the compact majority. (pp. 273–274)

For James, character, by which I believe he was referring to identity, is mental and moral, comes over you almost as a surprise, and is virtually palpable. For Freud, identity involves ethnic origins, is both personal and cultural, and is known to and shared by those who belong to a common community or group. For both, it comes about through recognition and reflection, not aspiration, and it is experienced as enlivening, vitalizing, and deeply authentic.

Erikson (1968), in keeping with the elusiveness and complexity of the concept, described it, all at once, as a conscious sense of individual uniqueness, an unconscious striving for a continuity of experience, and a solidarity with group values and ideals. He suggested that identity begins very early in life, somewhere in the first genuine meeting of the mother and her child, reaches a normative crisis in adolescence, and ends only when the individual's need for mutual affirmation wanes.

Most agree that a sense of professional identity is a highly important, however difficult, goal of assessment training. In practice, however, comparatively little direct and overt attention is paid to professional values and attitudes. Although training programs tend to emphasize the content of our work (i.e., techniques of assessment, issues of test reliability and validity, diagnostic classification systems, in some instances clinical thinking and clinical skills, etc.), little emphasis is accorded *how* we work—the professional attitudes, and manner in which we work and the underlying values.

In assessment, professional identity, in part, consists of ethical standards and one's theoretical orientation (i.e., psychoanalytic, cognitive-behavioral, etc.). There is another component, however, that extends beyond ethical guidelines and cuts across theoretical persuasions. It is that aspect of identity that is not formalized, but instead, is transmitted, unwittingly, through students' and supervisees' identification with their teachers. What I am referring to here is professional identity as reflected in one's attitude toward and approach to patients, clients, and so forth.

As a teacher and supervisor, both in words and in actions, I attempt to impart to students and beginning psychologists an approach to assessment based on a humanistic-clinical attitude. By humanistic, I am referring to the humanness of the assessor as expressed in his or her compassion, concern, and therapeutic intent toward the patient. This involves the continuous awareness that the individuals who seek our help are in pain and are suffering, and that our task is to understand the nature of their difficulties and to assist them to get well. Students ought to know that regardless of how provocative, obnoxious, or alienating a patient behaves or how repulsive we experience their past behavior, as a professional psychologist one attempts to maintain a concern for the patient's self-esteem, self-regard, and dignity.

A humanistic attitude is further expressed in our belief that the patient has rights in the assessment situation—the right to remain separate, the right to confidentiality, and the right to be helped. Students ought to know that it is because of these rights that one explains to patients why they are being assessed and the nature of the assessment procedures. Such rights are further expressed in our practice of judiciously sharing assessment findings and recommendations with patients.

For me, respecting patients' rights also means that mechanical devices such as audio or visual taping have no place in assessment, even for teaching or supervisory purposes. I recognize my stance runs counter to current training practices.

It has become commonplace in many teaching settings for patients to expect and accept that their privacy and the privacy of the assessment and treatment processes will be intruded upon for training needs. Even though these breaches do not violate issues of confidentiality in a legal-ethical sense, they do violate the spirit of confidentiality. As important, such practices convey to students that their own training needs take priority over the needs of patients. Also conveyed to students is the idea that under certain circumstances it is acceptable to compromise the structure of the clinical relationship.

There is another issue at stake here too. The issue is one involving mode of observation and data collection. Kohut (1959/1978), in his seminal article "Introspection, Empathy, and Psychoanalysis," argued that access to psychological depths can be obtained only through specific modes of observation: introspection into one's own subjective state, vicarious introspection, and empathy into that of another. Unlike Kohut, I believe that information obtained through external observational modes is valid and useful. It should, however, be integrated with empathically derived information. Audio and visual taping, implicitly and unfortunately, tilts the balance toward external observation.

A humanistic attitude also finds expression in the quality of our assessment reports and the type of report we teach students to write. We are all familiar with reports that describe individuals, not in human terms, but in diagnostic terms (i.e., manic depressive, depressive disorder, etc.), test-based terms (i.e., extratensive, high T, etc.), or technical terms with a heavy lacing of psychological jargon.

For example, in one report a patient was simply and succinctly referred to as a "narcissistic personality with schizoid features." In a second report the same patient was described as follows: "Like Holly Go Lightly, the main character in Truman Capote's *Breakfast at Tiffany*, the patient blyfully glides through life allowing little to touch or affect her. Her seeming imperviousness, while both enticing and alienating, serves as protection against profound fears of loss."

Clearly, lost in the first report but captured in the second was the patient's uniqueness, complexity, and humanness, together with a sense of her inner experience. Assessment reports written descriptively and humanely and pitched at an experiential level convey more useful information about a patient and more readily grab hold of the reader. Even more important, they reflect how we regard and think about our patients and train students to think about patients.

With respect to the clinical component of a humanistic-clinical attitude, this first includes a stance of receptive openness and nonjudgmentalness. The term *analytic neutrality* has been incorrectly taken to mean abstinence and deprivation. Rather, the concept has to do with an "even hovering attention," openness if you will, to the full array of an individual's productions and then a striving to understand, not judge, those productions.

A second aspect of a clinical attitude involves one's willingness and capacity to accord each session with a patient full importance. In assessment, this means that the examiner is patient oriented and not test oriented. As Mayman (1964) put it, testing should be automatic and familiar enough to the examiner that he or she is free to engage with the patient rather than the tests and is empathically attuned to the emotional nuances of the relationship.

In assessing with a clinical attitude one is emotionally available, not hindered by internal and external distractions. Such availability allows the examiner to take stock of all aspects of a patient's behavior, including, for example, the careful avoidance of blackness on the Rorschach cards, impatience in solving math problems, excessive precision and conciseness in developing TAT stories, and a tendency toward undue self-criticalness in an interview.

A third feature implicit in a clinical attitude is a heightened and continuous attunement to boundaries. Several authors (Chassequet-Smirgel, 1992; Greenson, 1967) have written of the "therapeutic frame," by which they meant the structural features that provide the framework for treatment to occur. Like treatment, assessment, too, has a frame. That frame includes the assessment procedure and the attendant assessment (i.e., test) directions. However, it also involves the way in which the assessor and assessee refer to each other, the assessor's dress and demeanor, how appointment times are set and held to, the matter of fees, and the assessor's awareness of the assessment setting and its meaning for the patient.

It is my experience that whereas we expend much time and energy to teaching the mechanics of testing and of inference building, we tend to be negligent in alerting students to the importance in establishing and maintaining the assessment frame. For example, a supervisee began a testing session by introducing himself by his title and referring to the patient by her last name. She immediately reacted by first pointing out the formality and distancing of titles and surnames and then suggesting they relate on a first-name basis. He hesitantly agreed. Only later in supervision could he appreciate her assault on the assessment structure, his willingness to bend with it, and its subsequent impact on the entire assessment.

The final element of a clinical attitude is the clinician's meaning-seeking orientation. I am referring here to the assessor's unwavering pursuit of meaning, understanding, and truth. In training, such an orientation is encouraged by the types of questions we ask of our students and suggest they ask of themselves. Meaning seeking goes beyond the "whats" and "hows" of behavior; it also includes the "whys."

A humanistic-clinical attitude, as both a way of working and as an aspect of professional identity, does not easily lend itself to formalized teaching. Instead, it is expressed in how clinical courses are taught, the manner of conducting supervision, and the way we ourselves relate to and regard students. For example, in a course in psychopathology or in an assessment practicum one can unwittingly devalue patients by discussing them exclusively as examples of specific diagnostic categories. Or, conversely, one can consider the individual with respect and concern by presenting an even-handed view of the individual in which symptoms and troubling personality characteristics are balanced with a consideration of the person's pain and adaptive strengths. Too often, both in and outside of the classroom, I have heard colleagues and students alike refer to patients flippantly and pejoratively in ways such as, "oh, she's just another narcissistic princess." Such a phrase is not just depreciatory; it also reflects an obliviousness to the individual's sense of vulnerability, naggingly low self-esteem, and defensive self-enhancement.

As illustrated by Kevin Arnold and Mr. Collins, the teaching relationship and the clinical relationship share much in common. It is because of their similarities that the former can be an unspecified training ground for the latter. In the laboratory of the teacher–student relationship students informally learn important lessons relevant to their future clinical work—how to (or how not to) set and keep boundaries, how a relationship with an imbalance in power can be used constructively or destructively, and how relationships are tended.

Those who work with children are especially aware of the child's tendency, for both defensive and adaptive purposes, to turn passive experiences into active ones. In relational terms, the child regards and treats others as he or she feels treated. Not unlike the child, students too, at various levels of training, will regard and react to patients not only as they have been directly taught, but also in ways expressive of how they have been regarded and responded to. Students cannot be expected to develop a humanistic-clinical attitude with patients if they, themselves, are regarded and dealt with otherwise.

CONCLUSION AND POSTSCRIPT

In this chapter I have stressed the importance of and role of object relations. I have suggested that internalization, of which learning is one form, takes place in an interpersonal context and is governed by several of the same principles found earlier in the parent–child relationship. Professional identity, too, develops in a relational matrix and is dependent on the teachers, supervisors, and mentors one has available to identify with.

In recent years many of what were once regarded as quintessential tenets and propositions of psychoanalytic theory have been dramatically reformulated. Although instinct theory and later ego psychology once held sway, psychoanalytic theory has increasingly become a psychology of object relations. This shift in emphasis within psychoanalysis from drive theory to object relations theory is part of what Stone (1954) labeled as the "widening scope of psychoanalysis." Accompanying this shift is the view that instinctual drives constitute one aspect of experience that must be integrated with other dimensions whether they be of an internal or environmental origin.

Contemporary object relations theory represents an integrative thrust including a confluence of attachment theory (Bowlby, 1969), cognitive psychology (Piaget, 1937/1954; Werner, 1948), and traditional ego psychology (Hartmann, 1939/1958; Rapaport, 1957/1967) all within a broadened developmental framework (Mahler et al., 1975). The major focus within object relations theory is on the development of a differentiated, cohesive, and integrated representational world that unfolds and molds in the context of a maternal or primary matrix, termed by Winnicott (1960) a "holding environment." The primary caretaker is conceived as the mediator of psychological organization.

These developments in psychoanalytic theory are in concert with movement away from an experience-distant metapsychology couched in the language of structures, forces, and energies and movement toward an experience-near clinical theory that focuses on self, other, and representations, and uses the language of experience. Fuller consideration is given the experiences of an individual within an interpersonal matrix and the ways in which these eventuate and are structured into representations of the self and of others. The developmental level of the organization of self- and object representations are seen as structures that evolve from the internalization of early, formative interpersonal interactions with significant others. In turn, these psychological structures, these representations of self and other, shape and direct later interpersonal relations.

The origins of these contemporary developments in psychoanalysis can be traced to the early work of Ferenczi and Abraham and the crucial contributions of Melanie Klein. Collectively, these writings have helped articulate the concept of an "internal world" which develops object relationally.

A major consequence of this shift in theoretical focus has been to decenter (Piaget, 1937/1954) psychoanalytic theory from an exclusive intrapsychic frame of reference to one that includes interpersonal phenomena in the formation and development of psychological structures. These advances have dramatically altered classical psychoanalytic notions concerning biological influences on behaviors, early developmental stages, the pivotal role of the mothering agent and early environment, and the impact on growth and learning of object relations.

From a psychoanalytic perspective, applying object relations theory to the issues of learning and identity formation is relatively contemporary. In terms of our current professional climate, simply discussing and focusing on these matters is anything but contemporary.

This is to say, at a time when courses in psychopharmacology and service delivery for managed care are being considered for inclusion in graduate training programs; when the language of diagnosis, behavioral description, and target symptoms has replaced an earlier language of experience and dynamics; when the clinical relationship, its meaning, value, and role as a vehicle of change is under attack; and when genuine change is regarded as magical, quick, effortless, and painless, an emphasis on learning as an interpersonal process and a concern with professional values and ideals may appear peculiarly outdated.

Clearly, I think not. Indeed, now, more so than at other times, a restating and revisiting of traditional professional concerns such as identity and humanistic-clinical values is called for. Implicit in biological psychiatry is an attempt to render meaning meaningless, and implicit in managed care is an attempt to commercialize assessment. Confronted with these challenges students need to be steeped in their professional roots. At issue here is integrity and "generational continuity."

With reference to generational continuity, there is one final point. Thirteen-year-old Kevin Arnold learned, as many of us have, that teachers, supervisors, and mentors never need to die; they can live on in our memories forever. There are several we believed in; however, if we were lucky, there were one or two who believed in us. Those individuals we not only remember, but cherish too.

REFERENCES

Bloom-Feshbach, J., &Bloom-Feshbach, S. (1987). *The psychology of separation and loss.* San Francisco: Jossey-Bass.

Bowlby, J. (1969). *Attachment and loss: Vol. 1. Attachment.* New York: Basic Books.

Chasseguet-Smirgel, J. (1992). Some thoughts on the psychoanalytic situation. *Journal of the American Psychoanalytic Association, 40,* 3–26.

Cohen, C., & Sherwood, V. (1991). *Becoming a constant object.* Northvale, NJ: Jason Aronson.

Erikson, E. (1968). *Identity: Youth and crisis.* New York: Norton.

Frankiel, R. (1994). *Essential papers on object loss.* New York: New York University Press.

Freud, S. (1917). Mourning and melancholia. *Standard Edition, 14,* 243–258.

Freud, S. (1923). The ego and the id. *Standard Edition, 19,* 12–66.

Freud, S. (1926). Address to the Society of B'nai B'rith. *Standard Edition, 20,* 273–274.

Greenson, R. (1967). *The technique and practice of psychoanalysis.* New York: International Universities Press.

Hartmann, H. (1958). *Ego psychology and the problem of adaptation.* New York: International Universities Press. (Original work published 1939.)

James, W. (1920). *The letters of William James.* Boston: Atlantic Monthly Press.

Kernberg, O. (1976). *Object relations theory and clinical psychoanalysis.* NewYork: Jason Aronson.

Kohut, H. (1978). Introspection, empathy, and psychoanalysis. In P. Ornstein (Ed.), *The search for the self: Selected writings of Heinz Kohut: 1950–1978* (Vol. 1, pp. 205–212). Madison, CT: International Universities Press. (Original work published in 1959.)

Lerner, H., & Lerner, P. (1986). Contributions of object relations theory toward a general psychoanalytic theory of thinking. *Psychoanalysis and Contemporary Thought, 9,* 469–513.

Loewald, H. (1962). Internalization, separation, mourning and the superego. *Psychoanalytic Quarterly, 31,* 483–504.

Mahler, M., Pine, F., & Bergman, A. (1975). *The psychological birth of the human infant.* New York: Basic Books.

Mayman, M. (1964). *Some general propositions implicit in the clinical application of psychological tests.* Unpublished manuscript, The Menninger Foundation, Topeka, KS.

Piaget, J. (1954). *The construction of reality in the child.* New York: Basic Books. (Original work published in 1937)

Rapaport, D. (1967). The theory of ego autonomy: A generalization. In M. Gill (Ed.), *The collected papers of David Rapaport* (pp. 722–744). New York: Basic Books. (Original work published in 1957)

Schwaber, P. (1971). Freud and the twenties. *Massachusetts Review, 10,* 133–147.

Stone, L. (1954). The widening scope of indications for psychoanalysis. *Journal of the American Psychoanalytic Association, 2,* 567–594.

Werner, H. (1948). *Comparative psychology of mental development.* New York: International Universities Press.

Winnicott, D. (1960). The theory of the parent infant relationship. *International Journal of Psychoanalysis, 41,* 385–395.

8

Interpersonal and Actuarial Dimensions of Projective Testing

Joseph M. Masling
State University of New York at Buffalo

An instructor teaching a course in projective techniques encounters almost as much ambiguity as a subject responding to inkblots or TAT stimuli. I assume that most classes in projective assessment will include some elementary material about test construction and assessment and most students will be expected to acquire basic knowledge about the various types of test reliabilities and validities. Beyond that, the field of teaching projective methods seems ill defined, allowing each instructor to bring something unique and valuable to the task.

In addition to teaching the basic facts about tests in general and projective tests in particular, when I taught such a course I tried to accomplish two other goals with first-year graduate students: to develop understanding of the demands and forces acting on a subject who must respond to projective stimuli, and to write a coherent, integrated report describing a unified human being functioning at some level of efficiency rather than portraying the subject as essentially a series of discrete pathological responses.

To help the new examiner empathize with the test subject's situation I had my students play the role of test taker. To be confronted by a stranger equipped with stopwatch, clipboard, and inkblots is stressful, especially when test takers, with few cues provided to guide their performance, are aware that important decisions will be made about them based on their responses. Beginning students are much less likely to overgeneralize from the subject's responses if they are mindful that for the most part subjects behave realistically to a stressful, ambiguous situation.

The most difficult task for me in teaching projective methods, and one in which I was ordinarily hugely unsuccessful, was training students to be sensitive to indications of health and integration in projective protocols. It is easy to notice signs of pathology in test responses, sometimes even when they are not there to begin with. Poor form responses, constricted and unimaginative re-

119

sponses, easy responses, confabulations, contaminations, illogical thinking, egocentric responses to the stimuli, card rejection, perseveration, seeing sexual images where others do not or not reporting sexual images where others do, and generally behaving in ways that the examiner finds inappropriate are easily spotted and easily classified as pathological. The literature is rich with examples of test responses showing pathology in one form or another. Beginning graduate students are being exposed to this material at the same time they are also reading intensively in psychopathology courses. Little wonder they are likely to pounce on any minor (or major) signs of disorganized thought in a protocol and construct interpretations based almost exclusively on them (Soskin, 1954, 1959).

Less easily discovered is evidence that the test taker is functioning adequately, shows ability to integrate complex material, can provide a coherent, meaningful narrative to ambiguous stimuli, and can perform well in the stressful conditions of the testing session. I found, for instance, that beginners almost always ignore humor in test responses because they do not know what to do with it, aside from interpreting it as a defensive maneuver. The grim task of learning to be a clinical psychologist somehow leads the new graduate student to expect nothing but sobriety from their test subjects as well. As one antidote to the tendency to invent or magnify pathology, I would have graduate students test undergraduates drawn from the Psychology 101 subject pool. Even with these subjects, generally healthy and well functioning, it is easier to spot and describe pathology than to see evidence of integration. It is apparent in this instance, and probably others as well, that psychology as a profession attends more to pathology than to health.

Because they do not yet know how to grasp gestalts but instead see only parts, beginning students sometimes construe specific responses to indicate the whole, generalizing from one response to an entire person. This is extremely concrete thinking, easily adopted when more complex modes of thinking have not yet been acquired. Akin to this illogic is a kind of analogical reasoning that can sometimes be seen in the clinical literature. For example, it is sometimes argued that human figures drawn without feet represent lack of contact with reality, that white space responses represent oppositional behavior because most people see figure rather than ground, that reporting eyes on the Rorschach indicates paranoia, and so forth. Empirical research does not support any of these assertions (see G. Frank's 1993 review of the literature on the validity of interpreting the white space response as oppositionalism). These three examples make sense if one accepts reasoning by analogy, but the lack of demonstrated validity of such propositions is disconcerting. Beginning students should also be made aware that statements that can be found in fortune cookies; for example, descriptions that sound universally true and could describe almost anyone are like empty calories that contribute little to nourishment. Such undiscriminating comments as "His performance is sometimes hampered by anxiety," "She is ambivalent about her relationships with her parents," and "He is uncomfortable acknowledging his anger," although sounding both profound and plausible, should be avoided (see Handler, Fowler, & Hilsenroth, chap. 24 of this volume).

Working with projective protocols allows clinicians to form high-strength verbal associations between a response and some form of human behavior. For example, in a Rorschach study L. J. Chapman and J. Chapman (1969) found that clinicians developed a strong association between buttock responses and percepts that include both male and female parts with the prediction of male homosexuality. Not only was this plausible inference incorrect, but the responses that did predict homosexuality, monsters and part human/part animal percepts, went undetected. This is yet another instance where a strongly held, incorrect intuition can be maintained because it is not checked against the target. Reading lists in graduate courses in projective techniques, no matter how brief, should include the Chapman and Chapman article, followed by class discussion of its implications.

I view the interaction between examiner and test subject as a special form of therapeutic encounter between therapist and client (see Finn, chap. 20 of this volume). Clients enter the professional relationship unsure of what is expected, uncertain about how to behave, perhaps ambivalent about being in the psychologist's office to begin with, and fearful about the interpretations that may be placed on their behavior. Therapy and testing sessions are both marked by ambiguity and are highly interpersonal, calling forth private, idiosyncratic responses from each participant.

Over 50 years ago, Schachtel (1945) commented on the interpersonal characteristics of the testing interaction. Schafer (1954) extended this notion and provided a detailed, sophisticated elucidation of the testing encounter, emphasizing both the idiosyncratic personal history each of the participants brings to the testing session as well as the constants found in the roles of examiner and subject.

In Schafer's (1954) view, administering a projective test puts the examiner in four different roles:

1. Testing allows the examiner to gratify *voyeuristic* needs, peeping into areas of another person's life that the person would prefer to keep secret.

2. In determining most of the circumstances of the session, the examiner acts *autocratically*, telling "the patient what to do, when to do it and when to stop, sometimes how to do it. ... He often demands to know why the patient did what he did, when he did, and the way he did" (p. 22).

3. The examiner must seem like an *oracle* to test takers, with the ability to "draw momentous and portentous inferences from signs or symbols. He 'sees into' hidden meanings, predicts turns of events ... " (p. 23).

4. In agreeing to help test takers with their problems and dilemmas, the examiner takes on a *saintly* aspect, "implicitly promising psychological salvation" (p. 24), subduing "his own needs and resentments and selflessly trying to understand and feel the tragedy of the patient" (p. 24).

In addition to these roles, which Schafer (1954) posited as invariant in the projective assessment encounter, he also described unique, highly personal needs that testers may bring to the testing interview:

5. Some testers may have an "uncertain sense of personal identity," entering psychology as a way of solving personal problems. Testing allows the examiner "to pick up such fragments from the total personality pictures of various patients as seem usable in his personality integrative efforts. ... As a way of finding out how other persons manage or mismanage, testing is therefore relatively safe and inexpensive, even though not too personally rewarding in actuality" (pp. 26–27).

6. For "the socially inhibited or withdrawn tester ... testing may become an avenue toward human contact, and in some respects toward interpersonal intimacy. ... The controlled, temporary, one-way intimacies in the tester's professional life will have appeal to the extent that the tester's personal relationships are fraught with compulsive, schizoid or paranoid anxieties and inhibitions" (p. 27).

7. For "the dependent tester ... looking and controlling become a kind of feeding on the patient. ... He will want to stay on the patient's good side, i.e., his generous, indulgent, supportive side. In response to discomfort in the patient, the dependent tester may not press inquiries or demand for continued effort even though such pressure is clearly indicated. He may defensively rationalize this gingerly policy by asserting the necessity of maintaining good rapport" (p. 28).

8. "The tester with rigid defenses against dependent needs ... [may be] dominated by a defensive imperative always to give and never to receive [and will] in a too cold, too maternal, too saintly or too syrupy way try to force the patient into a passive receptive role. Patients long for this role but are typically terribly afraid of it" (p. 29).

9. "The rigidly intellectualistic tester ... is necessary and probably present in all psychologists. ... Testing may tend to become too much of a detached, 'logical', verbalistic, puzzle-solving affair ... he will interpret everything in sight, and substitute quantity for quality, doubt for responsibility, and overabstractions for descriptions. He may go blithely and pretentiously on and on about castration fears, incestuous wishes, sadistic fantasies ... and with absolutely no 'feel' for the unique, emotionally tangible qualities of the specific patient" (pp. 29–30).

10. "The sadistic tester ... will tend to write one-sided reports that sound like exposes or denunciations; he will be insensitive to or ignore signs of strength, adaptability and appeal in the patient" (p. 30).

11. "The tester with rigid defenses against hostility ... may, on the one hand, blind the tester to malignant implications of the test results or lead him to minimize them or undo them by qualifications. ... A saintly attitude ... will justifiably put the patient on guard in the test relationship and will very likely increase his sense of guilt" (p. 31).

12. "The masochistic tester ... may relish the patient's narcissistic demands, abuse and non-compliance. He may even do much to exacerbate such behavior. He may, for example, let control of the testing slip out of his hands and allow the entire situation to become relatively disorganized. ... Inasmuch as masochism has its accusing, hostile aspect, his pleasures in interpretation may consist in exposing just how 'bad' people 'really' are" (p. 31).

Schafer's (1954) conjecture that each of us brings a good deal of personal baggage to the testing session can be confirmed by anyone who has supervised beginning students and has seen how their personalities influence both the way they interact with subjects and how they score and interpret test responses. It would be comforting to believe that even if these rather obvious personal motives characterized beginners, they would be nicely controlled and sublimated in older, more experienced clinicians. It is equally plausible, however, that a student, once out of the supervisor's sight, might "act out" and rationalize these motives. In the psychotherapy session it is likely that more sexual acting out occurs with older, unsupervised clinicians than with beginners. For some psychologists, experience and self-confidence, however ill-founded, may not lead to greater wisdom and discretion but to lessened inhibitions. It is curious that although the therapy literature is filled with self-reports and extensive discussions of acting out in the transference and acting out in the countertransference, there are scarcely any self-reports about acting out in test administration, scoring, or interpretation. Moreover, there is no evidence that experienced clinicians make more accurate predictions than those with less experience (Garb, 1989), nor is confidence in one's clinical judgments related to accuracy of prediction (Fischoff, Slovic, & Lichtenstein, 1977; Kelly & Fiske, 1951).

Considerable empirical evidence supports the importance of the examiner's personality on professional performance. Although this literature is too extensive to summarize here (see Masling, 1960, 1966 for reviews of these studies) I describe several representative experiments to provide examples of how these issues have been investigated and the results obtained.

To judge the effect on scoring and interpreting psychological tests when graduate student examiners were treated warmly or coolly by a female subject, I trained two attractive accomplices to act as test subjects. They memorized their test responses, giving identical answers in both the experimental manipulations. Each examiner tested two accomplices, one of whom acted warm, interested, and friendly, and the other more formal and removed. The results showed that the experimental manipulation affected the examiners' judgment. The first experiment studied the effects of a warm or cold examiner–subject interaction on the interpretations of an incomplete sentences protocol (Masling, 1957) and the second experiment examined this interaction on the administration and scoring of an intelligence test (Masling, 1959). In both cases, the responses of the subject who interacted positively with the examiner were scored more favorably, both on the projective test and the IQ test, compared with the responses of the subject who behaved politely, but distantly. Other studies (Sattler, Hillix, & Neher, 1970; Sattler & Winget, 1970) have also reported that examiners give "better" scores to subjects they like than to those they like less, an effect that occurs even when the responses are unambiguous (Donahue & Sattler, 1971).

A voyeuristic aspect of testing has been described by Schafer (1954): " ... our knowledge of primitive, affect-laden levels of thinking suggests that psychological voyeurism may be unconsciously elaborated as an act of hostile, sexual intrusion. That is to say, even if the tester did not, to begin with, choose testing in part as a more or less sublimated outlet for his infantile voyeuristic inclinations, these inclinations may well seize on the looking-in-secret aspects of testing and thus may invade the professional role" (p. 21).

This observation prompted Masling and Harris (1969) to investigate a voyeuristic motive by inspecting the frequency with which four sexual-romantic cards of the TAT (numbers 2, 4, 10, and 13MF) were selected by graduate student clinicians in our Buffalo clinic to administer to male and female clients. During a 5-year period, nine male clinicians and five females tested both a male and female client, allowing us to employ a within-subject analysis. As expected, the results showed that male clinicians administered the sexual-romantic cards significantly more frequently to female subjects than to males. Female clinicians did not treat these stimuli differentially but either used them with both genders or did not use them at all. Clearly, male clinicians, but not females, wanted to see how female clients responded when faced with sexual-romantic stimuli. Harris and Masling (1970) then turned to the Rorschach session to examine the effects of the gender of the clinician on the test subject. Again we searched the files of the Psychological Clinic in Buffalo, obtained Rorschach records gathered over a 10-year period, and located 23 instances when a clinician administered the Rorschach to both a male and female client. We found that female subjects reported significantly more responses than males did when both were tested by a male examiner; the protocols submitted by female examiners showed no such differential productivity. When the data were examined using gender of subject as the base, we found that females gave significantly more responses to male clinicians than to females, whereas male subjects responded with equal productivity to both male and female clinicians.

Projective tests are designed to encourage subjects to interpret minimal cues, but the extent to which the personality of the examiners contributes to the subjects' responses was neither desired nor intended. That examiners differ in their stimulus qualities is well established empirically. Baughman (1951), Gibby (1952), Gibby, Miller, and Walker (1953), Lord (1950), Miller, Sanders, and Cleveland (1950), among others have documented examiner differences in subjects' responses to projective stimuli. Lyles (1959) found that the children tested on the Rorschach and Children's Apperception Test produced responses so characteristic of the six school psychologists who administered the tests that there was a 79% accuracy in matching the protocols to the examiner. Although many studies of this question can be faulted for using small sample sizes, Meyer and Partipilo (1961) examined the Rorschach protocols of 375 college students who had been tested by 25 different examiners. Ten variables were significant at the .05 level or better as a function of examiner differences, among them R, D, Dd, Ad, and P.

Rosenthal's (1966) summary of the pertinent literature concerning experimenter effects on the psychological experiment shows that examiner effects are not limited to projective testing. How examiner and experimenter qualities are communicated to the subject is a matter of speculation, but it is likely that a subtle form of mutual shaping of responses takes place, though neither partner in the dyad may be aware of it.

It is easily demonstrated that examiners can condition a subject to produce desired responses. Wickes (1956) used 30 homemade inkblots and three groups of subjects to determine whether subjects could be influenced to produce movement responses. In the two experimental groups, the first 15 cards were administered normally, but movement responses in the second set of 15 blots were reinforced verbally for some subjects and by smiling and postural changes by the examiner for other subjects. The verbal reinforcement resulted in significantly increased movement responses from the first half of the test to the second, the postural and smiling reinforcement resulted in significantly increased movement responses, whereas the control group subjects did not change in the number of movement responses they reported. In a similar study, Gross (1959) reinforced human movement responses by saying "good" to some subjects, and nodded his head for human movement responses for other subjects. Both groups of subjects produced significantly more human movement responses than control subjects.

Similar results were obtained by Dinoff (1960), Magnussen (1960), and Simkins (1960), all of whom successfully reinforced selected responses to ink-blots. Content responses are apparently more readily influenced than location (Simkins, 1960). None of these experiments found any subject awareness of examiner influence. Dinoff, in fact, not only reported that none of his 28 subjects could verbalize the contingency between examiner behavior and their own response but that only 2 of them were even aware that the examiners sometimes said "uh huh" during the test administration.

To determine if examiners could *unintentionally* reinforce a particular class of responses, I described to one group of seven graduate students a series of experiments demonstrating that experienced, competent Rorschach examiners obtained more animal than human responses from their subjects (Masling, 1965). To another seven graduate students, I described studies demonstrating that experienced, competent examiners obtained more human than animal responses. Of course, all the "studies" were bogus. The graduate students then each tested two subjects and tape recorded the sessions. The hypothesized results were obtained; examiners who had been led to expect that animal responses were more valued produced protocols containing significantly more animal responses than those examiners who were told that human responses were more valued. Analysis of the taped sessions did not, however, show the expected signs of verbal conditioning. In fact, the examiners said very little during the testing sessions. The methods by which the examiners communicated their expectations remain unclear, though the absence of verbal reinforcement suggests that postural and gestural cues must have been utilized. When the subjects were interviewed following the testing, none was aware that the examiners had done anything to influence their responses.

Given the ubiquity of examiner and situational influence on the projective protocol, it is not surprising that clinical predictions based on projective test results have an unimpressive history of validity. When a psychologist is asked to score, interpret, and organize a complex set of responses into an integrated description of a human being the possibility, indeed the likelihood, exists that the psychologist's own personal history will help select which variables are emphasized and which are ignored. The complexity of the task and the number of variables the examiner must keep in mind can scarcely be exaggerated. Little wonder that each examiner seems to work with a finite number of personality dimensions, trying them for goodness of fit on projective protocols.

In a sense, the actual practice of interpreting a projective test is similar to the work habits of the mythological Greek robber, Procrustes, who solved the problem of fitting victims of different sizes to his iron bed by either stretching or amputating their limbs until he got the desired size. Empirical evidence strongly suggests that most examiners can consider only a limited number of dimensions when they are required to assemble and integrate the huge number of cues produced by responses to inkblots. Subjects are then measured against these dimensions, with the dimensions either made salient or irrelevant by the examiner's training, experience, personality theory, and defenses. Some examiners approach every protocol looking for signs of repressed hostility (or sexual confusion, dependence, autonomy, indications of childhood abuse, depression, etc.), whereas others are more sensitive to signs of ego confusion (or incestuous fantasies, separation anxiety, need for succor, fear of intimacy, etc.).

The situation is made even worse by the failure of most graduate programs to provide novice examiners with a report of the accuracy of their assessment comments. Their competence to use projective materials is not based on how close they come to the target but on the extent to which they pleased an authority—their instructor. Knowledge of results is as essential in learning to use projective tests as it is in learning to type, pronounce a foreign word, or hit a curve ball. Blindfolding a student does not aid the learning process.

Examiner effects, although inevitable and ubiquitous, do not constitute a major portion of the variance in protocols (Masling, 1966). Some clinicians apparently show remarkable skill in using clinical material, recognizing the most telling and meaningful information and discarding the rest. Clinical psychologists of a certain age are all aware of the instance of a "magical" interpretation made by Theodore Reik (1948) to a female analysand:

> One session at this time took the following course. After a few sentences about the uneventful events of the day, the patient fell into a long silence. She assured me that nothing was in her thoughts. Silence from me. After many minutes she complained about a toothache. She told me she had been to the dentist yesterday. He had given her an injection and then had pulled a wisdom tooth. The spot was hurting again. New and longer silence. She pointed to my bookcase in the corner and said, "There's a book standing on its head." Without the slightest hesitation and in a reproachful voice I said, "But why did you not tell me that you had had an abortion?" (p. 263)

That interpretation was correct and influenced not only that particular patient but a whole generation of psychologists who wanted to believe they, too, had the ability to listen with a "third ear."

Some individual clinicians undoubtedly have the capacity to divine such truths from scattered and disguised cues. One must infer the existence of these talented people from informal, anecdotal reports because by and large the literature does not provide evidence of the validity of projective tests used holistically and intuitively. Although there are scattered case reports of wonderfully insightful predictions made by gifted clinicians (Cronbach, 1970, e.g., described an instance where a psychologist predicted with impressive accuracy the vocational interests of a test subject), the well-prepared student would be wise to recall Malcolm's (1984) cynical caveat about case reports: "Certainly the self-congratulatory clinical histories in the analytic literature cannot be regarded as evidence of anything beyond the writer's self-regard" (p. 18).

The success of Reik's (1948) interpretation reinforces the seer and oracular motives Schafer (1954) described. Shakespeare described the same motive in "Henry IV", Part I, when he had Glendower boast, "I can call spirits from the vasty deep," to which Hotspur, evidently an empiricist, replied, "Why, so can I, or so can any man; But will they come when you do call for them?" How wonderful it must be to believe that one can penetrate a subject's defenses and disguises and get straight to the inner secret! Every meek, mild, bespectacled clinician can become a Superman or Superwoman, able to leap tall defenses in a single bound by deciphering the mysterious symbol of the inkblot response. It is a heady attraction that for a short time I could not resist until cold reality created by some truly awful attempts at interpretation forced me to recognize the sad truth that I did not have Theodore Reik's skills. Even so, this need to see oneself as gifted intuitively does not yield easily to sweet reason or reports of the lack of validity of clinical, impressionistic predictions.

Any system that allows the tracking of particular responses (e.g., oral responses to the Rorschach) to specific units of behavior (e.g., obesity, alcoholism, asthma) has both the virtue and disadvantage of not allowing the clinician's judgment to influence the prediction. In a mechanical, statistical approach bad predictions can quickly be discovered and either altered or discarded and correct predictions can be retained. In fact, research has demonstrated that the Rorschach protocols of obese and alcoholic subjects contain a great many oral images, but those of asthmatics do not (Masling, 1986). Any procedure that allows feedback from prior predictions to correct future predictions will be more effective than a system that rewards students for writing reports that please the instructor.

The message in Meehl's (1954) important book, *Clinical Versus Statistical Prediction*, was offensive to those who hold the motives Schafer (1954) described. It was Meehl's thesis that simple, mechanical rules of using test data were superior to a highly trained clinician's intuition. He reported that in 16–20 studies all but 1 showed that actuarial predictions were either superior to, or equal to, those made intuitively. Eleven years later, Meehl (1965) reported that in 50 studies of this issue all either favored an actuarial approach or did no worse than a clinical approach, a conclusion essentially supported by Gough's (1962) and Sawyer's (1966) reviews. More recently, Marchese (1992) reviewed this issue and confirmed the superiority of actuarial prediction. These arguments naturally did not (and do not) sit well with clinicians, who felt that after years of learning their craft the numbers and statistical crowd would have them displaced by a simple prediction machine.

The counterarguments, summarized by Holt (1978), took issue with the claims of those advocating actuarial methods. Reviewing the same literature covered by Meehl (1965) and Sawyer (1966), Holt found serious deficiencies in many of the studies and thus his conclusions differed from theirs. Even Holt, however, had to acknowledge that, *under some conditions*, the actuarial use of projective data was superior to the clinical:

> I believe that one point has been conclusively established: there is no magic in clinical intuition that enables a clinician to predict a criterion about which he knows little, from data the relationship of which to the criterion he has not studied, and to do so better than an actuarial formula based on just such prior study of predictor-criterion relationships. In retrospect, it seems absurd to have expected that it could have been done. The cockiness and naive narcissism of some clinicians were nourished by a fallacious conception of the nature of science given respectability and wide currency by Allport. Today, it can surely be of little further interest that a person without an expert's level of ability, training, or experience cannot surpass a good actuarial formula, and usually does worse. Let us therefore flog this dead horse no longer. (p. 120)

Little more need be said about this definitive statement, except to note that when Holt (1978) excluded those with "an expert's level of ability, training, or experience" from clinicians who cannot do as well as an actuarial formula, he did so without a solid base of empirical support. Experts with superior accomplishments in utilizing projective data impressionistically have largely failed to demonstrate these talents in refereed journals where their reports would have been available for examination and replication. For whatever reason, those who espouse the value of intuitive clinical skills have been either unable or uninterested in buttressing their claims in the empirical literature.

In the next section I selectively review a portion of the many actuarial procedures for scoring responses to inkblots and TAT stimuli. Methods and theories using other projective devices like human figure drawings represent entirely different issues and are not discussed here (see Handler & Riethmiller, chap. 16 of this volume).

Of the two measures, objective scoring methods have been applied much more frequently to responses to inkblots than to the TAT. In fact, an entire book (Goldfried, Stricker, & Weiner, 1971) is devoted exclusively to descriptions of objective scoring methods of inkblot responses. These include schemes for scoring for developmental level (Friedman, 1952, 1953; Phillips, Kaden, & Waldman, 1959), Elizur's (1949) guide for scoring anxiety and hostility, Fisher and Cleveland's (1968) body image scoring method, the Wheeler signs (1949) for detecting male homosexuality, at least a dozen methods of using Rorschach responses to predict suicide, five different scoring guides to predict signs of neurosis, four different procedures for using Rorschach responses to assess schizophrenia, seven different attempts to score inkblot responses for evidence of brain damage, and five different efforts to predict therapy outcome and prognosis. It is instructive to note that 25 years later not much remains of the

38 actuarial methods, once used so frequently, described by Goldfried et al. Only the body image scoring approach of Fisher and Cleveland is still being used, the others losing favor for a variety of reasons.

It is a testament to the actuarial method that it permits efforts to replicate, unlike the clinical use of test data, and hence is subject to verification, modification, and disconfirmation. Some scoring systems, like the Wheeler signs (1949), the Elizur signs (1949), the several efforts to predict neurotic symptoms, and the Blacky Test (Blum, 1950) failed ultimately to be easily replicated. Indeed, Goldfried et al. (1971) said of the attempt to relate inkblot responses to neurotic symptoms that it "represents a brief and inglorious chapter in Rorschach research" (p. 252). The same could be said about the well-intentioned but poorly conceived research conducted with some of the other actuarial approaches. Yet other scoring schemes fell out of favor because of paradigm shifts, the victims of changes in styles and fashions in psychology. Such once popular concepts as Gestalt psychology, the Szondi test, Freud's energy theory, the G spot, and massed versus distributed learning have had their 15 minutes of fame and have now faded from view. Much of the early work with actuarial methods seems to have stemmed from fascination with the Rorschach test, followed by subsequent efforts to discover how it could be used. Although this did no noticeable harm, it was not a particularly useful way to spend time. In the past, the absence of rigorous criteria for test construction and sophisticated theory for guiding actuarial scoring methods provided a climate where the chic could safely graze. At present, more meaningful applications of actuarial methods of scoring projective responses are employed to study the dynamics of borderline phenomena, primary process in creativity and with children, and interpersonal functioning.

Today the most commonly employed actuarial method is Exner's Comprehensive System (1986, 1991) with over 500 separate references (Ritzler, 1996). The boundary and penetration score of Fisher and Cleveland (1968) have been used successfully in several hundred investigations of personality and body image variables. Bornstein (1996) has estimated that 50 separate investigations have demonstrated the validity of a simple lexical method for assessing oral-dependent responses to the Rorschach (Masling, Rabie, & Blondheim, 1967).

As interest in object relations has grown, so have efforts to assess this variable from the Rorschach test. As might be expected, most of these methods have borrowed heavily from psychoanalytic theory. A survey by Stricker and Healey (1990) of objective methods for scoring projective protocols to assess object relations lists about a dozen reports using the Developmental Analysis of the Concept of the Object Scale of Blatt, Brenneis, Schimek, and Glick (1976). P. Lerner and H. Lerner's (1980) Rorschach scoring system for object relations is reported by Ritzler (1996) to have been used in 186 separate validation studies. Still another Rorschach measure of object relations, Urist's Mutuality of Autonomy Scale (1977, 1980), has been employed at least 15 times to investigate various pathological groups and aspects of interpersonal functioning. Krohn and Mayman (1974) reported a valid scale for assessing object relations from Rorschach responses. Other Rorschach measures to assess various aspects of object relations have been developed by Burke, Friedman, and Gorlitz (1988), Coonerty (1986), and H. D. Lerner, Sugarman, and Barbour (1985). A Rorschach measure (Cooper, Perry, & Arnow, 1988) is now available to assess defense mechanisms and the borderline personality. The TAT has also been found to supply responses that can be scored for object relations (Thompson, 1986; Westen, Lohr, Silk, Gold, & Kerber, 1990).

Holt's (1966, 1970, 1977) measure of primary process in Rorschach responses has been widely employed. Russ (in press) has used the Holt system in seven experiments, including six with children as subjects. Several studies have investigated the utility of administering the Ego Impairment Index of Perry and Vigilone (1991) to psychiatric patients. A computer search of the literature for the years 1991–1995 found 46 different reports of experiments using a number of different schemes for objectively scoring TAT and inkblot responses to predict many aspects of behavior.[1] Cramer estimated that the TAT has been used actuarially in about 1,400 studies.

All told, there must be close to 2,500 published empirical studies, as well as untold numbers of unpublished dissertations and master's theses, based on mechanical, inflexible rules for scoring responses to inkblots and TAT stories. The early proponents of projective tests might have been quite surprised to see how extremely useful these tests are for investigating developmental processes, psychopathology, psychotherapeutic change, and personality variables. In regard to the once important controversy that pitted clinical methods against the actuarial, it can be safely concluded that the hurly-burly is done and the battle won. As Holt (1978) indicated, it was no contest from the start, though it was difficult to recognize that outcome at the time the battle was being waged.

Even so, attitudes toward projective tests held by academic psychologists have not changed much over the years, even in the face of such frequent (actuarial) use of these tests. Undergraduate text book writers continue to describe projective tests as they might have years earlier: "Projective tests tend to have problems of reliability and validity. ... The validity of projective tests is also low, because they are not very effective in predicting behavior" (Bootzin, Bower, Crocker, & Hall, 1991, p. 511); "The validity and reliability [of the Rorschach and TAT] have been questioned ... Perhaps as a result, their use has declined since the 1970s" (Morris, 1996, p. 479); "Although projective tests such as the Rorschach and TAT are widely used and have a loyal following among some psychologists and psychiatrists, attempts to determine whether they reliably measure aspects of personality have yielded mixed results. ... The TAT is open to similar criticism of low reliability and validity" (Goldstein, 1994, pp. 623–624). The evaluation of psychoanalytic theory has encountered the same stubborn reluctance to acknowledge change. It is ironic that American psychology, so proudly empirical and behavioral, tends to cling to stereotypes and attitudes long after the world has changed (see Piotrowski & Keller, 1992, for more data on this topic).

---

[1] I am indebted to Bernard O'Connor for providing me with a computer search of the current relevant literature.

Another symptom of the lack of respect given projective techniques is the extent to which they are no longer required as part of the doctoral program in clinical and counseling psychology. Piotrowski and Zalewski (1993) reported that directors of clinical training expect projective tests to be deemphasized in the next few years. Kinder (1994), too, discovered that not a single academic position advertised in a recent APA Monitor listed teaching of assessment skills as an important component of the job, even though 64% of the ads for clinical positions stressed competence in assessment. There is apparently a clear disjunction between what academic departments are training students for and the skills new psychologists are expected to have when they apply for clinical positions. Watkins (1994) agreed that "projective techniques just get a 'bum rap' from a fair number of clinical training directors" (p. 388).

Suggestions for Teaching a Graduate Course in Projective Techniques

It is evident that even after having established highly respectable reliability and validity qualities, and having proven to be vigorously heuristic projective tests, like King Lear, are more sinned against than sinning. What's to be done? My suggestions follow directly from the research I have summarized:

1. Reading lists should include material emphasizing the two-person situation in projective testing. Schafer's (1954) theoretical descriptions of the examiner's needs and the research literature documenting the extent to which the examiner influences the administration, scoring, and interpretation of test responses should be required reading. The well-prepared student should know the advantages and disadvantages of both intuitive, global interpretations and actuarial methods of employing projective test responses. Students should be required to use some of the more popular actuarial procedures.

2. Graduate students should be sensitive to the situational stress imposed by diagnostic testing. Having students role play a naive, easily threatened test subject required to respond to TAT and inkblot stimuli helps accomplish this goal.

3. Graduate students should score and interpret the protocols of healthy, functioning people in addition to the protocols of the more disturbed subjects. Further, I would ask the students to learn how to recognize signs of health as well as signs of pathology. All test reports, even of the most deteriorated, regressed patient, should include some discussion of the patient's strengths and coping skills.

4. I would also use protocols from known diagnostic groups, for example, borderlines, and require the students to employ some validated actuarial method of scoring and interpreting the responses. As far as possible, I would avoid blind interpretation in favor of providing students with as much knowledge of results as possible.

REFERENCES

Baughman, E. E. (1951). Rorschach scores as a function of examiner differences. *Journal of Projective Techniques, 15,* 243–249.

Blatt, S. J., Brenneis, C. B., Schimek, J. G., & Glick, M. (1976). Normal development and psychopathological impairment of the concept of the object on the Rorschach. *Journal of Abnormal Psychology, 85,* 364–373.

Blum, G. S. (1950). *The Blacky pictures and manual.* New York: Psychological Corp.

Bootzin, R. R., Bower, G. H., Crocker, J., & Hall, E. (1991). *Psychology today: An introduction* (7th ed.). New York: McGraw-Hill.

Bornstein, R. F. (1996). Construct validity of the Rorschach oral dependency scale: 1967–1995. *Psychological Assessment, 8,* 200–205.

Burke, W. F., Friedman, G., & Gorlitz, P. (1988). The psychoanalytic Rorschach profile: An integration of drive, ego, and object relations perspectives. *Psychoanalytic Psychology, 5,* 193–212.

Chapman, L. J., & Chapman, J. (1969). Illusory correlations as an obstacle to the use of psychodiagnostic signs. *Journal of Abnormal and Social Psychology, 74,* 271–280.

Coonerty, S. (1986). An exploration of separation-individuation themes in the borderline personality disorder. *Journal of Personality Assessment, 50,* 501–512.

Cooper, S. H., Perry, J. C., & Arnow, D. (1988). An empirical approach to the study of defense mechanisms: I. Reliability and preliminary validity of the Rorschach defense scales. *Journal of Personality Assessment, 52,* 187–203.

Cramer, P. (1996). *Storytelling, narrative, and the Thematic Apperception Test.* New York: Guilford.

Cronbach, L. J. (1970). *Essentials of psychological testing* (3rd ed.). New York: Harper & Row.

Dinoff, M. (1960). Subject awareness of examiner influence in a testing situation. *Journal of Consulting Psychology, 24,* 465.

Donahue, D., & Sattler, J. M. (1971). Personality variables affecting WAIS scores. *Journal of Consulting Psychology, 36,* 441.

Elizur, A. (1949). Content analysis of the Rorschach with regard to anxiety and hostility. *Rorschach Research Exchange and Journal of Projective Techniques, 13,* 247–284.

Exner, J. E., Jr. (1986). *The Rorschach: A comprehensive system: Vol. 1. Basic foundations* (2nd ed.). New York: Wiley.

Exner, J. E., Jr. (1991). *The Rorschach: A comprehensive system.* (Vol. 2, 2nd ed.). New York: Wiley.

Fischoff, B., Slovic, P., & Lichtenstein, S. (1977). Knowing with certainty: The appropriateness of extreme confidence. *Journal of Experimental Psychology: Human Perception and Performance, 3,* 552–564.

Fisher, S., & Cleveland, S. (1968). *Body image and personality* (Rev. ed.). New York: Dover.

Frank, G. (1993). On the validity of Rorschach's hypotheses: The relationship of space responses (S) to oppositionalism. *Psychological Reports, 72,* 1111–1114.

Friedman, H. (1952). Perceptual regression in schizophrenia: An hypothesis suggested by use of the Rorschach test. *Journal of Genetic Psychology, 81,* 63–98.

Friedman, H. (1953). Perceptual regression in schizophrenia: An hypothesis suggested by the use of the Rorschach test. *Journal of Projective Techniques, 17,* 171–185.

Garb, H. N. (1989). Clinical judgment, clinical training, and professional experience. *Psychological Bulletin, 105,* 387–396.

Gibby, R. G. (1952). Examiner influence on the Rorschach inquiry. *Journal of Consulting Psychology, 16,* 449–455.

Gibby, R. G., Miller, D. R., & Walker, E. L. (1953). The examiner's influence on the Rorschach protocol. *Journal of Consulting Psychology, 17,* 425–428.

Goldfried, M. R., Stricker, G., & Weiner, I. B. (1971). *Rorschach handbook of clinical and research applications.* Englewood Cliffs, NJ: Prentice-Hall.

Goldstein, E. B. (1994). *Psychology.* Belmont, CA: Brooks/Cole.

Gough, H. G. (1962). Clinical versus statistical prediction in psychology. In L. Postman (Ed.), *Psychology in the making: Histories of selected research problems* (pp. 526–584). New York: Knopf.

Gross, L. (1959). Effects of verbal and nonverbal reinforcement in the Rorschach. *Journal of Consulting Psychology, 23,* 66–68.

Harris, S., & Masling, J. M. (1970). Examiner sex, subject sex, and Rorschach productivity. *Journal of Consulting and Clinical Psychology, 34,* 60–63.

Holt, R. R. (1966). Measuring libidinal and aggressive motives and their control by means of the Rorschach test. In D. Levine (Ed.), *Nebraska symposium on motivation* (pp. 1–47). Lincoln: University of Nebraska Press.

Holt, R. R. (1970). *Manual for the scoring of primary process manifestations in Rorschach responses* (10th ed.). New York: New York University, Research Center for Mental Health.

Holt, R. R. (1977). A method for assessing primary process manifestations and their controls in Rorschach responses. In M. P. Rickers-Ovsiankina (Ed.), *Rorschach psychology* (pp. 375–420). New York: Krieger.

Holt, R. R. (1978). *Methods in clinical psychology: Vol. 2. Prediction and research.* New York: Plenum.

Kelly, E. L., & Fiske, D. W. (1951). *The prediction of performance in clinical psychology.* Ann Arbor: University of Michigan Press.

Kinder, B. N. (1994). Where the action is in personality assessment. *Journal of Personality Assessment, 62,* 585–588.

Krohn, A., & Mayman, M. (1974). Object representations in dreams and projective tests. *Bulletin of the Menninger Clinic, 38,* 445–466.

Lerner, H. D., Sugarman, A., & Barbour, C. G. (1985). Patterns of ego boundary disturbance in neurotic, borderline, and schizophrenic patients. *Psychoanalytic Psychology, 2,* 47–66.

Lerner, P., & Lerner, H. (1980). Rorschach assessment of primitive defenses in borderline personality structure. In J. Kwawer, H. Lerner, P. Lerner, & A. Sugarman (Eds.), *Borderline phenomena and the Rorschach test* (pp. 257–274). New York: International Universities Press.

Lord, E. (1950). Experimentally induced variation in Rorschach performance. *Psychological Monographs, 64*(10, Whole No. 316).

Lyles, W. K. (1959). The effects of examiner attitudes on the projective test responses of children. *Dissertation Abstracts International, 19–11,* 3024–3025.

Magnussen, N. G. (1960). Verbal and non-verbal reinforcers in the Rorschach situation. *Journal of Clinical Psychology, 16,* 167–169.

Malcolm, J. (1984). *Psychoanalysis: The impossible profession*. New York: Random House.

Marchese, M. C. (1992). Clinical versus actuarial prediction: A review of the literature. *Perceptual and Motor Skills, 75,* 583–594.

Masling, J. M. (1957). The effect of warm and cold interaction on the interpretation of a projective protocol. *Journal of Projective Techniques, 21,* 377–383.

Masling, J. M. (1959). The effect of warm and cold interaction on the administration and interpretation of an intelligence test. *Journal of Consulting Psychology, 23,* 336–341.

Masling, J. (1960). The influence of situational and interpersonal variables in projective testing. *Psychological Bulletin, 57,* 65–85.

Masling, J. M. (1965). Differential indoctrination of examiners and Rorschach responses. *Journal of Consulting Psychology, 29,* 198–201.

Masling, J. M. (1966). Role-related behavior of the subject and psychologist and its effect upon psychological data. In D. Levine (Ed.), *Symposium on motivation* (pp. 67–104). Lincoln: University of Nebraska Press.

Masling, J. M. (1986). Orality, pathology, and interpersonal behavior. In J. M. Masling (Ed.), *Empirical studies of psychoanalytic theories* (Vol. 2, pp. 73–106). Hillsdale, NJ: Lawrence Erlbaum Associates.

Masling, J. M., & Harris, S. (1969). Sexual aspects of TAT administration. *Journal of Consulting Psychology, 33,* 166–169.

Masling, J., Rabie, L., & Blondheim, S. H. (1967). Relationships of oral imagery to yielding behavior and birth order. *Journal of Consulting Psychology, 32,* 89–91.

Meehl, P. E. (1954). *Clinical versus statistical prediction*. Minneapolis: University of Minnesota Press.

Meehl, P. E. (1965) Seer over sign: the first good example. *Journal of Experimental Research in Personality, 1,* 27–32.

Meyer, M. L., & Partipilo, M. (1961). Examiner personality as an influence on the Rorschach test. *Psychological Reports, 9, 221–222.*

Miller, D., Sanders, R., & Cleveland, S. E. (1950). The relationship between examiner personality and obtained Rorschach protocols: An application of interpersonal relations theory (Abstract). *American Psychologist, 5,* 322–323.

Morris, C. G. (1996). *Psychology: An introduction* (9th ed.). Upper Saddle River, NJ: Prentice Hall.

Perry, W., & Vigilone, D. (1991). The Ego Impairment Index as a predictor of outcome in melancholic depressed patients treated with tricyclic antidepressants. *Journal of Personality Assessment, 56,* 487–501.

Phillips, L., Kaden, S., & Waldman, M. (1959). Rorschach indices of developmental level. *Journal of Genetic Psychology, 94,* 267–285.

Piotrowski, C., & Keller, J. W. (1992). Psychological testing in applied settings: A literature review from 1982–1992. *Journal of Training and Practice in Professional Psychology, 6,* 74–82.

Piotrowski, C., & Zalewski, C. (1993). Training in psychodiagnostic testing in APA-approved PsyD and PhD clinical psychology programs. *Journal of Personality Assessment, 61,* 374–405.

Reik, T. (1948). *Listening with the third ear*. New York: Farrar, Strauss.

Ritzler, B. (1996). Personality assessment and research: The state of the union. *SPA Exchange, 6, 1, 15.*

Rosenthal, R. (1966). *Experimenter effects in behavioral research*. New York: Appleton–Century–Crofts.

Russ, S. W. (in press). Psychoanalytic theory and creativity: Cognition and affect revisited. In J. M. Masling & R. F. Bornstein (Eds.), *Empirical studies of psychoanalytic theories: Vol. 6. Psychoanalysis as developmental psychology*. Washington, DC: American Psychological Association.

Sattler, J. M., Hillix, W. A., & Neher, L. A. (1970). Halo effect in examiner scoring of intelligence test responses. *Journal of Consulting and Clinical Psychology, 34*, 172–176.

Sattler, J. M., & Winget, B. M. (1970). Intelligence testing procedures as affected by expectancy and IQ. *Journal of Clinical Psychology, 26*, 446–448.

Sawyer, J. (1966). Measurement and prediction, clinical and statistical. *Psychological Bulletin, 66*, 178–200.

Schachtel, E. G. (1945). Subjective definitions of the Rorschach test situation and their effect on test performance. Contributions to an understanding of Rorschach's test, III. *Psychiatry, 8*, 419–448.

Schafer, R. (1954). *Psychoanalytic interpretation in Rorschach testing*. New York: Grune & Stratton.

Simkins, L. (1960). Examiner reinforcement and situation variables in a projective testing situation. *Journal of Consulting Psychology, 24*, 541–547.

Soskin, W. F. (1954). Frames of reference in personality assessment. *Journal of Clinical Psychology, 10*, 107–114.

Soskin, W. F. (1959). Influence of four types of data on diagnostic conceptualization in psychological testing. *Journal of Abnormal and Social Psychology, 58*, 69–78.

Stricker, G., & Healey, B. J. (1990). Projective assessment of object relations: A review of the empirical literature. *Psychological Assessment, 2*, 219–230.

Thompson, A. E. (1986). An object relational theory of affect maturity: Applications to the Thematic Apperception Test. In M. Kissen (Ed.), *Assessing object relations phenomena* (pp. 207–244). Madison, CT: International Universities Press.

Urist, J. (1977). The Rorschach test and the assessment of object relations. *Journal of Personality Assessment, 41*, 3–9.

Urist, J. (1980). Object relations. In R. H. Woody (Ed.), *Encyclopedia of clinical assessment* (Vol. 1, pp. 821–833). San Francisco: Jossey-Bass.

Watkins, C. E. (1994). Do projective techniques get a "bum rap" from clinical psychology training directors? *Journal of Personality Assessment, 63*, 387–389.

Westen, D., Lohr, N., Silk, K., Gold, L., & Kerber, K. (1990). Object relations and social cognition in borderlines, major depressives, and normals: A TAT analysis. *Psychological Assessment: A Journal of Clinical and Consulting Psychology, 2*, 355–364.

Wheeler, W. M. (1949). An analysis of Rorschach indices of male homosexuality. *Rorschach Research Exchange, 13*, 97–126.

Wickes, T. A. (1956). Examiner influence in a test situation. *Journal of Consulting and Clinical Psychology, 20*, 23–26.

9

Assessing the Social Subject

Herbert M. Potash
Fairleigh Dickinson University, Madison

When graduate students are first exposed to projective instruments, they expect to achieve mastery in assessment by using the same study techniques that gained them entry into graduate school. By reading and memorizing texts and journals, they plan to learn the necessary content to guide the assessment process. In other words, they expect that expertise in projective instruments will be acquired by using the same methodology that one uses with objective tests. Specifically, graduate students seek objective scoring systems that possess high test reliability and validity, which will thereby minimize errors of interpretation. The students both hope and expect psychological assessment to be a process that can be readily mastered with intelligence and hard work.

Normative data, objective scoring systems, and traditional hypotheses all play important roles in projective assessment, but fully effective clinicians often complement this kind of knowledge with other forms of data interpretation. I believe the most effective assessment is a complex process that utilizes subjective, objective and idiosyncratic methods to apprehend most fully the person under study. Handler (1996) made a parallel point, advocating multidimensional methods when he discussed effective interpretation of figure drawings.

When I teach the Introduction to Projective Assessment course, my aim is to elicit and foster this kind of apprehension in the students. To do so I first try to reactivate the students' intellectual curiosity that initially led them to pursue graduate training in clinical psychology. Individuals who have been effective in understanding and assisting others in managing their personal lives are the ones who gravitate toward careers as mental health professionals.

All too often graduate training programs operate under the implicit assumption that students lack such interpersonal skills or successful experiences. Instead, the predominant training philosophy assumes the student is a *tabula rasa* and that textbooks, lectures by professors, and insights from clinical supervisors will offer the only path to wisdom. Students are to rely on professionals as the only valid experts whose function is to teach them whatever they need to know to be successful psychologists (Potash, 1981).

When graduate students enter their first assessment course, most of them have been fully indoctrinated into this *tabula rasa* philosophy and have accepted it as fact. They have learned to disregard their personal reactions and intuitions and instead to substitute objective methods for understanding individuals and their psychopathology.

In order to assist students to most fully understand patients, it is important to reacquaint them with the fundamental truth that they already possess expertise in understanding people that predates their graduate training. This skill in understanding others is their core strength, and it can be enhanced with the addition of formal training in projective assessment. However, if students do not possess any fundamental effective knowledge of people that predates graduate training, they will not learn to be effective in assessment no matter how skillful their professors are.

When professors can acknowledge that students enter a course in personality assessment with a certain level of expertise, two positive consequences ensue. First, the relationship between professor and student is redefined. It is no longer one between the expert and the novice; but rather, it becomes a relationship between a teacher and a student who possesses certain intermediate-level skills. The professor's recognition of this skill level is ego building for the students; they know they are seen as capable of making significant contributions to the classroom task of understanding individuals through the assessment process.

The second and more important consequence of recognizing the student's skill in interpersonal assessment is that it frees the student to use diverse methods of understanding others. When the professor effectively makes the point that students have already been assessing others for most of their lives, they take notice. When students are reminded that their informal assessments of others have proven trustworthy and have guided their actions over the course of their lifetime, they feel reassured about themselves. When they are told to draw on these same skills in the process of projective assessment, they feel encouraged.

When the teacher emphasizes the fact that students already possess requisite skills in understanding people, the students are less likely to fault *subjective assessment*, because they personally know the value of such judgments. This pedagogic strategy minimizes the threat that students, indoctrinated with the purported value of objective methods, feel when asked to participate in what has often been called inferior and unreliable subjective assessment.

Although most students have been quite effective in their informal assessment of other people, they have rarely paid systematic attention to the cues used in making their judgments. In order to enhance their skill at understanding others, it is vital to discuss both the verbal and nonverbal cues emitted by others that provide crucial diagnostic information. For example, students have learned not to take the statement "I love you" at face value and have learned to attend to voice tone and body language to "read" intentions in order to interpret the meaning of that communication.

Furthermore, it is also helpful for students to observe their own personal reactions to the behaviors of other people. These personal reactions comprise crucial diagnostic data about the nature of the other person. Accordingly, in teaching the Introduction to Projective Assessment course I first focus our attention on the interpersonal behavior of people undergoing projective testing.

A typical projective battery is administered over several hours, usually involving two separate sessions in a one-to-one setting. Consequently, the projective testing is conducted in the context of a limited interpersonal relationship that has a specific task focus. The task of understanding the patient becomes a twofold process. Graduate students obviously must make sense of the patient's formal responses to the various test stimuli. However, the students also need to examine the interpersonal behavior of the patient during testing for this, too, gives vital data about the person.

In nontesting situations graduate students, just like everyone else, routinely assess other people. They decide who is warm and who is cold, who is lazy, who is a jerk and who is worth pursuing. They generate these hypotheses and many others as a result of the behavioral cues given by people. Even though graduate students routinely make such implicit judgments in their personal lives, they do not often communicate these judgments to others. Because these personal evaluations are rarely communicated, students typically believe they have formed unique and probably idiosyncratic hypotheses about other people. Most students do not even consider, and therefore do not believe, that their personal reactions to certain people are common reactions that are routinely elicited by these people.

We attend to both verbal and nonverbal cues as we generate hypotheses about the other person. Before computerized scoring of projective instruments, it was usually expected that the individual who wrote the psychological assessment also administered the tests. It was believed that additional important information could be obtained through interaction with a patient, data that would not be available in the test protocol. This information was impressionistic in nature and focused on the patient's style of interaction and his or her attempts at influencing the examiner.

When the professor begins to teach projective assessment by describing these behavioral cues given by others, the graduate students are asked to verbalize the kind of judgments they have been implicitly making during much of their lives. If the professor starts in this manner, the students will not be on totally alien ground and can draw on the successful assessment skills they already use routinely.

One effective place to begin is with a discussion of a patient's manner of dress. I point out that psychological reports that describe a subject's appearance as "neat and clean" are using a poor communication strategy. Our usual expectation of others is that they will at least be "neat and clean" in interpersonal situations; and if they are not, that fact is the unusual occurrence.

Graduate students are typically aware of the value of specific dressing for different occasions. The chosen mode of dress is believed to be one particular method of impression management. Therefore, when the patients know in advance that they are to undergo psychological testing their manner of dress obviously needs to be studied. The questions to be raised are: *Do they dress for the occasion?* and *Does the manner of dress change from the first to the second testing session?*

I ask students what their first impressions of this person would be if they met him or her in another situation. Would they want to talk with the person or avoid contact and why or why not? Probing questions asked in the classroom setting are soon perceived as "safe" because the students quickly begin to recognize that their personal reactions to a patient are the same as the reactions of their classmates to that patient.

As students begin to recognize their consensus of opinions about a patient, they become receptive to the idea that they function as the *generalized other*. The concept of the generalized other is used both by sociologists and social psychologists to acknowledge that individuals are representatives of a common culture. As a result, personal reactions to certain stimuli and behavior are common reactions and are representative of the values and mores of the culture. When graduate students accept that their personal reactions to a patient are indeed the common reactions to a patient's behavior, they become more open to engaging in additional self-disclosure.

Recognizing that one functions as the generalized other is crucial in the training of a clinician. It enables graduate students to trust significantly their own personal reactions to other people. Such trust is especially necessary because too often graduate students have become oversensitized to the possibility of countertransference reactions. The taboo against countertransference often inhibits students from acknowledging their personal reactions when they function as professionals, thereby losing valuable data.

Once students have accepted the fact that they function as the generalized other, they become more adept at predicting the nature and degree of interpersonal success the patient will have in the world. By asking themselves if this person is boring, annoying, sexy, dumb, interesting, scary, or offensive, they can begin to *know* the patient in ways that transcend the specific hypotheses generated by different test responses.

When the projective testing situation is described as a specific form of social interaction, the students can more readily acknowledge that the interaction could satisfy the needs of both patient and examiner. The assessor needs the patient to cooperate with him or her and to follow test instructions; the assessor hopes that the patient will comply in a manner that is neither troublesome nor problematic. The patient can acknowledge the presence and needs of the assessor or the patient can choose to function in a way that disregards the social interaction.

The testing situation can be viewed as a sample of the patient's interpersonal behavior, at least in regard to how he or she deals with authority figures and stress. When the patient behaves in ways that disregard the social interaction between examiner and patient, the hypothesis then becomes that the patient would disregard the social interaction when dealing with other authority figures. Patients can show a wide range of behavior, ranging from overly attentive to extremely defiant; it is expected that the range represents the behavior the patient is likely to show in other settings.

Consider the interaction between subject and examiner when the Object Assembly subtest of any form of the Wechsler Intelligence Test is administered. In the proper administration of the test, the examiner places a screen in front of the patient and simultaneously arranges the test pieces in the correct order. To understand the interpersonal behavior of the patient, it is important to attend to how he or she behaves when the examiner holds the screen up with one hand while maneuvering object pieces with the other hand.

Some patients try to peek over the screen, others act oblivious to the examiner's struggle with administration, and yet others seem to delight in the examiner's discomfort. Some patients spontaneously offer to help by holding up the screen. After asking the graduate student to describe the behavior of the patient in this situation, it is easy to create interpersonal scenarios, with the class predicting the patient's behavior elsewhere. One such situation is imagining the patient driving a car and coming on an individual who had a flat tire on the side of the road. Graduate students are asked to hypothesize what they think certain patients would do in this situation. The students soon characterize those patients who would stop to assist, those who would slow down but not stop, and those who would act oblivious to the motorist's distress. Similar questions in which the students are asked to generalize from the test situation to other life situations help them to realize that the test behavior may be quite informative about the patient's social self.

Parallel data are available by addressing the patient's behavior during the administration of the TAT. Virtually all assessors attempt to write the patient's stories in longhand and therefore they struggle to keep pace with the patient's verbal output. When graduate students recognize that their own reactions to a patient are an important source of data, they will attend to any aspect of their own personal discomfort during TAT administration. For example, as students feel the frustration of not being able to keep pace with the patient's verbal output, they soon understand that the patient is causing their frustration.

If the patients are at all attentive to their external world, it must be readily apparent that the examiner is struggling to write down their stories. In this situation the patient holds potential power to make life easy or difficult for the examiner. The graduate student can then assess the likely motives of the patient by posing the following questions: Does the patient independently slow down the speed of storytelling or is it necessary for the examiner to ask the patient to slow down? After requesting the patient to slow down does he or she then speak slowly or is fast speech quickly resumed? Does the patient speak articulately, making it easy for the examiner to take dictation, or does the patient mumble? Does the patient follow the initial directions and give a complete story or is it necessary to remind him or her to follow directions?

Specific questions such as those just mentioned may be followed by the more general question: Is the patient likeable or frustrating? It becomes easy for students to recognize that their personal reactions to the patient's behavior are the common responses of the generalized other.

Another parallel classroom strategy is to ask students whether they would hire this patient as an employee. Here the patient's actions during testing are viewed as behavioral samples that can be used to predict his or her behavior in other interpersonal situations. As class members voice their opinions, a consensus is very quickly established, which once again reaffirms that the class members function as the generalized other.

The graduate student's ability to function as the generalized other is also quite useful during the Inquiry phase of the Rorschach. When the student recognizes the necessity of conducting a full inquiry in order to be able to unequivocally score determinants, the relationship between the patient and the examiner undergoes an important shift. The examiner usually must become more demanding and persistent in questioning style in order to obtain the necessary information.

When examiners engage in such behavior, they raise the stress level in their patients. Many beginning graduate students are quite reluctant to be so demanding because it violates their desired role of empathic helper. It is necessary to insist that students persevere in their inquiry until the patient says magic words such as *form* or *shape*. Because the assessor seems *persistently unreasonable* until the basic determinant is directly specified, the patient begins to feel frustrated. If the patient is not a quick learner or does not stumble upon the magic words that end the inquiry, his or her stress level will continue to rise.

Faced with the difficulties of satisfying a recalcitrant examiner, patients use a myriad of coping techniques. The graduate student needs to carefully attend to both the verbal and nonverbal behaviors of the patient in this situation, for they indicate how the patient deals with the demands of others. The patient's voice tone can range from the intrapunitive, signaling withdrawal or depression, to the extrapunitive, where the patient may castigate the examiner or, in one case I remember, actually tear the Rorschach card in half.

Once students become comfortable in being persistently unreasonable, they can much better attend to their personal reactions to the patients during the Inquiry phase of the Rorschach. They can see the patients' angry reactions as reflecting problems with impulse control rather than as justified anger. The patients' dealings with the world of authority unfold before the students' eyes during the Inquiry phase of the Rorschach. Even though many students attempt to reduce the demanding quality of their inquiry through nonverbal cues, such as smiling or by the use of a gentle voice tone, such behavior may come to naught with patients who must reenact long-standing transference reactions.

Other insights into the interpersonal style of the patients become clear during the administration of the House-Tree-Person Test. I find the best way to generate insight is first by asking questions, particularly those that tap one's experiential world. Not only is this approach vital in psychotherapy (Potash, 1994), but it is also the basis for understanding the "other" in the assessment process (Potash, 1981).

First I ask graduate students if they would feel comfortable drawing figures, and the group almost universally answers "no." I then ask if they would tell an examiner "I can't draw." Most acknowledge that they would not, and then they are asked "Why wouldn't you say this?" As they explain further that they would not feel comfortable making excuses or that excuses are unnecessary, they begin to see that the patient is attempting to manipulate the examiner. They perceive the pleas for special consideration and the attempts to ward off criticism as reenactments of the child–adult interaction. Furthermore, they can understand that the patient does not give the examiner full credence. The examiner can compare the quality of the drawing with the patient's statement "I can't draw." If the patient is singularly untalented in graphic skills, that will be readily apparent. Often the patient who complains about lack of drawing skills is not truly ungifted at drawing.

By attending to the patient's overall style of interacting with the examiner, one can achieve a good sense of the degree to which the patient cooperates in the interpersonal world. Some patients simply comply with the requests of the examiner but their nonverbal style can signify resentment, intimidation, or willing cooperation. Others may ask questions or require clarification; the intent behind the request can again be best revealed by the nonverbal cues of vocal tone and body posture. Other patients will be minimally compliant with the demands of testing (e. g., by drawing stick figures). By asking the students what feelings they have regarding these behaviors, the generalized other is once again brought into play. Students can then recognize how patients may alienate or attract others, and the students therefore perceive why these people fail or succeed in their social interactions.

It is very important to launch a classroom discussion about the nature of verbal communication before proceeding to teach the interpretation of projective instruments. Students hope that the patients' communications are truthful. Yet they also know from functioning in the world that only rarely can we accept communications at face value. There are different degrees to which we will trust others, and our degree of trust will vary across people and situations. For example, one does not expect to hear the truth from a used-car salesman.

A useful technique in teaching students how to interpret the communication of others is to ask the class what is meant when a person says "I love you." It does not take very much time for students to compose a lengthy list of diverse and contradictory motives that may lead a person to make this statement. When students recognize that verbal communication cannot be accepted at face value, they are ready to hypothesize and entertain the different intentions that produce certain verbalizations. People have three basic kinds of intentions that lead them to speak. They talk in order to communicate a message; they talk as a way of practicing self-deception; and they talk because they wish to produce certain effects on other people.

The clinician must ascertain the intentions of others as the first step toward understanding their verbal messages. Because communication is an interpersonal process, it has an interpersonal intention. Even when we speak to practice self-deception, the deception often works because it first deceives others. People typically wish to influence others and their communications will reflect this desire. Psychologists cannot afford to be naive and neglect the basic truth that patients are communicating much more than simply verbalizing open and direct truths each time they speak.

Because people regularly engage in impression formation, it is natural to expect that they will engage in impression formation during the assessment process as well. When students are learning to work with projective techniques, they must also regularly answer two questions regarding each patient. They need to ask what does the patient want them to believe and what are the real, underlying truths about him or her. By studying the patient's attempts at impression formation, it becomes possible to see how successful he or she is at influencing others. Subsequently, it becomes easier to see beneath the patient's efforts at impression formation and to detect the patient's underlying personality dynamics.

For example, in the original Miale–Holsopple Sentence Completion Test (Holsopple & Miale, 1954) and retained in my unpublished revision of this test, is the stem *A woman's body*. If a male patient answers the stem with *really turns me on*, the examiner must first consider if the patient is engaging in impression formation. The examiner will undoubtedly see an attempt at impression formation and realize that the patient wants others to believe that he is quite a virile male. Although it may certainly be true that the patient *is* a virile male, students can ask themselves why he needs to make such an emphatic statement. It then will not be much of a leap in logic to generate the hypothesis that the patient is probably not a particularly virile male because if he were, he would not need to proclaim the fact so strongly.

The ability to engage in impression formation is a necessary skill that enables people to be successful in the interpersonal world. Students need to be reminded that people do not always want to generate positive impressions. Some individuals may desire to create negative impressions and can be quite successful in getting others to dislike them. It is also important to inform students that individuals who can effectively engage in impression formation cannot be psychotic because psychosis represents a significant retreat from the interpersonal world.

Class discussion of the possible intentions that lead individuals to say certain things enables students to become more skeptical of the patient's statements. As the students become less gullible, they will draw on their reactions as the generalized other. They start to question whether their sympathetic feelings toward a patient were deliberately evoked by him or her. They may also ask if their budding sexual interest in the patient was deliberately evoked. They also question whether the patient wanted to generate the angry feelings they currently experience.

Once students accept that test subjects will engage in impression formation, they are better prepared to work with the two projective instruments that deal directly with the interpersonal world—the TAT and the Sentence Completion Test. Interpretations of patients' responses to both instruments will be enhanced if graduate students draw on their generalized other reactions to the patients' stories and sentence completions.

When teaching students how to interpret responses to the TAT, it is of course necessary to begin with basic questions, such as "Does the patient follow directions?" Students must then be taught to recognize the stimulus pull of the cards (Murstein, 1963) and to evaluate whether the patient's stories were consistent with the stimulus pull.

I find it helpful to have students take the TAT during class time without signing their names to the stories. Later the class generates interpretive hypotheses to different students' stories. Being a "patient" in this classroom experience helps students better understand the possible interpersonal worlds of their own patients. Having open class discussion, while preserving anonymity, enables students to learn that their dynamics are often shared by many of their classmates, which is personally quite reassuring.

There is no better way to teach students the reality of repression than to have them discover that half the class does not see either the gun on Card 3BM or the rifle on Card 8BM of the TAT. Before I interpret the graduate students' stories to Card 18GF, described as a woman, both strangling and pushing another woman backward over the banister of a stairway, I ask two class volunteers to position themselves in front of the classroom, portraying the exact physical interaction of the two women depicted on the card. The class immediately recognizes the marked contrast between the stories they composed about the very helpful daughter, on the one hand, and the hostile strangulation depicted on the card, that is about to take place in front of them, on the other hand. We then discuss the frequent use of reaction formation to cover up underlying hostile feelings.

Students can best begin TAT interpretation by reacting to the patients' stories as if they (the students) were actually engaged in the relationships and conversations described in the stories, as the generalized other, rather than as psychologists. I ask students to listen to the patient's stories and to ask themselves to what degree the patient really understands the needs, feelings, relationships, and behavior of other people. When patients tell illogical stories or those with magical endings, they are clearly conveying that they do not know why relationships succeed or fail. When they cannot relate a story that begins with a motive and has related consequences, they will not be able to anticipate effectively or deal with other people's reactions to their behavior.

One particular technique I use in the class concerns possible interpretation of the stories given to Card 4 of the TAT. In this card, which depicts a man and woman in conflict in the foreground and a half-clothed woman in the background, men and women typically will give very different stories. It is expected that individuals will identify with the same gender figure and, therefore, will tell a story in which the figure of their gender is behaving reasonably and the other figure is being unreasonable. For example, a woman usually describes the man in the card as impulsive, unreasonable, and out of control, and the woman as rational and hopefully capable of controlling the man. On the other hand, men will describe the man as strong and powerful, whereas the woman is depicted as excessively worrying or controlling. The men's stories will involve the man hopefully triumphing over the woman. By showing students how differently the two genders typically interpret the card, the students' generalized other is educated to view people from the vantage point of both genders.

Sentence completion tests elicit more direct impression formation statements than do other projective instruments. Once students are aware of this fact, they can try to see beneath the impression formation to the patient's underlying emotions and dynamics. It has been my personal observation that college students' attempts at impression formation have diminished over the past 30 years, as reflected in their sentence completion responses. The best example of this trend are the reactions to the Miale–Holsopple Sentence Completion stem *The easiest way to get money*. At least a third of the college students who today answer this stem propose antisocial solutions. These strategies involve selling drugs, selling one's body, or stealing. Such responses were extremely rare 30 years ago and may reflect different social priorities in how to present oneself. These test responses do not necessarily imply that individuals who offer antisocial verbal responses will actually engage in antisocial behavior.

When graduate students allow themselves personal reactions to subjects' TAT stories or to sentence completions, these reactions will typically reflect those of the generalized other. As a result, the emotions generated in assessors will reflect how most people in the world will feel toward the patient. Knowing these reactions tells the examiner the degree to which the patient will have or keep friends or lovers, what behaviors will get the patient in trouble, and which behaviors will produce success.

It is, of course, crucial for assessors to know the personality dynamics of their patients. However, unless one understands how these dynamics are expressed and how they impact others, this clinical knowledge is quite incomplete. Some people with inadequacy feelings are endearing and elicit assistance from many people. Other individuals with inadequacy feelings manage to alienate and repel many people. Only by knowing one's own feelings as a generalized other can the clinician make a fully effective assessment. Therefore, it is vital to stress the interpersonal dimension in an assessment course.

REFERENCES

Handler, L. (1996). The clinical use of drawings. In C. S. Newmark (Ed.), *Major psychological assessment instruments* (2nd ed.), (pp. 206–293). Boston: Allyn & Bacon.

Holsopple, J. Q., & Miale, F. R. (1954). *Sentence completion: A projective method for the study of personality*. Springfield, IL: Charles Thomas.

Murstein, B. I. (1963). *Theory and research in projective techniques: Emphasizing the TAT*. New York: Wiley.

Potash, H. M. (1981). *Inside clinical psychology: A handbook for graduate students and interns*. Madison, NJ: Gordon Handwerk.

Potash, H. M. (1994). *Pragmatic-existential psychotherapy with personality disorders*. Madison, NJ: Gordon Handwerk.

IV

TEACHING AND LEARNING SPECIFIC TEST INSTRUMENTS

In this part we have included chapters on teaching and learning selected self-report measures, projective measures, and a chapter on the interpretation of the Wechsler tests as personality instruments.

The chapter by Roger L. Greene and Poupak Rouhbakhsh, "Teaching the MMPI–2," focuses on well-developed strategies for teaching the details of MMPI-2 interpretation, using empirically driven interpretive approaches. Greene and Rouhbakhsh's chapter teaches the student how to use the entire pattern of scores rather than focusing only on peak scores or two-point scores. In this way they describe a more focused, individualized interpretive approach. The authors emphasize that students often use "canned statements," typically obtained from computer printouts, in their written reports, leading them to overpathologize the patient. Knowledge of how each scale is constructed and the multiple reasons for scale elevations should be communicated to students to avoid this pitfall. The authors also suggest teaching the limitations of the test. Greene and Rouhbakhsh also discuss teaching interpretation using a codetype-based approach or a content-oriented approach, and the use of the MMPI–2 Structural Summary in the interpretive process.

The chapter by Roger D. Davis and Theodore Millon, "Teaching Assessment With the Millon Clinical Multiaxial Inventory (MCMI–III)," begins with a directive to challenge students by asking them to discuss how they would design an instrument to assess personality, as well as challenging them to discuss the nature of personality and its development. For these authors, teaching the Millon begins by questioning theory and by a discussion of the model of Axis II personality development. Davis and Millon suggest that Loevinger's and Jackson's three-stage models of test construction should be taught, followed by a detailed discussion of the MCMI. They also discuss methods of communicating such important issues as base rates, reliability, and validity, and then they present an illustrative case.

Leslie C. Morey's chapter, "Teaching and Learning the Personality Assessment Inventory (PAI)" describes a relatively new self-report measure of personality. Morey outlines a five-step program beginning with a description of the conceptual rationale of the test, followed by a detailed examination of the individual scales of the PAI. Morey then describes his approach for teaching students about norms and reliability of the PAI. This is followed by a discussion of teaching profile validity, and finally, he introduces a configured interpretation, where students are taught ways to combine information gathered across the entire inventory, to address specific referral questions.

Irving B. Weiner's chapter, "Teaching the Rorschach Comprehensive System," describes in detail the conceptual issues involved in teaching students to score the Rorschach, using Exner's Comprehensive System. Weiner discusses the origins of the Comprehensive System and the reasons a standardized approach was necessary in administration and scoring, as well as the necessity for the establishment of a normative database. He discusses in some detail the empirical and conceptual features of Exner's interpretive approach, using a system that clusters variables and that describes a sequential search strategy.

"Teaching That First Rorschach Course," by Virginia Brabender, describes in detail the way in which she goes about teaching an introductory Rorschach course, emphasizing three areas of skill development: administration, scoring, and interpretation. Brabender describes a number of important strategies to facilitate students' learning in each area, also stressing ethical issues. She discusses many important details in communicating concepts to students, including those involved in the interpretation of the Structural Summary. She also includes information concerning the evaluation of performance.

Phebe Cramer's chapter, "Approaching the Thematic Apperception Test (TAT)" focuses on teaching the illumination of personality structure and dynamics using the TAT. Cramer describes quite innovative techniques for teaching the TAT, using students' own TAT responses as an initial starting point. The course not only teaches students to use the TAT clinically, but it also often provides the students with striking personal insights from their self-administered TATs and autobiography data. The students also get a chance to evaluate the data from a variety of other self-administered tests, comparing them with their TATs and autobiographies. Cramer discusses ways in which she addresses students' biases about the TAT, as well as their defensiveness and resistance to the notion that the TAT can reveal anything meaningful about a person's life. She discusses the use of multiple perspectives in teaching the interpretation of TAT stories, as well as a discussion of research with the test.

Leonard Handler and Robert J. Riethmiller's chapter, "Teaching the Administration and Interpretation of Graphic Techniques," illustrates for the student and the teacher an experience-near approach to the interpretation of the graphic techniques, Draw–A–Person (DAP), House–Tree–Person (HTP), and Kinetic Family Drawing (KFD). The authors emphasize that these techniques have not been well respected by researchers, because the research techniques used to validate them typically do not match the way in which clinicians use them in clinical practice. Handler and Riethmiller describe both research and application approaches that are quite similar to each other, and that seem to enhance the validity of these drawing techniques.

Leonard Handler's chapter, "Teaching the Interpretation of Wechsler Intelligence Tests as Personality Instruments," describes several methods of teaching students how to use these tests as personality assessment instruments. The chapter focuses on ways in which the instructor can help students learn to make individualized, experience-near personality interpretations rather than focus on inaccurate but popular subtest interpretation labels discussed in the literature. The techniques described in the chapter are borrowed from the Inquiry and the Testing of the Limits approaches to Rorschach administration, first described by Bruno Klopfer, employed here to discover personal meanings of the items and subtests, in collaboration with the patient. The chapter also includes instruction on how to use content interpretation to derive hypotheses about personality functioning, and techniques that allow the student to understand the relationship between cognition and personality functioning.

10

Teaching the MMPI–2

Roger L. Greene
Poupak Rouhbakhsh
Pacific Graduate School of Psychology

Personality assessment usually is one of the primary activities that distinguish psychologists from other clinical disciplines, and personality assessment is traditionally one of the core courses in any graduate program in psychology. The Minnesota Multiphasic Personality Inventory/Minnesota Multiphasic Personality Inventory–2 (MMPI: Hathaway & McKinley, 1940; MMPI–2: Butcher, Dahlstrom, Graham, Tellegen, & Kaemmer, 1989) has been one of the most widely used personality tests in a variety of situations, ranging from personnel selection to the clinical setting. According to a survey by Piotrowski and Zalewski (1993), the MMPI/MMPI–2 was ranked first among the objective assessment instruments in terms of training emphasis in both PsyD and PhD programs.

Nearly all graduate programs in psychology undertake the teaching of the MMPI–2 in the following areas: administration and scoring of the test, various strategies for profile interpretation, diagnostic issues in clinical cases, integration into psychological reports, and use with other objective and projective tests to assist in treatment planning.

Despite the importance of personality assessment in graduate training, however, teaching assessment courses, such as those focused on the MMPI–2 is often relegated to junior faculty who have little choice in what courses to teach, or to faculty members who are fundamentally opposed to personality assessment. For personality assessment to be a viable part of a graduate program, the courses should be taught by an individual who is steeped in and committed to personality assessment, and who has extensive experience with the MMPI–2 in a variety of clinical settings. It also is important for graduate programs to allocate adequate course time for students to gain basic mastery of the material. For example, a program that dedicates 3 weeks of class time to the MMPI–2 in a course that covers both objective and projective techniques is unlikely to provide students with an in-depth understanding of these instruments. Consequently, training programs must decide whether they prefer their students to have basic familiarity with a wide variety of instruments, or an in-depth understanding of a single or few instruments. It probably is more effective for students to become very familiar with a single instrument such as the MMPI–2, Rorschach, MCMI–III (Millon Clinical Multiaxial Inventory–III), or 16PF (Sixteen Personality Factor Questionnaire), rather than to be presented with a survey of numerous instruments. The skills learned with a specific instrument or technique can be generalized quickly to other instruments as the student chooses or the circumstances dictate.

Purpose of This Chapter

This chapter highlights some common problems encountered by students in learning the MMPI–2. Also, the common frameworks used by psychology programs in the training of the students in using the MMPI–2 in clinical settings are discussed. Finally, several strategies for teaching profile interpretation with the MMPI–2 are outlined.

CHALLENGES IN TEACHING AND LEARNING THE MMPI–2

One of the most common concerns of graduate level students in learning the MMPI–2, or any other personality assessment instrument, in a psychology program is the issue of time. This concern was expressed by Silverstein (1996): "the best work in psychological testing, as in psychotherapy, requires ... extended time for incubation" (p. 359). Devoting one term, or less, to teaching the administration, scoring, and interpretation of the MMPI–2, as well as one or two other assessment instruments, is not realistic, because no instrument can be mastered in such limited time. Most students report that a minimum of one full term is needed to familiarize themselves thoroughly, and to feel comfortable, with one assessment instrument. As a result of insufficient time being devoted to learning the MMPI–2 or any other personality assessment instrument, students feel that they do not possess a true knowledge and understanding of complexities of the instrument.

Possessing only a superficial knowledge of the MMPI–2 scales forces beginning students to resort to using "canned" statements in written reports. When students do not have a knowledge of how each scale is constructed, and the multiple reasons for scale elevation are not explored, students are more likely to overpathologize the client and produce written reports that are filled with canned, meaningless, and overly generalized statements. For example, when Scale 4 (Pd) is elevated, a typical statement is that the person has "difficulty in incorporating the values and standards of society" (Graham, 1993, p. 63), or the person is "fighting against something, which is usually some form of conflict with authority figures" (Greene, 1991, p. 155). Unless students realize that Scale 4 also contains content that assesses family problems (Pd2: Familial Discord) and alienation (Pd4: Social Alienation; Pd5: Self-Alienation), they may mis-assess/misdiagnose persons who have elevations on these subscales. Similar interpretive problems can be raised for the other MMPI-2 validity and clinical scales and most of the MMPI-2 content scales because of their heterogeneity of content(see Ben-Porath & Sherwood, 1993). Thus, it is important that students understand the major correlates of the scales as well as the types of item content that are contained within each scale that may impact its interpretation. Most graduate students report that when instruction begins by prescribing that students memorize the scales (clinical, content, and supplementary scales), followed by a test on the names, functions, and construction of the scales, their understanding of the MMPI-2 is increased significantly. Profile interpretation follows only after a thorough understanding of the MMPI-2 has been achieved. A majority of students believe that report writing per se does not assist them in their understanding of the scales, mainly because the information most often is looked up in reference books. Being tested on the material, however, encourages the students to examine the scales more thoroughly.

One of the major issues in teaching the MMPI-2 is the degree of emphasis on its limitations. For instance, it is important to emphasize that the number of scales exceeded the number of items on the original MMPI, all of which cannot be reliable or valid. Also, the problem in getting students to appreciate the difficulty that lies in taking the names of the scales literally is extremely challenging. More specifically, demonstrating that an individual who obtains a high score on Scale 8 (Sc) is not necessarily schizophrenic often is complex. It usually is extremely difficult to stop the student from looking at a certain scale and labeling the person who scores high on that scale as being a member of that diagnostic group, that is, schizophrenic, rather than as endorsing the items like a member of that diagnostic group. Again, the heterogeneity of item content within a given scale complicates its interpretation as noted previously.

Another issue that makes the teaching of the MMPI-2 particularly difficult is the sheer number of scales that are available for potential interpretation. If the National Computer System's Extended Scale Report is used as the standard, there are a total of 136 different scales and indexes that can be interpreted. It often is difficult for students to understand which of the clinical, supplementary, or content scales are to be the focal point in profile interpretation. If the standard validity and clinical scales are to be used in a codetype analysis, students need to know which of the supplementary and content scales should be reviewed to facilitate their interpretation. In a codetype that involves Scale 8 (Sc), for example, it is important to know whether the content scale of Bizarre Mentation (BIZ) is elevated. When BIZ is elevated, the person is more likely to have endorsed the psychotic items on Scale 8 than when BIZ is not elevated. Students also need to know whether similar scores among a set of scales reflects important clinical features of the person or merely redundancy among the scales due to item overlap and common sources of variance. An excellent example of this latter problem can be found by considering the First Factor scales of the MMPI-2 Structural Summary (Table 10.1) that reflect an individual's reported degree of general distress. This large factor reflects the primary character of the MMPI/MMPI-2; that is, it is an inventory of psychopathology designed to detect pathologic facets of symptomatology and personality. The First Factor is

TABLE 10.1
The MMPI-2 Structural Summary (First Factor Scales)

First Factor Scales (General Distress)
_____ A (Welsh Anxiety)
_____ Pt (Psychasthenia)
_____ PS (PTSD-Schlenger)
_____ PK (PTSD-Keane)
_____ Mt (College Maladjustment)
_____ WRK (Work Interference)
_____ ANX (Anxiety)
_____ TRT (Negative Treatment Indicators)
_____ LSE (Low self-esteem)
_____ DEP (Depression)
_____ K (Correction) [Low]
_____ Es (Ego Strength) [Low]

Note. From Greene and Nichols (1995). Copyright 1995 by Psychological Assessment Resources, Inc. Lutz, Florida. Reproduced by permission.

a unipolar dimension, ranging from no (or abnormally low) distress at the low end to an overwhelming level of psychological discomfort at the high end. These scales, despite their different names, are essentially interchangeable with correlations ranging between .75 to .96 (see Nichols & Greene, 1995). They merely provide a reliable estimate of the person's level of general distress and cannot be interpreted directly as measuring the construct indicated by the scale's name.

Practically all graduate students assert that they possess only a superficial knowledge of MMPI-2 codetypes. This superficial knowledge can result from students simply looking up the codetype in the standard MMPI-2 references (Butcher & Williams, 1992; Graham, 1993; Greene, 1991) and ignoring the information contained in the remaining scales. Thus, it is very easy for students, by looking through the lenses of codetypes, to overpathologize patients. For example, if students do not truly understand that Scale 8 (Sc) contains items measuring social alienation, poor family relationships, difficulties in memory and concentration, problems with impulse control, and sexual difficulties as well as bizarre thought processes, it is highly probable that they will label an individual with a 6-8/8-6 codetype as being schizophrenic, without considering whether these other areas of item content are elevating Scale 8 rather than bizarre thought processes. In addition, response styles such as excessive overreporting of psychopathology ("faking bad"), yea-saying (endorsing the items "true" regardless of their content), and inconsistent patterns of item endorsement (VRIN > 80T) routinely produce 6-8/8-6 codetypes.

One method for assisting students in recognizing whether other scales need to be examined carefully is to have them plot the prototypic profile for the codetype. The prototypic profile provides the pattern of interscale relationships that are found for a given codetype, and can give the student a frame of reference for deciding whether a specific scale is unusual or atypical for this specific person. Greene (1991) has provided the prototypic scores for all spike and 2-point MMPI and MMPI–2 codetypes. The prototypic T scores for Scales 2 (D) and 0 (Si) for a 4-9/9-4 codetype are 53 and 45 (Greene, 1991), respectively. A person with a 4-9/9-4 codetype who has T scores of 72 and 70, respectively, on these same two scales is much less likely to act out in a group of other individuals than a person with the prototypic scores. Students also can be provided with a computer or automated interpretation of the MMPI–2. They can then adapt this prototypic interpretation to fit the specific client's history and the changes that must be made because his or her profile varies from the prototypic profile.

Figure 10.1 provides an example of a profile of a client who has a 7-2 codetype (dark circles) and the prototypic 2-7-/7-2 codetype (hatched rectangles). In matching the client's codetype to the prototypic codetype, several points become apparent. The client had lower elevations than the prototype on Scales 1 (Hs) and 3 (Hy), and higher elevations on Scales 5 (Mf) and 6 (Pa). In comparing the client's codetype to the prototypic 2-7/7-2 profile, it becomes evident that this client would probably behave very differently in a clinical interview, and would have different reasons for being referred for treatment, than a person whose profile elevations match the prototypic 2-7/7-2 elevations. The prototypic individuals with 2-7/7-2 codetypes tend to be classically depressed and they are anxious, tense, and typically constant worriers. They complain of difficulties in concentration and thinking. The client's profile, however, is much lower on Scales 1 and 3, reflecting fewer somatic symptoms than would be expected, and it is likely that the depressive and anxious features are not significant enough or persistent enough to be producing physical symptoms. Students are encouraged to match the client's codetype to the

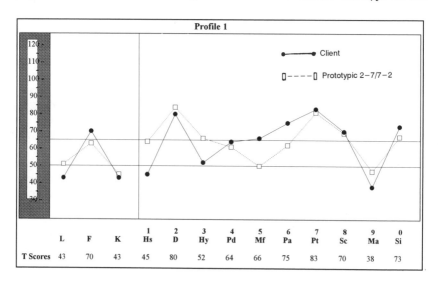

FIG. 10.1. Matching an MMPI–2 profile to the prototypic codetype.

prototypic profile for the standard validity and clinical scales. Any score that varies by more than 1 standard deviation (SD) (approximately 10 T = points) from the prototypic score for that scale should be evaluated carefully to determine whether and how it might modify the standard interpretation of that codetype. A wealth of information is readily available for students by merely matching a profile to a prototype. Appendix D of the MMMPI–2/MMPI Manual and/or the MMPI–2 Adult Interpretive System (Greene & Brown, 1998) provide the prototypic scores for all spike and high-point pair codetypes on the MMPI–2 and the MMPI.

Another challenge in teaching the MMPI–2 is the dearth of interpretive literature for MMPI–2 codetypes. Although very little was changed in terms of item composition between the standard validity and clinical scales of the MMPI and MMPI–2, research on codetype comparability has been very popular, with over 40 published studies since 1990. There are a wide range of opinions on the degree of codetype comparability between the MMPI and MMPI–2, ranging from 50% to 90% using "well-defined" codetypes, and 40% to 70% for "nonrestrictive" codetypes (cf. Dahlstrom, 1992; Edwards, Morrison, & Weissman, 1993a, 1993b; Graham, Timbrook, Ben-Porath, & Butcher, 1991; Morrison, Edwards, Weissman, Allen, & DeLaCruz, 1995). Well-defined codetypes have at least 5 T points between the second and third highest clinical scale; that is, the two scales defining the codetype are clearly distinct from the other clinical scales. Nonrestrictive codetypes have no requirements for differences in elevation between the clinical scales. Rarely do these researchers report whether the degree of concordance varies as a function of specific codetypes, although it does (see Greene, 1991), and none of the studies of the comparability of the MMPI and MMPI–2 actually has examined the empirical correlates of the two instruments, despite calls for such research (W. G. Dahlstrom, 1992). This lack of literature on codetype comparability between the MMPI and the MMPI–2 has the potential to complicate MMPI–2 profile interpretation, because the correlates of an MMPI codetype may not be totally applicable to the corresponding MMPI–2 codetype.

Finally, students strongly advocate the incorporation of practicum experience into their assessment training. By interpreting actual clinical cases students encounter in their practicum placements, their knowledge of the MMPI–2, as well as their conceptualization of their clinical cases, can be enhanced. A potential problem with evaluating the student's own clinical cases is the reluctance of some supervisors to allow the student therapists to test their own clients. In those cases, where the testing of the students' own clients is viewed as being inappropriate, interpreting a profile of a client that is seen by a student colleague can be beneficial to all parties involved.

CODETYPE- VERSUS CONTENT-BASED INTERPRETATION

The decision of whether to interpret an MMPI–2 profile empirically by emphasizing a traditional, codetype-based approach or utilizing a content-based approach is a complex issue. The emphasis on a codetype-based interpretation reflects the long tradition of the MMPI/MMPI–2 to ignore the actual content of the person's responses and to rely on the known, empirical correlates of the scales and codetypes. Despite this empirical tradition, clinicians were unable to ignore the actual item content and developed critical item sets (e. g., Koss & Butcher, 1973; Lachar & Wrobel, 1979), and then entire scales based on item content (Butcher, Graham, Williams, & Ben-Porath, 1989; Wiggins, 1966).

Wiggins' (1966) Content scales represented the first systematic attempt to develop a means of examining the client's responses to the items of the MMPI, and the Butcher et al. (1989) content scales reflect a similar approach on the MMPI–2. Butcher and colleagues began to develop the MMPI–2 Content scales by sorting the 704 items of the AX booklet (the original 550 items from the MMPI plus 154 additional new items that were under consideration for inclusion in the MMPI–2) into possible categories based on their item content. These initial groupings of items were refined statistically to ensure their psychometric homogeneity. Finally, only those items whose content was homogeneous with the rest of the items were retained. This procedure resulted in 15 Content scales: ANX (Anxiety), FRS (Fears), OBS (Obsessiveness), DEP (Depression), HEA (Health Concerns), BIZ (Bizarre Mentation), ANG (Anger), CYN (Cynicism), ASP (Antisocial Practices), TPA (Type A), LSE (Low Self-Esteem), SOD (Social Discomfort), FAM (Family Problems), WRK (Work Interference), and TRT (Negative Treatment Indicators). Ben-Porath and Sherwood (1993) have developed Component scales for most of the MMPI–2 Content scales that can be used to enhance and refine the interpretation of an elevation on the parent scale.

Most of the items on the MMPI–2 Content scales are from the original MMPI item pool, except for the LSE, WRK, and TRT scales. That is, the MMPI–2 Content scales are not composed primarily of new items. There also is substantial item overlap within the MMPI–2 Content scales. Only three scales (FRS, HEA, and SOD) have no items in common with the other Content scales. Four scales (OBS, CYN, WRK, and TRT) have almost one half of their items in common with the other Content scales. There also is significant overlap among the standard validity and clinical scales and the MMPI–2 Content scales. Some of the scales that share items make good intuitive sense: HEA with Scales 1 (Hs) and 3 (Hy), BIZ with Scales 6 (Pa) and 8 (Sc), and SOD with Scale 0 (Si).

However, other relationships among these scales would not be expected: DEP has only nine items in common with Scale 2 (D) and shares items with most of the other clinical scales; ASP, CYN, and ANG have few items in common with Scale 4 (Pd), and CYN and ANG share few items with any of the standard validity and clinical scales. ANX shares items with 11 of the standard validity and clinical scales. Students need to be aware of these interrelationships or lack thereof because they can impact the interpretation of a given profile.

The MMPI–2 Structural Summary (Greene & Nichols, 1995; Nichols & Greene, 1995) is a systematic method for content-based, profile interpretation. The MMPI–2 Structural Summary can assist students in organizing MMPI–2 observations, in facilitating the generation of interpretive hypotheses, and in expediting interpretation and report writing. The Structural Summary seeks to relieve some of the burden of MMPI–2 interpretation, especially those owing to the large numbers of scales, the varying appropriateness of scale names, and unanticipated patterns of intercorrelation among the scales. The Structural Summary facilitates the efficient review of MMPI–2 findings by providing a set of clinically relevant categories into which scales of disparate names, types, and origins can be stored. This organization maximizes the extraction of test information, while minimizing the amount of time required to do so. It achieves these goals by enabling the most salient factors in test performance to stand out, allowing a rapid appraisal of the robustness of trends in MMPI–2 data, and by following a sequence of topics that facilitates the preparation of interpretive reports. The MMPI–2 Structural Summary is structural in the sense that most of its categories reflect known (multiply replicated) dimensions of variation within the total item pool, and these categories are composed of scales possessing relatively high intercorrelations and relatively high amounts of similarity in terms of item content and overlap. By contrast, relations between scales and/or indices in different categories are characterized by generally lower correlations and more dissimilar item content. Students can see these relations or lack thereof for themselves by looking at Appendix A in the *MMPI–2 Structural Summary Interpretive Manual* (Nichols & Greene, 1995).

The MMPI–2 Structural Summary serves several purposes with respect to clinical practice with the MMPI–2. First, it functions as a mnemonic for MMPI–2 scores, arranging them in patterns that maximize the likelihood that their interpretive significance, when present, will be noticed. Second, in cases that produce a well-known profile pattern, the Structural Summary is intended as a supplement to the traditional codetype interpretive strategy. Structural Summary findings can be used to call attention to aspects of MMPI–2 performance that have not been included in the usual sources of codetype information (Butcher, 1990; Butcher & Williams, 1992; Dahlstrom, Welsh, & L. E. Dahlstrom, 1972; Duckworth & Anderson, 1986; Friedman, Webb, & Lewak, 1989; Gilberstadt & Duker, 1965; Graham, 1993; Greene, 1991; Gynther, Altman, & Sletten, 1973; Lachar, 1974; Marks, Seeman, & Haller, 1974). Finally, for codetypes that occur infrequently or whose empirical correlates have not been established, information provided in the Structural Summary may serve as the primary basis for interpretation.

Proper use of the MMPI–2 Structural Summary requires that students are familiar with the MMPI–2's rationale and construction, the most commonly used scales and indices, codetype correlates, and similar basic information. Therefore, the content or structural teaching of the MMPI–2 cannot be divorced from empirical instruction. However, the Structural Summary takes students a step further by assisting them in making an idiographic, content-based interpretation of each profile.

Teaching a content-based approach to the MMPI–2 is a three-step process. First, students learn the interpretation of the MMPI–2 Content scales which is relatively straightforward because the scales consist of primarily homogeneous sets of items. For example, a person who elevates ANX to a T = score of 65 or higher is saying that he or she is anxious. Because the Content scales utilize uniform T scores, they also can be ranked from high to low to illustrate what areas of content the person sees as most to least descriptive of him or herself, which also assists students in deciding what content areas to emphasize in the interpretation. Second, once students understand the interpretation of the Content scales, the Content Component scales (Ben-Porath & Sherwood, 1993) are introduced to refine the interpretation of the parent scale. This step proceeds quickly because it is simply an elaboration of the first step. Finally, students are introduced to the MMPI-2 Structural Summary, which adds the other MMPI-2 scales into areas of homogeneous content. Once students have been taken through several cases in this pattern, the content-based interpretation of the MMPI-2 is understood easily.

One solution to the issue of whether to use a traditional, codetype-based interpretation and/or a content-based interpretation for the MMPI-2 can be arrived at by considering the validity of the test and the client's response style. When, in studying a profile, questions surrounding test validity are raised such as extensive overreporting ("faking bad") or underreporting ("faking good") of psychopathology, the clinician probably will benefit from undertaking an empirically based interpretation of the profile. Greene (1991, 1997) has provided numerous scales and indexes that can be used to identify overreporting and underreporting of psychopathology. If no validity issues are evident, then a content-based interpretation not only is justified, it probably will be more accurate. Finn (1996) described the use of therapeutic assessment in which the client becomes an active participant in the assessment process that decreases substantially the potential for the client to distort his or her responses. A content-based interpretation can be particularly useful within this framework of a therapeutic assessment.

When the decision is made to use a content-based interpretation of the MMPI-2, several issues should be considered. First, clients have to have insight into their behavior and be willing to share these insights in order to have an accurate evaluation. Because the MMPI-2 Content scales are obvious measures of psychopathology, it is very easy for clients to present an inaccurate self-appraisal. Thus, low scores on the MMPI-2 Content scales (T scores less than 45) could represent the absence of the specific descriptors characteristic of high scorers, or their refusal to acknowledge the presence of such item content. Similarly, high scores on the MMPI-2 Content scales may reflect the presence of the actual item content that has been endorsed, or the client's overreporting of psychopathology. The clinician, therefore, should assess the accuracy of item endorsement when overreporting or underreporting of psychopathology is suspected. Second, the deviant response for a majority of the items on the MMPI-2 Content scales is "true," so a raw score of 12 or higher on the True Response Inconsistency scale (TRIN) would be expected to produce elevations on most of these scales. Third, a number of the items on these scales are clustered in the last 100 items so any waning of the client's motivation toward the end of the test could adversely affect these scales.

TEACHING PERSONALITY ASSESSMENT:
A SUGGESTED FORMAT

In teaching personality assessment, assuming that only one formula or procedure works is risky, because to date there is not one correct way of teaching
personality assessment. The following suggestions are merely examples of
several teaching methods that have been used with the MMPI–2 in the context
of a graduate training program. The first assignment for students in the MMPI–2
course is to take the MMPI–2 themselves, and then to select a specific
diagnostic category from the DSM–IV (*Diagnostic and Statistical Manual of
Mental Disorders*, 4th ed.) and complete the MMPI–2 like a client with that
diagnosis. The students are required to hand score and profile all of the MMPI–2
scales for both administrations, but only the simulated MMPI–2 is turned in.
The simulated profile will be used later in the course when validity issues are
discussed. Computer scoring is used for other MMPI–2s, specifically the NCS
Extended Score Report, because it scores all scales on the MMPI–2. It is
inefficient for students or clinicians to devote their time, or anyone else's, to
hand scoring and profiling the MMPI–2. Hand scoring and profiling is prone to
introduce errors unless students are extremely careful, and it encourages
students to score only the basic scales rather than using all of the information
that is readily available in the MMPI–2 when all 567 items are administered.
Students are required, however, to hand score and profile their first MMPI–2
so that they have the requisite skills if it ever becomes necessary to hand score
the test because of the unavailability of computer scoring. Also, administering
only the first 370 items of the MMPI–2 is discouraged, because of the loss of
information noted previously; it should be a rare circumstance in which a client
can complete the first 370 items, but not the entire test.

The *MMPI/MMPI–2 Manual* (Greene, 1991) is used as a general framework
for teaching interpretation of the MMPI–2. In general, 6–8 weeks are devoted
to covering the first five chapters of the *Manual*. Each scale is discussed
individually, as well as what specific elevations on each scale might mean for a
specific client. As might be expected, a considerable amount of time is spent
discussing how to assess the validity of the MMPI–2, and the effects that
test-taking attitudes will have on various scales. It also is extremely helpful to
spend some time in each class period discussing what scores would be expected
on one scale, given the score on a second scale and a consideration of what
type(s) of client(s) might produce such a pattern of scores on these two scales.
Using Scales 9 (Ma) and 0 (Si) as examples, if the client has a T score of 75 on
Scale 9, what would the client be expected to have on Scale 0? And, if the client
has a T score of 75 on both Scales 9 and 0, what types of psychopathology would
be expected, compared to a client that has T score of 75 on Scale 9 and a T
score of 30 on Scale 0?

Profile or codetype interpretation is covered first as a general process, and
then specific case examples are used for commonly occurring codetypes (e.g.,
1-3/3-1, 2-4/4-2, 2-7/7-2, 4-9/9-4, 6-8/8-6, and 6-9/9-6 codetypes). The students then are divided into small groups of two to four students and are given

about 2 weeks to develop a "blind" interpretation for an MMPI–2 Extended Score Report. Blind interpretations are emphasized initially so that the students are required to use the data provided by the MMPI–2 and to learn what additional clinical information or background material would be invaluable in understanding why a specific scale is or is not elevated. The first two interpretations are evaluated, but are not graded.

Once students understand codetype interpretation, they are introduced to content-based interpretation as described earlier. The students then complete two or three blind interpretations for the MMPI–2 Extended Scale Report and MMPI–2 Structural Summary that are graded. They are encouraged to argue and debate among themselves over potential interpretations to ensure that significant data are not being overlooked. The students are required to divide their interpretation into specific sections (test-taking attitude [validity]; presence of and degree of distress; cognition; mood; interpersonal, treatment, and DSM–IV diagnoses [Axis I and II]) and to indicate parenthetically the source for each statement that they make. Chapter 7 of the MMPI/MMPI–2 Manual (Greene, 1991) provides two examples of this procedure. Each student also is required to evaluate one or two patients with a clinical interview and the MMPI–2 so that they learn how to integrate the specific case material into an interpretation. By the end of the term each student has interpreted from five to seven MMPI–2s. The midterm and final examinations consist essentially of the students interpreting specific aspects of several MMPI–2 Extended Score Reports and MMPI–2 Structural Summaries. They are allowed to use their notes, books, and so on for these examinations.

A number of caveats are repeated continually throughout the course:

1. Elevations on a specific scale indicate that the client takes the scale *like* a member of the criterion group, not that the client *is* a member of the criterion group. This point also emphasizes the use of scale numbers rather than scale names to avoid such potential errors in interpretation.

2. In a clinical setting, scores in the normal range on most scales are *not* normal; rather, they are likely to be indicative of serious psychopathology that is not disturbing or upsetting to the client. For example, it would be rather unusual for a client requesting psychotherapy to have T scores of 50 on Scales 2 (D) and 7 (Pt). In fact, these two scales should rarely be low points (T scores of 50 or lower) for any clinical client. As an example, an MMPI–2 was obtained recently from a client at a state hospital who believed that he was "God" (Fig. 10.2, dark circles). This client's MMPI–2 was paired with the MMPI–2 of an age- and gender-matched, normal adult (Fig. 10.2, open circles), and the students are to select which profile was given by the client. The two MMPI–2 profiles are virtually indistinguishable! The client's Rorschach is clearly psychotic, which provides the students with additional information on the different ways patients may describe themselves on these two instruments. Examples of such clear false negatives on the MMPI–2 are readily available in any clinical setting.

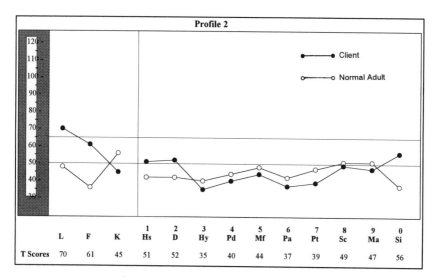

FIG. 10.2. "God's" MMPI–2 and an age-matched, normal man's MMPI–2.

Several exercises are first covered in class, with the professor modeling the response, that are then practiced by the students in small groups:

1. A brief case history is provided for the client and then the client's codetype, low-point clinical scales, accuracy of item endorsement, supplementary scales (A and R only), and content scales are predicted (Table 10.2). After consensus is reached or clear points of divergence are identified, the client's actual scores on the MMPI–2 are reviewed. Students are encouraged to get into the habit of predicting the MMPI–2 scores for each new client they encounter so they can identify areas that differ from how the client describes him or herself on the MMPI–2. If the student encounters a mismatch between the predicted scores and reported scores of the person, then issues such as overreporting or underreporting of psychopathology and response style of the person taking the test must be considered. In other words, when a person in a clinical setting produces a profile that is different from the common profile produced by that group (i .e., a person seeking treatment for depression that does not produce a 2-7/7-2 profile), then issues such as possible alternate diagnoses, response style, and motivation for seeking treatment must be strongly considered. On the other hand, when a match exists between the predicted scores and the scores produced by the person, then the profile interpretation can be approached with a baseline knowledge of the person's primary symptoms and characteristics.

2. A client's MMPI–2 is provided and, based on these scores, the client's reasons for seeking treatment and primary problem areas are predicted. These predictions then are verified against the client's actual case history.

3. Other MMPI–2 experts are invited to demonstrate their approach to interpreting the MMPI–2, so that the students appreciate that there are

TABLE 10.2
Format for Predicting MMPI–2 Performance

Clinical scales:

Codetype: _____

Lowest two or three scales: _____

Accuracy of item endorsement:

1	5	10	25	50	75	90	95	99

Percentile

Underreporting   Accurate   Overreporting

First-Factor and Second-Factor Scales:

[Anxiety (A), Repression (R)]

First Factor [high or low]: _____

Second Factor [high or low]: _____

Content scales: [ANX, FRS, OBS, DEP, HEA, BIZ, ANG, CYN, ASP, TPA, LSE, SOD, FAM, WRK, AND TRT]

Highest two or three scales: _____

Lowest two or three scales: _____

different ways of using the data. These experts do not have to have authored books (or chapters!) on the MMPI–2, because most clinical settings will have a clinician who is known as the local MMPI–2 "guru."

4. The students are provided with a computer interpretation of the MMPI–2 and asked to deduce the scores that served as the basis for each statement that is generated in the report. The *Minnesota Report*, authored by Jim Butcher, and the *Caldwell Report*, authored by Alex Caldwell, are particularly good for this task. This task also can be used as part of the final exam in the course.

5. A seminar on advanced interpretation of the MMPI–2, or other personality assessment instruments and techniques, can be an added benefit for students who desire more advanced training, and who plan to undertake assessment as their area of specialty.

SUMMARY

Teaching the MMPI–2, like any other personality assessment technique, is a complex task that requires that the professor be thoroughly familiar with the MMPI–2 and the variety of ways in which the data can be interpreted. A professor who is only familiar with traditional codetype interpretation cannot facilitate students' awareness or even make students aware of content-based approaches to profile interpretation, or vice versa. In addition, teaching the MMPI–2 is enhanced by the use of numerous clinical examples that require extensive experience in the use of the MMPI–2 in a clinical setting, and it is hoped a number of different clinical settings, because the MMPI–2 varies, sometimes rather drastically, as a function of the setting. These goals of providing an in-depth understanding of the MMPI–2 will not be attainable by a new assistant professor who tries to cover the MMPI–2 in a few weeks, in a survey course.

As clinical psychology moves increasingly to outcome-based treatments as a result of managed care, accurate assessment and diagnosis actually become more, rather than less, important so that patients will be receiving the appropriate treatment. It should be apparent that it does little good to know that a specific type of treatment is the treatment of choice for a specific disorder unless we have an accurate means of diagnosing that disorder. Clearly, teaching and learning personality assessment has a viable future.

REFERENCES

Ben-Porath, Y. S., & Sherwood, N. E. (1993). *The MMPI–2 content component scales: Development, psychometric characteristics, and clinical application.* Minneapolis: University of Minnesota Press.

Butcher, J. N. (1990). *MMPI–2 in psychological treatment.* New York: Oxford.

Butcher, J. N., Dahlstrom, W. G., Graham, J. R., Tellegen, A. M., & Kaemmer, B. (1989). *MMPI–2: Manual for administration and scoring.* Minneapolis: University of Minnesota Press.

Butcher, J. N., Graham, J. R., Williams, C. L., & Ben-Porath, Y. S. (1989). *Development and use of the MMPI–2 content scales.* Minneapolis: University of Minnesota Press.

Butcher, J. N., & Williams, C. L. (1992). *Essentials of MMPI–2 and MMPI-A interpretation.* Minneapolis: University of Minnesota Press.

Dahlstrom, W. G. (1992). Comparability of two-point high-point code patterns from original MMPI norms to MMPI–2 norms for the restandardization sample. *Journal of Personality Assessment, 59,* 153–164.

Dahlstrom, W. G., Welsh, G. S., & Dahlstrom, L. E. (1972). *An MMPI handbook: Vol. I. Clinical interpretation* (Rev. ed.). Minneapolis: University of Minnesota Press.

Duckworth, J. C., & Anderson, W. (1986). *MMPI interpretation manual for counselors and clinicians* (3rd ed.). Muncie, IN: Accelerated Development.

Edwards, D. W., Morrison, T. L., & Weissman, H. N. (1993a). The MMPI and MMPI–2 in an outpatient sample: Comparisons of code types, validity scales and clinical scales. *Journal of Personality Assessment, 61,* 1–18.

Edwards, D. W., Morrison, T. L., & Weissman, H. N.(1993b). Uniform versus linear T scores on the MMPI–2/MMPI in an outpatient psychiatric sample: Differential contributions. *Psychological Assessment, 5,* 499–500.

Finn, S. (1996). *Using the MMPI–2 as therapeutic assessment.* Minneapolis: University of Minnesota Press.

Friedman, A. F., Webb, J. T., & Lewak, R. (1989). *Psychological assessment with the MMPI.* Hillsdale, NJ: Lawrence Erlbaum Associates.

Gilberstadt, H., & Duker, J. (1965). *A handbook for clinical and actuarial MMPI interpretation*. Philadelphia: Saunders.

Graham, J.R. (1993). *MMPI-2: Assessing personality and psychopathology* (2nd ed.). New York: Oxford University Press.

Graham, J. R., Timbrook, R. E., Ben-Porath, Y. S., & Butcher, J. N. (1991). Code-type congruence between MMPI and MMPI-2: Separating fact from artifact. *Journal of Personality Assessment, 57*, 205–215.

Greene, R. L. (1991). *MMPI/MMPI-2: An interpretive manual*. Boston: Allyn & Bacon.

Greene, R. L. (1997). Assessment of malingering and defensiveness by multiscale inventories. In R. Rogers (Ed.), *Clinical assessment of malingering and defensiveness* (2nd ed.) (pp. 167–207). New York: Guilford.

Greene, R. L., & Brown, R. C. (1998). *MMPI-2 adult interpretive system* (Version 2.0). Lutz, FL: Psychological Assessment Resources.

Greene, R. L., & Nichols, D. S. (1995). *MMPI-2 Structural Summary*. Odessa, FL: Psychological Assessment Resources.

Gynther, M. D., Altman, H. F., & Sletten, I. W. (1973). Replicated correlates of MMPI two-point code types: The Missouri actuarial system. *Journal of Clinical Psychology, 29*, 263–289.

Hathaway, S. R., & McKinley, J. C. (1940). A multiphasic personality schedule (Minnesota): I. Construction of the schedule. *Journal of Personality, 10*, 249–254.

Koss, M. P., & Butcher, J. N. (1973). A comparison of psychiatric patients' self-report with other sources of clinical information. *Journal of Research on Personality, 7*, 225–236.

Lachar, D. (1974). *The MMPI: Clinical assessment and automated interpretation*. Los Angeles: Western Psychological Services.

Lachar, D., & Wrobel, T. A. (1979). Validating clinicians' hunches: Construction of a new MMPI critical item set. *Journal of Consulting and Clinical Psychology, 47*, 277–284.

Marks, P. A., Seeman, W., & Haller, D. L. (1974). *The actuarial use of the MMPI with adolescents and adults*. Baltimore: Williams & Wilkins.

Morrison, T. L., Edwards, D. W., Weissman, H. N., Allen, R., & DeLaCruz, D. (1995). Comparing MMPI and MMPI-2 profiles: Replication and integration. *Assessment, 2*, 39–46.

Nichols, D. S., & Greene, R. L. (1995). *The MMPI-2 structural summary manual*. Lutz, FL: Psychological Assessment Resources.

Piotrowski, C. & Zalewski, C. (1993). Training in psychodiagnostic testing in APA-approved PsyD and PhD clinical psychology programs. *Journal of Personality Assessment, 61*, 394–405.

Silverstein, M. L. (1996). Teaching the Rorschach and learning psychodiagnostic testing: A commentary on Hilsenroth and Handler (1995). *Journal of Personality Assessment, 66*, 355–362.

Wiggins, J. S. (1966). Substantive dimensions of self-report in the MMPI item pool. *Psychological Monographs, 80*(22, Whole No. 630).

11

Teaching Assessment with the Millon Clinical Multiaxial Inventory (MCMI–III)

Roger D. Davis
Institute for Advanced Studies in Personology and Psychopathology
Theodore Millon
Harvard University Medical School, University of Miami,
and Institute for Advanced Studies in Personology and Psychopathology

The Millon Inventories may be taught as part of an introductory or advanced personality assessment course, as part of a seminar series, or as part of a course specifically devoted to the personality disorders. Because of its more focused character, the third option probably presents the best opportunity for discussion of the issues involved in the development of the inventories. The first and second, however, are probably more common. This chapter presents an approach to teaching the MCMI (T. Millon, C. Millon, & Davis, 1994) that the authors have found to be effective over the course of many years, in a variety of different venues, with a variety of time constraints. Particular sections may be expanded or contracted, depending on the level of the audience, their interests, and the focus of the class or seminar. With some practice, the material may be introduced in as little as 3 hours, or expanded to fill several weeks.

The focus of this chapter is not on material of a theoretical nature, for which abundant references are already available (T. Millon, 1969, 1981, 1986a, 1986b, 1990; T. Millon & Davis, 1996), but instead on a progression of themes that challenge students to learn the inventory as they think cogently about fundamental issues that cut across all of assessment, and sometimes, across the entire field of clinical psychology. Unfortunately, space does not permit us to touch on all of the numerous subtleties that might be presented. Teachers are directed to original sources for such material.

All readers of this text are likely to have had courses in personality assessment. And although readers may disagree concerning the best aspects of these courses, they are likely to agree on one important point: that any lecture(s) that approaches a number of personality assessment instruments in series by reviewing first the scales of each instrument, then their reliability and validity, then common codetype configurations, and so on, is absolutely deadly. Attention will not be sustained for long. Such information has its place, but it could as easily be entered into a database for automatic retrieval. A personality assessment course cannot be allowed to degenerate into a list of tests and statistics.

When teaching personality assessment, it is necessary to bring each instrument to life, by discussing the spirit of the times, that is, issues that were being actively discussed in the field, problems that the authors thought it important to address, and even the personalities of the developers. Just as each individual human personality has its own developmental path that inclines it toward particular strengths and pathologies rather than others, so each clinical assessment instrument has its own unique idiography, which accounts for the strengths and pathologies of the test. Far from being simply filler, these historical and contextual particularities are as essential to an informed use of an instrument as history and context are to the individual personality to be assessed.

CHALLENGE YOUR STUDENTS TO QUESTION SACRED NOTIONS

Most students, especially those in an introductory assessment class, tend to accept the categories of the DSM and the instruments used in assessment as if they were handed down from the gods, sacred and unassailable, of ineffable significance. Many clinicians take the same approach. Although such an attitude may be motivated by respect for authority or for the pristine structures of science, it is unfortunately a barrier to critical thinking, approaching the official nosologic categories and the instruments that assess them as an exact reflection of nature, rather than evolved and biased social documents. The implicit assumption is: Here are the disorders, and here is how we assess them. If students are to become critical thinkers, aware of the margins of established knowledge, able to improvise when some aspect of the individual case deviates from formula, this mind-set must be defeated early. Thus disabused, students are free to transform themselves from passive beings, whose purpose is to osmose the dispensations of authority, into active creatures capable of intelligent criticism.

Often, it is helpful to challenge the students at the outset with a simple question: "If you were going to design an instrument to assess personality, how would you do it?" A period of silence usually follows, after which some of the students will tentatively venture their thoughts. Not surprisingly, many students are ready to vent their frustrations with the diagnostic system. They may, in fact, be confused on points and issues about which there are no easy answers, but that they hesitate to raise, either again out of respect, or worse, because they feel their confusion reflects some deficit in their own knowledge or range of experiences and do not wish to be embarrassed in front of their classmates. By establishing the instructor's openness to intelligent criticism of established, institutionalized ways of thinking and doing, an atmosphere of openness is established for remaining class sessions. Most students find such sanctioned criticism of authority and tradition to be empowering, although, depending on the size and level of the class, the variety of issues raised can sometimes be difficult to contain and coordinate. When this is the case, it is usually helpful to attempt to remember the concerns raised by each student and return to these over the course of the lectures where appropriate. Students are often surprised when they hear their initial objections sharpened and linked to fundamental issues hours or even days into the discussion of the inventory. Students who are not especially confident in their own capacities may be repeatedly drawn into discussions and validated in this manner.

Depending on the scope of the discussion, the lecturer may wish to raise some of the following issues, if they are not first touched on and elaborated by the class. A helpful, but deep, question is: "If you were going to design Axis II, choosing the constructs that would be included as personality disorders, of all the possibilities, how would you decide what to keep and what to discard?" Because few students are in a position to appreciate the significance of the issues involved, it is useful to paint a picture for them and then pose the question again. The lecturer may note, for example, the literally thousands of trait terms that exist in the language (Allport & Odbert, 1936). Scales could be developed for any of these and drawn together to form an inventory. The question then becomes: "On what logical basis would you cull from the thousands of possible descriptors only those necessary for an inventory?" Moreover, the issue of the level of abstraction of each construct can be raised, which sets the stage for distinguishing between personality traits and personality disorders. Pensiveness, for example, is a trait of such limited scope that it is not really useful in a personality inventory. Obviously, because the test author only has so many items to work with, the scales of an inventory must be geared to constructs of breadth sufficient to characterize large numbers of persons. The purpose of raising issues such as these is to help the students appreciate that any intelligent construction of Axis II requires some logical basis for generating its constituent disorders.

CHALLENGE YOUR STUDENTS
ON THE NATURE OF PERSONALITY

To make the issue even more compelling, it is useful to review various perspectives or domains that represent traditional approaches to personality. Previous publications (T. Millon, 1990; T. Millon & Davis, 1996), remarked on behavioral, phenomenological, biological, and intrapsychic approaches to personality (see Fig. 11. 1). Our experience is that it is often helpful to spend a half hour reviewing the tenets of each data level and the propositions offered by the more important writers and theoreticians. This can be extremely helpful in opening the minds of those in the audience who may be more doctrinaire to the utility of alternative views. Figures for review would potentially include Watson,

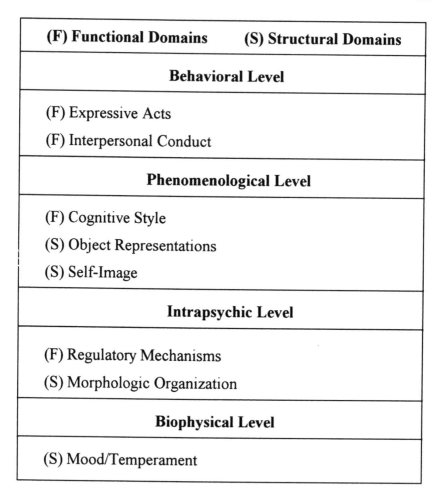

FIG. 11.1. Functional and structural domains of personality.

Skinner, and perhaps Hull, for the behavioral level; Eysenck, Gray, and perhaps Kretschmer and Sheldon for the physiological level; Freud, Jung, Abraham, and Horney for the intrapsychic level; and Beck and Ellis for the cognitive domain of the phenomenological level. Where time is extremely limited, it may be useful to forego a superficial review that merely mentions a series of names, and instead compare and contrast two historical models. Our choices have often been the psychodynamic and behavioral approaches, because these contrast sharply, and yet both make definite claims about the content of human nature.

After introducing the schematics of these diverse perspectives, the lecturer may wish to ask the class such rhetorical questions as: "So, coming back to our original question, and knowing that all of these approaches have had something to say about personality or human nature, how would we draw from these to produce an inventory? Should we believe that personality is exclusively behavioral? Or exclusively cognitive? Or exclusively the product of biological drives?" Again, it may be best to let the class chew on these questions for a while, so that the depth of the issues sinks in. What should be avoided, however, is letting the discussion somehow get caught up in the positives or negatives of any one approach. Although all of these authors and perspectives are interesting on their own terms, the point of this review when teaching the MCMI is to establish one important truth about personality and its disorders: that personality regards the entire matrix of the person, that personality is an intrinsically multioperational phenomenon, expressed across all domains or perspectives. This prepares the students for the two sections that follow: First, some theory must be found for the personality disorders that transcends any of these more narrow views, laying the groundwork for the introduction of the evolutionary theory of personality disorders (T. Millon, 1990). Second, when the test is actually to be constructed, its scales should ideally not be biased toward one domain or another, but must instead possess content validity by drawing on as many domains as possible, within the limitations of the self-report format.

INTEGRATIVE EVOLUTION
OF THE HEALTH SCIENCES

This part of the class presentation will be more of a narrative; it is oriented toward an explanation of the historical and conceptual basis of the multiaxial model, and an explanation of the nature of personality disorders. The presenter will link back to this portion of the presentation when discussing actual clinical cases. The movement toward integrationism in the conception of disease is not just an ideal; it is also an empirical, historical fact, illustrated by the evolution of the health sciences through two paradigm shifts, neither of which has yet been completed in psychopathology. The series of concentric circles comprising Fig. 11.2 represents changes that have evolved in medicine over the past century; they mirror, as well, shifts that must advance more rapidly in our thinking about the nature of psychopathology and psychotherapy. In the center of the figure we find Axis I, the so-called clinical syndromes, for example, depression and anxiety. The parallel to Axis I in physical disorders characterizes the state of medicine a hundred and more years ago; in the early and mid-19th century, physicians defined their patients' ailments in terms of their manifest symptomatology—their sneezes and coughs and boils and fevers—labeling these "diseases" with terms such as consumption and smallpox.

In contrast, the outer ring of Fig. 11. 2 parallels Axis IV of the *DSM*. The related medical paradigm shift occurred approximately a century ago, when illnesses began to be viewed as the result of intrusive microbes that infect and disrupt the body's normal functions. In time, medicine began to assign diagnostic labels to reflect this new etiology, replacing old descriptive terms. "Dementia paralytica," for example, came to be known as neurosyphilis.

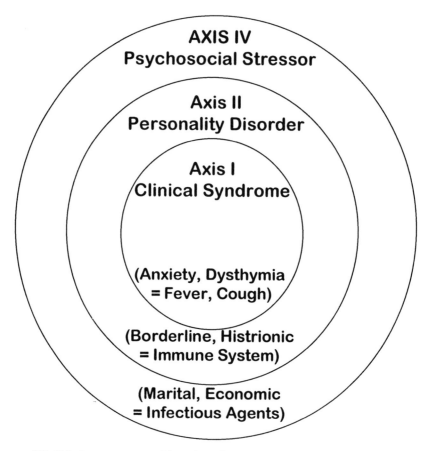

FIG. 11.2. Interactive nature of the multiaxial system (progression of health sciences).

Our understanding of psychopathology has progressed in making this shift from symptom to cause all too slowly. Our attention remains focused on depression or anxiety, the superficial symptoms comprising the syndromes of Axis I. As the psychic response to life's early or current stressors, such as those that comprise the DSM–IV's (DSM, 4th ed.) Axis IV—marital problems, child abuse, and the like—they represent the results of psychic intruders that parallel the infectious microbes of a century ago.

Fortunately, medicine has progressed in the past decade or two beyond its turn-of-the-century "intrusion disease" model, an advance most striking these last 15 years, due to the AIDS epidemic. This progression reflects a growing awareness of the key role of the immune system, the body's intrinsic capacity to contend with the omnipresent multitude of potentially destructive infectious and carcinogenic agents that pervade our physical environment. Medicine has learned that it is not the symptoms—the sneezes and coughs—or the intruding infections—the viruses and bacteria—that are the key to health or illness. Rather, the ultimate determinant is the competence of the body's own intrinsic defensive capacities. So too, in psychopathology, it is not anxiety or dysthymia, or the stressors of early childhood or contemporary life that are the key to psychic well-being. Rather, it is the mind's equivalent of the body's immune system—that structure and style of psychic processes that represents our overall capacity to perceive and to cope with our psychosocial world—in other words, the psychological construct we term personality. The multiaxial model has been specifically composed to encourage integrative conceptions of the individual's psychic symptoms in terms of the interaction between long-standing coping styles and psychosocial stressors. As such, its philosophy intrinsically favors therapies that appreciate and follow from the nature of the personality construct itself. Accordingly, any attempt to treat the Axis II disorders should not err at the outset by reducing Axis II to Axis I, that is, by regarding personality styles as reified entities that can themselves be symptomatized as disorders that inhere within the matrix of the person—for this is exactly what the personality disorders prototypally are, disorders of the entire matrix of the person.

INTRODUCE THE EVOLUTIONARY THEORY

Presenting personality as anchored across a variety of perspectives paves the way for the introduction of the evolutionary theory. The problem, as it was earlier framed, is to provide a logical basis for constructing the personality disorders. The presenter should point out that, because we know personality is not merely behavioral, or cognitive, and so on, there are two options: first, to invent some additional perspective on personality, or second, to appeal to some set of organizing principles that transcend any particular domain of personality. The first option can be disqualified on its own terms, because it simply repeats the error of the previous approaches by attempting to conceptualize the whole of personality through one narrow part or perspective. A detailed treatment of the evolutionary theory is available as a systematic treatise in T. Millon's 1990 book, *Toward a New Personology: An Evolutionary Model*. Alternatively, it is also discussed in T. Millon and Davis' 1996 volume, *Disorders of Personality: DSM–IV and Beyond*. Because space is lacking, the model is presented in the following discussion in an incomplete and highly abstracted form. Teachers are advised to consult original sources for more in-depth discussions. A minimal presentation of the theory should include, first, each of the fundamental stages or tasks of evolution—existence, adaptation, and replication—and the content domains to which these are coupled—pleasure–pain, active–passive, and self–other—and second, the derivation of the personality disorders from the deficiencies, imbalances, and conflicts of these polarities. Figure 11. 3 derives the personality disorders schematically; it is likely to be useful as a handout, as it gives the students a concrete anchor for this fairly abstract material.

The theoretical model that follows is grounded in evolutionary theory. In essence, it seeks to explicate the structure and styles of personality with

	Existential Aim		Replication Strategy		
	Life Enhancement	Life Preservation	Reproductive Propagation	Reproductive Nurturance	
Polarity	Pleasure - Pain		Self - Other		
Deficiency, Imbalance, or Conflict	Pleasure - Pain - +	Pleasure Pain (Reversal)	Self - Other +	Self + Other -	Self - Other (Reversal)
Adaptation Mode	DSM Personality **Disorders**				
Passive: Accomodation	Schizoid / Depressive	Masochistic	Dependent	Narcissistic	Compulsive
Active: Modification	Avoidant	Sadistic	Histrionic	Antisocial	Negativistic
Structural Pathology	Schizotypal	Borderline, Paranoid	Borderline	Paranoid	Borderline, Paranoid

FIG. 11.3. Polarity model and its personality disorder derivatives.

reference to deficient, imbalanced, or conflicted modes of ecological adaptation and reproductive strategy. The proposition that the development and functions of personologic traits may be usefully explored through the lens of evolutionary principles has a long, if yet unfulfilled tradition. Spencer (1870) and Huxley (1981) offered suggestions of this nature shortly after Darwin's seminal *Origins* was published. In more recent times, we have seen the emergence of sociobiology, an interdisciplinary science that explores the interface between human social functioning and evolutionary biology (Wilson, 1975, 1978).

Four domains or spheres in which evolutionary principles are demonstrated are labeled as existence, adaptation, replication, and abstraction. The first relates the serendipitous transformation of random or less organized states into those possessing distinct structures of greater organization; the second refers to homeostatic processes employed to sustain survival in open ecosystems; the third pertains to reproductive styles that maximize the diversification and selection of ecologically effective attributes; and the fourth concerns the emergence of competencies that foster anticipatory planning and reasoned decision making. Polarities derived from the first three phases (pleasure–pain, passive–active, other–self) are used to construct a theoretically embedded classification system of personality disorders.

The first phase, existence, concerns the maintenance of integrative phenomena, whether nuclear particle, virus, or human being, against the background of entropic decompensation. Evolutionary mechanisms derived from this stage regard life enhancement and life preservation. The former are concerned with orienting individuals toward improvement in the quality of life, the latter with orienting individuals away from actions or environments that decrease the quality of life, or even jeopardize existence itself. These may be called *existential aims*. At the highest level of abstraction such mechanisms form, phenomenologically or metaphorically expressed, a pleasure–pain polarity. Some individuals are conflicted in regard to these existential aims (e. g., the sadistic), whereas others possess deficits in these crucial substrates (e. g., the schizoid).

Existence, however, is but an initial phase. Once an integrative structure exists, it must maintain its existence through exchanges of energy and information with its environment. The second evolutionary stage relates to what is termed the *modes of adaptation*; it is also framed as a two-part polarity, a passive orientation, a tendency to accommodate to one's ecological niche, versus an active orientation, a tendency to modify or intervene in one's surrounds. These modes of adaptation differ from the first phase of evolution, because they regard how that which *is*, endures. Unlike pleasure–pain and self–other, the active–passive polarity is truly unidimensional; one cannot be both active and passive at the same time.

Although organisms may exist well adapted to their environments, the existence of any life form is time limited. To circumvent this limitation, organisms have developed *replicatory strategies* by which to leave progeny. These strategies regard what biologists have referred to as an "r" or self-propagating strategy at one polar extreme, and a "K" or other-nurturing strategy at the second extreme. Psychologically, the former strategy is disposed toward actions that are egotistic, insensitive, inconsiderate, and uncaring; whereas the latter is disposed toward actions that are affiliative, intimate, protective, and solicitous (Gilligan, 1982; Rushton, 1985; Wilson, 1978). As shown in Fig. 11. 3, various imbalances and conflicts on these fundamental polarities allow for a deduction of the personality disorders.

CHALLENGE YOUR STUDENTS
ON ITEM WRITING AND SELECTION

At this point, the teacher has established the need for a coherent theoretical approach to personality disorders that transcends and integrates particular perspectives on personality, and has introduced Millon's evolutionary theory of personality. The instructor may wish to challenge the students with a question: "Now that we have the constructs our inventory will measure, and an adequate scientific basis, how are we going to write the actual items, and where will these items come from?" To answer this question, the presenter should take the students back to the domain model, linking this with issues of content validity, the foundation of construct validity. In other words, if personality is a multioperational phenomenon anchored across behavioral, phenomenological, physiological, and intrapsychic domains, then items should be written to tap these various expressions.

A common question often raised at this stage concerns the intrapsychic domain and projective techniques, such as the Rorschach and TAT. The thrust of this objection is that because psychodynamic theory is by definition concerned with unconscious contents, whereas the MCMI is self-report, how can the MCMI assess defense mechanisms. This is a valid concern that should not be dismissed. Instead, it should be used to discuss limitations that are generic to the self-report, and can even be used as a lead-in to the idea of method variance (Campbell & Fiske, 1959), depending on the level of the audience. If no one raises the issue, it can usually be prompted by asking "Do you think we'll be able to write items for all of these domains? What domains do you think it would be difficult to get at with self-report items?"

INTRODUCE LOEVINGER'S THREE-STAGE MODEL OF TEST CONSTRUCTION

This portion of the presentation is again mainly narrative, rather than Socratic. The lecturer should note that up to this point, personality has been discussed from the standpoint of theory, but that, although theory can be used to suggest the structure of an inventory, its scales, and so on, the actual items written must be tested empirically. Our experience is that it is useful to review the history of personality assessment at this point, building toward Loevinger's (1957) and Jackson's (1970) three-stage model of test construction (see Fig. 11. 4). In classes that focus exclusively on objective assessment, this portion of the presentation provides useful points of contrast between the MCMI, and two other classic instruments, the MMPI and Cattell's 16PF (Cattell, Eber, & Tatsuoka, 1970). Figure 11.4 may be used as a handout at this point.

Briefly, in the beginning stages of personality assessment, instruments were constructed on a purely rational basis, as with the Woodworth Personal Data Sheet. That is, items were formulated according to the author's theory of the construct concerned. A test developer literally sat down and wrote out as many items as were desired, and that was the test. Eventually, the numbers of scales assessing similar constructs multiplied as various researchers developed their own measures. However, the scales often did not agree with each other, as evidenced by low correlations among them. This shows that in and of itself,

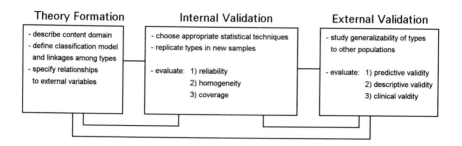

FIG. 11.4. Framework for classification research. From Skinner (1986). Adapted with permission.

theory is a necessary, but not a sufficient basis on which to select the items of an inventory. By the time the MMPI was designed, in the late 1930s and early 1940s, the pendulum had swung completely in the other direction. The philosophy of logical positivism was in its ascendancy, and theory was viewed as being too weak to inform test construction. Accordingly, the MMPI items were chosen according to an external method, the ability of items to separate normal and clinical groups, regardless of item content. This procedure had the unfortunate by-product of producing heterogenous scales, and made the MMPI more difficult to interpret, because clinicians could not be certain which variance components accounted for any particular scale elevation. Eventually, the construct nature of the scales was abandoned completely and the scales relabeled Scale 1, Scale 2, and so on. In addition, the Harris and Lingoes (1955, 1968) subscales were devised to provide a more molecular interpretation of the inventory. This illustrates a second fundamental point: that in and of itself, external methods are necessary, but not sufficient as a basis on which to select items for an inventory. The 16PF may be viewed as conceptually opposite the MMPI, because its scales were constructed on the basis of factor analytic methods, which guarantee internal consistency. In contrast to these three instruments, the items of the MCMI have been validated rationally, internally, and externally. Further information concerning the development of the MCMI is best sought in the manual for the MCMI–II (T. Millon, 1987), or MCMI–II (Millon, Millon, & Davis, 1997).

INTRODUCE THE STRUCTURE OF THE MCMI

At this point, the presenter is prepared to introduce the actual scales of the MCMI, along with information concerning reliability and validity. As noted at the beginning of this chapter, this material, which consists of lists and numbers, can be deadly. The presenter should note that the inventory consists of 175 items, grouped into 24 scales. The MCMI can be completed by most subjects in 20–30 minutes, and requires an eighth-grade reading level. Further information is available in the MCMI–III manual (T. Millon et al., 1997).

A common question at this point concerns the number of scales in the MCMI, compared with the number of items. Astute listeners inevitably note that items must be assigned to multiple scales. If this issue is not raised by the audience, it should be raised by the teacher, because it is a feature that distinguishes the MCMI from other inventories. Two important points should be made: First, the nature of the multiple item assignments accords with what would be expected on the basis of the evolutionary model. In other words, the item overlap reflects nature's structure rather than imposing its own, or being an artificial product of some statistical methodology. Second, the items in the – are weighted either 2 points or 1 point (items in the MCMI–II were weighted 3, 2, or 1), depending on the extent to which they are central to their respective constructs. This weighting system is intended to accord with the prototypal model first adopted in DSM–III (DSM, 2rd edition). The prototype construct recognizes that although all diagnostic syndromes represent a cluster of attributes, some attributes are more central than others, although no one attribute is necessary or sufficient to the diagnosis.

INTRODUCE THE IDEA OF BASE RATES

The idea of base rates (BR) is the logical next step in teaching the MCMI. Some teachers prefer to discuss base rates in the abstract, and then present an actual clinical case, whereas others prefer to present an MCMI profile and anchor the base rates discussion to a concrete audiovisual aid: "Let me show you now the profile of a client I saw several years ago. One of the first things to notice here is that the scale scores are presented as something called BR score. ... " Either works, if it is done right.

Most students are familiar with T-scores and percentile ranks, and these form a useful point of departure when explaining BR scores. Because most students will be involved in clinical practice, the essence of the BR concept can be sought in their own personal experience by asking such questions as "In your own work, do you see more Depressives or more Thought Disorders? Which disorder do you think is more common in an outpatient setting?" The answer, of course, is that Depressives are far more common; that is, the base or prevalence rate of Depression is simply higher than that of Thought Disorder. Having established this empirical fact, the presenter can now turn to the idea of T-scores: "But when you give a test that is normed using T-scores, where do you draw the line between normality and pathology?" Students acquainted with the MMPI are usually proud to give the answer. This question can be followed up with another: "What percentage of the population is assumed to fall above this cutting score?" After this answer is given, the presenter is free to draw his or her conclusion:

> Well, if a T-score of 65 or higher represents pathology, and if the scales are normed so that a fixed percentage of the population always falls above this mark, then we are implicitly assuming that the base rate of any given pathology is the same across all disorders. But we know that is not the case, because, as you just said, Depressives are more common than Thought Disorders. The idea behind base rate scores is to norm the instrument so that the number of individuals diagnosed by the test equals the number of individuals that actually have the disorder. So if 20% of the individuals seen in a clinical setting are depressed, then the test should diagnose 20% as depressed.

Both T-scores and BR scores are a transformation of the raw scores, and each has the purpose of putting the raw scores on a common metric. Unlike T-scores or percentile ranks, however, the BR scores are created such that the percentage of the clinical population deemed diagnosable with a particular disorder falls either (a) at or above a particular threshold, for the clinical scales, or (b) falls at a particular rank order in the profile, for the personality scales.

Another explanation of the BR concept concerns the definition of personality pathology and its relation to the amount of a trait possessed by an individual. This explanation is more complex, and is intended for more professional audiences. Let us consider some definitions of personality pathology. Personality disorders are defined as clinical syndromes composed of intrinsic, deeply embedded, and pervasive ways of functioning (Millon, 1981). According to the *DSM*, it is personality traits that are inflexible and maladaptive, causing "significant functional impairment or subjective distress" that are considered to be in the disordered range. When constructing an inventory, then, the problem is to separate scale elevations that have become inflexible or pervasive from those that have not. However, the degree to which a trait is problematic is not a direct function of the quantity of the trait, but instead is a function, first, of its interaction with other characteristics of the organism in which the trait is embedded, and second, the interaction between the organism and the context in which the organism exists. Thus not one, but two interactions separate the quantity of a trait and its flexibility or pervasiveness. Schizoid individuals, for example, are notable for their lack of emotional reactivity. Such individuals not only function well in, but actively seek out, environments that make few interpersonal demands. An accountant whose job requires long hours of tedious work may be well served by such characteristics. If this individual were suddenly thrust into a management position, difficulties would likely ensue. The fact that the quantity of a trait is not directly related to its functional consequences necessitates a transformation that more directly assesses its clinical implications.

The aforementioned examples may be followed up with a discussion of diagnostic efficiency statistics—positive predictive power, sensitivity, specificity, and negative predictive power—but many beginning students, and many professionals as well, are simply lost by the mathematical focus of this material. This is not to dismiss its importance, because it forms an important component of the external validity of an instrument. Nevertheless, where the audience consists of students in an introductory assessment class or where time is limited, this section is best omitted entirely, or prefaced by saying: "Let me now present to you now some statistics that form a part of the external validity of the MCMI, but that I don't want to spend too much time on. ... " The danger, of course, is that time will be wasted explaining novel material that will be easily forgotten, disrupting the easy flow of themes, and taking time away from illustrating an interpretation of the instrument.

PRESENT THE FACTS OF AN ACTUAL CLINICAL CASE

At this point, the students have been acquainted with the underlying theoretical model and structure of the instrument. Now they are ready to learn its interpretation, a process greatly facilitated through the use of one or more actual clinical cases. In general, it is best if the case chosen is from the presenter's own clinical experience, where the MCMI was used as part of a comprehensive assessment, or at the beginning of a course of therapy. Of the two, the latter may be the more valuable, because here the presenter can speak to traits uncovered by the inventory that were well managed in the impressions formed in the first few sessions. This illustration further gets at the issue of method variance and the importance of testing in assessment, because the test reveals valid information not accessible in early sessions or interviews.

To aid the presenter in teaching the interpretative process, we present the following case, for which an MCMI–III profile is presented in Fig. 11.5. Maria, a 31-year-old female graduate student from Venezuela, majoring in English literature, presented at the outpatient center of a large psychiatric hospital with tiredness and difficulty falling asleep as her primary complaints. In her words, " …my mind just doesn't want to shut down, so I only get about five or six hours [of sleep] each night," a pattern she had endured for the last 5 years, and that she was at a loss to explain. A medical examination suggested no relevant physiological problems. She was referred for psychiatric impressions and treatment recommendations.

Maria responded easily during the interview, readily offering psychologically salient information. She noted that her first graduate major was chemical engineering, from which she was forced to withdraw "when I found out I wasn't intelligent." She stated that she had difficulty understanding some of the more abstract course work, as well as describing an embarrassing incident in which an expensive apparatus in her charge was damaged.

Maria is an oldest child, with one sister 4 years younger than she. She reported that her parents at one time feared she was autistic, and that she was examined by a child psychologist at her mother's request when she was 6. Her father, a physicist, passed away when she was 11. Maria regrets that they were not able to spend more time together. As an undergraduate, she attended a small and exclusively female liberal arts college in the Northeast. She confided that she has never had a boyfriend. When asked if she ever felt lonely, she replied, "It's always been that way, you get used to it." Her family remains in Venezuela.

Diagnostic testing revealed a WAIS–R Verbal IQ of 128 and a Performance IQ of 115 with relative strengths in Vocabulary and Comprehension. The Spanish-language version of the MCMI revealed three basic personality scales in the disordered range, Schizoid (BR = 90), Avoidant (BR = 78), and Dependent (BR = 77), with a subthreshold Axis I peak on the Dysthymia scale (BR = 74). The Rorschach Inkblot Test, scored according to the Comprehensive System, revealed positive Schizophrenia and Depression Indexes, many Level 1 Deviant Verbalizations, and a high X-percent, indicating numerous violations of the contours of the blots. Her TAT responses emphasized facial expressions and sensitivity to the motives of others, and featured quick and almost magical endings. Several of her responses to the Incomplete Sentences Blank (ICB) are notable: #1, "I like to lie in bed with my dog and my cat"; #2, "The happiest time I can remember is playing with my little sister"; #10, "People are not nearly as enjoyable or comfortable to be around as animals"; #11, "A mother is someone who makes you a part of herself"; #16, "Sports are wonderful except for team sports"; #28, "Sometimes I long for someone to spend my life with"; #29, "What pains me is not feeling cared for"; #32, "I am very dreamy and think more about love than a career"; and #39 "My greatest worry is the future."

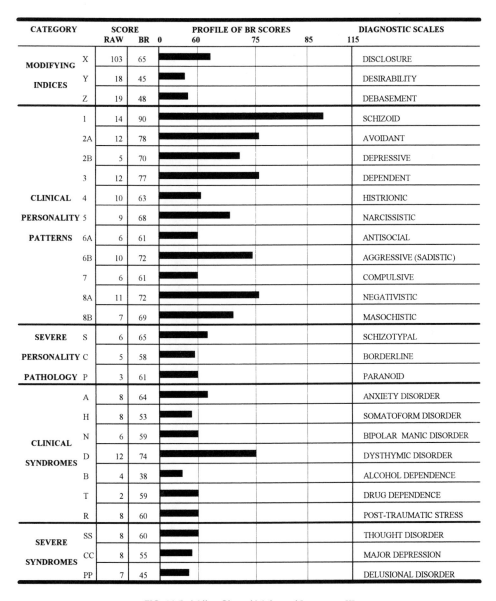

CATEGORY		SCORE		PROFILE OF BR SCORES					DIAGNOSTIC SCALES
		RAW	BR	0	60	75	85	115	
MODIFYING	X	103	65						DISCLOSURE
INDICES	Y	18	45						DESIRABILITY
	Z	19	48						DEBASEMENT
	1	14	90						SCHIZOID
	2A	12	78						AVOIDANT
	2B	5	70						DEPRESSIVE
	3	12	77						DEPENDENT
CLINICAL	4	10	63						HISTRIONIC
PERSONALITY	5	9	68						NARCISSISTIC
PATTERNS	6A	6	61						ANTISOCIAL
	6B	10	72						AGGRESSIVE (SADISTIC)
	7	6	61						COMPULSIVE
	8A	11	72						NEGATIVISTIC
	8B	7	69						MASOCHISTIC
SEVERE	S	6	65						SCHIZOTYPAL
PERSONALITY	C	5	58						BORDERLINE
PATHOLOGY	P	3	61						PARANOID
	A	8	64						ANXIETY DISORDER
	H	8	53						SOMATOFORM DISORDER
CLINICAL	N	6	59						BIPOLAR MANIC DISORDER
SYNDROMES	D	12	74						DYSTHYMIC DISORDER
	B	4	38						ALCOHOL DEPENDENCE
	T	2	59						DRUG DEPENDENCE
	R	8	60						POST-TRAUMATIC STRESS
SEVERE	SS	8	60						THOUGHT DISORDER
SYNDROMES	CC	8	55						MAJOR DEPRESSION
	PP	7	45						DELUSIONAL DISORDER

FIG. 11.5. Millon Clinical Multiaxial Inventory–III
(confidential information for professional use only).

INTERPRET BASIC SCALE ELEVATIONS

After presenting the basic facts of the assessment, the teacher may wish, depending on the level of the audience, to briefly discuss profile interpretation in the abstract. This portion of the presentation can be linked back to that which dealt with the integrative evolution of the health sciences, as the purpose is to evolve an integrated, or multiaxial, conception of the individual. First, there is the most basic level of interpretation, that which deals with the "boils and pustules" of the person who is the presenting complaints and symptoms. Here we are only interested in determining which scales are elevated and what diagnoses should be made. For the MCMI, this involves examining which scale elevations exceed the BR 75 cutting score across all scales. These form diagnostic hypotheses that can then be considered in the context of other information outside the inventory (presenting complaints, the therapist's "feel" for the client, reports of significant others, background clinical information, etc.). In view of the end goal, the integrated understanding of the person, this level of interpretation must be considered simplistic. This is especially true for the personality disorders, which, as we have seen, are not disorders at all, but instead reified constructs that act as the contexts through which the underlying meaning of the boils and pustules, the individual's presenting Axis I symptoms, must be understood.

A better approach interprets scale elevations *dimensionally, configurally,* and *contextually.* A dimensional interpretation is necessary to model clinical experience about real cases. Individuals may be somewhat anxious, or somewhat depressed, and so on, without actually meeting diagnostic criteria. On other hand, even among patients that meet criteria, some are more severely disordered than others. In contrast, a strictly diagnostic approach results in a loss of information about the person by dichotomizing scale scores into present or absent judgments. A configural interpretation is necessary for the same reason. Individuals almost never present as pure prototypes; instead, each person is likely to combine aspects of a variety of personality styles. For the Axis II scales, this configuration becomes one half of the context in which the Axis I boils seek their explanation (the other half being Axis IV, the situational factors that interact with Axis II to produce the presenting symptoms).

In Maria's case, the test results already suggest several diagnoses and other characteristics, each being a hypothesis about the nature of her pathology. The MCMI–II Schizoid (BR = 90) scale argues for an apathetic attitude and an absence of emotionality, that Maria functions as a passive observer, detached from rewards and affections as well as the demands of human relationships. The Avoidant (BR = 78), Dependent (BR = 77) scales and ICB findings (e. g., # 34, "I wish I could find true love"), however, argue against such procrustean first-order interpretive logic, and show that she is not a prototypal schizoid. Although configural logic asks for a level of sophistication, in return it breaks the pattern of labeling clients and fitting them to strict categories. Diagnosis, then, is viewed as the beginning of an assessment rather than its endpoint. A narcissistic-antisocial pattern, for example, is somewhat different from either the purely prototypal narcissistic pattern or the purely prototypal antisocial pattern.

A question that is sometimes raised at this point concerns the comorbidity of personality disorders, a phenomenon that is often manifest in terms of the *DSM–IV*, where an individual may meet criteria for three or even more personality disorders, and the MCMI, where an individual may elevate many scales above the BR 75 cutting line. This question, of course, is more often received from professional-level audiences or in advanced assessment classes, rather than from introductory courses, where the students are likely to have never before used the instrument in actual practice. Several points should be made when answering this issue. The first is that comorbidity is a medical term. As such, it again approaches the Axis II constructs as disease entities. However, it is the qualitative characteristics of the profile, not how many scales exceed some cutting score, that is really most important in deriving a concerption of the whole person. Thus, for interpretive purposes, a more undesirable situation for any inventory occurs when a large number of personality scales are approximately equally elevated, where no one personality style appears to dominate in the individual. In this case, the clinician is left with the hypothesis that it is the lack of a consistent coping style that may be responsible for the individual's current difficulties. Second, we are mainly interested in the highest two or three personality scales, not in all of them.

INTERPRET THE THREE SEVERE PERSONALITY SCALES

In making configural personality interpretations, a separation should be made between those scales pertaining to the *basic* clinical personality pattern (1–8B) and those pointing to the presence of more *severe* Axis II pathology, the borderline (C), schizotypal (S), and paranoid (P). These structural pathologies differ from the other clinical personality patterns by several criteria, notably deficits in social competence and frequent (but readily reversible) psychotic episodes. Less integrated in terms of their personality organization and less effective in coping than their milder counterparts, these people are especially vulnerable to decompensation when confronted with the strains of everyday life.

In terms of the theoretical model, these patterns are significantly less adaptable in the face of ecological vicissitudes. They are dysfunctional variants of the more moderately pathological patterns, a feature that leads to several predictions concerning these patterns and MCMI profiles. First, we noted earlier that at least two interactions mediate the role of a single personality trait for psychological functioning, and that for this reason, the quantity of that trait constrains but does not determine the level of personality pathology. The elevation of S, C, and P may be used as a rough index of the degree to which the client's basic personality pattern has become structurally compromised. If, for example, a client receives BR 105 on the narcissistic scale, but S, C, and P are low, then structurally the personality appears to be fundamentally intact, despite the elevated BR score. If, on the other hand, a client receives BR 80 on the narcissistic scale, but scale P is also at BR 75, this suggests a basic narcissistic pattern with paranoid tendencies, possibility an incipient structural pathology.

In Maria's case, a somewhat elevated (BR = 69) schizotypal scale was achieved. This finding corroborates those obtained with the basic personality scales, that is, her schizoid-avoidant-dependent pattern. Interestingly, this appears to converge with her response to ICB #11: "A mother is someone who makes you a part of herself." Accordingly, we may expect that in the face of severe stressors, Maria may evidence the schizotypal's somewhat autistic ideations, mixed perhaps with personal irrelevancies and magical thinking, depending on the nature and intensity of the stressors. The positive schizophrenia index obtained on the Rorschach with the Comprehensive System further supports this interpretation.

GENERATE DOMAIN HYPOTHESES
FOR ELEVATED PERSONALITY SCALES

Not all clients with the same personality diagnosis have the same problem. A single diagnostic label rarely if ever provides information specific and comprehensive enough to serve as a sound basis for intervention efforts. Not only do clients differ with respect to the magnitude of their pathology within a diagnostic kind, but they also differ in the features with which they approximate the kind. Whether diagnostic taxons are derived through clinical observation, mathematical analyses, or theoretical deduction, clients differ in *how* they meet taxonic requirements, a fact institutionalized in *DSM–III* with the adoption of the polythetic model. In and of itself, then, diagnosis *underspecifies* pathology, especially with regard to treatment considerations. Moreover, the vast majority of clients do represent so-called mixed types. In moving toward an integrated conception of the person, then, we must ask how each elevated personality scale is relevant to the interpretation of the individual case.

One option is to systematically investigate characteristics associated with each MCMI-suggested personality prototype in a *domain-oriented* fashion. These characteristics have been usefully organized in a manner similar to distinctions drawn in the biological realm, that is, by dividing them into *structural* and *functional* attributes. This distinction was alluded to earlier, when it was recommended that the teacher review various perspectives on personality. Functional characteristics represent dynamic processes that transpire within the intrapsychic world and between the individual's self and psychosocial environment. They represent "expressive modes of regulatory action." Structural attributes represent a deeply embedded and relatively enduring template of imprinted memories, attitudes, needs, fears, conflicts, and so on, which guide experience and transform the nature of ongoing events in accord with these imprintings. Obviously, this distinction is rooted in integrative logic. No organism exists that is composed exclusively of functional or exclusively of structural domains. Both are required if the organism is to exist as a self-regulating whole: Function animates structure; structure undergirds or substratizes function.

These domains are further grouped according to their respective data level, either biophysical, intrapsychic, phenomenological, or behavioral, reflecting four historic approaches that characterize the study of psychopathology. The grouping of functional-structural clinical domains within the four traditional data levels of psychopathology was previously schematized in Fig. 11.1.

Several criteria were used to select and develop the clinical domains that comprise this assessment schema: (a) that they be varied in the features they embody; that is, not to be limited just to behaviors or cognitions, but encompass a full range of clinically relevant characteristics, (b) that they parallel, if not correspond, to many of our profession's current therapeutic modalities, as evidenced by the four data levels, and (c) that they not only be coordinated with the official DSM schema of personality disorder prototypes, as well as the guiding model of evolutionary polarities, but also that each disorder be characterized by a distinctive feature within each clinical domain. Brief descriptions of these functional and structural domains have been given in several publications (T. Millon, 1986a, 1986b, 1987, 1990; T. Millon & Davis, 1996), and are printed in the MCMI manual as well.

In the context of the individual case, the question then becomes: "Which functional processes and structural attributes are necessary for the client's personality pattern to exist as the organic whole represented by the codetype?" Answering this question engages a synthetic process of clinical inference for which the endpoint is the mutual corroboration of parts and whole, a picture of the organism as a totality. If the personality assessment is to be exhaustive, then, with the guidance of the codetype, a description of the client in each clinical domain should be formulated. Each domain description may be said to represent a within-domain hypothesis about client functioning in that circumscribed clinical area, and these hypotheses should be evaluated and amended as needed until they fit with auxiliary data and represent what is indeed believed to be the facts of the case. For any given case, there are several possibilities. For a 2-point code, client functioning may be prototypal of the domain description for the primary code, prototypal of the domain description for the secondary code, or lie somewhere in between. Obviously, when presented with a 3-point code, matters become more complex.

By following this procedure, we are now in a position to advance a remarkably detailed assessment of the individual. We illustrate this process with regard to the featured case: Structural attributes and functional processes relevant to the schizoid-avoidant-dependent pattern are reprinted in Table 11.1. We simply move down the chart from domain to domain, asking ourselves which description the client most resembles, synthesizing these descriptions when needed. Behaviorally, Maria's presentation during diagnostic testing strongly suggested a dependent-avoidant behavioral style with its incumbent passivity, docility, immaturity, and heightened awareness of others' reactions to her, seen especially

TABLE 11.1

Comparison of Schizoid, Avoidant, and Dependent Clinical Domains

Schizoid Prototype	Avoidant Prototype	Dependent Prototype
Behavioral Level		
(F) Expressively Impassive (e.g., appears to be in an inert emotional state, lifeless, undemonstrative, lacking in energy and vitality; is unmoved, boring, unanimated, robotic, phlegmatic, displaying deficits in activation, motoric expressiveness, and spontaneity).	(F) Expressively Fretful (e.g., conveys personal unease and disquiet, a constant timorous, hesitant, and restive state; overreacts to innocuous events and anxiously judges them to signify ridicule, criticism, and disapproval).	(F) Expressively Incompetent (e.g., withdraws from adult responsibilities by acting helpless and seeking nurturance from others; is docile and passive, lacks functional competencies, and avoids self-assertion).
(F) Interpersonally Unengaged (e.g., seems indifferent and remote, rarely responsive to the actions or feelings of others, chooses solitary activities, possesses minimal "human" interests; fades into the background, is aloof or unobtrusive, neither desires nor enjoys close relationships, prefers a peripheral role in social, work, and family settings).	(F) Interpersonally Aversive (e.g., distances from activities that involve intimate personal relationships and reports extensive history of social pan-anxiety and distrust; seeks acceptance, but is unwilling to get involved unless certain to be liked, maintaining distance and privacy to avoid being shamed and humiliated).	(F) Interpersonally Submissive (e.g., needs excessive advice and reassurance, as well as subordinates self to stronger, nurturing figure, without whom may feel anxiously alone and helpless; is compliant, conciliatory, and placating, fearing being left to care for oneself).
Phenomenological Level		
(F) Cognitively Impoverished (e.g., seems deficient across broad spheres of human knowledge and evidences vague and obscure thought processes, particularly about social matters; communication with others is often unfocused, loses its purpose or intention, or is conveyed via a loose or circuitous logic).	(F) Cognitively Distracted (e.g., warily scans environment for potential threats and is preoccupied by intrusive and disruptive random thoughts and observations; an upwelling from within of irrelevant ideation upsets thought continuity and interferes with social communications and accurate appraisals).	(F) Cognitively Naive (e.g., rarely disagrees with others and is easily persuaded, unsuspicious, and gullible; reveals a Pollyanna attitude toward interpersonal difficulties, watering down objective problems and smoothing over troubling events).
(S) Complacent Self-Image (e.g., reveals minimal introspection and awareness of self; seems impervious to the emotional and personal implications of everyday social life, appearing indifferent to the praise or criticism of others).	(S) Alienated Self-Image (e.g., sees self as socially inept, inadequate, and inferior, justifying thereby his or her isolation and rejection by others; feels personally unappealing, devalues self-achievements, and reports persistent sense of aloneness and emptiness).	(S) Inept Self-Image (e.g., views self as weak, fragile, and inadequate; exhibits lack of self-confidence by belittling own attitudes and competencies, and hence not capable of doing things on one's own).
(S) Meager Objects (e.g., internalized representations are few in number and minimally articulated, largely devoid of the manifold percepts and memories of relationships with others, possessing little of the dynamic interplay among drives and conflicts that typify well-adjusted persons).	(S) Vexatious Objects (e.g., internalized representations are composed of readily reactivated, intense, and conflict-ridden memories of problematic early relations; limited avenues for experiencing or recalling gratification, and few mechanisms to channel needs, bind impulses, resolve conflicts, or deflect external stressors).	(S) Immature Objects (e.g., internalized representations are composed of infantile impressions of others, unsophisticated ideas, incomplete recollections, rudimentary drives, and childlike impulses, as well as minimal competencies to manage and resolve stressors).

(F) Intellectualization Mechanism (e.g., describes interpersonal and affective experiences in a matter-of-fact, abstract, impersonal, or mechanical manner; pays primary attention to formal and objective aspects of social and emotional events).

(F) Fantasy Mechanism (e.g., depends excessively on imagination to achieve need gratification, confidence building, and conflict resolution; withdraws into reveries as a means of safely discharging frustrated affectionate, as well as angry impulses).

(F) Introjection Mechanism (e.g., is firmly devoted to another to strengthen the belief that an inseparable bond exists between them; jettisons independent views in favor of those of others to preclude conflicts and threats to relationship).

(S) Undifferentiated Organization (e.g., given an inner barrenness, a feeble drive to fulfill needs, and minimal pressures either to defend against or resolve internal conflicts or cope with external demands, internal morphologic structures may best be characterized by their limited framework and sterile pattern).

(S) Fragile Organization (e.g., a precarious complex of tortuous emotions depend almost exclusively on a single modality for its resolution and discharge, that of avoidance, escape, and fantasy and, hence, when faced with personal risks, new opportunities, or unanticipated stress, few morphologic structures are available to deploy and few back-up positions can be reverted to, short of regressive decompensation).

(S) Inchoate Organization (e.g., owing to entrusting others with the responsibility to fulfill needs and to cope with adult tasks, there is both a deficient morphologic structure and a lack of diversity in internal regulatory controls, leaving a miscellany of relatively undeveloped and undifferentiated adaptive abilities, as well as an elementary system for functioning independently).

Biophysical Level

(S) Apathetic Mood (e.g., is emotionally unexcitable, exhibiting an intrinsic unfeeling, cold and stark quality; reports weak affectionate or erotic needs, rarely displaying warm or intense feelings, and apparently unable to experience most affects—pleasure, sadness, or anger—in any depth).

(S) Anguished Mood (e.g., describes constant and confusing undercurrent of tension, sadness, and anger; vacillates between desire for affection, fear of rebuff, embarrassment, and numbness of feeling).

(S) Pacific Mood (e.g., is characteristically warm, tender, and noncompetitive; timidly avoids social tension and interpersonal conflicts).

185

in her attentiveness to facial expressions on the TAT, and her willingness to self-disclose in the interview. Interpersonally, she seems to alternate between the schizoid and the dependent-avoidant styles, perhaps as a defense against the feared rejection and helplessness that typify the latter. If what one desperately desires appears completely unobtainable, then one solution is to deny that such needs exist at all, remaining aloof from others as well as from oneself. Such an analysis conceptualizes this schizoid feature as a compromise that reflects conflictual dispositions, but has nevertheless taken on characterological pervasiveness. Her ICB responses corroborate this interpretation: Animals are more enjoyable and comfortable than people, but wouldn't true love be nice! Here one sees the avoidant's view that others are critical and humiliating, the dependent's desire to be rescued, and a blunting of affect typical of the schizoid. Cognitively, the intrusive and perplexing quality of Maria's ideations appear more like the avoidant, possibly even the schizotypal, than it does the schizoid or the dependent. Maria herself noted that her parents at one time believed she was autistic. Moreover, the large number of poor form responses in her Rorschach protocol as represented by the inflated X-percent argue for poor reality testing and perceptual distortion. Defensively, Maria appears to combine the mechanisms of the avoidant with that of the dependent. Although her TAT stories possess nearly magical endings, she seems incapable of separating her goals for herself from those of her introjected father image. Although her affective expression is blunted in an effort to avoid pain, lending her presentation a numb or flattened quality, Maria's mood resembles more the avoidant's anguished desire for affection and constant fear of rebuff. As for her self-image, much like the dependent-avoidant, Maria sees herself as weak and inadequate, belittles her own intelligence and achievements, and regards herself as a failure in her chosen profession. Her internalizations and intrapsychic organization resemble more that of the avoidant and dependent than the schizoid (ISB #2: The happiest time I can remember was playing with my little sister when I was a child).

Often the yield of domain hypotheses will be much richer than can be practically evaluated with data internal to the MCMI, especially if the codetype pattern is complex. As seen earlier, we have readily drawn on TAT and Rorschach data, as well as the interpersonal impressions of the examiner. Some domain hypotheses will be thoroughly corroborated, as for example, by a therapist's own clinical observations. Others will be only partially corroborated, perhaps because the evidence simply suggests something else, but more often because not enough data exist to make an informed judgment. Evaluation of such hypotheses must await the accrual of extra-MCMI data, whether through additional testing or from impressions gained across therapy sessions. As with any form of clinical inference, the combination of various gauges from diverse settings provide the data aggregates (Epstein, 1979, 1983) necessary to increase the likelihood of drawing correct inferences, especially when coupled with multimethod approaches (Campbell & Fiske, 1959).

DEVELOP A LOGIC THAT RELATES SYMPTOMS
AND PREDISPOSING PERSONALITY PATTERNS

At this final stage of MCMI interpretation, the proper question to be asked is not "whether," but "how"— how the interaction of individual characteristics and contextual factors, that is, the interaction of Axis II and Axis IV, produces Axis I, classical psychiatric symptomatology. How do Axis II and Axis IV interact to produce the bedtime worries observed in the current case? The teacher will likely wish to point out that this final synthesis requires a certain amount of clinical imagination on the part of the test user, regardless of the inventory used. This requires that the symptom complaint and psychosocial history and functioning be integrated with the personality style explicated earlier.

For the case presented here, Maria emerges as a basically avoidant-dependent individual, someone who is far from home in Venezuela, who feels herself to be a failure at her chosen career, who questions her intellectual competency, and desperately longs for companionship (ISB #34: "I wish I could find true love"). If what one desperately needs or desires is believed to be completely unattainable, too painful to pursue, yet too painful to exist without, one solution is to deny that the need or desire exists at all. Thus it appears that Maria is socially inhibited and self-doubting. She is also secretive and intellectualizing. In part due to the enmeshment of her family system, she is probably less individuated and more developmentally immature than what is required for the professional life she is ostensibly seeking. Anchored in another culture, away from friends and family who could be relied on to gratify affectionate needs, a failure at what she values most, she longs to return to the security of an earlier developmental epoch, a security that, in all likelihood, now sadly perpetuates the very immaturity and impoverishment of interpersonal abilities that it originally engendered. As noted on the ICB, "The happiest time I can remember is playing with my little sister." Given the lack of reinforcers in her current setting, Maria is likely to turn inward, depending excessively on imagination to achieve need gratification and conflict resolution, withdrawing into reverie to discharge occasionally overwhelming affectionate needs (and perhaps aggressive impulses as well) when these can no longer be readily denied or intellectualized. In fact, this mechanism may have achieved pathological proportions, suggesting that she may be predisposed to temporary, but readily reversible, episodes of an almost psychotic nature. Depending on the intensity of stressors, her cognitive-ideational state may vary along a continuum of disruptive and irrelevant intrusions, but generally with good reality testing at the more normal end, to more schizotypal and schizophenic ideations at the other. During these episodes reality testing will be poor. Given the client's high intellectual level, her position on this continuum at any one moment may be difficult to judge. She is intelligent enough to know what constitutes a good presentation.

No less problematic in sustaining Maria's psychopathology is a generally inept, alienated, and devalued self-image. Her dependent style, specifically her generally fragile and inchoate intrapsychic organization, likely inclines her toward globalized beliefs of inefficacy rather than more realistic and differentiated appraisals of her performance in more narrow domains of competency. Her implicitly dichotomous conception of intellectual ability ("When I found out that I was not intelligent") supports this interpretation. In her eyes, her "failure" in chemical engineering likely validates her belief in her incompetency. Perhaps if she were not somewhat dependent, she could generate her own solutions and work toward realizing her possibilities. Perhaps if she were not somewhat avoidant, she could pursue whatever solutions and possibilities she envisioned. As a dependent-avoidant, however, she can do neither, creating and sustaining her dysthymic mood. Undistracted by the events of the day, a bedtime ruminative cycle begins, which focuses on present unfulfilled needs and future impossibilities.

REVIEW THE PRESENTATION

After the presentation has been completed, it is important to summarize what was accomplished. A helpful review will simply go section by section through the main body of the lecture. At a minimum, this review should proceed in the context of the overall goal that was desired, that of establishing a theoretical context that would allow for the individual and his or her pathologies to be understood as an organic whole. To accomplish this goal, a theoretical model was posited, based on the fundamentals of evolutionary theory. The polarities of this theory allowed for the deduction of the essential dimensions on which personality may be deficient, imbalanced, or conflicted, thus laying the foundation for the development of an instrument to assess these constructs, and provide a context for understanding the nature of the individual's more superficial or symptomatic disorders, those of Axis I.

Resources that may be of further interest to presenters include McCann and Dyer's 1996 book, *Forensic Assessment With the Millon Inventories*; Craig's 1993 book, *Psychological Assessment With the Millon Clinical Multiaxial Inventory (II): An Interpretive Guide*; and Choca & Ven Denburg's 1997 *Interpretive Guide to the Millon Clinical Multiaxial Inventory*. Additional works are available in *The Millon Inventories: Contemporary Clinical and Personality Assessment* (1997).

REFERENCES

Allport, G. W., & Odbert, H. S. (1936). Trait names: A psycholexical study. *Psychological Monographs*, 47 (Whole No. 00).

Campbell, D., & Fiske, D. (1959). Convergent and discriminant validation by the multitrait-multimethod matrix. *Psychological Bulletin*, 58, 81–105.

Cattell, R. B., Eber, H. W., & Tatsuoka, M. M. (1970). *Handbook for the Sixteen Personality Factor Questionnaire* [16PF]. Champaign, IL: Institute for Personality and Ability Testing.

Choca, J. P., & Van Denburg, E. (1997). *Interpretive guide to the Millon Clinical Multiaxial Inventory*, 2nd edition. Washington, DC: American Psychological Association.

Craig, R. J. (1993). *Psychological assessment with the Millon Clinical Multiaxial Inventory (II): An interpretive guide*. Odessa, FL: Psychological Assessment Resources.

Epstein, S. (1979). The stability of behavior: I. On predicting most of the people much of the time. *Journal of Social and Personality Psychology, 37*, 1087–1126.

Epstein, S. (1983). Aggression and beyond: Some basic issues on the prediction of behavior. *Journal of Personality, 51*, 360–382.

Gilligan, C. (1982). *In a Different Voice*. Cambridge, MA: Harvard University Press.

Harris, R. E., & Lingoes, J. C. (1955, 1968). *Subscales for the MMPI: An aid to profile interpretation*. Unpublished manuscript. The Langley Porter Neuropsychiatric Institute.

Huxley, T. (1981). Mr. Darwin's critics. *Contemporary Review, 18*, 443–476.

Jackson, D. (1970). A sequential system for personality scale development. In C. Spielberger (Ed.), *Current Topics in Clinical and Community Psychology* (Vol. 2) (pp. 61–92). New York: Academic Press.

Loevinger, J. (1957). Objective tests as instruments of psychological theory. *Psychological Reports, 3*, 635–694.

McCann, J. T., & Dyer, F .J. (1996). *Forensic assessment with the Millon inventories*. New York: Guilford.

Millon, T. (1969). *Modern psychopathology: A biosocial approach to maladaptive learning and functioning*. Philadelphia: Saunders.

Millon, T. (1981). *Disorders of Personality: DSM-III, Axis II*. New York: Wiley.

Millon, T. (1986a). Personality prototypes and their diagnostic criteria. In T. Millon & G. Klerman (Eds.),*Contemporary Directions in psychopathology: Toward the DSM–IV* (pp. 67–71). New York: Guilford.

Millon, T. (1986b). A theoretical derivation of pathological personalities. In T. Millon & G. Klerman (Eds.), *Contemporary directions in psychopathology: Toward the DSM–IV* (pp. 639–670). New York: Guilford.

Millon, T. (1987). *Millon Clinical Multiaxial Inventory DSM– II manual*. Minneapolis: National Computer Systems.

Millon, T. (1990). *Toward a new personology: An evolutionary model*. New York: Wiley-Interscience.

Millon, T. (Ed.). (in press). *The Millon inventories: Contemporary clinical and personality assessment*. New York: Guilford.

Millon, T., & Davis, R. D. (1996). *Disorders of personality: DSM–IV and beyond*. New York: Wiley-Interscience.

Millon, T., Millon, C., & Davis, R. D. (1994). *Millon Clinical Multiaxial Inventory – III manual*. Minneapolis: National Computer Systems.

Millon, T., Millon, C.., & Davis, R. (1997). *Millon Clinical Multiaxial Inventory Manual*, 2nd edition. Minneapolis: National Computer Systems.

Rushton, J. P. (1985). Differential K theory: The sociobiology of individual and group differences. *Personality and Individual Differences, 6*, 441–452.

Skinner, H. (1986). Construct validation approach to psychiatric classification. In T. Millon & G. L. Klerman (Eds.), *Contemporary directions in psychopathology: Towards the DSM–IV* (pp. 307–329). New York: Guilford.

Spencer, H. (1870). *The principles of psychology*. London: Williams & Norgate.
Wilson, E. O. (1975). *Sociobiology: The new synthesis*. Cambridge, MA: Harvard University Press.
Wilson, E. O. (1978). *On human nature*. Cambridge, MA: Harvard University Press.

12

Teaching and Learning the Personality Assessment Inventory (PAI)

Leslie C. Morey
Vanderbilt University

The *Personality Assessment Inventory* (PAI; Morey, 1991) is a self-administered, objective test of personality and psychopathology designed to provide information on critical client variables in professional settings. From its inception, it was constructed to provide measures of constructs that are central in treatment planning, implementation, and evaluation. Although it was introduced fairly recently, the PAI has already generated considerable attention from clinicians and researchers, and the various applications of the test have generated several important findings.

Because the knowledge base of the PAI is evolving, I find that the way that I teach others about the use of the PAI also evolves to accommodate this growing body of knowledge. Although different users of the test will typically be employing it in very diverse settings, there are certain core issues central to the clinician and the researcher across most of these settings. The topics covered in this chapter are those that frequently arise in teaching about the use of the PAI in many different contexts.

To teach the PAI, access to two source books is critical. One is the manual for the test (Morey, 1991). It provides an extensive documentation of the process of development of the test and the theoretical basis of the constructs that it was designed to measure. As is described herein, understanding this basis of the test is fundamental to its successful use. A second important source volume is the *Interpretive Guide* (Morey, 1996). This book is focused on the clinical use of the PAI to address specific questions, and was written primarily to teach clinicians and researchers to use the test effectively. The *Interpretive Guide* also provides information about research findings that have accumulated since the PAI was published. Familiarity with both of these source books is critical for a sophisticated understanding of this instrument.

191

There are five basic steps that I follow in teaching others to use the PAI. The first step involves an understanding of the *conceptual rationale* of the test. This includes a discussion of the philosophy of test development followed in the construction of the PAI, and the ways in which this approach differs from the test validation philosophy used in the development of other instruments. The second step involves an examination of the *individual scales* of the PAI. This stage introduces the trainee to the framework of the test as well as to some of the relevant validity evidence. The third step addresses the *norms and reliability* of the PAI scales. This step explains how the theoretical constructs surveyed in Step 2 are translated into quantitative scores and how those scores should be interpreted. The fourth step involves an introduction to the assessment of *profile validity*, an exercise that is critical in the evaluation of any PAI protocol. The fifth and final step introduces the *configural interpretation* of the PAI. At this stage, the trainee learns to combine information gathered across the entire inventory to address specific referral questions.

The sequence of these five steps is hierarchical and as such it is recommended that they be taught in the order described. For example, in understanding the influence of context on normative data (Step 3), illustrative examples with reference to particular scales (Step 2) are needed. The following sections provide a detailed examination of each of these five steps in training, with particular focus on those topics that are essential prerequisites for subsequent training and use of the test.

STEP 1. CONCEPTUAL RATIONALE OF THE PAI

The first step involved in using the PAI effectively is to understand how the instrument was developed and why it has the characteristics that it has. The development of the PAI was based on a construct validation framework that emphasized a rational as well as quantitative method of scale development. This framework placed strong emphasis on a theoretically informed approach to the development and selection of items, as well as on the assessment of their stability and correlates. The constructs assessed by the PAI were selected on the basis of two criteria: the stability of their importance within the conceptualization and nosology of mental disorder, and their significance in contemporary clinical practice. These criteria were assessed through a review of the historical and contemporary literature. In generating items for these syndromes, the literature on each construct was examined to identify those components most central to the definition of the concept, and items were written that were directed at providing an assessment of these components. The theoretical articulation of the constructs to be measured was assumed to be critical, because this articulation had to serve as a guide to the content of information sampled and to the subsequent assessment of content validity, as described later. To understand how the PAI operates, it is important for the trainee to understand the distinction between this approach and one that is more purely empirical, such as a criterion-keying approach, or a factor analytic approach to item selection. As such, my approach to teaching this test may involve more emphasis on psychometric theory than is typical of other authors.

To provide a solid foundation for understanding the construct validation process, it is often useful for the trainee to supplement their reading with some of the classic works in construct validation (e.g., Cronbach & Meehl, 1955; Jackson, 1971; Loevinger, 1957). Such readings reinforce the appreciation that the validation of an instrument is a complex process that cannot be reduced to a single coefficient. It also helps to underscore the fact that assessment techniques must be evaluated within the context of a theoretically informed network that makes explicit hypotheses about interrelationships among indicators of various constructs. The key point to understand is that, on instruments developed according to these principles, the scales are designed to measure particular constructs, represented by the names of the individual scales. This contrasts with instruments where scale names are task descriptions (such as the subscales on the Wechsler intelligence scales), factor names (as on the 16PF), or even numerals (such as the MMPI).

There are two facets of construct validity that played a particularly important role in the development of the PAI: *content validity* and *discriminant validity*. In teaching the conceptual rationale for the instrument, it is worth reviewing the importance of these two elements of construct validity and their implications for the interpretation of a psychological test. The following paragraphs summarize the influence of these aspects on the development of the PAI.

Content Validity

The content validity of a measure involves the adequacy of sampling of content across the construct being measured. Often, trainees confuse this characteristic of a test with face validity, referring to whether the instrument appears to be measuring what it is intended to measure, particularly as it appears to a lay audience. These are not synonymous terms; a test for depression that consists of a single item such as "I am unhappy" may appear to be highly related to depression (i.e., high face validity) but it provides a very narrow sampling of the content domain of depression (i.e., low content validity). The construction of the PAI sought to develop scales that provided a balanced sampling of the most important elements of the constructs being measured. This content coverage was designed to include both a consideration of *breadth* as well as *depth* of the construct. The breadth of content coverage refers to the diversity of elements subsumed within a construct. For example, in measuring depression it is important to inquire about physiological and cognitive signs of depression as well as features of affect. Any depression scale that focuses exclusively on one of these elements at the expense of the others will have limited content validity, with limited coverage of the breadth of the depression construct. The PAI sought to ensure breadth of content coverage through the use of subscales representing the major elements of the measured constructs, as indicated by the theoretical and empirical literature on the construct. Thus, in teaching the structural composition of the PAI scales it is useful to supplement this structure with the relevant literature that provides the basis for this structure, such as the importance of cognitive features in depression, the distinction between positive and negative symptoms of schizophrenia, or the differential contribution of behavior and personality in the diagnosis of antisocial personality. Useful references for these structures are provided in the *Professional Manual* (Morey, 1991) and in the *Interpretive Guide* (Morey, 1996).

The depth of content coverage refers to the need to sample across the full range of severity of a particular element of a construct. To assure adequate depth of coverage, the scales were designed to include items that addressed the full range of severity of the construct, including both its milder and its most severe forms. One aspect of the instrument that resulted from this consideration was the item response scaling; the test items are answered on a four-alternative scale, with the anchors "Totally False," "Slightly True," "Mainly True," and "Very True." Each response is weighted according to the intensity of the feature that the different alternatives represent. Thus, a client who answers "Very True" to the question "Sometimes I think I'm worthless" adds 3 points to his or her raw score on the Depression scale, whereas a client who responds "Slightly True" to the same item adds only 1 point. As a result, each item can capture differences in the severity of the manifestation of a feature of a particular disorder. The use of this four-alternative scaling is further justified psychometrically in that it allows a scale to capture more true variance per item, meaning that even scales of modest length can achieve satisfactory reliability. It is also justified clinically, because sometimes even a "slightly true" response to some constructs (such as suicidal ideation) may merit clinical attention. Furthermore, clients themselves often express dissatisfaction with forced choice alternatives, expressing the belief that the true state of affairs lies somewhere "in the middle" of the two extremes presented.

In addition to differences in depth of severity reflected in response options, the items themselves were constructed to tap different levels of severity in the manifestation of a problem. For example, cognitive elements of depression can vary in severity, from mild pessimism to severe feelings of hopelessness, help- lessness, and despair. Through an examination of the item characteristic curves of potential items, the final items were selected to provide information across the full range of construct severity. The nature of the severity continuum varies across the constructs. For example, for the Suicidal Ideation (SUI) scale, this continuum involves the imminence of the suicidal threat. Thus, items on this scale vary from vague and ill-articulated thoughts about suicide to immediate plans for self-harm.

Discriminant Validity

A test is said to have discriminant validity if it provides a measure of a construct that is specific to that construct; in other words, the measurement is free from the influence of other constructs. Although discriminant validity has been long recognized as an important facet of construct validity, it traditionally has not played a major role in the construction of psychological tests. This is unfortunate, because discriminant validity represents one of the largest challenges in the assessment of psychological constructs.

There are a variety of threats to validity where discriminability plays a vital role. One such area of great importance involves *test bias*. Simply put, a test that is intended to measure a psychological construct should not be measuring a demographic variable, such as gender, age, or race. This does not mean that psychological tests should never be correlated with age, or gender, or race. However, the magnitude of any such correlations should not exceed the theoretical overlap of the demographic feature with the construct. For example, nearly every indicator of antisocial behavior suggests that it is more common in men than in women. Thus, it would be expected that an assessment of antisocial behavior would yield average scores for men that are higher than those for women. However, the instrument should demonstrate a considerably greater correlation with other indicators of antisocial behavior than it does with gender; otherwise, it may be measuring gender rather than measuring the construct it was designed to assess.

While learning the PAI it is important to understand the steps that were taken to minimize the likelihood of test bias. First, every item on the PAI was reviewed by a bias panel (consisting of lay and professional individuals, both men and women, of diverse racial and ethnic backgrounds) to identify items that, although written to identify emotional and/or behavioral problems, might instead reflect other factors, such as sociocultural background. This panel represented a conceptually based approach to this particular aspect of discriminant validity. A second, empirical strategy for eliminating test bias involved the examination of item psychometric properties as a function of demography. In particular, associations between a given item and its corresponding full scale were evaluated using regression models, and items were chosen to display minimal variation in slope or intercept parameters as a function of demographic variables. The intent of this approach was to eliminate items that had different meanings for different demographic groups. For example, if an item inquiring about crying seemed to be related to other indicators of depression in women but not in men, then that item was eliminated because interpretation of the item would vary as a function of gender. Note that this strategy will not eliminate mean demographic differences in scale scores. For example, an item that inquires about stealing may have a similar meaning for identifying antisocial personality for both men and women, yet still be more common among men. In this example, the resulting gender difference is not a function of test *bias*; rather, it is an accurate reflection of gender differences in the disorder. Working a few examples of such regression models can help trainees understand that demographic differences are *not* necessarily a sign of bias, and that a test with no such differences can in fact be quite biased.

The issue of test bias is one that is particularly salient in light of past abuses of testing and current legislation designed to prevent such abuses. However, such bias is just one form of potential problem with discriminant validity. It is particularly common in the field of clinical assessment to find that a measure that supposedly measures one construct (such as anxiety, or schizophrenia) is in fact highly related to many constructs. It is this tendency that makes many instruments quite difficult to interpret. How does the clinician evaluate an elevated score on a scale measuring "schizophrenia" if that scale is also a measure of alienation, indecisiveness, family problems, and depression? At each stage of the development of the PAI, items were selected that had maximal associations with indicators of the pertinent construct and minimal associations with the other constructs measured by the test. By emphasizing the importance of both convergent and discriminant validity in selecting items for inclusion on the PAI, the interpretation of the resulting scales is straightforward because they are relatively pure measures of the constructs in question. For example, an elevation on the DEP (Depression) scale may be interpreted as indicating that the respondent reports a number of experiences consistent with the symptomatology of clinical depression.

The Construct Validation Approach and Item Interpretation

In the development of the PAI, both the conceptual nature and empirical adequacy of the items played an important role in their inclusion in the final version of the inventory. The goal was to include items that struck a balance between different desirable item parameters, including content coverage as well as empirical characteristics, so that the scales could be useful across a number of different applications. Of paramount importance in the development of the test was the assumption that no single quantitative item parameter should be used as the sole criterion for item selection. An overreliance on a single parameter in item selection typically leads to a scale with one desirable psychometric property and numerous undesirable ones. Thus, the construct validation approach intends to avoid the pitfalls associated with "naive empiricism" in test construction.

In contrast to the "empirical" approach, the content of each item was assumed to be critical in determining its relevance for the assessment of the construct. For example, each item was reviewed by a panel of experts to ensure that its content was directly relevant to the clinical construct in question. As a result, an interpretation of PAI responses at the item level is entirely consistent with the development philosophy of the test, and a review of item content can provide specific information about the nature of difficulties experienced by the respondent. For example, 27 PAI items were identified as "critical items" based on the importance of their content as an indicator of potential crisis situations, and their very low endorsement rates in normal individuals. Endorsement of these items can be followed by more detailed questioning that can clarify the nature and severity of these concerns. Although item-level interpretation can be useful, it should be recognized that the reliability of individual items is limited and greater caution must be exercised in such efforts than would be merited in interpreting full-scale scores.

STEP 2. INDIVIDUAL SCALES
AND THEIR CORRELATES

The starting point in interpreting the PAI lies at the level of the individual scales, which were developed to measure the construct implied by the scale name. A brief description of the full scales of the PAI is provided in Table 12.1, whereas Table12. 2 presents a description of the PAI subscales. Although there has been a great deal of discussion about the importance of "configural" interpretation of multiscale inventories, most of the validity literature in this area supports relatively simple linear models (Dawes & Corrigan, 1974) over

TABLE 12.1

The 22 Full Scales of the PAI

Scale (Designation)	Description
Validity Scales	
Inconsistency (ICN)	Determines if client is answering consistently throughout inventory. Each pair consists of highly correlated (positively or negatively) items.
Infrequency (INF)	Determines if client is responding carelessly or randomly. Items are neutral with respect to psychopathology and have extremely high or low endorsement rates.
Negative Impression (NIM)	Suggests an exaggerated unfavorable impression or malingering. Items have relatively low endorsement rates among clinical subjects.
Positive Impression (PIM)	Suggests the presentation of a very favorable impression or reluctance to admit minor flaws.
Clinical Scales	
Somatic Complaints (SOM)	Focuses on preoccupation with health matters and somatic complaints associated with somatization and conversion disorders.
Anxiety (ANX)	Focuses on phenomenology and observable signs of anxiety with an emphasis on assessment across different response modalities.
Anxiety-Related Disorders (ARD)	Focuses on symptoms and behaviors related to specific anxiety disorders, particularly phobias, traumatic stress, and obsessive-compulsive symptoms.
Depression (DEP)	Focuses on symptoms and phenomenology of depressive disorders.
Mania (MAN)	Focuses on affective, cognitive, and behavioral symptoms of mania and hypomania.
Paranoia (PAR)	Focuses on symptoms of paranoid disorders and more enduring characteristics of paranoid personality.
Schizophrenia (SCZ)	Focuses on symptoms relevant to the broad spectrum of schizophrenic disorders.
Borderline Features (BOR)	Focuses on attributes indicative of a borderline level of personality functioning, including unstable and fluctuating interpersonal relations, impulsivity, affective lability and instability, and uncontrolled anger.
Antisocial Features (ANT)	Focuses on history of illegal acts and authority problems, egocentrism, lack of empathy and loyalty, instability, and excitement-seeking.
Alcohol Problems (ALC)	Focuses on problematic consequences of alcohol use and features of alcohol dependence.
Drug Problems (DRG)	Focuses on problematic consequences of drug use (both prescription and illicit) and features of drug dependence.

TABLE 12.1 (cont.)

Treatment Scales

Aggression (AGG)	Focuses on characteristics and attitudes related to anger, assertiveness, hostility, and aggression.
Suicidal Ideation (SUI)	Focuses on suicidal ideation, ranging from hopelessness to thoughts and plans for the suicidal act.
Stress (STR)	Measures the impact of recent stressors in major life areas.
Nonsupport (NON)	Measures a lack of perceived social support, considering both the level and quality of available support.
Treatment Rejection (RXR)	Focuses on attributes and attitudes theoretically predictive of interest and motivation in making personal changes of a psychological or emotional nature.

Interpersonal Scales

Dominance (DOM)	Assesses the extent to which a person is controlling and independent in personal relationships. A bipolar dimension with a dominant style at the high end and a submissive style at the low end.
Warmth (WRM)	Assesses the extent to which a person is interested in supportive and empathic personal relationships. A bipolar dimension with a warm, outgoing style at the high end and a cold, rejecting style at the low end.

more complicated, configural/interactional strategies. Such results underscore the central importance of understanding the meaning of individual scales before concerning oneself with scale configuration. This is not to say that configural information is irrelevant in PAI interpretation; in fact, it is useful even at the level of the individual scales. Each scale on the test was designed to measure the major facets of different clinical constructs, as determined by current theoretical and empirical work on those constructs. Because most of the clinical scales offer subscales, configural interpretation of the test is possible even at the level of the individual scales, because two identical elevations on a particular scale may be interpreted quite differently, depending on the configuration of the subscales.

The PAI subscales were constructed as an aid in isolating the core elements of the different clinical constructs that the test measures. These subscales can serve to clarify the meaning of full-scale elevations, and may be used configurally in diagnostic decision making. For example, many patients typically come to clinical settings with marked distress and dysphoria, often leading to elevations on most unidimensional depression scales. However, unless other manifestations of the syndrome are present, this does not necessarily indicate that Major Depression is the likely diagnosis. In the absence of features such as vegetative signs, lowered self-esteem, and negative expectancies, that diagnosis may not be warranted, even with a prominent elevation on a depression scale. On the PAI, such a pattern would lead to an elevation on DEP-A, representing the dysphoria and distress, but without elevations on DEP-P (the vegetative signs) and DEP-C (the cognitive signs). As a result, an overall elevation on DEP in this instance would not be interpreted as diagnostic of Major Depression because of the lack of supporting data from the subscale configuration.

TABLE 12.2

PAI Subscales and Their Descriptions

Subscale (Designation)	Description
Somatic Complaints	
Conversion (SOM-C)	Focuses on symptoms associated with conversion disorder, particularly sensory or motor dysfunctions.
Somatization (SOM-S)	Focuses on the frequent occurrence of various common physical symptoms and vague complaints of ill health and fatigue.
Health Concerns (SOM-H)	Focuses on a preoccupation with health status and physical problems.
Anxiety	
Cognitive (ANX-C)	Focuses on ruminative worry and concern about current issues that results in impaired concentration and attention.
Affective (ANX-A)	Focuses on the experience of tension, difficulty in relaxing, and the presence of fatigue as a result of high perceived stress.
Physiological (ANX-P)	Focuses on overt physical signs of tension and stress, such as sweaty palms, trembling hands, complaints of irregular heartbeats, and shortness of breath.
Anxiety-Related Disorders	
Obsessive-Compulsive (ARD-O)	Focuses on intrusive thoughts or behaviors, rigidity, indecision, perfectionism, and affective constriction.
Phobias (ARD-P)	Focuses on common phobic fears, such as social situations, public transportation, heights, enclosed spaces, or other specific objects.
Traumatic Stress (ARD-T)	Focuses on the experience of traumatic events that cause continuing distress and that are experienced as having left the client changed or damaged in some fundamental way.
Depression	
Cognitive (DEP-C)	Focuses on thoughts of worthlessness, hopelessness, and personal failure, as well as indecisiveness and difficulties in concentration.
Affective (DEP-A)	Focuses on feeling of sadness, loss of interest in normal activities, and anhedonia.
Physiological (DEP-P)	Focuses on level of physical functioning, activity, and energy, including disturbance in sleep pattern and changes in appetite and/or weight loss.
Mania	
Activity Level (MAN-A)	Focuses on over involvement in a wide variety of activities in a somewhat disorganized manner and the experience of accelerated thought processes and behavior
Grandiosity (MAN-G)	Focuses on inflated self-esteem, expansiveness, and the belief that one has special and unique skills or talents.
Irritability (MAN-I)	Focuses on the presence of strained relationships due to the respondent's frustration with the inability or unwillingness of others to keep up with their plans, demands, and possibly unrealistic ideas.
Paranoia	
Hypervigilance (PAR-H)	Focuses on suspiciousness and the tendency to monitor the environment for real or imagined slights by others.
Persecution (PAR-P)	Focuses on the belief that one has been treated inequitably and that there is a concerted effort among others to undermine ones interests.
Resentment (PAR-R)	Focuses on a bitterness and cynicism in interpersonal relationships, and a tendency to hold grudges and externalized blame for any misfortunes.

TABLE 12.2 (cont.)

Schizophrenia

Psychotic Experiences (SCZ-P)	Focuses on the experience of unusual perceptions and sensations, magical thinking, and/or other unusual ideas that may involve delusional beliefs.
Social Detachment (SCZ-S)	Focuses on social isolation, discomfort and awkwardness in social interactions.
Thought Disorder (SCZ-T)	Focuses on confusion, concentration problems, and disorganization of thought processes.

Borderline Features

Affective Instability (BOR-A)	Focuses on emotional responsiveness, rapid mood changes, and poor emotional control.
Identity Problems (BOR-I)	Focuses on uncertainty about major life issues and feelings of emptiness, unfulfillment, and an absence of purpose.
Negative Relationships (BOR-N)	Focuses on a history of ambivalent, intense relationships in which one has felt exploited and betrayed.
Self-Harm (BOR-S)	Focuses on impulsivity in areas that have high potential for negative consequences.

Antisocial Features

Antisocial Behaviors (ANT-A)	Focuses on a history of antisocial acts and involvement in illegal activities.
Egocentricity (ANT-E)	Focuses on a lack of empathy or remorse and a generally exploitive approach to interpersonal relationships.
Stimulus-Seeking (ANT-S)	Focuses on a craving for excitement and sensation, a low tolerance for boredom, and a tendency to be reckless and risk-taking.

Aggression

Aggressive Attitude (AGG-A)	Focuses on hostility, poor control over anger expression, and a belief in the instrumental utility of aggression.
Verbal Aggression (AGG-V)	Focuses on verbal expressions of anger ranging from assertiveness to abusiveness, and a readiness to express anger to others.
Physical Aggression (AGG-P)	Focuses on a tendency to physical displays of anger, including damage to property, physical fights, and threats of violence.

To teach the interpretation of an individual scale, the best starting point is an overview of the construct that the scale attempts to measure. For those scales that have subscales, this discussion will cover the construct at both the subscale as well as full-scale level. Thus, learning about the interpretation of DEP requires the trainee to have some familiarity with the overall clinical syndrome of depression as well as its most important elements, such as the typical physiological signs in depression, or the cognitive distortions manifested by these patients. Within the construct validation framework, the construct itself is the key to interpreting the scale. Thus, if the literature indicates that vegetative signs of depression are often responsive to psychopharmacologic treatment, a scale that measures these signs may be interpreted as a potential indicator for such an intervention. As such, the best groundwork for individual scale interpretation is a foundation in basic psychopathology.

Once the trainee has an understanding of the construct, the discussion can turn to specific examples of this construct on the PAI by an examination of the items used on the PAI for a particular construct. Such an approach is consistent with the construction of the test, where it was assumed that the content of an item would be a critical determinant of its utility to assess clinical problems. The examination of the items may remedy any mistaken assumptions that trainees often bring to the instrument. As an example, the subscale on the PAI that assesses "phobias" (ARD-P) includes items that tap feared objects and/or situations that are commonly a focus of clinical concern. However, unless the specific items are examined, the trainee may not realize that the scale includes many questions directed at the assessment of "social phobia," or marked social anxiety in certain public situations. An inexperienced interpreter might assume that an ARD-P elevation indicates a fear of snakes or spiders—fears that are stereotypic phobias but are rarely a focus of clinical concern—and miss the social dysfunction that contributed to the elevation.

The final aspect of introducing the individual PAI scales involves providing an overview of some of the validity evidence bearing on the scale. To date, a number of studies have been conducted examining correlates of various PAI scales; the PAI manual alone contains information about correlations of individual scales with over 50 concurrent indices of psychopathology (Morey, 1991), and numerous validity studies have been conducted since the publication of the test, many of which are summarized in the *Interpretive Guide* (Morey, 1996). It may seem a bit premature to discuss validity evidence before discussing norms or reliability, but often this helps the trainee to understand what the scale measures (convergent validity) as well as what it does not measure (discriminant validity). As an example, the SOM-C (Somatic Complaints:Conversion) and SOM-S (Somatic Complaints:Somatization) subscales both make reference to different types of somatic complaints, and at first glance it might not be clear how the scales differ in an interpretive sense. However, examining validity correlations of these scales reveals that SOM-S tends to yield substantial correlations with measures of distress (such as depression or anxiety) whereas SOM-C has negligible associations with such measures (Morey, 1991). This pattern of validity correlations reveals that SOM-C tends to involve unusual and rather isolated sensorimotor dysfunction, whereas SOM-S elevations are typically part of a more general picture of malaise and complaintiveness. Thus, here the validity correlations help to sharpen the meaning of the different constructs addressed by these two subscales.

STEP 3. NORMATIVE AND RELIABILITY DATA

At this point in the process, the trainee has an understanding of the approach of the test and also has a grasp of the meaning of the concepts that the scales seek to measure. The third stage in the training process involves the "quantitative product" of the PAI: learning to interpret the numbers yielded by the scoring of the test. To use these numbers adequately, one must understand the reference framework for the scores (i.e., the normative data) as well as the margin of error inherent in their use (i.e., the reliability data).

The PAI was developed and standardized for use in the clinical assessment of individuals in the age range of 18 years through adulthood. The initial reading level analyses of the PAI test items indicated that reading ability at the fourth-grade level was necessary to complete the inventory. Subsequent studies of this issue (e.g., Schinka & Borum, 1993) have supported the conclusion that the PAI items are written at a grade equivalent lower than estimates for comparable instruments. Nonetheless, it is important to impress on the trainee that the client's reported level of educational attainment may be a limited predictor of their reading ability. In cases where the respondent cannot read, or has limited visual acuity, an audiotaped version of the PAI is available.

PAI scale and subscale raw scores are transformed to T-scores in order to provide interpretation relative to a standardization sample of 1,000 community-dwelling adults. This sample was carefully selected to match 1995 U.S. census projections on the basis of gender, race, and age; the educational level of the standardization sample was selected to be representative, given the required fourth-grade reading level. The only stipulation for inclusion in the stand-ardization sample (other than stratification fit) was that the subject had to answer more than 90% of PAI items; in other words, no more than 33 items could be left blank. No other restrictions based on PAI data were applied in creating the census-matched standardization sample. Using this sample, the PAI T-scores were calibrated to have a mean of 50 and a standard deviation (SD) of 10, using a standard linear transformation from the community sample norms. Most trainees will immediately recognize that a T-score value greater than 50 lies above the mean in comparison to the scores of subjects in the standardization sample. However, it is important to understand the dispersion of PAI scores as well; roughly 84% of nonclinical subjects will have a T-score below 60 (1 SD above the mean) on most scales, whereas 98% of nonclinical subjects will have scores below 70 (2 SDs above the mean). Thus, a T-score at or above 70 represents a pronounced deviation from the typical responses of adults living in the community. If the trainee is familiar with other instruments that had very homogeneous normative samples and hence yield dramatic elevations with regularity, he or she may need some convincing to recognize that a score of 65T may indeed represent a problem because such scores are so commonplace on those instruments. In such instances, I find it useful to use the "IQ" scale to emphasize the significance of such a score, because most individuals will have little difficulty accepting the importance of a difference between an IQ of 100 and one of 78.

For each scale and subscale, the T-scores were linearly transformed from the means and standard deviations derived from the census-matched stand-ardization sample. Unlike many other similar instruments, the PAI does not calculate T-scores differently for men and women; instead, the same (com-bined) norms are used for both genders. Separate norms are only necessary when the scale contains some bias that alters the interpretation of a score based on the respondent's gender. To use separate norms in the absence of such bias would only distort natural epidemiological differences between genders. For example, women are less likely than men to receive a diagnosis of Antisocial Personality, and this is reflected in lower mean scores for women on the Antisocial Features (ANT) scale. A separate normative procedure for men and women would result in similar numbers of each gender scoring in the clinically significant range, a result that does not reflect the established gender ratio for this disorder. The PAI included several procedures designed to eliminate items that might be biased due to demographic features, such as gender, race, or age, and items that displayed any signs of being interpreted differently as a function of these features were eliminated in the course of selecting the final items for the test. As it turns out, with relatively few exceptions differences as a function of demography were negligible in the community sample. Table 12.3 lists all PAI variables for which any of three demographic variables (age, race, or gender) accounted for more than 5% of the variance in the PAI score, and the resulting effect (in terms of T-score units) of that variable.

Because T-scores are derived from a representative community sample, they provide a useful means for determining if certain problems are clinically significant, because relatively few normal adults will obtain markedly elevated scores. However, other comparisons are often of equal importance in clinical decision making. For example, nearly all patients report depression at their initial evaluation; the question confronting the clinician considering a diagnosis of Major Depression is one of *relative* severity of symptomatology. Knowing that an individual's score on the PAI Depression scale is elevated in comparison to the standardization sample is of value, but a comparison of the elevation relative to a clinical sample may be more critical in forming diagnostic hypotheses.

To facilitate these comparisons, the PAI profile form also indicates the T-scores that correspond to marked elevations when referenced against a representative *clinical* sample. This profile "skyline" indicates the score for each scale and subscale that represents the raw score that is 2 SDs above the mean

TABLE 12.3
Summary of Significant Gender, Race, and Age Influences on PAI Scale Scores

PAI Scale	Demographic Influences	Primary Subscales Affected
PAR	Nonwhite: + 6T	PAR-H
	18–29 years: + 5T	PAR-P
	60+ years: – 4T	PAR-R
BOR	18–29 years: + 6T	BOR-I
	60+ years: – 4T	BOR-I
ANT	Male: + 3T	ANT-A
	18–29 years: + 7T	ANT-S
	60+ years: – 4T	ANT-A
AGG	18–29 years: + 5T	AGG-V
	60+ years: – 4T	AGG-P
STR	18–29 years: + 4T	(no subscales)
	60+ years: – 4T	

for a clinical sample of 1,246 patients selected from a wide variety of different professional settings. Thus, roughly 98% of clinical patients will obtain scores below the skyline on the profile form. Scores above this skyline thus represent a marked elevation of scores relative to those of *patients in clinical settings*. Thus, interpretation of PAI profiles can be accomplished in comparison to both normal and clinical samples.

Interpretation of PAI scale and subscale scores is aided by comparison to these two referents. The similarity of expected scores for these two populations varies a great deal across scales. For example, the interpersonal scales DOM (Dominance) and WRM (Warmth) have distributions that are quite similar in both community and clinical samples; thus, marked elevations (or very low scores) are noteworthy regardless of the nature of the client. On the other hand, the RXR (Treatment Rejection) scale, which was designed to identify risk for early treatment termination, has a markedly different distribution in clinical and community samples. The majority of clinical subjects (who are in treatment) obtain scores that are considerably below those of community subjects, who are typically not in psychological treatment and have little interest in it. Thus, a T-score of 50 on RXR in a client presenting for psychotherapy, although "average" for a community sample, is actually considerably above the expected score for clients in clinical settings. In this instance, this score should be interpreted as indicating potentially significant resistance to change for this client. In contrast, an RXR score of 50T in an individual who was administered the PAI for personnel selection purposes would be unremarkable. In these two cases, the differences in the assessment question leads to differences in the interpretation of the information yielded by a normative transformation.

Once the quantitative referents for the T-score are described, it is important to examine the effects of reliability on the meaning of the score. Such reliability effects are typically expressed in terms of the *standard error of measurement* (SEM) and are a direct function of the reliability of the scale. Many trainees confuse the SEM with the standard deviation of a test, and it is important that they recognize the distinction between variability of observations within a group of people (the standard deviation) and variability of observations within a given individual (the SEM). The SEM is very useful in the evaluation of change over time in a respondent (such as those resulting from therapy), because it provides a yardstick for gauging the magnitude of change that might be expected simply from measurement error.

The reliability of the PAI scales and subscales has been examined in a number of different studies that have evaluated the internal consistency (Alterman et al., 1995; Boyle & Lennon, 1994; Morey, 1991; Rogers, Flores, Ustad, & Sewell, 1995; Schinka, 1995), test–retest reliability (Boyle & Lennon, 1994; Morey, 1991; Rogers et al., 1995), and configural stability (Morey, 1991) of the instrument. Internal consistency alphas for the full scales are generally found to be in the .80s, whereas the subscales yield alphas in the .70s. Although these numbers are reasonable, internal consistency estimates are generally not the ideal basis for deriving the SEM in clinical measures, because temporal instability is often of greater concern than interitem correlations.

The temporal stability of PAI scales has been examined by administering the test to subjects on two different occasions. For the standardization studies, median test–retest reliability values, over a 4-week interval, for the 11 full clinical scales was .86 (Morey, 1991), leading to SEM for these scales on the order of 3–4 T-score points, with 95% confidence intervals of $+/-$ 6–8 T-score points. Examination of the mean absolute T-score change values for scales also revealed that the absolute changes over time were quite small, on the order of 2–3 T-score points for most of the full scales (Morey, 1991). The test–retest reliability of the subscales tended to be lower, resulting in SEMs of 4–5 T-score points and 95% confidence intervals of 8–10 points. These results should serve as a guide to the trainee in evaluating repeated administrations of the instrument. For example, a change of 15 T-score points on either a scale or a subscale is unlikely to be due solely to the effects of unreliability, whereas a change of 5 points (particularly on the subscales) must be considered within the realm of measurement error.

STEP 4. THE PAI AND RESPONSE SETS

One of the difficulties that has beset the field of psychological assessment since its inception concerns the accuracy of self-reported information as an indication of psychological status. The reasons offered as to why self-report may be distorted are myriad. One source of distortion may arise from an intention to deceive the recipient of the information; such examinees may attempt to distort their responses to appear either better adjusted or more poorly adjusted than is actually the case. A second source of distortion may arise from limited insight or self-deception. These examinees may genuinely believe that they are doing quite well or quite poorly, but this belief might be at odds with the impression of objective observers. A third source of distortion can also arise from carelessness or indifference in taking a test; examinees who answer questions with little reflection (or even randomly) may yield results that do not accurately mirror their experiences.

A consideration of profile validity is typically the first step in interpretation of a particular protocol. The importance of item content in PAI interpretation makes it essential that potential distortion arising from response sets be considered. The stigma of mental illness, the possibility of secondary gain, and the limitations of psychological insight in most people can all potentially distort the accuracy of self-reported information. The distorting factors can be quite diverse. They may result from personality traits or from situational influences on a respondent; they may involve intentional distortion or a genuine lack of insight; and they may involve selective distortions in some problem areas (e.g., substance abuse) but not others (e.g., depression). For this reason, the PAI does not include any "correction" factors of the sort employed by other inventories; these corrections invariably fail to enhance validity, mostly due to the reliance on one omnibus correction that cannot discriminate among such varied influences. Nonetheless, it is clear that the assessment of such potential distortions is an important part of interpreting any self-report instrument, and identifying them has arguably been the most difficult assessment task for researchers and clinicians. Fortunately, there are a variety of ways to detect such distortion with the PAI.

The first step in establishing profile validity involves using the PAI scales designed for this purpose. The PAI offers four scales that are designed to provide an assessment of factors that could distort the results of a self-report questionnaire. Two of these scales, Inconsistency (ICN) and Infrequency (INF), were developed to assess inconsistent or idiosyncratic responding, whereas the other two validity scales, Negative Impression (NIM) and Positive Impression (PIM), were developed to provide an assessment of efforts at impression management by the respondent.

Elevated scores on any of these scales suggest that other scales should be viewed with caution and any interpretation of results should be tentative. In general, if a subject obtains a score that is more than 2 SDs above the mean of the standardization *clinical* sample on any of these scales or indices, the profile is likely to be seriously distorted by some test-taking response style. Such a result casts serious doubt on all other information derived from the test, and under such conditions the necessity of considering the PAI protocol in light of information derived from other sources becomes particularly critical.

The trainee can draw on the results of a number of correlational and simulation studies to interpret these validity scales. For ICN and INF, the simulations have involved the generation of random responses to the PAI, and the manual describes cutoff scores that will successfully identify the vast majority of such profiles as invalid (Morey, 1991). For the NIM and PIM scales, a number of studies have been performed in which subjects were instructed to manage their impressions in either a positive or negative direction. Comparison of profiles for actual respondents (normal subjects or clinical subjects) and the response style simulation groups generally demonstrates a clear separation between scores of the actual respondents and the simulated responses (Cashel, Rogers, Sewell, & Martin-Cannici, 1995; Morey, 1991; Rogers, Ornduff & Sewell, 1993). However, these simulations studies often indicate that the recommended cutoffs for NIM and PIM (92T and 68T, respectively) may be somewhat conservative when the base rate of distortion is relatively high. Under such conditions, Morey identified an optimal cutoff of 84T for NIM and 57T for PIM.

A second strategy for the evaluation of profile validity is based on the consideration of various configural elements of the PAI profile. For example, the Defensiveness and Malingering Indices (Morey, 1996) consist of features that tend to be observed only in distorted profiles. Use of discriminant function analysis to identify defensive (Cashel et al., 1995) and malingered (Rogers, Sewell, Morey, & Ustad, in press) responding has also been found to yield good identification rates that cross-validate across different studies (Morey, 1996). Finally, the specific issue of defensiveness about alcohol and/or drug use has been addressed with a regression-based strategy that seeks to identify underreporting of substance use, based on various configural predictors (Morey, 1996).

Each of these strategies should be used to supplement the validity scales to ensure that the PAI profile can be interpreted in a straightforward manner.

In teaching the art of detecting distorted profiles, I often find it necessary to reintroduce trainees to Bayes Theorem and the classic article by Meehl and Rosen (1955) on the importance of situational base rates. In order to use the strategies described previously, the trainee must understand the influence that the a priori probability of distorted responding will have on the utility of any decision rules for the identification of such responding. There are several situations where the likelihood of distorted responding is quite high; these situations include (but are not limited to) preemployment screenings, fitness-for-duty evaluations, child custody suits, criminal dispositions, and involuntary hospitalization or treatment decisions. In such situations, the examiner must be particularly alert to the possibility of distortion, and should be willing to use more liberal cutting scores (such as the empirically derived PIM cutting score of 57T) in drawing conclusions about profile validity. In such instances, the supplementation of PAI profile information with concurrent reports from family members, peers, documents or records, and other psychological and/or laboratory testing is of particular value.

STEP 5. CONFIGURAL USE OF THE PAI

The highest level of interpretation of the PAI lies at the level of the profile configuration. Traditionally the premise behind multidimensional inventories such as the PAI has been that the *combination* of information provided by the multiple scales is greater than any of its parts. Because of the complexity of the myriad of potential interactions within this configural information, the mastery of configural PAI interpretation tends to come largely from experience and it is quite difficult to teach in a didactic fashion. It is at this point in learning the PAI that case studies become informative; without a solid grasp of the material described in the previous four steps, the trainee is not prepared to make use of case data. However, I find that in using case material for training purposes, it is important to specify precisely what questions the PAI needs to address for that case. In this way, the trainee will learn to recognize how different elements of the profile configuration can be used to address diverse referral issues.

One of the simplest and most time-honored approaches to teaching profile configuration is the codetype, a shorthand code that refers to the two highest scale elevations obtained in a given protocol. In my opinion, this is one of the *least* useful ways to approach profile configuration. Such codes provide an exhaustive but poorly focused way to understand test results. Two-point codes also ignore the wealth of information provided by other test scales. These codes fail to capture the heterogeneity of individuals who manifest the same code, particularly given the myriad number of PAI subscale configurations that might underlie elevations on any two particular full scales. Finally, the reliability of the small differences that can determine a 2-point code on any multiscale psychological instrument is typically suspect. As a result, I encourage a more focused use of scale configuration information, using this information to address specific questions rather than providing an omnibus catalog of possible outcomes. The following sections describe some of these specific issues and provide examples of relevant configural information for each.

Diagnosis.   One of the critical tasks of any clinical instrument is provide information relevant to clarifying potential diagnoses. Because of its subscale structure, the PAI is a rich source of diagnostic hypotheses for many emotional disorders, even where there is no direct scale counterpart. For example, although there is no PAI scale for the diagnosis of "Dependent Personality Disorder," the major elements of this disorder, such as interpersonal submissiveness (low DOM) and poor self-esteem (low MAN-G), can be ascertained quite clearly from the PAI profile. Providing a description of all possible diagnostic inferences is beyond the scope of this chapter. However, in learning to make such inferences from the PAI, three sources of information are particularly useful: diagnostic group mean profiles; actuarial functions; and configural decision rules derived from the *DSM–IV* (*Diagnostic and Statistical Manual of Mental Disorders*, 4th ed.) criteria.

With respect to mean profiles, the PAI manual (Morey, 1991) presents the average profiles derived from 24 different groups, isolated on the basis of a particular diagnosis. The similarity of any individual's PAI to these mean profiles can be calculated, and in fact the PAI interpretive software performs these calculations. However, trainees need to be cautioned against an overreliance on mean diagnostic profiles for interpreting the PAI, because they do not represent a "prototypic" profile for a diagnosis, but rather they present the "lowest common denominator" for the diagnosis. Because of the extensive comorbidity among emotional disorders and the inherent heterogeneity of individuals with any given diagnosis, the resulting mean profile for a given diagnosis may not fully capture the elements of the PAI that most reflect that disorder. Thus, the mean profile is only a beginning point in understand the relationship between diagnoses and profile configurations.

Various analyses have also been conducted to identify actuarial decision rules for diagnostic assignment. In one example of such efforts, LOGIT analyses were performed to construct models of diagnostic decisions provided by clinicians on patients who completed the PAI. These LOGIT functions, described in Morey (1996), were incorporated into the PAI computer interpretation program in an attempt to realize the promise of computerized actuarial interpretation. However, only diagnoses where adequate numbers of subjects (at least five for each predictor variable) were investigated with LOGIT analyses. In addition, the calculations are sufficiently complex to hinder use of such functions in routine clinical contexts outside of their use in computer interpretation. Nonetheless, the composition of such functions is often informative in illustrating important points about the diagnosis and its PAI profile. One important aspect of these functions is that they involve contrasts between a particular diagnostic group, compared to clinical subjects as a whole, rather than comparing them to normal controls. Thus, the parameters of these functions can be useful guides to make discriminations among different clinical groups, facilitating the discriminant validity of any resulting diagnoses.

Finally, conceptual configural rules have also been developed for a number of the *DSM–IV* diagnostic categories; these rules were designed to match the *DSM* criteria with corresponding constructs on the PAI, and were also incorporated into the computer interpretation program. By tapping many key elements of psychopathology, the subscale structure of the test is well-suited for application to the diagnostic criteria in the *DSM–IV*. For example, the criteria for Avoidant Personality Disorder involve chronic social withdrawal driven by marked social anxiety, features that may be directly ascertained from combinations of ARD-P, WRM, ANX (Anxiety), and/or SCZ-S (Schizophrenia: Social Detatchment). Morey (1996) provided summary tables that list relevant scales to be considered for each major diagnostic category. It should be recognized that certain aspects of these decision rules were also based on trends observed in the standardization samples of the PAI and there is clearly a need for cross-validational research. However, these rules are in keeping with the nature of the symptomatology specified in the *DSM* and as such they provide a useful starting point in identifying particular disorders.

Self-Concept. The view that people have of themselves can play a critical role in determining their behavior. On the PAI, there are three clinical subscales that are valuable to assess different important facets of the self-concept, and trainees are encouraged to examine the configuration of these scales. One such facet, *self-esteem*, reflects the evaluative component of the self-perception: Do people like themselves or do they dislike themselves? Are they the way they want to be, or would they prefer to be very different? The most direct measure of this self-facet on the PAI is the MAN-G subscale, with high scorers manifesting high, perhaps even inflated self-esteem. A second facet, *self-efficacy*, reflects a sense of personal competence and perceived control (Bandura, 1977). The DEP-C (Depression:Cognitive) scale provides information relevant to the person's perceived effectiveness; high scorers see themselves as ineffective in controlling the environment to meet their needs. The third facet involves the *stability* of the self-concept; is it fixed and enduring, or is it unstable and highly vulnerable to environmental events? For example, two people who each have quite high self-esteem may differ substantially in the secureness of this esteem; one person may be capable of maintaining high self-esteem in the face of considerable evidence to the contrary, whereas the other's self-esteem may be quite vulnerable to even the slightest "blow to the ego." BOR-I (Borderline Features:Identity Problems) provides a measure of the stability of the self, with high scorers having the more variable and vulnerable self-concepts. Different configurations of these three scales have quite different meanings; for example, an individual with both MAN-G and BOR-I elevated may have an inflated self-image that is fragile and very responsive to external insult, whereas if BOR-I were within normal limits, the self-esteem would most likely be impervious to feedback from others.

Interpersonal Style.   An individual's interpersonal style constitutes a significant portion of their personality. The way that a person relates to others is certainly associated with overall adjustment, although there are a variety of ways in which people interact with one another and there is no one "healthy" style that is necessary for personal effectiveness. However, a person's style can interact with aspects of the situation to produce outcomes both desirable and undesirable; for example, a person who is aloof and retiring may do quite well in a job requiring computer-programming skills, but the same person may be uncomfortable and ineffective at cocktail parties. In a clinical context, this person might respond quite differently to some therapies or therapists than another person, who is more outgoing. The interpersonal style thus represents a significant aspect of the personality that can mediate a number of clinical concerns.

The two interpersonal scales, DOM and WRM, represent the core of the assessment of interpersonal style with the PAI. The selection of these two dimensions was based on the interpersonal circumplex model originally formulated by Leary (1957) and elaborated on by many others. This model of interpersonal behavior involves two orthogonal dimensions that, considered in combination, characterize one's preferred manner of interacting with others. Typical configural use of such scales involves combining them into four "quadrants": a warm, dominating quadrant; a cold, dominating quadrant; a cold, submitting quadrant; and a warm, submitting quadrant. For each of the quadrants, stereotypic behaviors can be described for trainees; for example, a prototype for the "warm control" quadrant would be parenting behavior, where typically some degree of control is exerted, but the person is also interested in maintaining the attachment relationship. A particularly interesting aspect of circumplex theory is the principle of *complementarity*, which should be described to the trainee. This principle governs the expected nature of interpersonal transactions within the circumplex; every interpersonal behavior has a complement, which is the natural interpersonal reaction to a given event or transaction. Complementary behaviors are the same on the warmth dimension, and on the opposing end of the dominance dimension. For example, if a person controls people (high DOM) in a friendly (high WRM) way, the complementary reaction is for people to submit in a friendly way. On the other hand, if a person controls others in a hostile and uncaring way, the complementary reaction is to submit, but in a hostile manner. This property of the interpersonal dimensions is useful in allowing one to predict the types of interpersonal behaviors a person is likely to evoke in others.

The DOM and WRM scales have nearly identical distributions in clinical and normal subjects. Thus, trainees should understand that these two scales capture variation across normal personality traits, and that normals vary widely on these dimensions, as do individuals presenting for treatment. On these scales, high scores may be problematic, and low scores may also reflect problems; the interpersonal scales are probably the most bipolar of all PAI scales in that the low and high extremes are equally interpretable, and have equal potential for problems. Generally, it appears that obtaining higher scores on WRM are preferable, because this scale is typically correlated with indicators of favorable adjustment. However, high scores on WRM could well reflect a person who is sacrificing too much to maintain attachment relationships, and is thus ineffective in interpersonal relationships in many ways. Low scores on WRM could indicate a variety of interpersonal problems, and there are several other PAI referents that can further clarify the nature of these problems, including BOR-N (Borderline Features:Negative Relationships, for marked interpersonal conflict), SCZ-S (Schizophrenia:Social Detachment, for social disinterest), ARD-P (Anxiety-Related Disorders:Phobias, for social anxiety), ANT-E (Antisocial Features:Egocentricity, for capacity for empathy), PAR-R (Paranoia:Resentment, for interpersonal bitterness), and PAR-P (Paranoia:Persecution, for suspiciousness and touchiness).

Environmental Perception.   Personality assessment instruments have typically focused on identifying internal aspects of the individual, and yet it is clear that a person's behavior is substantially influenced by aspects of the environment. Unfortunately, assessment of the situational environment is very difficult because situations can vary in nearly infinite ways. The constructs underlying the two PAI scales that assess environmental influences were selected on the basis of the research literature studying these influences on physical and mental health, as well as the examination of the factor structure of the relatively few scales available for the assessment of the environment. Two aspects of environment emerged from these investigations. One aspect involved the predictability, organization, and structure of the person's surroundings, ranging from fairly predictable environments to highly changeable and very stressful kinds of environments. The second aspect involved the availability and quality of supports in the environment.

The STR (Treatment:Stress) and NON (Treatment:Nonsupport) scales provide an assessment of respondents' perception of their environment. It is useful to think about these scales as a configuration, because their combination can reveal whether the social support system is seen as an asset in coping with a stressful environment (high STR, low NON) or conversely, whether it is the primary source of stress (high NON, lower STR) for the respondent. In the latter instance, it is helpful to supplement this configuration with indicators of more generalized resentment, such as PAR-R or PAR-H (Paranoia:Hypervigilance) to clarify whether the current conflicts are situational, or whether they may perhaps represent a more enduring perceptual style.

Harm to Self or Others.   The assessment of suicide and/or assaultive potential are perhaps the most critical of all clinical evaluation tasks. Unfortunately, they are also some of the most difficult tasks, because both involve the prediction of imminent and rather low base rate behaviors, which are extremely difficult for instruments with anything short of perfect validity (Meehl & Rosen, 1955). The PAI provides several types of information that represent a valuable beginning point for identifying such behaviors, but given the difficulty of the task and the critical nature of the issue, it is particularly important that trainees understand the need to supplement the PAI with additional information for clinical decisions in this area.

The obvious starting points on the PAI for evaluating potential for self-harm or for violence are the SUI (Treatment:Suicidal Ideation) scale and the AGG (Treatment:Aggression) scale, respectively. Each of these scales provides information about behavioral history and ideation related to these issues. Although such information is central in the evaluation of risk for suicide or assault, there are other elements in the PAI profile that can also be helpful in assessing acute risk for these behaviors. Morey (1996) provided two indices, the Suicide Potential Index and the Violence Potential Index, that operationalize various features from the research literature that are empirically or conceptually related to such behaviors. For example, a lack of social support, operationalized by NON, is included on the Suicide Potential Index because this factor exacerbates the risk represented by suicidal ideation due to the lessened likelihood of intervention during times of particular crisis. The configurations represented in these indices are good illustrations to the trainee of the utility of going beyond single-scale elevations in making clinical inferences.

Treatment Issues. Treatment planning is a critical issue for psychological assessment, yet it is a daunting one because there is little empirical evidence to definitively support specific treatments for specific problems or patient types. However, as noted by Morey and Henry (1994), the PAI has particular promise for refining treatment-related decision making because it provides important information relevant to the treatment process —choice of setting, need for medications, suitability for psychotherapy, selection of therapeutic targets, and assessment of change. The Morey and Henry chapter offers a number of guidelines to help the clinician use PAI data to make many commonly faced treatment-related decisions.

The starting point in treatment planning with the PAI is the RXR (Treatment: Rejection) scale, because this scale assesses a variety of aspects of motivation for treatment: recognition of a need for change, candidness about one's difficulties, introspectiveness, and an openness to new ideas or approaches. High scorers on RXR are likely to show little interest in or commitment to treatment. It is important that the trainee understand that the normative referent for RXR (as for all PAI scales) was a *community* sample, where general interest in psychological treatment would be expected to be low relative to most clinical settings. As a result, a score of 50T on this scale is substantially above the mean of what would be expected in clinical situations, where mean scores are typically around 40T. Thus, scores that may appear to the novice to be within normal limits (such as 50T) will in fact indicate a very tenuous commitment to treatment.

Although motivation for treatment is an important factor in treatment outcome, the novice user will often inaccurately interpret RXR as a straightforward indicator of treatment prognosis. However, there are countless patient, treatment, and interaction variables that will determine treatment outcome, of which motivation is merely one. Many individuals with very low RXR scores will be at great risk for poor treatment outcome. For example, a person can recognize their need to change, and can be quite desperate for help, yet they can have problems such as chaotic social environments, marked interpersonal dysfunction, and poor impulse control that combine to yield a guarded prognosis. Morey (1996) described a number of these features, which are combined into an aggregate form, and are known as the Treatment Process Index, that can constitute considerable challenges to successful treatment.

CONCLUSION

Learning to use the PAI is relatively simple in certain respects and yet difficult in other respects. The emphasis on content and discriminant validity makes the meaning and interpretation of the scales relatively straightforward; the content of scale items generally corresponds to the name of the scale, so if a person obtains an elevated score on DEP it is safe to conclude that the person is reporting experiencing signs and symptoms of depression. However, because of the relatively recent introduction of the PAI, the configural power of the instrument is only beginning to be understood and tapped. As this chapter is written, actuarial checklists are being introduced that may be of assistance in identifying individuals who are attempting to distort their self-presentation, those who deny substance misuse, those at risk for suicide or violence, and those who may be particularly difficult to engage in therapy. As these indices gather cross-validation support, they may provide a valuable supplement to the standard PAI scales, in many cases providing alternative means of answering some of the most challenging issues in assessment.

Ultimately, the experienced user should become increasingly prone to viewing clinical problems within a PAI framework. When listening to a discussion of a clinical case for whom no PAI was available, they should consider what particular aspects of the case that PAI profile data could be helpful in addressing. When reading a research article about the description, etiology, or treatment of some clinical condition, they should translate the relevant variables into the language of PAI scales. In doing so, their skill in the application of the PAI will increase commensurate with their knowledge base of clinical problems. In this way, the personal database of the interpreter can grow, along with the empirical literature on the test itself. One hopes the developing skills of the trainee will serve as a catalyst for these new developments, because there are as many hypotheses remaining to be tested as there are clients in need of assessment.

REFERENCES

Alterman, A. I., Zaballero, A. R., Lin, M. M., Siddiqui, N., Brown, L. S., Rutherford, M. J., & McDermott, P.A. (1995). Personality Assessment Inventory (PAI) scores of lower-socioeconomic African American and Latino methadone maintenance patients. *Assessment, 2*, 91–100.

Bandura, A. (1977). Self-efficacy: Toward a unifying theory of behavioral change. *Psychological Review, 84*, 191–215.

Boyle, G. J., & Lennon, T. J. (1994) Examination of the reliability and validity of the Personality Assessment Inventory. *Journal of Psychopathology and Behavior Assessment, 16*, 173–188.

Cashel, M. L., Rogers, R., Sewell, K., & Martin-Cannici, C. (1995). The Personality Assessment Inventory and the detection of defensiveness. *Assessment, 2*, 333–342.

Cronbach, L. J., & Meehl, P. E. (1955). Construct validity in psychological tests. *Psychological Bulletin, 52*, 281–302.

Dawes, R., & Corrigan, B. (1974). The robust beauty of improper linear models in clinical decision making. *Psychological Bulletin, 81*, 95–106.

Jackson, D. N. (1971). The dynamics of structured personality tests. *Psychological Review, 78*, 229–248.

Leary, T. (1957). *Interpersonal diagnosis of personality*. New York: Ronald.

Loevinger, J. (1957). Objective tests as instruments of psychological theory. *Psychological Reports, 3*, 635–694.

Meehl, P. E., & Rosen, A. (1955). Antecedent probability and the efficiency of psychometric signs, patterns, or cutting scores. *Psychological Bulletin, 52*, 194–216.

Morey, L. C. (1991). *The Personality Assessment Inventory professional manual*. Odessa, FL: Psychological Assessment Resources.

Morey, L. C. (1996). *An interpretive guide to the Personality Assessment Inventory*. Odessa, FL: Psychological Assessment Resources.

Morey, L. C., & Henry, W. (1994). Personality Assessment Inventory. In M. Maruish (Ed.), *The use of psychological testing for treatment planning and outcome assessment* (pp. 185–216). Hillsdale, NJ: Lawrence Erlbaum Associates.

Rogers, R., Flores, J., Ustad, K., & Sewell, K. W. (1995). Initial validation of the Personality Assessment Inventory-Spanish version with clients from Mexican American communities. *Journal of Personality Assessment, 64*, 340–348.

Rogers, R., Ornduff, S. R., & Sewell, K. (1993). Feigning specific disorders: A study of the Personality Assessment Inventory (PAI). *Journal of Personality Assessment, 60*, 554–560.

Rogers, R., Sewell, K. W., Morey, L. C., & Ustad, K.L. (in press). Detection of feigned mental disorders on the Personality Assessment Inventory: A discriminant analysis. *Journal of Personality Assessment*.

Schinka, J. A. (1995). Personality Assessment Inventory scale characteristics and factor structure in the assessment of alcohol dependency. *Journal of Personality Assessment, 64*, 101–111.

Schinka, J. A., & Borum, R. (1993). Readability of adult psychopathology inventories. *Psychological Assessment, 5*, 384–386.

13

Teaching the Rorschach Comprehensive System

Irving B. Weiner
University of South Florida

The Comprehensive System developed by Exner (J. E. Exner, 1991, 1993; J. E. Exner & Weiner, 1995) is a psychometrically sound and interpretively rich approach to Rorschach assessment that takes time to master but repays many times over an investment in doing so. Those who teach the Comprehensive System should prepare their students for both the pain and the gain that await them. Teachers can also help to focus and sustain their students' commitment to learning this Rorschach approach by informing them of how and why the Comprehensive System originated, what purposes it serves, the way in which it generates both empirically and conceptually based interpretations, and the directions it is likely to take in the future.

These items of information touch on the nature, history, rationale, psychometric foundations, utility, and future of the Comprehensive System and elucidate the many reasons why it is worth learning and using. The present chapter is designed as an outline of these topics to assist instructors in introducing the Comprehensive System to their students, delineating the basic principles of this approach to the inkblot method, documenting its value and utility, and citing relevant sources in the literature. The discussion focuses on what students ought to know and will benefit from learning, and the chapter concludes with a few teaching tips that may help instructors promote the enthusiasm and effectiveness with which their students absorb, remember, and utilize information about the Rorschach.

ORIGINS OF THE COMPREHENSIVE SYSTEM

The Rorschach Inkblot Method was first published as a formal assessment procedure in 1921 by Hermann Rorschach, a Swiss psychiatrist, in a book titled

Psychodiagnostics: A Diagnostic Test Based on Perception (1921/1942). Although the Rorschach has come to be known as a "projective test," the instrument was designed and intended for use primarily as a perceptual task and not as a means of analyzing fantasy. Rorschach was concerned mainly with using the ways in which subjects organize and structure their perceptual impressions of the inkblots to identify personality characteristics and types of mental disorders. Although he was psychoanalytically informed and in fact served as vice-president of the Swiss Psychoanalytic Society, he paid little attention to the content of what subjects saw in the blots and did not invoke the concept of projection in his work. To the contrary, Rorschach (1921/1942) stated that "The test cannot be considered as a means of delving into the unconscious" (p. 123).

Nevertheless, Rorschach raised the possibility of using the inkblots to measure associational as well as perceptual processes by also saying, "Certain tendencies in the subconscious are occasionally revealed by comparison of the content of the interpretation with the rest of the findings" (Rorschach, 1921/1942, p. 123). Aronow, Reznikoff, and Moreland (1995) recently suggested that Rorschach would have shifted from his primarily structural approach to a more thematic approach to his measure had he not died at the age of 37, just 1 year after *Psychodiagnostics* appeared. However this may be, the point is that Rorschach did not survive to direct and systemize the further development of his measure. Instead, in 1922 the future of the Rorschach Inkblot Method fell into other hands in which, over the next 50 years, the instrument was promulgated in many different ways, in many different parts of the world.

Stories of Hermann Rorschach as a person and of the development and dissemination of his inkblot method are fascinating bits of history that fortunately have been well told (see Ellenberger, 1954; J. E. Exner, 1993; Schwarz, 1996). Lacking information about this history, many psychologists in the United States grew up professionally thinking of the Rorschach as an American product, as if the inkblots lay in some dusty Swiss drawer from 1922 until they saw daylight in a 1930 article by Beck, which was the first English-language publication on the instrument. In truth, however, word of Rorschach's method spread to many corners of the globe during the 1920s, and professionals came to Zurich from far and wide to talk with Rorschach's colleagues and take a set of plates home with them. As a consequence, Rorschach publications appeared not only in German but also in Spanish, Russian, and Japanese prior to Beck's 1930 article in English. Discussions of the history and use of Rorschach assessment in many different countries can be found in the 1993 to 1997 volumes of *Rorschachiana: Yearbook of the International Rorschach Society*.

Initially, most of the early Rorschach scholars in various parts of the world hewed closely to Hermann Rorschach's methods, as did Beck in the United States. However, as Rorschach acknowledged in his text, the method was far from complete when he published it. Hence it was not long before influential persons who were now determining the destiny of the instrument began to modify and supplement it to accommodate new research findings and advances in conceptualization. These revisions and additions produced differences between countries in preferred ways of using the Rorschach and led in the United

States to the emergence of five distinct systems of administering, scoring, and interpreting the test, namely, the systems of Beck, Klopfer, Hertz, Piotrowski, and Rapaport/Schafer. The basic features of these five systems were described by J. E. Exner in a 1969 book called *The Rorschach Systems*, a recent review of which by Handler (1996) provides an excellent summary of Exner's observations at the time and the impact they had on the development of the Comprehensive System.

In comparing these five American Rorschach systems and talking personally with their authors, Exner discovered substantial differences in their approach to the Rorschach. He also learned, to his dismay, that there was little prospect of these systematizers reconciling their differences to produce an integrated Rorschach system they would all endorse. To make matters worse, survey data collected at the time indicated that differences among psychologists in how they were actually using the Rorschach extended far beyond allegiance to one or another of these five incompatible systems (J. E. Exner & D. E. Exner, 1972). A substantial percentage of Rorschach assessors were not following any of the five systems faithfully, but instead were employing idiosyncratic combinations of elements selected from various systems on the basis of what they personally considered worthwhile. Hence, there were not just five Rorschach systems in use in the United States, but instead almost as many Rorschach methods as there were psychologists using the instrument.

Exner found further that many assessors had discarded any coding system at all in favor of relying on an exclusively thematic approach in their Rorschach interpretation. This abandonment of formal evaluation of the perceptual characteristics of Rorschach responses was typically tied to a psychoanalytic emphasis on the associational characteristics of responses. Psychoanalytic perspectives on the Rorschach emerged in the United States in the 1940s and 1950s, following the first description of the inkblot method as a "projective" test by Frank in 1939. Significantly, however, none of the pioneering figures in psychoanalytic approaches to the Rorschach subscribed to sole reliance on thematic imagery in the interpretive process. To the contrary, Klopfer (B. Klopfer, Ainsworth, W. G. Klopfer, & Holt, 1954), Lindner (1950), Rapaport (Rapaport, Gill, & Schafer, 1946/1968), Schafer (1954), and Schachtel (1966) all firmly endorsed careful consideration of both the structural-perceptual and thematic-associational features of Rorschach responses. Combined structural and thematic analysis has continued to the present day to characterize leading psychoanalytic contributions to the Rorschach literature, both in the United States and abroad (e.g., Baba, 1995; Blatt, 1990; Giambelluca, Parisi, & Pes, 1995; Leichtman, 1996; Lerner, 1991; Lunazzi de Jubany, 1992; Smith, 1994).

At any rate, troubled by what he had learned and concerned that the day was approaching when one psychologist's Rorschach would no longer be recognizable to any other psychologist, Exner came to this preliminary conclusion in his 1969 book: "It seems more reliable to approach the Rorschach problem through a research integration of the systems if the test is to survive and flourish in psychodiagnostic work" (p. 251). He subsequently set out to achieve this end, and thus originated the Comprehensive System. But why, one might ask, was Exner so concerned, and why was there need for change? What fault is there in the Rorschach Inkblot Method having proliferated during its first 50 years into numerous systems and countless individual variations on these systems? If assessors feel satisfied with their individual way of using the Rorschach and are able to form clinically relevant impressions of the people they examine, what does it matter that very few of them use the test in quite the same way?

The answer to such questions lies in the generally recognized value of combining idiographic and nomothetic perspectives in the practice of clinical psychology. Both the subjectivity of random individual impression and the objectivity of systematic group comparisons contribute essential information in efforts to understand and help people. Although subjective impressions of individual uniqueness enrich clinical practice and enhance psychologists' capacities to be helpful, subjectivity alone is insufficient to sustain clinical psychology and psychodiagnosis as a science as well as a profession (Weiner, 1983, 1991). To avoid foundering in subjectivity and being mistaken for artists or philosophers, then, assessment psychologists need to introduce a substantial modicum of objectivity into their projective testing.

The Rorschach was created as an objective measure of perceptual structuring, and Rorschach's original monograph contains numerous tables of data indicating the obtained frequencies of his coded variables among various subject groups. However, aside from the countless variations in Rorschach technique based on examiners' individual preferences, prior to 1974 even the major Rorschach systems included many features of administration and scoring that had been adopted on the basis of subjective impression rather than objective evidence. Worse yet, many features of these systems that did have a demonstrable empirical basis differed from one system to the next. The general lack of objectivity with which the Rorschach was being used was thus compounded by an almost total lack of systematic objectivity.

Psychodiagnosticians paid a very steep price for this lack of systematic objectivity during the first 50 years of Rorschach testing. Perhaps only because of its superb capacities to identify psychological structures and tap personality dynamics did the instrument survive the chaos that characterized its use. Most important, the absence of systematic objectivity in Rorschach administration and coding severely limited cumulative research. Exner's examination of the Beck, Klopfer, Hertz, Piotrowski, and Rapaport/Schafer systems revealed that differences among them led to variations in response totals, types of responses given, and obtained summary scores. The Rorschach must be administered and coded in exactly the same way in research studies if there is to be any reasonable basis for comparing, contrasting, or combining their results. Rarely was such uniformity in place on which researchers could depend in trying to learn from and build on the published work of their colleagues.

The constraints on cumulative research imposed by randomness and subjectivity in Rorschach methodology was thus responsible over the years for restricted opportunities to examine the psychometric properties of the instrument. Without standardization to promote systematic objectivity, there was little chance of demonstrating the reliability of the Rorschach, validating the meaning and utility of its variables, or amassing a useful normative database. In the absence of such psychometric foundations for Rorschach testing, credibility as a scientific procedure and respectability as a professional endeavor were elusive, and generations of Rorschach enthusiasts, unless talking to each other, spent much of their time warding off criticism, attack, and even ridicule. That is why Exner was rightly concerned, and that is why something had to be done.

PURPOSES OF THE COMPREHENSIVE SYSTEM

Exner developed the Comprehensive System specifically to establish the systematic objectivity previously lacking in Rorschach assessment and thereby to put an end to 50 years of brilliant promise dimmed by chaotic implementation. He focused first on establishing three essential pillars of the Comprehensive System: standardized administration, objective and reliable coding, and a representative normative database.

Beginning with administration, Exner examined the methods used in the major systems and determined that the spare and simple approach originally employed by Hermann Rorschach was sufficient to generate an adequate protocol and was also likely to minimize unintended examiner influence (J. E. Exner, 1993). He then provided detailed guidelines for conducting the free association and inquiry phases of the administration. Examiners may prefer other methods, but there is extremely little room in the Comprehensive System for variability or examiner discretion in administration: You either use the Comprehensive System administration exactly as prescribed, or you are not using the Comprehensive System. This means that practitioners and researchers can expect that Rorschachs administered according to the System will in fact be the same test and will contain essentially the same responses as would have been obtained by any examiner using the System.

Turning to the coding of responses, Exner drew on past contributions by assessing the adequacy of scoring categories and indices proposed by many different Rorschach scholars. For inclusion in the Comprehensive System, these categories and indices had to be sufficiently objective to lend themselves to clear statements of criteria for scoring them, and they had to achieve substantial interrater agreement among independent scorers who had received a moderate amount of training. In its present form, the Comprehensive System comprises (a) many codes originally proposed by Rorschach and other early systematizers, (b) numerous codes previously developed as features of specific Rorschach scales, such as developmental quality scoring, and (c) various new and revised codes originally developed for or subsequently added to the Comprehensive System (J. E. Exner, 1993).

With a standardized administration and an objective and reliable coding scheme in place, the way was prepared for collecting reference data on various populations. Over time the Comprehensive System database grew to include information on 700 adult nonpatients stratified to represent the 1980 U.S. census; 1,390 nonpatient children and adolescents ages 5 to 16 years; and patient reference groups of 320 hospitalized schizophrenics, 315 hospitalized depressives, 440 diagnostically unspecified outpatients, and 180 outpatients with character disorders (J. E. Exner, 1993).

Hence the main purpose served by the Comprehensive System is the embodiment of the Rorschach Inkblot Method in a systematically objective procedure for collecting, codifying, and standardizing test responses. Achieving this end overcame previous obstacles to cumulative research and made possible studies with the Comprehensive System that have demonstrated beyond a doubt that the Rorschach is a reliable assessment instrument with considerable validity for many important purposes (see Weiner, 1996, 1997). With reliability, validity, and a normative database in hand, Rorschach assessors at last gained some psychometric respectability for their instrument, and they also became able to formulate clinical conclusions with more confidence than was previously possible and to communicate these conclusions with greater effect. Nowhere is this progress more visible than in the area of forensic practice, where survey data indicate that Comprehensive System Rorschach testimony is rarely challenged and almost always admitted into evidence (Meloy, 1991; Weiner, Exner, & Sciara, 1996).

The preceding observations indicate why assessment psychologists should bother to learn the Comprehensive System, conform slavishly to its guidelines for administration, and struggle to master its detailed and complex scoring. Succinctly put, doing so provides a systematically objective approach to the Rorschach that can be utilized productively in research, applied with confidence in clinical practice, and endorsed professionally in the expectation of thereby gaining respect from colleagues and appreciation from service users. Beyond systematic objectivity in administration and scoring, moreover, a fully coded set of Comprehensive System data, appropriately arrayed in a Sequence of Scores and Structural Summary, facilitates an efficient, incisive, and wide-ranging interpretive process that generates a great deal of information about personality functioning.

The next section of this chapter describes the empirical and conceptual foundations of Comprehensive System interpretation. Before proceeding, it should be noted that the emphasis to this point on systematic objectivity does not mean that Rorschach assessment necessarily ends with the Comprehensive System. There are structural indices not included in the Comprehensive System that have shown promise of being reliable and useful, and there are approaches to thematic analysis beyond Comprehensive System guidelines that can generate intriguing speculations about personality functioning. However, in whatever way examiners choose to develop their work with a Rorschach protocol, they do well to begin with the psychometrically sound foundation that Comprehensive System procedures provide.

EMPIRICAL AND CONCEPTUAL FEATURES
OF INTERPRETATION

The Comprehensive System was initially designed to emphasize empirically based guidelines for administering, coding, and interpreting the Rorschach.

Nevertheless, subsequent development of the System has involved equal attention to conceptualizing both the response process and various strategies for administration, scoring, and interpretation. With respect to the response process, J. E. Exner (1993) used information-processing and decision-making models to describe how subjects formulate and articulate their impressions of what the inkblots might be. According to this conceptualization, subjects deliver responses after a series of mental events in which they (a) encode the stimulus properties of the blots, (b) compare a gestalt of these stimulus properties with gestalts stored in their memory to determine which ones they resemble, (c) select from these resemblances those having the closest fit, (d) decide which of these close fits to report and which to censor for some reason, and (e) then express these possible and acceptable responses in a manner shaped by their state and trait personality characteristics. This modeling of the response process helps to explain in psychological terms how the Rorschach works and to suggest lines of general psychological research with the instrument, especially from a cognitive frame of reference (see Acklin, 1994).

The Comprehensive System administration was developed not only with an eye to standardization, but, as previously mentioned, also as a conceptually sensible way of minimizing examiner influence on subjects' responses. Avoiding the subject's direct line of vision by using a side-by-side or catty-corner administration is a case in point. As for the coding scheme adopted in the System, the search for objectively defined and reliably scorable categories was accompanied by an emphasis on codes that have meaningful correlates in aspects of personality functioning. Texture (T) is scored because it is known to relate to the capacity for intimate attachment to others, Anthropology (Ay) is scored because it is associated with intellectualization, Aggressive (AG) is scored because it suggests physical or verbal assertiveness, and so forth. Some presently coded variables are better understood than others with respect to the personality processes they measure, and efforts are ongoing to narrow existing gaps in conceptualization. In the past, such easily codeable content categories as Vocation (Vo) and Architecture (Ar) were discarded because no reliable corollaries could be found for them. Similarly, it is unlikely that any new scores or scoring refinements will be added to the System until they have clearly demonstrated both interscorer agreement and some personality correlates that are not already adequately measured by existing System variables.

As these observations indicate, the Comprehensive System has never been a closed or static approach to the Rorschach. Just as Rorschach had done in 1921, Exner in 1974 published the first edition of his basic text with the notation that his system was by no means finished. Over the years new data and improved conceptualization have led to numerous revisions in Comprehensive System coding, and there will no doubt be further revisions in the future. As has always been the case, however, changes in the System will never be casual or whimsical, but instead formal, gradual, systematic, data based, and conceptually informed.

For interpretation as well as administration and coding, the essence of the Rorschach Comprehensive System is an unflagging commitment to empirically documented inferences that also make conceptual sense and serve some useful purpose (see Weiner, 1986). The interpretive process begins with an objective determination of whether a protocol is valid. Retest data indicate that stability coefficients for Rorschach trait variables fall below an acceptable level for reliability when records contain fewer than 14 responses. Like any measure that is too short to be reliable, a brief (R < 14) Rorschach protocol does not provide an adequate basis for valid interpretation. This does not mean that brief records are necessarily worthless. Exner and Weiner (1995) pointed out that certain dramatic features of brief records may in some cases provide important information about a subject's personality functioning. Generally speaking, however, empirical evidence provides compelling reason to refrain from interpreting brief protocols along the same lines that have been validated for records with 14 or more responses.

The validity of Comprehensive System interpretation springs from the emphasis on coding only variables for which behavioral correlates can be empirically demonstrated. This requirement promotes valid inferences when the presence or frequency of a particular coded variable is taken as evidence of a personality characteristic with which it is known to be associated. Thus the fact that W is coded for a global focus of attention in articulating a response means that a notable frequency of W responses in a record is likely to identify preference for a global approach to experience; the fact that minus form-quality is coded for responses involving gross misperception of the correspondence of a blot to the object it is said to resemble means that a notable frequency of minus form-quality responses is likely to identify inaccurate or distorted perception of reality; and so on.

Going beyond these basic empirical foundations, sophisticated clinical interpretation of Comprehensive System Rorschach variables requires clear understanding of how such composite indices as SCZI, DEPI, and CDI relate to various patterns of normal and abnormal behavior; how patterns of interaction among variables, such as the balance between Vista (self-criticism) and Reflections (self-aggrandizement), help to reveal complex aspects of personality dynamics; and how the kinds of overarching dispositions manifest in a high Lambda or a pervasively introversive or extratensive style can influence the import of many other features of a protocol. Such matters are elaborated in the Comprehensive System volumes, and students should be helped to appreciate that adequate attention to these complexities is part of the challenge of mastering the Comprehensive System and part of the reward of being consequently able to provide rich, relevant, and useful personality descriptions.

The guidelines addressed thus far in the chapter for an empirically justified and conceptually informed administration, coding, and interpretation of the Rorschach constitute the basic features of the Comprehensive System. Having followed these guidelines, examiners could continue with their interpretation in many different ways and still have in place a Comprehensive System foundation. However, they may want to take advantage as well of some further interpretive guidelines developed by Exner for applying the Rorschach in clinical practice. As first elaborated in 1991 (J. E. Exner, 1991), these guidelines involve (a) the grouping of Rorschach variables into clusters and (b) the formulation of interpretations according to a sequential search strategy.

Grouping Variables Into Clusters

The grouping of Rorschach variables into clusters emerged initially from a formal cluster analysis that identified seven groups of intercorrelated variables. On inspection, each of these seven clusters appeared related to a distinct aspect of personality functioning. Thus was born the Comprehensive System clustering of variables into (a) an *information-processing* section, which concerns how people pay attention to their world, (b) a *mediation* section, which involves how people perceive the objects of their attention, (c) an *ideation* section, which consists of how people think about what they perceive, (d) a *control* section, which has to do the psychological resources people have available for coping with their experience and managing stress, (e) an *affect* section, which comprises how people deal with emotional situations and how they experience and express feelings, (f) a *self-perception* section, which pertains to how people view themselves, and (g) an *interpersonal* section, which addresses how people perceive and relate to others.

Along with identifying clusters of intercorrelated structural variables that measure each of these seven components of personality functioning, Exner concluded that a subject's thematic imagery as well can shed light on some of them, especially in responses involving projection. Having previously analyzed the extent to which projection is likely to have occurred in different kinds of responses (J. E. Exner, 1989), Exner recommended close attention to the content of responses containing movement (especially human movement), perceptual distortions (i.e., minus form-quality responses), and embellishments (especially those with themes of morbidity or aggression). The thematic content of these kinds of responses was included with structural variables in the various clusters, most conspicuously in those concerned with self-perception and interpersonal perception.

Although not anticipated at the time, two very important conceptual implications emerged from this clustering of structural and thematic variables. First, the cluster approach to interpreting the Rorschach fosters a focus on describing people and personality functions rather than on test findings. Traditional Rorschach interpretation addressed a protocol with test-centered questions concerning how the subject deals with color, what the form level is, whether the record includes any striking thematic imagery, and the like. By contrast, examiners versed in a cluster-based approach to the data organize their interpretive process around such questions as "What does this Rorschach protocol indicate about how the subject is likely to manage stress and handle interpersonal relationships?" This interpretive focus on personality functions rather than on test characteristics helps prevent examiners from enshrining their techniques while losing sight of the person for whose benefit the techniques are being used. The person-centered approach fostered by a cluster-based interpretation also provides a useful guide for communicating test results. An orderly presentation of how a person attends, perceives, thinks, copes, feels, views self, and regards others constitutes a comprehensive report of personality functioning that is usually easy to understand, has obvious implications for the referral questions at issue, and demonstrates the utility of an adequate psychodiagnostic examination.

As for its second important conceptual implication, cluster-based interpretation provides for an integrated analysis of the structural and thematic data in a Rorschach protocol. Prior to 1991, traditional Rorschach interpretation as practiced according to Beck, Klopfer, Hertz, Piotrowski, and the Comprehensive System itself employed a segmented approach to interpretation. Initially the structural summary would be examined for whatever inferences it seemed to suggest, then the sequence of scores would be used to amplify these inferences, and finally the responses would be read to identify further implications of the thematic imagery in the record. In the classic literature, only Schafer in his 1954 book, *Psychoanalytic Interpretation in Rorschach Testing*, deviated from this compartmentalization of the data by attempting to look jointly at structural and thematic aspects of individual responses.

With the formal introduction of cluster-based interpretation in 1991, the Comprehensive System interpretive process changed in this respect, as did the manner in which illustrative cases are presented. Consistent with the already noted focus on personality functions rather than on test characteristics, each cluster calls for consideration of all available information relevant to the function with which the cluster is concerned. Thus, in determining what can be inferred about a subject's self-perception, all of the structural data and all of the thematic imagery bearing on feelings and attitudes toward oneself are examined conjointly. This integrative approach means that contemporary Comprehensive System interpretation of valid protocols begins with examining the first cluster and ends with examining the seventh cluster, at which point all of the test data will have been utilized. Looking separately at the structural summary, the sequence of scores, and the content of responses and presenting cases in this way have thus passed into the history of the Comprehensive System, replaced by a seven-cluster integrated analysis of all three in relation to assessing particular personality functions.

Employing a Sequential Search Strategy

With the structural and thematic data of the Rorschach grouped into clusters concerned with particular personality functions, interpretation could conceivably consist of searching these clusters in any sequence. Eventually, regardless of the order in which the clusters are searched, everything that a protocol says about a subject's personality functioning will become known. However, searching clusters randomly or routinely in the same sequence typically proves less efficient than employing a protocol-specific sequence dictated by salient features of the record itself.

For example, if there is reason to be concerned about a possible schizophrenic disorder, beginning with the affective cluster, even though often informative, will initially overlook the most critical and defining characteristic of schizophrenia spectrum disorders, namely, problems in thinking logically and coherently. If schizophrenia is at issue, the most relevant place to begin searching the data is with the ideational cluster of variables. Conversely, if there is reason to suspect a depressive disorder, the critical place to begin is not with ideational variables, although these often play a role in affective disorder, but with the affective cluster of variables.

Employing this kind of clinically informed reasoning, the sequential search strategy in the Comprehensive System was formulated around a series of key variables that, if positive, dictate a specific sequence for searching the seven clusters. The key variables themselves were identified by an empirical analysis in which they were found to be prominent in records that generated large numbers of interpretive statements related to particular clusters. After these experimental records were sorted into groups according to an identified key variable for its most interpretively prolific cluster, these several groups were examined further to determine which key variable/cluster combination yielded the second most frequent number of interpretive statements, which the third, and so on (see J. E. Exner, 1991).

Thus there emerged in association with each key variable a sequence of clusters in which it can generally be expected that the first will yield the greatest amount of interpretive information and the remaining six will yield a gradually diminishing amount of information as the search proceeds. As the final step in formulating this sequential search strategy, empirical and clinical analysis of the import of the key variables was used to establish the following order of priority for them: Schizophrenia Index (SCZI) of four or more, Depression Index (DEPI) of six or more, D score less than the $AdjD$ score, Coping Deficit Index (CDI) of four or more, $AdjD$ less than zero, Lambda of 1.00 or more, presence of Reflection responses, Introversive or Extratensive EB style, passive movements more numerous than active movements by two or more, and Hypervigilance Index (HVI) positive.

As an illustration of the sequential search strategy in practice, a record in which the Schizophrenia Index (SCZI) is four or more is interpreted by examining first the three cognitive clusters of variables (ideation, mediation, and processing) and then continuing with the control, affect, self-perception, and interpersonal perception clusters. If SCZI is less than four but the Depression Index (DEPI) is six or seven, the search begins with affect and proceeds through controls, self-perception, interpersonal perception, and the cognitive clusters. Thus, as elaborated and illustrated in current editions of the Comprehensive System texts (J. E. Exner, 1991, 1993; J. E. Exner & Weiner, 1995) the interpretive process is guided by a list of positive findings, designated as key variables, that identify a specific sequential search strategy tailored to the implications of the particular positive finding.

The sequential search strategy guided by key variables fosters a systematic but also flexible and clinically relevant approach to interpretation. With few exceptions, the initial key variable by itself directs examiners to what prove to be the most salient characteristics of a protocol and accordingly of the subject's personality functioning. Moreover, because the key variables are ordered in terms of priority, the indicated point of entry into a record appears to have some diagnostic implications in its own right. Positive findings on any of the first three key variables to be examined—SCZI > 3, DEPI > 5, and $D < AdjD$—are typically associated with symptomatic disorders involving schizophrenia spectrum, affective spectrum, or anxiety spectrum disorders, respectively. The next four key variables (CDI > 3, $AdjD < 0$, Lambda > 0.99, and Reflections > 0) tend to identify persistent and potentially maladaptive developmental or characterological orientations. The remaining key variables in the list tend, in the absence of any of the first seven key variables, to identify personality preferences or variations within the normal range. The same is true for a supplementary list of "tertiary" variables provided by Exner (1991) for working with the occasional record that does not contain any the previously noted positive key variables.

This grouping of the key and tertiary variables into three categories is by no means discrete and should not be taken as an absolute basis for distinguishing symptomatic from characterological psychopathology or abnormal from normal personality functioning. Clinically, we know that persons with symptomatic disorders in remission may show primarily characterological problems, that persons with developmental arrest or personality disorders may respond to stressful situations with symptoms of anxiety and depression, and that the boundaries between states of normal and abnormal psychological functioning are often blurred and permeable. Rorschach indices of these phenomena can be expected to reflect similar variability. Furthermore, research has not yet assessed the validity of grouping key and tertiary variables in the manner suggested here. Nevertheless, clinical conceptualization of what is known about these key variables provides some reason to believe that the point of entry into a Rorschach protocol has implications for a subject's general level of adjustment and for distinguishing between symptomatic and characterological disorders.

FUTURE DIRECTIONS

The past and present status of work with the Comprehensive System suggests that future developments involving this approach to the Rorschach will proceed in four directions: refinements and elaborations in the scoring, utilization in combination with other Rorschach scales, conjoint interpretation with other assessment instruments, and expansion of cross-cultural normative standards and applicability.

Regarding refinements and elaborations in scoring, Comprehensive System coding has been altered and expanded considerably since its introduction in 1974. Now as then, however, it can accurately be said that the System is incomplete. Numerous questions about the most reliable and useful way of coding certain kinds of responses remain unanswered, and research has suggested various amendments to the System that might eventually meet criteria for incorporation within the basic scoring scheme. Prominent examples in this regard are the Ego Impairment Index developed by Perry, Viglione, and Braff (1992) and the Aggressive Potential (AgPot) and Aggressive Past (AgPast) special content scores used by Gacono and Meloy (1994).

As for using the Comprehensive System along with other specific scales, the Rorschach Defense Scales of Cooper, Perry, and Arnow (1988) and various scales developed within an object relations frame of reference, such as Urist's (1977) Mutuality of Autonomy (MAO), appear to provide useful information in addition to interpretive statements presently gleaned from the Comprehensive System cluster search. These and other specific scales that demonstrate adequate psychometric properties may well see increased use as valuable adjuncts to a Comprehensive System interpretive process.

Traditionally, Rorschach authorities have focused their textbooks exclusively on Rorschach assessment, and only rarely has a systematic effort been made to integrate Rorschach interpretation with the findings of other assessment instruments. Such efforts at conjoint interpretation as have been made have been limited largely to clinical integration with Wechsler scales and other projective instruments, as in the work of Rapaport et al. (1968), Weiner (1966), and Hurt, Reznikoff, and Clarkin (1991). More recently, Rorschach assessors have extended integration of their findings with other test data to include relatively structured self-report inventories, especially the MMPI/MMPI–/MMPI–A. The potential benefits of integrating projective and objective test findings, long appreciated by practitioners but given little attention in the literature, have recently been addressed in numerous journal articles (Acklin, 1993; Archer & Krishnamurthy, 1993; Weiner, 1993) and in an important new book by Ganellen (1996), *Integrating the Rorschach and MMPI–2 in Personality Assessment.*

Finally, because of the systematic objectivity on which it is based, the Comprehensive System seems destined to make the Rorschach an internationalized instrument that will foster advances in both cross-cultural assessment and comparative personality research. In the United States the Comprehensive System has become the most widely used approach to Rorschach assessment. Hilsenroth and Handler (1995) reported that 75% of students learning the Rorschach in graduate programs are being taught the Comprehensive System, and Piotrowski (1996) found, in a search of recent literature, that the Comprehensive System is by far the method most commonly employed in Rorschach research studies. Abroad, the Comprehensive System is the prevalent approach in most countries in which the Rorschach is used, and assessment psychologists in many of the remaining countries are in the process of changing to the System from some previously preferred approach. Evidence to this effect can be found in contributions from around the world appearing in the volumes of *Rorschachiana* and in the published proceedings of the Paris (1990), Lisbon (1993), and Boston (1996) Congresses of the International Rorschach Society.

Worldwide application of the Rorschach is appropriate to the fact that the structural variables and the personality dimensions they measure are universal phenomena. Regarding dimensions of personality, for example, people everywhere include some who prefer to deal with their experience in a deliberative, ideational way and others who prefer instead an expressive, affective way of responding to situations. Correspondingly, wherever and to whomever the Rorschach is administered, those subjects who show a clearly introversive Experience Balance (EB) are likely to be relatively ideational people in their coping style, and those with a clearly extratensive EB are likely to be relatively expressive individuals.

However, the universal relationship between EB style and coping style does not mean that particular coping styles or other personality characteristics identified by the Rorschach will have the same implications for adjustment and adaptation from one culture to another. At present, international applications of the Comprehensive System are based mainly on the normative data collected from subjects in the United States. To the extent that certain patterns of Rorschach performance and the personality characteristics they reflect vary in frequency in different cultures, comparisons with Comprehensive System norms may be misleading with respect to the nature and adequacy of subjects' adjustment within their own culture.

For example, if the frequency of Popular responses in a record is to be taken as an indication of the subject's inclination to view the world in conventional ways, examiners need to recognize that there are some national differences in which responses are Populars (e.g., Fried, 1981). Because the cultural surroundings to which people have been exposed are likely to influence what they see frequently when they look at inkblots, a response that is quite common and conventional in one culture may be unusual and idiographic in another, and vice-versa, which means that Populars need to be coded in light of culture-specific standards if they are to be used as an index of conventional perception.

Because of its systematic objectivity, the Comprehensive System provides a basis for collecting cross-cultural normative data that will enhance the accuracy and cultural sensitivity of Rorschach interpretation and thereby broaden the applicability of the instrument. Large-scale normative data collection studies with the Comprehensive System are in fact presently underway in many countries of the world, and the results of these studies are likely to play an important role in shaping the future of cross-cultural assessment with the Rorschach.

SOME TEACHING RECOMMENDATIONS

As in the teaching of other complex procedures, effective pedagogy can help instructors produce capable and devoted students of the Rorschach method. Three teaching techniques that often help to clarify and enrich presentation of the Comprehensive System consist of elucidating the conceptual basis of the coding scheme, providing prototypical examples of alternative codes, and translating interpretations into simple language and everyday examples.

Regarding the conceptual basis of coding, the Comprehensive System has since its inception paired an empirical approach to the coding process with equal attention to the meanings that attach to various codes. In teaching the formal guidelines for assigning codes, instructors should also address the conceptual basis of these codes and the purposes they serve. Knowing why certain codes are used eases the dull rote of learning criteria bereft of meaning, and knowing what the codes signify promotes understanding of rules that may otherwise seem arbitrary or ambiguous. It is important to explain, for example, the conceptual basis for scoring various locations, and the various determinants.

With respect to rules that may seem arbitrary, for example, why should examiners avoid scoring both Botany and Landscape in the same response and both Art and Anthropology in the same response? Concerning the first instance, Botany and Landscape are two of the five variables that load on the Isolation Index (the other three being Nature, Clouds, and Geography). These five contents share similar conceptual significance by virtue of depicting a depopulated environment, and elevation of the Isolation Index to which they contribute suggests that the subject is in fact an interpersonally isolated individual. However, the corollary data on this variable indicate that coding both Botany and Landscape in a single response overloads the Isolation Index and tends to exaggerate the extent of a subject's isolation.

Similarly in the second instance, Art and Anthropology both load on the Intellectualization Index, which when elevated identifies prominent recourse to intellectualization as a defense against affect and intimacy. Coding both Art and Anthropology in the same response tends to overload this index and overstate the extent of a subject's reliance on intellectualizing defenses. Information of this kind can help students appreciate why they do what they do when they code responses in certain ways and gives them the satisfaction of functioning intelligently rather than as automatons.

As for ambiguities, consider the question of how a response of "crown" should be coded. Is a crown a decorative object that should be scored Art, or is it a covering of the body that should be scored Clothing? The choice can be formulated conceptually by noting that a coding of Art loads on the Intellectualization Index, as just mentioned, whereas a coding of Clothing loads on the Hypervigilance Index. Knowing this, an examiner can seek to answer the question by ascertaining whether the response speaks mainly to intellectualization or to hypervigilance; in plainer words, is this an artistic crown or a paranoid crown? The answer to such a question typically depends on how the response is elaborated. A crown described as "a beautiful crown with shiny jewels in it" would seem to be a decorative object that should be scored Art; a crown described as "like kings wear to show how important they are" would seem to have more in common with concerns about power and protection than with decoration and should probably be scored Clothing. As this example shows, a clear conceptual grasp of what alternative codes signify can help students make informed choices between them. Such knowledge also sharpens students' inquiry skills by helping them recognize when to solicit further comments (e.g., by saying "I'm not sure how you're seeing it") as a means of resolving coding ambiguity.

Turning to prototypical examples, well-chosen sample responses often prove effective in helping students grasp the underlying principles that guide certain subtle coding distinctions. Such prototypical examples facilitate remembering scoring guidelines and applying them accurately to other similar responses. The following are four examples of prototypical responses that serve these purposes well:

1. The "stepdown" hypothesis calls for coding what might otherwise be a *Pure* C response (e.g., "blood") as a CF on the basis of its being integrated with a response that has some form demand. The purpose of this scoring guideline is to monitor accurately the level of intensity of the emotional experience represented by a chromatic color response: The more color stands alone and the less it is integrated within a response that has some form demand, the more intense is the affective response it suggests, and conversely, the more color phenomena are integrated within responses having form demand, the less intense is the affect they reflect. Hence, even in an integrated response, use of a nonadjacent detail for a formless color response is coded C and not "stepped down" to CF. The intricacies of this coding guideline can be boiled down to two prototypical responses that capture clearly what it involves. On Card II, by virtue of an integration involving adjacent details, "Bears fighting with blood on them" is an FM.CF response. On Card III, because the chromatic and achromatic portions of the blot are not contiguous, the integrated response of "People fighting and this is some of their blood" is coded M.C.

2 The coding of Cooperative (COP) movement is intended to reflect a positive or helping relationship between figures. At times examiners will need to distinguish carefully between people who are doing one thing together (which is COP) and people who are doing the same thing, but separately (which is not COP). As prototypical examples, "Two women picking up a pot" on Card III is COP, because the women are jointly engaged in a single effort; "Two women picking up pots" is not COP, because each woman is engaged in her own activity. Similarly, "Two people dancing together" is COP, but "Two people doing a dance" is not yet a COP, pending some elaboration of whether the dancing is a joint or solitary activity.

3. Ordinarily, responses involving figures with inappropriate or supernumerary parts are coded as Incongruous Combination (INCOM), which signifies some breakdown in logical reasoning. However, most such responses are not coded INCOM if the figures are specified as being imaginary and the content is therefore (H) or (A); in the imaginary world, almost any combination can exist without violating principles of logic. On the other hand, even parenthesized contents can be coded INCOM if the figure as described would be as improbable in the imaginary world as in the real world. As prototypical examples, "Person with two heads" is an INCOM; "Creatures from outer space with two heads" is an (H) and not an INCOM, because such creatures could presumably have any imaginable characteristics; and "Batman with two heads" is an (H) but still an INCOM, because Batman is a familiar imaginary figure with well-specified characteristics, which do not include having more than one head.

4. In some instances use of white space in a whole or usual detail response involves a synthesis that identifies integrative processing of stimuli and should be coded WS+ or DS+. In other instances white space is used merely as a blank portion of the percept without identity in its own right, in which case it does not indicate any integration and should be coded WSo or DdSo. As prototypical responses, a Card I "Butterfly with holes in its wings" is a WSo, whereas a Card I "Butterfly with white spots on its wings" is a WS+.

Finally, with respect to the language of interpretation, every effort should be made to impress on students that Rorschach information about personality functioning serves a useful purpose only when it is communicated clearly and effectively (see Ritzler, chap. 23 of this volume). As examples of translating test findings into comprehensible English, students should be capable of saying that people who give numerous *m* responses are worried about being at the mercy of forces over which they have no control and concerned about being helpless to prevent bad things from happening to them. They should know that people with a high X-% are more likely than most people to perceive events inaccurately, to form mistaken impressions of what is happening around them, and to have difficulty anticipating the consequences of their actions. They should recognize that a complete absence of texture in a record ($T = 0$) suggests limited capacities to form close attachments to other people and little inclination to anticipate or reach out for mutually supportive relationships with others.

In addition to briefing their students with such generally comprehensible ways of formulating Rorschach interpretations, instructors should also help them identify everyday illustrations of the kinds of behavior that can be inferred from their test data. For example, most people to whom Rorschach examiners communicate their results readily recognize that some individuals are contemplative by nature and inclined to be thinkers rather than doers (introversive EB); that some individuals are self-centered and pay more attention to themselves than to others (high Egocentricity Index); that some individuals are relatively flexible and open-minded in their thinking, whereas others are relatively rigid and narrow-minded (nature of *a:p* ratio and level of Lambda); and so on, for each of the interpretable percentages, ratios, and indices in the Comprehensive System. Although merely illustrative, these examples and the three teaching suggestions presented here can contribute to the pleasure and effectiveness of teaching and learning the Rorschach Comprehensive System.

REFERENCES

Acklin, M. W. (1993). Integrating the Rorschach and the MMPI in clinical assessment: Conceptual and methodological issues. *Journal of Personality Assessment, 60,* 125–131.

Acklin, M. W. (1994). Some contributions of cognitive science to the Rorschach test. *Rorschachiana, 19,* 129–145.

Archer, R. P., & Krishnamurthy, R. (1993). Combining the Rorschach and the MMPI in the assessment of adolescents. *Journal of Personality Assessment, 60,* 132–140.

Aronow, E., Reznikoff, M., & Moreland, K. L (1995). The Rorschach: Projective technique or psychometric test? *Journal of Personality Assessment, 64,* 213–228.

Baba, R. (1995). A comparative study of the Comprehensive System and a psychoanalytic sequence analysis. *Rorschachiana, 20,* 64–92.

Beck, S. J. (1930). Personality diagnosis by means of the Rorschach test. *American Journal of Orthopsychiatry, 1,* 81–88.

Blatt, S. J. (1990). The Rorschach: A test of perception or an evaluation of representation. *Journal of Personality Assessment, 55*, 394–416.

Cooper, S. H., Perry, J. C., & Arnow, D. (1988). An empirical approach to the study of defense mechanisms: I. Reliability and preliminary validity of the Rorschach Defense Scales. *Journal of Personality Assessment, 52*, 187–203.

Ellenberger, H. F. (1954). The life and work of Hermann Rorschach (1884–1922). *Bulletin of the Menninger Clinic, 18*, 173–219.

Exner, J. E., Jr. (1969). *The Rorschach systems.* New York: Grune & Stratton.

Exner, J. E., Jr. (1989). Searching for projection in the Rorschach. *Journal of Personality Assessment, 53*, 520–536.

Exner, J. E., Jr. (1991). *The Rorschach: A comprehensive system: Vol. 2. Interpretation* (2nd ed.). New York: Wiley.

Exner, J. E., Jr. (1993). *The Rorschach: A comprehensive system: Vol. 1. Basic foundations* (3rd ed.). New York: Wiley.

Exner, J. E., Jr., & Exner, D. E. (1972). How clinicians use the Rorschach. *Journal of Personality Assessment, 36*, 403–408.

Exner, J. E., Jr., & Weiner, I. B. (1995). *The Rorschach: A comprehensive system: Vol. 3. Assessment of children and adolescents* (2nd ed.). New York: Wiley.

Frank, L. K. (1939). Projective methods for the study of personality. *Journal of Psychology, 8*, 389–413.

Fried, R. (1981). Christmas elves on the Rorschach: A popular Finnish response and its cultural significance. *Rorschachiana, 14*, 114.

Gacono, C. B., & Meloy, J. R. (1994). *The Rorschach assessment of aggressive and psychopathic personalities.* Hillsdale, NJ: Lawrence Erlbaum Associates.

Ganellen, R. J. (1996). *Integrating the Rorschach and the MMPI-2 in personality assessment.* Mahwah, NJ: Lawrence Erlbaum Associates.

Giambelluca, F. C., Parisi, S., & Pes, P. (1995). *L'interpretazione psicoanalitica del Rorschach* [Psychoanalytic interpretation of the Rorschach]. . Rome: Edizioni Kappa.

Handler, L. (1996). John Exner and the book that started it all: A review of *The Rorschach Systems. Journal of Personality Assessment, 66*, 650–658.

Hilsenroth, M. J., & Handler, L. (1995). A survey of graduate students' experiences, interests, and attitudes about learning the Rorschach. *Journal of Personality Assessment, 64*, 243–257.

Hurt, S. W., Reznikoff, M., & Clarkin, J. F. (1991). *Psychological assessment, psychiatric diagnosis, and treatment planning.* New York: Brunner/Mazel.

Klopfer, B., Ainsworth, M. D., Klopfer, W. G., & Holt, R. R. (1954). *Developments in the Rorschach technique: Vol. I. Technique and theory.* Yonkers-on-Hudson, NY: World Book.

Leichtman, M. (1996). *The Rorschach: A developmental perspective.* Hillsdale, NJ: Analytic Press.

Lerner, P. M. (1991). *Psychoanalytic theory and the Rorschach.* Hillsdale, NJ: Analytic Press.

Lindner, R. M. (1950). The content analysis of the Rorschach protocol. In L. E. Abt & L. Bellak (Eds.), *Projective psychology* (pp. 75–90). New York: Knopf.

Lunazzi de Jubany, H. (1992). *Lectura del psicodiagnóstico* [Lectures in psychodiagnosis]. Buenos Aires: Editoral de Belgrano.

Meloy, J. R. (1991). Rorschach testimony. *Journal of Psychiatry & Law, 8*, 221–235.

Perry, W., Viglione, D., & Braff, D. (1992). The Ego Impairment Index and schizophrenia: A validation study. *Journal of Personality Assessment, 59*, 165–175.

Piotrowski, C. (1996). The status of Exner's Comprehensive System in contemporary research. *Perceptual and Motor Skills, 82*, 1341–1342.

Rapaport, D., Gill, M., & Schafer, R. (1968). *Diagnostic psychological testing* (Rev. ed., R. Holt, Ed.). New York: International Universities Press. (Original work published in 1946).

Rorschach, H. (1942). *Psychodiagnostics: A diagnostic test based on perception.* Bern: Hans Huber. (Original work published 1921)

Schachtel, E. G. (1966). *Experiential foundations of Rorschach's test.* New York: Basic Books.

Schafer, R. (1954). *Psychoanalytic interpretation in Rorschach testing.* New York: Grune & Stratton.

Schwarz, W. (1996). Hermann Rorschach, M.D.: His life and work. *Rorschachiana, 21*, 6–17.

Smith, B. L. (1994). Object relations theory and the integration of empirical and psychoanalytic approaches to Rorschach interpretation. *Rorschachiana, 19*, 61–77.

Urist, J. (1977). The Rorschach test and the assessment of object relations. *Journal of Personality Assessment, 41*, 3–9

Weiner, I. B. (1966). *Psychodiagnosis in schizophrenia.* New York: Wiley.

Weiner, I. B. (1983). The future of psychodiagnosis revisited. *Journal of Personality Assessment, 47*, 451–461.

Weiner, I. B. (1986). Conceptual and empirical perspectives on the Rorschach assessment of psychopathology. *Journal of Personality Assessment, 50*, 472–479.

Weiner, I. B. (1991). Theoretical foundations of clinical psychology. In M. Hersen, A. E. Kazdin, & A. S. Bellack (Eds.), *The clinical psychology handbook* (2nd ed., pp. 26–44). New York: Pergamon.

Weiner, I. B. (1993). Clinical considerations in the conjoint use of the Rorschach and the MMPI. *Journal of Personality Assessment, 60*, 148–152.

Weiner, I. B. (1996). Some observations on the validity of the Rorschach Inkblot Method. *Psychological Assessment, 8*, 206–213.

Weiner, I. B. (1997). Current status of the Rorschach Inkblot Method. *Journal of Personality Assessment, 68*, 5–19.

Weiner, I. B., Exner, J. E., Jr., & Sciara, A. (1996). Is the Rorschach welcome in the courtroom? *Journal of Personality Assessment, 67*, 422–424.

14

Teaching That First Rorschach Course

Virginia Brabender
Institute for Graduate Clinical Psychology, Widener University

This chapter considers the various dimensions of the design of the basic Rorschach course within a doctoral training program in professional psychology. The challenge that arises for instructors who wish to share ideas in regard to Rorschach instruction is that across various programs, the Rorschach is given highly varying treatment concerning where it appears in the assessment curriculum and the time devoted to its presentation. As a recent survey has shown, academic programs vary widely in terms of the time devoted to the Rorschach (Hilsenroth & Handler, 1995). Some programs accord to the Rorschach Inkblot Method its own course; others include it along with a number of other personality instruments; still others offer no Rorschach instruction. Some programs offer advanced courses on the Rorschach after the basic course, whereas others do not. To some extent, this great variability has hindered instructors' engagement in a dialogue about teaching philosophies and methods within Rorschach courses. However, surveys conducted with internship training directors over the past 25 years show consistently that these directors see students as being poorly prepared to utilize core psychological tests such as the Rorschach during their internship (e. g, Tipton, Watkins, & Ritz, 1991). Moreover, on completion of Rorschach courses, students feel that they had difficulty communicating the Rorschach results in terms that would be useful and descriptive in a psychological report (Hilsenroth & Handler, 1995). These facts indicate that despite the impediments to carrying on an intellectual discussion about pedagogical techniques, it is high time such a dialogue begin so that our students can become more competent users of the Rorschach Inkblot Method.

This chapter focuses primarily on the one-semester Rorschach course, but it may have implications for the briefer Rorschach exposure. It follows the typical chronology of the Rorschach course through five steps: (a) setting the stage, (b) teaching administration, (c) teaching scoring, (d) teaching interpretation, and (e) the evaluation of students. This author relies on Rorschach courses she has taught at various universities, but primarily at Widener University in the Institute for Graduate Clinical Psychology. This course comes after the student has been exposed to the concept of a psychological battery and a number of other instruments in that battery, such as the WAIS–R and WISC–III, the Thematic Apperception Test, the Bender-Gestalt, figure drawings, and so on. Following this course, a year later, students take a required advanced course on psychodynamic differential diagnosis in which the author has an opportunity to discuss concepts not covered in the basic course. Students may also take a variety of electives on the Rorschach following the basic course, such as "Content Analysis and the Rorschach" and "Rorschach Research Methodology."

SETTING THE STAGE

The framework that is established in the beginning of the course is critically important to the degree and quality of learning that occurs throughout. A solid framework also ensures that the student will be able to assimilate effectively knowledge pertaining to the Rorschach with other assessment-related knowledge. There are three principles whose underscoring at the beginning of the course and emphasis throughout the course enhances greatly the likelihood that students will use the Rorschach Inkblot Method competently and responsibly.

The first principle is that in the course syllabus and opening lectures the instructor should be as specific as possible about course goals and should clearly indicate to students what in all likelihood can and cannot be achieved in the period of a semester. Certainly, specificity of objectives is desirable for any academic course but in relation to mastery of Rorschach skills it possesses special significance. Achieving proficiency in use of the Rorschach is formidable because it requires competence in the related but nonetheless separate areas of administration, scoring, and interpretation. Over the course of a single semester, with the appropriate opportunities for practice, a student can become reasonably skilled in administration. Although considerable development can also occur in the area of scoring, at the end of the course most students will still have difficulty with the subtle discriminations demanded by complicated protocols. Of the three areas, interpretive skills are likely to be least developed. Generally, students can perform a sequential analysis and generate reasonable hypotheses given the data at hand. Yet, they often fail to achieve the rich ideographic interpretations that require a more integrative use of the data, for example, integrating content and structural measures (Lovitt, 1992). As Silverstein (1996) has pointed out, the capacity to think and write about assessment data in a refined, sophisticated way often requires years of postdoctoral study. Students should be apprised of this fact, for reasons discussed later.

By delineating highly specific goals and by yoking the course's evaluative instruments to these goals, the instructor accomplishes several missions. In conveying to students that they still will be at a fairly early point of skill development, instructors inoculate students against the disappointment and dismay that sometimes occurs when students continue to struggle with the material at the end of the semester. Instructors also "pave the way" for the students' continuing education involvement, particularly if the instructor identifies postcourse opportunities for students. In this way, instructors foster students' observance of the ethical requirement to remain current in terms of developments in assessment (Weiner, 1989). As a corollary to this point, the instructor also sends out an important message that without additional supervision and instruction beyond that first Rorschach course, this instrument is better left in the hands of more experienced assessors.

The second principle is that from the beginning, the instructor should keep in mind that he or she is not teaching mere proficiency in use of this particular assessment method, but is also providing training in the ethical and professional use of assessment instruments in general. Although students in their doctoral courses typically take courses in ethics and professional issues, frequently these courses are general in nature and cannot possibly cover the panoply of issues that are specific to assessment, and in some instances, personality assessment. Moreover, the instructor may not safely assume that such ethical training will occur in the practicum or internship setting (Berndt, 1983). Invariably, practical problems will emerge in the Rorschach course that will provide the instructor an opportunity to model ethical decision making. For example, early in the Rorschach course (and sometimes prior to the course) students often indicate that they would like to take the Rorschach before learning its mechanics. The arguments that are raised in favor of this opportunity is that it would provide the basis for an empathic grasp of the subject's reactions, a fuller understanding of the response process, and self-knowledge, which might no longer be available once naiveté about the test is forever lost.

If an instructor elects to encourage students to obtain their own Rorschach protocols, he or she must recognize that as the conditions under which this might be done are specified, an attitude toward the Rorschach and its use is being conveyed. For example, the instructor (out of concern for students' often-limited financial resources) may suggest that students arrange to have more advanced students administer to them the test and submit it to them unscored. In so doing, the instructor is modeling a casual attitude toward the Rorschach by failing to recognize the dual role problem inherent in this arrangement. Such an instructor may believe that because the advanced student did not score the protocol, therefore that student is not in possession of clinical information. Yet, many examiners know before the formal scoring whether it is likely that Vista, Texture, or Reflection responses are present, as well as whether there are manifestations of serious cognitive slippage. The dual relationship is created because the advanced student, on the one hand, possesses information that typically emerges within a protected clinical/professional relationship and on the other hand, relates to the subject as a peer. Casualness is also demonstrated in bypassing the feedback process, which is critical to any assessment. In contrast, an instructor who recommends that students take the

Rorschach only under conditions in which they have the controls and protections of any subject, communicates a far more responsible attitude toward the use of the instrument.

This particular problem of students taking the Rorschach is given merely as an example. Other problems will invariably arise that involve careful decision making on the part of the instructor. For example, the instructor may be asked whether class participants can test their own psychotherapy patients as additional practice opportunities, or they inquire whether they may practice with one another. Who is going to supervise all aspects of the Rorschach learning and practice is a critical concern. Unless the class size is exceptionally small, rarely can an instructor serve as the formal supervisor with all that implies legally and ethically to every member of the class, although often the instructor can provide some supervisory input. If students are required to assess clinical subjects, the issues of secure storage and maintenance of protocols and feedback to subjects also emerge (Trenerry, 1989). If students present clinical protocols, the confidentiality of subjects is also of concern. In any problem that arises, it is important that the instructor both be careful in his or her decision making and also articulate the reasoning underlying the decision, ideally with reference to the ethical principles and code of conduct established by the American Psychological Association (1992), so that students can internalize not simply a solution but a process of ethical decision making.

The third principle is that from the inception of the course, the instructor should plant the notion of the necessity of integration: the integration of various types of Rorschach data with one another, the integration of Rorschach data with history, and the integration of Rorschach data with the data from other instruments. Assessors who have had the opportunity to read the reports of colleagues will have had the experience of coming across those reports that were based on data from a single instrument, although an extensive battery was administered. As students take their introductory course in the Rorschach, they may be swayed in this direction, not only because of the extensive information often provided by a Rorschach protocol, but also because the sequential cluster analysis provides a convenient means of organizing that information into a report. Therefore, it is essential that at the outset, the student should be presented with the concept of using a battery of tests, and should be helped to understand that rarely will the Rorschach or any one instrument be sufficient to answer the kinds of referral questions about personality functioning that one gets in contemporary assessment practice. Then, throughout the course, the instructor should reinforce the importance of integration by pointing out circumstances in which the Rorschach data may lead to the generation of competing hypotheses, which could then be evaluated, using data from other instruments. Some examples of this might be the use of history to clarify the meaning of multiple texture responses, clarified by history of loss; an elevated somatization index, clarified by history of recent illness; or the use of the validity scales of the MMPI to shed light on possible malingering efforts on the part of the subject. It may also be shown how the data from other instruments might be used to refine further a hypothesis generated from Rorschach data.

In addition to the instructor's observance of the three points relevant to setting the stage, it is also helpful to students for the instructor to provide some attention to the history of the Rorschach, which is better told than read. Fortunately for the instructor, the history of the Rorschach is a vibrant one, involving the interplay of some of the most colorful personalities to enter the theater of professional psychology (see Exner, 1993; Handler, 1994, 1995, 1996). However, the most important reason for covering history is that the unfolding of events highlights some of the core conflicts and tensions that are very much part of the contemporary Rorschach landscape. Even Hermann Rorschach's own personal history illustrates these profound forces. By enabling the student to see how inherent certain problems (such as the reliance on content vs. structural data) are in the understanding and use of the Rorschach, the student is led to devise a perspective that is truly comprehensive, in keeping with the system they are about to master.

TEACHING ADMINISTRATION

In teaching administration and scoring, there is somewhat of a cart-and-horse problem. It is reasonable to begin with administration in order both to follow the chronology of the testing process and to enable the student to know how the to-be-scored material was obtained. One problem is that some aspects of administration, especially the Inquiry, have little substantive meaning unless students become aware of the importance and the meaning of location and determinant variables (see Weiner, chap. 13 of this volume). In addition, however, although students may grasp the general principles of administration, the specifics may elude them until they are fairly conversant with the scoring categories. Therefore, it is useful for students to appreciate that the administrative process will become clearer as the course progresses into other areas. It is also incumbent on the instructor to revisit administration once certain scoring decisions have been made. For example, when the instructor distinguishes between the perception of depth based on shading, compared with the perspective of depth based on form, the instructor should discuss what kinds of queries might assist the student in making this distinction.

In presenting the basics of administration, it is essential that the instructor impress on students the rationale for a standard administration, specifically in terms of the examiner's ability to use norms. The instructor should troubleshoot for students all of the challenges they are likely to encounter in a standard administration. Within the Comprehensive System, what is particularly helpful is the list of questions and responses found in chapter 3 of *The Rorschach: A Comprehensive System* (Exner, 1993). However, students must also know that patients are multifarious in their strategies to reduce ambiguity, so that the principles for examiner intervention must always be available to inform new replies.

One technique that this Rorschach instructor has found to be effective in furthering students' administrative skills is to have them critique an incomplete inquiry. A protocol is created that incorporates many of the common omissions noted by Ritzler and Nalesnik (1990). Students work in small groups, dissecting the protocol line by line and developing more appropriate interventions. This type of exercise, wherein the instructor presents for critique an avowedly flawed product, can be introduced at many points in the Rorschach course. It is useful because when students examine another's work, they are less fettered by the enormous self-criticalness that often restricts their learning in this course. However, it is best to present this exercise following their exposure, through reading and lecture, to all scoring categories.

Students should not complete a basic Rorschach course or even begin to test clinical subjects without having their administration checked out (Yalof, 1996). This writer has experimented with various formats for doing so and has found the most useful one is to involve the employment of a confederate subject who has memorized a script. Ideally, the confederate is a course assistant who can evaluate the administration and provide detailed feedback. The advantages of this format are the following: First, the protocol can be pitched to the appropriate level of difficulty, an especially important consideration if part of the course requirement is for students to go on and score the garnered protocol. Second, the instructor can plant various "challenges" in the protocol (e.g., giving only one response to Card I, rejecting a card, rendering a brief protocol), that call on the student to intervene appropriately. Third, the use of the confederate bypasses the difficulties created concerning the trustworthiness of the data obtained by a totally inexperienced examiner. It also eliminates the confidentiality, dual role, and other ethical issues arising when friends, relatives, and other students are used as subjects. It is important that the check-out occur after the student has a sufficient grasp of scoring principles to be able to formulate appropriate questions in the Inquiry phase.

TEACHING SCORING

Instructors generally select from one of two formats in teaching scoring. The first format relies exclusively on exercises and the scoring of protocols (see DeCato, 1992). The second involves the delivery of formal lectures on all or most of the scoring categories before the applied segment is begun. This author has experimented with both approaches and has found that for a one-semester course (in contrast to a workshop), the second format is more suitable, for several reasons. Even the most diligent student will find the amount of information overwhelming and is likely to profit from its repetition in a systematic way. Moreover, in a lecture, the instuctor is more readily able to emphasize certain principles that run across scoring categories. The lecture is often a better place to highlight some of the aspects of scoring that often elude students or that give rise to confusion. Multiple examples can be given to highlight a particular scoring distinction (e.g., between T and V). In the lecture situation, students can listen somewhat dispassionately without having the distraction of comparing their own performance with a standard. Finally, with the advantages of the readings and the lectures, students enter the applied phase in a stronger position and therefore experience much less unproductive exasperation as they begin to do exercises and score protocols.

Organizing the lecture presentation is relatively straightforward. As does the text, the instructor can follow the Sequence of Scores sheet from left to right, presenting the score categories as they would arise in the scorer's decision making. This format has the beauty that some of the easier scoring categories, for example, location and developmental quality are presented first, giving students an easy entrance into this new task. The effectiveness of the lectures is augmented by interspersing miniexercises frequently, which test the students' ability to make certain distinctions, such as those between active and passive movement, or Level I and Level II Special Scores.

Teaching scoring is often a tedious aspect in Rorschach teaching, for both student and instructor. Students are called on to make a series of distinctions without always knowing their significance (see Weiner, chap. 13 of this volume). Some instructors attempt to enliven the discussion of scoring by interweaving it with interpretation. In the experience of this instructor, who has experimented with the two methods, for several reasons learning is seriously compromised when scoring and interpretation are presented together. First, students find interpretation so much more compelling than the rigors of scoring that they make short shrift of the latter. Second, combining the two areas is confusing because whereas the scoring criteria are highly precise, interpretation, even with the interpretive rules, is a more complicated, integrative activity (DeCato, 1992). Third, when students are performing in clinical situations, one would want them to be doing scoring independently of interpretation. Certainly, scoring is inherently more anxiety producing in that students are called on to compare their performance with an exact standard. Rather than intermingle the two areas, where each is worthy of separate treatment, the instructor should make some of the frustrating reactions that students have to scoring more bearable by their anticipation.

Once the instructor has concluded the presentation of the scoring segment, students may begin the scoring exercises in the back of the *Rorschach Workbook* (Exner, 1990). At some point, however, it is important for students to have the experience of scoring actual protocols. Relative to the exercises, most protocols will contain many ambiguities and it is essential for students to learn to grapple with these. Because scoring is a skill and any skill requires practice, the more opportunity students have to practice on an array of protocols, the more proficient they will be. The protocols should be carefully chosen so that they progress from those that are easy to those that are more difficult (DeCato, 1992). To accomplish this, the instructor may need to create the protocols by drawing responses from a set of protocols. The protocols should also be edited for those ambiguities that are simply a result of flaws in administration. As these protocols are reviewed in class, students will find that they make a variety of mistakes. Scoring errors vary in their level of seriousness. The instructor should point out errors that represent a lack of knowledge of basic principles versus those that involve the misplacement of a response on a continuum (e.g., categorizing as

Level I an example of cognitive slippage that the instuctor would deem a Level II response).

TEACHING INTERPRETATION

Students are best served in the acquisition of interpretive skills if they have a clear grasp of what the Rorschach task represents. To achieve such an understanding, the instructor should give special attention to a careful description of the response process, at least to the extent that it can be characterized given extant research. The instructor should delineate the various processes that are activated by the Rorschach task and the way in which the response fits into this array. Although chapter 2 of *The Rorschach: A Comprehensive System: Vol. 1: Basic Foundations* (Exner, 1993) provides superb coverage of this topic, in my opinion, students make better use of the material and understand it more fully after they have received the presentation on scoring. Therefore, I assign chapter 2 after the scoring chapters and I also highlight aspects of it in my lecture. The material in this area is sufficiently complicated that students never complain about the repetition. To appreciate the fact that projection has a role, albeit a limited one, in the determination of responses, it is critical that students come to recognize how important the stimulus characteristics are in response determination. As time has permitted, I have had the students create their own inkblots using both chromatic and achromatic colors. Poster paints work well for this activity. Once the inkblots are created, we discuss how different inkblots have different *pulls* for location scorings, determinants, and so on. Although the actual inkblots could be used in the same way, they provide less vivid contrasts than the blots the students generate. This activity also provides a regressive release, which is much valued by students, coming as it does on the heels of the course's most challenging segment, "Mastering Scoring."

As part of the introduction to interpretation, students should also be helped to understand how validity considerations apply to the Rorschach. Graduate students doing their beginning clinical work are often asked by cynical supervisors or faculty about the validity of the Rorschach. Students have found Weiner's 1994 article emphasizing that the Rorschach is a method and not a test (given that it does not measure anything) extremely helpful. They find his point that validity considerations pertain to particular hypotheses rather than to the method in toto, clarifying. Moreover, his argument that the Rorschach does not require the use of a particular theory increases the students' receptivity to learning it, especially if they had worried that their particular theoretical orientation may be incompatible with that of either the instrument or the instructor.

Having established the nature of the Rorschach task, the instructor has sufficient basis to proceed step by step through the interpretive process, beginning first with considerations in relation to the validity of a protocol. The limits of R and response omissions on the interpretability of a response should be discussed. Although the topic of malingering is important, the literature is too complicated and extensive to treat it more than superficially in a one-semester course. Instead, students should be referred to the literature on this topic for future consideration.

At this point, the coverage of the Suicide Index is also important and students are likely to have many concerns about clinical decision making in relation to positive values. This provides a natural point to talk about how other instruments, such as the Hopelessness Scale (Beck, Weissman, Lester, & Trexler, 1974), or other methods such as clinical interviewing, can help to clarify Rorschach findings. Through an even brief discussion on this point, the value of integration of data is promoted. The Suicide Index also provides an opportunity for the discussion of another important point. Given the nature of the information that the Rorschach provides, I share with students my perception of the existence of an obligation on the part of all examiners to score a protocol in a timely manner. I present to them a guideline of scoring the protocol within 24 hours after its administration and urge them to have a system in place for contacting their supervisor if the Suicide Index is significant. In this way, the ethical awareness of the student, as it pertains to assessment practice, is heightened.

Certainly the sequential cluster analysis provides a useful pedagogical tool for organizing the presentation of measures. Its utility is likely to be particularly appreciated by those instructors who, like the author, taught the Comprehensive System before it became readily available. At this point in the course, case presentations by the instructor are a very convenient means of familiarizing the students both with the individual measures and with the overall interpretive process. Case presentations are also helpful in showing how history can be integrated with Rorschach data to get an enriched picture of the person.

Instructors and supervisors continually lament that statements made in psychological reports, especially those made in relation to the structural measures, sound technical and textbooklike. This problem occurs because students do not acquire a feel for the measures they are considering. They cannot translate Rorschach terms into everyday language because they understand them in such a limited way (see Fischer, chap. 19 of this volume). There are two ways in which the instructor can deepen the student's understanding of the Rorschach measures. The first is for the instructor himself or herself to have as full a grasp as possible of the psychological correlates of these measures and this can be achieved in part by delving into the writings that predated the Comprehensive System, but on which the Comprehensive System was based. For example, this author's understanding of the connection between diffuse anxiety and Y has been forever enriched by Schachtel's (1966) phenomenological writings about the perceptual dimensions of the experience of anxiety. Without some grasp on the part of the students concerning why it might be that a particular variable may reflect a certain psychological process, the learning that occurs is on a paired-associate level, admitting of no flexibility in its expression.

Another means to both expand and concretize students' knowledge of the psychological correlates of the Rorschach measures is to present them in the context of the experiments that established their validity. This is done elaborately in Exner's (1993) volume, but it bears repetition in the classroom. To support this same conclusion, Hilsenroth and Handler (1995) cited the results of their survey showing that graduate students generally see themselves as being insufficiently grounded in Rorschach research and methodology. But the emphasis here is that the research can bring the measures alive to students. For example, if students can see the connection between the presence and number of T and the distance from other people a subject elects to maintain in a waiting room, then the psychological process that T reflects becomes more accessible to them.

As in all other phases, throughout the presentation of interpretation it is important that students have active engagement with the material. As each cluster is presented, the students are given an exercise in which a clinical question is posed and students are asked to generate hypotheses from the data in the cluster. The nature of the question is such that the information in the cluster is highly relevant to its answer. For example, after the Information-Processing cluster has been presented, the students are given a problem of a man who worked in a company on an assembly line. Because of his excellent work, he was promoted to a higher-level position involving his checking others' work. He felt extremely unhappy in the position and wanted to return to his former job. The class examines the various measures in the Information-Processing cluster and discovers that this individual is a very simple processor of information, one who does not have a propensity to integrate, particularly to the extent that would be required by his new position. We learn how this new job would go against his processing grain. The students are then asked to consider how the data from previously presented clusters might further illuminate the case. In the prior example, the students look at the Situational Stress cluster to see that this man's report that he is struggling in the new position, given an elevated number of m and Y responses, is probably accurate. Students are also asked to speculate on what additional information they would like concerning the case and this often serves as a transition to the next clusters.

EVALUATING PERFORMANCE

It is a paradox in clinical practice that although great care is given in the construction of instruments to assess the subject, virtually no attention is given to the development of tools to assess the assessor who uses clinical instruments. The field has failed to recognize adequately that the assessor's competence in administration, scoring, and interpretation is the glass ceiling on the reliability and validity of clinical tools. For this reason, how students are assessed in their first Rorschach course is of utmost importance.

From this author's perspective, three performance evaluations are optimal during a one-semester course. The first is the administrative check-out described earlier. The second is a scoring examination administered when two thirds of the course have been completed. This examination involves the scoring of a protocol from easy to moderate-level difficulty. Each score category, for example, location, determinants, and so on, is compared with a standard and any departure, be it an omission or comission, is counted as an error. Feedback from the results of this examination should be timely and detailed. Rather than merely receiving a grade, the student should be given feedback in the areas that are posing a difficulty for him or her, as well as suggestions for remediation.

The final examination, the third evaluative tool, should be comprehensive. This instructor has found that students benefit from revisiting the administrative procedures. Students are given a number of short-answer questions in which they are asked what intervention they would make in a vareity of situations, for example, brief protocol, refusal of a card. For the scoring component, students are asked to score a protocol with items that range from easy to difficult. The interpretive component involves the generation of a personality description based on a sequential cluster analysis. This examination takes approximately 3 hours. Again, a grade should be produced from this examination, along with a set of recommendations to each student concerning where his or her efforts should be concentrated in correcting systematic errors. Some students may make such basic mistakes as to warrant a rereading of the text in identified areas. Other students may need more practice in doing more of the exercises in the back of the workbook. Other students are clearly ready to move on to the regular use of the Rorschach in supervised settings. However, all students are strongly urged to obtain response-by-response scoring supervision of the Rorschachs. This point is made explicitly because so often the supervision a student is offered is one wherein he or she identifies to the supervisor where their scoring problems lie. Almost all students will have inappropriate biases and misconceptions lying outside of their awareness. Through this exhortation, students are encouraged to lobby for more intensive supervision than might occur otherwise. When the demands of the students' placement site preclude this type of close monitoring, our program has arranged to have other practitioners in the field, often graduates of the program, provide adjunctive supervision.

SUMMARY

This chapter follows the chronology of a semester-long introductory Rorschach course in the Comprehensive System. Five elements were covered: establishing a course framework, teaching administration, scoring, interpretation, and evaluating students. A theme running through this presentation is that the attitudes toward assessment in general and the Rorschach specifically that the instructor cultivates, primarily through modeling attitudes leading to ethical and reponsible testing practices, are as important as the particular Rorschach skills developed.

REFERENCES

American Psychological Association (1992). Ethical principles of psychologists and code of conduct. *American Psychologist, 47*, 1597–1611.

Beck, A. T., Weissman, A., Lester, D., & Trexler, L. (1974). The measurement of pessimism: The Hopeless Scale. *Journal of Consulting and Clinical Psychology, 42*, 861–865.

Berndt, D. J. (1983). Ethical and professional considerations in psychological assessment. *Professional Psychology: Research and Practice, 14*(5), 580–587.

DeCato, C. M. (1992). Development of a method for competency-based training in Rorschach scoring. *The Journal of Training and Practice in Professional Psychology, 6*(2), 59–66.

Exner, J. E. (1990). *The Rorschach workbook for the comprehensive system* (3rd ed.). Asheville, NC: Rorschach Workshops.

Exner, J. E. (1993). *The Rorschach: A comprehensive system: Vol. 1. Basic foundations* (3rd ed.). New York: Wiley.

Handler, L. (1994). Bruno Klopfer, a measure of a man and his work: Developments in the Rorschach technique, Volumes I, II, and III. *Journal of Personality Assessment, 62*(3), 562–577.

Handler, L. (1995). Maria Rickers-Ovsiankina: A Russian expatriate in America. *Journal of Personality Assessment, 65*(1), 169–185.

Handler, L. (1996). John Exner and the book that started it all. *Journal of Personality Assessment, 66*, 650–658.

Hilsenroth, M. J., & Handler, L. (1995). A survey of graduate students' experiences, interests and attitudes about learning the Rorschach. *Journal of Personality Assessment, 64*(2), 243–257.

Lovitt, R. (1992). Teaching the psychology intern assessment skills in a medical setting. *The Journal of Training and Practice in Professional Psychology, 6*(2), 27–34.

Ritzler, B., & Nalesnik, D. (1990). The effect of inquiry on the Exner Comprehensive system. *Journal of Personality Assessment, 55*(3 & 4), 647–656.

Schachtel, E. (1966). *Experiential foundations of Rorschach's test.* New York: Basic Books.

Silverstein, M. L. (1996). Teaching the Rorschach and learning psychodiagnostic testing: A commentary on Hilsenroth and Handler (1995). *Journal for Personality Assessment, 66*(2), 355–362.

Tipton, R. M., Watkins, C. E., & Ritz, S. (1991). Selection, training, and career preparation of predoctoral interns in psychology. *Professional Psychology: Research and Practice, 22*(1), 60–67.

Trenerry, M. R. (1989, March). Ethical problems in the use of volunteer practice subjects in psychological assessment training. Paper presented at the mid-winter meeting of the Society for Personality Assessment, New York.

Weiner, I. B. (1989). On competence and ethicality in psychodiagnostic assessment. *Journal of Personality Assessment, 53*(4), 827–831.

Weiner, I. B. (1994). The Rorschach Inkblot Method (RIM) is not a test: Implications for theory and practice. *Journal of Personality Assessment, 62*(3), 498–504.

Yalof, J. (1996, March). *Assessing classroom learning of the Rorschach test.* Paper presented at the 1996 mid-winter meeting of the Society for Personality Assessment, Denver.

15

Approaching the Thematic Apperception Test (TAT)

Phebe Cramer
Williams College

Skillful use of the TAT for personality assessment, as with any assessment approach, depends in considerable part on one's personal conviction about the importance and utility of the approach. This belief in the merits of the assessment procedure is not a blind acceptance, but rather a confidence that it will reveal something meaningful about the individual being studied. One of the important tasks in teaching assessment is to help the student develop such a conviction.

My approach to this task is threefold. First, I try to enlist and encourage the development of the students' creative, clinical sensitivity, and to loosen them from inhibiting skepticism and prejudice regarding projective assessment techniques. Second, through a series of workshops, each student has personal experience with the TAT as well as with other approaches designed to assess similar personality constructs. Third, I introduce the students to the research literature that supports the clinical assumption that the TAT stories reveal important information about personality that may or may not be consciously available to the storyteller. I prefer to begin on a more global level, looking at broad life themes and story lines, with the goal of showing convergence between life history and TAT stories. This is followed by a focus on particular aspects of personality, as these are revealed in TAT stories—features such as motives, gender identity, defense mechanisms, and object representations. Although I discuss these three approaches to learning the TAT separately in this chapter, in my teaching they are intertwined, so that the areas of theory, clinical practice, research, and personal experience are used continually to illustrate and to inform each other.

THE BEGINNING

Because I believe in the importance of understanding the historical context in which any behavior occurs, I begin the course with a brief history of psychological assessment, from ancient China through World War I, World War II, and the OSS (Office of Strategic Serivces; now Central Intelligence Agency) operation, and the dispersion of this operation after World War II to various academic centers throughout the United States. Discussing the role of Henry Murray, both prior to and post-World War II, as the person who introduced to the United States the approach to personality assessment in which a small group of individuals is studied intensively by a staff of psychologists, leads to a description of the development of the TAT—how and why the pictures were chosen, how the test is administered, and Murray's ideas about the discovery of needs, press, and thema in TAT stories. At this beginning point in the class, students self-administer five TAT-like research cards, writing out their own stories.

ADDRESSING THE BIASES

Many students approach the TAT with strong biases, developed from previous courses in which the "unscientific" nature of projective techniques was stressed and/or in which principles of logical empiricism and operational definitions were ingrained into their thinking to such an extent that their imagination has become curtailed and they are fearful of speculation. Sometimes, this armamentarium of biases they carry is expressed in polite skepticism; in other instances, it takes the form of more defensive animosity.

Among the skeptics are the students who ask, "Isn't it just a story?", or "Isn't the story determined by the picture?", reflecting the narrowing of their psychological experience. More adversarial comments take the form of: "I imagine a lot of people just borrow a plot from a movie, or a book they are reading, so how does this say anything about them?", or, "Doesn't everyone say this [tell this story]?", or the variant, "If there are usual themes for each picture, what can you find out about the individual?", or, "A person could make up anything, it doesn't necessarily mean anything."

Other students, when faced with the TAT, are less biased than apprehensive. They fear that they won't "get it right." Drawing on the knowledge that different people see different things in the pictures, and different interpreters may reach different conclusions about the meaning of a story, they wonder how anyone can ever arrive at a reliable interpretation.

It is important to respond to each of these doubting questions—or to raise them if they are not asked overtly—in a considered manner. It is necessary to recognize both their validity as inquiries as well as the mistaken assumptions on which they are based. For example, to the question, "Isn't it just a story?", I would reply "Yes, it is a story, but not *just* a story," for this is an idea that presupposes that stories are without psychological importance. To the question "Isn't the story determined by the picture?", I would draw attention to the fact that although there is one picture, different people see the same picture in different ways, as having different interpretations. At this point, it is often informative to present a TAT picture, such as 17BM, which shows a man clinging to a rope, and to ask the students to determine what is going on in the picture. Their subsequent discovery that some of them see the man as climbing *up* the rope, whereas others see him as climbing *down*, is a good demonstration of the point that different people, looking at the same picture, see different things.

The more adversarial comments are also deserving of serious consideration. The main thrust of these questions is often to deny the possibility of personal relevance in the stories told: thus the suggestion that the plot is borrowed from somewhere else, or is so common that it is personally meaningless. A similar attempt to deny personal meaning is expressed in the comment that an infinite number of different stories might be told; with such a muddle, what meaning could be found?

My approach here is to agree with the particular statement—for example, that the plot could be borrowed—but to point out that the storyteller is personally choosing *which* plot to borrow, and that this is important information in the process of trying to understand his or her personality. More generally, in responding to these negatively questioning statements, my emphasis is on what the storyteller has done, how he or she has responded to the request to tell a story. It is important to note, for example, that this person, when asked to tell a story, does *not* tell their own story, but borrows one from someone else. What could this mean? Why would the person avoid their own story, substituting someone else's? By raising these questions, I use the students' doubts to introduce a major tenet of TAT interpretation, namely, that the way in which a storyteller responds to the task of storytelling will itself say something about that individual's personality, and as such is useful information, not meaninglessness. In every opportunity possible, I stress that what the storyteller does and does not do, or say, is determined by that individual and so reflects something of personal importance.

A potentially sensitive issue here is that the comments of doubting students are not dissimilar to those of resistant storytellers. Stressing the importance of how the storyteller reacts to the task is similar to noting the way in which the student is responding to the test. The defensive storyteller is similar to the defensive student; both wish to avoid the possibility of personal meaningfulness or personal revelation through stories.

Defensiveness of this magnitude on the part of students is to be respected. Attacking such resistance head on is as ineffective as is such an attack in psychotherapy. Rather than pushing defensive students into yet further stances of disbelief, I try to create a bridge that will keep the student attached, by indicating, for example, that it is possible that for certain individuals there is really nothing to be learned from their stories, but in the large majority of cases, the information turns out to be personally meaningful.

QUESTIONS OF MEANING

In recognizing the validity of students' questions and doubts regarding the TAT, the discussion inevitably turns to issues of meaning: What does the story "mean"? In a more extreme form, this questions becomes: How does one find the "right" interpretation?

This line of questioning leads to a consideration of a theoretical, or even philosophical orientation that is helpful, perhaps even required, when working with the TAT. It is important to understand that TAT interpretation does not assume that there is but one right or correct interpretation. Different interpretations of the same story are not only possible, but often desirable, depending on the interest of the storyinterpreter. However, this is not to say that *any* interpretation is meaningful, or that all are equally satisfactory, for some interpretations will "fit" better than others.

To begin a discussion of fit, we consider first whether a story fits with the TAT picture to which it is told. Thus, for Card 1 (the boy with violin), the story will fit if it includes some relationship between the boy and the violin. This kind of fit is easily understood by students. Questions involving the fit of interpretations are more difficult to decide. One criterion of fit is based on a consideration of whether the resulting personality characterization is cohesive and noncontradictory; or, if there are contradictions, whether they are made explicit and discussed? Another aspect of fit is external to the story: Does the interpretation fit with other information available about the storyteller, from life history or from different assessment methods. For example, good fit would be demonstrated if the interpretive themes discovered in the TAT could be successfully matched with independently derived themes that characterize the individual's life history. Evidence for the success of this matching task has been provided by Morgan and Murray (1935) and more recently, in a more systematic manner, by Demorest and Alexander (1992), and can be presented to students, if proof of fit seems necessary.

As an example of this match between story and life history themes, let us consider materials from a male college student, "Don." In his autobiography, Don wrote about his relationship with his older brother, and the repeated upset that occurred throughout his life whenever his brother was absent from home. At these times, Don became very anxious because he could not remember what his brother looked like; only when his mother showed him his brother's photo was his concern relieved. Don wrote in his autobiography that this early concern about his brother's absence seemed to foreshadow what was to come. Tragically, while away at college, his brother fell to his death in an apparent accident. Don experienced great pain over this loss, and made a suicide attempt on his own life by jumping from a ledge. Don remained bitter and cynical, feeling that no one cared about his brother. After a period in which he engaged in self-destructive activities, Don made an important connection with a baseball team, and his social and academic life improved.Don's projective story to a picture showing two people sitting on a bench near a river, which was spanned by a large bridge, was as follows:

> This is Mr. and Mrs. James Smith. Their son Bill committed suicide almost seven years ago, by jumping off this bridge. This is the first time they have been able to come here and really think about their son. They are torn by

emotions and memories of the happy times they spent with their son. Their one overriding fear is for their youngest son, Donald, who has turned very depressed and has trouble making friends since his older brother's suicide. The Smiths are extremely worried that Donald may also take his own life in a fit of deep depression. The thought of losing a second son in this way tears at their souls. Donald refuses professional help and seems angry with his mother often. Even in this hour of stress, as his parents attempt to finally accept their son's death, Donald is off playing baseball with his friends from college.

In this story are numerous autobiographical events: death of a brother from a fall, the (attempted) suicide by jumping, the psychological disturbance of the younger brother over the older brother's death, and the solace found in the association with the baseball team.[1]

Although one can provide such evidence to demonstrate matching between autobiography and stories, I prefer to approach the question of fit in a more intuitive fashion, as discussed later. At this point in the discussion about "rightness" ("How do I know if the interpretation is right?"), I encourage students to formulate creative hypotheses, to put aside the concern about rightness, and to consider questions such as "What does this bring to mind?", or "Have you heard anything like this in the other stories?"

Once the student has discovered/created a set of hypotheses for each story, the next step is to look for convergences across stories, or across situations represented by a subset of stories (e. g., stories involving men, or stories involving aggression), and to consider what it might be about the situation depicted in those particular TAT cards that would elicit similar reactions from the storyteller. In this way, some hypotheses will be kept, others discarded. In the end, a series of cohesive propositions should result, which the interpreter should be able to fit together into a coherent picture of a personality.

Multiple Perspectives; Narrative Theory

Raising the issue that there is no one right interpretation—that different interpretations are possible and useful—provides the opportunity to present the idea of multiple perspectives regarding meaning, and to introduce some ideas from narrative theory (Bruner, 1986; Sarbin, 1986; Schafer, 1992; Spence, 1982). This way of thinking about experience may be foreign to many students. It is, however, critically important for working with the TAT. A general comprehension of the basic tenets of narrative theory will enhance the clinical sensitivity and enrich the interpretive capacity of the students.

In discussing the relevance of narrative theory for the TAT, we begin with the self-evident observation that the TAT story is itself a narrative. What may be less obvious to the beginning student is that every individual has developed, or constructed certain narratives, or storylines, which are used to organize,

---

[1] This case and TAT stories are discussed in greater detail in Cramer (1996).

summarize, and perhaps explain his or her important life experiences. These personal narratives are not replicas of historical "truths"; they are constructions that help individuals make sense out of their own experience. In turn, these narrative story lines direct the person's behavior, either consciously or unconsciously, and are at the basis of what we call personality.

To be skillful in using the TAT, possessing narrative sensitivity is important. This includes a recognition that stories refer to something more than, and different from, the surface content—that stories have implicit as well as explicit meanings. In this sense, narrative sensitivity is similar to clinical sensitivity. One way of approaching the idea of implicit meaning is to think of the process involved in creating the story. In this process, the storyteller *transforms* experience into storylines—that is, represents his or her personal experience in a way that can be communicated to others. The importance of stories, then, is not to discover discrete historical events of the past, although these events, in transformed form, may be present in the stories. Rather, it is the way in which these experiences, including affective experiences, are transformed into narrative story lines that we try to understand.

An example of this idea—that the storyteller transforms experience into a form that can be communicated—may be seen in a series of TAT stories told by a woman hospitalized for severe psychological problems. The patient was diagnosed as having a schizoaffective disorder, and was characterized by regressive behavior, extreme dependency, multiple physical and psychological complaints, and proclaimed helplessness. In contrast to the patient's stance, her female therapist increasingly indicated that it was the patient's job to care for herself and to assume responsibility for her behavior. The patient improved and returned home, only to collapse again after several personal losses. She returned to the hospital and was assigned to a male therapist, although her original female therapist was still present.

In the following three TAT stories, all told to the same card (18GF: two women standing close) at different points in the patient's hospital stay, we can see how the patient expressed her experience of her female therapist. That is, we see the nature of the patient's felt relationship with the therapist as revealed in the stories.

The first story was told after the patient had been in therapy for 4 months. During this time, she maintained a helpless, dependent stance, which the therapist challenged as seen in the following story, in which one woman insists that the other tell her something: "She's making her tell her something but she doesn't understand what she wants to know and she says, 'Tell me.' And she says, 'I don't know.' And she keeps saying, 'Tell me' over and over. She doesn't know and now she's gotten so mad that she's choking her."

As an interpreter, one senses the patient's experience of being forced to do something that she, by virtue of being mentally incapacitated—for example, not understanding, not knowing—is helplessly unable to do, and her further experience of the therapist being angered by this stance of helpless passivity. The story also portrays the therapeutic situation in the woman's insistence that the patient talk—that is, make explicit her thoughts, feelings, and behavior.

The second occasion for the patient telling a story to this TAT card occurred at the point that she was readmitted to the hospital: "Oh no! She's trying to make her come back to life, and, she loves her in some sort of capacity. I don't know what kind of way and they've been really close for a long time and, she's, she doesn't know whether she wants to come back to life or not." Here one senses a distinct change in the representation of the relationship between the patient and therapist. Their closeness is recognized, and the therapist is felt to be loving and helpful. The patient, however, is ambivalent about whether she wants to assume responsibility for her life or not.

The third occasion for telling a story to this picture occurred after the patient had transferred to a new therapist, but was hoping to resume work with the original therapist: "These pictures are so disturbing. She's choking her. She can't take her anymore. She's just choking her. She loves her but she can't take her any more so she's choking her." In this story, one feels a reemergence of the relationship with the therapist expressed in the first story, in which the passivity of the patient is felt as angering the therapist. In addition, because this story was told in the context of the patient wanting to return to the therapist after having lost her, the story may also be understood as the patient's experience of that loss. That is, although the patient recognizes the therapist's positive regard, she also believes that her passivity has angered the therapist to the point of rejecting her—"she just can't take her any more."[2]

Important life experiences, when transformed into thematic material, may be presented in multiple variations in the stories. Narrative sensitivity involves being alert to these repetitions, to the recurring patterns that reveal the storyteller's way of organizing experience. Thus the "meaning" of a TAT story is found in the patterns of experience that are both revealed by the storyteller and discovered by the interpreter.

Another aspect of narrative theory that critically informs work with the TAT is the recognition of the importance of context—both situational and personal. Important factors in the situational context include the TAT pictures themselves and issues of *card pull*, discussed later. Also, the place in which the testing occurs, the reason for the testing, and personal characteristics of the examiner are important aspects of context. Although these situational features are significant in all methods of personality assessment, the interpersonal features of the testing context are especially important for the TAT. This is seen in the following story told to Card 12M, in which the patient expressed her experience of being with an examiner who is presenting a series of projective tests, the implications of which are difficult to figure out:

The man is casting some kind of spell. That sounds a little peculiar but—in order to make her—speak freely to him without her being aware of it at all after it is done. She is a very reserved woman and she never speaks to him of what she's thinking or hearing. She tries hard not to tell him anything and he is very curious about her. Guess that is it.

---

[2] This case, with additional TAT stories is discussed in greater detail in Cramer (1996).

The salient features of the psychological testing situation are presented in this story. She, the patient, is reticent; she does not like to reveal anything about herself. He, the examiner, is curious about her and keeps asking her to do things, the import of which she cannot decipher. Throughout the testing, she senses that she is being made to reveal something about herself that she otherwise would not do. Although she tries not to expose herself, she believes it is happening anyway.

Personal context, too, is important; the personal features of the storyteller, including age, gender, ethnicity, educational/career background, as well as the psychological reaction of the storyteller to the situational context are all information to be considered in the process of story interpretation. Although, for research purposes, there are times when contextual or personal information may be appropriately withheld, in general attempting "blind" analysis is like trying to decide if someone is overweight without knowing how tall they are.

The preceding discussion is meant to illustrate how some of the tenets of narrative theory are relevant for TAT interpretation. The purpose of this semiphilosophical discussion is to enhance the students' sensitivity to narrative themes and to increase their capacity for creative speculation. A more complete explication of the relevance of narrative thinking for working with the TAT may be found in Cramer (1996).

CASE STUDIES

At this point in teaching the class, I return from the excursion into narrative theory to a consideration of TAT fit as exemplified in a series of case studies. The selection of these cases requires only sufficient biographical information and that a reasonably full set of TAT stories is available. Ideally, for me, this would include Cards 1, 6BM, 7BM, 7GF, 8BM, 12MF, 13MF, 14, and 17BM. However, less than ideal circumstances often prevail; a selection of stories to any six of these cards provides a reasonable basis for discussion.

Beyond these requirements, the particular cases selected may vary with the purpose of the class; with clinical psychology students, for example, the cases might include examples of different diagnoses. These cases may be drawn from one's personal files, or there are published cases available that include both basic TAT and biographical information, as well as the thematic interpretation of an expert. I have found these published case studies to be particularly useful for introducing students to the idea of thematic analysis.

The first case study I present to the class is that of a college student with the pseudonym of "Earnst," a case published in Murray's (1938) *Explorations in Personality*. This case, presented as part of the discussion about Murray and the creation of the TAT, contains extensive background information as well as an autobiography and TAT stories, and provides an excellent illustration of discovering common themes (or thema, as Murray called them) in autobiographical and story material and of linking these thema into a coherent personality description. The four thema extracted from the material—summarized in the case analysis as "oral succorance," "quest for provisions," "predator," and "forced robbery"—are seen as uniquely representing the narrative storylines that Earnst has created to organize and make sense of his life experience. The extensive material available for this case allows a discussion not only of broad themes but also permits attention to be directed to the use of particular words and phrases. An example is the frequent references to water and thirst which, when compared to the students' own TAT stories, are recognized as being unusual, and thus a significant feature in this case protocol.

The second case study is that of another college student, "Inburn" (Keniston, 1963). Again, extensive autobiographical information is available, as is a set of TAT stories. The case analysis also provides a skillful linking of life history with story material, again summarizing four underlying narrative themes that link together what might at first appear to be a series of unconnected story lines.

These two cases are also used as an occasion to discuss the influence of social context on storytelling. Earnst comes from the generation whose late adolescence and young adulthood coincided with the Great Depression. His TAT themes of deprivation, although they have early life history precedents, are also congruent with the social milieu in which he was living. Inburn, who could be Earnst's son, was part of the alienated youth of the 1950s—the Beat generation—and strongly portrays the existential alienation of that time and social group.

A third case study is that by Murray of "Grope," subtitled "American Icarus" (in Shneidman, 1981). Murray's analysis of the autobiographical and TAT materials again results in four descriptive life thema. For this case, I prefer to present the case materials without expert analysis, and to have the students work on their own to arrive at descriptive thema, and then to discuss the reasons for these choices, and to consider if some fit better than others. This case, with its emphasis on the Icarus theme, also serves as a prologue to a subsequent discussion of a particular interpretive perspective that has been used in research studies of gender identity (see later discussion).

A fourth case study, of a female college student, provides the opportunity to identify life thema from two different types of narrative material, as well to compare the personality picture that emerges from these sources with that derived from other assessment methods. The case study of "Janus" (Barron, 1972) provides not only TAT stories, but also an extended dramatic scenario produced in connection with the use of miniature props (the Dramatic Construction Test). In addition to these two sources of narrative material, the results from the MMPI, the CPI, the Adjective Check List, and other personality assessment approaches are published with the case. From these materials, and especially the narrative materials, students discover the reason for the choice of this woman's pseudonym.

SELF-STUDY: DISCOVERY OF PERSONAL THEMES IN TAT STORIES

At the beginning of the semester, students write five TAT stories. Several weeks later, each student writes a brief autobiography. After the practice, described earlier, of identifying life thema in the TAT stories of published case studies, students' TAT stories and autobiographies are returned to them, and they are now asked to identify their own life thema. More specifically, they are asked to locate thema that appear in both autobiography and TAT stories, and to write a brief paper describing these thema. This is often a very important experience for students. Many are very surprised to discover how the TAT stories they wrote at the beginning of the semester, and that were described by them as "just stories" are in fact replete with personal significance.

At this time I have an individual conference with each student. Prior to the conference, I study their autobiography and TAT stories in order to identify what I see as the central thema in the material. Then, with each student, I discuss the thema they have identified, noting the supporting evidence as well as any inconsistencies or contradictions in their formulations. I then go over the entire process of thema identification as I experienced it using their materials. My approach, I explain, is to read the TAT stories first, then the autobiography, and then the TAT stories again. When reading the stories, I indicate that I am first alert to any indications of uniqueness—in perception, plot, word use, or other aspect of the story. I explain that this aspect of TAT interpretation—the awareness of uniqueness—depends on having an internal standard for knowing the usual—that is, for recognizing what one commonly, or usually finds in a story told to a particular picture. This internal standard is based on experience with many stories and storytellers. Beginning students are not expected to have yet developed such a standard. Still, by this time in the course, they have had experience with other students' stories (see later discussion), and with the protocols of the published cases. They also have experience with literary prose and the use of the English language. I encourage them to call on this background, from which they have a preliminary basis for making judgments about usualness, or, more important, about uniqueness. In discussing the nonusual aspects of their stories, I like to use this concept of "uniqueness," rather than, for example, "difference" or "idiosyncrasy," which may carry connotations of being peculiar or somehow pathological.

In addition to the unique aspects of their stories, I discuss with students how, when I discover thema that are repeated in the stories, I look to the autobiography for related material. If possible, I also demonstrate how certain thema are linked, or how they lead to similar outcomes.

Students differ in their capacity to engage in this process. Generally, I have some indication of the degree of their capacity for this enterprise from the paper they have written, in which they identify their own thema. Those who show insight and capability in this process are able to easily engage. Others, however, may show resistance; this is often foretold in the rather limited and vapid result of their self-analysis. For all students, I stress that my formulations are hypotheses, and that other interpretations are possible. For further examples of how students' autobiographical and TAT thema coincide, I refer the interested reader to *Storytelling, Narrative and the Thematic Apperception Test* (Cramer, 1996).

There are times when the attempt to identify some common theme in students' TAT stories and autobiography is not successful. Although the student may have located some points of similarity for the written exercise, I am primarily struck, when reading the material, by the absence of common themes. Most often, this takes the form of themes of aggression, conflict, or other negative emotions being expressed in multiple TAT stories but being entirely absent from the autobiography. My approach to this situation is to point out the discrepancy and to wait to see if the student wishes to explore this observation. Most often, they do not. The defensiveness that has produced the discrepancy between the autobiography and the stories continues to be present, impeding exploration. In this case, I acknowledge once again that the thema from the two different sources do not seem to coincide, and I place this result in a group of "unusual occurrences," thereby letting the student know that something is a little off here.

"LISTENING"

Throughout, I refer to the importance of "listening" to the story. This is a metaphorical listening, of course, because at the point of studying the story it is generally in written form. By listening, I have in mind the kind of free-floating attention exemplified in Theodore Reik's concept of "listening with the third ear." For some people, this capacity is ever present, even to a distracting degree. For others, it is a learned skill. But it is clear that clinical astuteness, whether in psychological interviews or TAT interpretation, is significantly based on this capacity to listen, to hear the usual and to note the unusual, to register the explicit and to wonder about the implicit, to sense the hesitations, to recognize cliches and creativity, and to be as much aware of the innuendoes, asides, unspoken implications and resistances as of the manifest content. One also listens for cognitive style: Is the story logical, cohesive, with a beginning, middle, and end, or is it fragmented, beginning in obscurity and ending in oblivion? Are the characters well defined, or are they vague, amorphous, difficult to tell apart? Is there sufficient detail to create a clear scene of action; or, does an obsessive accounting of a myriad of trivia overwhelm and destroy the story line? Is the story organized or rambling? Is the language flexible or dogmatic? Sensitivity to all of these stylistic issues is part of the listening process.

This process will also be affected by the listener's own narrative, and it is this part of listening that is most directly related to the learning process. The listener has the opportunity to choose from among different interpretive stances or perspectives, from which the TAT story may be understood. These interpretive perspectives may be taught and then used to explicate TAT stories. This kind of listening differs from the more open, free-floating activity described previously, for it imposes a particular structure on the story from which it is then evaluated. The use of such structured interpretive perspectives is discussed in the following section.

RESEARCH WITH THE TAT

To create confidence in students regarding the validity of the TAT, a discussion of selected research studies is helpful. At the same time, the discussion of research with the TAT introduces students to systematic interpretive approaches, and demonstrates how multiple interpretations can be made from the same story material. Further, research findings can demonstrate that each of these interpretations is valid, supporting the position that multiple perspectives are enriching, not contradictory. The discussion of research with the TAT, as with the case studies, is intertwined with the other material in the course. For example, as the students are introduced to research methods for coding motives in TAT stories, they apply these coding systems to their own stories.

The first research study I introduce is the early work by Sanford (1936, 1937) and by Atkinson and McClelland (1948), which demonstrated that a physiological need may be expressed in TAT stories. In these studies, the degree of hunger in subjects was systematically manipulated by withholding food for varying intervals of time. Students can easily empathize with this situation and are able to accept the proposition that the longer the food deprivation, the stronger the hunger need. These research studies demonstrate that the occurrence of food-related TAT imagery increased as a function of the strength of the hunger need, a finding that generally convinces even the most skeptical students that physiological needs can be expressed in TAT stories. It is then just a small step to move to the idea that psychological needs may also be expressed in the stories. For this reason, it is helpful to present these studies close to the beginning of the course.

Subsequently, I present McClelland's work on achievement motivation (McClelland, Atkinson, & Lowell, 1953) with a focus on how a reliable coding system was developed to assess the presence of this motive in story material. I point out how the basic approach here is similar to that for developing criterion-keyed scales: that is, identify a group of subjects who are known to be high on the motive in question (e. g., achievement) and a group who are low, and have both groups write TAT stories; then identify the themes or content in the stories that differentiate the high-motive group from the low-motive group. These differentiating themes are assumed to reflect motive strength. An alternate approach to developing these coding systems is to take a single group of randomly selected subjects, and expose them to an experimental manipulation that is designed to produce a change in motive strength; subsequently compare the pre- and postmanipulation TAT stories of the same subjects. Content or themes that appear in the postmanipulation stories, but were not present in the premanipulation stories, are assumed to reflect an increase in the strength of the motive, and thus serve as a measure of that motive. Examples of how this approach was used to establish coding systems for the motives of achievement (McClelland et al., 1953) affiliation (Shipley & Veroff, 1952), power (Winter, 1973), and intimacy (McAdams, 1988) are presented. (For a single reference presenting the coding approaches, see Smith, 1992.) At the same time, in a workshop, students apply these coding systems to their own stories, as discussed later.

With this background on the development of coding systems, students then examine the application of these approaches, with a focus on the success of the assessment of TAT-based motives for predicting real-world behavior. This includes McClelland's early work on the relationship between the achievement motive and national economic development (McClelland, 1953). It also includes Winter's (1982) studies on the role of the power motive in politicians' behavior, showing, for example, that political leaders with strong power motives exercise their power in different ways than do leaders with strong achievement motives, who in turn are different from leaders with strong affiliative motives. Based on studies of real-life political figures and the application of the TAT motive-coding system to their political speeches, this research also demonstrated that the three motives predict different kinds of campaigning behavior—for example, differences in when the candidate enters the political campaign, how long he or she remains in the race, and how he or she reacts to changing information from the polls regarding his or her probability of success. The power motive has also been used to predict presidential behavior. This section of the course is augmented by a discussion of motives in a case study of Richard Nixon (Winter & Carlson, 1988).

Evidence for the importance of TAT motives in predicting real-world behavior is also seen in the research on intimacy motivation. For example, in one research study (see McAdams, 1988) college students carried electronic beepers around with them for an entire week. Seven times during the waking day, at random intervals, they were "beeped" and asked to record their thoughts, feelings, and behaviors at that moment. This *experience sampling method* revealed that the students who were known, from their TAT stories, to be high in intimacy motivation spent more time during the week thinking about people and relationships, feeling good about interactions with people, and took more time talking with people or writing to them than did students who were low in intimacy motivation.

Further information on research demonstrating the success of systematically assessed TAT motives for predicting behavior may be found in McAdams (1988), Stewart (1982), and Winter (1973). A detailed discussion of the methods for assessing motives from TAT stories is given in Smith (1992).

Through the discussion of these research studies, which are examples drawn from a much larger research literature, students see that the assessment of psychological motives in TAT stories can be demonstrated to predict real-world behavior. From this discussion of the assessment of motives, students also see a demonstration of the possibility of multiple interpretations of the same story material. This idea—that more than one interpretation of the same story is possible—is stressed throughout the course, along with the notion that the interpretation made will reflect the perspective of the interpreter.

In addition to these motivational perspectives, students are introduced to other interpretive perspectives that may be useful when working with the TAT. One of these perspectives is May's (1980) approach to assessing gender identity through TAT stories. The development of this approach was based on the observation that the pattern, or story trajectory, of male and female stories is frequently different. Men's stories tend to begin on a high note, with things going well, but then, after a critical, or pivotal incident, the story goes downhill, ending on a negative note, a pattern May characterized as enhancement followed by deprivation. For women, the reverse pattern is found: The story begins with some hardship, or difficulty; following the pivotal incident, things look up, and the story ends on a positive note, a pattern characterized as deprivation followed by enhancement.

Students can readily identify these two patterns from myth and fairy tales. The masculine pattern occurs in the myths of Icarus and Phaethon, both of whom flew too high, only to fall to their deaths, and has been previously encountered by the students in the case study of Grope. Likewise, the feminine pattern, of deprivation followed by enhancement, is easily identified in the fairy tales of Cinderella and Snow White.

Students are introduced to the coding system to identify the masculine and feminine pattern, along with a discussion of what the existence of these patterns might indicate about masculine and feminine personality. This discussion may be enriched by reading May's (1980) book, *Sex and Fantasy*. Also, research showing consistent gender and age differences in these fantasy patterns is discussed (Cramer, 1987). In the workshops, students apply this coding system to their own TAT stories (see later discussion).

Another interpretive perspective, the assessment of defense mechanisms from TAT stories, is also presented (see Cramer, 1991, for a full discussion of this approach). By first identifying the components of defenses and considering how these might be manifest in story protocols, students are introduced to the idea that stories provide information not only about life themes and motives, but also about personality dynamics—how the individual deals with anxiety or conflict created by the arousal of these motives or life themes. This idea has been presented earlier, as it has occurred in the case study protocols. Now, students are introduced to a systematic coding procedure to identify the presence of three defenses—denial, projection, and identification—chosen to represent three points on a developmental continuum. A consideration of the developmental maturity/immaturity of these defenses is related to the implications of their use by persons of different ages. For example, the use of the immature defense of denial is to be expected in young children, but its extensive use by an adult would be indicative of psychological difficulties. Research demonstrating a developmental progression in defense use is considered, along with experimental and real-world demonstrations of the utility of this approach to assessing defenses in the TAT (Cramer, 1995, 1997; Cramer & Block, in press).

The following three vignettes exemplify the expression of the defense mechanisms of denial, splitting, and projection in the TAT stories. Further examples may be found in Cramer (1991, 1996). The use of the defense of denial is characteristic of the stories of young children, although it occurs also in adult stories. The following brief story from a 5-year-old girl to TAT Card 17BM illustrates several uses of denial: "This is a statue, climbing down a rope. (What happens?) He falls and then breaks. And then somebody builds him back up and he does the same thing over again."[3]

To begin with, turning the man who is clinging to the rope into a statue represents an aspect of denial (not seeing what is there), the purpose of which becomes apparent almost immediately. The story conveys anxiety about the possibility of falling. If the figure is not real, it cannot be hurt. Thus, the possibility of pain is denied. Even when the statue does fall and break, the implications of this are quickly denied, through the reconstruction of the figure.

The primitive defense of splitting is also seen in TAT stories, as in the following story to Card 12F told by a patient hospitalized with a diagnosis of borderline personality disorder.

> The picture in the background, the character in the background represents one facet of the young man's personality. I guess that facet would be insanity. Oh, the character in the background looks foolish and simpering. He or she, uhm, I can't tell, it has no look of understanding or recognition of an external reality, the young man who is looking in the opposite direction from the picture in the background and he does not even realize that this side of him exists. He has lots of ambitions and hopes for the future and but, ah, he will be dragged down and have to struggle with the insanity that's within him.

This story clearly portrays the good–bad, healthy–sick split-off self-representations of the storyteller. The functioning of the defense itself is described in the statement, "he does not even realize that this side of him exists."

Here is an example of the defense of projection in a story told to Card 18GF by a 26-year-old man, hospitalized with an initial diagnosis of schizophrenic disorder, chronic undifferentiated type: "This is a picture of two people: a mother and a son, and the … er … what's the mother doing … uhm. The mother, in fact, seems to be hurting the son. She has tension on her face and there is anger on her face and she is squeezing the … face of her son." The misperception of one of the figures as being male is extremely unusual. It sets the scene, however, for the patient to engage in multiple projections of hostility onto the "mother" figure, including the peculiar idea of "squeezing the face of her son."

In addition to looking at TAT stories from the perspective of the expression of defense mechanisms, another interpretive perspective that may be introduced is an approach designed to assess the storyteller's level of object relations, as demonstrated in TAT stories (see Westen, 1991, see also Russ, chap. 25 of this volume). This approach may be of particular interest to students who would use the TAT as a tool for differential diagnosis. Because the distortion of object relations is one of the central features of many borderline personality disorders as well as other serious psychopathological disorders, this approach offers a systematic method for assessing an individual's level of functioning in a diagnostically important area. In this coding approach, extensive guidelines are

---

[3] This, and following examples, are taken from Cramer (1996).

provided for using the TAT to assess the nature of the storyteller's internal representation of others, the quality of affect in interpersonal relationships, the capacity for and the quality of emotional investment in relationships, moral standards and values, and the degree to which the individual understands interpersonal motivation.

WORKSHOPS

The third component in teaching the TAT, which is again intertwined with the previous two foci, consists of a series of workshops, in which students self-administer the TAT and then apply the various interpretive perspectives discussed in class to their own protocols.

In the first workshop, five TAT-like cards (the research series; see McClelland & Steele, 1972) provide the basis for self-administering the written form of the TAT. This workshop also provides the occasion for discussing differences between written and oral administration of the TAT, and how certain types of information are lost when using the written presentation method.

In the second workshop, students are provided with the coding schemes for the motives of achievement, affiliation, and power. TAT stories from previous students are provided and used to demonstrate the scoring criteria for these motives. Students then score their own stories, with the opportunity for discussion of questions, problems, and uncertainties.

A third workshop consists of students exchanging their stories. Now that they have developed some proficiency in using the motive-coding schemes, they apply these schemes to score the stories of another student and then exchange scores, discussing disagreements and reaching some final consensus about the evaluation of each story.

This exercise introduces the topic of interrater reliability. It also provides the setting for a discussion of *card pull*. By totaling up the motive scores for each picture card, it becomes apparent that some cards elicit stories that produce high scores on the achievement motive, whereas other produce high scores on affiliation or power. For example, the third picture in this research series, which shows a man boxing in the foreground and another in the background, typically elicits high scores on the achievement motive, with a secondary score on the power motive. In contrast, Picture 2 (a man and woman sitting on a bench by a river) and Picture 5 (a man and woman at a restaurant table, with guitar player) typically elicit strong scores on the affiliation motive, with very weak scores on achievement and power. Noting the consistency of this card pull across students' stories demonstrates that this is a result of the pictures themselves, not of some intraindividual personality factor.

Understanding this issue of card pull then forms the basis for a discussion of why traditional methods for determining test reliability, if they depend on measuring internal consistency, are not appropriate for the TAT. That is, insofar as the TAT pictures were initially selected by Murray (1938) to represent different intrapsychic conflicts, and to the extent that they are demonstrated to assess different motives, there is no reason to expect consistency in scores across pictures. Thus reliability measures that are based on determining this kind of internal consistency (e. g., Cronbach's alpha) are inappropriate for the TAT.

Subsequent workshops involve the students' application of alternative coding systems to their own TATs. These include the coding system associated with gender identity, developed by May (1980), the method used to assess defense mechanisms (Cramer, 1991), and the approach used to assess the level of object relations present in the stories (Westen, 1991).

In addition, when the TAT is taught as part of a more general course in personality assessment, additional workshops are held in which students self-administer other assessment techniques that are designed to measure personality constructs similar to those assessed though the TAT coding schemes. These include measures of the motives of achievement, affiliation and power, as assessed from scales derived from the Adjective Check List (ACL; Gough, 1952), as well as from the Personal Research Form (PRF; Jackson, 1987). Measures related to the construct of gender identity include Bem's Sex Role Inventory (SRI; Bem, 1978), and the Femininity scale of the California Psychological Inventory (CPI; Gough, 1986). Alternative measures of defense mechanisms include the Defense Mechanism Inventory (DMI; Gleser & Ihilevich, 1969), the Coping Operations Preference Enquiry (COPE; Schutz, 1962), the Defense Style Questionnaire (Bond, 1986), and the Joffe-Naditch CPI-derived defense scales (in Haan, 1977).

A comparison of students' ranking on these various measures of the same-named construct leads to a discussion of different levels of personality assessment, and to the idea that although two measures from different levels may not correlate with each other, both may predict some third variable in a systematic and meaningful fashion (see Handler & Meyer, chap. 1 of this volume). This discussion is amplified by reading McAdams' (1995) article on levels of personality, and McClelland, Koestner, and Weinberger's (1989) article on the differences between self-attributed and implicit motives.

McAdams (1995) addressed the question, "What do we know when we know a person?" by differentiating between different levels of personality. He discussed how the assessment of traits (Level 1) yields a very different kind of information than the assessment of motives or defenses (Level 2), which in turn provides a different kind of information from the discernment of life themes, or identity of an individual (Level 3). It is thus not surprising if measures of different levels of personality do not correlate, although all levels may contribute to predicting some other behavior. McClelland et al. (1989) made the same point when they differentiated between self-attributed motives (which are at the same descriptive level as traits) and implicit motives (of which the individual may or may not be aware). McClelland et al. demonstrated that although these two levels of motives may not intercorrelate, each may independently predict the same behavior; additionally, prediction is improved by combining the measures from the two different levels.

SUMMARY

One approach to developing skill in personality assessment using the TAT is described in this chapter. This approach consists of developing clinical sensitivity, providing research evidence for the validity of systematic TAT coding schemes, and having personal experience with the TAT through a series of workshops. In these ways, the students' confidence in the value of this assessment approach is increased.

REFERENCES

Atkinson J. W., & McClelland, D. C. (1948). The projective expression of needs: Vol. 2. The effects of different intensities of the hunger drive on thematic apperception. *Journal of Experimental Psychology, 38,* 643–658.

Barron, F. (1972). *Artists in the making.* New York: Seminar Press.

Bem, S. L. (1978). *Bem Inventory.* Palo Alto, CA: Consulting Psychologists Press.

Bond, M. (1986). Defense style questionnaire. In G. E. Vaillant (Ed.), *Empirical studies of ego mechanisms of defense* (pp. 146–152). Washington, DC: American Psychiatric Press.

Bruner, J. (1986). *Actual minds, possible worlds.* Cambridge, MA: Harvard University Press.

Cramer, P. (1987). The development of sexual identity. *Journal of Personality Assessment, 44,* 604–612.

Cramer, P. (1991). *The development of defense mechanisms.* New York: Springer-Verlag.

Cramer, P. (1995). Identity, narcissism and defense mechanisms in late adolescence. *Journal of Research in Personality, 29,* 341–361.

Cramer, P. (1996). *Storytelling, narrative and the Thematic Apperception Test.* New York: Guilford.

Cramer, P. (1997). Evidence for change in children's use of defense mechanisms. *Journal of Personality, 65,* 233–247.

Cramer, P., & Block, J. (in press). Preschool antecedents of defense mechanisms use in young adults. *Journal of Personality and Social Psychology.*

Demorest, A. P., & Alexander, I. E. (1992). Affective scripts as organizers of personal experience. *Journal of Personality, 60,* 645–663.

Gleser, G. C., & Ihilevich, D. (1969). An objective instrument for measuring defense mechanisms. *Journal of Consulting and Clinical Psychology, 33,* 51–60.

Gough, H. G. (1952). *The Adjective Check List.* Palo Alto, CA: Consulting Psychologists Press.

Gough, H. G. (1986). *The California Psychological Inventory.* Palo Alto, CA: Consulting Psychologists Press.

Haan, N. (1977). *Coping and defending.* New York: Academic Press.

Jackson, D. N. (1987) *PRF–Form E.* Goshen, NY: Research Psychologists Press.

Keniston, K. (1963). Inburn: An American Ishmael. In R. White (Ed.), *The study of lives* (pp. 40–70). New York: Atherton.

May, R. R. (1980). *Sex and fantasy: Patterns of male and female development*. New York: Norton.

McAdams, D. P. (1988). *Power, intimacy and the life story*. New York: Guilford.

McAdams, D. P. (1995). What do we know when we know a person? *Journal of Personality, 63*, 365–396.

McClelland, D. C., Atkinson, J. W., Clark, R. A., & Lowell, E. L. (1953). *The achievement motive*. New York: Appleton-Century-Crofts.

McClelland, D. C., Koestner, R., & Weinberger, J. (1989). How do self-attributed and implicit motives differ? *Psychological Review, 96*, 690–702.

McClelland, D. C., & Steele, R. S. (1972). *Motivation workshops*. Morristown, NJ: General Learning Press.

Morgan, C. D., & Murray, H. (1935). A method for investigating fantasies: The Thematic Apperception Test. *Archives of Neurological Psychiatry, 3*, 115–143.

Murray, H. A. (1938). *Explorations in personality*. New York: Oxford University Press.

Sanford, N. (1936). The effect of abstinence from food upon imaginal processes: A preliminary experiment. *Journal of Psychology, 2*, 129–136.

Sanford, N. (1937). The effect of abstinence from food upon imaginal processes: A further experiment. *Journal of Psychology, 3*, 145–159.

Sarbin, T. R. (1986). *Narrative psychology: The storied nature of human conduct*. New York: Praeger.

Schafer, R. (1992). *Retelling a life: Narration and dialogue in psychoanalysis*. New York: Basic Books.

Schutz, W. (1962) *COPE. A FIRO Awareness scale*. Palo Alto, CA: Consulting Psychologists Press.

Shipley, T., & Veroff, J. (1952). A projective measure of need for affiliation. *Journal of experimental psychology, 43*, 349–356.

Shneidman, E. S. (Ed.) (1981). *Endeavors in psychology: selections from the personology of Henry A. Murray*. New York: Harper & Row.

Smith, C. P. (Ed.) (1992). *Motivation and personality: Handbook of thematic content analysis*. New York: Cambridge University Press.

Spence, D. P. (1982). *Narrative truth and historical truth. Meaning and interpretation in psychoanalysis*. New York: Norton.

Stewart, A. J. (1982). *Motivation and society*. San Francisco: Jossey-Bass.

Westen, D. (1991). Social cognition and object relations. *Psychological Bulletin, 109*, 429–455.

Winter, D. G. (1973). *The power motive*. New York: Free Press.

Winter, D. G. (1982). Motivation and performance in presidential candidates. In A. J. Stewart (Ed.), *Motivation and society* (pp. 244–267). San Francisco: Jossey-Bass.

Winter, D., & Carlson, L. (1988). Using motive scores in the psychobiological study of an individual: The case of Richard Nixon. *Journal of Personality, 56*, 75–103.

16

Teaching and Learning the Administration and Interpretation of Graphic Techniques

Leonard Handler
University of Tennessee
Robert Riethmiller
University of Tennessee

Despite a continuing controversy that questions whether drawings can divulge anything important about an individual's personality, practicing clinicians continue to use drawing techniques as an integral part of their assessment battery (Handler, 1995). For years this has frustrated critics of the technique who believe that these clinicians either ignore or do not read the bad press that drawing techniques have received. Polarization seems to be the problem here, as adherents line up against naysayers, each often citing different supporting literature. In this chapter we address this issue and describe how attention to the research, both pro and con, has led us to methods of interpreting figure drawings, and teaching others to do so, that we find useful.[1]

The first author (Handler) described his initial approach to figure drawing assessment in the following statement:

> I have been using and researching figure drawings for more than 30 years. I began in graduate school to examine discrete drawing variables such as size, erasure, shading, line quality, distortion, omission, and the like. Although each variable was considered individually, there was also an attempt to summarize subgroups or groups of variables (Handler & Reyher, 1964, 1965, 1966) with the use of a rating scale for anxiety/conflict (Handler, 1967). Similar work has been done by Koppitz (1968, 1984). This validation research yielded a number of positive results, but over the years I have come to see

---

[1] For those who are unfamiliar with drawing techniques, detailed instructions given to the client are provided in Handler (1995), for the Draw-A-Person Test (DAP), the House-Tree-Person Test (H-T-P), and the Kinetic Family Drawing technique (K-F-D).

this method as counterproductive to an experiential approach in clinical application, and to validation research. I have come to believe that the usefulness of drawing techniques seems to be limited by the interpreter's ability to make experiential judgments about the drawings, and depends less on objective evaluations of the content of the drawings themselves, or on the stylistic variables often measured (e.g., shading, erasure, line pressure, etc.).

As I read the research and taught classes on drawing techniques over the years, I found that the focus on discrete variables seemed to encourage a molecular approach to interpretation. Students would focus on one or another variable, examining each in turn, and would be led to hypotheses that seemed far from the patient's experience. Similarly, researchers would repeatedly attempt to validate specific variables by correlating each one separately with one or another criterion. This research has been largely disappointing because it tends to be simplistic and to lack an experiential basis (see Riethmiller & Handler, in press). The inconsistent findings using this method have greatly damaged the reputation of graphic techniques within the field.

So why do we continue to be optimistic about the use of figure drawings for personality assessment? Primarily because in addition to being researchers we are also assessors and therapists with a predominantly psychodynamic orientation. We believe that attention to one's own reactions to the client are more useful than a detached cataloguing of observable behavior. Indeed, empathic attunement to the patient through "loss of distance" and "regression in the service of the ego," identification, and introspective attention to countertransference are the primary tools used in psychodynamic psychotherapy to gain a better understanding of the client. In addition, Winnicott (1971) reminded us that an approach to the patient and to his or her productions is facilitated by a "playful" attitude. Play transcends the boundary between self and other. It allows the interpreter to provide a "trying out ground for proceeding onward" (Grolnick, 1990).

Fortunately, the bulk of research has shown that interpretations guided by impressions and emotional reactions to drawings are superior to current sign approaches and objective scoring systems. For example, Tharinger and Stark (1990) tested this hypothesis in a clear and controlled way. They were careful to take full advantage of the raters' abilities to be empathically attuned to the drawings. They had two doctoral students sort drawings into five piles, with the pile scored with a 1 representing a general absence of psychopathology and the pile scored 5 representing severe emotional distress. The raters were then interviewed and were asked to describe the aspects of the drawings that led them to make their choices. These aspects were based on the raters' affective experience when "placing oneself in the place of the individual depicted [in the drawing] (p. 369)." The four criteria were (a) feelings of inhumanness, whereby one would feel animalistic, grotesque, or missing in essential body parts, (b) lack of agency, whereby the drawing gave the rater the feeling of being unable to make changes in the environment, (c) lack of well-being, which is highly related to the facial expressions in the drawing, and (d) a hollow, vacant, or stilted feeling. After these criteria were made explicit, a new rater and one of the original raters again rated the drawings using these criteria. These criteria successfully differentiated children with mood disorders from children in a control group. The exact procedure was also used with the Kinetic Family Drawings, with the same result. Meanwhile, none of the 30 individual, objective signs on the Koppitz Scale for figure drawings, and none of the 37 objective signs on a Kinetic Family Drawings rating scale differentiated among these groups. Thus, the experience-near approach was more successful than an individual sign approach.

It is important to note that although the approach used in this study was subjective and experiential, the raters were still able to achieve a high level of reliability. This high reliability of general impressions was also shown by Guinan and Hurley (1965), who found that PhD clinicians were able to match an average of 19 out of 20 drawings from individuals that were produced 5 weeks apart. Thus, we have reason to expect that when individuals stay close to their reactions to the drawings, and do not engage in free associations about the drawing details, they should make valid interpretations. We also believe this because of the consistency of interpretations seen among students in the classroom, a perfect place to informally test this hypothesis, if the atmosphere in that setting allows the students to risk creative play (see Fowler, chap. 2 of this volume; Handler, Fowler, & Hilsenroth, chap. 24 of this volume; Waehler & Sivec, chap. 6 of this volume). In such a setting students making blind interpretations, where they knew nothing about the patient but age and gender, consistently made correct, detailed interpretations 81% of the time, over a 6-year period.

Kot, Handler, Toman, and Hilsenroth (1994) used the same experiential approach to the one used by Tharinger and Stark (1990). In this study raters were asked to evaluate drawings of homeless men, inpatient psychiatric patients, and unemployed individuals who were enrolled in a vocational rehabilitation program. There were four criteria, posed as questions, used to rate the drawings for level of psychopathology: (a) Is the person in the drawing frightened of the world? (b) Does the person drawn have intact thinking? (c) Is he comfortable with close relationships? and (d) Would you feel safe being with the drawn person? Again, an objective scoring system did not differentiate these groups of individuals, but the rater's sum on the four experiential criteria did. On a scale from 1 to 5 (1 = no impairment, 5 = most impairment), the psychiatric patients all scored in the most impaired categories (4 and 5) and the vocational rehabilitation group had more scores in the mild range (1 and 2) than either of the other groups.

Another relevant study has demonstrated that accurate drawing interpretations are reached through qualities needed in clinical inference, namely empathy, intuition, and cognitive flexibility. This was demonstrated by Burley and Handler (1997), who tested the accuracy of drawing interpretations of undergraduate and graduate students. They found that those who were more accurate in their interpretations tended to score higher on the Hogan Empathy Scale, the Intuition scale of the Myers–Briggs, and on the Remote Associates Test, a measure of cognitive flexibility and/or creativity. Scribner and Handler (1987) found that affiliative interpreters were significantly more accurate in their interpretations, compared with those who were disaffiliative. In addition, interpreters who were unconsciously affiliative were significantly more accurate in their analysis of figure drawings, compared with those who were only consciously affiliative. The poor interpreters' approach to life emphasized power, dominance, order, and precision, whereas good interpreters saw themselves as responsible and cooperative in their relationships (Scribner & Handler, 1987).

Of course these studies do not suggest that drawing interpretation cannot eventually become a more objective enterprise through continued research. We may in time become more aware of the objective aspects in a drawing that tend to make it look distant, or friendly, or intimidating. However, success will require more complex drawing research than has been done thus far. For example, in order to identify drawings that would all tend to seem distant to good interpreters, one would need to look for combinations of features in drawings rather than individual signs. In other words, configural scoring approaches would be optimal with this method (Riethmiller & Handler, in press). Another approach to the validation of various drawing techniques is to focus not on the drawings themselves, but rather, on the clinician who is doing the interpretation. As indicated previously, not every interpreter can use figure drawings effectively in their clinical work; some prefer a variety of other techniques. To paraphrase Emanual Hammer, a long-time expert in figure-drawing assessment, "In the hands of some, figure drawings are like disconnected telephones." Therefore, if one wants to do good drawing interpretation research, one should first validate the interpreter (make certain he or she is skilled at making accurate interpretations).

TEACHING DRAWING INTERPRETATION

The similarity between teaching and learning assessment, on the one hand, and conducting psychotherapy, on the other hand, is aptly stressed throughout this book. Both endeavors are designed to help individuals expand their level of expertise, confidence, and ability. Not surprisingly, many of the technical advances made through the evolution of psychoanalysis are directly relevant to teaching, and particularly to the teaching of projective techniques. Some of these advances are: Gertrude Blanck's (1966) widely accepted notion that the analyst should support the currently highest level of ego functioning and should actively work with the patient's ego strengths, the Kohutian belief that interpretations should be kept close to the patient's experience lest they be misunderstood or completely lacking in impact (Kohut, 1984), and the familiar notion that when the therapist enables insight and interpretations to come from the patient, this facilitates a sense of agency and increased confidence in the patient. In the approach we describe in this chapter, figure-drawing interpretation becomes a cooperative enterprise between instructor and students, similar to that between therapist and patient. That is, interpretations that are reached in the classroom should be kept close to the students' experience. In addition, ideally, either interpretations should come from other students, or they should be a clarification of the students' experience. This process, by supporting the students' highest level of ego functioning, allows them to experience their own interpretive abilities. This experience can be understood as one that builds confidence and perhaps also builds something akin to psychic structure, thereby enhancing the students' interpretive ability using their own personal reactions. These concepts are all utilized in a teaching method that specifically attempts to build on the student's skills, and that emphasizes the student's trust in and use of his or her experience.

Research demonstrates that many students have the ability to interpret figure drawings fairly well before they receive any training in the technique, or even any training in personality theory (Albee & Hamlin, 1950; Burley & Handler, 1997; Levenberg, 1975; Schmidt & McGowan, 1959; Scribner & Handler, 1993). This finding is not surprising if we recognize the parallels between skill in figure-drawing interpretation and basic interpersonal skills. To do this, it is helpful to remember Harry Stack Sullivan's postulate that humans are, by nature, social beings. We communicate often despite ourselves, and all of our actions, gestures, facial expressions, and so on, in some way show others who we are. For example, when a deep relationship forms between two people they often feel that they "know" each other. This knowing involves, in part, an ability to intuit a friend's experience by recognizing, often without realizing it, subtle signs such as tension in their voice or uncharacteristic fidgets seen in the other. Similarly, figure drawings can be seen as a special mode of communication, which is largely unconscious, implicit, tacit. Individual differences in the natural ability to attend to and correctly perceive these communications of other people have been reflected in several studies discussed earlier in this chapter (Burley & Handler, in press; Scribner & Handler, 1987). This skill, however, appears to be amenable to training (Murray & Deabler, 1958), particularly if teachers actively encourage students to be open to exploration and flexible in their thinking. As Grolnick (1990) stated in his discussion of Winnicott's work concerning the child's adventures with creativity : "To take a creative leap, or even a little skip, off the beaten track, one must feel that the base of operation is a stable one, that experience has been continuous enough to tolerate the risk of discontinuity "(p.32). In this case we would substitute the term *stable, harmonious classroom holding environment* for stable base of operation.

Of course, we are not saying anything new here. Individuals' natural attunement to subtle communication has always been the key to empathy or, as Kohut referred to it, "vicarious introspection," which is the most basic ingredient in contemporary psychodynamic psychotherapy. We, however, want to explicitly state not only that this natural ability is the key to drawing interpretation, but also that it is an ability that the students already possess to a greater or larger extent when they first enter the assessment class. Thus, the initial and most crucial task in teaching students how to interpret drawings is to help them recognize their own abilities and to trust and use them (see Potash, chap. 9 of this volume; Handler, Fowler, & Hilsenroth, chap. 24 of this volume).

Part of this process will be to create an open forum in the classroom where voicing immediate reactions, which may at first seem uncomfortable, is actively encouraged. Often, when looking at drawings from a clinical sample, students will respond to the strangeness or uncanniness of the drawings. This experience is often expressed in the classroom through exclamations such as "wow" or "that's bizarre." It is the teacher's job, at this stage, to encourage students to direct their attention to these immediate reactions. They need to describe the uncanny, or sometimes subtle feelings that the drawings evoke, and aspects of the drawings that seem to stand out as most evocative. Some drawings may seem distant or mechanical, some may seem friendly, and others may evoke feelings of intrusion. Some drawings may seem bizarre in their deviance from reality, whereas others may seem rigidly conventional. All these factors evoke an initial emotional reaction in students; the trick is to describe these reactions in a careful and precise way.

When we interpret figure drawings, we are essentially analyzing an intense interpersonal interaction between the patient and the assessor. In this situation, the assessor simply asks the patient to "draw a person," and the patient knows that the assessor seeks to know him or her in a very real and personal way. The patient is asked to be open and vulnerable, as he or she realizes that the drawing created will be scrutinized as a representation of who he or she is. Thus, is there any doubt that this interpersonal situation will lead the patient to make use of his or her defensive structure, which is designed to shape the reactions of those who are seeking to know him or her?

The first technique we describe asks students to function as a *generalized other*. By this we mean that by carefully observing their own reactions to the drawings, students can obtain information about the reactions of others who encounter the patient interpersonally. The training focus becomes the dyadic unit formed by the clinician and the drawing itself. Questions such as "what would it be like to be this person's friend, child, or employer?" should be asked. But unlike many lay people, students trained in psychodynamic theory are able to recognize that their initial reactions are shaped by the defensive structures of the patient. In other words, the patient has tried to portray a particular persona through the drawing that is in some ways protective. But the drawings are like real life in that the defensive portrayal is rarely, if ever, completely successful. By examining the reactions with scrutiny, we are able to see not only the identity that the patient seeks to portray, but also the weaknesses that the defenses are designed to protect. We hope this is better shown in the examples provided later.

The next step in the interpretive process is somewhat more active, but equally important. The patient has presented us, through the drawing, with a representation of his or her experience. As assessors, our job is to become as closely acquainted with this presentation as we can. If the student can experience what it is like to *be* the person drawn, he or she will be better able to understand the artist. Getting "in touch" with the person in the drawing facilitates the student's identification with the artist. Students are thus in-structed to identify with the character in the drawing, and to ask themselves a number of questions: "How do I feel about myself"? "How do I approach the world"? "What is going on with me right now"? "What am I lacking and what do I need, or yearn for, in order to feel comfortable (safe)"? To answer these and other similar questions the students must experience a "loss of distance" of personal boundaries with the drawings. That is, the student must be free to imagine him or herself as the person drawn. He or she must then allow these experiences to become focal and then to articulate these evoked feelings, attitudes, needs, and desires. Using a qualitative approach, the good interpreter is able to engage fully in order to transcend mechanistic patterns of thinking. This approach sounds very much like the concept of psychoanalytic listening, developed by Kohut, as well as by other analysts (Kohut, 1959, 1977). Handler (1995) noted:

> Although this process is in part similar to the concept of "adaptive regression in the service of the ego," described by Kris (1952), it goes beyond the emphasis of the dynamic aspects of regression and the primitive, immature content of thoughts and feelings. What is added here is openness in turning toward the object and the ability to approach it with freshness, spontaneity, and interest. Introspection and self-reflection in the regressive process is probably not enough to achieve valid interpretation. What is needed, in addition, is the ability to become again reconnected, with cognitively reor-ganized creative understanding. (p. 238)

Although all of us regularly identify with characters when we watch televi-sion and film, and even in our daily interactions, some students may find it difficult to identify with a static drawing. To facilitate this process the students can be instructed to imitate the drawings as closely as possible. They should imitate the character's posture and facial expression. To the extent that the student is able to identify with the character in the drawing, to *become* that character, by allowing themselves to momentarily transcend ordinary self-boundaries, the student is likely to get a deeper understanding of the experience of the patient. Kris (1952) described this phenomenon when he wrote about a person viewing a work of art:

> Looking long enough, one tends to become aware of a kinesthetic reaction, however slight; it may be that one tries, at first imperceptibly and later consciously, to react with one's own body, or it may be that the reaction remains unconscious. We know that our ensuing emotional experience will still be colored by the reflection of the perceived posture, that our ego has in the process of perception utilized a complex apparatus, the body scheme, or ... the image of the body. ... On the second stage of reaction we identify ourselves with the artist's model. (pp. 55–56)

A Case Example

For example, suppose you show students the drawings in Figs. 16. 1 and 16.2, the male and female drawings of a 33-year-old male. You ask the students for reactions to the drawing, not psychological interpretations or theoretical constructs, but just reactions. It is easy to imagine that some students would respond

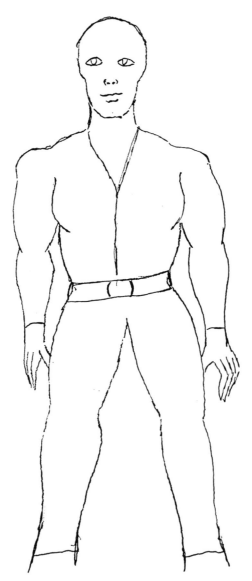

FIG. 16.1. Male figure drawing of a 33-year-old male patient.

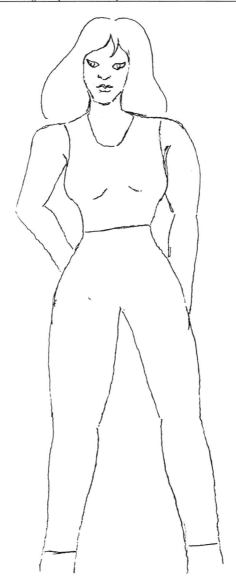

FIG. 16.2. Female figure drawing of a 33-year-old-male patient.

emotionally to these drawings. When they were shown to a group of graduate students, many of the students registered at least surprise, and many were startled. Why such reactions? Because the figures look superhuman; the portrayal of power and strength in these two drawings is very salient. "They look like superheroes out of a comic book," says one student. "Yes, how strange that they are both wearing tights" and "the male figure in particular looks almost inhuman" say two other students. Thus, the reactions have led us to recognize in the drawings a bold expression of power that lacks realism. In contrast to many other drawings, these portrayals do not seem to be of this world. Rather, they are likely to be rooted primarily in fantasy.

When identifying with the drawings, the male drawing looks benevolent, yet strong. He looks like he is ready for a fight if he is faced with one; he is hypervigalent, but he comes in peace. The aspects of the drawing that seem to suggest this are the man's open stance, his mouth, which moves upward at the ends into almost a smile, and his wide eyes. In contrast, when one stands in the posture of the female drawing and imitates her facial expression, the affects evoked are clearly more negative. Most of the students imagine that she feels angry or contemptuous. Her stance is slightly tilted and perhaps a bit cocky, her eyes are sharp and intimidating, and the hands behind her back look almost secretive (notice in the male drawing that the subject is able to draw hands well). So in our analysis of the drawings thus far we are pretty safe in assuming that this man regards strength highly and the ability to protect himself quite highly. In fact, we would guess that this man wants others, including the assessor, to see him as extremely strong, and at the same time, as peaceful. Yet despite this emphasis on strength we already see a hint of vulnerability, most notably the feelings of intimidation evoked by women. The feelings of intimidation that the female drawing evokes in us are likely to reflect this man's feelings about women. We would hypothesize that he finds women threatening. We would suspect, through our identification with the figures, that this man often does feel very strong, but this feeling of strength is clearly defensive, because it is not rooted in real-life interactions. The lack of realism in the drawings suggests that this strength is restricted to fantasy life.

Figure 16.3 is the drawing that this man produced when asked to "draw a family, doing something." The reaction in the students is visible as soon as the picture is shown. You see a class full of puzzled facial expressions, many of them wondering whether this was a particular test that they neglected to study. "What is the matter?" you ask. "Are those figures supposed to be interacting?" asks one student. "It looks like three separate scenes" says another student. "And two of the figures are doing solitary activities" says a third student. The reactions then start pouring in: "They don't have faces," "Their bodies don't have any detail," "They look like statues," "Are those three separate people or all the same person,?" and "That picture just looks eerie." You ask the students to tell you more about the affects associated with these reactions. The students tell you the lack of detail makes the drawing feel "eerie" because the figures look expressionless, inanimate, distant, inhuman, empty, and stiff. One student remarks that the fact that the figures are not interacting, when the instructions imply they should, gives her a cold feeling. It is a very impersonal drawing in many ways. "What kind of person would create this kind of drawing?" you ask. "Someone who spends a great deal of time alone, using the computer and writing music" one student responds. Not surprisingly, most of the class agrees that it

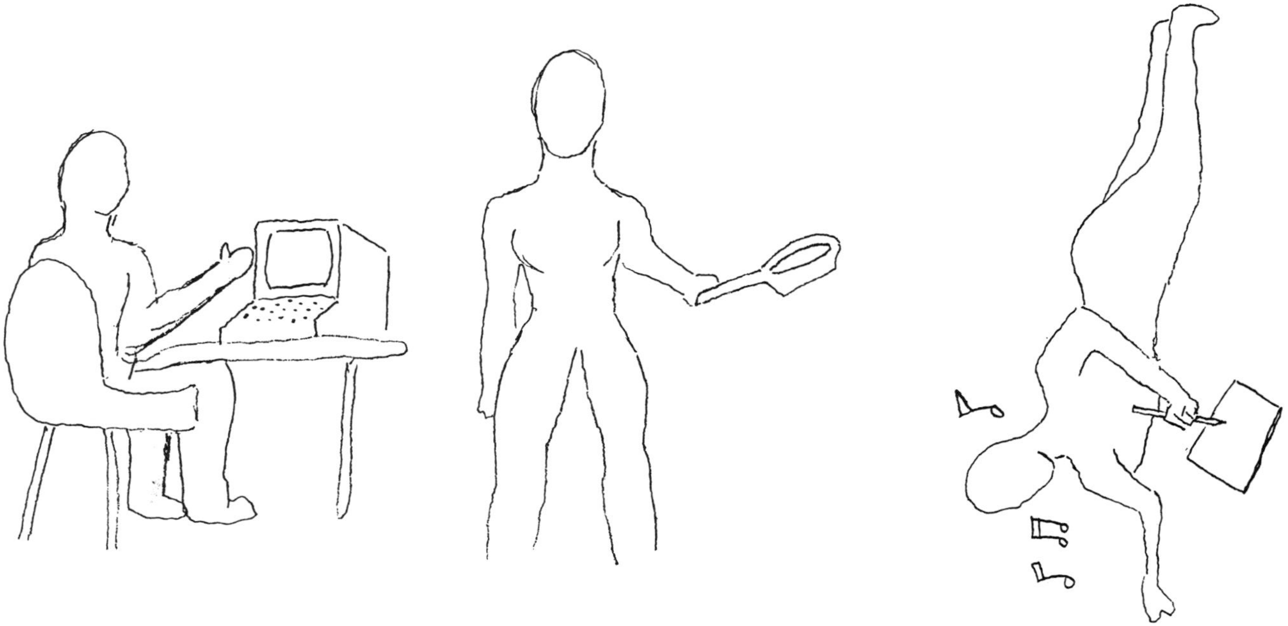

FIG. 16.3.   Kinetic family drawing of a 33-year-old male patient.

277

is unlikely that a person who is well connected with others, and whose life and world are "peopled" would produce this type of drawing.

These characters are difficult to identify with because they do not have faces. Yet the postures of the individuals portray activity, just like the male and female drawings. The music that is around the head of one figure gives the picture a lively feel, as if the figures seem to be somewhat engrossed in what they are doing. The integration of the common reactions suggests that this man probably tends to be very isolated; he is a loner. The fact that he even had to disregard the instructions that imply drawing a family "in some type of interaction" suggests that he feels very uncomfortable interacting with other people. Yet, he is likely to fill his life with solitary activities that make him feel engrossed, but do not eradicate his lack of vitality. At a very basic level this man is likely to feel isolated, dead, mechanical.

Notice that this method does not preclude the need for the interpreter to eventually explain the reasoning behind interpretations. Interpretations are *not* explained merely with the statement, "It just feels that way." Rather, one's reactions lead him or her to evocative aspects of the drawing, which can then be identified and then connected with affective responses. This interpretative strategy is not magic. For example, thus far we have made claims that the lack of facial features in the family drawing made the drawing feel distant, the upturned mouth and wide eyes in the male drawing made it seem friendly, and so forth. These inferences are amenable to consensual validation within the classroom. And if the context within which these features appear is carefully taken into account, we believe that these impressions are amenable to research validation as well.

Figure 16.4 is the man's animal drawing. It is not surprising that the animal comes out of pure fantasy. Again we see well-defined muscles and strength. However, our reaction here is a bit different than with the superhero drawings. The students respond, saying that this animal is much more vulnerable; it is beautiful and sensitive. One student says he is reminded of the benign look on the male figure's face. This drawing acccentuates the idea that a powerful figure, with a potentially deadly spear coming out of its head, is peaceful and loving. None of the students sees the unicorn as threatening. Much to the contrary, the hearts around this unicorn make it seem romantic, in a childish sort of way. And the childlike nature of the drawing leads us to take another look at the people drawings. They *do* look like comic book characters; they *are* expressing an almost preadolesent type of idealized power and strength. This animal, on the other hand, is showing an idealized, childish view of love and sexuality. By this time several students have commented on the unicorn's horn piercing the heart as an evocative symbol of sexuality. Thus, when integrating the reactions to these drawings, we would anticipate that this is a man who has difficulty participating in the real world because it clashes so starkly with the idealized and childlike fantasy world that he has created. The real world makes him feel vulnerable and threatened, which is something he is unable to tolerate. And relationships in the real world do not match his fantastical concepts of love and

FIG. 16.4. Animal drawing of a 33-year-old male patient.

sexuality, which is why he needs to represent them to us through symbols that only exist in pretense.

When examining the other testing and social history for this man we find some corroborating data. According to his assessor, who administered a full battery of tests, this is a man who is extremely anxious around others. His anxiety seems to be closely related to past romantic relationships that have led to his exploitation. For example, in a recent marriage, this man's wife asked to be able to sleep with other men, and he eventually discovered that she had been cheating on him. In a current relationship he became annoyed when his girlfriend repeatedly bit him, and he eventually bit her back. He felt very guilty about this event. It seems that he opens himself up to these exploitations because he has a very difficult time expressing his own aggression. Yet, these events seem to affect him; he has his guard up currently, and he is hypervigalant to prevent them from happening again. His Paranoia score on the MMPI (Minnesota Multiphasic Personality Inventory) is a T-score of 80 (second only to the Social Introversion Scale ($T = 82$). Yet, despite this hypervigalance, the assessor notes that this man tends to ignore the abuse of his current girlfriend, and to idealize her in a very childish and dependent way.

His high Social Introversion scale score reflects his tendency to deal with the threat of others through avoidance and escape. This man says that ever since preadolescence, when he reports an upsetting event where he was sexually fondled by an older female, he has spent most of his time in his room reading, listening to music, or drawing. He came to the psychological clinic because of an inability to express himself and to connect with other people.

In this demonstration we attempted to portray not only an interpretive process, but also a pedagogical technique. Notice in these examples that the psychological interpretation was tied closely to the students' reactions, so that the expression of these reactions almost seemed to be interpretations in themselves. In addition, students were encouraged to be very candid with their reactions without making an effort to fit them immediately into a theoretical framework. Thus, like the interpretive technique, this form of teaching is very experience-near; the teacher attempts to understand the students' reactions and experiences as closely as possible. These experiences and reactions are then used and built upon to develop well-formed interpretations in the classroom, because all of the students' reactions will have some basis in that of a generalized other (see Potash, chap. 9 of this volume). As I (Riethmiller) have been trained through this technique, I can attest to the experience that it evokes for the students. Interpretations raised and accepted in the class that were kept close to our reactions as students felt different than ones based on formulas or reached solely by professors. When interpretations were kept close to my experience I felt that I grasped them better. They were more understandable to me and felt less foreign. This procedure also allowed me to feel my own strength as an empathic interpreter, which was immensely important when I later began seeing patients as a therapist. And finally, expressing my reactions within a group setting and under the supervision of a professor gave me some understanding of my biases and countertransferential issues, which can lead to empathic failures. I have thus come to believe that this is an effective teaching method, both because of my own positive experience with it and because of its consistency with contemporary psychodynamic concepts regarding the facilitation of personal growth.

Additional Examples

Strangely enough, Fig. 16.5 was drawn by a 43-year-old man. What are the reactions that it evokes, and what are the feelings experienced through identification? This is a boy who is glowing while he is jumping through the air saying "look at me." The drawing has a fun-loving, boyish quality to it, but at the same time it feels intrusive. The boy seems to be forcing himself on us in a very grandiose, presumptuous, and phallic way.

The mere fact that this was drawn by a 43-year-old adult gives one an uncanny feeling, because the drawing is so clearly childish and full of a narcissistic naiveté. Interestingly, this man came for psychological assistance after he had been arrested for repeatedly prank calling an escort service, and initiating sexual discussions with the receptionist. This is a man who came to all of his appointments wearing jeans, T-shirts, and sandals. This drawing, much like this man's behavior and dress, clearly suggests that he either has never grown up, or is attempting to recapture his childhood in a very forced and maladaptive way.

FIG. 16.5. Figure drawing of a 43-year-old male patient.

Another example, one that was memorable for me (Handler), was a situation in which I was challenged by a student who was psychometrically oriented, who offered me a protocol to interpret. He believed nothing important could be said about the protocol that was of any significance concerning the drawer's person-ality. The adult female patient drew what appeared to me to be a rather seductive-looking female, and I reported to the student that I felt she would be somewhat harsh with men, would insist on being in control, and would want to be dominant in her relationship with males. I told him that I arrived at that conclusion by attempting to allow myself to feel as *she* would feel, to become *her* for a moment or two, and then report my feelings. This impression was enforced, I continued, when I could change my stance and could imagine myself being *with* her—being in her presence. I felt impressed by her power, strength, and attractiveness, but as a passive admirer rather than as an equal participant. I felt rather powerless under her searching gaze, and I verbalized that to the class. To the students' and my amazement, I saw that she had drawn the second figure, a male, nude, looking down at the floor, crouched in a submissive position. He felt powerless and exposed, compared to her stylishly clothed presence, further enhancing my initial feelings "in her presence." I repeated my feelings of vulnerability, and of weakness, exposed in her presence. She had drawn a phallic looking sportscar for her third figure, when she was asked to draw an automobile. Many years ago women did not draw sportscars when they were requested to draw automobiles. I rounded out my impressions by adding that I felt she was identified more with males than with females and that she was an art student (because of the crouched nude male drawing, in a studio art pose), who had recently been divorced. The latter was only a guess, because I believed that she would be having trouble in heterosexual relationships. The surprised student insisted that I knew the person who had done the drawings. They apparently were made by someone he knew well, and not by a patient. It was difficult to dissuade him from the notion that I knew the person when I attempted to interpret her drawings, he said, because I was correct in my interpretations.

The students were able to follow my approach in this classroom demonstration. They were able to comprehend the empathic intuitive experience, first of being the person drawn, and then of being a person who would interact with the person drawn. The final interpretation, of course, involved an integration of these two approaches. In addition, this is the time to help students sharpen their interpretations through a more detailed examination of various drawing details. This should not be done before the intuitive, experiential approach has been learned well, because it teaches the students to focus on details, thereby preventing them from using the preferred empathic, experiential approach to fully comprehend the patient. Now, however, attention to symbolic and stylistic aspects of the drawings will assist the students in their ability to generate more detailed, specific interpretive statements about the patient. A detailed discussion of these variables and their possible meanings can be found in a number of sources (e.g., for the DAP, Hammer, 1958, 1968; Handler, 1995; Handler & Reyher, 1964, 1966; Koppitz, 1968, 1984; Machover, 1949; Ogdon, 1977; for the K-F-D, Burns, 1982, 1987; Burns & Kaufman, 1970, 1972; Handler, 1995; Handler & Habenicht, 1994; for the H-T-P, Buck, 1948, 1966; Hammer, 1958; Handler, 1995). Care must be taken to ensure that students do not learn to interpret these symbols and signs in a rigid, or fixed manner, because the signs often have numerous alternative meanings, for different patients, and in different contexts. For example, shading and erasure, often interpreted as signs of anxiety and conflict, can also be interpreted as indications of adaptability and flexibility, denoting good ego functioning. In fact, in certain assessment situations, where the patient feels the atmosphere or the situation is tense, the *absence* of shading and erasure can be an indication of anxiety (see Handler & Reyher, 1964, 1965, 1966; Riethmiller & Handler, in press).

Concerning the issue of drawing styles, Handler and Reyher (1964, 1966) have described two drawing patterns: (a) a coping pattern, where the drawings are typically small, well-executed, with much detail, and heavy line quality, suggesting that this patient copes with the stress of the assessment situation by focusing on the task in a somewhat constricted manner, and (b) an avoidant pattern, where the drawings are typically large, diffuse, poorly articulated, with light lines, and missing body parts, suggesting that under the stress of the testing situation this person withdraws and/or avoids dealing with the situation.

Drawings and Artistic Ability

Many colleagues have been quite negative about the usefulness of figure drawings in the assessment battery, because they believe that the interpretation of the drawings is thoroughly confounded by the artistic ability variable. However, recently it has been demonstrated that artistic ability itself is an important factor in reflecting the degree of psychopathology rather than being a source of error, as indicated in the research literature. We are not here speaking of the differences between drawings of gifted artists, compared with those who have average artistic ability. Rather, the fact that clinicians tend to attribute drawings that are poorly executed to poorly adjusted people and drawings that are well executed to well-adjusted individuals (e.g., Cressen, 1975) may actually reflect clinicians' accurate diagnostic ability. Note the drawings of a random sample of patients on a hospital psychiatric ward in Fig. 16.6; they demonstrate severe body image distortion and reality-testing problems.

Lewinsohn (1965) also found that the overall quality of the drawings was related to measures of patients' adjustment, whereas Maloney and Glasser (1982) reported that the overall quality of the drawings differentiated various patient populations. The study by Yama (1990) supports this finding. He found that ratings of overall artistic quality, a rating of bizarreness of the figures, and a drawing estimate of overall adjustment of Vietnamese foster children were all related to the frequency of foster home placement, indicating that the child had severe emotional problems and therefore could not adjust, and had to be moved a number of times.

Students should be shown that in general the more emotionally disturbed a patient is, the more his or her drawings will demonstrate body image disturbances and major distortions, omissions, and a sense of instability and poor balance. Clinical and research evidence for this relationship can be seen in the work of Robins, Blatt, and Ford (1991). Several examples are included in this chapter. Note Fig.16. 7, the "before therapy" male drawings and the drawings after 15 months of therapy, obtained from a 24-year-old male patient. Figure 16.8 contains the "before" and "after" female drawings of the same male patient, done after 15 months of therapy. Note that the before-therapy drawings are simplistic and primitive; they are grossly distorted, devoid of detail, and they lack well-defined boundries.

Note the dramatic improvement in these drawings after about 15 months of inpatient psychotherapy at the Austen Riggs Center. The before-therapy drawings lack important body parts that deal with self-definition and communication with others (e.g., face, mouth, hands, fingers).

The first drawing of the female lacks sexual differentiation, whereas the second drawing has definite sexually defined body areas. The first male drawing

FIG. 16.6. Drawings from patients in a psychiatric hospital.

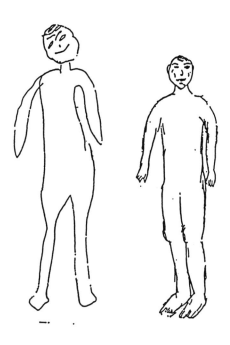

FIG. 16.7. Before and after 15 months of therapy:
male drawings of a 24-year-old male patient.

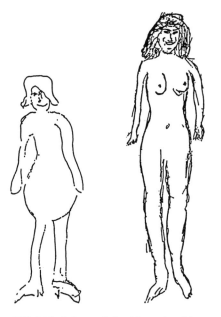

FIG. 16.8. Before and after 15 months of therapy:
female drawings of a 24-year-old male patient.

is quite similar to the first female drawing in that it is primitive and childlike in its
execution, with poor boundaries, poorly articulated hands and arms, and a posture
that seems to reflect dependency and passivity. The head and body of the before-
therapy drawings are quite distorted, and lack detail. The very significant change
in the posture, to what appears to be a more assertive stance, and the major
improvements in drawing quality, which seems to reflect a sense of adequacy and
activity, were also found in the drawings of other improved patients. The facial
features are now clearer, and more realistic, and the hands are better defined,
suggesting better ability to communicate and to interact with others. There is a
sense of self-definition in the drawings done after 15 months of treatment that was
not present in the before-therapy drawings. It is emphasized to the students that
the drawings of patients who are not improved do not change appreciably, and they
are helped to learn the distinction between distortions produced due to poor artistic
ability, and those that reflect severe emotional problems.

In another example of drawing changes during psychotherapy, Handler
(1995) described the drawing of a 34-year-old man who was facing a prison
sentence for theft (see Fig. 16.9).

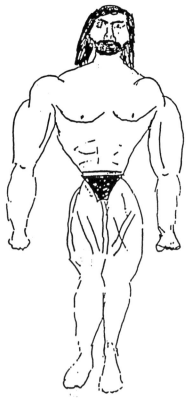

FIG. 16.9. Drawing of a 34 year-old man who committed a crime
and was awaiting sentencing.

FIG. 16.10. Drawing of the same 34-year-old man, after 2 years of therapy.

Although his anger was easily seen in the demeanor of the figure, he denied feeling angry, even when the examiner attempted to discuss the figure with him. Despite requests to describe the look on the man's face, his piercing eyes, his clenched fists, or his body stance, the patient insisted that he had drawn a happy man, with a smile on his face. After additional questioning, the patient asserted that the smile was not evident, because it was underneath the beard.

After 2 years of therapy, which is still ongoing, where the patient and the therapist have dealt with denial, false-self issues, as well as many self-defeating, narcissistic issues, the patient was more open about his dependency and neediness, and his immaturity in some areas. He drew a quite different drawing this time (Fig. 16.10).

In a discussion with the patient about this drawing he requested that it be titled, "Working Toward Getting Better." He was now able to immediately recognize the differences between this drawing and the one he had done 2 years before: "This shows how I really feel underneath, where I'm really not sure of myself," he said, "I don't feel grown up, so I don't draw as well," and "he looks like he's falling over."

To deal with moderate artistic ability problems, Handler and Reyher (1964, 1966) developed a control figure for artistic ability, an automobile drawing, which was found to be an emotionally neutral stimulus, to get an initial gauge of the individual's artistic ability. This estimate should then enable the clinician to separate artistic ability from psychopathology in the more emotionally laden drawing responses. A number of studies validated the use of this control measure (Handler & Reyher, 1964, 1965, 1966) and therefore, students are asked to use it when the issue of artistic ability presents itself in doing an assessment. It is often possible to differentiate between those patients who draw poor figures and a poor automobile, and are therefore rated as having poor artistic ability, and those patients who draw the people poorly, because of the conflictual emotional content aroused by doing the drawing, and, in contrast, produce a good automobile drawing.

In Fig. 16.11 we see the male figure drawing, and in Fig. 16.12 we see the female figure drawing of a highly schizoid individual, compared to his house drawing (Fig. 16.13).

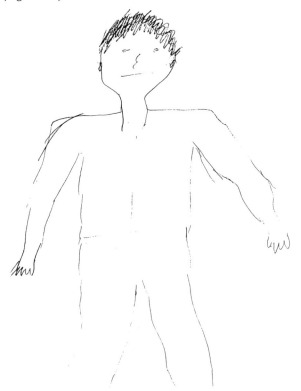

FIG. 16.11. Male figure drawings of a highly schizoid patient.

FIG. 16.12. Female figure drawing of a highly schizoid patient.

FIG. 16.13. House drawing of a highly schizoid patient.

The well-drawn house precludes our ability to explain away the bizarreness of the person drawings by suggesting a global deficit in drawing ability. Perhaps the house, because it is drawn with some intellectualized distance, arouses less internal conflict, compared with the figures. However, this pattern clearly indicates that the patient possesses adequate artistic ability, but that his severe emotional problems result in a distortion or fragmentation of the self. Thus students, when they begin to become somewhat comfortable in their interpretive skills, should be encouraged to be vigilant to these discrepancies.

The Unique Contribution of Drawings

In those training programs that still maintain an emphasis on assessment, students may often feel like they are being hit by a barrage of new tests and they may have trouble distinguishing their purposes. Thus, it is important that the unique contributions of drawing tests be discussed. Often, when asked, students will recognize the key contribution drawing approaches make to the test battery. Drawing is the only task in the battery that does not involve copying or describing an external stimulus. Therefore, the patient is required to create an image without the aid of external structure or direction. In order to complete this task without unmanageable anxiety and confusion, a patient needs to rely on internal structure. Thus, in the absence of either external or internal structure patients whose sense of self is fragmented or damaged will tend to draw strangely distorted or uncanny images. Therefore, it is through the drawing techniques that we begin to see, with these patients, the full depth of their psychopathology. Students can be sensitized to this phenomenon if they are shown samples of drawings from psychotic and severely disturbed inpatients. They can readily see that these distortions transcend the issue of poor artistic ability as a confounding variable in drawing interpretation.

Another reason drawings are valuable, which may seem objectionable to many researchers, is that they allow the clinician to obtain a nonverbal understanding of the patient. When a clinician reaches an interpretation by verbalizing and making explicit his or her reactions, this clinician will necessarily only be able to partially describe his or her emotional experience. Nevertheless, the unarticulated aspects of these reactions are an important form of knowledge about the patient. They contribute to a "working model" that one has and uses in one's work with a client. The working model, as it has been described by Greenson (1960), is the representation of a patient that a clinician has within his or her psyche. It is an intimate, nonverbal understanding of the client that enables one to anticipate the patient's actions, reactions, and experience. Indeed, the working model is similar to, but more primal, than one's theoretical conceptualization of the patient. And it is the development of this structure that allows for a gradual increase in empathic understanding of the client. We hope the demonstrations in this chapter have allowed teachers and students to recognize that the interpretation of drawings has a more intimate feel to it than the interpretation of other tests. We believe that this feeling is evoked because of the largely nonverbal nature of the task, and of the interpreter's understanding.

There are a number of additional reasons that drawing techniques are useful in the assessment battery. They require a minimum amount of time to administer (5 to 10 minutes, typically); they yield a great deal of information about self-concept and the patient's view of their role "in the world." The various drawing techniques have few age and intelligence limitations; they are often useful with patients who are guarded, evasive, or otherwise nonverbal, or those who cannot comprehend the more complex instructions of other tests. Drawing techniques also offer an excellent springboard for discussions with the patient of problem or conflict areas. They are also quite useful in illustrating change in psychotherapy (see Blatt & Ford, 1994; Handler, 1995), especially in charting changes in sex therapy (see Hartman & Fithian, 1972; P. Sarrel & L. Sarrel, 1979; P. Sarrel, L. Sarrel, & Berman, 1981), in illuminating relationship patterns and areas of difficulty in families (see Burns, 1982, 1987; Burns & Kaufman, 1970, 1972; Handler, 1995), and in illuminating object relations issues (Kissen, 1986).

Special Populations

The discussion of children's drawings in the classroom allows students to recognize how stages of development are reflected in figure drawings. Therefore, it is important to describe the development of drawing ability in children, beginning with the primitively drawn circle, which at first represents the entire person to the child, to the gradual development of a body concept and the refinement of drawing details as the child's observational and representational abilities improve. These gradual changes, which mirror the continued awareness of self and body, should be illustrated with many examples, and the students should be given additional normative data (see Handler, 1995; Koppitz, 1968, 1984; Machover, 1949) to help them understand age-related norms. Students are then quite able to internalize the norms and standards needed to interpret childrens' drawings. Thus, an understanding of the vast differences in the representation of the body at various ages makes students less likely to interpret children's drawings from the vantage point of an adult, enabling them to more effectively take the child's perspective.

One misconception about drawing techniques is that, because they do not involve language, they are culture free. This is incorrect; there are a number of large differences in the quality and content of drawings from different ethnic and cultural groups. These differences must be addressed by the instructor. The work of Dennis (1966) and Handler and Habenicht (1994) illustrate the cultural variation quite well and can be very helpful to students.

SUMMARY

Through the discussion and examples in this chapter we have attempted to demonstrate the usefulness of figure drawings for personality assessment when they are used experientially by skilled interpreters. Currently, research suggests that an experiential approach, which utilizes the interpreter's emotional responses to the drawings, is the most appropriate way of reaching accurate interpretations. Consequently, the teaching method offered in this chapter focuses on enabling students to trust, and clarify their own emotional reactions. Through this method students should get a sense of how their patients function in the absence of external structure, and they should be able to enhance the nonverbal working model which is used to understand the patient's emotional life. In this chapter we have also addressed other important issues, such as the unique contributions of drawings in a battery, how interpreters, students, and teachers can deal with the issue of artistic ability, and the use of drawings with children and cultural minorities. Overall, we hope this chapter encourages teachers and students to think about the usefulness of figure drawings as one test in the battery that is experiential, completely lacking in structure, and often very intimate in its portrayal of the patient's experience.

REFERENCES

Albee, G., & Hamlin, R. (1950). An investigation of the reliability and validity judgements inferrred from drawings. *Journal of Clinical Psychology, 5*, 389–392.

Blanck, G. (1966). Some technical implications of ego psychology. *International Journal of Psycho-Analysis, 47*, 6–13.

Blatt, S., & Ford, R. (1994). *Therapuetic change*. New York: Plenum.

Buck, J. (1948). The H-T-P. *Journal of Clinical Psychology, 4*, 151–159.

Buck, J. (1966). *The House-Tree-Person technique, revised manual*. Los Angeles: Western Psychological Services.

Burley, T., & Handler, L. (1997). Personality factors in the accurate interpretation of projective tests: The Draw-A-Person Test. In E. Hammer (Ed.), *Advances in projective drawing interpretation* (pp. 359–377). Springfield, IL: Thomas.

Burns, R. (1982). *Self-growth in families: Kinetic Family Drawings (K-F-D) research and application*. New York: Brunner/Mazel.

Burns, R. (1987). *Kinetic-House-Tree-Person Drawings (K-H-T-P)*. New York: Brunner/Mazel.

Burns, R., & Kaufman, S. (1970). *Kinetic Family Drawings (K-F-D): An introduction to understanding children through kinetic drawings*. New York: Brunner/Mazel.

Burns, R., & Kaufman, S. (1972). *Actions, styles, and symbols in Kinetic Family Drawings (K-F-D)*. New York: Brunner/Mazel.

Cressen, R. (1975). Artistic ability of drawings and judges' evaluations of the DAP. *Journal of Personality Assessment, 39*, 132–137.

Dennis, W. (1966). *Group values through children's drawings*. New York: Wiley.

Greenson, R. (1960). Empathy and its vicissitudes. *International Journal of Psychoanalysis, 41*, 418–424.

Grolnick , S. (1990). *The work and play of Winnicott*. Northvale, NJ: Jason Aronson.

Guinan, J. F., & Hurley, J. R. (1965). An investigation of the reliability of human figure drawings. *Journal of Projective Techniques, 29*, 300–304.

Hammer, E. (Ed.). (1958). *The clinical application of projective drawings.* Springfield, IL: Thomas.

Hammer, E. (1968). Projective drawings. In A. Rabin (Ed.), *Projective techniques in personality assessment.*(pp. 366–396). New York: Springer.

Handler, L. (1967). Anxiety indexes in projective drawings: A scoring manual. *Journal of Projective Techniques and Personality Assessment, 31,* 46–57.

Handler, L. (1995).The clinical use of drawings. In C. Newmark (Ed.), *Major psychological assessment instruments* (pp. 206 –293). Boston: Allyn & Bacon.

Handler, L., & Habenicht, D. (1994). The Kinetic Family Drawing technique: A review of the literature. *Journal of Personality Assessment, 63(3),* 440–464.

Handler, L., & Reyher, J. (1964). The effects of stress on the Draw-A-Person Test. *Journal of Consulting Psychology, 28,* 259–264.

Handler, L., & Reyher, J. (1965). Figure drawing anxiety indexes: A review of the literature. *Journal of Personality Asessment, 29,* 305–313.

Handler, L., & Reyher, J. (1966). Realationship between GSR and anxiety indexes in projective drawings. *Journal of Consulting and Clinical Psychology, 30,* 605–607.

Hartman, W., & Fithian, M. (1972). *Treatment of sexual dysfunction.* Long Beach, CA: Center for Marital and Sexual Studies.

Kissen, M. (1986). Object relations aspects of figure drawings: Structural and graphic characteristics. *Psychiatric Quarterly Supplement, 38,* 76–110.

Kohut, H. (1959). Introspection, empathy, and psychoanalysis. *American Psychoanalytic Association Journal, 26,* 21–47.

Kohut, H. (1977). *The restoration of the self.* New York: International Universities Press.

Kohut, H. (1984). *How does analysis cure?* Chicago: University of Chicago Press.

Koppitz, E. (1968). *Psychological evaluation of children's human figure drawings.* New York: Grune & Stratton.

Koppitz, E. (1984). *Psychological evaluation of human figure drawings by middle school pupils.* New York: Grune & Stratton.

Kot, J., Handler, L, Toman, K., & Hilsenroth, M. (1994, April). *The psychological assessment of homeless men.* Paper presented at the meeting of the Society for Personality Assessment, Chicago.

Kris, E. (1952). *Psychoanalytic explorations in art.* New York: International Universities Press.

Levenberg, S. (1975). Professional training, psychodiagnostic skill, and Kinetic Family Drawings. *Journal of Personality Assessment, 34,* 389–393.

Lewinsohn, P. (1965). Psychological correlates of overall quality of figure drawings. *Journal of Consulting Psychology, 29,* 504–512.

Machover, K. (1949). *Personality projection in the drawings of the human figure.* Springfield, IL: Thomas.

Maloney, M., & Glasser, A. (1982). An evaluation of the clinical utility of the Draw-A-Person Test. *Journal of Clinical Psychology, 38,* 183–190.

Murray, D. C., & Deabler, H. L. (1958). Drawings and diagnoses, and the clinician's leaning curve. *Journal of Projective Techniques, 22,* 415–420.

Ogdon, D. (1977). *Psychodiagnostics and personality assessment: A handbook* (2nd ed.). Los Angeles: Western Psychological Services.

Riethmiller, R., & Handler L. (in press). Problematic methods and unwarranted conclusions in DAP research: Suggestions for improved research procedures. *Journal of Personality Assessment*.

Robins, C., Blatt, S., & Ford, R. (1991). Changes in human figure drawings during intensive treatment. *Journal of Personality Assessment, 57*, 477–497.

Sarrel, P., & Sarrel, L. (1979). *Sexual unfolding*. Boston: Little, Brown.

Sarrel, P., Sarrel, L., & Berman, S. (1981). Using the Draw-A-Person (DAP) Test in sex therapy. *Journal of Sex and Marital Therapy, 7*, 163–183.

Schmidt, L., & McGowan, J. (1959). The differentiation of human figure drawings. *Journal of Consulting Psychology, 23*, 129–133.

Scribner, C., & Handler, L. (1987). The interpreter's personality in Draw-A-Person interpretation: A study of interpersonal style. *Journal of Personality Assessment, 51*, 112–122.

Scribner, C., & Handler, L. (1993). *Intuitive DAP interpreters: An investigation of lifestyles of good and poor interpreters*. Paper presented at the mid-winter meeting of the Society for Personality Assessment, San Francisco.

Tharinger, D., & Stark, K. (1990). A qualitative versus quantitative approach to evaluating the Draw-A-Person and Kinetic Family Drawing: Study of mood- and anxiety-disorder children. *Psychological Assessment, 2*, 365–375.

Winnicott, D. W. (1971). *Playing and reality*. New York: Basic Books.

Yama, M. (1990). The usefulness of human figure drawings as an index of overall adjustment inferred from human figure drawings. *Journal of Personality Assessment, 54*, 78–86.

17

Teaching and Learning the Interpretation of the Wechsler Intelligence Tests as Personality Instruments

Leonard Handler
University of Tennessee

Students often wonder why I include the Wechsler tests (WISC–III, WAIS–R, WAIS–III) as personality assessment instruments. My reply is that Wechsler understood that intelligence and personality were not separate aspects of functioning. His definition of intelligence indicated that he viewed intelligence and personality as overlapping and interconnected concepts: "The aggregate or global capacity to act purposefully, think rationally, and to deal effectively with his [or her] environment" (Wechsler, 1958, p. 7). This definition says nothing about such concepts as, for example, verbal ability, abstract ability, concept formation, or visual-motor functioning, some terms that are typically used in describing WISC and WAIS performance.

Daniel Goleman, in his recent book, *Emotional Intelligence* (1995), highlighted the importance of emotional and social factors as measures of intelligence. He described an expanded model of what it means to be intelligent, which "puts emotions at the center of aptitudes for living" (p. xiii). Goleman pointed to the importance of such personal characteristics as: being able to motivate oneself and persist in the face of frustration; the ability to control impulses, and delay gratification; the ability to regulate one's moods and keep distress from interfering with the ability to think; and the ability to empathize and hope, as characteristics of emotional intelligence, which are central to living an intelligent life. Gardner (1993) and Salovey (Mayer & Salovey, 1993; Salovey & Mayer, 1989–1990) have discussed similar issues, such as the importance of *interpersonal* intelligence ("the ability to understand other people; what motivates them, how they work; how to work cooperatively with them"; Goleman, 1995, p. 39), as well as *intrapersonal* intelligence, "the capacity to form an accurate, veridical model of oneself and to be able to use that model to operate effectively in life" (Goleman, 1995, p. 43).

I ask students to focus their attention on such related areas of functioning on the Wechsler tests as stylistic and characterological variables (e.g., the manner in which patients approach the various subtests, how they deal with success and failure, the style of approach to each item, and ego function variables, all defined and discussed later. This approach is very difficult to communicate to students because they have been indoctrinated with the psychometric approach to intelligence testing, which they find is a reassuring alternative to the typically subjective approach to the interpretation of projective data. To bolster interest in this somewhat experiential approach, I deemphasize the importance of obtaining an IQ score. Instead, I emphasize a rationale that describes the use of the test to obtain a view of the patient as he or she functions on a variety of tasks (the subtests), in order to make generalizations from this performance to the patient's functioning in a variety of everyday situations. It is also possible to make predictions concerning the patient's functioning in therapy, because the experience of interpersonal stress in the assessment setting is often similar to the stress experienced in many approaches to psychotherapy (Zetzer & Beutler, 1995). For example, Zetzer and Beutler stated, "The patient's response to the time demands of the Digit Symbol (DS), Block Design (BD), Object Assembly (OA), and Arithmetic subtests provide an opportunity for the clinician to observe, in the analogue test environment, how the patient responds to the imposition of combined time, role and structure pressures that may characterize different forms of therapy" (p. 141).

We also focus on the assessment of ego functions. For example, it is possible to determine whether the patient can, when necessary, perform adequately while ignoring extraneous stimulation. This stimulation can be external (e.g., annoyances such as noises), or internal (interfering thoughts, fantasies). This ego function is called *stimulus barrier* (Bellak, Hurvich & Gediman, 1973). Other ego functions tapped by various parts of the WAIS–R and WAIS–III include *reality testing* (accuracy of perception), *judgment* (including appropriateness of behavior and awareness of consequences), *sense of reality of the world and the self* (clearness of demarcation of self from outside world, extent to which external events are experienced as real, extent to which body is experienced as familiar and as belonging to the self), *regulation and control of drive, affect, and impulse* (the directness of impulse expression, the effectiveness of delay and control mechanisms, degree of frustration tolerance), *object relations* (the degree and kind of relatedness to others, the extent to which others are seen as separate from the self, the extent to which object constancy is present), *thought processes* (the ability to use reasoned concepts, the degree to which language is based on secondary process thinking, the degree of adaptiveness in memory, concentration, and attention), *defensive functioning* (the extent to which anxiety or repression are present, the degree to which the defense mechanisms have maladaptively affected relationships, behavior, and adaptation), *autonomous functioning* (degree of impairment in attention, concentration, memory, learning, perception; degree of disturbance in habit patterns and learned complex skills, routines, hobbies), *synthetic-integrative functioning* (degree to which discrepant or contradictory attitudes, values, emotions, behaviors are reconciled or integrated; degree to which intrapsychic and behavioral functioning are integrated), and *mastery-competence* (how well a patient performs, especially compared with his or her ability to actually master the environment; patient's feeling of competence with respect to mastery; Bellak et al., 1973). Space does not permit examples of test indications for each of these ego functions. Data come from performance on the various subtests, from content of the responses, or from extratest verbalizations. Students easily learn that the WISC–III, WAIS–R, and WAIS–III are rich sources of hypotheses about psychopathology (Blatt & Allison, 1981, Matarazzo, 1972; Rapaport, Gill, & Schafer, 1968) and that data from the Wechsler tests are also an excellent source of information about emotional control, areas of conflict, and coping strategies (Kaufman, 1990; Zetzer & Beutler, 1995).

Allison, Blatt, and Zimet (1968) viewed the use of the WISC and WAIS in a similar fashion, which they also conceptualized from an ego psychology point of view:

> The primary function … of the Wechsler tests is to assess … adaptive potentials of the individual, namely, his [or her] ability to function effectively in relatively impersonal situations which involve past achievements and current problem solving efforts. The Wechsler tests play a unique role in the … battery of presenting the subject with a number … of situations with the request that he [or she] respond in as organized and realistic a way as possible and remain relatively unaffected by … conscious fantasy life. Adequate functioning demands the maintenance of ego boundaries, so that primitive fantasies and wishes do not invade reality oriented thought.…Excursions into fantasy on the Wechsler tests, therefore, represent at least a momentary loss of reality focus and orientation and suggest that to some degree secondary process thinking can be infused by more archaic modes of thought. (p. 21)

More recent approaches to conceptualization stress the importance of object relations in the analysis of Wechsler data. There are a number of ways in which the patient's object relations (a person's thoughts, feelings, and mental representations of self and others, as well as the pattern of relationships they establish) can be tapped by Wechsler analysis. For example, Allison et al. (1968), Rapaport et al. (1968), and Wechsler (1958) all recommended that patients should be asked to tell a story about each of the Picture Arrangement (PA) items after the patient has arranged them, in order to provide projective data concerning the way in which the patient experiences relationships. Segal, Westen, Lohr, and Silk (1993) found a strong relationship between nearly all the object relations scales used to rate the PA stories and the patients' social adjustment in their love relationships. Even more important, the authors found that the patients' capacity to offer coherent and integrated accounts of events in their stories and to attribute plausible causes of events to the characters in their stories correlated highly with measures of social adjustment. To tap these aspects of object relations, students are therefore taught to obtain stories to each of the PA items.

One aspect of object relations theory focuses on the *interpersonal* sphere. The patient's reactions to the examiner, and the relationship established with the examiner are in some sense similar to the relationships the patient establishes in situations outside the testing session. It is important to fully understand the quality of this relationship. This information will, in turn, illuminate the meaning and quality of the test responses and will provide data concerning the generalizability of the reactions called forth. The manner in which the patient responds to support and encouragement is important. Does it facilitate the patient, or does he or she ignore it? Does it appear effective in motivating him or her? Perhaps this is symbolic of the manner in which the patient responds to similar support in the environment, or of how he or she would respond to the therapist (see Potash, chap. 9 of this volume). Another issue concerns the degree to which the patient will allow the examiner to participate in reducing their level of tension. That is, does the patient allow the examiner to soothe him or her, and does the patient work to soothe himself or herself? (Winnicott, 1971, 1975). Students are taught to pay special attention to this interaction, as a possible key to how the patient may later deal with a therapist.

The ego function rationale described earlier is based on the work of David Rapaport and his associates (Rapaport, Gill, & Schafer, 1946; Schafer, 1948). Rapaport emphasized that a great deal could be learned about patients from an analysis of their intelligence test scores and responses. He felt it was important to consider "not only every subtest score, but every single response and every part of every response, as significant and representative of the subject. ... Where the response deviates from the conventional, the deviation does not merely fail to add to his score; it must also be considered as a characteristic which may give us material toward the understanding of the subject" (Rapaport et al., 1946, p. 67). Rapaport also stressed the importance of comparing the successes and failures on a given type of test item in order to gain some understanding of the subject (intratest scatter): "If a subject knows how many pints there are in a quart, but does not know what the Koran is, this will give us merely an idea of his range of information. But if he knows what the Koran is and asserts that a quart has four pints, we must consider the presence of a temporary insufficiency; and if he insists that the capital of Italy is Constantinople or the Vatican is a robe, psychotic maladjustment will have to be considered" (Rapaport et al., 1946, p. 66).

Another major part of Rapaport's orientation to intelligence test interpretation is the analysis of the relationship of the score of one subtest to the scores of other subtests (intertest scatter). Rapaport made much of the importance of scatter patterns associated with various diagnostic groups. However, emphasis on scatter does not seem to be an effective teaching strategy because it focuses on nomothetic rather than on ideographic and experiential aspects of the test, reifying a sign approach as an interpretative style. In addition, Piedmont, Sokolove, and Fleming (1989a) found no evidence for the utility of many of Rapaport's diagnostic hypotheses using WAIS and WAIS–R subtest scatter patterns. Other findings (Boone, 1992, 1993; Mittenberg, Thompson, Schwartz, Ryan, & Levitt, 1991; Ryan, Paolo, & Smith, 1992) also call into question many popular and long-held interpretations based on intertest scatter. The research data concerning the meaning of differences among subtest scores for an individual protocol are reviewed with the students to facilitate subtest scatter interpretation. They are alerted to data that indicate that in most cases these differences are due to chance or represent normal individual differences in ability (e.g., Piedmont, Sokolove, & Fleming, 1989b; Schinka, Vanderploeg, & Curtiss, 1994).

In his revision of Rapaport's two-volume series Holt (in Rapaport et al., 1968) suggested that clinicians have misinterpreted Rapaport's approach, ignoring the very creative ideographic emphasis he pioneered. Instead, subtest scores and patterns became associated with specific interpretations and with specific diagnostic entities [e.g., "a Similarities score three points below Vocabulary is suggestive of psychosis (or brain damage); paranoid trends are often indicated (except in chronic or deteriorated schizophrenics) by well-retained Similarities rising above Vocabulary and the Verbal mean"] (p. 105)]. In teaching Wechsler interpretation it is important to discourage students from reliance on these misleading and often irrelevant subtest labels and subtest relationships to describe intellectual functioning. Students cling tenaciously to these trait labels, often employing them in meaningless fashion in test reports (e.g., "She had good judgment and ability to maintain attention and concentration, but her ability to utilize abstract reasoning and her visual-motor coordination are below average, as is her ability to define words").

Except for his emphasis on subtest scatter, this writer feels that Rapaport's insights are still quite germane in establishing an understanding of the WAIS–R, WAIS–III, and WISC–III for an individual patient. Yet, it is just this emphasis on scatter that has been highlighted by applied clinicians. In this chapter an attempt is made to utilize Rapaport's original insights as a starting point, in an effort to describe to students and teachers alike an approach to the interpretation of Wechsler data that includes a modification and extension of administration procedures. The suggestion of a change in the administration procedure often results in a great deal of resistance from students, who believe that this procedure might compromise present and future administration (see H. Lerner, chap. 3 of this volume). Therefore, as an introduction, we discuss the standardization approach to the Wechsler tests, and the fact that this standardization did not focus on a variety of situational, experiential, or personality variables. Both the importance and the pitfalls of the psychometric approach are emphasized. The standardization implies a nomothetic orientation, despite the fact that individual scores are generated. Research on the factor structure of these tests also implies a nomothetic approach, because only two or three factors are typically reported.

In addition, the Wechsler tests are standardized on the general public and not on the populations we typically test. We primarily test people who self-select with various emotional and/or educational problems. There are problems of style and approach with these patients, and a host of other potential idiosyncratic problems that can adversely affect performance. For example, nowhere in factor analytic studies do we see such idiosyncratic issues mentioned as concerns about body integrity, fear of failure, fear of success, compulsive needs to be accurate, or diffuse thinking/perception, to name just a few of the problems that have been demonstrated to interfere with efficient performance. These and other interfering factors are undoubtedly less of a problem in people whose emotional adjustment is typically good, compared with those who typically self-select for assessment. If this is the case, it behooves us to make an effort to determine which of these factors, if any, and which others not yet mentioned, interfere with adequate performance. Without such an analysis major errors are made in the interpretation of findings.

Students are initially confused when I decry the overemphasis on objectivity, standardization, and structure in much of present-day IQ testing. It is difficult for them to understand that in most instances reliance on scores alone, to the exclusion of experiential data, often results in quite erroneous and misleading conclusions. We often "lose" the "person" in our overzealous attempts to obtain reliable and objectively scored protocols. I give them an example of a recently tested patient who spent 8 years in a class for the mentally retarded, based on a very low WISC–R IQ score. It was obvious from reading a brief summary of the assessment that his attention and motivation were minimal during the testing session. The report described such behaviors as fidgeting, looking out the window, and refusal to respond to a number of rather easy questions. Yet, the IQ score was reported as if it alone were objective fact; no allowance was made for possible interfering factors. I obtained an IQ for this patient that was well within the Average range. As he took the test the patient repeated again and again, "I'll show them—I'm not retarded!" The first examiner made the obvious mistake of "believing the number" while ignoring the circumstances of the testing, the child's willingness to communicate, and the quality of rapport established.

Such a procedure may be more widespread than at first imagined. Garfield and Affleck (1960) reported a study concerning 24 individuals committed to a state home for the retarded who were later released as not mentally defective. They stated, in part:

> We were impressed ... with the tendency of some examiners to report psychometric data and IQ scores with little sensitivity to other non-cognitive factors which may affect intellectual performance. ... Little allowance was made ... for emotional factors which ... might have contributed to the lowered level of performance. ... *In the desire to appear "objective," great reliance was placed on test scores alone. This ... was ... evident in the reports [and] in the reaction of social agencies and the courts ... Credence is readily* granted a reported test score because of its *seeming objectivity.* (pp. 907, 911–914 [emphasis added])

Again and again, I emphasize that the IQ score is not an end in itself and that a person's approach to the test and his or her various attempts to deal with the problems it poses are far more important. The IQ score merely provides a guideline and is just one additional piece of data that should be used to draw conclusions about the patient. In fact, in the *DSM–IV* Mental Retardation is based on two criteria: IQ *and* (often forgotten) social competence. The students are therefore challenged to look beyond the standardized approach, focusing instead on a more experiential, less formalized approach.

LABELS AND FABLES

As indicated earlier one of the major problems in teaching the use of the WISC–III, WAIS–R, and WAIS–III as assessment instruments is that clinical lore has labeled the functions supposedly tapped by each of the subtests. Despite research evidence to the contrary, a single descriptive label is often assigned to a specific subtest by students, in spite of my efforts to discourage such procedures. To discourage such concrete application, we analyze the skills necessary for good performance on each subtest. For example, I emphasize that the WAIS–R Comprehension subtest is not *necessarily* a test of judgment, nor *solely* a test of judgment, and that some people do poorly on it for other reasons. The subtest contains three items that seem to require concept formation ability. ("One swallow doesn't make a summer;" "Strike while the iron is hot;" "Shallow brooks are noisy"). Numerous studies of the Comprehension and PA subtests have reported significant correlations of these subtests with a variety of personality measures, such as Introversion/Extraversion (Schill, 1966; Schill, Kahn, & Meuhlman, 1968 for PA only), ego maturity (Browning & Quinlan, 1985), and need for approval (Dickstein & MacEvitt, 1971; Nobo & Evans, 1986; Ramos & Die, 1986). However, Lipsitz, Dworkin, and Erlenmeyer-Kimling (1993) found that their data did not support the hypothesis that the Comprehension or PA subtests reflect *social functioning*.

Clinical lore still labels the Similarities subtest as a measure of abstract ability or concept formation, the Digit Symbol (DSY) subtest as a measure of visual-motor coordination and concentration. As an antidote to the use of these subtest labels, I might focus on the possible meanings of poor performance on one specific subtest. For example, Kamphaus (1993) indicated that among the hypotheses to investigate when a child does poorly on Picture Completion (PC) are such factors as having an adequate knowledge base about the objects, simultaneous processing ability, the ability to cope with novelty, perceptual organization, spatial ability, adequacy of perceptual speed, anxiety related to being timed, willingness to venture a response or to guess when uncertain, attention span, degree of impulsivity, and visual acuity and discrimination.

This is not to say that, for example, the Similarities subtest is *never* a measure of abstract ability or concept formation, or that the DSY subtest is *never* a test of visual-motor functioning. Rather, they may be measuring something else for a specific patient. It is misleading to merely apply the label, without trying to understand the behavior. For example, it is possible that for some, the Similarities subtest (or any other verbal subtest) may be a measure of willingness or ability to communicate, and/or of the presence of suspicion.

Furth and Milgram (1965) disagreed with Wechsler's assertion that the Similarities test is not generally influenced by language usage and knowledge of unfamiliar stimulus words. They concluded instead that the data suggest the requirement to respond verbally is the more cogent consideration. These authors suggested that the Similarities subtest is not an adequate measure of verbal conceptual ability in children. Their conclusion suggests that the results on the Similarities subtest may be greatly influenced by the ability or willingness to communicate rather than by concept formation ability or ability to abstract.

Concerning the relationship between suspiciousness and scores on the Similarities subtest, Wiener (1957) found that subjects who were distrustful scored significantly lower on both the Similarities and PC subtests of the WAIS compared with a low distrustful group. In a follow-up study Levine (1958) found that subjects who stated that the paired Similarities items were not alike, when the examiner suggested that they *were* alike, had a significantly lower mean IQ than control subjects who did not make this response. This difference was considerably greater than could be accounted for only on the basis of the "not alike" error. This study further emphasizes that the distrustful attitude serves to reduce *overall* effectiveness in intelligence test performance.

The Similarities subtest is said to measure the ability to function on an abstract level, a level of thinking said to be more difficult, compared to an approach based on facts and details, called concrete functioning. Yet, both seem necessary in everyday living. But the Similarities subtest seems to consist of two somewhat different tasks. In the earlier, easier items a person is asked how two somewhat similar objects are alike (e.g., orange and banana), asking the patient to make a second-order generalization about their similarity (both fruit), as the most desirable response. Later items, however, are quite different from each other (e.g., praise and punishment). Here the task is to determine how two very *different* items can be classified as similar, using a second-order generalization. This task is very similar to S. Mednick and M. Mednick's (1967) Remote Associates Test (RAT), a test of convergent thinking, except that in the Mednicks' test three items are employed rather than two. The RAT is essentially a test of cognitive flexibility, and it is directly related to various aspects of the creative process.

The ability to think convergently is no doubt impaired in a variety of psychopathological syndromes (e.g., schizophrenia, obsessive-compulsive and paranoid syndromes) and possibly in certain hysteroid patients. There are many hints available to the assessor concerning these problems in the content of the individual responses. For example, the person who says an orange and banana are alike because "you eat them both" seems to be functioning on a more oral, need-focused level, compared with the person who answers "fruit," or even the more concrete person who says "you peel them both." At any rate, it is easy to see that various degrees of creative flexibility in thinking, associated with personality style and with psychopathology, can affect performance quite significantly. These effects must be seen as separate from any general intelligence factor or one that emphasizes a verbal factor, or from any specific difficulties in the ability to function on an abstract level. Whether or not the person can function on an abstract level is usually of little relevance in personality assessment, but whether the person can creatively and flexibly use associational thinking is often a more relevant issue.

Over and over again I present examples of possible reasons for success or failure on the Wechsler subtests other than those that center around the labeled abilities supposedly tapped by those subtests. For example, students are asked to generate hypotheses on the observation that some patients do well on BD and DSY, but they perform rather poorly on OA. One hypothesis that has been generated to account for this discrepancy is that in the BD and DSY subtests there is a very definite model in front of the patient. However, in the OA subtest no model is available to the patient, who is not told in advance what the completed object is to be. To support this hypothesis I quote Lanfeld and Saunders (1961) who stated: "Object Assembly confounds at least two variables: a "performance" component held in common with Block Design and, as Rapaport has suggested, an anxiety component. … The potentially anxiety-provoking feature of the OA task is that the subject is not given any model to copy; he or she must manipulate and organize the pieces of each puzzle in order to learn what it makes. If this ignorance proves bothersome to the subject, we may call him or her anxious" (pp. 238–239).

We discuss research evidence to indicate that performance on the OA subtest is affected by concerns and preoccupations about body intactness. For example, Blatt, Allison, and Baker (1965) found that children with intense bodily concerns had significantly lower scores on the WISC OA subtest, compared with a matched sample of children without bodily concern. Subjects with low OA subtest scores also had a significantly greater indication of bodily concerns in their Rorschachs compared with those subjects who had high OA subtest scores. In discussing the reason that the OA subtest is particularly susceptible to concerns about body intactness, Blatt et al. (1965) stated: "These seemingly dismembered pieces involve specific content—whole bodies or parts of bodies—which are likely to stimulate preconscious thought derivatives to a greater degree than more neutral stimuli. For these reasons, this test may bring into focus more sharply concerns about bodily integration" (p. 228).

I indicate to the students that two subsequent studies did not support Blatt et al.'s (1965) findings (Marsden & Kalter, 1969; Rockwell, 1967), but that subsequent reports (Blatt, Baker, & Weiss, 1970; Chain, reported in Blatt et al., 1970) support the original findings. Chain found that obese children (whom he assumed had bodily concerns because of their overweight problem) had lower OA subtest scores compared with matched controls. Blatt et al. (1970) found that, in three independent samples, adults whose Wechsler profiles had OA as the first or second lowest subtest "had a significantly greater number and percentage of Rorschach responses which indicate bodily concern than subjects whose OA was the first or second highest subtest" (p. 269). These data offer additional support for the notion that personality variables influence the results of various subtest scores. The premise emphasized to the students is that the manner in which the person approaches a problem, the kinds of situations and tasks that facilitate and inhibit the person, the methods of problem analysis the patient employs, and the ways in which he or she responds (or adapts) to the reality demands presented by the various subtests are more meaningful and descriptive than the actual subtest scores and/or IQ values.

As an illustration, we consider a hypothetical patient who has earned a low score on the DSY subtest of the WAIS–R. Because this subtest is *presumed* to reflect visual-motor functioning, a student might conclude that the patient's visual-motor functioning is rather poor or is impaired. The point is developed during the discussion that not only may such a conclusion be completely unwarranted, but it may also be quite meaningless in helping to understand the patient and quite meaningless to the reader who is left to interpret the relevance of the phrase "visual-motor coordination." At this point I suggest that an investigation of the patient's approach to the task, and the possible alternative reasons for poor performance might yield relevant and meaningful information concerning his or her characteristic "style of life."

As we reason out the possible causes of poor performance on this subtest, it becomes clear that there are many possible reasons for poor performance on the DSY subtest, reasons perhaps only tangentially related to visual-motor functioning. The students are then asked how it is possible to draw more relevant conclusions. Eventually, after some discussion, they conclude that it is possible to do so by observing the *quality of performance*. This information might be more meaningful to the patient, the examiner, and the referring agency. I point out that a prospective employer would most probably be more interested in learning more about the patient's rate of efficiency and the style and quality of approach under pressure than he or she would be in visual-motor coordination. Such a consideration may also be more important to a therapist who wants to evaluate ego functioning under stress. In this case, qualitative factors are often much more important than the score the patient earned on the subtest. Not that these scores are unimportant. Qualitative indications of obvious stress under the pressure of the testing situation, coupled with a low DSY score, may be suggestive of inability to deal with certain everyday pressures and tension situations (poor adaptive efficiency). These same indications of stress accompanied by a DSY subtest score within the range of the other subtests might indicate that although the person is made anxious under minimal stress, his or her performance is not impaired. A high DSY subtest score, coupled with the same set of observations, might indicate that this subject functions best (at highest efficiency) in stress situations; his or her efficiency is enhanced in such situations.

At this point I raise a related issue, concerning the route to *good* performance on this subtest. Eventually students recognize that if one asks people who do well how they did it, they emphasize the importance of rapid learning under time stress. Those who learn quickly to associate each symbol with the appropriate number can place the proper marks in the blank spaces rapidly. Is the DSY subtest therefore a measure of "rapid learning?" I ask. Well, perhaps in part, it is, the students eventually conclude. "What about the type of material to be learned?" I ask. Many people who learn meaningful verbal material rapidly do poorly when they must learn meaningless material, such as the DSY marks that correspond to the various numbers. Instead, they view each symbol placement as a discrete task, even though they repeat it again and again, and thus they respond more slowly. One patient told me she could learn many lines of a script quite rapidly because of the context, but she could not efficiently master the symbol-number pairings on the DSY subtest. Therefore, important factors other than visual-motor ability are all involved here, such as association learning, the ability to deal with time pressure, the ability to size up task requirements quickly, and the ability to learn nonverbal material. Finally, the point is made: The factors just listed are all related to various aspects of personality functioning, and should be considered in the evaluation process.

CLUES FROM FACTOR-ANALYTIC STUDIES

Factor analytic studies also strongly refute the breakdown of subtests according to the abilities attributed to them by clinical lore. In fact, some studies indicate that certain abilities ascribed to single subtests on the WISC and WAIS are scattered through a number of subtests.

A host of studies and reviews report that factor analyses of the Wechsler tests report a two- or a three-factor solution (Verbal Comprehension, Performance/Perceptual Organization, and Memory/Freedom from Distraction; e.g., Atkinson & Cyr, 1984; Beck, Horwitz, Seidenberg, T. Parker, & Frank, 1985; Leckliter, Matarazzo, & Silverstein, 1986; Matarazzo, 1972; K. Parker, 1983; Reynolds & Kaufman, 1990; Ryan, Rosenberg, & DeWolfe, 1984; Siegert, Patten, Taylor, & McCormick, 1988; Silverstein, 1982; Waller & Waldman, 1990) and some even report a one-factor solution (O'Grady, 1983). This finding holds up even for learning-disabled children (Juliano, Hadded, & Carroll, 1988; Naglieri, 1981;) and in mildly mentally retarded children (Cummins & Das, 1980). Similar findings were obtained for the WISC–III, although the findings for PA and Digit Span are not entirely clear, and a fourth factor emerged with the addition of the Symbol Search subtest, called "processing speed" (Wechsler, 1991). The PA and Digit Span subtests do not seem to load heavily on any factor.

It is possible, however, that the two- or three-factor solution is an artifact of the factor analytic approach used. As Beck et al. (1989) pointed out, they could find no studies that factored the entire matrix of individual items rather than subtest intercorrelations. When a subset of items from the WAIS Information and Arithmetic subtests were factor analyzed (Saunders, 1960a) *six* factors emerged: General Information, Contemporary Affairs, Cultural Knowledge, Scientific Generalizations, Numerical Information, and Numerical Operations. Therefore students are urged to examine each subtest to see which items are passed and failed, in order to discover if any pattern exists among the passes and failures on a particular subtest. For example, Karson (1986) stated,

If a child with average overall [intelligence] shows particular difficulty with knowing the number of days in a week, the number of items in a dozen, the seasons of the year, the direction in which the sun sets and, at a higher level, the distance from New York to Los Angeles and the number of pounds in a ton, [such misses may be] clues about the child's stability in locating herself in time and space, as well as her capabilities in regard to numerical concepts. The child who is uncertain about the environment and shows low awareness of relational, number and physical properties may well be a child who is having ego difficulties. (p. 215)

Saunders' (1960b) factor analysis of the WAIS PC subtest yielded three factors: (a) "maintenance or loss of contact," which is much the same as Rapaport's "increase of distance from the picture" or "impaired contact with reality," (b) "maintenance or loss of perspective," and (c) "the effect of uncertainty," much like Rapaport's "loss of distance" (the subject's loss of appreciation that he or she is dealing with a picture and not with the real thing). Poor scores may be due to difficulties tapped by any of the three factors, or a combination of several factors. It also seems possible for a person to earn a low (or a high) score on PC for several other reasons. For example, Cohen (1952) reported that PC measures *both* verbal and nonverbal organizational factors, and added that it measures two abilities simultaneously, making it extremely ambiguous in pattern analytic interpretation. A low score may be a result either of low verbal or low nonverbal organizational ability, or of both.

A factor analysis (Klingler & Saunders, 1975) that factor analyzed items from nine WAIS subtests resulted in 15 factors. In addition, factor analysis of the WAIS and its subtests by Saunders and Gittinger (1968) report as many as 18 factors, whereas several doctoral dissertations of WAIS factor analyses have reported 10 or more factors (Krauskopf & Saunders, 1994). In addition, a review of WISC and WISC–R factor analytic studies by Blaha and Wallbrown (1984) indicates that with some subgroups the expected factor structure did not appear and a more differentated factor structure appears in some specialized groups, such as reading-disabled and retarded children and children referred for psychoeducational evaluation. Although factor analyses of Wechsler scores for brain-damaged and emotionally disturbed patients often result in the typical two- or three-factor solution, the evidence cited previously nevertheless indicates that a research methodology that examines Wechsler performance in a more detailed manner will find results that will be more differentiating, just as the clinician who examines individual items on the WISC–III or the WAIS–R will often find a number of reasons to explain good or poor performance. The students are taught that procedures described later in this chapter will allow them to determine which of a host of many possible factors has caused the patient's imparied functioning.

STYLISTIC CLUES

In most cases the items on the Wechsler subtests are graded for difficulty, the easiest items placed at the beginning and the hardest items at the end. The items are supposed to gradually increase in difficulty. Thus, for the most part, patients should earn full credit for earlier terms, and no credit for items close to their maximum level of intellectual ability, the level of consecutive failures, which indicates termination of that subtest. Of course there are occasional zero credit and partial credit scores for some early and middle items, because many people have small gaps in their knowledge and some items are not placed accurately in the sequence of difficulty. However, when there is a pattern to these missed items, analysis of this pattern will help explain reasons for impaired performance. For example, on the Information subtest there are a number of items that deal with time, distance, and numerical estimates. It is possible that the patient's poor performance comes from the inability to focus on these details, a pattern of unawareness that is typically prevalent in a more hysteroid approach to the world, marked by vagueness and lack of detail in the respondent's experienced world, focusing instead on emotional components. Students are taught to examine the items a patient misses within each subtest, to search for patterns such as the one just indicated. Although it is true that a patient who does poorly on Information has a poor fund of knowledge, it is not this fact that is the critical clinical issue being assessed in this subtest, but rather, a stylistic approach to the world that results in less general knowledge than would otherwise be had. If one wanted to utilize this explanation for poor performance, he or she would examine performance for this patient on subtests that are heavily based on material that requires specific knowledge (e.g., Information) and compare that performance with the performance where this style will not penalize performance (e.g., Similarities). For example, the writer had a hysteroid patient who was convinced she was "stupid" because she knew so little about many topics. Of course she made no active attempt to learn about her world; she did not read, watch TV news, or invest herself in the details of her environment. Although she scored below average on the Information subtest, she was very significantly above average on the Similarities subtest, indicating that she was capable of far better intellectual performance when her personality disorder did not impair her functioning. The test results were used by us to help her explore her intellectual ability in a variety of ways. She began reading and learning about her environment and the world, and also about herself, in an attempt to modify her approach. This led to a very significant reduction in her self-devaluation.

It is important to note that when a Wechsler record contains a number of missed easy items, when more difficult items are passed, as indicated previously (clusters of zero-point scores in a string of 1- or 2-point scores), and no meaningful pattern emerges as an explanation, it is possible that the problem centers around damage to the integrity of the patient's cognition, and not just impaired attention/concentration, stylistic problems, or anxiety. For example,

Feinberg and McIlvried (1991) found that the presence of such scatter was found to correlate with psychotic behaviors.

PERCEPTUAL STYLE AND WECHSLER PERFORMANCE

Witkin, Dyk, Faterson, Goodenough, and Karp (1962) report that: "There is a general cognitive style which runs through perceptual and intellectual function-ing. ... This common ... style underlies the observed relation between extent of field dependence and performance on standard tests of intelligence" (p. 69). Thus, one may approach a problem, organize a field, or perceive in an analytical (field independent) or a global (field dependent) manner. What makes Witkin's work especially meaningful to the clinician is his demonstration of the relation-ship between field dependence-independence and a number of personality variables centering around differentiation and articulation (or lack of it) of the self from the environment. "Highly differentiated" children had a more realistic impression that their opinions were of value, were realistic in their self-appraisal, and did not engage in unrealistic bragging about accomplishments, as did some of the less differentiated children. They exhibited a well-developed control structure, a clear sense of responsibility, and had well-developed interests, in contrast to the less differentiated children. Finally, these children demonstrated a tendency to be too perfectionistic, overcontrolled, or emotionally distant, and tended to evidence an obsessive-compulsive personality structure.

Children who demonstrated limited differentiation had a poorly developed sense of separate identity, relied on others to define their attitudes and feelings, and in general seemed rather dependent. Many demonstrated a "poorly devel-oped self-concept" (Witkin et al., 1962, p. 262), and role confusion. They had few lasting friendships, and those friendships they did establish were casual and transient. These children responded to questions only tangentially, and their replies tended to be vague and overinclusive. They had poorly developed controls, demonstrated an inability to assume responsibility, and tended to be babyish and demanding with their parents. The difficulties of the group centered about impulse control problems and a poorly developed sense of responsibility.

The two extremes are meaningful in terms of their expected performance on the BD, PC, and OA subtests of the WISC. Children who score lower on these subtests tend to be dependent, demonstrate difficulty with control and respon-sibility, do not attend to the details of the environment, and tend to be more affectively labile.

VERBAL–PERFORMANCE DICHOTOMY: ANOTHER UNWARRANTED ASSUMPTION

Even the Verbal–Performance dichotomy on the Wechsler tests is somewhat misleadingly accepted as fact. The two parts of the test are typically viewed as quite separate entities, but a number of writers disagree and feel that the breakdown is artifical. In this regard, Freeman (1962) stated that the ability to verbalize and to make abstractions is not necessarily involved in the nonverbal subtests, but it has often been observed by examiners that this ability facilitates and expedites performance of the nonverbal subtests: "*Even though a test is nonverbal, the ability to verbalize and abstract may be one of the psychological functions involved*" (p. 250[emphasis added]).

Additional evidence for the partial communality of the Verbal and Perform-ance subtests of the WAIS comes from factor analytic studies by Cohen (1957) and Shaw (1966). Shaw found that OA, BD, and Arithmetic formed a single factor, despite the fact that the first two subtests were from the Performance portion of the WAIS and the third subtest was from the Verbal section. Shaw viewed all three subtests as demanding tasks, requiring perserverence. High scorers on this factor are said to have realistic appraisals of their abilities, and tend to be confident, calm, and willing to tackle any task within reason. They are slow to panic when confronted by seemingly insoluble problems.

Students are instructed to interpret only very large Verbal–Performance differences (about 15 points), but they eventually recognize that the interpre-tation of the difference must be investigated separately for each patient because there are many reasons for such a difference. Only some of these differences are caused by personality problems, because other factors, such as poor education, cultural background, language and reading problems, and socioeconomic status are often at the root of such Verbal-Performance differences.

THE INQUIRY PHASE

It is at this point that I introduce a new idea: "Observe people as they perform the task and ask them how they approached it. Ask about their experience of responding to each subtest and their experience of the entire test as well." For example, the efficient mathematician quickly sized up the DSY task as a memory-association task, smoothly and efficiently inserting the proper marks in the blank spaces. She hardly had to glance up at the model above, because she had memorized all the symbols after doing only a small number of them.

These questions provide a measure of patients' feelings about their intellec-tual ability and their ability to function effectively when their intellectual ability is "challenged" by questions from the examiner. The Wechsler tests are experi-enced as interpersonally stressful by many patients (Kaufman, 1990; Zetzer & Beutler, 1995). The source of this anxiety probably comes from the fact that the examiner imposes directions, pressing for compliance and discouraging devia-tions from the procedure. The examiner controls the type of task and the type of response, and judges the correctness or appropriateness of the responses. He or she places pressure on the patient to respond with precision and speed, pressing for focused attention and concentration (Sprandel, 1985; Zetzer & Beutler, 1995). The patient is required to reorient him or herself over and over again, for each subtest, to still another highly structured situation. The patient's response to the structure and to the sudden shifts in focus provides a great deal of data concerning how they might respond in similar situations outside the testing situation. It is important to question the patient about their thoughts and feelings concerning the testing situation, the test itself, and the various subtests.

For example, a patient did extremely poorly on the Arithmetic subtest because he could not remember the details of the problems. At first he asked again and again for the details, attempting to group them and keep them in mind long enough to respond correctly. When he saw that he could not do so successfully, he merely shrugged and said "I don't know" to subsequent questions. When, after the subtest was completed, the examiner wrote the question out for the patient to read, he was capable of doing the necessary arithmetic to obtain the correct answer. When his response was questioned later, it became clear to the examiner that the patient's level of anxiety was debilitating, interfering with short-term memory. He demonstrated similar problems in several other subtests. The student was able to understand the debilitating role of anxiety in this patient's approach to the subtests, and the degree to which it impaired both cognitive and interpersonal functioning. The student then felt more secure in generating a hypothesis about the debilitating effects of anxiety on the patient's life outside the testing situation.

We often do not realize that the assessment setting, especially the assessment of IQ, represents a quite stressful situation for the patient. The clinician is evaluating the "patient," which sets up a status difference; the clinician has the manual in hand, ostensibly knowing the correct answers. This is an anxiety-provoking situation for the patient, and it will often have a significant effect on the process and outcome of the test. Students are often not sensitive to the patient's feelings because they are too concerned with the mechanics of the test and its administration. Even when the examiner is supportive and encouraging, the setting is a challenging situation for many people, because most people have some concern about their intellectual ability. Although one person might respond to the test administration as a productive challenge, others might perceive it as an aggressive or destructive challenge to their sense of self. Others may feel intimidated and frightened, withdrawing interest and involvement, fearing to take a chance and to engage fully with the examiner. They may, for example, be hesitant to explore their responses in any great depth, refusing the opportunity to "explain further," or they may say "I don't know" to a question rather than take a chance and respond to an item. Others may view the testing with suspicion, also withdrawing involvement and responding minimally to questions, with terse responses that typically result in lower scores on many subtests. Then there are those people who respond to this challenge by becoming anxious and/or diffuse, giving vague answers that miss the mark, when they might otherwise be able to answer correctly. Least affected is the person who copes with the challenge by using an obsessive and overly intellectualized style, although these patients sometimes also lose credit when they spoil a response through contradiction, and also because they are too slow on certain timed tests. They make too much of being correct and must check and recheck their work, despite an already slow and overly careful approach to the task. Thus, it is an illusion that the Wechsler tests are objective tests for many patients.

To understand the effects of the factors just discussed, students are encouraged to obtain additional information from the patient concerning their attitude toward the subtests and their feelings about the test and the testing situation itself. An approach that can be a useful adjunct to interpretation concerns detailed discussion of each subtest (and of the total testing situation) with the patient. This procedure is similar to the Inquiry procedure of the Rorschach, where emphasis is placed on seeking the reason(s) a patient responded the way they did to each of the cards. I make it a point to encourage students to investigate the patient's attitude toward the test and the testing situation and toward each subtest whenever their performance is atypical (good, bad, or unusual in some other manner), or whenever more information is required concerning their functioning. Such questioning serves the purpose of illuminating the reason that this particular patient had difficulty with the task. The first question might be "What do you think of that test (subtest)?," or "Which test(s) did you like best (least)?" "Why?", or "What did you think of that test with the blocks (puzzles, pictures with missing parts, etc.)?" Often the first question will bring an evasive or an empty and seemingly meaningless reply. Persistence is important. Additional, more specific probing is often necessary. Students are eventually aware that the task of assessment with the Wechsler tests is to describe the processes by which the patient thinks through an answer rather than using the labels supposedly assigned to the subtests to identify traits.

TESTING OF THE LIMITS (TOL)

After the test is completed, the students are asked to return to each subtest at the point where the patient began doing poorly, in an effort to discover the reason(s) for failure. This approach was pioneered by Klopfer (B. Klopfer, Ainsworth, W. Klopfer, & Holt, 1954). TOL is done by using a variety of questions (e.g., How did you begin that problem?). As part of the administration the student is also taught to begin the TOL approach by systematically modifying the task or question the patient failed until the patient catches on and can respond successfully. For example, if the patient states "I'd yell fire and run like hell" when asked, "What should you do if while in the theater you are the first person to see smoke and fire?" the examiner might merely repeat the question, this time emphasizing *should*, so the patient would not respond with an impulse-oriented self-referent answer. If this does not produce a correct response, the examiner might ask the patient what might happen if he or she did as they had indicated. If a patient tends to answer impulsively throughout most or all of the test, it is probably true that the poor response is due in part to an impulse-oriented approach to life in which personalized thinking prevails over logical analysis. Although this will undoubtedly impair social judgment, it will impair other cognitive processes as well. Rather than focus on social judgment, it makes more sense, instead, to focus on the personalized impulsive style. Several examples of additional questions that may be appropriate in a particular case are: "You seemed to be having some trouble with that test. What was wrong? What caused the difficulty?" "How did you feel while you were taking that part of the test?"

To introduce this procedure I ask the students what they can learn about a patient if he or she misses a question on a subtest. After some discussion they conclude that not a great deal of information is communicated to the examiner from this information. Two possibilities present themselves. First, the answer may be in the patient's repertoire, but he or she did not choose to offer it as a response. For one reason or another they offered an alternative, incorrect response. A second alternative is that the answer is not in the patient's repertoire. The students are taught that one method of differentiating between the two alternatives is to ask the patient to generate another possible response to the question. Thus, the examiner might say, "Give me another (a different) answer to that question." If this response is also wrong, the examiner might want to press further, making certain to be supportive and encouraging in order to maintain interest and motivation. A patient who offers correct responses to questions he or she initially got wrong would probably have potential for higher level intellectual functioning than a patient who cannot generate correct responses in any case. Patients with severe incapacitating emotional problems, and perhaps patients who feel insecure about their intellectual ability, might well show large IQ discrepancies when tested with this method of "maximal facilitation," compared with the administration according to standardized procedures, which stresses "typical responsiveness." The greater the interference of ego function impairments and stylistic impairments, the greater the difference would be in each of these two methods. Using both approaches not only yields a measure of cognitive impairment, but in addition, allows the assessor to describe the quality of these impairments with increased clarity.

Some examiners might want to provide as many hints as necessary to secure a correct response on an item of a subtest. The number of hints provided and the type of hints employed might communicate more information to the examiner than a mere statement that the patient failed the item. Different types of hints (assistance) could be offered, and again, the more effective types of hints could provide additional information concerning missing cognitive or emotional factors in a person's intellectual functioning. For example, a low score on PA might indicate difficulties with anticipatory planning, but there are other possibilities. However, if hints that provide structure in the PA subtest are effective, whereas those that suggest attention to the details of the stimulus material prove ineffective, it would then be possible to hypothesize: (a) The patient's inability to structure situations will at times interfere with logical anticipatory planning, or (b) the patient's ability to function will be enhanced if he or she is provided with minimal (or maximal, depending on the degree of structure provided by the examiner) structure. A selection of one or the other of these two similar alternatives depends in part on the initial level of performance on PA. Also, more explicit statements concerning the types of situations that interfere with functioning can be obtained from the rest of the data. In this way the examiner provides a host of miniature test situations that are potentially capable of reflecting the subtleties and nuances of the patient's functioning. By *systematically* providing additional cues, the examiner can thereby make clearer, more explicit inferences from the patient's resultant pattern of functioning (Handler, 1988, 1993).

The value of such a procedure is to help the examiner understand and interpret a specific failure or difficulty in the test protocol. Students soon learn that using the TOL approach also allows them to describe the *quality* of the impairments with increased clarity and accuracy, and to provide suggestions for amelioration. Students also enjoy an opportunity to describe the patient's cognitive response difficulties and strengths using experiential language. They find it easier with this approach to provide meaningful information to their patients concerning cognitive and personality problems, both during the assessment and in the feedback sessions. In addition, the procedure helps to establish rapport, and allows the patient to see that the examiner is a supportive person who is interested in helping him or her achieve at a maximal level. In this respect the approach is similar to the assessment approach developed by Fischer (1985; and see chap. 19 of this volume) and by Finn (1996; Finn & Tonsager, 1992; and see chap. 20 of this volume). This facilitative procedure is also quite therapeutic. I have noticed that many parents have verbalized that their child's behavior changed considerably, even before the formal treatment had begun, but after the facilitative assessment had taken place. Similar feedback has been obtained from adults about their own assessment experience (Handler, 1988, 1993). The procedure is also useful in helping to determine whether the test is a true indication of a person's potential level of intellectual functioning. If the hints provided by the examiner do not result in a substantial increase in IQ, then it is probably safe to say that the score is accurate—providing, of course, that problems concerning attention, rapport, and so on, are not interfering with performance. The data obtained may then provide information that would allow the clinician to modify his or her conclusions in light of the additional information. Other modifications in administration are also suggested, such as allowing some patients to continue working past a time limit, in order to determine whether time alone is the problem, and testing past the required cut-off point on a subtest, to determine whether a patient can respond correctly to more difficult items. In both cases the responses are scored according to the instructions in the manual, but a facilitated score is also obtained. Of course, as Zetzer and Beutler (1995) pointed out, if possible, the TOL procedure should *probably* be done after the entire administration is completed in order to minimize the possibility that the results could assist the patient in other subtests.

CUES FROM CONTENT ANALYSIS

It is a relatively easy task to teach students to use the content of a patient's responses as a source of clinical interpretations. To sensitize students to the use of content in this manner I begin with a few examples: What is the difference between a patient who, on the WAIS–R Vocabularly subtest, defines the word *consume* as "to use up" and one who defines the same word as "devour"? Both these responses get full credit. Recently, one group of students focused on the *activity* communicated in the latter definition. They also saw this response as indicating that the person giving it was more dependent, primitive, aggressive, and impulsive, compared with the first example, especially because the response consisted of one word, as if it were more like a free assocation.

The second example is the patient mentioned previously, who when asked "What should you do if you are the first person to see smoke or fire?" answered, "I'd yell fire and run like hell." It was easy to see that this patient would probably be impulsive and that under pressure he might act without thinking, possibly risking his life and the lives of others. Perhaps this person was made so anxious by a consideration of the danger in the situation that he did not even hear the question accurately. He responded with what he *would* do rather than what he *should* do. Although he recognized a need to warn others, his own needs took precedence. I then describe another patient who responded to the same question with, "One should always be aware of the possibility of courting danger and, therefore, one should carefully think through a plan." The students could readily see that this man's obsessive, intellectualized nature would preclude him acting quickly and efficiently under pressure, whereas they also easily understand that the patient who answered, "I'd stand up on the seat and ask everyone to pay attention to me and tell them I will guide them out" had distinct grandiose and/or narcissistic problems.

A third example, also from the Vocabulary subtest, is the definition of *sanctuary* as "a place where religious objects are in the church," as "a safe place," or as "a place to hide." The three definitions are scored alike, but the third one suggests a more pressing need for emotional protection, and, depending on the situation, for physical protection as well.

The content of children's responses can also be used to obtain important clinical information. On the WISC–III, for example, a child who, on the Vocabularly subtest, defines *mimic* as "to repeat what someone does" or "to mock," both receive full credit. Yet, the child who choses the latter response perhaps feels a sense of shame. Other examples include the word *nonsense*, defined either as "acting foolish," acting silly," or "acting stupid," the latter response being the harshest evaluation of self or other; and *seclude*, defined as "be away from everything," " to draw away," "to go by yourself;" and "to be put alone— by yourself," suggesting interpersonal withdrawal. In addition, the child who defines *thief* as a "burgler," or "criminal" is not feeling as vulnerable and defensless as the child who defines the word as "someone who breaks into your house and takes your things." Each of these definitions earns full credit. I ask students to discuss the difference between a patient who defines "terminate" as "to end" and one who defines *terminate* as "to kill," in terms of the type of object relations patterns suggested by the two different definitions.

In another Vocabulary example, a rather direct and inappropriate young woman told her assessor that she became upset when a young man she recently met rebuffed her when she expressed very directly her intense interest in him.

On the WAIS–R Vocabulary subtest she defined matchless "as not having a mate. Not being able to get a mate." It became clear after she began treatment that his refusal to return her interest was a major narcissistic injury to her.

There are a number of responses on each subtest that offer clues concerning emotional issues. For example, even on the PC subtest, completions that indicate missing or broken items could suggest issues of depression and accompanying lack of agency, and responses that focus on the inclusion of people, such as the response indicating that there is no hand holding the water pitcher on the WAIS–R, might suggest dependency problems. Responses on other subtests often yield information that is quite telling about family dynamics. For example, Karson (1986) told of a 10-year-old boy who responded on the "first–last" item of the Similarities subtest of the WISC–R with "It's like my family—the same as my brother and me. He's always first and me last." (pp. 216–217). Students are instructed that each of these telling responses should be followed up and discussed with patients whenever it is appropriate to do so.

Karson (1986) offered examples of personal references to Vocabularly subtest items that obviously reveal personal and family problems: "Nonsense": "What my mother says I am filled with"; "Gamble": "What my father shouldn't do"; "Nuisance": "What I am in school"; "Join": "The other kids never ask me" (p. 221); "Brave": "Some girl who is not afraid to stay alone at night" (p. 224). This child gave numerous responses that indicated "fear about her female status" (p. 224), and her obsessive, phobic, and ritualistic behavior about bedtime suggested to the examiner that she was dealing with fantasized or real experiences of inappropriate sexual behavior. The assessment helped focus the therapist on the overly close relationship with an older male sibling, and after 8 months of therapy her symptoms disappeared.

Waite (1961) presented many examples of content analysis from the WAIS. These examples, interpreted from an ego-psychological point of view, are quite helpful to new students, who might otherwise overlook valuable interpretive material. Finally, Zetzer and Beutler (1995) described a case in which the patient perceived the "Escape" scene from the PA subtest "as an abortive rape attempt," and other PA tasks "as inherently violent and threatening" (p. 138). In her response to the "Robber" item she said, "If I had a gun, I would have shot that guy" (p. 138). In their analysis of these responses the authors stated: "B.W.'s responses gave evidence of a negatively toned bias in her perceptions that led her to be excessively quick to perceive danger and unhappy consequences to social interactions. She ... saw most social situations as adversarial, depressing and negative" (p.138). Zetzer and Beutler concluded that because of her "proclivity to foresee maleficence in others' intentions and her tendency to resolve social conflicts with imagined forms of violence" (p. 138), it was almost certain that this attitude would hamper the development of a strong therapeutic working alliance. Therefore, they stated that any type of confrontational or intense form of individual therapy would not be indicated.

SUMMARY

I hope the reader can see from this chapter that although a standardized approach to assessment is quite valuable in its own right, one who would be competent in assessment must go beyond standardized guidelines to develop a more ideographic, experiental understanding of the person they are testing. This is not to suggest that standardized approaches should be ignored. Rather, they should be supplemented by judicious inquiry and exploration *with the patient* in order to grasp more fully the meanings of the responses for that individual. These data, along with the standardized scores, the clinical observations and impressions of the assessor, and the stylistic approach of the patient to the test and to the clinician, taken together, should result in a more meaningful picture of the individual than one obtained with only standardized methods. In addition, such collaboration typically results in a more positive experience for the patient, an experience that is quite often therapeutic in its own right.

REFERENCES

Allison, J., Blatt, S., & Zimet, C. (1968). *The interpretation of psychological tests*. New York: Harper & Row.

Atkinson, L., & Cyr, J. (1984). Factor analysis of the WAIS–R psychiatric and standardization samples. *Journal of Consulting and Clinical Psychology, 52*, 714–716.

Beck, N., Horwitz, E., Seidenberg. M., Parker, J., & Frank, R. (1985). WAIS–R factor structure in psychiatric and general medical patients. *Journal of Consulting and Clinical Psychology, 53*, 402–405.

Beck, N., Tucker, D., Frank, R., Parker, T., Lake, R., Thomas, S., Lichty, W., Horwitz, E., Horwitz, B., & Merritt, F. (1989). The latent factor structure of the WAIS–R: A factor analysis of individual item responses. *Journal of Clinical Psychology, 45*(2), 281–293.

Bellak, L., Hurvich, M., & Gediman, H. (1973). *Ego functions in schizophrenics, neurotics and normals*. New York: Wiley.

Blaha, J., & Wallbrown, F. (1984). Hierarchical analyses of the WISC and WISC–R: Synthesis and clinical implications. *Journal of Clinical Psychology, 40*, 556–571.

Blatt, S., & Allison, J. (1981). The intelligence test in personality assessment. In A. Rabin (Ed.), *Assessment with projective techniques* (pp. 187–232). New York: Springer.

Blatt, S., Allison, J., & Baker, B. (1965). The Wechsler Object Assembly subtest and bodily concerns. *Journal of Consulting Psychology, 29*, 223–230.

Blatt, S., Baker, B., & Weiss, J. (1970). Wechsler Object Assembly subtest and bodily concerns: A review and replication. *Journal of Consulting Psychology, 34*, 269–274.

Boone, D. (1992). WAIS–R scatter with psychiatric inpatients:I. Intersubtest scatter. *Psychological Reports, 71*, 483–487.

Boone, D. (1993). WAIS–R scatter with psychiatric inpatients: II. Intersubtest scatter. *Psychological Reports, 73*, 851–860.

Browning, D., & Quinlan, D. (1985). Ego development and intelligence in a psychiatric population: Wechsler subtest scores. *Journal of Personality Assessment, 49*, 260–263.

Cohen, J. (1952). A factor-analytic based rationale for the Wechsler-Bellevue. *Journal of Consulting Psychology, 16*, 272–277.

Cohen, J. (1957). The factorial structure of the WAIS between early adulthood and old age. *Journal of Consulting Psychology, 21*, 283–290.

Cummins, J., & Das, J. (1980). Cognitive processing, academic achievement and WISC–R performance in EMR children. *Journal of Consulting and Clinical Psychology, 48*, 777–779.

Dickstein, L., & MacEvitt, M. (1971). Comprehension subtest of the WAIS and need for approval. *Psychological Reports, 28*, 482.

Feinberg, J., & McIlvried, E. (1991). WAIS–R intratest scatter in a chronic schizophrenic population: Is it an attentional problem? *Journal of Clinical Psychology, 47*(3), 327–335.

Finn, S. (1996). *A manual for using the MMPI as a therapeutic intervention.* Minneapolis: University of Minnesota Press.

Finn, S., & Tonsager, M. (1992). Therapeutic effects of providing MMPI–2 test feedback to college students awaiting therapy. *Psychological Assessment, 4*, 278–287.

Fischer, C. (1985). *Individualizing psychological assessment.* Hillsdale, NJ: Lawrence Erlbaum Associates.

Freeman, F. (1962). *Theory and practice of psychological testing.* New York: Holt, Rinehart & Winston.

Furth, H., & Milgram, N. (1965). Verbal factors in performance on WISC Similarities. *Journal of Clinical Psychology, 21*, 424–427.

Gardner, H. (1993). *Multiple intelligences: The theory in practice.* New York: Basic Books.

Garfield, S., & Affleck, D. (1960). A study of individuals committed to a state home for the retarded who were later released as not mentally defective. *American Journal of Mental Deficiency, 64*, 907–915.

Goleman, D. (1995). *Emotional intelligence.* New York: Bantam.

Handler, L. (1988, March). *The use of inquiry and testing of the limits in WISC and WAIS interpretation.* Paper presented at the annual meeting of the Society for Personality Assessment, New York.

Handler, L. (1993, April). *Teaching personality assessment.* Paper presented at the symposium "Teaching and Learning Personality Assessment," annual meeting of the Society for Personality Assessment, San Francisco.

Juliano, J., Haddad, F., & Carroll, J. (1988). Three year stability of WISC–R factor scores for Black and White, female and male children classified as learning-disabled. *Journal of School Psychology, 26*, 317–325.

Kamphaus, R. (1993). *Empirical assessment of children's intelligence.* Boston: Allyn & Bacon.

Karson, M. (1986). Projective and clinical aspects of intelligence tests. In A. Rabin (Ed.), Projective techniques for adolescents and children (pp. 212–235). New York: Springer.

Kaufman, A. (1990). *Assessing adolescent and adult intelligence.* Boston: Allyn & Bacon.

Klingler, D., & Saunders, D. (1975). A factor analysis of the items for nine subtests of the WAIS. *Multivariate Behavioral Research, 10*(2), 131–153.

Klopfer, B., Ainsworth, M., Klopfer, W., & Holt, R. (1954). *Developments in the Rorschach technique: Vol. I. Technique and theory.* New York: Harcourt, Brace, & World.

Krauskopf, C., & Saunders, D. (1994). *Personality and ability: The personality assessment system.* Lanham, MD: University Press of America.

Lanfeld, E., & Saunders, D. (1961). Anxiety as "effect of uncertainty": An experiment illuminating the OA subtest of the WAIS. *Journal of Clinical Psychology, 17,* 238–241.

Leckliter, I., Matarazzo, J., & Silverstein, A. (1986). A literature review of factor analytic studies with the WAIS–R. *Journal of Clinical Psychology, 42,* 332–342.

Levine, M. (1958). "Not alike" responses in Wechsler's Similarities subtest. *Journal of Consulting Psychology, 22,* 480.

Lipsitz, J., Dworkin, R., & Erlenmeyer-Kimling, L. (1993). Wechsler Comprehension and Picture Arrangement subtests and social adjustment. *Psychological Assessment, 5,* 430–437.

Marsden, G., & Kalter, N. (1969). Bodily concerns and the WISC Object Assembly Subtest. *Journal of Consulting and Clinical Psychology, 33,* 391–395.

Matarazzo, J. (1972). Factoral structure of the WB–I and WAIS. In J. Matarazzo (Ed.), *Wechsler's measurement and apprasial of adult intelligence* (5th ed., pp. 261–276). Baltimore: Williams & Wilkins.

Mayer, J., & Salovey, P. (1993). The intelligence of emotional intelligence. *Intelligence, 7*(4), 433–442.

Mednick, S., & Mednick, M. (1967). *Examiner's manual: Remote Associates Test.* Boston: Houghton Mifflin.

Mittenberg, W., Thompson, G., Schwartz, J., Ryan, J., & Levitt, R. (1991). Intellectual loss in Alzheimer's dementia and WAIS–R intrasubtest scatter. *Journal of Clinical Psychology, 47,* 544–547.

Naglieri, J. (1981). Factor structure of the WISC–R for children identified as learning disabled. *Psychological Reports, 49,* 891–895.

Nobo, J., & Evans, R. (1986). The WAIS–R Picture Arrangement and Comprehension subtests as measures of social behavior characteristics. *Journal of Personality Assessment, 50,* 90–92.

O'Grady, K. (1983). A confirmatory maximum liklihood factor analysis of the WAIS–R. *Journal of Consulting and Clinical Psychology, 51,* 826–831.

Parker, K. (1983). Factor analysis of the WAIS–R at nine age levels between 16 and 74 years. *Journal of Consulting and Clinical Psychology,. 51,* 302–308.

Piedmont, R., Sokolove, R., & Fleming, M. (1989a). An examination of some diagnostic strategies involving the Wechsler Intelligence scales. *Psychological Assessment: A Journal of Consulting and Clinical Psychology, 1,* 181–185.

Piedmont, R., Sokolove, R. & Fleming, M. (1989b). On WAIS–R difference scores in a psychiatric sample. *Psychological Assessment: A Journal of Consulting and Clinical Psychology, 1*(2), 155–159.

Ramos, M., & Die, A. (1986). The WAIS–R Picture Arrangement subtest: What do scores indicate? *Journal of General Psychology, 113,* 251–261.

Rapaport, D., Gill, M., & Schafer, R. (1946). *Diagnostic psychological testing* (Vol. 1). Chicago: Year Book.

Rapaport, D., Gill, M., & Schafer, R. (1968). *Diagnostic psychological testing* (2nd ed., editied by R. Holt). New York: International Universities Press.

Reynolds, C., & Kaufman, A. (1990). Assessment of children's intelligence with the Wechsler Intelligence Scale for Children–Revised (WISC–R). In C. Reynolds & R.

17. Teaching Interpretation of Wechsler Tests 319

Kamphaus (Eds.), Handbook of psychological and educational assessment of children: Intelligence and achievement (pp. 127–165). New York: Guilford.

Rockwell, G. (1967). WISC Object Assembly and bodily concerns. Journal of Consulting Psychology, 31, 221.

Ryan, J., Paolo, A., & Smith, A. (1992). WAIS–R scatter in brain-damaged patients: A comparison with the standardization sample. Psychological Assessment, 4, 63–66.

Ryan, J., Rosenberg, S., & DeWolfe, A. (1984). Generalizations of the WAIS–R factor structure with a vocational rehabilitation sample. Journal of Consulting and Clinical Psychology, 52, 311–312.

Salovey, P., & Mayer, J. (1989–1990). Emotional intelligence. Imagination, Cognition & Personality, 9(3), 185–211.

Saunders, D. (1960a). A factor analysis of the Information and Arithmetic items of the WAIS. Psychological Reports, 6, 367–383.

Saunders, D. (1960b). A factor analysis of the PC items of the WAIS. Journal of Clinical Psychology, 16, 146–149.

Saunders, D., & Gittinger, J. (1968). Patterns of intellectual functioning and their implications for the dynamics of behavior. In M. Katz, J. Cole, & M. Barton (Eds.), The role and methodology of classifications in psychiatry and psychotherapy (pp. 377–390). Washington, DC: U. S. Public Health Service.

Schafer, R. (1948). The clinical application of psychological tests. New York: International Universities Press.

Schill, T., (1966). The effects of MMPI sosical introversion on WAIS PA performance. Journal of Clinical Psychology, 22, 72–74.

Schill, T., Kahn, M., & Meuhlman, T. (1968). WAIS PA performance and participation in extracurricular activities. Journal of Clinical Psychology, 24, 95–96.

Schinka, J., Vanderploeg, R., & Curtiss, G. (1994). Wechsler Adult Intelligence Scale Revised subtest scatter as a function of maximum subtest scaled score. Psychological Assessment, 6(4), 364–367.

Segal, H., Westen, D., Lohr, N., & Silk, K. (1993). Clinical assessment of object relations and social cognition using stories told to the Picture Arrangement subtest of the WAIS–R. Journal of Personality Assessment, 61(1), 58–80.

Shaw, D. (1966). A factor analysis of the collegiate WAIS. Paper presented at Midwestern Psychological Association Meeting, Chicago.

Siegert, R., Patten, M., Taylor, A., & McCormick, A. (1988). Factor analysis of the WAIS–R using the factor replication procedure, FACTOREP. Multivariate Behavioral Research, 23, 481–489.

Silverstein, A. (1982). Factor structure of the Wechsler Adult Intelligence Scale–Revised. Journal of Consulting and Clinical Psychology, 50, 661–664.

Sprandel, H. (1985). The psychoeducational use and interpretation of the Wechsler Adult Intelligence Scale–Revised. Springfield, IL: Thomas.

Waite, R. (1961). The intelligence test as a psychodiagnostic instrument. Journal of Projective Techniques, 25, 90–102.

Waller, N., & Waldman, I. (1990). A reexamination of the WAIS–R factor structure. Psychological Assessment: A Journal of Consulting and Clinical Psychology, 2(2), 139–144.

Wechsler, D. (1958). The measurement and appraisal of adult intelligence (4th ed). Baltimore: Williams & Wilkins.

Wechsler, D. (1991). *Wechsler Intelligence Scale for Children, Third Edition: Manual*. New York: The Psychological Corp.

Wiener, G. (1957). The effects of distrust on some aspects of intelligence test behavior. *Journal of Consulting Psychology, 21*, 127–130.

Winnicott, D. (1971). *Playing and reality*. New York: Routledge.

Winnicott, D. (1975). Psychosis and child care. In D. Winnicott (Ed.), *Through paediatrics to psychoanalysis* (pp. 219–228). New York: Basic Books.

Witkin, H., Dyk, R., Faterson, H., Goodenough, D., & Karp, S. (1962). *Psychological differentiation: Studies in development*. New York: Wiley.

Zetzer, H., & Beutler, L. (1995). The assessment of cognitive functionins and the WAIS–R. In L. Beutler & M. Berren (Eds.), *Integrative assessment of adult personality* (pp. 121–186). New York: Guilford.

V

TEACHING AND LEARNING
SPECIALIZED ISSUES IN ASSESSMENT

In this section we have included several chapters that allow the reader to view information on testing procedures from a quite different vantage point than is traditionally described in the assessment literature. Although the topics are all quite varied, they also are all quite similar in that they attempt to refocus our approach to assessment data, or they attempt to suggest ways in which traditional measures can be used in very innovative ways. For example, Dana asks us to consider looking at test data through a different lens, that of the patient's prevailing culture; Fischer suggests that we may "re-view" Exner's scoring system from an experiential vantage point, and that we should approach assessment in a collaborative manner with the patient; Finn convinces us that the assessment procedure itself can and should be therapeutic; Wagner gives us an entirely new way in which to conceptualize special scores; whereas Ritzler describes ways in which to disseminate assessment findings; and Hilsenroth describes a very clever method of helping students conceptualize assessment data using metaphor. A brief discussion of the contents of each of these chapters follows.

Richard H. Dana's chapter, "Personality Assessment and the Cultural Self: Emic and Etic Contexts as Learning Resources," explains the need to include culture-specific personality and psychopathology information in personality assessment courses and in assessment practice, to discover "the cultural self." Dana describes both culture-specific (emic), and culture-general (etic) sources of information to inform clinical diagnosis and personality description. He emphasizes the importance of acculturation and racial identity measures to help decide when, how, and to what extent these information sources should be used. He believes that ethical practice requires the assessor to use caution in constructing experiential realities of persons with markedly different world views, self-concepts, behaviors, and symptomatologies. Using a fictitious case study, Dana outlines steps the student should take in determining, during the assessment process, when external sources of cultural information are required.

"The Rorschach and the Life World," by Constance T. Fischer, focuses on teaching the Exner system, but from a very different vantage point. Fischer emphasizes the translation of the Exner variables into familiar experiential and interpersonal terms, which she terms the "life-world orientation," using a variety of quite innovative methods to communicate them to students. In addition, she describes a very valuable assessment technique, teaching students how to collaborate with patients/clients in the assessment process. Fischer describes approaches she has developed to ask clients directly about the possibilities raised by their Rorschach responses, and together they refine the assessor's impressions.

Stephen E. Finn's chapter, "Teaching Therapeutic Assessment in a Required Graduate Course," teaches beginning graduate students to use assessment as therapy, in addition to its traditional information-gathering focus. Finn emphasizes teaching an approach in which the client and the assessor together define the questions to be addressed. He then describes an approach in which the assessment of clients is first done under standardized conditions, followed by an exploration with clients concerning the meanings, for them, of the test findings. In addition, he describes alternatives to problem behaviors. Students are also taught the value of asking clients to read and comment upon a written report, before it is sent to the referring professional.

In a chapter titled "A Logical Analysis of Rorschach Autisms," Edwin Wagner focuses on the problem area of "special scores" and the confusion that surrounds their interpretation. Wagner's system attempts to clarify and reclassify these scores, in order to improve students' understanding of their special meaning. He describes a system he calls TRAUT, or Tripartite Classification of Autisms, to include situations where the blot shape is ignored altogether, situations in which the perceptual rules are disregarded altogether, and situations in which counterfactual percepts are rationalized by spatial juxtaposition. Wagner illustrates his system with many clinical examples.

Mark J. Hilsenroth's chapter, "Using Metaphor to Understand Projective Test Data: A Training Heuristic," describes a method in which projective data are conceptualized as metaphorical expressions of experience, thoughts, feelings, and relationship patterns. Students are instructed, through clinical example, to use metaphor in building an interpretive framework of the individual, understanding both relational paradigms and emotional experience. The chapter describes methods by which the instructor can encourage students to employ the data to become phenomenologically involved in the patient's world and to vicariously explore how the patient experiences various aspects of his or her world.

Barry A. Ritzler's chapter, "Teaching Dissemination of Personality Assessment Results in Graduate Programs," includes a discussion of how to teach the dissemination of assessment results to patients and/or their families in feedback sessions, as well as ways to teach students to give oral and written feedback to referral sources. Ritzler recommends role playing and other techniques (e.g., modeling) to give students practice in verbal dissemination of results. He outlines the steps involved in dissemination of results, so that students can understand the complexity of the process, and he places special emphasis on suggestions and directions for crafting the written report, stressing the use of understandable language.

Ritzler discusses the purpose of assessment, emphasizing his view that assessment should *not* be used for generating a *DSM–IV* diagnosis. He clearly outlines his reasons and cites research to support his view. The reader should be aware that this view is quite controversial, and that many assessors believe that an approach that carefully integrates test results with detailed history, observational data and behavioral data are typically adequate to make a DSM–IV diagnosis.

18

Personality Assessment and the Cultural Self: Emic and Etic Contexts as Learning Resources

Richard H. Dana
*Regional Research Institute, Portland State University
and Southern Oregon University*

Interpretation of standard psychological test data from culturally diverse assessees for clinical diagnosis and personality description is difficult due to bias and deficits in cultural competence. This chapter presents a process for learning to use credible and available emic and etic sources for culture-personality information that can increase cultural sensitivity by reducing bias. Emic sources originate in communities representing one culture, or group within a culture (e.g., Native American Navajos), and are called *culture-specific*. Etic sources are intended to be *universal* and hence applicable to *all* cultural groups. However, many so-called etics, including psychological tests and structured interviews, come directly from our Anglo-American culture and have not been cross-culturally validated for equivalence before being used with other cultural groups. As a consequence, these measures are pseudoetics because their generality has not been established empirically. Personality theories and research may also be pseudoetic because of their Euro-American, male origins and subsequent inappropriate applications to persons from diverse cultural groups.

A second purpose of this chapter is to reduce bias that can occur whenever information from pseudoetic sources is accepted uncritically, or in the absence of corroborating emic content. Bias appears in psychological assessment reports as stereotypy, caricature, pathologization, or failure to diagnose. Systematic attention to potential cultural influences during the process of interpretation can reduce bias.

We have the requisite tests, research, and theory to understand persons who are like ourselves, but this information is not readily available for persons unlike ourselves. There are profound dfferences in world view, life histories, health/illness beliefs, expectations for services, values, first languages, self-concept, and encounters with oppression. Nonetheless, Anglo-Americans still have primary responsibility for assessment of all individuals regardless of cultural identity or national origins. As a consequence, there have been negative reactions to inappropriate or misleading research conclusions by Anglo social scientists that would also apply to assessment reports prepared by Anglo psychologists (Mio & Iwamasa, 1993).

This review of emic and etic sources of personality information begins with an acknowledged purpose of describing the cultural self, a necessary objective to provide relevant content for clinical diagnosis and/or personality description. Information resources on acculturation evaluation, racial identity models, and other sources of culture-specific information are included. Learning how to use information in a responsible manner can be accomplished by awareness of one's own cultural identity, by examining both emic and etic perspectives, and by self-study to increase cultural sensitivity. A fictitious case example included later in this chapter suggests helpful steps, appropriate questions to ask, and sources of relevant information to assist the student.

THE CULTURAL SELF

Each of us has a cultural self that provides a contextual reality for our life experiences. Until recently this cultural self has not been widely recognized as a formidable clinical resource for understanding clients. Many assessors have learned an impersonal behavioral-cognitive service delivery stance that diminishes human complexity in order to control the response process and provide more reliable sources of data. Concomitantly, this stance also reduces awareness of individual and cultural differences. Now that there are new expectations for assessment and psychotherapeutic responsibilities with at least one third culturally diverse clients, we must understand how culture contributes to interpretation of assessment data.

An encounter with one's own cultural identification is at first a solitary and intuitive journey, but should be supplemented by shared perspective during supervised experience. Mock interviews or therapy/counseling sessions with clients who have different cultural origins and different outcomes of acculturation can be used as sources of information for discussion of how and to what extent a person who differs from the therapist is accepted and acknowledged in words, feelings, facial expressions, and other inadvertent actions. An ethnocentrism–ethnorelativism or rejection–acceptance dimension has been described (Bennett, 1986) that can foster understanding of how an assessor's behaviors become a major source of a client's subsequent willingness to be sufficiently task oriented for a reliable assessment process to occur. This is especially important when the Rorschach is used because one form of refusing to cooperate lies in giving only a very small number of responses, which may then be overinterpreted in spite of Exner's caveat that 14 responses are required for interpretation.

A cultural self for Anglo-Americans has been described as self-contained individualism with "firm boundaries, personal control, and an exclusionary concept of the person" (Sampson, 1988, p. 15). Markus and Kitayama (1991) also described a self-contained individualism with a unique configuration of behavior-inducing traits, abilities, motives, and values.

Sampson (1988) contrasted self-contained individualism with an ensembled individualism or collectivist self common to many other cultures in which self–other boundaries are more fluid and control over the contents admitted to the self is minimal. Markus and Kitayama (1991) described a collectivist self predicated on interconnectedness among persons. The social milieu for the collectivistic self relies on perceived "thoughts, feelings, and actions of *others* in relationships" (p. 227), whereas situation-specific and secondary internal activities are always experienced in context with others and voluntarily controlled to ensure harmony.

The collective self can be explored by the Individualism–Collectivism Scale (INDCOL) (Hui, 1988) that looks at feelings, beliefs, behaviors, or behavioral intentions as enacted in contexts with spouse, parents, kin, neighbors, friends, and co-workers. Collectivism includes feelings of involvement in others' lives, self-presentation, susceptibility to social influence by sharing material and nonmaterial resources and outcomes, and consideration in decisions and actions of costs-benefits to others.

INDCOL was administered to a Japanese student as part of counseling. The extent to which the self dealt with interpersonal influences was suggested by score discrepancies from cultural expectations. This self wanted to make her own decisions regarding occupation, religion, and friendships, but was conflicted and confused as to how she should behave in situations calling for independent behavior in the United States that violated Japanese norms.

By means of INDCOL, Asian and Asian-American assessees can provide a situation-specific description of the self emphasizing a cultural contribution to acculturation issues, culture shock, and various problems-in-living. The behavior and psychopathology of Asians can only be understood within a self that incorporates other persons, the life situation, and ultimately the natural world. This dimension is composed of etic constructs that have received a significant amount of research attention (Triandis, 1990).

General statements can be made concerning the cultural specificity of the self, but each culture, including Anglo-American society, has within-group differences of unknown magnitude (Dana, 1993). There are, for example, Anglo-American within-group world view differences by gender. Women are generally more collectivist than men, especially with regard to preferences for cooperativeness instead of competition, helping rather than controlling, and compromise in lieu of power (L. C. Jensen, McGhie, & J. R. Jensen, 1991). Most Anglo-American men display individualism, although men who are less traditional display more elements of collectivism in their selves (Lykes, 1985).

The self can be examined using several hypothesized criteria that should have a characteristic range for each cultural group, overlap between cultural groups, and differ by cultural orientation status as described in the following section.

These criteria include (a) permeability of boundaries, (b) contents that may be admitted: human, animal, plant, natural and supernatural forces, affective/spiritual, behavioral, cognitive, social/environmental, (c) concept of person: exclusionary or including few or many other persons in particular relationships, and (d) control, organization, and relative importance of contents within the self. These criteria may be compared with individualist and collectivist selves (Markus & Kitayama, 1991). An individualized locus includes a self separated from others by rigid boundaries with a unique, private, goal-oriented, self-actualization agenda. Self-evaluation is by reflected appraisal and is validated by self-expression. An interdependent locus requires flexible boundaries for a personhood contextualized with others and containing appropriate acts toward realizing the goals of others. Self-definition occurs through relationships in specified contexts with a continuous adaptation of the self to ensure harmony.

Traditional American Indians/Alaska Natives may have the most permeable boundaries with inclusion of family, extended family, and tribe, natural and supernatural contents, with relatively little control over these contents. African Americans also have permeable boundaries that include a range of family and nonfamily members, although there is a person-centered focus with only vestiges of natural or supernatural contents and some control over contents. Asian Americans have very extended selves that include family but may or may not include supernatural forces, depending on the particular group and country of origin. Control by the person is secondary and ordinarily preempted by family members. Hispanic Americans typically also have extended selves and more permeable boundaries than Anglo-Americans. If their cultural origins are Mexican, Central, or South American, there may be infusions of Indian or African belief systems that result in only minimal personal control over contents that may include natural and supernatural forces. Traditional persons may experience no clear separation of affective/spiritual, behavioral, cognitive, or social/environmmental domains (Choney, Berryhill-Papke, & Robbins, 1995).

As an example, the Card I Rorschach W response of an Apache shaman was "the birds in the cloud … an enemy in the cloud … giant bat … he resemble the traveling star" (Klopfer & Boyer, 1961, p. 171). In interpreting this response, it is not helpful to even consider possible psychopathology without knowledge of behaviors and reputation in the community over time. We know the shaman is a traditional person because the Rorschach was administered using an interpreter. This Rorschach response illustrates that everything is indeed interrelated; the self is transmuted into a living vehicle without discrete boundaries, permeated by natural and supernatural fluxes that embody his cultural identity. There is space to encompass animals, clouds, and stars. Animal helpers and adversaries have origins in tribal symbols and myths to provide the dimensions of an internal cosmology that guides his everyday actions. These symbols and myths can be discussed during feedback of test findings in a cultural learning experience during which the assessee continues to be a teacher as he has presented himself in the Rorschach responses. If this seems to be a giant step from the Rorschach data, this interpretation also requires the previously described cultural elaboration of the self for credibility.

As this discussion suggests, the magnitude and kinds of differences in self-structure and contents belie any universality of Anglo-European assumptions concerning the self, particularly as expressed in the DSM. Research in this area is required to examine within-group and between-group differences in self-contents. A comparative normative basis for describing these criteria for the cultural self also needs to be developed.

Understanding culturally different others is dependent not only on a goodness of fit between provider and client world views, but awareness of their similarities and differences as well as a detailed knowledge of the assessee's culture (Grubb, 1989). This juxtaposition of different belief systems requires assessors to be motivated by curiosity and to be open to what may be unfamiliar and ambiguous. An awareness of Anglo cultural identification has importance for providers by encouraging them to label their own health/illness beliefs, self-concept parameters, and assumptions concerning reality as culture-specific and not universal (e.g., Helms, 1993; Ponterotto, 1988).

SOURCES OF INFORMATION ON CLIENT CULTURAL IDENTITY

Acculturation

Acculturation refers to a process of attitudinal/behavioral changes induced by cross-cultural contact (Casas & Pytluk, 1995). There are very large within-group differences in acculturation outcomes. Recognition of within-group differences can lessen stereotypy and lead to more careful definition of traditional, transitional, bicultural, marginal, and assimilated cultural orientations (e.g., Choney et al., 1995). An acculturation instrument or interview content should be used to describe cultural orientation status and provide additional culturally relevant personality information (for review with Hispanics, see Dana, 1996).

At present, I recommend routine use of instruments including the Acculturation Rating Scale for Mexican Americans (ARSMA, ARSMA–II) (Cuéllar, Arnold, & Maldonado, 1995), the African-American Acculturation Scale (AAAS) (Landrine & Klonoff, 1996), the Suinn–Lew Asian Self-Identity Acculturation Scale (SL–ASIA) (Suinn, Rickard-Figueroa, Lew, & Vigil, 1987), and the Northern Plains Bicultural Immersion Scale (NPBI) (J. Allen & French, 1994). Each of these instruments has a construction and validation history providing relevant content for elaborating dimensions of a cultural self. It is now vitally important and I believe ethically necessary to have this acculturation content prior to assessment for use in selection of appropriate tests and to inform test interpretation. Estimates of normative expectations for cultural orientation categories may be found elsewhere (see Dana, 1997).

Racial Identity and Oppression

An insistence on recognition of African-American racial identity emerged from a history of slavery, emancipation, and oppression during a 100-year struggle for civil rights. Beginning in the early 1970s, African-American psychologists interpreted their history using Nigrescence theories, theories of the development of African-American identity (Cross, 1971; Thomas, 1971). These theories described a sequence of stages with only minor differences between theories and the tests that were developed subsequently from them—the Racial Identity Attitude Scale (RIAS; Helms, 1990) and the Developmental Inventory of Black Consciousness (DIB–C; Milliones, 1980).

For simplicity here, I call these stages denial, awakening, internalization, and identity. The first stage, denial, describes acceptance of a White world view that served to minimize or denigrate their race and has been equated by some authors with psychopathology. This experience of denial was poignantly described in *The Invisible Man* by Ellison (1952), who said, "the invisibility to which I refer occurs because of a peculiar disposition of the eyes of those with whom I come in contact" (p. 3). Not existing in the world of other persons is akin to hibernation and the only recourse was the self-determined awakening described in subsequent Nigrescence stages.

Denial was followed by awakening with anger and anxiety as individuals learned who they were and shared their experiences in what became a transformation of consciousness. This frequently explosive self-discovery of racial attitudes induced by adaptation to oppression was exemplified by Nat Turner, W. E. B. DuBois, and Marcus Garvey (Cross, 1995).

Internalization, an incorporation and acceptance of change, stimulated pride in a newly recovered identity that could be sustained and developed over time. Finally, consolidation of a new Afrocentric identity provided confidence and an experience of increasing control over individual lives as well as renewed hope for African Americans as a group.

It is also feasible and necessary to evaluate the extent to which Nigrescence has had an outcome in racial or cultural identity. This can be done using a measure of racial identity as an outcome of oppression (Baldwin & Bell, 1985) or using a measure of African-American acculturation status (Landrine & Klonoff, 1996).

Historically, the predominantly Anglo healing professions apparently missed the potential pathology of absolute acquiescence and saw nothing remarkable in persons who conformed to an external, caricatured image of themselves. Anglo-American views of Blacks were tempered by their role-playing survival tactics to counter the immediate effects of oppression. Stereotypes were accepted as accurate and group differences were labeled as deficits (Wyatt, Powell, & Bass, 1982). Psychologists rarely looked beneath the surface in formal cross-racial encounters to glimpse the shrouded humanity and intensely cultural lives of individuals. The impact on personality of an oppressive system that sought to create second-class citizens was largely ignored.

African Americans have had to literally rewrite their history in the United States to provide a more accurate rendition of many lives beggared not by poverty alone but by denial of their own racial and cultural identities. Nigrescence can now be viewed as a resocializing process that can transform an existing negative identity into an Afrocentric identity (Cross, 1995) to provide an internalized source of strength and pride in a worldview and concommitant behaviors and beliefs that are valued for themselves. It is now necessary for assessors to examine the process of racial identity development and outcomes, the presence of oppression-derived pathologies (Akbar, 1991) and positive alternatives expressed by psychological health (Hayles, 1991; Ramseur, 1991).

Moreover, there is a growing conviction that "race" is a political category responsible for a history of invidious group comparisons in the name of science (for review, see Okazaki & Sue, 1995). Landrine and Klonoff (1996) preferred to talk about ethnicity and cultural differences among ethnic groups, or simply cultural differences. Nonetheless, R. T. Carter (1995) favored use of race because that perspective "transcends/supercedes all other experiences in the United States" (p. 3). Although this is indeed true, the persistent denial and denigration of African-American culture by mainstream psychology strongly suggests that an emphasis on culture, in addition to racial identity, can serve as a corrective by providing more accurate personality and psychopathology information.

In spite of the emergence of Afrocentrism, it would be an egregious mistake to assume that oppression does not leave intergenerational scars. African Americans have experienced a history of trauma that has been reaffirmed in the life experience of each individual and may be expressed as posttraumatic stress disorder (I. M. Allen, 1996). Countee Cullen (1947), for example, described in his poem, "Incident," an 8-year-old boy rebuffed by insult, leaving only a solitary, denigrating memory of a time from May until December that should have been "heart-filled, head filled with glee" (p. 9). This is not an isolated incident that violated one child's expectations for a responsive humanity in everyday life. Rather it represents a reiterated and sometimes daily occurrence for persons of color in this society. The potential impact as trauma in the developmental process is very great, particularly in a context of ghetto life that includes high risk for drug addiction, violence, and family disorganization.

How to Become Aware of the Cultural Self

I encourage awareness of the cultural self by using a series of steps: (a) examination of students' own cultural selves, (b) exposure to measures of acculturation outcomes, (c) describing the cultural self in general terms for various cultural groups, (d) using the criteria previously discussed as a framework for describing the cultural self, and (e) applications to case history materials or to client assessment data, depending on the course.

First, an example of how the student's cultural self can be examined. The first 2 weeks of a course on Native-American Mental Health became increasingly strident as American-Indian students vented their concerns about racism and Anglo students became increasingly defensive and angry. To help understanding on both sides of this chasm, I described two culture-specific approaches to the development of cultural identity, an Anglo model (Sabnami, Ponterotto, & Borodovsky, 1991) and an American-Indian model, which I prepared as a consequence of the feelings aroused in this class (see Dana, 1997). These models were similar and the class was able to process with me the content of the separate stages essentially paralleling the stages of denial, awakening, internalization, and identity described for African Americans. What happened as a consequence was that Anglo students began to appreciate what it means to be American Indian, the genocidal impact of Anglo conquest and the sequences for individuals across generations of repeated experiences with racism. Anglo students also began to acknowledge how their own cultural development had minimized the impact of their own stereotypes and prejudices on others, the conflict between their norms and humanitarian values, the privilege of being White, and the denied experiences of guilt, depression, and anger. This stimulated interest in an immersion in American-Indian cultures and provided a new meaning for the course. American-Indian students began to feel that White students were capable of understanding their histories of grief and loss and no longer felt compelled to use the classroom as a personal forum for confrontation. This process occupied two 3-hour classes and was followed up by a Psi Chi presentation and discussion with all psychology undergraduate and graduate students.

Exposure to acculturation measures uses those measures that actually describe the self rather than provide only categorization of acculturation outcomes or cultural orientation. For example, I would go over the kinds of information available for Mexican Americans from ARSMA–II (Cuéllar, Arnold, & Maldonado, 1995), the Cultural Life Style Inventory (Mendoza, 1989), and the Bicultural/Multicultural Experience Inventory (Ramirez, 1984). These contents are useful for describing the cultural self in considerable detail. Although these contents are not organized into the previously discussed criteria for describing the cultural self, they can also provide data for using these criteria.

Finally, in an assessment course it is necessary to have examples of clients who have responded to various acculturation measures prior to the administration of standard psychological tests. The use of these moderators to describe the cultural self can then illustrate how the interpretation of subsequent tests is altered by this information. In other courses, published case materials can be reexamined after discussion of hypothetical data from acculturation measures.

EMIC CONTRIBUTIONS

A variety of emic, or culture-specific resources predate the development of genuine etic resources and, at present, are more reliable and persuasive. These emic sources include constructs and less formal descriptive vocabularies, culture-specific measures, case studies, reviews, theory, and examples from literature contained in novels, short stories, and poetry. These sources suggest culture-specific personality, psychopathology, and life history characteristics, and also illustrate the extent of within-culture variability and can supplement information obtained from etic measures.

Constructs and Descriptive Vocabulary

Two examples illustrating different methodologies and research purposes expose core constructs and develop descriptive vocabularies from interviews with informants. One construct approach identified familism, fatalism, machismo, and folk beliefs related to generation and acculturation status (Cuéllar, Arnold, & González, 1995). These constructs have indigenous validity because group members not only identify the dimensions but provide reliable rank ordering of individuals on these dimensions (Irwin, Klein, & Townsend, 1982).

Traditionalism was examined in the lives of women from seven distinct Canadian cultures including three Indian/Eskimo groups, Jamaicans, Mennonites, Chinese, and Ukrainians (Billson, 1995). A potpourri of methods, including participant observation and recorded interviews, were used to develop social or group portraits individualized by verbatim quotations. The participants shared all phases of the discovery process, from community entrée to reviewing drafts of the findings. The author clearly described her differences and similarities from the persons and cultures she visited, living both "inside and outside" simultaneously, with a conspicuous and intense emotional investment and advocacy. A formal set of eight questions were addressed to acknowledge these women "are the true experts of their own lives" (p. 8). Issues of powerlessness and power regained, oppression, cultural supports, control over resources, role definitions, and decision making were addressed in historical and culture-difference contexts. Because much of what we know about other cultures is developed by men and is a product of empirical research or description without methodological substance, her book and a forthcoming companion volume on French and British cultural origins in Canada are unique expositions of feminist scholarship.

Culture-Specific Instruments

Emic information may also be found in culture-specific instruments. Between 1976 and 1986, approximately 10% of *Journal of Counseling Psychology* studies used such instruments, whereas an expanded journal base for 1983–1988 yielded nearly 31% (Sabnani & Ponterotto, 1992).

Problems-in-living and hassles differ across groups due to prejudices, discrimination, and local conditions. As a result, standard measures of these problems have only limited applicability because they omit culture-specific sources of distress and fail to acknowledge the pervasiveness and intensity of particular stressors. Not only do these stressors differ between American Indians and Anglo-Americans, they also differ among tribes. For example, urban and rural Anglos ranked marital problems most highly, while for American-Indian people being fired from a job, jail, family illness/injury, and sexual problems have the highest rankings. When reservation tribal groups were compared, the urban Washoe were less impacted as crime victims and by repossession of household goods, but ranked arrests of family members, incidents of racism, and being on welfare as more salient than for Sioux (Dana, Hornby, & Hoffmann, 1984).

Case Studies

Although case studies can provide new understanding of how cultural knowledge informs descriptions of personality and psychopathology, there are only a small number of available examples. Most of these examples provide too little information and serve primarily as stimuli for considerations of how to apply this information in a useful manner. An exception is found in recent case descriptions of the effects of World War II incarceration of Japanese Americans on their children and grandchildren (Nagata, 1991). Case studies are minimized here because they require careful scrutiny within a seminar setting rather than a simple listing of references.

Reviews

Reviews are selectively reported without intending to slight any author by omission or minimize available resources for any particular group. For example, Chinese personality, primarily in terms of test scores, was examined by Hwang (1982), and Bond (1986, 1991) has contributed a broad base of relevant information. General information on Asian groups in the United States was provided by Min (1995) on an introductory level. Uba (1994) organized content that is descriptive of Eastern versus Western differences, as well as differences within groups of Asians that include acculturation, personality patterns, and psychopathology.

African Americans have been described in many volumes by psychologists and others who have made significant but controversial contributions to personality study (e.g., Robinson, 1995; Steele, 1990). Jenkins (1995) is a place to begin self-education for Anglo psychologists because of the careful treatment of self-concept, competence, Black English, identity development, and psychopathology. Books by White (1984) and Kochman (1981) should be supplemented by *Black Psychology* (Jones, 1991) for multiauthored perspectives on personality, particularly as impacted by racism. Finally, the research-based volumes, *Life in Black America* and *Mental Health in Black America* (Jackson, 1991; Neighbors & Jackson, 1996, respectively) provide an introduction to quality of life issues.

The relatively large numbers of research studies with Hispanic populations have been reviewed in many sources within a mental health framework (e.g., Malgady & Rodriguez, 1994; Marín & VanOss Marín, 1991; Padilla, 1995). These books should be examined after some immersion in history (e.g., Acosta-Belen & Sjostrom, 1988). It is of critical importance to recognize the magnitude of differences among Hispanic subgroups and to focus on book-length examinations of each subgroup (e.g., Canino, Earley, & Rogler, 1988; Keefe & Padilla, 1987; Koss-Chioino, 1992).

American Indians have a research literature that has been developed historically and contemporaneously largely by Anglo-American anthropologists. Trimble (1977) has described many of these social scientists as sojourners who leave with something of value for themselves but give nothing back to the community. Furthermore, personality research methods are often alien, uninformed by native contributions, and their findings have been taken out of tribal cultural contexts and reported using Anglo-European theoretical conceptualizations, also without local interpretation (Trimble & Medicine, 1976). More recently, however, there has been some collaborative research, although outsiders remain suspect. This distrust presents a problem for professional psychologists requiring ethnographic information and case studies of particular tribes, either historic or contemporary. Although I am informed by anthropological accounts, I try to focus on American-Indian authors and am particularly impressed by long-term time commitments within a community (e.g., Weibel-Orlando, 1991).

Theory

Some culture-specific theory is available, but remains largely unexamined by research process. For example, Ramirez (1983) presented Mestizo perspectives on personality theory, a profound and compelling encounter with a non-Eurocentric world view. The anthropologist F. L. K. Hsu (1971) combined classical psychoanalytic layers of unconscious, preconscious, unexpressed unconscious, and expressible conscious with additional outer layers of intimate society and culture, operative society and culture, wider society and culture, and outer world for an Asian expanded self-concept of Jen. Jen functions for psychosocial homeostasis or a satisfactory level of psychic and interpersonal equilibrium.

Literature

Literature can divulge life scenarios by telling life stories and exposing human dilemmas in their cultural contexts. Assessors who work with a particular client group should immerse themselves in this literature. I have done this, especially with the American-Indian, and to a lesser extent with African-American literature, because my passion for poetry and literature parallels strong relationships and life experiences in learning about cultural and racial identities.

How much immersion is sufficient can only be answered by example. For Native Americans, it is necessary to have very precise knowledge of the real historical events in conquest and colonization, the magnitude of mass murder, disease, coerced education, imposed religion, and deliberately created dependence on commodities and alcohol. This factual information was obscured by minimization and distortion in the absence of a cadre of American-Indian scholars (e.g., Jaimes, 1992; Welch, 1994). It requires knowledge of both the unvarnished historical events and the poetic/literary accounts of the consequences of contact and conquest to gain a perspective on the extent of demoralization and despair as well as the courage and integrity that have found expression in cultural resources used to foster survival.

However, this historical context is not adequate without supplemental tribe-specific histories and contemporary status information. For example,

Blackfeet images of past and present were given life by James Welch (Welch, 1975, 1986, 1990). Forrest Carter, a Cherokee, has described his boyhood (F. Carter, 1990). To understand something of Chippewa people, read Louise Erdrich's books. An Osage history lesson is graphically retold in *Mean Spirit* (Hogan, 1990), whereas *River Song* and *Winterkill* describe contemporary life and historic identities of many Columbia River peoples and the Nez Percé (Lesley, 1989; Leslie, 1984). The impact of urban life on a displaced Pueblo Indian has been described by Momaday (1968).

Genocide, racism, and forced acculturation provided the genesis for inter-generational posttraumatic stress disorder (Choney et al., 1995). Grief is always present on American-Indian reservations, as a result of untimely deaths due to accident, violence, murder, disease, infant mortality, and the frequency of drug- and alcohol-related lifestyles. Similarly, depression is endemic, whether de-scribed by Anglo psychiatric conditions or culture-specific and often reserva-tion-specific syndromes (e.g., D. L. Johnson & C. A. Johnson, 1965; Topper & Curtis, 1987).

For example, a *Poem for James who Asked Me Why Everything Hurts So Much*, by Sherman Alexie (1993), describes his 10-year-old brother "killing wasps by proxy," to flail against the BIA (Bureau of Indian Affairs), reservation life, and his own powerlessness. When Alexie said, this behavior was "an ornamental medicine because there was nothing left to heal," the enormity of pain, ex-pressed and unexpressed, that burdens daily experience is exposed.

It is my belief that with an unknown Anglo assessor, these unverbalized feelings of pain resulting from oppression and genocide overshadow the rela-tionship and often minimize productvity with subsequent overinterpretation of available data. For this reason, assessors must beware of an exhorbitant and potentially stigmatizing role their own fantasies can have in extrapolating from insufficient data, particularly without recourse to extratest information.

More elusive than general historical information or tribal histories is reading that invokes an awareness of the cultural self. A self that is not only part of nature but resonant to natural and supernatural power sources is alien to most Anglo-Americans. When F. Carter (1978) described Geronimo, an Apache shaman and warrior, we behold a self that is literally beyond our comprehension and even transcends compelling fiction. When Klopfer and Boyer (1961) used psychoanalytic theory to interpret their Apache shaman Rorschach record, the cultural self was unbelievable to these Euro-Americans and was pathologized as a consequence.

Mowat (1975) provided an Ihalmiut Eskimo example of extended self in the form of a "song-cousin". A song-cousin embodied an unconditional relationship gift that for an Ihalmiut was an immutable acknowledgment of inseparability that included shared welfare and survivial. This "gift" was an inclusion of someone outside the kinship group in the selves of these people. Song-cousin Mowat could not reciprocate by a similar extension of self and consequently was unwilling to relinquish the ammunition necessary for group survival when he left. In spite of this abrogation of expectations, the Ihalmiut were also unable to even consider withdrawing this gift as a consequence.

I have described self-differences of indigenous people at length because of the extreme divergence from an Anglo-American self. However, the indigenous African self can also place the individual in an enlarged human context of community that at one time included a force field containing plants, animals, and natural phenomena (Dana, 1993). Although it is unknown to what extent Afrocentrism has enlarged the self beyond the collectivity of extended family, African-American natural consciousness has been described as the equivalent of an altered state for most Anglo-Americans (McGee & Clark, 1974).

ETIC CONTRIBUTIONS

Leung and Bond (1989) proposed three levels of analysis for cross-cultural comparisons: cultural, intercultural, and etic. Using an example in which two variables are applied to 100 individuals in 10 cultures, they derived pancultural correlations (or factor analyses) based on all individuals, cross-cultural correlations based on countries of origin, and intracultural correlations based on within-culture comparisons between variables. A within-culture standardization was used to correct for response sets, vitiating the pancultural and cross-cultural analyses. Culture-specific influences on item endorsement can be detected from the average patterning of item relationships and the average relative location of responses or positioning. Only the etic level of analysis allows for cross-cultural comparisons of individuals.

Etic contributions can occur at group and individual levels (Triandis, Bontempo, Leung, & Hui, 1990). A group identity level includes cultural and demographic constructs to comprise "subjective culture" (Triandis, 1972). Demographic constructs further break down cultural constructs into particular groups, such as age or gender, whereas personal constructs provide for examination of individual uniqueness. Triandis (1996) proposed identification of cultural syndromes or "dimensions of cultural variation ... used as parameters of psychological theories" (p. 407) or "pattern(s) of shared attitudes, beliefs, categorizations, self-definitions, norms, role definitions, and values ... organized around a theme that can be identified among those who speak a particular language"(p. 408). Examples include collectivism and individualism, active-passive, cultural complexity, and vertical/horizontal relationships. Triandis offered a methodology for studying cultural syndromes and future research will determine a constellation of syndromes usable for personality and psychopathology descriptions.

Personal identity, or uniqueness at an individual level, was identified by a methodology that extracts shared elements of subjective culture from culture-specific samples (Triandis et al., 1990). Ultimately it will be necessary to separate aspects of group and personal identity in our descriptions of persons. The complexity of these method issues and distinctions among kinds of constructs during this early research period requires reduction for practical use to inform interpretation. For the present, cross-culturally valid constructs from existing tests provide the primary sources of etic data.

Research Definition of Constructs

An etic assessment perspective examines psychological tests as genuine etics or pseudoetics (Dana, 1993). Gray-Little (1995) has correctly commented that emic techniques often rely on subjective interpretation, whereas demonstrations of cultural sensitivity in etic tests has been a research priority. Clearly, although this is the primary reason professional psychologists prefer etic resources, the status of cross-cultural construct validation remains a major problem with some of these tests. Many standard tests are pseudoetics, or Anglo-American emics, although they have been applied as if they were universal measures. Few standard tests meet consensual criteria for cross-cultural construct validation and these tests are not among the most widely used standard tests, such as the MMPI (Dana, 1993). How to use the MMPI, for example, with multicultural populations in the United States remains a source of controversy, although recommendations are available, at least for Hispanic populations (e.g., Dana, 1995). Diaz-Guerrero and Diaz-Loving (1990) reviewed examples of possible universal assessments that represent cross-culturally validated constructs, including the Holtzman Inkblot Technique, the Spielberger State-Trait Anxiety Inventory, Osgood's Semantic Differential Technique, Hofstede's Cultural Dimensions, and Witkin's laboratory procedures. Unfortunately, these measures are not frequently used in assessment practice and can only provide examples of methodology.

CULTURALLY COMPETENT
ASSESSMENT PRACTICE

Some suggestions are offered for teaching and learning culturally competent assessment practice. Following these suggestions, a flow chart is included for organizing the different kinds of information presented in this chapter. The use of this flow chart can increase the reliability and the accuracy of interpreting psychological test data.

Teaching and Learning How to Become Aware
of Etic and Emic Perspectives

I can recommend a process used by Steve López et al. (1989) to increase awareness that both etic and emic perspectives provide useful lenses to increase cultural sensitivity. López et al. proposed considering a balancing of etic norms, emic norms, and individual norms to differentiate between normal and abnormal behaviors, to evaluate etiologic factors, and to implement appropriate interventions. A comparison of the hypotheses generated by these different perspectives, in addition to suggesting alternative hypotheses, can facilitate the processing of assessment data. Learning to balance these different sets of normative expectations and incorporating the client's own view may confirm or deny specific expectations.

How to Become Culturally Sensitive:
Suggestions and Caveat

1. Students should be taught that self-monitoring is required in compliance with the APA ethical code (Dana, 1994). Assessors should be clear with clients that they are in the process of learning to understand cultural backgrounds and feedback should be encouraged from clients as teachers. Students should be taught not to expect too much from standard tests. Even their own life experiences, if limited to Anglo-American settings, may be misleading. Similarly, they should be urged to be cautious in using DSM categories and recognize practical and culture-specific limitations in their assessment recommendations resulting from a Eurocentric world view.

2. Students' professional reading should focus on the cultural group(s) encountered in their client population. Culture-specific journals should be read including, for example, the *Hispanic Journal of Behavioral Sciences, Journal of Black Psychology*, the *American Indian and Alaska Native Mental Health Research Journal*, and the *Journal of Cross-Cultural Psychology*. Asian-American publications appear primarily in mainstream journals. Clinical psychology students should be urged to read counseling psychology journals, which contain an overwhelming percentage of the relevant papers, particularly the *Journal of Multicultural Counseling and Development*.

3. Small study groups can be organized to read and review several new books per month. It is of particular importance to balance books primarily focused on intervention (e.g., Pedersen, Draguns, Lonner, & Trimble, 1996; Ponterotto, Casas, Suzuki, & Alexander, 1995) with culture-specific assessment contributions (e.g., R. T. Carter, 1995; Landrine & Klonoff, 1996) because the cultural self will be exposed in these interdependent contexts.

4. For each assessment, the students should be asked to consider whether they have followed a process that is culturally competent by using racial identity and/or acculturation measures, a culture-specific style of service delivery, selection of tests in accord with acculturation status, test interpretation using some materials contained in this chapter, culture-specific formulations for DSM–IV diagnosis, and provision of feedback to clients and significant others that recognizes self-concept parameters.

Each of these steps can increase the reliability of personality statements or clinical diagnosis (Cuéllar, 1996; Cuéllar, Dana, & González, 1995).

An Example of Use of Cultural Information
During the Assessment Process

An example is provided to help the student and the teacher to anticipate when, during an assessment process, the particular kinds of cultural information described in this chapter can be used. For a fictitious case example, a 27-year-old man born in El Paso, Texas, of Mexican-origin parents was committed by police to a psychiatric ward after appearing out of control with possible hallucinations in a bar disturbance in which he physically assaulted his wife and others.

During the interview (Step 1, Table 18.1), the initial stage in an assessment process, the assessor was able to be simpatico and thus establish suffcient task orientation for subsequent testing. The patient protested in reasonably accurate English that he was not "loco," did not need to be locked up, and wanted to talk with someone who spoke Spanish. He did feel badly at having hit people, particularly his wife. Interview information and reports from others should be compared with demographic information, including social class, religion, education, and occupation. This is done to suggest his health/illness beliefs, the diagnostic significance, if any, of his symptoms, and his expectations for treatment. He has already stated that he is not crazy and therefore should neither be locked up, nor treated like a sick person. Step 2 (Table 18.1) would be an administration of a cultural identity measure, preferably ARSMA or ARSMA–II, to provide information on cultural orientation status. Because it is likely that he will be either marginal or traditional, hypotheses regarding relatively traditional health/illness beliefs should be supported. There is also an indication that his cultural self would be extended to include family members.

TABLE 18.1

Steps During an Assessment Process When Relevant Questions May Require External Sources of Cultural Information

Assessment Steps	Relevant Questions	Sources of Cultural Information
1. Interview	English language fluency? Demographics? Exposure to discrimination?	Research on services in client second language Census information/Public health statistics Possible use of test
2. Cultural/racial identity evaluation	Acculturation status? Racial identity status? Description of cultural self?	Use of acculturation measure Use of racial identity measure
3. Standard psychological tests	Are tests etic or pseudoetic? Appropriateness of norms? Availability of culture-specific norms? Translations?	Cross-cultural linguistic, metric, construct validity research
4. Culture-specific measures	Needed? Available? Psychometric adequacy?	Research on culture-specific measures
5. Cultural formulation	Is there a culture-specific disorder?	DSM–IV glossary Relevant research literature
6. Report	How to describe culture-specific personality characteristics? Feedback of assessment findings: To client and/or family/significant others	Examine emic personality theories Examine emic literature reviews Examine research on validated emic personality constructs Examine relevant emic case studies Read relevant emic novels, poetry, etc.

If he is traditional and of lower class origin, especially with any Indian admixture, the self may also contain physical and magical forces.

Standard psychological tests (Step 3, Table 18.1) might include the Rorschach and MMPI–2. The Rorschach would provide content or structural indications of the organization and control over self-contents and also suggest any presence of physical and/or magical forces in his thought processes. Rorschach psychopathology indicators would be more persuasive if the patient had a marginal rather than a traditional cultural orientation. The MMPI–2 is skewed for higher socioeconomic classes and education, as well as underrepresenting Hispanics in the standardization (Dana, 1995). If this patient was traditional, the profile would be expected to have significant elevations on clinical scales that corresponded with Rorschach psychopathology indicators. If the patient was marginal, then the MMPI would still show some spurious elevation, but much less, and a depathologized interpretation could proceed by emphasizing personality characteristics and examining content suggestive of anger and physical symptomatology. Step 4 (Table 18.1) would require the administration of the Hispanic Stress Inventory (Cervantes, Padilla, & Salgado de Snyder, 1990), an emic measure, to delineate problems and stressors. This information would contribute to an understanding of the demographic information regarding the content of everyday life experiences. Step 5 (Table 18.1) would focus on a cultural formulation for diagnosis, using the DSM to examine the contribution of culture in the production of symptomatology and particularly to describe any culture-specific disorders such as *ataque de nervios* or *nervios*. If these and other disorders could be ruled out, then the subsequent reliability of any DSM diagnosis would be increased. If a culture-specific disorder could not be ruled out, then more information should be obtained by a Spanish-speaking professional and referral to a folk healer might need to be considered as an option. Step 6 (Table 18.1) , the report, should be separated into a section providing cultural influences on interpretations of symptoms and problems. I do this first section as a basis for any possible modification of test and interview findings on the basis of cultural materials. For this purpose, reference would be made to emic personality theories (e.g., Ramirez, 1983), literature on relevant constructs (macho, familism, etc.), and novels or case studies for additional information on relevant life experiences. Finally, the assessment results would be discussed with the patient and significant others in the family or extended family.

It is important for students to consider each of these six steps in an assessment process where cultural/racial identity issues can require additional sources of information, either by introduction of specialized assessment instruments/measures, or by awareness of specific research literature and other kinds of potentially helpful materials. All of these steps are necessary in order to produce a report that is accurate, relatively free from bias or stereotypy, culturally relevant for the assessee, and useful for subsequent treatment planning. The use of both etic and emic lenses in report preparation provides different but often equally helpful perspectives for understanding cultural issues.

REFERENCES

Acosta-Belen, E., & Sjostrom, B. R. (Eds.). (1988). *The Hispanic experience in the United States: Contemporary issues and perspectives.* New York: Praeger.

Akbar, N. (1991). Mental disorder among African Americans. In R. L. Jones (Ed.), *Black psychology* (3rd ed., pp. 339–352). Berkeley, CA: Cobb & Henry.

Alexie, S. (1993). *Old shirts and new skins.* Los Angeles: University of California, American Indian Study Center.

Allen, I. M. (1996). PTSD among African Americans. In A. J. Marsella, M. J. Friedman, E. T. Gerrity, & R. M. Scurfield (Eds.), *Ethnocultural aspects of posttraumatic stress disorder: Issues, research, and clinical applications* (pp. 209–238). Washington, DC: American Psychological Association.

Allen, J., & French, C. (1996). (Version 5). Northern Plains Bicultural Immersion Scale-Preliminary Manual and Scoring Instructions. Vermillion: University of South Dakota.

Baldwin, J. A., & Bell, Y. R. (1985). The African Self-Consciousness Scale: An Africentric personality questionnaire. *Western Journal of Black Studies, 9*(2), 65–68.

Bennett, M. J. (1986). A developmental approach to training for intercultural sensitivity. *International Journal of Intercultural Relations, 10,* 179–186.

Billson, J. M. (1995). *Keepers of the culture: The power of tradition in women's lives.* New York: Lexington.

Bond, M. H. (Ed.). (1986). *The psychology of the Chinese people.* Hong Kong: Oxford University Press.

Bond, M. H. (1991). *Beyond the Chinese face.* Hong Kong: Oxford University Press.

Canino, I. A., Earley, B. F., & Rogler, L. H. (Eds.). (1988). *The Puerto Rican child in New York City: Stress and mental health.* New York: Hispanic Research Center.

Carter, F. (1978). *Watch for me on the mountain.* New York: Dell.

Carter, F. (1990). *The education of Little Tree.* Albuquerque: University of New Mexico Press.

Carter, R. T. (1995). *The influence of race and racial identity in psychotherapy: Toward a racially inclusive model.* New York: Wiley.

Casas, J. M., & Pytluk, S. D. (1995). Hispanic identity development: Implications for research and practice. In J. G. Ponterotto, J. M. Casas, L. A. Suzuki, & C. M. Alexander (Eds.), *Handbook of multicultural counseling* (pp. 155–180). Thousand Oaks, CA: Sage.

Cervantes, R. C., Padilla, A. M., & Salgado de Snyder, N. (1990). Reliability and validity of the Hispanic Stress Inventory. *Hispanic Journal of Behavioral Sciences, 12,* 75–82.

Choney, S. K., Berryhill-Papke, E., & Robbins, R. R. (1995). The acculturation of American Indians: Developing frameworks for research and practice. In J. G. Ponterotto, J. M. Casas, L. A. Suzuki, & C. M. Alexander (Eds.), *Handbook of multicultural counseling* (pp. 73–92). Thousand Oaks, CA: Sage.

Cross, W. E., Jr. (1971). The Negro-to-Black conversion experience. *Black World, 20,* 13–26.

Cross, W. E., Jr. (1995). The psychology of Nigrescence: Revising the Cross model. In J. G. Ponterotto, J. M. Casas, L. A. Suzuki, & C. M. Alexander (Eds.), *Handbook of multicultural counseling* (pp. 93–122). Thousand Oaks, CA: Sage.

Cuéllar, I (1996). *Cross-cultural clinical personality assessment*. Manuscript under editorial review.

Cuéllar, I., Arnold, B., & González, G. (1995). Cognitive referrents of acculturation: Assessment of cultural constructs in Mexican Americans. *Journal of Community Psychology, 23*, 339–356.

Cuéllar, I., Arnold, B., & Maldonado, R. (1995). Acculturation Rating Scale for Mexican Americans–II: A revision of the original ARSMA scale. *Hispanic Journal of Behavioral Sciences, 17*, 275–304.

Cuéllar, I., Dana, R. H., & González, G. (1995). *Competent psychological assessment with Hispanics: A cultural formulation approach using* DSM–IV. Unpublished manuscript.

Cullen, C. (1947). *On these I stand*. New York: Harper.

Dana, R. H. (1993). *Multicultural assessment perspectives for professional psychology*. Boston: Allyn & Bacon.

Dana, R. H. (1994). Testing and assessment ethics for all persons: Beginning and agenda. *Professional Psychology: Research and Practice, 25*, 349–354.

Dana, R. H. (1995). Culturally competent MMPI assessment of Hispanic populations. *Hispanic Journal of Behavioral Sciences, 17*, 305–319.

Dana, R. H. (1996). Measurement of acculturation in Hispanic populations. *Hispanic Journal of Behavioral Sciences, 18*, 317–328.

Dana, R. H. (1997). *Understanding cultural identity in assessment and intervention*. Thousand Oaks, CA: Sage.

Dana, R. H., Hornby, R., & Hoffmann, T. (1984). Local norms of personality assessment for Rosebud Sioux. *White Cloud Journal, 3*(2), 17–25.

Diaz-Guerrero, R., & Diaz-Loving, R. (1990). Interpretation in cross-cultural personality assessment. In C. R. Reynold & R. W. Kamphaus (Eds.), *Handbook of psychological and educational assessment of children: Personality, behavior, and context* (pp. 491–523). New York: Guilford.

Ellison, R. (1952). *Invisible man*. New York: Random House.

Gray-Little, B. (1995). The assessment of psychopathology in racial and ethnic minorities. In J. N. Butcher (Ed.), *Clinical personality assessment: Practical approaches* (pp. 140–157). New York: Oxford University Press.

Grubb, H. J. (1989). The bi-polar prepubescent adolescent: A literature review and clinical case study of an eleven-year old Black female. *Journal of Black Psychology, 15*, 129–147.

Hayles, V. R., Jr. (1991). African American strengths: A survey of empirical findings. In R. L. Jones (Ed.), *Black psychology* (3rd ed., pp. 379–400). Berkeley, CA: Cobb & Henry.

Helms, J. E. (Ed.). (1990). *Black and white racial identity: Theory, research, and practice*. New York: Greenwood.

Helms, J. E. (1993). I also said, "White racial identity influences White researchers." *The Counseling Psychologist, 21*, 240–243.

Hogan, L. (1990). *Mean spirit*. New York: Atheneum.

Hsu, F. L. K. (1971). Psychosocial homeostasis and Jen: Conceptual tools for advancing psychological anthropology. *American Anthropologist, 73*, 23–44.

Hui, C. H. (1988). Measurement of individualism-collectivism. *Journal of Research in Personality, 22*, 17–36.

344 Dana

Hwang, C. H. (1982). Studies in Chinese personality: A critical review. *Bulletin of Educational Psychology (Taiwan Normal University), 15*, 227–242.

Irwin, M., Klein, R. E., & Townsend, J. W. (1982). Indigenous versus construct validity in cross-cultural research. In L. L. Adler (Ed.), *Cross-cultural research at issue* (pp. 23–29). New York: Academic Press.

Jackson, J. S. (Ed.). (1991). *Life in Black America.* Newbury Park, CA: Sage.

Jaimes, M. A. (Ed.). (1992). *The state of Native America: Genocide, colonization, and resistance.* Boston: South End Press.

Jenkins, A. H. (1995). *Psychology and African Americans: A humanistic approach* (2nd ed.). Boston: Allyn & Bacon.

Jensen, L. C., McGhie, A. P., & Jensen, J. R. (1991). Do men's and women's world views differ? *Psychological Reports, 68,* 312–314.

Johnson, D. L., & Johnson, C. A. (1965). Totally discouraged: A depression syndrome of the Dakota Sioux. *Transcultural Psychiatric Research, 1,* 141–143.

Jones, R. L. (Ed.). (1991). *Black psychology* (3rd ed.). Berkeley, CA: Cobb & Henry.

Keefe, S. E., & Padilla, A. M. (Eds.). (1987). *Chicano ethnicity.* Albuquerque: University of New Mexico Press.

Klopfer, B., & Boyer, L. B. (1961). Notes on the personality structure of a North American Indian shaman: Rorschach interpretation. *Journal of Projective Techniques and Personality Assessment, 25,* 170–178.

Kochman, T. (1981). *Black and White styles in conflict.* Chicago: University of Chicago Press.

Koss-Chioino, J. (1992). *Women as healers, women as patients: Mental health care and traditional healing in Puerto Rico.* Boulder, CO: Westview.

Landrine, H., & Klonoff, E. A. (1996). *African-American acculturation: Deconstructing race and reviving culture.* Thousand Oaks, CA: Sage.

Lesley, C. (1989). *Riversong.* New York: Dell.

Lesley, C. (1984). *Winterkill.* New York: Dell.

Leung, K., & Bond, M. H. (1989). On the empirical identification of dimensions for cross-cultural comparisons. *Journal of Cross-Cultural Psychology, 20,* 133–151.

López, S. R., Grover, K. P., Holland, D., Johnson, M. J., Kain, C. D., Kanel, K., Mellins, C. A., & Rhyne, M. C. (1989). Development of culturally sensitive psychotherapists. *Professional Psychology: Research and Practice, 20,* 369–376.

Lykes, M. B. (1985). Gender and individualistic vs. collectivist bases for notions about the self. *Journal of Personality, 53,* 356–383.

Malgady, R. G., & Rodriguez, O. (Eds.). (1994). *Theoretical and conceptual issues in Hispanic mental health.* Malabar, FL: Krieger.

Marín, G., & VanOss Marín, B. (1991). *Research with Hispanic populations.* Newbury Park, CA: Sage.

Markus, H. R., & Kitayama, S. (1991). Culture and the self: Implications for cognition, emotion, and motivation. *Psychological Review, 98,* 224–253.

McGee, D. P., & Clark, C. X. (1974, August/September). Critical elements of Black mental health. *Journal of Black Health Perspectives,* 52–58.

Mendoza, R. H. (1989). An empirical scale to measure the type and degree of acculturation in Mexican-American adolescents and adults. *Journal of Cross-Cultural Psychology, 20,* 372–385.

Milliones, J. (1980). Construction of a Black consciousness measure: Psychotherapeutic implications. *Psychotherapy: Theory, Research and Practice, 17,* 175–182.

Min, P. G. (Ed.). (1995). *Asian Americans: Contemporary trends and issues.* Thousand Oaks, CA: Sage.

Mio, J. S., & Iwamasa, G. (1993). To do, not to do: That is the question for White cross-cultural researchers. *The Counseling Psychologist, 21,* 197–212.

Momaday, N. S. (1968). *A house made of dawn.* New York: Harper & Row.

Mowat, F. (1975). *People of the deer.* Toronto: Seal Books.

Nagata, D. K. (1991). Transgenerational impact of the Japanese-American internment: Clinical issues in working with children of former internees. *Psychotherapy, 28,* 121–128.

Neighbors, H. W., & Jackson, J. S. (Eds.). (1996). *Mental health in Black America.* Newbury Park, CA: Sage.

Okazaki, S., & Sue, S. (1995). Methodological issues in assessment research with ethnic minorities. *Psychological Assessment, 7,* 367–375.

Padilla, A. M. (Ed.). (1995). *Hispanic psychology: Critical issues in theory and research.* Thousand Oaks, CA: Sage.

Pedersen, P. B., Draguns, J. G., Lonner, W. G., & Trimble, J. E. (Eds.). (1996). *Counseling across cultures* (4th ed.). Thousand Oaks, CA: Sage.

Ponterotto, J. G. (1988). Racial consciousness development among white counselor trainees: A stage model. *Journal of Multicultural Counseling and Development, 16,* 146–156.

Ponterotto, J. G., Casas, J. M., Suzuki, L. A., & Alexander, C. M. (Eds.). (1995). *Handbook of multicultural counseling.* Thousand Oaks, CA: Sage.

Ramirez, M., III. (1983). *Psychology of the Americas: Mestizo perspectives on personality and mental health.* New York: Pergamon.

Ramirez, M., III. (1984). Assessing and understanding biculturalism and multiculturalism in Mexican-American adults. In J. L. Martinez & R. H. Mendoza (Eds.), *Chicano psychology* (2nd ed., pp.77–94). Orlando, FL: Academic Press.

Ramseur, H. P. (1991). Psychologically healthy Black adults. In R. L. Jones (Ed.), *Black psychology* (3rd ed., pp. 353–378). Berkeley, CA: Cobb & Henry.

Robinson, J. L. (1995). *Racism or attitude? The ongoing struggle for black liberation and self-esteem.* New York: Plenum.

Sabnani, H. B., & Ponterotto, J. G. (1992). Racial/ethnic minority-specific instrumentation in counseling research: A review, critique, and recommendations. *Measurement and Evaluation in Counseling and Development, 24,* 161–187.

Sabnani, H. B., Ponterotto, J. G., & Borodovsky, L. G. (1991). White racial identity development and cross-cultural counselor training: A stage model. *The Counseling Psychologist, 19,* 76–102.

Sampson, E. E. (1988). The debate on individualism: Indigenous psychologies of the individual and their role in personal and societal functioning. *American Psychologist, 43,* 15–22.

Steele, S. (1990). *The content of our character: A new vision of race in America.* New York: Harper Perennial.

Suinn, R. M., Rickard-Figueroa, K., Lew, S., & Vigil, S. (1987). The Suinn-Lew Asian Self-Identity Acculturation Scale: An initial report. *Educational and Psychological Measurement, 47,* 401–407.

Thomas, C. S. (1971). *Boys no more*. Beverly Hills, CA: Glencoe.

Topper, M. D., & Curtis, J. (1987). Extended family therapy: A clinical approach to the treatment of synergistic dual anomic depression among Navajo agency-town adolescents. *Journal of Community Psychology, 15,* 334–348.

Triandis, H. C. (1972). The analysis of subjective culture. New York: Wiley. Triandis, H. C. (1990). Cross-cultural studies of individualism and collectivism. In J. Berman (Ed.), *Nebraska symposium on motivation* (pp. 41–133). Lincoln: University of Nebraska Press.

Triandis, H. C. (1996). The psychological measurement of cultural syndromes. *American Psychologist, 51,* 407–415.

Triandis, H. C., Bontempo, R., Leung, K., & Hui, C. H. (1990). A method for determining cultural, demographic, and personal constructs. *Journal of Cross-Cultural Psychology, 21,* 302–318.

Trimble, J. E. (1977). The sojourner in the American Indian community: Methodological issues and concerns. *Journal of Social Issues, 33*(4), 159–174.

Trimble, J. E., & Medicine, B. (1976). Development of theoretical models and levels of interpretation in mental health. In J. Westermeyer (Ed.), *Anthropology and mental health: Setting a new course* (pp. 161–198). The Hague, Netherlands: Mouton.

Uba, L. (1994). *Asian Americans: Personality patterns, identity, and mental health.* New York: Guilford.

Weibel-Orlando, J. (1991). *Indian country, L. A.: Maintaining ethnic community in complex society.* Chicago: University of Illinois Press.

Welch, J. (1975). *Winter in the blood.* New York: Bantam.

Welch, J. (1986). *Fools crow.* New York: Penguin.

Welch, J. (1990). *The Indian lawyer.* New York: Norton.

Welch, J. (1994). *Killing Custer: The battle of the Little Bighorn and the fate of the Plains Indians.* New York: Norton.

White, J. L. (1984). *The psychology of Blacks: An Afro-American perspective.* Englewood Cliffs, NJ: Prentice-Hall.

Wyatt, G. E., Powell, G. J., & Bass, B. A. (1982). The Survey of Afro-American Behavior: Its development and use in research. In B. A. Bass, G. E. Wyatt, & G. T. Powell (Eds.), *The Afro-American family: Assessment, treatment, and research issues* (pp. 13–33). New York: Grune & Stratton.

19

The Rorschach and the Life World: Exploratory Exercises

Constance T. Fischer
Dusquene University

The life world is where we go about our lives. It is the world as we live it prior to scientific conceptualizing, theorizing, and measuring. This chapter describes exercises undertaken by doctoral students in a Rorschach course to help them to *explore* and appreciate the general relations between Rorschach data and the life world. Students also learn to work collaboratively with clients to explore how Rorschach data might provide access to their everyday lives and options.

Our guiding principle is that "If we can't describe our findings in terms of the client's everyday life, then literally we don't yet know 'what *in the world*' we're talking about." We regard an assessment account that restricts itself to reporting scores, ratios, symptoms, constructs, hypothetical dynamics, and diagnostic impressions as having stopped short, being unfinished. The next step would be to inquire into and then to describe how our derived data point back to a particular person's ways of participating in actual situations. For example, we might say "Just as Mary sometimes bypassed the instructions to say what the blots could be, and instead addressed the white space (S = 5), so too she sometimes has ignored her supervisor's instructions and completed tasks her own way." We also describe whatever the client and assessor have learned about the client's personally viable options—alternative ways to continue his or her course more satisfyingly. For example: "We eventually agreed that Mary might bypass irritating her boss, first by reiterating his goal to him and then by proposing *her* plan of action. Mary already has followed this tactic successfully with an office mate."

The students in the Rorschach course are enrolled in Duquesne University's human-science psychology graduate program. They have completed a prerequisite course in which they learned standardized administration of the Wechsler intelligence tests, the TAT, Draw-A-Person Test, and the Bender-Gestalt. In that course they also conducted collaborative, interventional assessments through which they developed tailored suggestions for clients and their helpers. Clients review the students' reports and write a "Client's Commentary" section on the last page. The textbook, *Individualizing Psychological Assessment* (Fischer, 1985/1994a), was developed for this prerequisite course. See also Finn (1996, and chap. 20 of this volume), and Fischer (1979).

For the Rorschach course, students learn Exner's (1993) Comprehensive System, first preparing summary sheets by hand (to better appreciate the constitution of the various ratios), and then by computer program. They administer and score five practice Rorschachs, exchanging them to check scoring and to discuss impressions, before turning them in to me. In addition each student serves as a Rorschach subject, and then scores his or her own protocol. Students videotape their standardized administrations and discuss possible impacts of their styles. They conclude the course with two clinical assessments utilizing the Rorschach and other assessment materials. Reports are based on multiply grounded impressions. They specify any impressions that were not discussed with the client or about which assessor and client have agreed to disagree.

INTRODUCING DETERMINANTS
VIA GREETING CARDS

In the first class I present an overview of the history and present status of the Rorschach. Then I say that we will do an exercise using greeting cards to demystify the scoring process. I have already written the names of all the parts of the "scoring sentence" across the top of a black board: location ... developmental quality ... determinants ... form quality ... pairs ... content ... popular ... organization ... special scores.

I show the class a series of greeting cards, one at a time. Each time, I ask "As the artist what would you have to attend to in order to produce this image?" or "What do you find that you've attended to as you perceived this image?" The first card depicts the American Psychological Association building in Washington, DC. Someone quickly mentions "perspective," and in response to my questioning says that he meant by that the coming closer together of lines and planes of windows and walls to indicate a receding into distance. Now on the blackboard I draw a line from "determinants," and begin what will become a list of all determinants, in this case beginning with "FV" for form seen as vista. Someone mentions that perspective is also indicated by the depiction of a person walking in front of the building. Now I write "FD" for form dimensionality and explain its criteria. Someone else says she was struck at first by the grayness of the building. I add "C´F" to the list, explain about achromatic color, and ask whether I have accurately indicated the student's attention to the gray as more important than the form of the building. I explain the alternative scores of "FC'" and of "C´" to reflect differing attunements to the card's grayness. I point out that in one of my own gray moments, I might perceive the entire card as more or less gray (C´), and that I might or might not be interested in noting shading variations (C´.Y). A student comments that in *his* dark moods, as an artist he would render the building as dark, not as the color gray. Now we discuss YF, FY, and Y.

Next I display a card showing colorful flower beds, with individual flowers clearly represented in the foreground. We discuss the attunement that would lead us to score CF to represent color dominating form, and FC for the inverse. Someone provides a fortuitous example of a deviant verbalization by referring to "daffolillies," and I list "DV1" under the special scores and give an example of a "DV2." I happily acknowledge another student's observation that we could also score FD and FV on this greeting card.

I hold up a card that is just red, with no illustration. The class agrees that a viewer could only be attuned to color (C) on this greeting card. A brief discussion of the rarity of pure determinants, aside from F, ensues.

Now I hold up a children's Easter card with rabbits and chicks. We quickly score FCs and CFs, and then someone points out that on this card one could note fluffiness and softness. We go on to score FTs and TFs to represent texture. One person mentions that she could practically feel the silkiness of a tulip petal on the earlier greeting card. By now we can talk about how different cards invite or limit various attunements; I refer to Schachtel's (1966) book that discusses not only determinants but the differing stimulus qualities of each card. We note that just as we had not mentioned all that we saw, so too clients do not mention all that they see on Rorschach cards, even if the features stood out for them. We agree that "determinants" is a misnomer, that the card features themselves do not determine the response. "Determinants" might better be called "descriptors."

After we have noted examples of the remaining determinants, I point out how else we have been attending to the cards, such as mentioning the entire depiction (W), or an obvious feature noted by most of us (D), or a more obscure feature (Dd). I go back to write out the abbreviations for all the content that we have named.

By now we have shared some teasing and laughter as we recognize one another's styles of attending to and describing aspects of the greeting cards. I point out which of these features are scorable, which show up in later ratios, and which can be otherwise noted.

A postcard photo of a New England seafood dinner draws pained expressions of desire from a tired and hungry class. We note that our response would have been different that morning.

I conclude the first class with a demonstration of administering and enquiring cards I and II. We write out the scoring sentences that characterize how the subject encountered and responded to the two cards. Our volunteer subject tells us that her first responses for each card were ones she had heard on a TV show, and that in her long pauses after that she was trying to censor the sexual and aggressive themes that leapt out at her. She wound up reporting benign percepts. I remark that clients too select which meanings to report. I encourage the students to retain the commonsense understandings we developed through the greeting cards and through our volunteer demonstration as they go on to work with the Rorschach blots.

DEVELOPING LIFE WORLD INSTANCES
OF STRUCTURAL SUMMARY DATA

I emphasize that the summary sheet data do not present an X ray of psychic structure, but rather, summary notations by a participant observer of how a person took up the Rorschach task. To extrapolate meaningfully into other situations, we must bear in mind the testing situation's characteristics: A seated person is presented with unfamiliar and ambiguous visual material and is asked to tell a psychologist what it might be. The person cannot be sure what the psychologist is looking for or finds significant. This interpersonal encounter is regarded as one scene in the person's ongoing life. About midway in our graduate course the students talk about how their own Rorschachs reflected not only their trans-situational ways of coping, but also what was happening at this stage and day in their lives, the time of day and setting, and their relationship with the classmate test administrator. After that we often preface interpretations with "*On this day*, the client. ... "

We build a repertoire of events in life that are similar to those that during a Rorschach administration resulted in various codings and ratios. As an introduction we review some of the statistical studies that Exner has summarized (e.g., 1993). For example, inanimate movement responses increased as medical students awaited results of their gross anatomy exams, while survivors awaited burial of loved ones, and while sailors weathered a dangerous storm.

We add to this review events from our own lives that seem structurally similar: treading water, being stuck in traffic, being in a holding pattern above your airport, enduring a repetitive bad dream. We note what all these instances have in common: having to wait alertly due to circumstances beyond our control, while wanting to get on with life. I share other instances that clients have readily provided when I have wondered with them whether they might be in circumstances like some of the aforementioned: awaiting a bank's decision on a mortgage application, getting through 6 weeks before comprehensive exams are graded, trying to plan for the future, although the company has not committed to preserving one's job.

Throughout the course, students share new items contributed to their repertoires by assessees. We speak in terms of collecting a range of possibilities that any score or ratio may point to. For example, one student had asked a client what it was like to attend to white space rather than to the ink in "a vase" (VII) and "islands" (III). The man spoke of relief in getting away from complexity and nuances, and went on to say that he had about had it with trying to figure out what people wanted from him. Other possible instances of responding to white space developed with other clients: being attuned to emptiness, taking one's own stand, being playful. Similar repertoires are developed for all entries in the summary sheet.

We practice exploring life world instances of summary sheet constellations by imagining what it would be like to be in the shoes of a person recently featured in the news (e.g., man perched on a bridge tower for 3 hours), and then attempting to sketch his or her living of that situation in Rorschach terms. Our life world orientation helps students to be patient about learning how to inquire and code; they already see the interpretive implications.

DISCOVERING DYNAMICS
THROUGH SCORING DILEMMAS

In discussing scoring questions, we first determine how to follow Exner's advice to score conservatively. Often we then explore tensions the client may have experienced while coping with the cards, now reflected in our conflicting scoring inclinations. Some examples follow:

Scoring Dilemma: Shall I score COP here: "Two people holding something"? *Answer*: No, because the client does not specify cooperative effort. *Possible Dynamic*: Perhaps, like us, the client sees potential for the people to be working together, but hesitates to develop that option. Likewise on Card VII she reported, "Two girls on a playground [They're jumping—-hair up"], but she does not say that they are playing *together*. I wonder whether this woman similarly remains alongside of others, perhaps waiting to be invited in, or perhaps preferring the lesser involvement of "parallel play. "

Scoring Dilemma: How do I code color in this response: (Card X) "Oh, I just love the color! —Much more pleasant (than Card IX). I'll say a painting of beautiful flowers [the petals—shaped like the ones in Torm prints. Stems. The rest would be leaves. (?) Pleasant because of the balance of the composition]"? *Answer*: We seem to have F, with no scorable color. *Possible Dynamic:* In other situations, too, this fellow may find himself pulled powerfully toward an emotional stance, but then after initially responding to this evocation, backing off to offer evaluative commentary. I'm reminded of a person erupting with, "John, you're here! I'm so glad you came!!," then incongruously evading a potential hug, and after a pause remarking, "Did you notice that Donninger's has those leather book covers again? They look as well stitched as the ones at Hickston's."

Scoring Dilemma: Do I score DQ+ for "Animal climbing [its body is leaning this way. You can see it's straining because of the position of this bulging muscle in the back leg]"? *Answer*: Possibly FY or FV for "bulging," but DQo because what the animal is climbing is not mentioned. *Possible Dynamic:* I wonder if out in her daily life Charlene is focusing more on struggle and striving than on goals and context? I'll bet you could mention that you are wondering about this response, and directly ask her about that possibility. (See Fischer, 1994b, for further examples and discussion of how it is that scoring questions can provide access to possible dynamics.)

DESCRIBING ONE'S OWN LIFE EVENTS
IN RORSCHACHESE

As a take-home part of the final exam, students are asked to write a one- to two-page Rorschachese description of a recent personal event. Early in the course, I provided handouts describing several scenes from my own life. Knowing that this exercise is coming up, we all practice from time to time in our conversations: "Geez, my whole day has been Y, with hardly any F, and no S in sight." "You got the job?! Great! —Your CF must be way up!" "Let's take a break; our FM, m, and Fd are on the rise!"[1]

In the following five excerpts,[1] codes refer to the graduate student authors' experience as well as to the perceived scene:

1. About writing a late Rorschach report at 3 a.m.: "The formerly beautiful FV.FC MOR flowers are the only Bt in the room. ... As I realize how much more I still have to do, my Afr and Zd are sinking. My EA, which was so big this morning, is waning. My rising es seems to be looming in front of me. Isolate/R is climbing. I am aware mostly of shading blends. I want my EA back, so I can overcome the es that is oppressing me. ... "

2. A scored dream: "An H in the woods was M^aing toward me, his face illuminated with C´ light. A C´.FD light beams from his eyes. Although the Hx during the scene had been W_v, I was now frightened by the AG/MOR capabilities of this H/(H). ... "

3. An autumn walk to the river: "Every now and then m^a.FY (I feel compelled) to M^a (walk) down to the Na (river) to M^P (listen). Today is one of those decreased F+ %, increased Ls and Y, and wanting FD days. Cg (jeans, undershirt, flannel shirt, hiking boots) all TF FABCOM1 (feel like that spot down by the) Na (river). I M^a (go out) the Hh (door) and a certain Dd99 V.TF.m^P MOR (clogged heaviness) begins to FV.FT.M^a.m^a (flow productively again) as the slow descent m^P (draws) me to the Na. ... I M^a (turn) to W+ (Autumn) and am C (awash) in it. The Cls blanket the YF Ls (sky) in a C´Yish glow. ... The Bt (trees) Mª FABCOM1 (shout) MOR (the end of another vital cycle) while FABCOM1 M^Ping (basking) in Na's C´.YF (sky's iridescent glow)."

4. Preparing Thanksgiving dinner for an involved other, his family, and a sister: "As an ambitent, I don't even know how to begin cooking! I read recipes instructing how to combine Ds to make a W. Yet I vacillate between reading and being drawn out by the Cful Fd, desiring to learn by experimentation. As I switch between INT and EXT styles, others become HVI wondering if I'll really Zf and Zd+ enough to achieve a delicious W+ meal. Lots of Ds clutter the Hh: F recipes and spice containers, FC Fd, and Sc kitchen accessories.

"'What a mess!' my sister says, Zf-ing the room to see what needs to be done. I don't Zf in a P way. I feel L escalate. But resistant, I provide no R, and put on my apron as a Cg shield. Now I feel protected. My sister asks to COP. I refuse her help, in S style, reluctant to COP after her R. Besides, in a 3r + (2)/R way I wish to covet credit. AGly, she M^as out of the kitchen? ... My D momentarily dips to a −3 and I feel a CDI developing. When someone PSVing about FM appetite for the fifth time, asks "When's dinner?", I grunt. After my DVs and DRs, no one asks again. ... My glorious $\frac{3r+(2)}{R}$ fantasy evaporates. I feel MOR, and rub my soft Cg, yearning for T. "How will I get a W+ from all those Ds?,"

---

[1]Excerpts are drawn from papers by the following doctoral students (in alphabetical rather than sequential order): William Culley, Stacy Giguere, Alissa Perrucci, Rameshwari Rao, and Robert Sandford.

I weep to myself. What was my X+ % when I aspired to the W? Can I M^a enough to reach my W? … I become OBS, meticulously stuffing each squash with an equal number of cranberries, painstakingly counted in PSV style. People are no longer (H) but Hd—helping hands counting cranberries for me. … Attuned to my high es state, perhaps through my tears, my family provides a new FD, COPly reassuring me that they've come to see me, not my Fd. I feel my EA rise, and M begins to flow, meeting the challenge of the W. Less HVI and OBS, I become appreciative of the EA provided by special Hs and begin to remember what I forgot when I was lost in Hds and Dds—simply to give thanks. Together, we achieve a W+ through COP and the Hx of Thanksgiving."

5. Shopping for a Christmas gift for a friend: "I decide to M^a my friend a practical Hh rather than a sparkling FC Art. My C is diminishing and shortly pure F takes hold. Now more attuned to W and Z, I notice several FC´ Hhs (Teflon pans) are on sale. As I inspect one Hh, I M^p its usefulness in preparing Fd. Ah, but an Hh is such an impersonal ideo."

"Perhaps I can M^a her a book? I ALOG that she must enjoy reading because she studied English. In the bookstore I am confronted with AB and Dd books as well as FC INCOM figurines such as Santa wearing red swim trunks: FC (H), Cg. Tired of M^aing, my FM is quickly rising. I must M^a an ideo soon, for my X+ % is dropping."

"I approach a final D—Cg! After an H comments on the TF of a particular Cg, I try the Cg on my own Hds. The T, C, and F of the Cg are appealing. Hm, why not M^a this Cg for myself? Ah, my $\frac{3r+(2)}{R}$ must be up. As I focus my attention on W, Zf and Zd+ increase. I M^a the FC.TF Cg for my friend."

"As I leave the Sc, I hear several Hs joyfully M^aing carols. Having finally found the appropriate ideo, I recognize with cheerful Hx a similar CP; I feel TF by the holiday spirit, Hx—AB."

Even after the course we still find ourselves scoring our situations and experiences. Our own lives thus serve as a continuously developing resource for understanding clients' Rorschachs. Our growing repertoires also provide us with concrete life world examples to offer to clients as the ground for collaborative exploration.

COLLABORATING WITH CLIENTS

Students think their way through diagnostic ("thorough knowing") tasks by considering data in light of multiple developmental and personality theories, and in light of researched patterns of pathology and well-being. Theories and categories come to life as we wonder how a particular person might have come to the place of taking up the Rorschach in particular ways. Students always regard life as primary data and theories and scores as derivations. Life events are our point of departure into tests and theories, and life events are also our point of return.

We engage the client as a coassessor, moving the assessment beyond nomothetic and other general characterizations to discussion of concrete instances in that particular person's life. Through discussion, contexts also become apparent, as do "when-nots"—the circumstances in which the client has experienced or behaved in contrasting ways. In that the assessor also observes and inquires about *how* clients participate in getting themselves in and out of various situations, alternatives can be explored directly. In this process, clients become more keenly aware that they are active agents in "what happens" to them. Collaboration of this sort occurs during the initial interview and throughout the assessment process—with the Bender, MMPI, and so on. This collaboration is a far cry from unilateral "feedback" after completion of an assessment. In the illustrations of assessors' shared impressions that follow, the client's remarks are in brackets:

1. (P = 8; F+ % = 50) You know, there are things, like the bats, the bears, and the native dancers that most people notice. And you did too. I would guess that in your first scan of a situation, you read the scene the way most people do? [You mean like I get oriented first, like I'm good at maps, and like I can find the men's room in a new building without asking?] Good. That's more to the point than what I was thinking. Now, although I too could see everything you pointed out, because I'm familiar with the cards and because you helped me, a lot of the time what you said was unique, which leads me to wonder about times that other people find it difficult to follow you. [That's amazing! From this inkblot test?! Do you mean like my group not following my flip chart presentations? I have a hard time being patient when it's black and white to me.] Like you couldn't believe that I couldn't see your armadillo? [I wasn't impatient; I just couldn't believe you couldn't see it. Were you trying to test my patience?] No, I just needed you to "orient" *me* more, as you in fact did on the last card when you explained that the parachutist would either have to be seen as far away or as belonging to another scene. Should this be one of our suggestions for work? [Yes, write down that I should check with my "audience" to see if they need more orienting before I go on.]

2. (EB = 4:7.5; a:p = 8:2) It looks to me as though typically you've been a hands-on person—you like to figure things out by trying them out. Like with the blocks (WAIS–R), your hands just flipped the blocks until what you needed came up. Then when the designs became more difficult, you stopped and worked on figuring out a system. [What's wrong with that?] Nothing. I think that you enjoy that approach and that it works for you in most situations. When it wouldn't work is if you were to insist that some one solution *should* work, instead of backing off to see if a different system would work better. Oh, you told me that your wife says you get "obstinate." Tell me an example, and let's see if it fits. [Well, that was about Tim's curfew. But she was standing there, like testing me, to see if I'd check with her.] Ah, so it's been more difficult to check your own actions when someone's standing around judging you? [Yeah. —I guess that's what happens when Smitty's supervising]

3. (P = 3; F + % = 74) [Yes, I don't like for people to think I'm just ordinary; you're right, I try not to be trite.] Could you think of some examples? [At work all the other secretaries have pictures of their children on their desks or the cubical cork board; I put up my "rogues gallery" of losers I've gone out with. It's really creative, but I've been getting pressure about it.] Whoops. Maybe sometimes you're not ordinary enough—maybe in this instance you didn't pick up on the kind of atmosphere your co-workers prefer? [I just don't care to. The place, the people, are just too dumbly bland and conformist.]

The preceding excerpt points to the importance of checking out life referents of characterizations. Often the client's provision of examples points in different directions from what the assessor had in mind, and the assessor changes his or her formulation. In other instances examples provide refinements and differentiating contexts. Sometimes client and assessor wind up acknowledging certain differences in their understandings.

In a later course, students conduct part of an assessment in the client's home, where life contexts are more readily available for collaborative discussion. After that, students remain aware of the constraints imposed by office assessments.

WRITING REPORTS THAT CAN BE READ
BY PSYCHOLOGISTS, OTHER PROFESSIONALS,
AND CLIENTS

The closing exercise in the Rorschach course is writing clinical reports. We endeavor to write with multiple readers in mind: clinicians, other helpers and decision makers, the client, and possible future readers. The author *represents* the understandings developed through the collaborative assessment, by *re-presenting* illustrative assessment events and similar life events that they evoked. The report therefore may be read by all the aforementioned parties, who are then "on the same page" in regard to the client's life. For example, instead of reporting that "The F -% and low P indicate that this person has poor reality testing," we might say, "Joe acknowledged that just as he didn't pay attention to what most people notice on the inkblots (P = 4), he often has found himself trying to find something pleasant even when he knows his family and co-workers don't share his Pollyannish view (F+ % = 59, X+ % = 48, T = 2, FC = 6)."

The report's format is fairly standard, with the following exceptions:

1. The referral section contains not only the initial issue, but also the results of conferring with the referring party about the contexts in which the issue arose, and with the client, about his or her understanding of the referral. The referral section also includes what the client said he or she would like to learn from the assessment. Example: "*Referral:* Dr. Monte requested a psychological assessment to aid in developing a differential diagnosis between schizoid personality disorder and schizophrenia in remission following an acute episode. Dr. Monte

had found that medical records, family, and Mr. Jarak himself provided little history of help in deciding on medications and between individual psychother-apy and a group support program. The question is whether Mr. Jarak's present state is pretty much a life-long one, or whether neuroleptic medications might help him to regain a pre-episode level of interpersonal relating, which in turn might allow him to make good use of psychotherapy. Mr. Jarak's interest in the assessment was additionally in learning why his cousins think he's 'crazy' and whether he could qualify for a job retraining program. When we reviewed Dr. Monte's referral and the DSM–IV diagnostic criteria, Mr. Jarak thought that he fit the schizoid and avoidant personality disorder characteristics better, although he said that when he has become very agitated, other people say he's 'paranoid.'"

2. Unless there are particular reasons to do so, the report is not organized by instruments, but rather by referral-relevant themes, often highlighted by subheadings, such as "'Doing the Job' in Familiar Situations," and "Retrenching in Unfamiliar Situations"; or "Watching From the Outside," "Rushing Toward Safety," and "Risking Successfully."

3. We attach a technical appendix that reports additional data and reflec-tions to clinicians who may want to know more than was efficacious to include in the theme-oriented and already longish narrative report. (The appendix also lets me know how thoroughly the graduate student has studied the Rorschach and the other tests.) The form of the appendix is tailored for each case. Sometimes the appendix is a list of additional data that support themes, for example:

"Concrete intellectual style:
WAIS–R highest scale = Information (14);
lowest scale = Similarities (8)
Rorschach sequence: D, D, D; Approach: W = 2; D = 18
R = 20; Zf= 8; Zd = –2
16 P-F scale B (Concrete/Abstract Thinking) =7."

For other purposes, the author might comment on notable Rorschach summary sheet data, specifying how these items were discussed with the client. Excerpt[2]:

"R: 41 responses contrasts with the expected range of 17–27 responses for adults. The assessee and I discussed this in terms of 'giving 110%.'

"C´: The assessee's elevated achromatic responses (4 in contrast to a mean of 1.53 for 23 responses) reflects affective constraint or a psychological 'biting of the tongue.' We discussed this in terms of the assessee's 'gritting her teeth.'"

4. The final section of the report is "Client Comments" or "Mr. Jarak's Comments," where the client writes remarks about the report and signs and dates it. We regard our reports as progress reports—reports of progress-to-date for both parties in coming to understand the person's participation in his or her world. The comments indicate the degree to which the person has compre-hended and agreed with the author's written understandings. Often the review becomes an occasion for further clarification by both parties. Within reports,

---

[2]From a single-spaced 1½ page Rorschach Technical Appendix by Rameshwari Rao.

authors write in first person ("I" rather than "the examiner," or, "I administered the test," rather than using the passive voice ("the test was administered"). This style reminds readers that assessments occur in interpersonal contexts, and that our findings are necessarily grounded in personal perspectives. We use past rather than present tense, to indicate that the conduct may change ("Thus far Jayson has avoided situations in which he might fail," rather than "Jayson is risk-avoidant"). This last example also illustrates another writing principle: We try to bypass constructs, and instead describe in terms of specific actions. For example, instead of "His underlying hostility results in distorted human rela-tionships," we might say, "When insisting on being treated fairly, Thomas has not noticed that some people would be willing to help him." We also try to own our impressions rather than attribute them to the tests. In place of "Despite his denial, the Rorschach indicates that this person is depressed," we might say, "Although Ms Jamison said she was just tired, I saw her as being depressed as I witnessed her sighs and slouched posture, and when I reflected on her attune-ment to death and illness and to the dark and hidden aspects of the inkblots. This attunement was at the expense of noticing color and playful possibilities."

Finally, we regard the crafting of our reports as carefully grounded but creative exercises. We discover different meanings as we attempt to express our understandings to ourselves and to diverse readers. We carefully choose our language, images, juxtapositions, and inclusions to resonate with readers' lives so that those lives become a resource in evoking a sense of the client's life. Students find comparisons of Andrew Wyeth's disciplined representational art with the life-world assessment's disciplined description to be freeing and chal-lenging (Fischer, 1980, 1994a).

CONCLUSION: THE RORSCHACH EXPERIENCE LIVES ON

Graduates retain a collaborative, exploratory attitude in all of their work—as-sessment, teaching, psychotherapy, consulting, research. Whether or not stu-dents again use the Rorschach, they continue to see depth and dynamics more readily than before the course. They understand more fully that all test data, like other life tracks and outcomes, point to how a person took up a circum-stance and traveled through it. Knowing that a person's journey through Rorschach cards (or other material) is part of that person's journey through life, they ask what other situations might have been like this one for the client. With all tests, graduates strive to get from statistics (static) back to a person in motion—a person en route to goals, perceiving and acting in accordance with attunement to landmarks, invitations, dangers. Graduates respect the access to a person's life that a well-researched test provides, but they also respect life's inherent ambiguity; they know that numbers are more precise than life. They continue to measure the validity of their work in terms of the extent to which it has assisted clients and their other helpers toward revised comportment and decisions. In short, the Rorschach students go forth from the course knowing "what in the world they are talking about."

REFERENCES

Exner, J. E. (1993). *The Rorschach: A comprehensive system: Vol. 3. Basic foundations* (3rd ed.). New York: Wiley.

Finn, S. E. (1996). *Manual for using the MMPI-2 as a therapeutic intervention.* Minneapolis: University of Minnesota Press.

Fischer, C. T. (1979). Individualized assessment and phenomenological psychology. *Journal of Personality Assessment, 43,* 115–122.

Fischer, C. T. (1980). Phenomenology and psychological assessment: Re-presentational description. *Journal of Phenomenological Psychology, 11,* 79–105.

Fischer, C. T. (1994a). *Individualizing psychological assessment.* Hillsdale, NJ: Lawrence Erlbaum Associates. (Original work published 1985)

Fischer, C. T. (1994b). Rorschach scoring questions as access to dynamics. *Journal of Personality Assessment, 62,* 515–525.

Schachtel, E. G. (1966). *Experiential foundations of Rorschach's test.* New York: Basic Books.

20

Teaching Therapeutic Assessment in a Required Graduate Course

Stephen E. Finn
Center for Therapeutic Assessment

Therapeutic Assessment (Finn, 1996; Finn & Tonsager, 1997, in press) is an assessment model in which psychological testing forms the center of a brief psychotherapeutic intervention with clients. Resting on humanistic and phenomenological principles articulated by Fischer (1985/1994), Dana and Leech (1974), Pruyser (1979), and others, Therapeutic Assessment attempts to engage clients in a collaborative, exploratory process through which they learn about the factors maintaining their existing life problems and try out possible solutions to these problems. The techniques of Therapeutic Assessment can be applied to a wide variety of assessment questions and client populations. Several controlled research studies have demonstrated that clients receive lasting benefit from psychological testing conducted according to the principles of Therapeutic Assessment (Finn & Tonsager, 1992; Newman & Greenway, 1997).

As a member of the psychology faculty at the University of Texas at Austin from 1984 to 1992, I routinely taught the theory and techniques of Therapeutic Assessment to first-year clinical psychology graduate students in their required course on personality assessment. This course involved a theoretical/factual component as well as a practical/hands-on component. Students read research and theory about the major personality tests, learned the administration and scoring of each test, and conducted a number of practice assessments while being closely supervised. Early on it became clear to me that students in this course were not only learning how to assess clients; they themselves were also undergoing an important assessment—of their knowledge of psychological testing and their suitability to be clinical psychologists. Furthermore, the assessment to which my students were subjected was analogous to the most difficult of clinical assessment situations—in which clients are tested in part against their will, are ambivalent about self-disclosure, and are aware that assessment results will be used by others to make major decisions affecting their lives.

To be more specific, my observations about students' personality traits, clinical skills, and knowledge of assessment were often weighed heavily by the clinical psychology faculty in deciding whether to retain a student at the end of the first year. Students were well aware of this fact and felt great pressure to do well in my course. This pressure, in turn, had the potential to inhibit greatly students' comments in class and their willingness to take risks while practicing assessment. In effect, the evaluation component of the course tended to set up a transference situation where I was seen as a feared, omnipotent authority rather than as a benevolent, human instructor. I soon realized that I might best address this stressful assessment situation by applying the same principles and techniques to my teaching that I was educating my students to use in their clinical interactions with clients. In this way I would be "practicing what I preached," and students would have the benefit of experiencing Therapeutic Assessment at the same time that they were learning to do it themselves. I describe the course in its final form even though different elements were changed and added over the years.

Principles of Therapeutic Assessment as Applied to the Graduate Course in Personality Assessment

The underlying principles of Therapeutic Assessment in clinical assessment situations are articulated elsewhere (Finn, 1996; Finn & Tonsager, 1997, in press). A modified set of these principles—as applied to a required graduate course in personality assessment—guided my teaching:

1. A required graduate course in personality assessment is an unsettling and personally challenging experience for students. It demands interpersonal and emotional skills and ways of thinking that have not typically been required in other academic courses; also the instructor's ratings of students will be used by others to make major decisions regarding the students' lives. These factors can cause considerable anxiety for students.

2. A graduate course in personality assessment is also an interpersonally challenging situation for an instructor. It involves providing factual information, giving feedback to students about clinically relevant personality characteristics, modeling interactions with clients, and supporting students through their first interactions with clients. This multifaceted role has the potential to generate considerable anxiety in the instructor.

3. When students and instructors are anxious, they are prone to enact highly stereotyped roles in which instructors play all-knowing experts and students act the part of deferential, passive novices. Such roles interfere with active learning on the part of both students and instructors.

4. Students have the right to know, at the beginning of the course, what aspects of their performance will be evaluated, the procedures used to assess their performance, and how the results may affect them when the course is

completed. Providing such information may decrease students' feelings of powerlessness and lower their anxiety.

5. The instructor has the responsibility of clarifying with the students the goals, purpose, and requirements of the course.

6. Students become most engaged in and benefit most from a course when they are treated as collaborators whose ideas and cooperation are essential to the learning process.

7. Students become most invested in a course when it addresses, in part, their own personal and professional goals.

8. When a course addresses students' goals and students are treated as collaborators, their anxiety is lower and their motivation is high; thus, their course performance is more likely to reflect accurately their abilities and personal potential.

9. Giving students feedback about their course performance in a collaborative manner can help them understand and address any performance deficits.

10. When instructors discuss course ratings with students in an emotionally supportive manner, students often feel affirmed, less distressed, and more hopeful, even if the feedback is initially difficult for them to hear.

11. A course on personality assessment can have a lasting impact—both personally and professionally—on students' lives.

12. A collaborative approach to teaching personality assessment also creates opportunities for instructors to learn, hone clinical skills, and be challenged by their teaching.

Flow Chart of a Course in Therapeutic Assessment

Table 20.1 represents a flow chart of my course in Therapeutic Assessment.

Step 1: Assessment Questions Are Specified and Gathered. In Therapeutic Assessment, the assessor engages clients as collaborators at the beginning of the assessment by helping them identify personal goals and form questions to be addressed during the assessment (Finn, 1996; Finn & Tonsager, 1997, in press). In involuntary assessments (such as court-ordered assessments, disability evaluations, and personnel-screening evaluations), clients typically are reluctant to frame personal goals for an assessment; they may even feel that posing assessment questions is dangerous in that such information may be used against them. In such situations, assessors can often gain clients' cooperation by first sharing the referring persons' assessment questions with clients, and negotiating beforehand with the referring person for permission to keep the client's own questions confidential (Finn & Tonsager, 1997).

In my graduate course, I followed the protocol for involuntary assessments by reviewing at the first class meeting the questions the clinical psychology faculty members would ask me to answer about each student at the end of the course. These questions were:

1.

TABLE 20.1

Flow Chart of a Course in Therapeutic Assessment

Step 1–Assessment Questions Are Specified and Gathered

Step 2–Course Contract Is Finalized

Step 3–The Assessment Task Is Explained and Conceptualized

Step 4–The Assessment Task Is Demonstrated by the Instructor

Step 5–Students Rate and Give Feedback to the Instructor

Step 6–Students Role-Play Each Assessment Task

Step 7–Students Perform Each Assessment Task With a Client

Step 8–Students Are Given Feedback on Each Task

Step 9–Students Try Out Modifications of Each Task

Step 10–Students Repeat the Assessment Task With Another Client

Step 11–End of Course Feedback Session Is Given to Student

Step 12–Written Report Is Prepared and Student Comments Invited

Step 13–Students Anonymously Give Feedback to the Instructor

Step 14–Report and Student Comments Are Presented to Faculty

Note. Steps 3–10 are repeated through the course for each assessment (e.g., initial interview, Rorschach administration, feedback session).

Does this student have an adequate knowledge of the theory and research related to personality assessment?

2. How well was the student able to conceptualize clinical case material?
3. Has the student adequately mastered the administration and scoring of major personality tests?
4. How well did the student write assessment reports?
5. At what level are this student's basic clinical skills—for example, empathy, active listening, ability to maintain appropriate boundaries?
6. How did the student respond to supervisory feedback?
7. Did the student demonstrate any behavior that raises concern about her or his suitability to be a clinical psychologist?
8. Is this student ready to participate in a clinical practicum ?

I promised students that I would discuss my answers to these questions with each of them at the end of the semester before I gave my report to the clinical psychology faculty. I also stated that I would be very interested in their ideas and reactions to my answers and would incorporate their ideas in my report. I then invited students to pose additional individual questions that might be useful to them, for me to address during and at the end of the semester. I assured them that these questions (and my answers) would not be shared with the clinical training committee without their permission, and that their course evaluation would not be influenced by whether they came up with additional questions, or by the content of these questions. I gave examples of questions students had posed in previous years (e.g., "Why do I find it hard to talk about sexuality with clients?" "Am I too shy to be a good therapist?" "I've been told I need to be warmer with clients. How can I do this?") Last, I let students know that they could offer these questions at any point during the semester by discussing them with me, or jotting them down and putting them in my mailbox.

Step 2: Course Contract Is Finalized.   During the first class meeting I also handed out a detailed syllabus of the course requirements, including information about how each assignment would be graded. For example, as part of the course, students were required to learn the administration of the Rorschach according to the Comprehensive System (Exner, 1993). The course information specified when students would be tested on administration and included a rating sheet I used to grade the observed administration. Last, I answered any questions students had about the course structure and requirements until they and I were satisfied that we had a mutual understanding of the course contract.

The majority of the syllabus was structured to follow the flow of a standard Therapeutic Assessment of a client, that is, initial interview, standardized testing, assessment intervention session, feedback session, and written report (Finn & Tonsager, 1997). For each of these tasks, I would repeat the following steps (3–10) during the course.

Step 3: The Assessment Task Is Explained and Conceptualized.   First, I provided readings about each task, and students and I discussed the techniques and underlying principles involved. For example, we thoroughly explored the purpose of the initial interview of a Therapeutic Assessment, the types of problems that can arise, and how to handle these various complications.

Step 4: The Assessment Task Is Demonstrated by the Instructor.   Before the course began, I invited colleagues in the community to refer clients to be assessed by myself and the students as part of the course. (It was not difficult to find clients who would agree to such an arrangement in return for a free assessment.) I would select one of these clients to assess myself. Then, I demonstrated each assessment task in front of the class, before the students performed the task on their own. For example, after the students and I had discussed the initial session of a Therapeutic Assessment, I interviewed a volunteer client while students observed during a class meeting. Later, I worked with this same client to demonstrate other parts of the assessment. I videotaped some lengthy tasks, for example, the Rorschach administration, outside of class sessions. I then showed portions of the videotape during class periods and/or asked students to watch the tape on their own before we met. I openly discussed any anxiety I felt about such demonstrations, in order to normalize the students' anxiety about being observed. I also modeled steps I took to deal with my anxiety.

Step 5: Students Rate and Give Feedback to the Instructor.   While I demonstrated each assessment task, students rated me on the same form the teaching assistants (TAs) and I would later use to rate them. After I completed each task, I would also rate myself. Then students and I would discuss our observations and ratings of my performance. I would try to model a nondefensive receptivity to their feedback and to be open to learning from the students' observations. This was rarely difficult, as students generally made sensitive, accurate, and insightful comments.

I was repeatedly told by students that my willingness to demonstrate each assessment task was extremely valuable and greatly appreciated. It was also an important way to embody the collaborative principles underlying Therapeutic Assessment. By making myself vulnerable and openly acknowledging my anxiety, mistakes, and learning, I reduced the power imbalance between students and myself and helped to alleviate their anxiety. One can never completely eliminate this power imbalance, nor is it the goal of Therapeutic Assessment to do so. The instructor/assessor is still seen as an expert on assessment, but one who recognizes that no one person has the entire truth about any interpersonal situation and who is willing to learn from the student/client. By demonstrating my work, I also managed to engage the students as coassessors and collaborators in the course and in the observed assessment and thereby increased their excitement and motivation to learn. Last, my actions communicated my respect for students as individuals and as a group, and seemed to empower them to believe that they too could become skilled assessors.

Step 6: Students Role-Play Each Assessment Task. Following the observed demonstration, students would practice each task (e.g., the initial interview) in pairs or small groups—with myself, the TAs, or other students role-playing clients. I tried to encourage students to give each other feedback, based on their subjective experience of playing assessors or clients. By letting students supervise each other, I again tried to resist being viewed as the only expert.

Step 7: Students Perform Each Assessment Task With a Client. Next, students were individually observed while performing each assessment task (initial interview, Rorschach administration, feedback session, etc.) with a volunteer client. The TAs or I would observe these sessions and rate students on the appropriate rating form. Students would rate themselves on the same form after completing the task.

Step 8: Students Are Given Feedback on Each Task. The TAs and I compared our ratings and observations of the students' performance on each task with the students' own ratings. Both strengths and weaknesses were brought up for discussion, and we asked students to respond to our comments, rather than passively accept them as "ultimate truths." We paid special attention to issues students had identified in their individualized assessment questions (posed at the beginning of the course). This approach parallels the feedback process in Therapeutic Assessment, in which clinicians tie assessment findings to clients' individual goals and engage clients in discussing the accuracy and meaning of test findings, rather than acting as if such results represent absolute reality.

Step 9: Students Try Out Modifications of Each Task. In the assessment intervention stage of Therapeutic Assessment, clients and assessors use test behaviors as analogs of extratest problems in living. Then they search for new solutions to external problems by identifying new ways for the client to approach test materials (Finn & Martin, 1997; Finn & Tonsager, 1997, in press). For example, a client who has posed the question "Why do I have trouble completing my assignments at work?" may copy the Bender-Gestalt figures in an obsessive, painstakingly slow manner. After discussing with the client the similarities between his behavior in the two situations, the assessor might ask the client to draw the figures again, but more rapidly. By trying different ways to speed up the Bender-Gestalt copy, the client and assessor may identify ways that the client can complete more assignments at work.

In the assessment course, after students and I noticed problems in their performance of any assessment task, we would role-play the task again and again, identifying possible solutions and/or blocks to behavior change. For example, a student and I might discover that she failed to do an adequate Rorschach inquiry because she was afraid of annoying the irritable, easily offended client she had been assigned. The student and I would discuss ways to deal with such clients' annoyance, and would try out these strategies together until we were both reasonably confident that she could handle such situations in the future. In class, I would explicitly state my belief that such problems arise for all beginning assessors and that the purpose of the practice assessments was to identify such difficulties and address them before students went on to practicum placements. In rare instances, students and I found that they were unable easily to modify problem behaviors that showed up during their assessments. In such cases, I sometimes suggested to students that they consider psychotherapy.

Step 10: Students Repeat the Assessment Task With Another Client. By the end of the course, students observed me many times, and they, too, were observed many times, as they honed or modified their assessment skills, and repeated each assessment task with another client. Students generally completed two to three full personality assessments as part of the course requirements. Although I had no illusions that this amount of experience would identify and address all potential problems students might encounter, I felt fairly confident that students would have the chance to address most major clinical and characterological issues.

Step 11: End of Course Feedback Session Is Given to Student. When all course requirements were completed, I offered an individual feedback session to each student, which I conducted according to the techniques of Therapeutic Assessment, for example, addressing students' individualized goals, offering positive comments early in the session, beginning with feedback that was likely to fit students' self-concepts, allowing students to challenge my comments (Finn, 1996; Finn & Tonsager, 1997). As with earlier supervisory sessions, I tried to engage each student in a dialogue about my observations and I carefully listened to any disagreements or modifications of my feedback. Before the session ended, I told each student her or his grade and I invited feedback about the course and/or about me as an instructor. I let students know they would have another opportunity to give me feedback anonymously.

Step 12: Written Report Is Prepared and Student Has Option of Commenting. In Therapeutic Assessment, reports are written in language that clients can understand and are virtually always shared with clients. In addition, clients are given the chance to respond in writing to their reports (Finn & Tonsager, 1997). In my course, I followed this approach with students. Shortly after the feedback session, I prepared my written report about each student for the clinical psychology faculty, including modifications that came out of my discussions with students. I gave students copies of their reports and I invited them to put any reactions or disagreements in writing and give them to me. I promised to present such comments to the clinical psychology faculty at the same time I gave my own report. I believe that my commitment to showing students my reports helped keep my assessments precise and balanced. I avoided impressions and comments that I could not adequately support. Also, as in a clinical assessment, students' comments on my reports were often illustrative of my impressions, and were thereby useful to the other faculty.

Step 13: Students Anonymously Give Feedback to the Instructor. In our clinic, all clients are invited to rate their assessment experiences on a standardized form (the Assessment Questionnaire-2; Finn, Schroeder, & Tonsager, 1995) at the end of an assessment. My department routinely required students to anonymously complete course evaluations at the end of the semester. I always let students know that I paid careful attention to their ratings and comments in designing the course for the following year. I sometimes found that students were more forthcoming in their feedback on the anonymous course ratings than they were when discussing the course with me in their feedback sessions. I see this as an inevitable result of the distrust inherent in involuntary assessment situations.

Step 14: Report and Student Comments Are Presented to Faculty.
Finally, I shared my report about each student—along with any comments she or he had written—with the clinical psychology faculty. My observations were integrated with those of other faculty members to make recommendations about commendation, remediation, or dismissal of students from the department.

CASE EXAMPLE—ELIZABETH

Let me now illustrate the approach I have described with the case of one student, a 23-year-old woman who I name Elizabeth.

First Impressions

In the initial class session, Elizabeth impressed me as a bright, nervous woman. She asked several excellent clarifying questions about the course syllabus, but spoke in a rapid, breathless voice, sometimes stumbling over words. She repeatedly twisted a bead necklace that she wore throughout the class meeting, and several times I had a vision of its breaking and spilling all over the floor. I vaguely remembered meeting Elizabeth 4 months earlier, at the departmental party at the beginning of the first semester, where we chatted about our mutual interest in horseback riding. I also recalled Dr. Smith, the first-semester assessment instructor, telling me that Elizabeth seemed quite "anxious." In keeping with these experiences, I received the following note in my department mailbox the day after the class session:

> Dr. Finn,
>
> I have one additional question for us to consider during the course. Dr. Smith told me that I talk too much with clients and I haven't been able to stop this. I hope you and I can figure out why I do this and how to help me stop.
>
> Elizabeth

I was impressed by Elizabeth's awareness of a problem and her willingness to disclose it to me. I was also encouraged by the "you and I" phrasing in her note, which seemed to indicate her acceptance of the collaborative frame of the course.

Initial Interview

I briefly acknowledged Elizabeth's note at the beginning of the next class session, and she appeared calmer in this and the next several class meetings. She continued to ask excellent questions in class and made insightful comments about the readings I had assigned. I began to see her as a bright and very dedicated student who worked hard and prepared carefully for class sessions. She and I had a short meeting before her first client session, after I interviewed the client I was assessing in class. I took the opportunity to ask Elizabeth more about her "talking too much" with clients. I found out that Dr. Smith's observation reminded her of comments several friends had recently made—that she seemed "wound up." She confessed that this feedback had surprised her at first because she had often been told she was "too quiet" in college. When I asked Elizabeth what she thought about this discrepancy, she said it might be because she "tried too hard" with new things, but then calmed down after a while. I sympathized with the anxiety of doing new things and of overdoing as a result, and we agreed that Elizabeth should "do her best" but not "try too hard" in her first client interview. She also agreed to role-play an initial interview with one of the TA supervisors prior to meeting with her client. At the end of our meeting Elizabeth also asked me how I felt when the client I had interviewed in class began to cry.

Early Assessment Sessions

Elizabeth's first assessment client was a subdued, apparently chronically depressed young man who sought psychological testing to explore why he had so much trouble keeping friends. As I watched her initial interview I was struck by Elizabeth's calm firm demeanor with the client, and I wondered if Dr. Smith or Elizabeth's friends had misperceived her, or if she had simply corrected her tendency to "talk too much" and "try too hard." After the interview, we both agreed that the session had gone quite well and that Elizabeth had done a good job of both directing the client and letting him talk. I commended her for her poise; she said that she had felt in the interview as she did when riding a "good horse": "comfortable and not at all afraid." We sketched out the next steps in the assessment and scheduled a time for me to watch Elizabeth administer the Rorschach to her client several days hence. She had already watched me administer the Rorschach and had passed a trial administration during which one of the TAs played a client.

Part way into the observed Rorschach session, I noticed a marked change in Elizabeth's comportment, compared to the beginning of the Rorschach or the initial interview. She began to fidget in her seat, several times cut the client off in midsentence with questions, and her speech became rapid and breathy, as I had noted in the first class session. As I watched, I remembered that Elizabeth asked me about my experience of the client I had interviewed, and I developed a hypothesis about her apparent rise in anxiety. The young man Elizabeth was testing had become noticeably distressed on Card V of the Rorschach, after seeing "a bat flying home over a battlefield. His wings are burned and torn. He's been through something terrible and is just trying to make it through—to make it back to his cave." This response was followed by numerous morbid percepts, and the client's general flat affect became more and more depressed until, on Card IX, he began to cry.

Elizabeth reacted by becoming more and more directive and by speaking very rapidly, especially during the Inquiry. This seemed to confuse the client, and there was a rather tense ending to the Rorschach administration. After the session, Elizabeth herself was upset, and she commented that she was aware she had "talked too much." When I asked if she knew why, she said she had been anxious because this was her first Rorschach, and she felt she had once again "tried too hard." When I shared my hypothesis that she had gotten more active as her client got more distressed, Elizabeth paused to consider and then quickly agreed that this was so. She said she had been afraid the client was going to "fall apart" and she had no idea "how to put him back together again." This led to a fruitful dialogue, where I noticed that Elizabeth had seemed calmer in the initial interview, where the client was somewhat withdrawn and depressed, but not overtly upset. Elizabeth agreed and spontaneously noted that both of the clients she had tested in the previous semester (under Dr. Smith's supervision) had been highly emotional and very distressed. We concluded that Elizabeth got uncomfortable when clients showed painful emotions, and she tended to react by talking too much and becoming controlling. I reminded her of her question about how I felt when the client I interviewed began to cry, and we spent some time discussing my reactions and ways to handle such situations.

Assessment Intervention

The next day, Elizabeth and I met to role-play ways to handle distressed clients. I modeled simply acknowledging clients' pain, without trying to fix or control it. Elizabeth confessed that this was a novel idea for her; she tended to feel responsible for others' distress. At first, as I role-played a weeping client she reacted by trying to cheer me up. I drew an analogy to horseback riding, and we discussed how a rider must stay calm and unruffled if a horse is frightened by a sudden noise or event. At this point, Elizabeth seemed to catch on and she successfully handled several other situations that I presented to her. Last, we reviewed how she could have responded to her client when he began to cry during the Rorschach. Later that week, Elizabeth met with her client again to conduct the assessment intervention session for his assessment.

I had asked Elizabeth to begin by asking the client about his experience of the Rorschach administration. Not surprisingly, the client seemed even more subdued and withdrawn at the beginning of the session. However, he was able, with Elizabeth's help, to say that he felt upset after their previous meeting. I was pleased as Elizabeth calmly asked questions about his perception of her. Then, to my surprise, the client spontaneously offered, "You know, what happened with us happens with me and my friends all the time. That's part of the problem I've been having." The client went on to relate how his friends couldn't handle his depression, and how misunderstood he felt when they offered suggestions, told him to "stop moping," or suggested he "just go out and have fun." Elizabeth participated in this discussion beautifully, and was able to incorporate the client's observations later in the TAT testing we had planned. After the session, she and I joyfully discussed the client's learning and her ability to react well to his distress.

Later Assessment Sessions

For Elizabeth's second assessment, we both agreed that she would work with a middle-aged woman who was described by the referring therapist as "prone to fits of hysterical crying." I did not personally supervise this assessment, but the TA reported that Elizabeth handled the initial interview and early testing sessions quite well, even though the client became markedly distressed at several points. Then, during the feedback session, Elizabeth again became rather anxious and strident, and insisted on the rightness of several of her interpretations. Afterward, both she and the TA were puzzled about her behavior, because the client had not been markedly distressed during the feedback, and in fact, had seemed pleased and appreciative of the assessment.

I was concerned when Elizabeth came to see me during my office hours the next day, for she looked disheartened and a bit haggard. Once again, she was rather breathless as she talked about the feedback session with her client, speaking rapidly and stumbling over words. I gently probed about what might have made her anxious during that session, until Elizabeth broke down and began to cry. I remembered my advice to her and stayed calm and inquisitive, as Elizabeth finally disclosed another piece of the puzzle: Her mother had been diagnosed recently with ovarian cancer. In fact, Elizabeth had found out about her mother's illness only the morning before the first assessment class meeting. (No wonder she had been so anxious that day!) The day of the feedback session with her second client, Elizabeth had learned that her mother's cancer was not responding to chemotherapy. Furthermore, it came out that Elizabeth was extremely close to her mother, who was a highly emotional woman who had always looked to Elizabeth to help contain her depressed feelings.

I sympathized with Elizabeth's situation, recommended that she seek support during such a difficult time, and gave her the name of several good psychotherapists in the community. This event demonstrates the fine line that often exists between supervision and therapy. I do not inquire about students' personal issues during supervision unless there is an impasse in their ability to work with clients. Once personal issues are identified, I generally refer students to an outside therapist to explore them further.

Elizabeth calmed down considerably and appeared to leave my office with renewed hope and determination. I was left musing about how I too tend to avoid seeking help when I need it, and I realized that I had never discussed with students the impact that personal emergencies can have on an assessor's ability to be with clients. I resolved to add such a discussion to my course in the future.

In the following weeks, Elizabeth appeared calmer and happier in class sessions. She did an excellent third assessment on a difficult client, and showed no disabling anxiety or controlling behavior during that assessment. Her reports were well crafted and insightful. She also achieved the highest grade in the class on the written final exam.

Feedback Session

My feedback session with Elizabeth, held jointly with the TA supervisor, was smooth and productive. We reviewed Elizabeth's considerable strengths as an assessor and again discussed the difficulties she had shown earlier in the semester. I commended Elizabeth for her ability to improve her clinical skills, and Elizabeth thanked me for my support and responded briefly to my inquiries about her mother's health. She also shared, in an appropriate way, some additional insights she had discovered in therapy about her reactions to others' distress. The TA and I said a few words about our own learning process in this area and we all parted with warm feelings.

Written Report

My written report on Elizabeth's course performance (Table 20.2) was given to the clinical psychology faculty. I shared this report with Elizabeth several days before the faculty met to discuss her performance.

Elizabeth's Comments on the Report

Elizabeth wrote a brief response to my report, which I also shared with the clinical faculty:

> I agree with Dr. Finn's report and feel that I learned a lot about myself and about assessment through his course. Dr. Finn discreetly mentioned "family issues" that were troubling me during the semester. I want to clarify this. My mother was diagnosed with cancer earlier this year and her health is going down hill quickly. This has been quite upsetting for me and my family, but I think that I am handling it as well as can be expected and I have lots of support. I will be spending the summer with my mother and I plan to return to my studies in the fall.

SUMMARY AND CONCLUSIONS

In this chapter I have highlighted the similarities between a required graduate course in personality assessment and the clinical assessment of clients who are involuntarily referred for psychological testing. I have attempted to demonstrate how the same principles underlying clinical Therapeutic Assessment may also be applied to the educational setting. By minimizing any unnecessary power differential between themselves and students, addressing students' personal goals in course evaluations, modeling vulnerability and openness to feedback, and treating students as collaborators in the learning process, instructors of personality assessment may increase the professional and personal impact of their courses on students. Such an approach is challenging to instructors, in that it requires them to be aware of their own anxiety and to minimize defensive reactions to it. However, the rewards of this method are great. Over the years I have had the pleasure of receiving feedback from former students that my course in personality assessment was one of the most important in their graduate training. I am also very aware of how much I have learned about myself, about teaching, and about personality assessment from instructing others in Therapeutic Assessment.

ACKNOWLEDGMENTS

I am grateful to Jim Durkel for his comments on an earlier draft of this chapter and to the many students who instructed me in how to teach psychological assessment.

TABLE 20.2
Written Report Concerning Elizabeth's Course Performance

PSY389L–Theory and Technique of Assessment II–Spring 19XX

Course Evaluation

Student: Elizabeth J.   Course Grade: A

TA Supervisor: Mary Jones

Elizabeth impressed me as an intelligent, caring, responsible student who worked very hard on the course assignments and on improving her clinical skills. Both the TA supervisor and I feel Elizabeth has adequately addressed certain difficulties that Dr. Smith noted in her interactions with clients first semester.

1. *Does this student have an adequate knowledge of the theory and research related to personality assessment?*

Yes. Elizabeth obviously prepared each of the course readings with great care and made insightful and useful comments in class discussions. She received the highest grade in the class on the final exam, and her answers demonstrated a sophisticated knowledge of the theory and research regarding personality assessment.

2. *How well was the student able to conceptualize clinical case material?*

Elizabeth showed a good ability in supervision sessions to think psychologically about cases and to integrate theory and case material. She was more able than most first-year students to analyze clients' interactions with her during assessment sessions and to connect these with clients' problems in their outside lives.

3. *Has the student adequately mastered the administration and scoring of major personality tests?*

Yes. Elizabeth is able to adequately administer and score the tests covered in the course. She was precise and careful in her test scoring. However, like almost all students at her level of training, she will need ongoing assistance with the scoring of difficult Rorschach protocols.

4. *How well did the student write assessment reports?*

Elizabeth's reports were finely reasoned and elegantly worded. She always met deadlines for revisions, even when a quick turn-around was needed.

5. *At what level are this student's basic clinical skills–e.g., empathy, active listening, ability to maintain appropriate boundaries?*

At several points early in the semester, Elizabeth's clinical interactions were influenced by her anxiety and her attempts to manage it. At such points, Elizabeth tended to be overactive and controlling with clients–not listening well and imposing too much of her own agenda on sessions. Elizabeth was aware of this tendency from feedback she received last semester and she worked hard to overcome it during this course. I now feel that Elizabeth has adequately addressed the underlying issues contributing to her anxiety, and she now shows good empathy, listening skills, and appropriate flexibility with clients.

6. *How did the student respond to supervisory feedback?*

Elizabeth was receptive to supervisory feedback and was able to use it to improve her skills with clients. She also appropriately reached out for support from her supervisors when she was troubled by family issues that were influencing her course performance.

7. *Did the student demonstrate any behavior that raises concern about her suitability to be a clinical psychologist?*

8. *Is this student ready to participate in a clinical practicum?*

Elizabeth performed in an ethical and responsible way throughout the course. I have no concerns about her taking part in the second-year practicum. I believe that Elizabeth has the abilities, temperament, and dedication necessary to become an excellent clinical psychologist.

Stephen E. Finn

Course Instructor

REFERENCES

Dana, R. H., & Leech, S. (1974). Existential assessment. *Journal of Personality Assessment, 38,* 428–435.

Exner, J. E., Jr. (1993). *The Rorschach: A comprehensive system: Vol. 1. Basic foundations* (3rd ed.). New York: Wiley.

Finn, S. E. (1996). *A manual for using the MMPI–2 as a therapeutic intervention.* Minneapolis: University of Minnesota Press.

Finn, S. E., & Martin, H. (1997). Therapeutic assessment with the MMPI–2 in managed health care. In J. N. Butcher (Ed.), *Objective psychological assessment in managed health care: A practitioner's guide* (pp. 131–152). New York: Oxford University Press.

Finn, S. E., Schroeder, D. G., & Tonsager, M. E. (1995). *The Assessment Questionnaire–2 (AQ–2): A measure of clients' experiences with psychological assessment.* Unpublished manuscript, Center for Therapeutic Assessment.

Finn, S. E., & Tonsager, M. E. (1992). Therapeutic effects of providing MMPI–2 test feedback to college students awaiting therapy. *Psychological Assessment, 4,* 278-287.

Finn, S. E., & Tonsager, M. E. (1997). *Therapeutic Assessment: Using psychological testing to help clients change.* Manuscript in preparation.

Finn, S., & Tonsager, M. (in press). Information gathering and therapeutic models of assessment: Complementary paradigms. *Psychological Assessment.*

Fischer, C. T. (1994). *Individualizing psychological assessment.* Hillsdale, NJ: Lawrence Erlbaum Associates. (Original work published 1985)

Newman, M., & Greenway, P. (1997). Therapeutic effects of providing MMPI–2 test feedback to clients at a university counseling service: A collaborative approach. *Psychological Assessment, 9,* 122–131.

Pruyser, P. W. (1979). *The psychological examination: A guide for clinicians.* New York: International Universities Press.

21

A Logical Analysis of Rorschach Autisms

Edwin E. Wagner
Isle of Palms, South Carolina

In learning the Rorschach one of the most fascinating yet perplexing aspects of scoring and interpretation concerns the nature and meaning of the so-called *autistic response*. It is argued here that the major impediment to understanding Rorschach autisms is not the naiveté of the new graduate student but, rather, a lack of definitional precision; that is, the absence of an overall concept that explains what autisms have in common, which would therefore relieve the student of the burden of memorizing each variety of autism piecemeal. It is further contended that it is possible to logically deduce the underlying nature of autistic responses, thus providing the student with a more efficient approach to understanding and appreciating these powerful signs of cognitive distortion.

THE PROBLEM WITH AUTISMS

A major intuitive appeal of the Rorschach has always been the trenchant manner in which psychopathology is manifested via various perceptual anomalies. In a tour de force, Rapaport, Gill and Schafer (1968) catalogued a large number of such peculiarities, coining the term autistic to describe reactions to the Rorschach that reflected " ... cognitive processes that are not ruled by the laws and convention of logic" (p. 427). Later, Exner (1986) pared this list down to include, among his Special Scores, certain autisms deemed indicative of cognitive mismanagement, collectively designated as WSUM6.

Although WSUM6 could be reliably scored (indeed the components were selected for this reason!) and proved capable of distinguishing between normal and cognitively disturbed individuals, a disquieting study by Adair and E. E. Wagner (1992) demonstrated that the index was not stable over time for the individual case. Because outpatient schizophrenics were used in this research, some of the test–retest unreliability was attributed to the temporal variability of florid psychopathology in these patients. However, a subsequent perusal of the outpatient schizophrenic protocols revealed the presence of many strikingly aberrant percepts that could not be classified as a WSUM6. In fact, some conspicuous perceptual anomalies seemed to defy any extant scoring system for autisms. At least some of the test-retest instability noted in the study by Adair and Wagner was attributable to a shift from one type of perceptual aberration to another that WSUM6 was not broad enough to capture. The problem with current systems for listing autisms became painfully obvious. Without an overarching rationale, the inclusion of a specific response type was selective and arbitrary. Further, the lack of a guiding principle mitigated against discovering new and potentially useful autisms. It was therefore decided to search for a more rational method for defining autisms based on a compelling logical definition. A solution to the problem emerged once it was realized that perceptions should not be confounded with verbalizations and autisms are really perceptual absurdities.

PERCEPTION VERSUS VERBALIZATIONS

Many psychologists believe that the Rorschach is primarily a test of perception, although verbal elucidation is necessary to objectify what the subject sees. Although idiosyncratic expressions are important, they do not necessarily reflect the perceptions themselves. Neologisms, slips of the tongue, circumlocutions, and so forth, are diagnostically valuable but also detectable during interviews, therapy sessions, and even ordinary conversations. Strange verbalizations can be scrutinized and studied in their own right but the view taken here is that if a unifying logic is to be uncovered, autisms must be examined as aberrant perceptions and should not be confounded with verbal vagaries as important as the latter may be. This is sometimes difficult because percepts must be inferred from what the subject says, but this is a perennial problem for all Rorschach scoring.

THE AUTISM AS AN ABSURDITY

With the confounding effect of anomalous verbalizations removed, it becomes apparent that autistic perceptions are really absurdities. That is, they all entail assumptions that, if uncritically accepted, would place the percept beyond further scrutiny, thus defeating the purpose of a Rorschach evaluation (E. E. Wagner, 1994). Therefore, an autism can be viewed as a reductio ad absurdum, a percept with an underlying premise that leads to a contradiction and is self-defeating if taken to the logical extreme. If someone were asked to estimate the size of an object and replied, "It weighs 15 pounds," the answer would be rejected outright. It is absurd because it assumes that weight can be substituted for size. Further, if it were permissible to substitute weight for size, then any answer involving weight would be correct, whether it were 15 pounds or 15 tons.

A FABCOM such as "Two ducks stirring a pot of soup" would be an absurdity in this context because to accept such a counterfactual image would by extension and implication validate any factually impossible response and place it beyond critical evaluation. Suppose a subject sees "A snark and a boojum sipping tea." If the percept does not have to conform to reality, how can it be wrong? No one knows what snarks and boojums look like!

Once this principle is understood it becomes possible to recognize other autisms not included in any existing system. For instance, "card edging," or peering along the rim of the Rorschach plate in order to evoke private, unconfirmable images, which cannot be seen by the examiner, has long been regarded by Rorschach experts as a sign of psychopathology. It can now be recognized as an autism because a percept that no one else can discern is beyond appraisal and therefore an absurdity.

CLASSIFICATION OF AUTISMS

Rorschach absurdities appear to be created in at least three basic ways: (a) The blot shapes are ignored altogether, (b) implicit or explicit perceptual or procedural rules are violated, or (c) counterfactual percepts are rationalized by spatial juxtaposition. For purposes of exposition these autistic subdivisions can be referred to collectively and acronymically as TRAUT or a tripartite classification of autisms (E. E. Wagner, in press).

The Hypoattentional Autism (HYPO). The HYPO is so named because the patient responds as if he or she is not paying attention to the blot shapes. A purely imagined percept such as "The devil" may be envisioned, or the response may involve a highly subjective reaction such as "This feels like anger" or "Complete chaos at the end of the world." HYPOs are obvious autisms because they ignore the shapes of the blots, and therefore cannot be evaluated on any objective basis. It must be emphasized that the HYPO should not be categorized as merely a "poor form" or F– response. It has no form; that is why it cannot be evaluated.

The Hyperattentional Autism (HYPER). HYPERs are, in a sense, just the opposite of HYPOs, because the subject appears to be devoting too much effort and attention to discovering highly personalized images, as in the previously mentioned card edging where a seemingly deliberate attempt is made to see what no one else can. Many HYPERs involve intrinsically ambiguous details such as tiny dots seen as "islands," or rare configurations that overlook the natural gestalt configurations of the blots. HYPERs are absurdities because they circumvent the explicit or implicit assumptions of the Rorschach task and by doing so achieve idiosyncratic solutions that cannot be challenged. For example, a subject assiduously scans internal shading nuances and triumphantly disinters "Joseph Stalin's mustache." Because practically anything the respondent may be looking for can be found somewhere within the subtle variations in shading, such responses are autistic. The author once showed a picture of a duck-billed platypus to a class of graduate students and asked them to find one in the Rorschach. It turned out to be no problem if they were permitted to choose *any* area.

HYPERs are of two varieties: topographical, involving offbeat areas that ignore the natural gestalt properties of the blots; and procedural, where implicit task demands are circumvented, as in the previously mentioned card edging, where the subject's idiosyncratic way of looking at the blot precludes further evaluation because the percept cannot be seen by anyone else.

The Relationship Autism (RELER). RELERs are produced when spatial juxtaposition is used to justify a percept that is counterfactual and/or illogical. Those WSUM6 (Exner, 1986) scores that deal with *percepts* as opposed to strange verbalizations would fall into this category. For example, a subject perceives the center D on Card I as "Holy matrimony" and when queried further adds, "There's two and they're together, that means they're married." In Exner's system this would probably be scored an ALOG. For TRAUT it is a RELER autism because two entities are illogically interpreted as marriage based mainly on spatial proximity. Such responses are absurd because practically any percept can be rationalized by proximity if logically extended. Another example might be "Bat girl" (Card V), interpreted as such because the wings and head resemble a bat but the leg of a girl is also seen along the edge of the wing. In Exner's system this would probably be scored an INCOM.

DIAGNOSTIC IMPLICATIONS

Whereas logical and pedagogical considerations dictated subdividing autisms into the three major subtypes, a recent study indicated that HYPOs, HYPERs and RELERs may also be useful for purposes of differential diagnosis. E. E. Wagner, C. F. Wagner, Hilsenroth, and Fowler (1995) compared four clinical groups presumed to have varying degrees of thought disorder: inpatient schizophrenics, outpatient schizophrenics, borderline clients, and Cluster A clients. It was found that the three TRAUT scoring categories could be reliably scored and could also differentiate significantly among the four criterion groups. The inpatient schizophrenics, as expected, gave more total TRAUT and more HYPOs, but the borderline and Cluster A groups were higher on RELERs.

The three TRAUT categories were not highly correlated, confirming the implication of the postmortem analysis of the Adair and E. E. Wagner (1992) data that it is advisable to score as many types of autisms as possible in order to detect thought disorder over long intervals for the individual case. Even among the 30 inpatients, where overlap would be expected, there were eight protocols with no RELERs and five where only one type of TRAUT was evidenced. All 30, however, showed at least one TRAUT.

PLAYING THE GAME

Autisms are neither mysterious nor arcane and can be understood in a practical sense as responses that abrogate or at least bend the rules of the Rorschach game. They are absurdities in the same way that any rule that prevents a game from being fairly played would be absurd. Everyone would recognize as ridiculous a rule that permits one baseball team to decide unilaterally whether a hit ball lands fair or foul. An autism such as the HYPO that "allows" individuals to see whatever they wish, completely disregarding blot forms, is tantamount to playing the game without rules. It is self-contradictory and self-defeating; that is, an absurdity.

COMPARISONS WITH EARLIER SYSTEMS

Conceptual Underpinnings. Rapaport et al. (1968) presented 25 autisms that they conceptualized in terms of a " ... loss or increase of distance from the inkblot" (p. 428). By "distance" the authors were referring to opposite extremes in which subjects either "show too little regard for the inkblot" or relate to the blot " ... as an immutable reality, with its own real affective and logical propensities" (p. 429). Aberrant verbal expressions were included among their autisms although a certain conceptual discontinuity between the actual percept and the accompanying verbalizations appears to have been acknowledged: " ... [T]here is no explicit autistic reasoning in them, but rather verbal end products thereof" (p. 442). Further, in justifying the inclusions of the so-called queer verbalization, the concept of distance seems to have been abandoned altogether: "[O]ur baseline of evaluation was everyday verbal convention ... " (p. 443).

In his original formulation, Exner (1986) pared the autisms of Rapaport et al. (1968) down to 10, 6 of which, the Unusual Verbalizations, were regarded as being indicative of cognitive slippage. The basic rationale for Exner's selections appears to be scoring reliability. Interestingly, one of the bulwark's of the Comprehensive System's approach to autisms, interrater reliability, has been questioned recently because of the inflation caused by calculations of percentage agreements (McDowell & Acklin, 1996). Excellent descriptions of the six indices of cognitive mismanagement are provided but no unifying rationale is offered and the concept of distance appears to have been forsaken.

The TRAUT approach is logical rather than psychological. No attempt is made to explore the process of distantiation advocated by Rapaport et al. (1968). A response is deemed autistic if the percept leads to a contradiction; that is, by implication further evaluation would be abrogated or at least attenuated. Verbalizations per se are excluded from consideration because they are not percepts.

EMPIRICAL SUPPORT

Rapaport et al. (1968) supplied no normative data but acknowledged that the assertion that autisms are associated with a breakdown in reality testing must be validated against " ... the records of a large variety of normal subjects" (p. 429). Later, Johnston and Holzman (1979) showed conclusively that schizophrenics do indeed produce a greater number of autisms. Exner (1986) provided data for his six individual indices of cognitive mismanagement, along with their sums and weighted sums for samples of nonpatient adults, children, and adolescents, and for inpatient schizophrenics, inpatient depressives, and outpatient character problems.

Empirical support for the TRAUT system was obtained after examining the Rorschachs of over 800 individuals, including three groups of nonpatient adults and late adolescents, inpatient schizophrenics, and a variety of outpatients such as antisocial personality disorders, schizophrenics, anxiety reactions, and brain-impaired individuals (E. E. Wagner, in press). Percentage of interscorer agreements for HYPOs, HYPERs, RELERs and total TRAUT were computed and were all found to be in the 80s and 90s. Because percentage agreements can be artificially inflated, correlations among three raters on total TRAUT scores were also computed, yielding respective coefficients of .88, .77, and .73. In round figures, average TRAUT scores proved to be about six for recently admitted inpatient schizophrenics, three for thought-disordered outpatients, such as borderline personality disorders, and one for "normal" groups, such as college students and non-thought-disordered outpatients. Inpatient schizophrenics, as a group, gave all three TRAUT categories; outpatient thought-disordered groups tended more toward RELERs and HYPERs, and nonpatient subjects were more prone to HYPERs if they gave any TRAUT at all.

Today, most Rorschachers are guided in their scoring and understanding of autisms by the six types of Unusual Verbalizations included in Exner's (1986) Special Scores. Consequently, to highlight the differences and similarities between TRAUTs and Unusual Verbalizations, critical comparisons are summarized in Table 21.1.

ILLUSTRATIONS AND COMMENTARY

Pedagogically, the chief advantage of TRAUT is its conceptual clarity, but empirically the system's main contribution is that it casts a wider net. That is, TRAUT is likely to discern traces of thought disorder in a given patient from one testing period to another when specific signs may have changed. This is especially important in Rorschachs of limited length, where even one such index could at least alert the examiner to the possible presence of a thought disorder.

TABLE 21.1

Comparisons between TRAUT and Exner's (1986) Unusual Verbalizations

TRAUT	Unusual Verbalizations
Rationale: Autisms are logical fallacies that contravene the evaluative process. They are "absurd" in the sense that endorsement would lead to a contradiction. They are incongruent in the sense that reality cannot be inferred from the blot, and vice-versa.	Unusual Verbalizations reveal "cognitiveslippage" and "cognitive disarray" (p. 161). Autisms selected for inclusion were based on considerations such as interscorer reliability and validation data.
Verbalizations: Only percepts can be regarded as autistic.	Two of the six Unusual Verbalizations deal with idiosyncratic expressions as opposed to percepts.
Types: TRAUT is subdivided into HYPOs (disregard of form), HYPERs (use of unconventional blot areas and/or response modes), and RELERs (justifying illogical and/or counterfactual perceptions on the basis of spatial proximity).	There are three kinds of Unusual Verbalizations: Deviant Verbalizations (strange expressions), Inappropriate Combinations (unreal relationships), and Inappropriate Logic (strained reasoning).

Notes. Similarities: Exner's four perceptual autisms (INCOM, FABCOM, CONTAM, ALOG) could be subsumed under the RELER category because they all involve illogical or counterfactual spatial relationships. Another one of Exner's Special Scores, Confabulation (CONFAB), would also be classified as a RELER because an illogical/counterfactual nexus is established on the basis of spatial juxtaposition. A CONFAB is an overgeneralization that extrapolates from a detail to a larger adjoining area, for example, "There's his feet so the rest of it must be a man."

Differences: There is no equivalent to the HYPO in the Exner (1986) system. Exner does score for minus form level but lumps together responses that are "distorted, arbitrary [and] unrealistic" with those that reveal "a total or near total disregard for the structure of the area being used." (p. 148). For TRAUT, weak or poor form level cannot be equated with no form level. Further, HYPERs play no role in the Comprehensive System. Some HYPERs would receive Dd or DdS scores but are not necessarily regarded as autistic and, in fact, could represent "a form of respite from the ambiguities of the blot areas" (p. 359).

The following protocols are designed to illustrate the underlying principles of TRAUT scoring and to show how even brief records of thought-disordered patients will usually yield at least one TRAUT score. The subjects were all inpatients obtained from a state mental health institute serving a metropolitan community. All had received a schizophrenic diagnosis assigned by a multidisciplinary team based on case history, clinical interview, staff behavioral observations and psychological test data. Patients with a comorbid psychoactive substance abuse disorder or an organic mental disorder were excluded. The Rorschach was given shortly after admission to the facility and was administered according to Exner (1986). Most inpatient schizophrenics produce a large number and variety of TRAUT but some give only a few, and as is shown, it is important to score for all three categories—HYPOs, HYPERs, and RELERs.

Patient "V" is a 19-year-old single man with a 10-grade education, diagnosed as a paranoid schizophrenic, and tested after the sixth day of admission. He shows all three TRAUT categories, one of each, despite his short record (see Table 21.2).

A HYPO is awarded for Response 5 (Card II) where he states, "This one's dangerous to fool around with. It's hell," and adds, "Hell, hell is dangerous. Better not fool around with this one. It's hell!" He appears to be responding to

TABLE 21.2
Patient V's Rorschach

Card	Response	Inquiry
I.	1. A bat.	Wings, shape.
	2. A bird.	Wings, shape.
	3. A plane	Wings, shape, tail.
II.	I don't know.	
	4. A butterfly.	Wings, body.
	5. This one's dangerous to fool around with. It's hell.	Hell. Hell is dangerous. Better not fool around with this one. It's hell. (Seems to be responding to whole card.)
III.	6. An animal like a spider but a butterfly too.	A spider made into a butterfly's back. A spider and part of a butterfly. This part is a butterfly back. The rest here is the spider (excludes middle red D and top and side Ds).
IV.	7. A giant.	Big feet, body.
V.	8. A butterfly.	Wings, antennae.
VI.	I don't know.	
	9. A bumble bee.	Body, shape.
VII.	10. A spider.	Antennae, body, eyes, mouth (bottom D seen as part of body and mouth, top side Ds as antennae; vague and poorly seen).
VIII.	I don't know. I don't know.	
	11. A fish.	Head, tail, fins.
	12. A bat.	Shape (seen in space under middle blue).
IX.	13. A tortoise.	Green color, head, back.
	14. Two flies.	I don't know. Head (seen in two orange Ds).
X.	15. A bumblebee.	Center. Shape, wings (seen vaguely as two reds and inside space).

the whole card, and although something about the plate may have triggered his reaction, he is really not concerned about the shapes, and therefore, a HYPO must be scored. Note that a HYPO would not be scored for a response such as the one given to Card VI where the whole blot is seen as a "bumblebee." Although the resemblance is questionable, the subject does make some attempt to connect the shape with something real. Poor form level is not a reason to score a HYPO. An errant disregard for the shapes is typical of schizophrenics who are projecting their delusions and hallucinations onto the plate, whereas the painfully unsuccessful effort to match up the blot with an external object is more characteristic of low-IQ and brain-impaired individuals. Some schizophrenics will give HYPOs as well as "organic" signs.

In Response 6 (Card III) V sees a combination spider and butterfly. This response is morphologically counterfactual and predicated upon spatial juxtaposition. It is an obvious RELER. In Exner's (1986) system it would probably be scored an INCOM.

Response 12 (Card VIII) utilizes the space located in between the middle blue, side reds, and bottom orange-pink. It would be allocated an area score of S (for space) in most Rorschach systems, but for TRAUT it is also a HYPER (actually a HYPER:RAR) because it focuses on an out-of-the-way blot seldom seen by others. It is a violation of the natural gestalt properties of Card VIII to choose this interstice for interpretation. Again, such responses are deemed absurdities because practically anything a subject wishes to see can be found somewhere in an inkblot if one is permitted to use any area regardless of size, location, position, or natural conformation.

The HYPO alone would be sufficient to suggest schizophrenia, and the two additional TRAUTs provide confirmation despite the relative brevity of the record.

Patient "W" produced another abbreviated record, and as noted, at the end of the Rorschach, she simply refused to respond to Cards IX and X. Nevertheless, her one HYPO response is sufficient to diagnose a serious thought disorder. (See Table 21.3.)

W is a 31-year-old divorced woman with a hospital diagnosis of paranoid schizophrenia, who was administered the Rorschach the second day after her admission to the hospital. Her first response to Card VII is a classic HYPO: "Something evil. It's just evil. It represents pure evil." HYPOs can be subcategorized as completely subjective perceptions of nonexisting entities (e.g., "My old dog Scout come down from heaven to help me"); formless abstractions (e.g., "The end of the world"); emotional expressions (e.g., "My joy and happiness!"); or unwarranted sensual experiences (e.g., "I hear pure, sweet music"). W's response appears to be an abstraction and could be scored HYPO:ABS. It is a completely subjective reaction to the inkblots and is a hallmark of serious psychopathology.

Despite the limited number of responses and W's refusal to respond to the last two cards, the HYPO is an almost certain indicator of schizophrenia. To be sure, there are other qualitative signs that would suggest schizophrenia, but it is the HYPO that is pathognomic. Note that the idiosyncratic verbalizations do not count for TRAUT. For example, the comment about the "work of Satan" is certainly of interest but it is not a perception, and TRAUT deals with what subjects see in inkblots, not secondary verbal elaborations that can often be elicited during an interview, without the need of inkblots.

As mentioned previously, TRAUT categories can shift from one Rorschach administration to another. The reasons for these temporal fluctuations are unknown, but probably have something to do with the degree of floridity and deserve more research attention. HYPERs are usually the least virulent of the TRAUT categories, but in some ways they are the most interesting. They connote something idiosyncratic and very personal about the respondent, although the interpretive implication may be clothed in symbolism and may be

TABLE 21.3

Patient W's Rorschach

Card	Response	Inquiry
I.	1. A moth.	Shape.
	2. A butterfly.	Wings, body, head.
	3. A bumblebee.	Stinger at bottom, wings, head, body.
	4. Two men together with their arms around each other.	They have masks on. Large hands. Shape and position of their body. Masks are military masks. They're military men (Center D).
II.	I don't know.	
	5. Two bears dancing.	Shape and looks like they're dancing.
	6. Butterfly (laughs)	Wings, blending of colors. (Q) Black and red blended together (seen in center space and surrounding black—DS).
	7. A missile.	Shaped like a missile.
III.	8. Afro-Americans setting down buckets.	Black, shape. Looks like setting down buckets on ground the way their bodies are positioned (Q) of water.
IV.	I don't know.	
	9. A bat.	The size, color black, and the shape.
V.	10. Another bat.	Size, color black, shape.
VI.	11. A catfish on one side. I don't know what the other side is.	Sharp whisker things. Two eyes and you can see the bone down the center (usual top D).
VII.	(3 minutes elapse)	
	12. Something evil.	It's just evil. It represents pure evil (whole card).
	13. A cloud.	Looks like clouds I've seen with faces in them. It was the work of Satan. Other times I have seen myself in clouds as well.
VIII.	14. Two polar bears climbing up a mountain.	Shape of the body. Legs are moving climbing up a mountain.
IX.	I don't know (turns card, 3 minutes go by). I tried. I can't. I can't think of anything (pushes card away). I can't do this one.	
X.	Nothing. I don't see anything (2 minutes). I don't know. I have no idea what it could be (30 seconds). I don't know. I don't know. I don't know (pushes card away).	

Note. Patent adamantly refused to take another look at Cards IX and X, put her head down in her arms and said, "I'm done. I can't do this any more," and did not move or look up for a substantial amount of time.

difficult to decipher. The first HYPER given by patient "X" is transparent, however, and she even explains it for us: "Two eyes that are crying. I wish I could cry (Q). Maybe that's me."

X is a 55-year-old married woman with a high-school education. She was diagnosed as an undifferentiated schizophrenic and tested the sixth day after she was admitted. Response 8 (Card IV) is a HYPER because it is a rarely seen space response, located at the upper left and right corners of the blot, which actually has to be rotated to be seen as an "eye." Sometimes this space is combined with the surrounding blot area as a DS and perceived, for example, as "The heads of two ducks"; but when viewed only as an S, and inverted to boot, it is clearly rare. Likewise, the "cross" (Response 14, Card VIII), seen at the very tip of card VIII and hardly discernible, is an obvious HYPER. Such tiny protrusions could be "discovered" at myriad sites on all 10 cards. Responses 8 and 14 are inherently ambiguous and circumvent the compelling gestalt properties of the respective blots. With an assiduous search similar responses could be projected practically anywhere and, therefore, the "eye" and the "cross" must be classified as HYPERs. See Table 21.4 for details.

Our fourth inpatient, "Y," is a 45-year-old married woman with a college education. She received a diagnosis of paranoid schizophrenia and the Rorschach was administered 5 days after admission.

Patient Y illustrates the use of the third TRAUT category, the RELER, in screening for thought disorder. She only gives one RELER, but it is enough to at least raise suspicion that something is amiss in her cognitive processing. On Card III (Response 5) she says, "Two people facing each other with hats and bodices. They're swinging something. Buckets. Shoes, pants, jacket, nose." (See Table 21.5.) The response seems acceptable at first and scorable as a "Popular" because the two humans are seen in the two large Ds. On inquiry, however, she indicates that the bodice is " ... aligned with the body. It's where a bodice should go." The "bodice" is the middle red detail in between the two women. It should, of course, be on the women and part of their attire. Bodices cannot be suspended in midair. The response is counterfactual and determined by spatial proximity. It is therefore a RELER.

There are other suggestions of psychopathology in Y's record such as the two whole card "masks," the "belly-up rat," the vague "U" on Card VII, and remarks such as "The hunter and the hunted," but the RELER on Card III stands out as the most objective and reliable index of thought disorder. The protocol is short (13 responses) and some Rorschachers would be reluctant to venture an interpretation, but with the RELER, a substantial amount of diagnostic material can be gleaned from Y's Rorschach.

TRAUTs AND QUALITATIVE INTERPRETATION

TRAUT functions best as a rationally derived quantitative screening index for thought disorder but it can also be used with circumspection as an adjunct to qualitative interpretation. Although every Rorschach response is in some way

TABLE 21.4

Patient X's Rorschach

Card	Response	Inquiry
I.	1. Looks like a bat to me	The way the wings are, points on top, inkblot is dark.
	2. Moth	Way the wings are.
II.	Weird-looking design.	
	3. Could be a space ship in the middle.	
	4. Just looks dark with some red.	(Apparently meant as a response, not a comment.)
	5. Could be two things meeting, kissing or whatever.	Animals. Right here where mouths are touching
III.	6. Looks like two people on a teeter totter.	Head, neck, shape (teeter totter?) in middle. They're playing.
IV.	7. Looks like a monster.	Just looks ugly. Big blot.
	8. Looks like eyes that are crying. I wish I could cry.	Maybe that's me. (upper sides, white area only, seen vertically).
	9. Two big boots.	Those could be boots or shoes (points usual bottom Ds).
V.	10. Butterfly. Just not bright or pretty. It should be. That's all.	Antennae, wings, two things on back.
VI.	11. Bearskin rug. Why do they have them so gross like this?	Stretched out (whole).
	12. Could be a scarecrow on top, scaring away.	Arms out, standing up (top D).
VII.	13. Two faces. Two girls with pony tails or something. Like Siamese twins.	Because pony tails.
VIII.	14. Looks like a cross up here.	Because it's near Easter (tiny area at extreme tip of top gray)
	15. Looks like a couple seals or something.	Shape (usual side reds).
IX.	16. Looks like a couple dragons. That's all.	Like in a Disney film (orange).
X.	17. This one's got pretty designs. Has got flowers in there.	Yellow look like jonquils.
	18. Couple crabs on top.	They taste good. Lots of legs.

reflective of a subject's psychological functioning, percepts are not equal in this respect. Some responses seem laden with meaning, and TRAUTs, because they are so idiosyncratic, can often reveal trenchant and perhaps hidden aspects of an individual's psyche.

Interpretively, HYPOs are often blatant, as when a paranoid schizophrenic who believes people are out to get him or her sees "a trap" on every card. HYPERs are not as obvious but can be quite revealing, especially when integrated with the rest of the Rorschach and/or case history data. For example, a 22-year-old woman gives the following response to Card X: "There's a face in this one. He has yellow eyes, a green mustache, red hair, and a head thing. The top of his head is exploding. (Q) (Smiles) It's the form that I see in it, not really the color. (Q) Because the gray part on top of his head is going straight up" (Q) (subject delineates DS extending up middle of card. Blues, greens, browns are excluded from percept). The response is a HYPER because of the strange way in which selected center details and spaces are combined. Conceivably, it could also be identified as a RELER because the "exploding" part is differentiated from the head proper, proximity in space apparently dictating the illogical perception of an "exploding head." There is a thematic element to this response, because she also sees " ... a bell or something that's exploding, being fragmented" on Card VII. Several months after taking the Rorschach this young woman was hospitalized for a "nervous breakdown," the exploding head apparently presaging personality disintegration and a psychotic episode.

TABLE 21.5

Patient Y's Rorschach

Card	Response	Inquiry
I.	1. A scarab with wings open (looks at back of card and reads it).	The body in the center, insect wings on side.
	2. Butterfly.	Body, wings.
II.	3. A couple elves dancing with palms together.	Hats, bodies, palms, boots, robes. (Q) Hats in position where heads should be. (Q) Boots because on the bottom. (Q) Shape of robes.
	4. A mask.	Mouth, eyes, nose, rounded shape.
III.	5. Two people facing each other with hats and bodices. They're swinging something. Buckets. Shoes, pants, jackets, nose.	Legs, arm, body, head. (Q) Near head. Looks like they tumbled off due to the movement of the body (top side red are hats). (Q) The position, where it is. Aligned with body. It's where a bodice should go (middle red D is the bodice).
IV.	6. Looks like a dead animal, belly up. A rat.	Texture. Looks like fur is ruffled. Midline looks like sharp teeth. Dead because it's belly up.
V.	7. A butterfly.	Antennae, center body, two wings.
	8. A ballerina.	A tiara, head piece on top. Skirt, leg, shoes.
VI.	9. Looks like animal's hide hanging on a wall.	Texture of gray area's outline, shape of body. (Q) Because hold the card up so it's on the wall.
VII.	10. Looks like the letter "U,," a stylized letter "U."	Shaped like a "U."
VIII.	11. The hunter and the hunted. Rocks, two bears climbing up to find food. Hunting ground on top part.	Shape, body, legs, short tail, slick fur. (Q) Texture of color. (Q) Salad greens, berries and bushes.
IX.	12. (smiles, laughs) A mask.	Eyes, symmetrical shape, mirror image on other side. Squarish rounded shape. Nose, mouth.
X.	13. Underwater scene.	Sea creatures and coral reef. (Q) All the colors.

As another illustration, consider this response to Card VI from a male transvestite who was receiving psychotherapy for a pronounced gender role disturbance: "I see a snake's head here. (Q) Its eyes and a little face. (Q) (points to a very small detail at the tip of card) I see nothing in the rest." The entire elongation at the top of Card VI is often interpreted as symbolically representing the penis, and considering the case history, this HYPER might be construed as connoting feelings of inferiority in relation to a diminished sense of masculinity. This supposition appears to be confirmed by his response to Card X, which is another HYPER, because the percept involves the green area with the card held upside down: "I see a man here with a parachute. Nothing else. (Q) The shape looks like a man with a parachute that didn't open. (Q) The man is falling and I can't tell what's gong to happen. (Q) No, just the shape." This doleful response would seem to confirm the subject's vanished virility and also raises the disturbing questions as to the possibility of a psychotic break and/or suicide.

Obviously, interpreting TRAUTs qualitatively in terms of content, symbolism, and thematic material is a process that cannot be objectified and its efficacy will vary with the experience and acumen of the interpreter. The approach is intended to complement rather than supplant the simpler and more reliable quantitative procedure based on the logical classification and enumeration of the three TRAUT categories.

DISCOVERING NEW AUTISMS

An advantage of TRAUT's rational approach is that it permits the identification and utilization of new autisms. Every once in a while a strange percept is encountered, which if duly recognized as a TRAUT, can make a significant diagnostic contribution. Even if the autism is extremely rare and perhaps not worth formalizing with a brand new score, recognizing the response for what it is can help to assess an individual record.

A case in point is the Extrapolated Area Response that can be scored HYPER:EAR. Thus far it has only been found in bipolar disorders in a hypomanic state, and it may prove useful in diagnosing individuals who have not yet reached a level of excitement where the manic aspect of their behavior becomes obvious (E. E. Wagner & Rinn, 1994).

In the HYPER:EAR the subject starts out by selecting an identifiable blot area, usually an S, and then extrapolates beyond the visualized configuration into the empty space of the blot (and sometimes into the empty space of the room!) in order to complete what starts out as a well-seen percept. For example, on Card II, the space between the two top reds is seen fairly accurately by a patient as the base of a missile. Then, in order to visualize the entire missile, the percept is extended upward to encompass an imagined barrel and warhead. Although now dealing with empty space, the patient actually takes pains to describe the contours of the missile, apparently oblivious of the fact that he is talking about literally nothing!

This type of response was uncovered many years ago during research conducted on manic-depressive Rorschachs (E. E. Wagner & Heise, 1981), but with the advent of TRAUT, its autistic nature can now be deduced. The EAR is autistic because it deals with formless space. Obviously, if a subject is permitted to see a missile in empty space, then anybody can see anything, hence the absurdity. It is a HYPER because the patient breaks an implicit rule of the game when he or she assumes that, having begun with good form, it is allowable to end with no form at all. Interpretively, this type of response may incisively reflect the manic's tendency to expand beyond the constraints of reality in thought and behavior. There may well be additional autisms ready to be discovered, based on the absurdity priniciple.

Pedagogical Implications

For the teacher who wants to get down to basics, TRAUT provides an approach that is rooted in the underlying assumptions of the technique itself and therefore does not depend on some arbitrary and contestable list of autisms that will vary with a specific scoring system or theoretical orientation. Because the logic of TRAUT is derived from the Rorschach task, the teacher can appeal to reason rather than to authority.

For the student, TRAUT clarifies, classifies, and interrelates. Autisms are organized and interconnected and the student discovers what they have in common as well as their differentiating characteristics. The subject matter becomes more meaningful and is easier to retain.

Definitional imprecision retards scientific progress. When authors take refuge in examples rather than providing an explanatory principle, the student can surmise that a concept has not been properly defined. The fallacy of substituting an example for a definition, recognized as far back as Plato's Euthyphro, is amply illustrated in the short history of the Rorschach autism. Given the powerful diagnostic implications of autisms it is little wonder they were pressed into service before an underlying rationale could be formulated. The time has come, however, to relieve the long-suffering graduate student of the burden of memorization without explication. Autisms are neither mysterious nor arcane. They are Rorschach percepts that, if endorsed, will lead to a contradiction.

An autistic percept provides nonvalid information in the sense that an observer could not, reciprocally, derive an object in reality from the response, or infer the nature of the blot from a known object, and it is this incongruity between blot and reality that produces the absurdity. This knowledge should make life a little easier for the beginning Rorschacher.

REFERENCES

Adair, H. E. & Wagner, E. E. (1992). Stability of Unusual Verbalizations on the Rorschach for outpatients with schizophrenia. *Journal of Clinical Psychology, 48,* 250–256.

Exner, J. E. (1986). *The Rorschach: a comprehensive system: Vol. 1. Basic foundations.* (2nd ed.). New York: Wiley.

Johnston, M. H., & Holzman, P. S. (1979). *Assessing schizophrenic thinking.* San Francisco: Jossey-Bass.

McDowell, C., & Acklin, M. W. (1996). Standardizing procedures for calculating Rorschach interrater reliability: Conceptual and empirical foundations. *Journal of Personality Assessment, 66,* 308–320.

Rapaport, D., Gill, M. M. & Schafer, R. (1968). *Diagnostic psychological testing.* (Rev. ed., edited by R. Holt) New York: International Universities Press.

Wagner, E. E. (1994). Reductio ad absurdum: A formal analysis of Rorschach autisms. *Perceptual and Motor Skills, 79,* 912–914.

Wagner, E. E. (in press). TRAUT: A Rorschach index for screening thought disorder [Monograph]. *Journal of Clinical Psychology.*

Wagner, E. E. & Heise, M. R. (1981). Rorschach and Hand Test data comparing bipolar patients in manic and depressive phases. *Journal of Personality Assessment, 45,* 240–249.

Wagner, E. E., & Rinn, R .C. (1994). The Extrapolated Area Response: A pathognomic sign of mania on the Rorschach? *Perceptual and Motor Skills, 78,* 1025–1026.

Wagner, E. E., Wagner, C. F., Hilsenroth, M. J., & Fowler, C. (1995). A taxonomy of Rorschach autisms with implications for differential diagnosis among thinking disordered patients. *Journal of Clinical Psychology, 51,* 290–293.

22

Using Metaphor to Understand Projective Test Data: A Training Heuristic

Mark J. Hilsenroth
University of Arkansas

the weaver's masterpiece,
… a thousand threads one treadle throws,
Where Fly the shuttles hither and thither,
Unseen the threads are knit together,
And an infinite combination grows.

—Goethe, *Faust*

Metaphors express comparisons and highlight features or relational qualities that do not exist within the same domain. Yet these comparisons often aid in the comprehension and understanding of one or both of the concepts expressed in the metaphor. We may use the preceding quote from Goethe to help illustrate this point in that one way in which to understand an individual's personality is as an intricately woven tapestry, with each thread representing different experiences and traits. The many different qualities of each thread (i.e., length, texture, color, etc.) and the way in that they are combined produce a unique work. Although many single threads exist, these are subordinate to the coherent whole of the individual.

Langer (1976) considered metaphor to be both a process and a product of thought. Utilizing metaphor as a process enables us to understand one kind of thing or experience in terms of another (Johnson, 1981). A second important aspect of metaphor is the ability to embody and evoke feelings. Santostefano (1984) viewed metaphors as providing information on how actions and emotions are construed. Metaphors also appear to play a significant role in learning new material (Duit, 1991). The significance of metaphor to the learning process is most likely related to the process of generating associations between knowledge that is already available and concepts to be learned. Thus the process of metaphorical thought taps new, different, or deeper levels of meaning that aid in the synthesis of elements that are often disparate.

Many believe that the role of metaphor is essential to the learning process (Ballim, Wilks, & Barnden, 1991; Carbonell, 1982; Hobbs, 1983a, 1983b; Johnson, 1987; Lakoff, 1987; Lakoff & Johnson, 1980). Previous research has shown that the use of metaphors and an understanding of metaphorical interpretation significantly enhances the learning of new material (Evans, 1988; Evans & Evans, 1989; Gentner, 1982, 1983; Reed, Ernst, & Banerji, 1974; Rigney & Lutz, 1976; Royer & Cable, 1975, 1976; Russell, 1986; Schustack & Anderson, 1979). Recently there have been concerted efforts to supply teachers with recommendations for the design and use of instructional metaphors that highlight specific aspects of their curriculum (Bonnett, 1991; Duit, 1991; Nicola, 1992; Williams, 1988). Underlying the significance of metaphor in the learning endeavor is the notion that students construct their own understanding within the framework of existing cognitive structures, which can then be subsequently modified through experience.

Metaphor can also be a vehicle for experiencing the world and conveying those experiences to others and is therefore a prominent feature in various art mediums, such as theater, poetry, storytelling, and visual images (Langer, 1957). This occurs in a symbolic representation, through various mediums, of an individual's personal experience. The methods by which people organize this symbolic transformation of language, artistic expressions, or music is seen to be highly personal and may reveal patterns of that individual's thought. It is in this use of past associations and experiences to organize unstructured tasks or create images that the concept of metaphor is useful in projective test data interpretation.

Because new information is understood by relating it to previously comprehended material, metaphors are powerful devices for extending and understanding knowledge, as they build bridges from the known to the unknown through deep-level comparisons. It is in this capacity of exploring themes, the process of discovery, and the development of insight that the concept of metaphor has been most utilized by psychoanalytic theorists, therapists, and diagnosticians in the past.

The interpretation of projective test data is one of the most difficult tasks that students learn. Students typically struggle with the material, searching for a way to express their unformed thoughts, unable to find the elusive avenue to the patient's experience. Paradoxically, the more they struggle the less they can utilize intuition and are unable to gain a deeper understanding of the patient. The integration of metaphor and its relationship to psychodynamic psychology offer one method for the conceptualization of projective test data that utilizes a first-person proximal, precis approach. This approach advocates projective data be viewed as a metaphorical expression of the individual who produced it and emphasizes the development of empathic/inferential skills that students already possess (see Potash, chap. 9 of this volume).

PROJECTIVE TECHNIQUES
AND PSYCHOANALYTIC THEORY

Projective methods in personality assessment provide a clinician with a window through which to understand an individual, by the analysis of responses to ambiguous or vague stimuli. An individual's response(s) to the projective stimulus are thought to reflect his or her internal needs, emotions, past experience, thought processes, relational patterns, and aspects of behavior. Moreover, projective methods involve the presentation of a stimulus designed to evoke highly individualized meaning and organization. No limits on response are arbitrarily set, but rather, the individual is encouraged to explore an infinite range of possibilities in relating their private world of meanings, significance, affect, and organization (Frank, 1939).

A common example of how personality is expressed through projection, in the interpretation of a vague stimulus, can be observed when a young boy sees a shadow outside his window during a thunderstorm, which he perceives a monster trying to get into his room. This interpretation is a projection of his fear onto the shadow. The image itself is neutral, it is neither good nor bad, but to the child it is a projection of inner dynamics sitting alone in bed, afraid of the natural forces at work beyond his room, over which he has no control.

Although creativity and an understanding of the theory supporting the projective hypothesis can provide the clinician with an infinite number of ways in which projective data may be elicited, a complete enumeration of the various methods that provide a medium for projection is beyond the scope of this chapter. These methods are highly unstructured and also call on the individual to create the data from personal experience. It suffices to say that wheras the instruments may differ, the results of these methods provide ready access to rich unconscious material.

Rapaport was the first person to lay down an organized set of principles concerning the manner in which psychoanalytic theory could enrich test data beyond a simple evaluation of a set of scores. He did this by offering the clinician a way in which to conceptualize diagnosis and etiology of disorders that provide relevant clues to therapeutic material (Rapaport, 1942; Rapaport, Gill, & Schafer, 1945). Central to Rapaport's ideas was the interplay between theory and testing as a synergistic process by which each one has much to gain from the other. Where Rapaport led, others were quick to follow in further expanding the relationship between projective testing and psychoanalytic theory (Schafer, 1954). This movement has recently blossomed into a number of books and articles in which the relationship between projective testing and various aspects of psychoanalytic theory (e.g., object relation; self psychology; structural, drive, and defense paradigms). The integration of cognitive and analytic theory in the understanding of projective data (Westen, Lohr, Silk, & Kerber, 1985) have also been explored. Furthermore, many contemporary theorists have delineated the role that psychoanalytic theory can play in understanding an individual in the assessment process (Jaffe, 1990; Lerner, 1991; Smith, 1990; Sugarman, 1991; Willock, 1992). Projective testing has also provided an avenue to investigate diagnostic, etiological, and therapeutic constructs of psychoanalytic theory. Conversely, there has also been a significant contribution concerning the method(s) by which psychoanalytic constructs have aided clinicians in better understanding their test results.

However, little direction has been offered concerning the methods by which one can develop clinical-intuitive skills in students (Handler, 1985; Lerner, 1990). These skills would help link data and theory in an effort to forge a deeper understanding of the individual. Several recent attempts have been made in this direction through the format of symposia concerning the teaching of personality assessment (Brabender, 1992; Handler, 1992) and by a recent task force developing a set of guidelines for training in personality assessment (Ritzler, 1993). Although there can admittedly be no substitute for the experience of working with projective methods on clinical cases, a number of questions need to be addressed. They include the following: How can one foster the development of clinical skills in a way that maximizes learning opportunities? Can a teaching heuristic be developed that might help students to use projective data in a manner that enriches their knowledge of an indiviudal's experience? Are there some systematic strategies that illuminate the relationship between psychoanalytic theory and responses to projective techniques that are easily digestible to the novice and that may aid in the development of clinical skills?

Responding to the extant need for a formal approach in the training of diagnostic interpretation, this chapter presents one heuristic method to help students better understand the qualitative aspects of projective test data. This training heuristic utilizes the concept of metaphor as a vehicle to learn about the individual from an experience-near, psychoanalytically informed perspective. I first review the past use of metaphor in psychoanalytic theory, therapy, and projective testing. Having exposed the reader to the usefulness of metaphor in this context, I then describe the formal aspects of my thesis by presenting the theoretical rationale and a number of clinical examples for an interpretive heuristic that illustrate how the various aspects of metaphoric thought can aid in the deciphering of projective test data. Related to the use of metaphor is the concept of creativity on which I will comment before concluding with a summarization of how the nature of metaphor, both as a product and process of thought, lends itself to the conceptualization of projective material in a manner that aids in understanding interpretation.

PAST USE OF METAPHOR IN PSYCHOANALYTIC THEORY AND THERAPY

It is not surprising that the use of metaphor permeates many aspects of psychoanalysis when one considers that Freud employed metaphor in his writing quite frequently. Edelson (1983) pointed out that metaphor is a necessary part of Freud's formulation and exposition of his scientific theories. It is evident throughout his work that Freud used metaphors to explain (e.g., "The interpretation of dreams is the royal road to a knowledge of the unconscious activities of the mind," Freud, 1900/1959b, p. 608); to lend continuity (e.g., "there are paths along which wishful impulses may be dealt with,", Freud, 1915/1959c, p. 226); to integrate various aspects of his theory (e.g., "In its relation to the id it [the ego] is like a man on horseback, who has to hold in check the superior strength of the horse," Freud, 1923/1959a, p. 25); and to describe clinical examples (e.g., "if we throw a crystal to the floor, it breaks; but not into haphazard pieces. It comes apart along its lines of cleavage into fragments whose boundaries, though they were invisible, were predetermined by the crystal's structure. Mental patients are split and broken structures of this same kind," Freud, 1933/1959d, p. 59).

The concept and use of metaphor has also aided clinicians in the practice of therapy. The effectiveness of metaphors in psychotherapy has been elaborated by many clinicians over the years (Aleksandrowitz,1962; Ekstein, 1966; H. R. Pollio, Barlow, Fine, & Pollio, 1977; Reider, 1972; Sharpe, 1940; Shengold, 1981; Voth, 1970; Wright, 1976). The sum of this inquiry readily shows metaphor to be a rich vehicle of information through which the patient informs the therapist of inner states, experiences, struggles, and emotions. However, Arlow (1979) viewed the concept of metaphor as well as the use of metaphor as an integral feature of therapeutic communications, fundamental in the psychoanalytic process. Although he believed that metaphors are a vital source of information upon which essential reconstruction and insights may be built, Arlow also viewed the concept of metaphor as implicit in the psychotherapeutic process:

> Transference, perhaps the most significant instrumentality of psychoanalytic technique, and metaphor both mean exactly the same thing. They both refer to the carrying over of the meaning from one set of situations to another. The transference in the psychoanalytic situation represents a metaphorical mis-apprehension of the relationship to the analyst. The patient says, feels, and thinks one thing about a specific person, the analyst, although really meaning another person, an object from childhood. Thus meaning is carried over from one set of situations, from experiences or fantasies of the early years, to another situation, a current therapeutic interaction in which the old signifi-cance are meaningless and irrelevant. Transference in the analytic situation is a particularly intense, lived-out metaphor of the patient's neurosis. (p. 382)

Arlow (1979) interpreted aspects of the self to be metaphorically expressed via relationships in psychotherapy. In a similar manner productions elicited from projective tests can also be interpreted as metaphorical experiences, relation-ships, and feelings of the person's inner world.

PRECURSORS OF THE CONCEPTUALIZATION
OF PROJECTIVE DATA AS A METAPHOR
OF THE SELF

The idea of viewing responses to projective data as a metaphor of the self is not a new one. Similar to the metaphorical approach to projective data being presented here is the work of Piotrowski (1957, 1971) whose ideas on the interpretation of the Rorschach and dreams are particularly salient. In *Perceptanalysis* (1957) Piotrowski offered a reconceptualization of the human movement response (M) of the Rorschach. He defined M as reflecting an individual's "prototypal roles in life" (p. 141) meaning that a person will perceive M in a manner that is parallel to his or her own behavior and action tendencies. For example a 48-year-old woman gave the following response to Card III on the Rorschach:

> Free association: looks like two women talking while they are preparing dinner.
>
> Inquiry: Two women there and there. They are preparing dinner, adding ingredients, spices and such, stirring it up in a bowl. They're discussing the recipe and cooking in general.

The prototypal life role being exhibited in this response is not that this woman likes to cook. In fact, she may, but the prototypal role is of a person who will engage and interact with others in a cooperative and supportive manner. One can see how Piotrowski viewed the interpretation of M as that individual adding aspects of his or her self-experience in the organization of a response to an ambiguous form. Much like Piotrowski, Mayman (1977) and Blatt (1990) also suggested that M is directly related to an individual's self-experience and relational patterns.

Piotrowski (1971) also proposed two related axioms in which to approach the interpretation of dreams. He stated that every dream figure not only represents the dreamer, but also reflects that individual's attitudes, feelings, and thoughts. These dream axioms are also quite similar to the formulations of Jung (1953) who viewed dream content as symbolized aspects of the dreamer's own personality. I believe that these approaches to understanding dreams and the definition of M can be extended to aid in the interpretation of all projective data, including dreams, figure drawings, TAT responses, or early memories. The extension of these principles to all projective techniques may help the clinician better to understand that individual's experience, thoughts, and feelings. Psychoanalytic inquiry into early memories can also reveal a gold mine of themes that are representative of that individual's emotions and personality style as well as preconceptions of the self and others (Langs, 1965; Mayman, 1968; Mayman & Farris, 1960). Concerning interpretation Mayman stated "Character structure is organized around object-relational themes that intrude projectively into the structure and content of his early memories, just as they occur repetitively in his relations with significant persons in life" (p. 304).

Bruhn (1992) recently expanded upon the work of Mayman, advocating an interpretive precis for early memories. This approach utilizes thematic analysis to summarize the essential needs, wishes, expectations, major beliefs, and unresolved issues present in an individual's early memories into a short declarative self-statement (usually beginning with "I will", "I feel," or "I am"). The precis method can provide one way to clarify, understand, and simplify a basic process in the interpretation of early memories. An application of the precis method is: A young woman's earliest memory was of being on a playground and falling off a jungle gym in front of many other children who just stared at the foible silently, at that time she ran from the playground feeling stupid and embarrassed, not to return for the rest of the day. Bruhn's precis for this early memory goes as follows: "When I encounter difficulties with an achievement task, I feel embarrassed and self-conscious and (rather than continue to struggle) I withdraw [to avoid further risk of failing again] (p. 327).

As with Piotrowski's work, I believe that both Mayman's conceptualizations and Bruhn's precis for understanding early memories can be used effectively to provide a basic approach to the interpretation of all projective material. Also, one can again observe a parallel between the conceptualization of responses to projective methods and metaphor, both as a production and expression of the self.

However, it was not until the work of Miale (1977) that a clinician first labeled data from a projective technique, the Rorschach, as a metaphor of the self. Miale suggested that Rorschach symbols may be viewed as a self-referent, faithfully representing the inner states and character structure of that individual. She believed that "the clinician can understand an aspect of the symbol by treating it as though it were a metaphor for some aspect of the personality" (p. 441). In the same work, Miale undertook a study to determine whether her assumptions about the metaphoric nature of Rorschach symbols could aid novices' interpretations of personality attributes from a content analysis of Rorschach responses. Results showed that individuals who were instructed to interpret the content of a response as a metaphor reflecting the self produced more accurate descriptions of a subject's personality, and these individuals did significantly better than those who did not utilize a metaphoric approach to interpretation. This work mirrors that of educational researchers who have shown the concept of metaphor to be useful in understanding of projective data (see Handler, Fowler, & Hilsenroth, chap. 24 of this volume; Waehler & Sivec, chap. 6 of this volume). I also believe that the concept of metaphor can aid clinicians in the interpretation of narrative data obtained from projective stimuli as well as providing a conceptual framework for a training heuristic. This approach will integrate the various aspects of metaphor with a wide assortment of projective techniques.

METAPHOR AS PROVIDING AN INTERPRETIVE FRAMEWORK

Much of the recent work in psychoanalytic assessment has stressed the need for clinicians to utilize an experience-near approach when attempting to analyze projective data (Handler, 1985; Lerner, 1992). This experiential approach to the data can be summarized by the following axiom: *To understand an individual,* one must first adopt the mode of thought that allowed that person to produce his or her response. You must try to perceive the stimuli in the same manner in which the individual arrived at the response. However, statements like "adopt someone's mode of thought," "become intimately involved with the data," and "get into someone's head" may be perplexing to students if they are not provided with an example or frame of reference in which to understand these interpretive techniques. I believe that concept of metaphor may provide such a vehicle for students to develop and hone their inferential skills.

Metaphor has been described as a process where one thing or experience is understood through another, and therefore this is identical to the hypothesis underlying all projective interpretation. Metaphor can be understood as a product of an expression of the self via art. Likewise, many projective tests tap an individual's artistic expression through the drawing of figures, storytelling, and in the nature of unstructured situations or play. Also, these symbolic representations of art and projective data can reveal highly personal nuances of that individual's thoughts and experiences. In many ways the relationship between an individual and his or her responses to projective techniques can be considered metaphorical or *projective data can be viewed as a metaphor of the experiences, feelings, and relationships of the self.*

This way of conceptualizing projective data may be quite useful in that it directs the student to think of a response as representing some aspect of the person who gave it. Understanding the data as a self-referent is the first step before one can adopt an alternative viewpoint or become intimately involved with a response. I suspect it is at this point that many students run into their first obstacle in the interpretation of projective data, not because they cannot vicariously empathize with the experience of another, but rather, because they do not know how to frame the various responses in a manner that promotes this loss of distance. This is where I believe an expansion of Bruhn's (1992) precis system may prove useful in setting the stage for a clinician to enact the experiences that are communicated to him or her.

As I indicated previously, Bruhn (1992) examined an early memory, extracting from it the basic theme, and presented it in a self-statement (i.e., "When I encounter difficulties with an achievement task, I feel embarrassed and self-conscious ... "). I would likewise utilize this procedure with other projective methods as a starting point to an experiential interpretation. Some general precis stems that may aid in framing the themes encountered in projective tests would include, but are not limited to, "I am," "I feel," "I experience the world as," "My relationships with others are," and "I experience others as." Often it will be possible to frame a theme from a response in several different ways and this will reveal various aspects of the personality. Thus, the precis approach may aid students in generating hypotheses about a patient's personality organization.

Before presenting some examples, I would like to preface these with some cautionary notes on interpretation. First, although I will develop interpretive precis based on just one response, this is done for instructional purposes only. I would advocate developing an interpretive framework of themes that appear in a number of different responses and across different tests, as they would be most representative of that individual's personality (Brooks, 1983). Second, it is the purpose of this chapter to present a heuristic method designed to explain and utilize the qualitative aspects of projective data rather than quantitative scoring. However, I would strongly discourage the sole use of qualitative data in the overall diagnosis and formulation of a report. To effect a complete assessment one must also utilize the quantitative aspects of scoring as well as information gathered from the interaction during the testing procedures (Handler, 1985; Phillips, 1992; Schafer, 1954; Sugarman, 1981, 1991).

Let us now walk through an example of extracting various themes from some projective material that helps to construct an interpretive framework. A 32-year-old man seeks therapy at an outpatient clinic following a divorce. During an intake evaluation he responds to card 17BM of the TAT described by Murray (1943) as "A naked man … clinging to a rope. He is in the act of climbing up or down" (Murray, 1943) in the following manner:

> (58") Hummm, well this guy is a freshman in a high school gym class who tried to do that rope climbing thing. He was trying to climb it but the rope was too slick and he lost his grip and slid down. (29", prompt for thinking and feeling) he's thinking that it's just too hard to do and he feels like he doesn't want to try it again. (24' prompt for a long-term outcome or resolution) well, maybe he'll be able to climb it someday, … hopefully.

Understanding this story as a metaphorical expression of the self, one can glean a good deal of information as to how this man experiences not only himself but the world around him as well. I believe that most novices in personality assessment could develop the following list of precis for this man associated with his response: I have trouble trying to master tasks that are strenuous and demanding; I experience the world as a place that is hard to get a hold of and often it slips through my fingers or passes me by; I will avoid things at which I have failed previously.

Using this precis as a starting point, the student is provided with an idea of how to begin to conceptualize this patient's experience in the world and in effect is given a map to a "place" where this man's experience is to be found. Using these precis as a target, I believe most students could adopt this man's mode of thought and vicarious experience aspects of this individual. Most accessible in mulling over these statements is a sense of lethargy, malaise, futility, and withdrawal associated with depression. Feelings of not being able to effect the environment, failure in attempting to master tasks, and being ashamed of his inabilities abound in the "place" from which this response was given.

To become experience-near with this material, and subsequently with the patient, will require the student to search his or her past experience in order to recall when he or she has felt similarly. To share the patient's experience one must share the feelings of depression and failure by accessing one's own similar feelings. This "loss of distance" is an example of what Kris (1952) called "adaptive regression in service of the ego" (p. 177). The regression is adaptive because it will help one to empathize and understand the experience of the patient. It is regressive in that the clinician returns to a time when he or she felt similarly. Becoming reconnected to reality and organizing the information that has been obtained in a creative and meaningful manner is to accomplish this task in the service of the ego. If the clinician can experience the character in the story, he or she can also experience the person who told it (see Handler & Riethmiller, chap. 16 of this volume). The story, drawing, memory, or image is a metaphorical expression of the person producing it. Regarding this process Kris stated, "We started out a part of the world which the artist created; we end as cocreators: we identify ourselves with the artist" (p. 56) From this identification we are better able to reach the place of a patient's experience.

However, once in this place of shared experience, it is crucial that the student address such questions as: What issues will be important to work on in the therapy? How might these issues be addressed? and How might this individual respond to various therapeutic interventions? It is at this point of empathic attunement that a student may reconstruct as individual's experience and apply this knowledge to other situations. By engaging in this exercise, a student not only gains insight into the phenomenological experience of an individual via their projective productions, but will also develop clinical-intuitive skills.

METAPHOR IN UNDERSTANDING
· RELATIONSHIP PARADIGMS

At its most basic level metaphor expresses relational features between two objects or concepts, which at first glance appear dissimilar. As a product of thought, metaphor can also be viewed as a transformation of symbolic aspects within the self into an artistic creation. Central to the understanding of art as a metaphorical product of thought is the tenet that this external production is inextricably related to an internal representation of the artist. As I discussed earlier, this metaphorical approach to the interpretation of art is identical to the formulations of clinicians (Blatt, 1990; Mayman, 1977; Piotrowski, 1957) who interpret relational themes evinced on projective techniques to be representative of that individual's actual interaction patterns. In essence a person will perceive relationship paradigms in projective tests that most reflect their experience of relationships in their day-to-day life. I now present some examples that highlight the metaphorical approach to understanding relationship patterns and integrate these with the interpretive framework that was described in the preceding section.

For instance, an early memory of eating or being fed can aid in diagnosis and inform a clinician of important themes that may arise in the therapeutic relationship (Fowler, Hilsenroth, & Handler, 1995). Knowledge of certain aspects of object relations theory is helpful in answering this question. Within object relations theory, an eating metaphor is often used to conceptualize the incorporation or introjection of affectively laden memories. Imagine, if you will, a child at his or her birthday party with many guests, presents, and activities.

During the course of the party the child experiences a number of very emotional moments (i.e., receives a much desired toy, blows out the candles of his or her birthday cake, gets hugged and kissed by his or her mother, plays an especially fun game, etc.). During the day the child takes in these memories and incorporates these experiences as aspects of the self. In a metaphorical nature one could say the child "takes in," "eats," or "digests" more than just birthday cake, and these experiences help the child to develop a sense of identity in the same manner that a well-balanced meal helps to sustain and nurture the body.

Querying for early memories of "feeding, being fed, or eating" often stimulates important interpersonal conflicts or tensions around the acceptance of nurturance and dependency, which is an especially important theme in the patient–therapist relationship (Fowler et al., 1995). With this in mind, let us examine the eating/being fed early memory of a 16-year-old girl utilizing a metaphorical approach to understanding her relationship patterns and integrating this knowledge into an interpretive framework:

> The whole family was eating dinner one night, I was probably about five or six, and my mother put cream corn on my plate and it had run into my other food. I hated cream corn and she knew that but put it on my plate anyway. She told me I had to eat everything on my plate or I couldn't have dessert. So I just sat there and stared off into space. After about an hour she just got fed up with me and sent me to my room. (How did you feel when that happened?) Relieved, I got out of eating cream corn.

Some precis to be derived from this early memory would include: In my relationships I will often become embroiled in power struggles; if others do not give me what I want I will ignore their existence; and, I experience the world as an overbearing and intrusive place. With specific regard to the theme of accepting nurturance and dependence, one might develop the following statement: if I don't like any part of what you have to offer, I won't take any of it, nor will I show remorse when rejecting you. From these themes a student may begin to predict how a therapy might ensue and what problems would arise. The informed clinician would guess that this young lady's therapist will have a difficult time establishing rapport and a female therapist, in particular, would probably find herself caught in a quickly developing, aggressive transference. This girl was in fact on an inpatient adolescent unit and was being treated for anorexia nervosa when she was tested. Prior to admission she was vomiting into plastic zip-lock bags, which she would subsequently hide around the house for her mother to find while cleaning.

It is not always an easy task to place oneself in the phenomenological world of another, especially if that person is extremely disturbed. The following case illustrates how it is sometimes very difficult, even for experienced diagnosticians, to adopt the viewpoint of a very disturbed individual. The following is a response to Card III of the Rorschach by a 38-year-old female inpatient, diagnosed with Borderline Personality Disorder:

Free Association: It looks like two witches standing over a body, ... ripping it apart and throwing gobbets of blood at each other.

Inquiry: the corpse is in the middle, blood in the middle and at the top, two witches here and here (What about it makes it look like blood?) It's red. (Witches?) They're black and have pointy noses. (Throwing?) Yeah, they're sticking their hands into the body and scooping out blood to throw at each other. I guess they're having a blood fight.

In organizing a framework of the themes associated with this response, we immediately run into the problem concerning which perspective should be developed in the descriptive statements, that of the corpse or that of the witches? One answer to this question is provided by the work of Piotrowski (1971) and Jung (1953), who viewed every figure in a dream to be metaphorically representative of some aspect of the dreamer. Therefore, both the witches and the corpse can be viewed as representing aspects of the patient's personality. With this in mind, one can develop an interpretive framework for this woman's response that may be informed by the perception of the witches: My relationships are grossly violent, intense, and hostile; I view myself as wicked and barely human; I experience the world as an aggressive and dangerous place; and take what I want from others, only to throw it away. One can also hypothesize on how this woman has developed these self-representations by integrating the aspects of the corpse into the interpretation: Others have taken from me what I needed to survive; I am dead and drained of life; I have learned to take from others as I have been taken from; in my world I need to do things in order to survive, which has degraded my sense of humanity, respect for others and myself. A case could even be made that the blood also represents some aspect of the self. A precis underlying a thrown gob of blood might be: I am an unbounded and formless mass, which is out of control, an interpretation that is not incongruous with the rest of this patient's clinical picture.

After these precis have been organized it will be up to the clinician to dare to adopt such a primitive outlook of this patient. This is often only the first challenging task to be undertaken in work with patients suffering from severe character pathology (Kernberg, 1984). However, this loss of distance, although unpleasant, offers valuable information and insight into the patient's world. Specifically, a therapist will often experience aggressive countertransference feelings when working with this group of patients. One method that I have found useful in defusing this hostile affect is to remind myself that whereas I can imagine myself in their malevolent world and can then leave, they cannot leave their world. This realization restores my empathy with the patient and often redoubles my efforts to help the patient extricate him or herself from this destructive place.

Before leaving this example, it is instructive to the reader to turn back to the Rorschach response to Card III, given by the 48-year-old woman, earlier in this chapter (p. 396): Two women, who were preparing dinner, discussing the recipe, and so on. This woman responded to the same card (Card III) as the borderline patient just described, but their creations to explain the same stimuli are radically different. I would ask that you imagine how these women differ in the kinds of lives they lead, their experiences of the world, the type of relationships they have, how they might view themselves, and how they each experience emotions.

METAPHOR IN UNDERSTANDING
EMOTIONAL EXPERIENCE

The concept of metaphor can also be used to understand the emotional material that is contained in projective test responses. As Santostefano (1984) indicated, metaphors convey more than just information about a concept; they also impart the feeling and emotional content of the material. The emotional experience expressed in metaphorical representations may offer information not only about that individual's feelings, but also in determining the affective valence in his or her relationships. An example of this can be seen in a Kinetic Family Drawing (Burns & Kaufman, 1970) of a 9-year-old girl. In her drawing, this young lady placed her father away from the rest of the family, in a building "at work." Also of note was that her father was the only figure in the entire picture that was drawn in black crayon, whereas the other figures were drawn in various colors. When she was asked about this she replied, "Daddy doesn't have any colors in him." Developing an interpretive precis concerning this aspect of the drawing might go as follows: I experience my father as distant and lacking emotion (toward me and/or others). What is also significant to note in this case is that at the time of this drawing the parents of the girl had recently separated, with the father leaving the house. Her father would soon enter treatment and would be diagnosed with depression, that helps to explain why the girl drew him as colorless and distant.

As stated earlier, interpretative themes should be developed across a number of tests and those that are recurrent should be used to build an interpretive model. In this next example, I explore responses on two different projective tests from the same individual in order to show the continuity of emotional expression. A 37-year-old man at an inpatient hospital gave the following response to Card X of the Rorschach:

> (42") Free association: It looks like a futuristic machine, a carnival ride from the future, but it's not working, it's broken.
>
> Inquiry: It looks like something you'd see in a carnival, except it's from the future. It looks like if you pumped hot air through it, it would inflate and spin around. They probably play music that the children like while it's spinning. (What about it makes it look like a carnival ride?) All of the different colors. (What does it look like now?) It's all deflated and lying around on the ground, someone musta let all of the air out of it.

He also responded to Card 9BM of the TAT described by Murray (1943) as: "Four men in overalls are lying the grass taking it easy" (p. 19) in the following way:

(23") It's a bunch of cowboys sleeping. They were on one of those long cattle drives that take weeks to do. They worked hard day and night and didn't get much sleep until they finally made it to cattle town where they sold off the herd to be slaughtered. They went out and partied too after they got paid, they're pretty much out of it for a couple of days. (prompt for thinking and feeling?) They're glad to be done with the stampede and feeling tired and worn out. (long-term resolution/outcome?) They'll ride back home and next season do it all over again.

What themes indicative of this man's emotional experience can we generate that occur in both responses? The precis that best seems to summarize both is: I am drained and exhausted after a period of activity and fun. Also the potential for this pattern of behavior to be repeated is present in the themes of both responses; the carnival ride is most likely to be inflated again and the cattle drive will reoccur next season. Imagine yourself on a repetitive emotional roller-coaster rides of emotional highs and lows. This cyclical theme is consistent with the bipolar disorder diagnosis for which this man was being hospitalized.

This metaphorical approach in the development of a precis is but one training method with which to approach projective data and is designed to aid in the development of inferential skills. An expert in the interpretation of projective data would undoubtedly view the set of precis from the TAT example (Card 16BM) given earlier (p. 399), of the 32-year-old man seeking treatment at an outpatient clinic, to describe very general and basic elements of this individual's personality. The expert might point out that taking such a long time in responding to the task may indicate the delicate nature of the mastery issues presented in this response. In identifying the person in the picture as a freshman in high school, someone in early to midadolescence, one might consider the figural issue to be moving from a latency to genital level of development, which is also supported in this patient's inability to hold onto the rope and climb into the adult world to assert himself. His need to be prompted for the thoughts and feelings of the character may indicate a defensive style of withdrawal from painful situations, both cognitively and affectively. This interpretation is also supported by the subsequent behavior of the character in the story. It would also be important to note that even when prompted the patient still does not offer a feeling, but instead states, "He feels like he doesn't want to try it again." From a drive perspective he is sliding down the rope and doesn't have the energy or capacity to try to climb again. From a relational perspective, his story is devoid of others, which also adds support for the interpretation that he is feeling alone and isolated. A skilled therapist might also see the paradox that must be addressed in therapy as: In not trying to attain mastery I avoid taking the chance of feeling worse, but in doing so I also avoid the chance to succeed (Winnicott, 1971). Encouragingly, this man will probably benefit from therapy should an initial rapport be established, because he does have hope that some day he may succeed, although it is tentatively expressed.

All this information, and possibly more, might be readily apparent to the experienced clinician. However, it is not the purpose of this chapter to give an expert account of projective responses, but instead to outline a structured training heuristic that utilizes the concept of metaphor as an explanatory vehicle. It is not enough for experts to show students what they know. Rather, they need to show students how they arrived at their conclusions. The precis formulations that I have presented are basic and general descriptions of personality dynamics. These basic presentations facilitate understanding and outline a clear succession of steps that are easy to follow. It is important for teachers and supervisors not only to demonstrate their clinical prowess through a loss of distance with the projective material, but to also apply these same principles of vicarious empathy in order to present information to their students in a clear manner, and to facilitate students in their ability to use vicarious empathy in their clinical work.

Often it is the case that expert clinicians may not be expert instructors. Research in cognitive psychology suggests this problem may be endemic to expertise, as expert decision making is often carried out in a manner that is unconscious, automatic, and not mediated by verbal activity (Anderson, 1983; H. Dreyfus & S. Dreyfus, 1986; Fitts & Posner, 1967). One way in which to circumvent this breakdown in the learning process is to imagine what is described in Zen as the concept of "beginner's mind." In the state of beginners mind the Zen master suspends what he knows in order to place himself in the role of the student (Herrigal, 1981; Suzuki, 1970). From this position of empathy he can more readily evaluate how to present material to students in an orderly and logical progression, which facilitates understanding. Likewise, expert psychodiagnosticians must be able to use their intuitive abilities to understand what their students need throughout the training process and to provide them with clear structured principles.

Before moving on I would like to review the interpretive process being presented here. First, one utilizes the concept of metaphor to understand projective data as an expression of the self. From this conceptualization, the interpreter develops a number of self-statements or precis based on the salient themes observed in the data. After a number of precis are collected for responses in and across different measures, a list of those statements that occur with some frequency should be compiled. From this list of precis, the student is provided with a framework in which to imagine him or herself in the experience of another. After an alternative mode of thought has been adopted by a student, he or she is encouraged to explore an array of experiences from this perspective, especially aspects related to the therapeutic interaction. This ability to develop an interpretive framework by which to understand and engage the experience of another is a highly creative and dynamic process.

THE ROLE OF CREATIVITY
IN THE PRODUCTION AND INTERPRETATION
OF PROJECTIVE NARRATIVE DATA

The role of creativity from both a psychoanalytic and cognitive science perspective is important in the production and understanding of projective material.

From the psychoanalytic viewpoint, the work of Winnicott (1971) and Kris (1952) can be particularly helpful in understanding the creative mechanism that allows individuals to express themselves in a novel manner. Winnicott's concept of play and transitional phenomena can aid in understanding responses to projective stimuli. From this perspective, the response to a projective stimulus is carried out in a transitional sphere that represents "an immediate area of experience, to which inner reality and external life both contribute" (p. 2). In Kris' theory of creativity, the individual imbues an external stimulus with aspects of the self. This synthesis produces a novel creation that is a unique expression of that individual. Through both of these formulations, we can observe the creative aspects involved in the development of a response to a projective technique. In responding to the stimulus, the subject experiences various aspects of the test and assigns personal meaning to the stimuli, which are then relayed to the outside world via the mechanism of projection. Russ (1991) has reported a series of studies employing projective methods in which she documents the relationship between subjects' affective expression, creativity, and convergent and divergent thinking (see Handler, Fowler, & Hilsenroth, chap. 24 of this volume).

Creativity also comes into play when a clinician attempts to decipher the meaning of a projective test response. This act of comprehending is always a dynamic process in which the clinician joins the patient in a cocreative act. A psychodiagnostician's skill in comprehending and responding to an individual's projective responses will play a vital role in communicating a sense of empathy and understanding in the therapeutic alliance. Lakoff and Johnson (1980) noted: "Metaphorical imagination is a crucial skill in creating rapport and in communicating the nature of the unshared experience. This skill consists, in large measure, of the ability to bend your world view and adjust the way you organize your experience" (p. 231). Responses to projective data should not be regarded as any less of a communicative act than more direct, less symbolic forms of communication.

This skill of "metaphorical imagination" appears to be quite similar to recent work in cognitive psychology that views creativity from a problem-solving framework. Simon (1989) conceptualized creativity as arising from a good deal of refining, elaboration, and reformulization of a problem, as well as from unsuccessful attempts at a solution. This cognitive flexibility helps to generate abundant and unique ideas, which are a vital component in the creative process (Guilford, 1959).

These formulations concerning the problem-solving and cognitive flexibility aspects of creativity have been investigated in the area of psychodiagnostic interpretation (Burley & Handler, 1997; Mintz, 1959). Most salient to my thesis is the research conducted by Burley and Handler, who investigated the relationship between accurate DAP test interpretation and the variables of empathy, intuition, and cognitive flexibility. The findings of this study illustrate how an interpretive understanding of the patient is significantly related to all three of these variables, with cognitive flexibility being the best predictor of interpretive ability. The authors described a good interpreter as "an open, empathic person whose thinking is flexible, a person whose openness to the drawings (and through them to the artist) is evident as intuitiveness." Given this body of research it may be quite beneficial for graduate training to include seminars that hone divergent, and critical thinking, as this would aid students in the development of therapy, assessment, research, and theoretical skills.

Creative processes appear to be utilized not only in the use of metaphor, but also in the production and comprehension of responses to projective techniques. The patient and clinician engage in a cocreative act in which information is communicated and where the goal of the interaction is to deepen understanding and rapport. This experience can be likened to a cartographer showing a map to someone, who for the first time sees the origin and delta of the river that runs beside their home.

SUMMARY

A central problem in the education of students learning to use projective techniques has been the lack of well-defined strategies in which to understand content analysis and qualitative inferences. I have attempted to overcome this deficiency by presenting one method for setting up an interpretive framework that utilizes the various aspects of metaphor. The concept of metaphor aids students by emphasizing the conceptualization of projective data as an expression of the self. This, in turn, helps the student to understand various self, relational, and emotional themes that lay the foundation for an empathic connection in which the student may vicariously come to experience another individual's way of "being in the world." Both the production and interpretation of the projective material is seen as a creative process in which information is symbolically communicated.

The relevance of this method can be noted in a number of different ways. First, it is an attempt to distill the process of arriving at an interpretation of a sequence of steps designed to facilitate learning in the beginner. It is my belief that it will be easier for the student to understand the varying aspects of interpretation and methods designed to utilize this information if the process is presented with intermediate steps rather than going directly from the response to an interpretation of that response. Second, this approach is designed to aid students in the generation of possible hypotheses about a patient's character structure. These hypotheses may then be retained or discarded depending on whether or not they receive sufficient support from other assessment data. Third, this method explains how a student may approach an interpretation to initiate a loss of distance in order to experience the world as if he or she were the patient who generated the response. This step is important because achieving this vicarious empathy is facilitated by an organizing framework. Finally, this approach encourages the student to walk a while in the shoes of another, exploring how his or her world is experienced. This understanding is a vital activity, not only in making therapeutic recommendations, but also in developing intuitive skills for all aspects of clinical work.

This metaphorical analysis of projective test data is offered as a heuristic, not an algorithm, to interpretation. Therefore it can be expected that the formulations presented here may not always produce the level of intimacy and insight that one desires. Also, it is important to note that in a comprehensive assessment, precis should be generated for a number of responses across various tests and integrated with structural quantitative scores, countertransference reactions, and behavioral observations. However, I expect that this method may help students to approach projective material in an experiential manner, which will aid them in knitting the threads that contribute to a richer understanding of an individual.

REFERENCES

Aleksandrowitz, D. (1962). The meaning of metaphor. *Bulletin of the Menninger Clinic, 26*, 92–101.

Anderson, J. (1983). *The architecture of cognition*. Cambridge, MA: Harvard University Press.

Arlow, J. (1979). Metaphor and the psychoanalytic situation. *Psychoanalytic Quarterly, 48*, 363–385.

Ballim, A., Wilks, Y., & Barnden, J. (1991). Belief ascription, metaphor, and intentional identification. *Cognitive Science, 15*, 133–171.

Blatt, S. (1990). The Rorschach: A test of perception or an evaluation of representation. *Journal of Personality Assessment, 55*, 394–416.

Bonnett, M. (1991). Developing children's thinking. *Cambridge Journal of Education, 21*, 77–292.

Brabender, V. (1992, March). *Challenges in teaching the Rorschach test*. Symposium conducted at the Society for Personality Assessment mid-winter meeting, San Francisco.

Brooks, R. (1983). Projective techniques in personality assessment. In M. D. Levine, W. B. Carey, A. C. Crocker, & R. T. Gross (Eds.), *Developmental-behavioral pediatrics* (pp. 974–989). Philadelphia: Saunders.

Bruhn, A. (1992). The early memory procedure: A projective test of autobiographical memory part 2. *The Journal of Personality Assessment, 58*, 326–346.

Burley, T., & Handler, L. (1997). Personality factors in the accurate interpretation of projective tests: The Draw-A-Person Test. In E. Hammer (Ed.), *Advances in projective drawing interpretation* (pp. 359–377). Springfield, IL: Thomas.

Burns, R. C., & Kaufman, S. H. (1970). *Kinetic Family Drawings (K-F-D)*. New York: Brunner/Mazel.

Carbonell, J. G. (1982). Metaphor: An inescapable phenomenon in natural language comprehension. In W. Lehnert & M. Ringle (Eds.), *Strategies for natural language processing* (pp. 132–158). Hillsdale, NJ: Lawrence Erlbaum Associates.

Dreyfus, H., & Dreyfus, S. (1986). *Mind over machine*. New York: The Free Press.

Duit, R. (1991). On the role of analogies and metaphors in learning science. *Science Education, 75*, 649–672.

Edelson, J. (1983). Freud's use of metaphor. *Psychoanalytic Study of the Child, 38,* 17–59.

Ekstein, R. (1966). Interpretation with metaphor. In: *Children of time and space, of action and impulse* (pp. 158–165). New York: Appleton–Century–Crofts.

Evans, G. E. (1988). Metaphors as learning aids in university lectures. *Journal of Experimental Education, 58,* 5–19.

Evans, R., & Evans, G. (1989). Cognitive mechanisms in learning from metaphors. *Journal of Experimental Education, 58,* 5–19.

Fitts, P., & Posner, M. (1967) *Human performance.* Belmont, CA: Brooks Cole.

Fowler, J. C., Hilsenroth, M. J., & Handler, L. (1995). Early memories: An exploration of theoretically derived queries and their clinical utility. *Bulletin of the Menninger Clinic, 59,* 79–98.

Frank, L. K. (1939). Projective methods for the study of personality. *Journal of Psychology, 8,* 389–413.

Freud, S. (1959a). The ego and the id. *Standard Edition, 19,* 3–66. London: Hogarth Press. (Original work published 1923)

Freud, S. (1959b). The interpretation of dreams. *Standard Edition,* 4 & 5. London: Hogarth Press. (Original work published 1900)

Freud, S. (1959c). A metapsychological supplement to the theory of dreams. *Standard Edition, 14,* 217–235. London: Hogarth Press. (Original work published 1915)

Freud, S. (1959d). New introductory lectures on psycho-analysis. *Standard Edition, 22,* 3–182. London: Hogarth Press. (Original work published 1933)

Gentner, D. (1982). Are scientific analogies metaphors? In D. S. Mail (Ed.), *Metaphor: Problems and perspectives.* Atlantic Highlands, NJ: Humanities Press.

Gentner, D. (1983). Structure-mapping: A theoretical framework for analogy. *Cognitive Science, 7,* 155–170.

Guilford, J. (1959). *Personality.* New York: McGraw-Hill.

Handler, L. (1985). The clinical use of the Draw-A-Person Test (DAP). In C. Newmark (Ed.), *Major psychological assessment instruments* (pp. 165–216). Boston: Allyn & Bacon.

Handler, L. (1992, March). *Teaching and learning personality assessment.* Symposium conducted at the Society for Personality Assessment Mid-Winter Meeting, San Francisco.

Herrigal, S. (1981). *Zen and the art of archery.* New York: Random House.

Hobbs, J. R. (1983a). Metaphor interpretation as selective inferencing: Cognitive processes in understanding metaphor (Part 1). *Empirical Studies of the Arts, 1,* 17–33.

Hobbs, J. R. (1983b). Metaphor interpretation as selective inferencing: Cognitive processes in understanding metaphor (Part 2). *Empirical Studies of the Arts, 1,* 125–141.

Jaffe, L. (1990). The empirical foundations of psychoanalytic approaches to psychological testing. *Journal of Personality Assessment, 55,* 746–755.

Johnson, M. (Ed.). (1981). *Philosophical perspectives on metaphor.* Minneapolis: University of Minnesota Press.

Johnson, M. (1987). *The body in the mind.* Chicago: Chicago University Press.

Jung, C. G. (1953). *Two essays on analytical psychology.* New York: Pantheon.

Kernberg, O. (1984). *Severe personality disorders.* New Haven, CT: Yale University Press.

Kris, E. (1952). *Psychoanalytic explorations in art.* New York: International Universities Press.

Lakoff, G. (1987). *Women, fire, and dangerous things: What categories reveal about the mind.* Chicago: University of Chicago Press.

Lakoff, G., & Johnson, M. (1980). *Metaphors we live by.* Chicago: University of Chicago Press.

Langer, S. (1957). *Problems of art.* New York: Scribner's.

Langer, S. (1976) *Philosophy in a new key* (3rd ed.). Cambridge, MA: Harvard University Press.

Langs, R. (1965). First memories and characterological diagnosis. *Journal of Nervous and Mental Disorders, 141,* 319– 320.

Lerner, P. (1990). The clinical inference process and the role of theory. *Journal of Personality Assessment, 55,* 426–431.

Lerner, P. (1991). *Psychoanalytic theory and the Rorschach.* Hillsdale, NJ: Analytic Press.

Lerner, P. (1992). Toward an experiential psychoanalytic approach to the Rorschach. *Bulletin of the Menninger Clinic, 56,* 451–464.

Mayman, M. (1968). Early memories and character structure. *Journal of Projective Techniques and Personality Assessment, 32,* 303–316.

Mayman, M. (1977). A multidimensional view of the Rorschach movement response. In M. A. Rickers-Ovsiankina (Ed.), *Rorschach psychology* (2nd ed., pp. 229–250). Huntington, NY: Krieger.

Mayman, M., & Farris, M. (1960). Early memories as the expression of relationship paradigms. *American Journal of Orthopsychiatry, 30,* 507–520.

Miale, F. R. (1977). Symbolic imagery in Rorschach material. In M.A. Rickers-Ovsiankina (Ed.), *Rorschach Psychology* (2nd ed., pp. 421–454). Huntington, NY: Krieger.

Mintz, E. (1959). Relationships between diagnostic errors and personal anxieties of psychologists. (Doctoral dissertation, New York University, 1959). *Dissertation Abstracts, 1959 ,* 3370.

Murray, H. A. (1943). *Thematic Apperception Test.* Cambridge, MA: Harvard University Press.

Nicola, G. (1992). Conceptual content as generating the creative tasks. *Revue Roumaine de Psychologie, 36,* 29–38.

Phillips, L. (1992). A commentary on the relationship between assessment and the conduct of psychotherapy. *The Journal of Training & Practice in Professional Psychology, 6,* 46–52.

Piotrowski, Z. A. (1957). *Perceptanalysis: The Rorschach method fundamentally reworked, expanded, and systematized.* Philadelphia: Ex Libris.

Piotrowski, Z. A. (1971). A rational explanation of the irrational: Freud's and Jung's own dreams reinterpreted. *Journal of Personality Assessment, 35,* 505–518.

Pollio, H. R., Barlow, J. M., Fine, H. J., & Pollio, M. R. (1977). *Psychology and the poetics of growth: Figurative language in psychology, psychotherapy, and education.* Hillsdale, NJ: Lawrence Erlbaum Associates.

Rapaport, D. (1942). Principles underlying projective techniques. *Character and Personality, 10,* 213–219.

Rapaport, D., Gill, M., & Schafer, R. (1945). *Diagnostic psychological testing: The theory, statistical evaluation, and diagnostic application of a battery of tests* (Vols. 1–2). Chicago: Year Book.

Reed, S. K., Ernst, G. W., & Banerji, R. (1974). The role of analogy in transfer between similar problem states. *Cognitive Psychology, 6,* 436–450.

Reider, N. (1972). Metaphor as interpretation. *International Journal of Psycho-analysis*, 53, 463–469.

Rigney, J. W., & Lutz, K. A. (1976). Effect of graphic analogies of concepts in chemistry on learning an attitude. *Journal of Educational Psychology*, 68, 305–311.

Ritzler, B. (1993). SPA task force on training guidelines and credentialing in assessment: Recommendations for minimum standards. *SPA Exchange*, 3, 9–12.

Royer, J. M., & Cable, G. W. (1975). Facilitated learning in connected discourse. *Journal of Educational Psychology*, 67, 116–123.

Royer, J. M., & Cable, G. W. (1976). Illustrations, analogies, and facilitative transfer in prose learning. *Journal of Educational Psychology*, 68, 205–209.

Russ, S. (1991). *Affect and creativity*. Hillsdale, NJ: Lawrence Erlbaum Associates.

Russell, S. (1986). Information and experience in metaphor: A perspective from computer analysis. *Metaphor and Symbolic Activity*, 1, 227–270.

Santostefano, S. (1984). Cognitive control therapy with children: Rationale and technique. *Psychotherapy*, 21, 76–91.

Schafer, R. (1954). *Psychoanalytic interpretation in Rorschach testing*. New York: Grune & Stratton.

Schustack, M., & Anderson, J. R. (1979). Effects of analogy to prior knowledge on memory for new information. *Journal of Verbal Learning and Verbal Behavior*, 18, 565–583.

Sharpe, E. (1940). Psychophysical problems revealed in language: An examination of metaphor. *International Journal of Psycho-analysis*, 21, 201–213.

Shengold, L. (1981). Insight as metaphor. *The Psychoanalytic Study of the Child*, 36, 289–305.

Simon, H. (1989). The scientist as problem solver. In D. Klahr., & K. Kotovsky (Eds.) *Complex information processing: The impact of Herbert A. Simon* (pp. 191–217). Hillsdale, NJ: Lawrence Erlbaum Associates.

Smith, B. (1990). Potential space and the Rorschach: An application of object relations theory. *Journal of Personality Assessment*, 55, 756–767.

Sugarman, A. (1981). The diagnostic use of countertransference reactions in psychological testing. *Bulletin of the Menninger Clinic*, 45, 475–490.

Sugarman, A. (1991). Where's the beef? Putting personality back into personality assessment. *Journal of Personality Assessment*, 56, 130–144.

Suzuki, S. (1970). *Zen mind, beginner's mind*. New York: Weatherhill.

Voth, H. (1970). The analysis of metaphor. *Journal of the American Psychoanalytic Association*, 18, 599–621.

Westen, D., Lohr, N., Silk, K. & Kerber, K. (1985). *Measuring object relations and social cognition using the TAT: Scoring manual*. Ann Arbor: University of Michigan.

Williams, P. S. (1988). Going west to get eat: Using metaphors as instructional tools. *Journal of Children in Contemporary Society*, 20, 79–98.

Willock, B. (1992). Projection, Transitional Phenomena, and the Rorschach. *Journal of Personality Assessment*, 59, 99–116.

Winnicott, D. W. (1971). *Playing and reality*. New York: Basic Books.

Wright, K. (1976). Metaphor and symptom: A study of integration and its failure. *International Review of Psychoanalysis*, 3, 97–109.

23

Teaching Dissemination of Personality Assessment Results in Graduate Programs

Barry A. Ritzler
Long Island University

A DEFINITION

Dissemination refers to any communication of assessment results including report writing, formal verbal consultations, and less formal conversations. Formal consultations typically take place in sessions with professional colleagues, clients, and the clients' significant others in which information from assessment is used to promote understanding of the client's personality. Less formalized dissemination may occur in team meetings, therapy sessions, family meetings, or anywhere the client's personality is discussed.

In most graduate programs, report writing is the primary, and often the only form of dissemination taught. Students usually have several opportunities to practice and to be evaluated for report writing. Many programs, however, give little opportunity for verbal dissemination. Formal verbal presentations can be practiced if students are required to present cases in the assessment class and/or in an in-house clinic. Role playing of various clinical situations for dissemination of assessment results can provide practice in circumstances as close to real experience as possible. To guide the student in presenting results for a professional consultation, the instructor can provide an outline for formal presentations. Typical questions asked of the assessment psychologist during formal presentations also can be provided by the instructor to prepare students for the response to the formal presentation. Students should be discouraged from giving a mere reading of the written report. Written reports are usually too long and detailed for formal verbal presentations and do not allow for the kind of feedback from and exchange with the audience that makes formal verbal presentations more useful than written reports.

A special type of formal verbal dissemination practiced more and more often by assessment psychologists is structured feedback to the client and/or the

413

client's representative (parent, spouse, teacher, etc.; Lewak, Storms, Finn, & Meyers, 1995). Graduate students can be introduced to such dissemination through role-playing. Classmates can assume the roles of client or client representatives and a protocol can be discussed with feedback and inquiries provided by the classmate. Instructors, of course, also could provide such feedback, but it usually is meaningful for students to play roles of the recipients of assessment feedback as a way of learning to appreciate the client's position in such circumstances.

Less formal communication of assessment information can be promoted by encouraging students to engage in loosely structured conversations concerning a client's assessment data. The instructor may join such discussions when possible, but students can benefit by carrying on such interactions among themselves. When given such encouragement, their enthusiasm and curiosity usually motivate frequent exchanges outside of class. About all the instructor needs to add is a reminder about confidentiality to prevent such conversations from occurring in public places or when nonauthorized listeners are around.

DISSEMINATION INSTRUCTION

The training standards of the Society for Personality Assessment (Society for Personality Assessment, 1992) propose that the equivalent of two semesters is the minimum instruction necessary to prepare students for further development of assessment skills in practica, internships, and postdoctoral training. In a typical graduate program that meets these minimum standards, the first semester is primarily devoted to (a) the introduction of the assessment procedures taught in the program, (b) methods of administration, and (c) scoring. Because little time is left in the first semester, the second semester is typically devoted to teaching interpretation. Students are likely to be required to write reports and to discuss their interpretations in class from the beginning, but too much early emphasis on complete dissemination of results will only confuse most students, who are typically struggling with the intricacies of interpretation. Trying to teach dissemination in the first semester detracts from the time necessary to teach a basic understanding of the measurement properties of the assessment methods as well as adequate administration, scoring, and an introduction to interpretation. However, if students must wait too long before they are introduced to the issue of dissemination, their interest in the fundamentals of assessment may wane. Most students need to stay in touch with the practical application of methods and dissemination is the ultimate practical goal in any assessment situation. It cannot be neglected entirely in the first semester.

Dissemination can be introduced in the first semester through modeling. The instructor can discuss interpretation of actual test data in a formal demonstration of a case or two. Also, the instructor can provide written reports based on several protocols. Students are eager for such demonstrations and they usually find it easier to get their bearings when they have tangible examples of dissemination. However, because of time constraints, class presentations of dissemination by the instructor probably cannot occupy more than a class period or two and too many written reports will overwhelm the beginning student. Consequently, it is recommended that in the first semester, dissemination should be demonstrated in no more than two class periods and report examples should be limited to five or less.

Should students be required to present interpretations in the first semester? Probably not, but if an instructor disagrees with this opinion, then it may work to allow students an opportunity to make interpretations in class. If written dissemination is assigned, it probably should be limited to a simple listing of interpretive hypotheses (see later definition). Complete formal report writing probably should be avoided in the first semester. It is a complex, difficult task and most students will find it too aversive if they are asked to do it before they are ready. Most students will not be ready to write reports in the first semester.

SOME ASSUMPTIONS

Before more advanced dissemination instruction is discussed, some basic assumptions are important to note. First, these discussions assume the students have been trained adequately in the administration and scoring of the assessment methods they are being asked to use. Adequate reliability of assessment is essential and students should be graded on their ability to yield reliable results through competent administration and scoring (see Brabender, chap. 14 of this volume). Any students who do not attain basic levels of competence in the first semester should not be allowed to progress to the second semester. In other words, they should repeat or remediate the course if they can not administer and score the methods properly.

A second assumption is that students (and all psychologists) should use only valid methods of personality assessment. Validity, of course, is a matter of judgment and two psychologists may disagree about the validity of an assessment method, but an instructor should not teach a method or expect students to use one that he or she considers to be invalid. On the other hand, students should have some introduction to a method of disputed validity even if the instructor does not accept the method. A battery of acceptably valid methods can be designated for use in class exercises, but students need to have some basic knowledge of other methods in order to make their own judgments about validity.

Another assumption is that the students have good communication skills. Clear writing, articulate verbal presentations, and a knack for speaking extemporaneously are important for effective use of personality assessment. However, a psychologist who begins with adequate assessment data and makes accurate interpretations, but who writes a difficult-to-read report or stumbles over him or herself while trying to find the right words during a consultation, probably is less harmful than a glib, smooth-writing psychologist whose presentation skills make invalid data sound true and meaningful.

Report-writing skill can be improved with proper practice and instruction. Students should be encouraged to read sample reports written by experienced clinicians. As indicated earlier, the instructor might supply some of his or her own reports covering different types of cases. When students submit written reports, instructors should provide as much feedback as possible through notes and, if possible, through direct verbal feedback. Part of a class period can be used to go over a particularly important point regarding report writing. If students give verbal reports, the instructor can highlight points that are unclear or awkwardly worded by asking for clarification and/or by suggesting a different phrasing of the information. As students become more comfortable and fluent in their verbal presentations, their written reports tend to improve as well. Instructors also might want to schedule individual sessions with students who are having communication difficulties. The individual sessions provide sufficient privacy for discussion of flaws that might be embarrassing in a group context.

THE GOALS OF DISSEMINATION

Three simple, general goals are probably enough to summarize the purpose of personality assessment: (a) Get people to pay attention to the results; (b) help them to understand the results accurately; and (c) enable them to use their understanding effectively.

Although stated simply, these goals are not easy to achieve. They require a level of integration and amounts of practice that severely test the limits of time available to teach assessment. Too often, instruction in dissemination neglects integration, affords too little opportunity for practice, and focuses almost entirely on report writing to the exclusion of verbal reporting, which can be the most effective and frequently used form of dissemination. In order to teach students to achieve the goals of dissemination, instruction must include integration of assessment information, plenty of practice, and adequate emphasis on verbal, as well as on written dissemination.

Steps of Dissemination. The steps in the typical dissemination process are important for students to understand. They include (a) Specifying the purpose of the assessment, (b) formulating interpretive hypotheses, (c) integrating interpretive hypotheses from different sources of information into final interpretations, (d) translating interpretations into understandable language, (e) the written report, and (f) verbal consultation with mental health professionals, other professionals, the client, and the client's significant others.

PURPOSE OF ASSESSMENT

Even though the purpose of the assessment sounds like a simple issue, it is often difficult for students to understand at first. They have heard of referral questions and some may even have read some actual referral questions. The problem is that the referral question is an antiquated and nearly meaningless concept. It is far too limited and limiting to be helpful in the typical assessment situation. It is rare when the referral question turns out to be the actual purpose of the assessment. Students need to know that many people who request personality assessment do not know enough about it to know that a single referral question is usually inappropriate. Those who do know enough about assessment seldom phrase their request in a single question. Students must be taught to make certain that the client understands that assessment provides extensive information that can be useful for many purposes (see Blais & Eby, chap. 27 of this volume; Lovitt, chap. 26 of this volume).

Clarifying the purpose of assessment and responding to referral questions can be taught by exposing students to a variety of cases that were assessed for different purposes and that carried different initial referral questions. If the instructor has had much experience in a variety of clinical settings, he or she can give examples of the initial phase of the assessment process. For example, the instructor may discuss the typical clinical situation in which the assessment psychologist receives the simple referral question, "Is this patient schizophrenic?" An important, practical question to ask initially would be "Why do you want to know?" The referring colleague may answer, "Because I want to know if it would be helpful to prescribe certain medications." In response to this reply, the psychologist might say, "Then you probably want to know if the patient is a high-functioning (good premorbid) paranoid schizophrenic or a more marginal (poor premorbid) undifferentiated schizophrenic, because the latter is much more likely to respond favorably to medication than the former" (Goldstein, Judd, & Rodnick, 1969). If the colleague agrees, the psychologist might add, "The assessment results may also help to determine what auxiliary or alternative interventions might be useful" (Weiner & Exner, 1991). The psychologist might also suggest that a reassessment should be done after medication and/or other interventions have been implemented to determine their effects. In this way, the instructor can enable the student to see how developing a more extensive purpose out of the overly simplistic referral question can help the referring colleague to become a more sophisticated consumer of assessment. Also, of course, the more extensive purpose can act as a guide to the selection of methods to use in the assessment battery; a more complete statement of purpose will also help to structure the dissemination report.

Appropriateness of Purpose. To effectively structure the purpose of assessment, students must be able to distinguish between the many things assessment can do and the important things it cannot do. For example, primary among the purposes for which assessment usually is *not* appropriate are predicting specific behavior, and making most diagnoses in the American Psychiatric Association, *Diagnostic and Statistical Manual* (4th ed.; DSM–IV; American Psychiatric Association, 1993).

Specific Predictions. Personality assessment, when done properly, enables a psychologist to describe accurately the client's personality. To predict specific behavior it is usually important to have as much information about personality functioning as possible, even though it is not sufficient for highly accurate prediction. To predict behavior sufficiently, an adequately trained professional must add to the personality assessment report information about (a) the client's current life situation, (b) opportunities for certain behaviors, and (c) past behavior in similar situations. Only with these additional data can the clinician come up with accurate predictions of specific behaviors. Any element of this combination is less effective in prediction when taken alone and the elimination of any element typically will weaken accuracy of prediction.

Although clients cannot be promised *specific* predictions from assessment data alone, *general* predictions are not beyond the scope of these methods. For example, the Rorschach is quite good at indicating whether an individual is likely to emit aggressive behaviors (Kazaoka, Sloane, & Exner, 1978), exercise poor judgment (Exner, 1993), or respond favorably to insight-oriented psychotherapy (Weiner & Exner, 1991). Students must know the extent and limits of prediction from assessment methods when they approach dissemination and should be warned against doing more (or less) than the methods allow.

The Problem of Diagnosis.   Diagnosis is a form of prediction and it presents special problems for the assessment psychologist. When and if assessment clinician can make accurate guesses at the correct *DSM–IV* category for the client, such feedback is, at best, not very helpful and, at worst, harmful to the client. Diagnosis usually does not require the use of most of the rich information available from assessment. Unfortunately, if a diagnosis is given, it is about all some people see. It is important to include in the teaching of dissemination the caveat, "Do not predict specific behavior and avoid diagnosis whenever possible."

Students should learn that another problem in trying to determine *DSM–IV* diagnoses from personality assessment data is that assessment methods do not do very well in predicting the specific diagnosis given an individual on the basis of *DSM–IV* criteria. Ganellen (1996) reviewed numerous studies of the diagnostic validity of the Rorschach, MCMI–II, and MMPI–2 and concluded that these assessment methods do reasonably well at differentiating general classes of diagnosis (e. g.,determining if an individual is psychotic or has a major affective disorder), but such determinations can be made nearly as well from quick observations of the client's presenting symptoms. The studies cited by Ganellen (Archer & Gordon, 1988; Ben-Porath, Butcher, & Graham, 1991; del Rosario, McCann, & Navarra, 1994; Elwood, 1993; Exner, 1991, 1993; Fechner-Bates, Coyne, & Schwenk, 1994; M. Hesselbrock, V. Hesselbrock, Tennen, Meyer, & Workman, 1983; Libb, Murray, Thurstin, & Alarcon, 1992; Marlowe & Wetzler, 1994: Mezzich, Damarin, & Erickson, 1974; Nelson & Cicchetti, 1991; Piersma, 1991; Post & Lobitz, 1980; Wetzler, Kahn, Strauman, & Dubro, 1989; Wetzler & Marlowe, 1993) consistently show that personality assessment methods fail to discriminate effectively between specific *DSM–IV* diagnostic categories, such as unipolar and bipolar depression, and various Axis II personality disorders. This is no surprise because accurate *DSM–IV* diagnosis requires specific and comprehensive interview methods that are not very similar to the methods of personality assessment.

The real value in personality assessment is the more comprehensive, detailed, and individualized information yielded by the methods. Students need to learn that often, the most meaningful question is not "Is this person schizophrenic?", but "How does this person's cognitive disturbance impact on their capacity to adapt?" For the latter question, methods like the Rorschach and MMPI–2 are invaluable.

Of course, in some clinical settings, the psychologist will be required, or at least strongly encouraged, to give a *DSM–IV* diagnosis based on the assessment results alone. Students can be taught that if an adamant refusal seems inappropriate or ineffective, an approximate diagnosis can be given in the context of a report that elaborates on the relationship between the symptom patterns and the subject's overall personality functioning. Simple listing of diagnostic labels can be avoided in all but the most rigid settings. In addition, extensive interview and history data, collected by the clinician and by others, is quite helpful in reducing errors. In a case conference setting, these additional pieces of data are typically shared and discussed. In some instances, if there is some question concerning diagnosis, videotapes of the assessment sessions may also be shown.

Preparing the Client. An especially important part of the assessment process is preparing the client for the assessment sessions (Lewak et al., 1995; see also Finn, chap. 20 of this volume). Again, through the use of role-playing, students can be taught to truthfully and supportively inform the client of the general purpose of the assessment, while giving them a clear understanding of what they have to gain from participating. Also, students need to learn how to inform a client about what they will be asked to do without compromising the effectiveness of the procedures. For example, Exner (1995) provided guidelines for introducing the client to the Rorschach without giving away how the procedure works.

Students should be taught that assessment information has many practical applications, but also, some important limitations. They should finish their graduate assessment training with the appreciation that assessment results are not a dangerous secret that should be kept from clients and their representatives, but rather, they are useful, therapeutic information that, if delivered properly, can enable clients to work better in therapy and to more effectively structure their lives.

FORMULATING INTERPRETIVE HYPOTHESES

As much as students would like it to be, personality assessment is not a cookbook process. In most cases for all valid methods, single scores do not yield final interpretations. Interpretation is a process of setting forth "interpretive hypotheses" that eventually coalesce and come together to form a complete, integrated description of the personality. In learning *interpretation*, students must practice establishing hypotheses from individual data points and evaluating (or testing) them as more data are added (see Handler, Fowler, & Hilsenroth, chap. 24 of this volume). In learning *dissemination*, students must learn the skill of developing and refining interpretive hypotheses. In class, detailed, systematic discussions of data are useful in teaching students how to effectively refine their results into meaningful interpretations. The interpretive hypothesis must be understood clearly as an intermediate stage of interpretation and dissemination.

Computer Aids for Establishing Interpretive Hypotheses. Useful tools for learning about appropriate formulation of interpretive hypotheses are the computerized programs that print statements based on empirically validated test scores or combinations of test scores. These programs help the student learn how to precisely phrase accurate interpretive hypotheses. These computer programs, however, create at least two problems for teaching assessment. First, they produce interpretive hypotheses that are limited to modestly integrated data from a single assessment method. Although new, more sophisticated programs attempt to provide more integration within the method, they seldom combine all relevant information available from the method when stating an hypothesis. It seldom happens that a meaningful, maximally helpful report can be constructed by merely reproducing the computer printout (see Greene & Rouhbakhsh, chap. 10 of this volume). Students must be shown that the psychologist needs to augment and refine the computer statements into more comprehensive and accurate personality descriptions. Otherwise, they will be of limited value to the patient or to the referral source.

An even more critical problem with computer programs is that they very seldom integrate valid information from other sources. The psychologist is left with the important responsibility of integrating the method's computer interpretations with other meaningful information (see later discussion of integration of material from different sources).

Perhaps the most aggravating problem coming from computer assessment programs is that students tend to take such statements and weave them into the report in unedited form. Most of these statements are worded in the type of jargonistic, stilted language associated with the empirical foundations of the hypotheses. Consequently, unedited use of them in reports yields a description of the client that is difficult to comprehend for most readers. Translating interpretations into understandable language is a necessary step in the dissemination process that is discussed shortly.

INTEGRATION OF INFORMATION

There are three types of integration that go into personality assessment dissemination: (a) integration of interpretive hypotheses within the same assessment method, (b) integration of interpretations from different methods, and (c) integration of data from assessment methods and nonassessment information about the client.

Integration Within the Same Method. The Rorschach Comprehensive System (Exner, 1993) provides an illustration of integration within a method. The Comprehensive System interpretive method uses 83 data points, organized into eight clusters, corresponding to eight personality components, such as "Self Perception and Information Processing." Within each cluster, the clinician proceeds in a stepwise fashion, forming interpretive hypotheses at each significant data point. As the clinician proceeds with interpretation through the cluster, integration of interpretive hypotheses takes place until, at the end of the cluster, the psychologist formulates a summary of the information regarding the personality component assessed by the cluster. Because the clusters are not completely independent, information from earlier clusters may influence interpretations of later clusters. Because of this, the system provides a means of ordering the clusters so that the most critical clusters are assessed near the beginning of the interpretive process (see Weiner, chap. 13 of this volume). Such systematic coverage of the data within a single method is a good model for students in approaching other methods. Another example of progressive integration within an assessment method is the MMPI–2 interpretive method of profile analysis (Graham, 1990). Students should be taught not to leave their interpretation with a method until such intramethod integration has been done.

A useful class exercise is one in which students are given data from a Rorschach Comprehensive System cluster (e. g., the Affect cluster) or an MMPI–2 profile (e. g., the basic scales profile) and are asked to summarize their understanding of the person based on this subset of data before going on to other subsets (e. g., the Rorschach Controls cluster or the MMPI–2 Content Scales Profile). Generally, score-by-score interpretation should be discouraged, because it detracts from an integrated understanding of the individual. On the other hand, a single, overall summary of the results from an assessment method also should be avoided because it is likely to be insufficiently comprehensive.

Integration Between Methods. The second form or level of integration is among various pieces of information obtained from different assessment methods. The task is easy when two or more methods yield similar, consistent results and simply act to confirm each other. The task becomes more difficult (and is more typical) when the results are not the same when the results from the methods are compared. In fortunate cases, the results from one method will clarify and/or augment the results from another, enabling the psychologist to present a more complete description of the personality. In the more difficult cases, the results from different methods will seem to be contradictory. In such instances, the student must be encouraged to resolve the contradiction and explain the discrepancy in terms of the client's personality, or some aspect of the test itself, or both. Usually this can be done by referring to other data or information about the client from sources other than the assessment methods. It is not good practice, however, to overlook a contradiction by simply deciding between the two conflicting results. Instead, the students should be impressed with the complexity of personality functioning and they should be encouraged to at least consider ways in which the conflicting results can be explained with a more comprehensive, integrative interpretation (see Handler & Meyer, chap. 1 of this volume). Class exercises using test battery results in which such contradictions occur are valuable training for the advanced student. Early examples of complete test batteries, however, should be relatively free of such contradictions until the students are experienced enough to approach the more difficult, less consistent case.

Integration with Nonassessment Results.   In most clinical settings, written assessment reports include two sections that precede the presentation of the assessment results. These paragraphs usually are headed "Background Information" and "Behavioral Observations."

Background information usually includes a very brief personal history and selected demographic information. Behavioral observations are an equally limited summary of the client's appearance and some of his or her behavior during the assessment session. Rather than following the conventional insertion of this information in an unintegrated fashion at the beginning of the report, I recommend a different approach: (a) If you are confident that the background information and behavioral observation information are accurate, use it, but (b) do not put it in paragraphs separate from the test results. If such information is valid it will enable the psychologist to phrase the interpretations of assessment data more precisely and meaningfully. Also, integrating such information in the body of the report avoids creating a halo effect with such unstandardized and selected data. It is particularly upsetting to see a report beginning with a behavioral observation that the person is physically attractive. Although such an evaluation may have some relevance for assessment, empirical studies have shown that early statements about attractiveness often inaccurately bias a reader's subsequent evaluation of the client. To illustrate this point, simply ask students "How important do you think physical appearance is for really knowing a person? Is it the most important thing? If not, do not put it first" The same goes for much of the other information that is often placed in the background and in the behavioral observation sections of the report.

TRANSLATING DISSEMINATION
INTO UNDERSTANDABLE LANGUAGE

Usually, when students begin writing reports, especially with the help of interpretation-generating computer programs, they present information in a stilted, boring fashion—information that sounds little like the description of a real human personality. In trying to teach them otherwise, a particular didactic gimmick has proven effective: Students are encouraged to "Write the report for your grandmother" with the assumption that their grandmothers are intelligent women who know little about psychology, but who can be sensitive and empathic when they understand someone's personality. The assessment methods provide plenty of information to give to their grandmother, but it has to be in her language, not in the overly jargonistic language of the assessment text. Sometimes it may be useful to encourage students to actually talk to their grandmothers about their assessment clients before they write the reports. Roommates or other acquaintances will suffice as long as confidentiality is preserved by concealing the identity of the subject or client. Not only does this procedure enable the students to write more interesting and comprehensible reports, but it also assures that they understand the results well enough to make such a translation. With such increased understanding, their interpretations are likely to be more accurate and meaningful.

Another reader to keep in mind as a report is being formulated is the client. Not only will this promote effective translation, but it will also provide practice for verbal dissemination to the client.

THE WRITTEN REPORT

The first thing to learn about written dissemination is how to organize a report. There is a simple principle involved: An assessment report should be organized in the way personality functioning is organized. With this in mind, it is not correct to organize a report test by test. In other words, reports should not have separate sections on the Rorschach, MMPI, TAT, and so on. Such organization prohibits integration and unnecessarily increases redundancy. Instead, it is much better to organize a report "personality component by personality component" (e. g., a section on cognitive functioning, a section on emotions, a section on interpersonal relations, etc.). It is even better if the order of these sections varies from report to report, with the most salient personality components placed early in the report instead of beginning every report with a section on intelligence followed by defenses, and so forth. Assessment psychologists who use the Rorschach Comprehensive System often use the order provided by the "cluster search routine" of interpretation (Exner, 1993) to structure their reports. In other words, they place the personality component designated as the most important by the Comprehensive System at the beginning of the report. However, a meaningful order may be identified that is more appropriate for all the data from a particular client. Therefore, by exercising flexibility in this approach the psychologist will occasionally see that after other assessment data have been considered, the first Comprehensive System cluster is not always the most salient, and the more appropriate order can be substituted.

Another issue in organizing the report is to decide to what extent specific quantified (i. e., test score) data should be included. The best answer may be "not at all." Certainly, specific data should not be used to inform the reader about how interpretations were derived, as if it was a requirement to prove everything by submitting supportive data. Hopefully, enough integration has gone into each interpretation to mean that sufficient "proof" would require a report in the neighborhood of 40–50 pages—far too long to sustain the average reader's interest. Of course, the presentation of specific responses sometimes can clarify an interpretation better than any words the psychologist can write. In such cases, the student should be taught to present the example with enough clarification to make sure the reader (i. e., their grandmother) will understand its application.

Finally, there should be no summary section in the report. The entire report of four to seven double-spaced, typewritten pages is the briefest meaningful summary possible. Anything shorter would be leaving out critical information; many readers will go directly to the summary if one is available, and will ignore the rest of the report.

VERBAL CONSULTATION

The final and perhaps the most important topic for this presentation is about the verbal communication of results to clients. Each of the previous principles apply: understanding the purpose of the assessment, the selection of relevant data, the language used, and the general organization of the feedback. In most cases it was another professional who made the referral. Therefore, a written report has preceded the verbal exchange and the consultation will be an opportunity for this referral source to gain clarification, ask additional questions, and discuss intervention or disposition. Usually, the referral source will bring new information to the consultation that was not part of the test data or original background information. In particular, if information in the report does not agree with the professional's previous understanding of the client, the discrepancy can be discussed and can usually be resolved now that more data are available.

If the client is a lay person, that is, the patient or a significant other, such as a parent or spouse, it is neither advisable nor ethical to give them the report prior to the verbal feedback. Usually, when people get complete verbal feedback, they are not interested in seeing the written report and it can be provided only if specifically requested by the client, but not without first thoroughly explaining everything in it so the person seems to understand what is being communicated.

Communication of the results to the patient or the patient's representative can begin with the statement of some general interpretations indicated by the results and then asking for feedback from the client. In this way, it can be determined if the client understood the interpretation, considered it to be accurate, and related it to something else in their self-concept. In general, feedback should proceed from interpretations about which the patient is aware, to concepts about which the patient is less and less aware, making certain to also facilitate their active participation. Usually, such work takes several sessions to complete and it is not unusual for several weeks of therapy to center around assessment feedback and the client's association to it.

Students can be prepared for giving verbal feedback through role playing with their classmates, although a potentially better method is to require students to give feedback to undergraduate volunteers who have been administered practice test batteries.

PRACTICE

The final issue in this discussion of teaching personality assessment dissemination is how to provide adequate practice. Basically, there is not enough time for sufficient practice in a two semester course sequence. In the second semester, lab sessions directed by the instructor or advanced student assistants can help students get experience in making interpretations and conveying the results to others. Report-writing practice is a standard procedure for most assessment courses, but the work is labor-intensive for the instructor. Detailed feedback is essential, either in the form of extensive margin notes or direct verbal feedback, both of which take time. A strong assessment practicum sequence is very helpful in providing guided practice for assessment dissemination. It is a luxury for most graduate programs to have sufficiently competent practicum instructors for assessment, but when such individuals are available, they prove invaluable.

Practice in an in-house clinic can be effectively tailored to the students' needs. This is where verbal consultation can be most often practiced, as students test each other's clients and share results. Of course, a third semester or more advanced instruction in personality assessment can place a premium on dissemination practice, particularly on the verbal exchange and discussion of results.

Although a typical graduate program can do much to develop the assessment skills of its students, the time available is rarely enough to provide sufficient competence for postgraduate practice. Consequently, the concept of continuing education must be stressed for students who are serious about becoming assessment psychologists. Schedules of workshops, symposia, conventions, and other training experiences can be provided to students and they can be encouraged to check source material, such as the APA Monitor, for continuing education opportunities.

A final note: Teaching assessment dissemination may seem like an inordinantly time-consuming task for training programs already full of required courses and highly desired electives. It is important to realize, however, that a class in personality assessment training is not an isolated learning experience, but requires the student to use knowledge and skills learned in general courses such as psychopathology, personality theory, and psychotherapy. Consequently, an assessment course sequence that features instruction in dissemination can provide additional experience for the consolidation of important knowledge and skills in applied psychology.

REFERENCES

American Psychiatric Association. (1993). *Diagnostic and statistical manual of mental disorders* (4th ed.). Washington, DC: Author.

Archer, R., & Gordon, R. (1988). MMPI and Rorschach indices of schizophrenic and depressive disorders among adolescent inpatients. *Journal of Personality Assessment, 52,* 276–287.

Ben-Porath, Y., Butcher, J., & Graham, J. (1991). Contribution of the MMPI–2 content scales to the differential diagnosis of schizophrenia and major depression. *Psychological Assessment, 3,* 634–640.

del Rosario, P., McCann, J., & Navarra, J. (1994). The MCMI–II diagnosis of schizophrenia: Operating characteristics and profile analysis. *Journal of Personality Assessment, 63,* 438–452.

Elwood, R. (1993). The clinical utility of the MMPI–2 in diagnosing unipolar depression among male alcoholics. *Journal of Personality Assessment, 60,* 511–521.

Exner, J. (1991). *The Rorschach: A comprehensive system: Vol. 2. Current research and advanced interpretation* (2nd ed.). New York: Wiley.

Exner, J. (1993). *The Rorschach: A comprehensive system: Vol. 1: Basic foundations* (3rd ed.). New York: Wiley & Sons.

Exner, J. (1995). *A Rorschach workbook for the comprehensive system* (4th ed.). Asheville, NC: Rorschach Workshops.

Fechner-Bates, S., Coyne, J., & Schwenk, T. (1994). The relationship of self-reported distress to depressive disorders and other psychopathology. *Journal of Consulting and Clinical Psychology, 62,* 550–559.

Ganellen, R. (1996). Comparing the diagnostic efficiency of the MMPI, MCMI–II, and Rorschach: A review. *Journal of Personality Assessment, 67,* 219–243.

Goldstein, M., Judd, L., & Rodnick, E. (1969). Psychophysiological and behavioral effects of phenothiazine administration in acute schizophrenics as a function of premorbid status. *Journal of Psychiatric Research, 6,* 217–287.

Graham, J. (1990). *MMPI–2: Assessing personality and psychopathology.* New York: Oxford University Press.

Hesselbrock, M., Hesselbrock, V., Tennen, H., Meyer, R., & Workman, K. (1983). Methodological considerations in the assessment of depression in alcoholics. *Journal of Consulting and Clinical Psychology, 51,* 399–405.

Kazaoka, K., Sloane, K., & Exner, J. (1978). *Verbal and nonverbal aggressive behaviors among 70 inpatients during occupational and recreational therapy.* Unpublished Workshops Study No. 254, Rorschach Workshops.

Lewak, R., Storms, L., Finn, S., & Meyers, J. (1995, March). *Feedback with the MMPI–2: Practical guidelines: A symposium.* Symposium conducted at the Society for Personality Assessment Midwinter Meeting, Atlanta.

Libb, J., Murray, J., Thurstin, H., & Alarcon, R. (1992). Concordance of the MCMI–II, the MMPI, and Axis I discharge diagnosis in psychiatric inpatients. *Journal of Personality Assessment, 58,* 580–590.

Marlowe, D., & Wetzler, S. (1994). Contributions of discriminant analysis to differential diagnosis by self-report. *Journal of Personality Assessment, 62,* 320–331.

Mezzich, J., Damarin, R., & Erickson, J. (1974). Comparative validities of strategies and indices for differential diagnosis of depressive states from other psychiatric conditions using the MMPI. *Journal of Consulting and Clinical Psychology, 42,* 691–698.

Nelson, L., & Cicchetti, D. (1991). Validity of the MMPI Depression scale for outpatients. *Psychological Assessment, 3,* 55–59.

Piersma, H. (1991). The MCMI–II depression scales: Do they assist in the differential diagnosis of depressive disorders? *Journal of Personality Assessment, 56*, 478–486.

Post, R., & Lobitz, W. (1980). The utility of Mezzich's MMPI regression formula as a diagnostic criterion in depression research. *Journal of Consulting and Clinical Psychology, 48*, 673–674.

Society for Personality Assessment. (1992). *Standards for training in personality assessment.* Washington, DC: Author.

Weiner, I., & Exner, J. (1991). Rorschach changes in long-term and short-term psychotherapy. *Journal of Personality Assessment, 56*, 453–465.

Wetzler, S., Kahn, R., Strauman, T., & Dubro, A. (1989). Diagnosis of major depression by self-report. *Journal of Personality Assessment, 53*, 22–30.

Wetzler, S., & Marlow, D. (1993). The diagnosis and assessment of depression, mania, and psychosis by self-report. *Journal of Personality Assessment, 60*, 1–31.

VI

TEACHING AND LEARNING ASSESSMENT COURSES

We hope the reader can see that the chapters in Part IV, Teaching and Learning Specific Test Instruments, can be organized to form a specific introductory assessment course. Part VI includes the description of two courses, one by Handler, Fowler, and Hilsenroth, who describe an advanced course in assessment, and one by Russ, who focuses on the assessment of children.

Leonard Handler, J. Christopher Fowler, and Mark J. Hisenroth's chapter, "Teaching and Learning Issues in an Advanced Course in Personality Assessment," describes a course, taught by Handler, as a second assessment course in a two-course series. The authors describe a number of methods used to facilitate the interpretive process, including a discussion of divergent and convergent thinking, as well as an approach that stresses the combination of experiential and objective approaches. The authors stress the importance of dealing with students' restance to the interpretive process, resistance that is based in anxieties about their new role as an expert, as well as on their fears of doing harm to patients by saying negative things about them. Handler, Fowler, and Hilsenroth describe methods to deal with these anxiety-based resistances, including the use of research data, open discussions of these anxieties, use of the Socratic method, stressing the inclusion of patients' strengths as well as their weaknesses, individualized assistance in making interpretations, modeling, and facilitative instruction in crafting written statements that will be helpful to the patient. In addition, a method of facilitative testing is described, in which the patient is assisted in responding to test items he or she cannot do easily.

The chapter by Sandra W. Russ, "Teaching Child Assessment from a Developmental-Psychodynamic Perspective," describes a course designed to teach graduate students how to approach assessment of children, using a developmental-psychodynamic approach. Russ emphasizes research experience as a bridge between developmental theory and clinical-child issues. She highlights the use of various child assessment measures, especially object relations measures. Russ describes a general battery of child assessment tests and recommends their use with a play or interview session. In addition, she describes various methods to evaluate children's play. She suggests the use of case example presentations in helping students integrate developmental-psychodynamic theory with child assessment data. Russ lists 11 goals of training in child assessment, including such items as deciding when testing is necessary and knowing how to use assessment to evaluate treatment outcome.

24

Teaching and Learning Issues in an Advanced Course in Personality Assessment

Leonard Handler
University of Tennessee
J.Christopher Fowler
The Erik H. Erikson Institute of The Austen Riggs Center
Mark J. Hilsenroth
University of Arkansas

This chapter describes the teaching–learning process in a second (advanced) course in personality assessment, taught by the first author, from a psychodynamic-experiential approach, and informed by the second and third authors, when they were class participants. Although some aspects of the assessment process have been informed by research, presented later in the chapter, other aspects of the interpretive process have been informed by the work of Schachtel (1966), by the human science approach described by Polkinghorne (1983) and Fischer (1985), and by the psychodynamic approach to interpretation described by Rapaport (Rapaport, Gill, & Schafer, 1968), Mayman (1968, 1977), Schafer (1978), and P. Lerner (1991). Most of all, the approach to the course was determined by the work of Potash (1989).

Emphasis is placed on the communication of the experiential aspects involved in the *process* of assessment and on a group approach to help students master the process. In addition, a discussion is included concerning some of the cognitive processes involved in effective interpretation (e. g., convergent and divergent thinking approaches). The chapter also discusses the use of feedback from students concerning the problems involved in the teaching–learning process, in order to focus the teaching process more adequately.

The chapter begins with a brief discussion concerning the use of theory and the problems involved in teaching assessment, from both the teacher's and from the students' viewpoints. A discussion of the ways in which the first author's research has informed the interpretive process follows. A major focus of the chapter is a description of the development of an experience-near interpretive process, where the students mutually learn to interpret and integrate assessment data by group participation. The development of the experiential ability to explore the symbolic and narrative understanding of the data is described, emphasizing the stance of authentic openness to fully comprehend the patient's responses. The students' resistance to such openness is discussed, as well as a variety of approaches designed to deal effectively with these resistances. The importance of such an approach to the interpretation of projective tests has been emphasized by a number of writers (e. g., Lyons, 1967; Schachtel, 1966, 1967; see also H. Lerner, chap. 3 of this volume).

THE ROLE OF THEORY

An important part of instruction has been the effort made to help students understand how different aspects of personality assessment and personality theory fit together (Ritzler, 1993; Erdberg, chap. 4 of this volume; Smith, chap. 5 of this volume). By learning the concepts of themas, press, and the projective hypothesis, one can better understand the experiential world of an individual in ways that expand upon a solely quantitative or sign approach. Students report that learning how a theory can offer a foundation for clinical conceptualization has been one of the most helpful aspects in their attempts to understand an individual's experiences and their inner world, as well as offering the potential for greatly broadening and enriching test-derived inferences. Students typically report that the use of a theory in understanding test data has helped them to conceptualize, organize, and integrate data that are often complex, exceedingly rich, and at times inconsistent. The use of theory has proven helpful in a clinical setting because it allows the student to understand how the character structure has developed, and how to make specific treatment recommendations (Hilsenroth & Handler, 1995). The organizational principles of a theory make possible certain ways of thinking, or arranging the infinitely complex tapestry of human experience into consistent interpretive patterns.

Throughout the course the instructor made attempts to urge the students to make interpretive and predictive statements that incorporated theoretical concepts derived from various psychodynamic theoretical positions (e. g., object relations theory, ego psychology, self psychology). There has been a relatively recent paradigmatic shift from a psychodynamic approach that emphasizes drives and drive derivatives to an approach that emphasizes the ways in which "the individual constructs meaning and reality as a basis for living" (Tallent, 1992, p. 102). A number of writers (e. g., Blatt, 1986; Schafer, 1978) have emphasized the importance of cognitive processes and schemas that influence the ways in which individuals establish and maintain relationships, organize their lives, and interpret their interpersonal world. As Blatt (1986) noted, "Psychology has begun to shift from the view that reality is well defined and that we must understand how individuals come to perceive this reality veridically, to a view that reality is constructed by each individual. ... The task for psychology is to appreciate the individual's construction of reality and especially the assumptions on which the individual comes to create a conception of reality and construct meaning" (p. 345). This approach stresses the integration of traditional concepts of psychoanalytic theory with psychodynamically based developmental theory, object relations and self psychology (Blatt & H. Lerner, 1983, 1991). As Blatt indicated, "Experience-distant metapsychological concepts [have been] replaced by a more experience-near clinical theory concerned with concepts of the self and others in a representational world [through the systematic assessment of] the construction of the meaning of psychological events and the articulation of motives rather than trying to explain psychological functioning ... "(p. 5).

COURSE INTRODUCTION

The students are provided with an annotated bibliography, along with a list of articles and book chapters in an attempt to focus the learning process. The textbooks required for the course are discussed and a plan of reading is outlined in the syllabus. Assigned reading material (Exner, 1993; Greene, 1991; Handler, 1995; P. Lerner, 1991; Rapaport, Gill, & Schafer, 1968; various chapters from Rickers-Ovsiankina, 1977) help the students in their initial attempts to formulate hypotheses because the material provides a theory-based interpretive philosophy and many clinical examples. Additional research findings are brought into class and are discussed as the students are prepared to assimilate them (e. g., several of Westen's articles on the measurement of object relations from the Thematic Apperception Test [Westen, 1991a, 1991b]; Urist's [1977] work on the Mutuality of Autonomy scale for the Rorschach; Handler & Habenicht's [1994] article on the evaluation of the Kinetic Family Drawing Technique, and other newly published relevant articles). In addition, the students are given a very extensive bibliography that lists many assessment books, categorized as focused on either adults or children, and categorized according to the test or tests covered. They are encouraged to read in areas of their interest.

The students have taken or are taking courses in personality theory, descriptive psychopathology, and dynamic psychopathology, along with a variety of other related courses (e. g., social psychology, physiological psychology). The task in this class concerns the interpretation and integration of test findings, utilizing an experiential and psychodynamic theory-based approach, but also informed by interpretations of more objective and psychometric data.

PROBLEMS IN INTERPRETATION

One of the most plaguing problems in teaching personality assessment is the mechanistic manner in which many new students go about learning to interpret test data. No matter how much it is emphasized that cookbook interpretations do not yield accurate data, many students nevertheless start out by writing cookbook reports. There is no substitute for a firm grounding in empirically based scoring systems. Formal instruction should be quite extensive, including practice in the administration and scoring of intelligence tests, the Rorschach, and other projective tests. However, feedback from students indicated that although they could make distinct interpretations from the data (e. g., they could tell you if the protocol was produced by an extratensive, ambient, or introversive), unfortunately the usual result was merely a "laundry list" of distinct interpretations joined to each other to produce a somewhat mechanical and psychologically clumsy profile. The students recognized that something essential was lacking, something that could form the matrix into which these interpretations could be woven, to create a richer, more comprehensive narrative of the person. However, they were reluctant to enliven their written interpretations. Psychoanalytic concepts were often rotely applied, as were individual interpretations made from actuarial data.

Learning basic assessment techniques, such as test administration and scoring test data, are essential components to a solid grounding in psychological assessment. As Levinger (1977) pointed out, for example, "The psychogram and individual Rorschach scores allow the diagnostician to step back from the specific history and symptoms and gain a sense of the common threads of the life experience and the way the person approaches a variety of life situations" (p. 290). Fortunately, these skills are relatively easy to acquire because they are rule-based techniques with clear procedural guidelines. Learning an experiential, psychoanalytic method of interpretation is far more unwieldy and idiosyncratic. Content interpretation places novel demands on the students; for the first time they are being placed in the position of substantial authority as "experts." They are also being called on to use *themselves* as an assessment tool, in a manner that is similar to the approach required of students in learning to conduct psychotherapy. It is also difficult to teach students how to integrate the experiential data with more objective data, such as test scores and ratios. Because the task is quite complex, innovative teaching methods are needed to help the student overcome the difficulties inherent in the integration of the data. The complexity of the data is somewhat overwhelming for the students, further pushing them to rely on simplistic methodology and the use of signs. As Levinger (1977) noted, these initial problems in interpretation are ways in which "to cope with multiple threats of new ways of thinking" (p. 289) and also ways of dealing with pathological test material that can be anxiety producing.

CLUES FROM RESEARCH

To help resolve the problem of utilizing rigidly applied cookbook interpretations, the instructor avoided assigning materials that emphasize this approach. In addition, he set out to investigate the reasons that some students were quite able, from the beginning of the course, to generate complex and accurate psychodynamically based experiential interpretations, whereas others seemed to rely primarily on nomothetic data applied ideographically, or on cookbook interpretations. The more talented assessment students seemed more intuitive, more empathic, and they seemed to think in a more flexible manner, either searching for alternative interpretations when the one presented did not seem adequate, or in searching for ways in which various pieces of seemingly unrelated data could fit together.

These individual differences in assessment ability were observed many years ago by Henry Murray (1938, 1943) who classified psychological assessors as either centralists or peripheralists; the first group was said to emphasize feelings and an empathic approach to knowing, whereas the second group was said to be more objective, emphasizing more statistical and mechanical explanations (Tallent, 1992). The most recent mention of this difference in approach is by Blatt and Ford (1994), who drew attention to the differences in thinking patterns between those who place major emphasis on interpersonal relatedness and those who place more emphasis on self-definition. Those in the former group "are generally more figurative in their thinking, and focus primarily on affects and visual images. Their thinking is usually characterized more by ... reconciliation, synthesis and integration of elements into a cohesive unity rather than on a critical analysis of separate elements and details" (p. 11; see also Szumotalska, 1992). For these people *"thinking is much more intuitive and determined by feelings and personal reactions than by facts, figures and other details"* (p. 11; italics added). Blatt and Ford contrasted this group with the group of individuals who are primarily focused on self-definition. The thinking of these individuals is much more literal, with an emphasis on analysis rather than synthesis, on the "critical dissection of details ... rather than on achieving an integration and synthesis" (p. 12).

A series of studies was conducted to test the differences between those students who were talented in interpretation and those who seemed to possess little talent for a more experiential, intuitive interpretive approach (Burley & Handler, 1997; Handler & Finley, 1994; Scribner, 1989; Scribner & Handler, 1987, 1993), utilizing some of the observations described previously. Both undergraduate and graduate students were utilized in a series of studies of empathy (measured with the Hogan Empathy Scale; Hogan, 1969), intuition (measured with the intuition-sensation scale of the Myers–Briggs; Myers, 1962) and cognitive flexibility, defined as creativity (measured by the Remote Associates Test; S. Mednick & M. Mednick, 1967).

We observed that an important problem area in the interpretive process concerned the linking or association of bits and pieces of diverse test data to form a complex interpretation that meaningfully integrates all the data. Therefore we looked for a measure of cognitive flexibility based on both convergent and divergent thinking approaches. We have measured convergent thinking in our laboratory with Mednick's Remote Associates Test (S. Mednick & M. Mednick, 1967). In this test, the respondent is asked to come up with a word that is related to three other presented stimulus words. For example, take the following three words: *"base,""snow,""dance"*; the correct answer is *ball*. The interpretive process concerns "seeing relationships among seemingly mutually remote ideas" (S. Mednick & M. Mednick, 1967, p. 4). This is essentially the same type of task that is required in effective assessment interpretation, where it is necessary to take diverse pieces of data and fit them together to create an interpretive hypothesis. We found significant differences between accurate and inaccurate DAP (Draw-A-Person Test) interpreters; the good interpreters were more empathic, more intuitive, and more cognitively flexible, compared with the poor interpreters (Burley & Handler, in press). In another study, utilizing the Leary Interpersonal System, the accurate interpreters were significantly more affiliative, compared with the inaccurate interpreters (Scribner & Handler, 1987). Scribner and Handler (1993) found that the most salient feature that distinguished poor interpreters was the need for control in their activities and experiences, whereas the essential aspect of the good intuitive interpreters was their willingness and ability to relinquish any inclination to control what was experienced and simply to allow themselves to experience things freely and openly, just as Kris (1952) described the need to relax one's typical stance toward reality in order to permit ego regression to occur.

Burley and Handler (1997) found that there were even poor interpreters in a group of trained graduate students, whereas some of the undergraduates in a group who had no interpretive training made fewer errors than the graduate students. The fact that there were still significant differences in interpretive ability in the carefully selected, highly trained graduate group suggests that more systematic attention needs to be paid to the analysis of the skills involved in the process of interpreting assessment data. From the data reported by Scribner and Handler, and by Scribner (1989), the process of accurate interpretation using a qualitative approach may be described in the following manner: The good qualitative interpreter is an open, empathic person whose thinking is flexible, a person whose openness to the material (and through the material, to the person who generated it) is evident as intuitiveness. Empathy involves such attributes as being perceptive to a wide range of cues, having insight into one's own motives, and the ability to accurately evaluate the motives of others. The utilization of this approach to interpretation requires a certain amount of affective "tuning in" to one's own feelings and to the feelings of others; this description involves the creative "loss of distance" emphasized by Kris (1952) and the concept of "psychoanalytic listening" developed by Kohut (1959, 1977) and by other analysts. Although this process is in part similar to Kris' concept of adaptive regression in the service of the ego, it goes beyond the emphasis on the dynamic aspects of regression and the primitive, immature content of thoughts and feelings. What is added here is openness in turning toward the data and the ability to approach the responses with freshness, spontaneity, and interest (Schachtel, 1959). Introspection and self-reflection in the regressive process are probably not enough to achieve valid interpretation. What is needed, in addition, is the ability to become reconnected again with cognitively reorganized creative understanding.

Several other studies support this theorized relationship between good projective test interpretation and both creativity and adaptive regression in the service of the ego. For example, J. Murray and Russ (1981) reported a significant positive correlation between adaptive regression scores and the scores on the Remote Associates Test in college students. In addition, Domino (1976) and Martindale (1972) reported a similar significant correlation between the Remote Associates Test and the degree of creativity expressed in dreams. Domino found more primary-process thinking (e. g., more condensation and symbolization) in creative subjects compared with matched controls. Murry and Russ' data emphasize that both primary-process and secondary-process thinking are involved in adaptive regression, the former to provide access to creative material and the latter to evaluate the primary-process data. Thus, the picture of the effective interpretive process may be described as one in which the interpreter regresses in the service of the ego, experiences through regression and empathy the personality of the person who gave the response, and then cognitively reorganizes this knowledge in a creative and meaningful manner.

Russ (1993) emphasized the similarities between primary process thinking and creativity, and indicated that the concept of regression to an *earlier* mode of thinking is not necessary. Rather, she believed that the major issue is the ability to achieve access to the primary process content. Rothenberg (1994) also believed regression is unnecessary for creative work. His research focuses on the thinking processes involved in the creative process: the "homospatial process" defined as "actively conceiving two or more discrete entities occupying the same space"; the "janusian process," defined as "actively conceiving multiple opposites or antitheses *simultaneously*"; and "articulation," defined as "the joining of one element with another [producing] both a coming together and a separation at the same time" (pp. 208–209, 213). Rothenberg utilized object relations theory to conceptualize the creative process, which he believed is rooted in the transitional phenomena of childhood, described by Winnicott (1971) as "in the intermediate area of experience, unchallenged by inner or shared reality, [which] constitutes the greater part of the infant's experience, and throughout life is retained in the intense experience that belongs to … imaginative living" (p. 14). Our finding that the good interpreters were more cognitively flexible is consistent with Rothenberg's findings.

As important as convergent thinking is to model and to teach, it is also important to teach the students about divergent thinking, because emphasis on this type of thinking illustrates that there is typically more than one possible interpretation for any single test sign or symbol. Divergent thinking is often tapped in creativity research by asking the subject to list in how many different ways a specific object (e. g., a brick, a box) can be used (Torrance, 1966, 1974). Divergent thinking is highlighted in class by emphasizing that a single response can contain multiple and complex aspects of interpretation.

In an effort to determine whether a divergent thinking approach is indeed related to accurate interpretation, a group of undergraduates who were accurate DAP interpreters and a group of inaccurate DAP interpreters were tested with "The Unusual Uses Subtest" of the Torrance Tests of Creative Thinking and "The Test of Divergent Thinking" from the Williams' Creative Assessment Packet (Williams, 1980). The Torrance test requires subjects to list as many new and unusual uses for cardboard boxes as he or she can; the Test of Divergent Thinking requires subjects to produce drawings inside 12 different frames, each of which contains a line or form that must be incorporated into the drawing. The good DAP interpreters were significantly more creative on both tests of divergent thinking (Handler & Finley, 1994).

Rather than seek only one isolated interpretation for a specific test response, the students are able to see that *several* interpretations that fit the data can be simultaneously accurate and meaningful, as we often see from an analysis of the manifest and latent content of dreams. Emphasis on these cognitive processes in the classroom helps the student to conceptualize in a more flexible and creative manner, enhancing the effectiveness of the experiential-psychodynamic process. Although there is no additional literature concerning the use of these cognitive variables in teaching assessment, there is a large body of literature that emphasizes their use to enhance creativity in the classroom (e.g., Dirkes, 1977; Houtz & Denmark, 1983; Hyman, 1978; Weener & Tzeng, 1972; see also Waehler & Sivec, chap. 6, this volume).

ADMINISTRATION MODIFICATIONS:
INQUIRY AND TESTING OF THE LIMITS

It is also the students' perception that what makes learning assessment difficult is the need to integrate much diverse information, presented at different psychological levels. However, what makes learning assessment even more difficult than learning psychotherapy is the need to do this integration rather quickly, without additional patient input once the data are collected. In psychotherapy, by contrast, such exploration usually takes place at a more leisurely pace, as the various aspects of personality functioning and dynamic issues are explored. There is ample time to return again and again to the patient, for additional clarification. In the traditional assessment process, however, there is sometimes little or no opportunity to return to the patient for additional clarification, to explore the patient's frame of reference, and there is hardly any opportunity to learn the many details of a patient's life experience in order to place them in proper context.

In order to deal with this problem the students are taught to investigate with each patient the particular reasons for their good and poor performance on various tests and subtests, and to investigate the "set" or expectancy of the patient concerning the test itself, as well as for parts of the assessment battery in which the patient had trouble. Students are also taught to ask specifically how the patient felt and what he or she was thinking while taking certain tests or subtests. It is also suggested that they question the patient concerning the approach he or she used in doing the particular task. Thus, what the patient thinks the test or subtest is about, how the patient wishes to be seen or understood in this test setting, and what he or she expects to happen if their performance is good or poor are all relevant issues.

The students began to see that from questions such as these, from observations of the patient's general pattern of performance, as well as from clinical intuition, a picture emerges concerning the factors that are problems for the patient in his or her performance on any particular subtest or test. In this way the students begin to build a picture of the ideographic meaning of this task for the patient, of the skills involved in success on this task for the patient, and to understand what environmental stimulus changes are necessary for successful performance. They are taught that a similar approach should be taken with any test in which the meaning of a response is not entirely clear. They are asked to modify the question or the stimulus by systematically changing one specific problem element at a time, utilizing as many trials as necessary, until a correct or appropriate response is obtained, or until it is obvious that this is not possible. This approach, called testing of the limits, is a concept borrowed from Bruno Klopfer (B. Klopfer, Ainsworth, W. Klopfer, & Holt, 1954) in his approach to Rorschach psychology, and is utilized in the class actively for many tests in the assessment battery. The chapter titled "Teaching the Interpretation of the Wechsler Intelligence Tests as Personality Instruments" (Handler, chap. 17 of this volume), provides additional information concerning this approach. The information derived from this procedure provides the student with more precise, ideographic interpretations concerning the patient's strengths and weakness, and therefore, the student is required to make fewer "guesses" concerning the precise meaning of these findings for this patient.

THE GROUP INTERPRETIVE APPROACH IN THE CLASSROOM

The initial idea for the group approach to interpretation came from a discussion with a colleague, Herbert M. Potash, who employed the approach with his students; they were asked to interpret the data collectively, in class. A demonstration of this interpretive approach was held by Dr. Potash and some of his students at a symposium during the 1989 Midwinter Meeting of the Society for Personality Assessment. The course described in this chapter utilizes such an approach.

The goal is to encourage the students to "lose distance" from the data, a process suggesting an experiential openness to the data that enhances the ability to empathize. The students can then allow themselves to become intimately involved with the data, and from that stance they are asked to generate hypotheses concerning the analysis and integration of those data. During each class session one student provides a case he or she has recently assessed. Complete test protocols are provided for the students a week before they are due to be worked on in class. Neither the students nor the first author has any history, observation, or referral issue data, except for the gender and age of the patient.

At first, the focus is on the interpretation of the individual response, gradually branching out to include patterns of data from a series of responses, and finally, integrating these interpretations across the various tests administered. It is important, at first, to model an interpretive style for the students and to facilitate and direct the discussion in order to produce an interpretation that is specifically stated and is psychologically relevant. As a way of introducing the approach to be used, the instructor presents journal articles and vignettes from his work, and demonstrates the experiential method of interpretation. Russ (1978) emphasized the importance of providing such frequent illustrations by the instructor of the process of hypotheses formation, as well as allowing active practice by the students. To begin this process the students are introduced to interpretations derived from Rorschach and TAT protocols. Cookbook sign approach interpretations are discouraged because it is felt that they facilitate a more secondary process approach to the data, and reduce the much-desired cognitive flexibility. Instead, the emphasis in the class is on the development of keen awareness of and responsiveness to one's inner experience (Handler, 1993).

Through discussion and by demonstration, it becomes evident to the students that the exploration of symbolic and narrative understanding requires a certain sensitivity on the part of the interpreter, "intimate contact with the internal life that makes the [assessor] the same as his patients" (Bouchard & Guérette, 1991, p. 388). The students gradually become aware that a stance of authentic openness is required in order to comprehend fully the patient's responses, and that effective experiential interpretation cannot be done if the interpreter "stays enclosed in his or her own expectations of meaning"; under such circumstances "the many possibilities conveyed [by the data] will pass unnoticed and the patient will not have been truly understood" (Bouchard & Guérette, 1991, p. 388). The intent of the group participation process is to help the student develop the ability to be intuitive, cognitively flexible, creative, and empathic, at least with personality assessment data. Although everyone begins enthusiastically, and a few people initially do quite well, most people feel awkward, confused, and anxious, and a few even feel resentful. They try to focus on details—"She drew the hands behind her back"; "This Rorschach response is an F–"; "He forgot to say how the people in the TAT stories were feeling." To discourage this descriptive approach to the data, the student is asked to tell *all* the things that such observations *could* mean, thereby encouraging divergent thinking. If the student cannot come up with more than one possibility, other class members are asked to help. After a number of possibilities are generated, the student is asked which among these possibilities applies to this patient, with the following directions: "Let yourself become the person who gave that response," or "Let yourself become the person who was drawn," or "How would you relate to the world if you were this tattered moth? this colorful butterfly? this figure drawing?

In the next step in the familiarization and adaptation process to this "novel" approach the students begin to shift their interpretations, from a mere description of the response, as indicated previously, to a somewhat more descriptive, but still test-based type of interpretation. This is typically seen as a resistance to making *psychologically* meaningful interpretations. An example of such an interpretation is "She seems to be alternating between a more concrete level and an abstract level"; "He seems to respond to this card with anxiety." Again, the student is encouraged to make a *psychologically relevant* interpretation concerning the meaning of this observation, in reference to this person's life issues, especially in relation to the rest of the data we have discussed so far. Many students feel awkward with this approach, demonstrating resistance in their desire to avoid committing themselves to an interpretation, and expressing some difficulty in putting into words what they experience during the interpretive process.

Judicious questioning of the students about a response is necessary if each student's interpretive potential is to be developed. Everyone in class is asked to generate *possible* interpretations to a response given by the patient to a specific test. By continued questioning a series of responses is generated, and each one is written on the blackboard. Students often believe that one response among those generated has to be correct, to the exclusion of the others. It is helpful to illustrate how each of the responses generated can sometimes be correct or appropriate, each focusing on one or another aspect of the response.

Sometimes, it is possible to reject one or more interpretations generated and/or to endorse one or more of the others. To illustrate this validation procedure the student is asked to consider several other aspects of the response, usually one or more aspects of the scoring. For example, a Rorschach response in which the content suggests that the patient has extreme anxiety concerning the expression of emotion can perhaps be validated by examining the developmental level and/or the form level of the response, as well as the determinants used in the response. The intensity of disturbance generated, and the ability of the patient to come to terms with this emotion is sometimes illustrated by asking the student to consider the details of the responses that follow; do the content and the determinants utilized in these subsequent responses suggest adaptation or continued emotional upheaval? Also to be considered is whether there is a specific conflictual source of the anxiety generated or whether the problem centers around emotional stimulation in general. The task here is to model the gradual generation of hypotheses, finding additional data to support and or to focus and refine the hypotheses, demonstrating the experiential link among sequential hypotheses, rather than considering each response separately. We also consider data from other tests, compared with the test we are analyzing. For example, a hypothesis generated from a Rorschach response that illustrates the patient's imperfect ability to maintain reality testing was supported by an examination of the MMPI data where the elevation of the scales on the right side of the profile also illustrated such strain.

The instructor might ask a student if he or she agreed with the addition or clarification of a second student, throwing the question open to others in the class if the two participants cannot mutually appreciate the blend of the two ideas. Eventually, alterations and clarifications are made in the interpretation so that it is focused and sharpened, and reasons for these changes are offered, so that intuition is balanced with data, to allow the students to understand that the process is not based on magic, and therefore can be mastered. Vague interpretations, especially those that can apply to almost anybody, are either discouraged, or better yet, refocused and sharpened so that they now take on some meaning that is unique to the patient. When the student generates a statement that does not seem to fit the data, or perhaps is not phrased in a manner that is productive to be clearly understood in a report, he or she is asked if they would write that interpretation in the final report. That question is usually enough to make the student evaluate their interpretation and reconsider it, as other students assist with evaluative feedback. Sometimes, as in a group therapy process, a student and the teacher might dialogue concerning his or her thoughts about their interpretation, if the class does not understand either its source or its relevance. Eventually the class enters into this discussion. This is also done when a student is stuck and cannot offer an interpretation. Here the teacher might ask the student what they think the patient might be trying to tell us about them by offering this response.

As we begin to build a pattern of interpretations, the students are encouraged to relate their interpretations to other findings. Sometimes they are directed to specific details of a response other than the content, in order to sensitize them to the importance of quantitative data. For example, when a student tentatively interpreted a specific Rorschach response as indicating that the patient was experiencing anxiety concerning the expression of hostile impulses, she was asked what could be added to the content interpretation by an examination of the scoring for that particular response and by the other details of the structural summary. The student pointed out that according to the Exner system, the response was a CF-, indicating that the anxiety generated concerning the expression of these impulses caused an impairment in reality testing. Another student indicated that this impairment was only transitory, because the patient gave a well-articulated and well-organized M response as the next response to the same card. Other examples of similar response patterns were sought. Several other students began to search the structural summary for additional quantitative clues concerning this patient's ability to contain hostile impulses, such as the number of aggressive movement responses, the adjusted D score, Exner's Controls Cluster and the Coping Deficit Index (Exner, 1993), as well as signs of inadequate coping, hostility, and direct impulse expression from the analysis of other test data. The use of these objective findings makes it even easier for the students to legitimize their content interpretations. They are able to take some comfort in buttressing their idiosyncratic content interpretations with empirically validated data. This approach typically allows them to begin choosing among several alternative interpretations of a piece of test data. Thus, test scores, including individual Rorschach scores and ratios, other projective test data, various Wechsler items, subtest and IQ scores, MMPI data, and sequence data are all included in attempts to formulate and/or validate various hypotheses generated by the students.

When the students are having difficulty in verbalizing a coherent and usable interpretation of the patient's response I ask them, in class, to write several sentences or a paragraph interpreting the data, as if they were actually writing a report. Given these directions, they write interpretations that are integrated and quite profound, compared with the more descriptive and more superficial responses given orally. The students read their completions aloud immediately after writing them and they are typically impressed with each other's work. We often find that several of the written interpretations can be joined, offering a more detailed and expanded exposition of the response. An additional asset of this approach is that the students get practice in report writing so that this experience is less daunting and intimidating for them.

DISCOMFORT AND RESISTANCE

Students often become resistant to an interpretation that shows the patient as significantly impaired because they have become identified with the patient. As Yalof (1996) stated, "they empathize with the client's vulnerability and may identify with it" (p.178). Such identification comes about because the student feels transparent and believes that the teacher can see beneath the surface of their defenses, and is conducting a "silent analysis," just as the student is doing with the patient. Therefore, the student and patient both feel as if they are in the same naked and bare situation. Yalof noted that there is a "sense of passivity and even victimization that binds client and student" (p. 179).

Another major problem concerns the students' resistance to an experientially based interpretive approach, because they lack self-confidence with this approach. As Russ (1978) has noted, because students lack the experience that is necessary in order to have confidence in their clinical judgment, they are typically reluctant to state an interpretive hypothesis. Nevertheless, they are encouraged to do so despite their discomfort with the lack of objective data on which it was based. In addition, the students are asked why they do not trust themselves in making these experiential interpretive hypotheses. They typically respond in several different ways. Some students indicate that they had never been asked to trust themselves as they were growing up, adding that they were taught instead to trust authority figures. Some said they are more comfortable trusting something in print rather than trusting themselves, or trusting other people's interpretations. The students are extremely uncomfortable with introspection and self-reflection when they have to be responsible for the outcome. They are more comfortable with cookbook data, and that is one of the reasons they persist in writing such statements as "The patient has good visual-motor coordination but poor understanding of social situations and poor attention and concentration," rather than attempting to figure out alternative individualistic interpretations.

In discussing the difficulties in generating accurate interpretations the students express distrust for the process of content interpretation. Although they feel that the sign approach is lacking in some ways, they indicate that they can always take comfort in the empirical basis of the approach. On the other hand, content interpretations offer far less external validation and support, and there is little hard scientific foundation for their interpretive hypotheses. This brings about the sobering realization that the interpretations are solely their responsibility, and that they cannot take refuge behind empirical findings and percentages (Fowler, 1993; Russ, 1978).

WORKING WITH RESISTANCE

As an antidote to the resistance, data are presented that debunk the validity of cookbook statements (Handler, 1988); instead, the students are asked to list all the possibilities they can think of that could account for the obtained pattern, no matter how outlandish the interpretations sound. This is an attempt to encourage divergent thinking, described earlier in this chapter. Each statement is listed on the board, and the students are gradually able to eliminate some of them, using an examination of the content of other responses, along with other relevant data.

Several discussions usually take place concerning what some students still feel is a "reckless and irresponsible" approach to assessment. These people are concerned that we are saying less than positive things or possibly harmful things about people without adequate substantiation. This attitude toward the possible harmful effects of assessment has been noted by several writers (Rader & Schill, 1973; Russ, 1978). These students have not yet had the experience of seeing how these tests can be used in making meaningful decisions that are helpful in people's lives. Russ indicated that for students to have a positive attitude toward learning assessment, they must "experience for themselves that tests and diagnostic assessment can be used to make decisions that are helpful to people's lives" (p. 453). Russ also observed that students often have difficulty in taking the responsibility for making meaningful decisions about patients, especially when they "lack the experience necessary to have confidence in their own clinical judgments" (p. 453).

If students are to function well with projective techniques, the instructor must help them work through these personal defenses and resistances. Fears that students will project their own unconscious conflicts into the unfocused and confusing mass of data must be dealt with by helping them manage their fears of doing harm. Usually this resistance takes the form of refusing to state that the patient is emotionally disturbed; they condemn the entire testing process as discriminatory and as politically incorrect. One attempt to deal with this problem was an interaction in which the instructor compared ignoring existing pathology as similar to ignoring an X ray of a broken leg or a cancerous biopsy. When the student agreed that such a procedure would be negligent, the instructor compared the assessment process to that of a pathologist or radiologist, thereby communicating one vital role the students could play in assessment. Of course, with this comparison one must be careful to avoid the comparison of assessment as *merely* a static X ray rather than a fluid process (see Handler & Meyer, chap. 1 of this volume). Another way to deal with this problem is to clarify, again and again, that as assessors we are truly interested in the patient's *strengths* as well as their weaknesses. This truth can be demonstrated, for example, when the students are taught to do sequence and process analysis of the Rorschach, illuminating the ways in which patients deal with troublesome affects, relationships, and cognitions.

Students demonstrate their resistance by verbalizing fear of discussing dynamic interpretations in their reports; they actively voice their discomfort, often couched in terms of having ethical problems saying "bad things" about a patient. They argue with tenacity about whether it is ethical or moral to diagnose a patient, verbalizing how insecure they feel about applying such labels (see Ritzler, chap. 23 of this volume). Indeed, they are reflecting the huge amount of material they must master in order to do justice to the assessment process; they must be able to master psychopathology, psychodynamics, interviewing, and developmental psychology at the very least. Viewed from this perspective, it is quite understandable that the student of assessment is anxious, sometimes resistant to deeper level interpretations, often falling back on simple, rotely memorized fixed formulas to simplify the interpretive process.

In order to deal more actively with the problem of resistance, data are presented on the use of projective tests to make predictions concerning the therapist's initial approach in psychotherapy. One example is presented where the test data were ignored and the case went awry, and several examples where the test data informed the therapy, with an excellent outcome. (See Handler & Meyer, chap. 1 of this volume, for more details about these cases.) Additional case examples of the productive use of assessment to bridge the gap between assessment and psychotherapy help to give students more confidence that the assessment methods being taught can be of great benefit to the patient.

A number of discussions ensue as to what actually constitutes "proof." Although on the surface these issues are certainly relevant and deserve discussion, they seem, in part, to constitute intellectualized resistance to self-exploration. At any point during the class there is at least silent, if not open, opposition to the notion that it is possible to form accurate, meaningful interpretations from content by relying heavily on personal life experiences and knowledge of psychodynamics. The approach taken to deal with this resistance is to meet each student's defensive stance with a series of discussions concerning fear of making interpretive errors and emphasizing that the experiential approach includes the responsibility of the examiner not merely to generate hypotheses about the patient but also to make certain that these interpretations accurately reflect the patient. It is important to demonstrate that the interpretive process involves multiple sources and multiple examples of a specific interpretation. However, a number of students usually still fear that their interpretations will be wrong and will result in damage to the patient. They are asked whether an interpretation based on an invalid sign approach, or one based on nomothetic data that merely differentiated two extreme groups, would not also produce false or misleading interpretations. A method of multiple validation of test interpretations from other sources of data is described.

Attempts are made to help students tackle their resistances by employing the Socratic method of questioning, occasionally directly challenging the resistances, but all the while consistently supporting students' efforts to use their knowledge of psychodynamic theory and their idiosyncratic associative processes. They are drawn into a dialectic process whereby the skeptical, resistant students often find themselves able to transform their vague impressions into sound, dynamically relevant interpretations. For example, a student might allow him or herself to associate to the following response to Card IV of the Rorschach: "This is a picture of a monster—little head, big arms with claws and beady eyes. It's looking down at you—it's real tall and it's smiling." The inquiry exposed a duplicity in the characterization of this monster in that the subject attributed a "mean face" to the smiling monster. A typical reaction in the experiential connection with this response is to experience a degree of tension and anxiety. Therefore the initial interpretation might be: "This person is afraid of other people—sees them as malevolent and is confused about their intentions." Although this interpretive hypothesis may or may not be accurate, it does little to bring the subject's inner experience to life. Nevertheless, this interpretation was used as a point of departure by asking for more specific details, such as "How do you make sense out of the smiling, yet mean face of a monster? Why might this person see a monster instead of some other imposing figure? Why claws instead of hands?" These basic questions forced the students to consider ever more complex aspects of the personality dynamics and perspectives of the creator. Thus, the questions facilitated and encouraged greater depth and dimensionality to the interpretive hypothesis, and were intended to direct the students' critical faculties to issues relating to object relations, dynamic conflicts, and possible therapeutic stalemates. Other typical questions included: "What kind of early childhood experiences might be necessary to create such a perception of people in this way?" "What does this person expect from people?" "How might this person's expectations influence their behavior and attitudes toward people?" "What kind of reaction will this person have to a male or female therapist?" "What can this projective response tell you about possible transference developments?" "What therapeutic stance might help this person the most?" These questions gave the students a framework for developing other critical questions with direct relevance for conceptualizing and writing experientially based, psychodynamically oriented assessment reports.

When all the interpretations are generated and those that do not stand up to additional scrutiny are omitted, the intake history and observational data are given to everyone, along with any available psychotherapy process and content data. The classroom interpretations are repeated to the therapist or to the assessor, who provides feedback concerning their accuracy.

THE USE OF ENCOURAGEMENT

As indicated earlier, a problem in teaching assessment from the perspective just described and possibly from any other perspective, is that it creates anxiety in students; they often already have some doubts about their basic ability and adequacy to do clinical work because such work requires unusual and often undeveloped skills, talents, and responsibilities. Little experiential interpretation can be accomplished given the intense concern about adequacy with which these students are struggling.

To teach this type of interpretive process one must be extremely supportive and facilitative, offering hints and direction whenever the student cannot proceed further. The classroom must become a "holding environment," to borrow a term from Winnicott. This is accomplished in several different ways. First, I ask other members of the class to assist the struggling student, offering alternative, facilitative, or clarifying assistance. The group process is quite helpful to students because their assistance is usually experienced as supportive, whereas the teacher's efforts are sometimes experienced as more judgmental. Therefore, I try to offer more facilitative hints rather than clarifying interpretations, leaving it to the interpreter's peers to assist and clarify, much like the process one often sees in a group therapy session.

Another significant problem is that the teacher is often idealized and the students feel terribly inadequate when they compare their skills to the skills of the teacher (Yalof, 1996). This attitude makes creative expression difficult because the students view themselves in such a comparatively inadequate manner. Of course such idealization has its assets as well, because it allows the teacher a degree of influence to facilitate learning. However, the goal of the classroom interpretive experience is to *empower the students*, so that eventually they come to view their ability as less discrepant from the skill of the teacher. Therefore, it is vital that the students experience themselves making interpretations that they feel are as good as those made by the teacher, and that the teacher is active in highlighting these new skills, again and again, in each class. Gradually, as their skills increase, the students' anxiety about speculating is thereby reduced and they are free to tap into creative processes.

Carefully orchestrated success experiences allow the students to feel a sense of pride and assurance as they are amply rewarded for accurate, meaningful interpretations. What is needed, then, is a great deal of differential work with each student during the class to process, assist, bolster, guide, and focus the student according to his or her individual cognitive and/or emotional needs. Thus, for example, one student might need more structure, one an example, and another, just active support and encouragement. When the instructor is successful in supplying these needs, the student's ability to interpret the data is enhanced. When he or she is unsuccessful in these efforts, the student's performance suffers and a good deal of resistance becomes evident.

The students replace fear with increasing courage as they find themselves correct far more often than they are incorrect. It is important to be quite lavish with praise, providing a good deal of active support and feedback. The students are typically asked how well they think they performed with each case, in an effort to extract self-praise. Nevertheless, posing ever more detailed and complex questions, and asking for more specificity often results in feelings of frustration on the part of the students because their initial interpretations were not sufficient. It is important to be keenly aware of the students' reactions, and to offer support and encouragement, while directly challenging them to sharpen, add dimensionality, and enhance their initial interpretations. It is also important to deal with their frustrations, while offering "solutions" to overcome their self-doubts and reactive criticism. Fowler (chap. 2 of this volume) describes an example of this approach.

The students also derive a great deal of comfort and support from each other in the classroom setting, mutually assisting each other in their struggles to formulate relevant hypotheses. This step offers a transition point to the eventual time when they will be required to interpret protocols on their own, in order to complete the three assessment reports that are required for the course. The first report is evaluated and returned with comments concerning the appropriateness of the interpretations and the format of the report. The student is allowed to rewrite the report if it is not sound, to earn a better grade. Consultation with the instructor is encouraged in order to facilitate the transfer of training from a group process to a two-person collaborative process, and eventually to a time when the report will be written by the student him or herself. All these efforts are made to demystify the interpretive process and to allow the student to feel comfortable enough to interpret the data experientially.

Once some semblance of confidence is evidenced in generating focused clinical interpretations, the students are introduced to sequential interpretation. In addition, the process of searching the data for validating evidence of an interpretation is demonstrated and is routinely done for a number of hypotheses generated. From this point one final step is necessary: to integrate the different sources of data into a series of interpretations that explicate the dynamic interplay of all psychological components. When this process is completed, the writing of an integrated, dynamically rich psychological report is possible.

A FACILITATING TEACHING HEURISTIC

Recently, the third author developed a teaching heuristic as one way in which to help the students form meaningful hypotheses. They are taught to offer an interpretation of a projective response as though it were a metaphorical expression of an individual's experience (see Hilsenroth, chap. 22 of this volume). In this procedure the student is asked to summarize the essential needs, wishes, expectations, major beliefs, and unresolved issues of the patient through the use of a short declarative statement, usually beginning with "I will," or "I wish," "I feel," or "I am." The students are told that such data represent the patient's "metaphor of the self," and therefore, provide a unique understanding of the patient (Miale, 1977). This approach facilitates interpretation because it gives the interpreter a quick and easy way to frame the response in order to promote the loss of distance necessary to empathize vicariously with the patient.

The first author utilized the metaphor approach described by Hilsenroth in the classroom setting with quite encouraging and enthusiastic results. The students found that with this focusing method they were more quickly able to imagine themselves as the patient and to verbalize self-statements with greater ease and clarity. They were able to explore an array of experiences, especially aspects of the therapeutic interaction, as if they were the patient. The requirement of beginning each statement as a self-referent encourages the student to enter the experiental world of the patient with much greater ease, compared with a typically more cognitive approach to the data. The experience of the interpreter was enhanced when the first author, using the metaphor process, asked the students to imagine themselves being the person who generated the response, while answering such questions as, for example, "How do I feel when I get close to a man (woman)? when I am faced with responsibility (decisions)?" and so on.

Another method used to facilitate interpretation is to encourage the students to make "interpersonal statements" by asking them to consider how it would feel to interact with a person who gave a specific response or pattern of responses (e. g., What would this person be like on a date? What would it be like to work for this person?). Sometimes this task is easier for the students than the approach that emphasizes the generation of self-statements, because it requires less introspection. This approach could be used as a bridge from interpersonal assessment to intrapsychic assessment, and in relating the two approaches (see Potash, chap. 9 of this volume, for a more complete description). The two approaches just described should not be viewed as alternatives or substitutes for the configurational analysis described earlier in this chapter, because the former two approaches do not utilize all the data (e. g., test scores, sequence and pattern analysis). However, the step from conceptualization to the written report becomes a much easier task from this perspective. When the metaphor and interpersonal approaches are taught in conjunction with a quantitative analysis approach, the result can be a comprehensive description and understanding of the person being assessed. The student typically comes away with a feeling of competence concerning the interpretation of the assessment data. In addition, conceptualized in this manner, the student is able to make very useful recommendations to the prospective therapist concerning an initial approach to the patient. Much valuable time can be saved and therapy can be made more effective when the personality dynamics and recommendations are helpful to the therapist. Utilizing the methods of interpretation and conceptualization described previously, the students soon also learn that the processes involved in assessment and psychotherapy are quite similar. Therefore, these two major areas of clinical work are brought together more closely in training, and hopefully in later clinical practice.

REFERENCES

Blatt, S. (1986). Where have we been and where are we going? Reflections on 50 years of personality assessment. *Journal of Personality Assessment, 50,* 343–346.

Blatt, S., & Ford, R. (1994). *Therapeutic change.* New York: Plenum.

Blatt, S., & Lerner, H. (1983). The psychological assessment of object representation. *Journal of Personality Assessment, 47,* 7–28.

Blatt, S., & Lerner, H. (1991). Psychoanalytic perspectives on personality theory. In M. Hersen, A. Kazdin, & A. Bellack (Eds.), *Handbook of clinical psychology* (Rev. ed., pp. 147–169). New York: Pergamon.

Bouchard, M., & Guérette, L. (1991). Psychotherapy as a hermeneutical experience. *Psychotherapy. 28*(3), 385–394.

Burley, T., & Handler, L. (1997). Personality factors in accurate interpretation of projective tests: The Draw-A-Person Test. In E. Hammer (Ed.), *Advances in projective drawing interpretation* (pp. 359–377). Springfield, IL: Thomas.

Dirkes, M. (1977). Learning through creative thinking. *Gifted Child Quarterly, 21,* 526–537.

Domino, G. (1976). Primary process thinking in dream reports as related to creative achievement. *Journal of Consulting and Clinical Psychology, 44,* 929–932.

Exner, J. (1993). *The Rorschach: A comprehensive system. Vol. 1: Basic foundations* (3rd ed.) New York: Wiley.

Fischer, C. (1985). *Individualizing psychological assessment.* Monterey, CA: Brooks/Cole.

Fowler, C. (1993, April). First person proximal: A student's view of learning the process of assessment. In *Teaching and learning personality assessment.* Symposium conducted at the annual meeting of the Society for Personality Assessment Meeting, San Francisco.

Greene, R. (1991). *The MMPI–2/MMPI: An interpretive manual.* Boston: Allyn & Bacon.

Handler, L. (1988, March). The use of inquiry and testing of the limits in WISC and WAIS interpretation. Paper presented at the annual meeting of the Society for Personality Assessment, New York.

Handler, L. (1993, April). Teaching personality assessment. In *Teaching and learning personality assessment.* Symposium conducted at the annual meeting of the Society for Personality Assessment Meeting, San Francisco.

Handler, L. (1995). The clinical use of figure drawings. In C. Newmark (Ed.), *Major Psychological assessment instruments* (pp. 206–293). Boston: Allyn & Bacon.

Handler, L., & Finley, J. (1994). *Convergent and divergent thinking and the interpretation of figure drawings.* Unpublished manuscript.

Handler, L., & Habenicht, D. (1994). The Kinetic Family Drawing Technique: A review of the literature. *Journal of Personality Assessment, 63*(3), 440–464.

Hilsenroth, M., & Handler, L. (1995). A Survey of graduate students' experiences, interests and attitudes about learning the Rorschach. *Journal of Personality Assessment, 64,* 243–257.

Hogan, R. (1969). Development of an empathy scale. *Journal of Clinical Psychology, 33,* 307–316.

Houtz, J., & Denmark, R. (1983). Student perceptions of cognitive classroom structure and development of creative thinking and problem solving skills. *Educational Research Quarterly, 8,* 20–26.

Hyman, R. (1978). Creativity in open and traditional classrooms. *Elementary School Journal, 78,* 266–274.

Klopfer, B., Ainsworth, M., Klopfer, W., & Holt, R. (1954). *Developments in the Rorschach technique: Vol. I. Technique and theory.* New York: Harcourt, Brace & World.

Kohut, H. (1959). Introspection, empathy and psychoanalysis: An examination of the relationship between mode of observation and theory. *American Psychoanalytic Association Journal, 7*(3), 459–483.

Kohut, H. (1977). *The restoration of the self.* New York: International Universities Press.

Kris, E. (1952). *Psychoanalytic exploration in art*. Cambridge, MA: Harvard University Press.

Lerner, P. (1991). *Psychoanalytic theory and the Rorschach*. Hillsdale, NJ: Analytic Press.

Levinger, L. (1977). Schachtel's contribution to the teaching experience. *Contemporary Psychoanalysis, 13*, 287–295.

Lyons, J. (1967). Whose experience? *Journal of Projective Techniques and Personality Assessment, 31*, 4–10.

Martindale, C. (1972). Anxiety, intelligence, and access to primitive modes of thought in high and low scorers on the Remote Associates Test. *Perceptual and Motor Skills, 35*, 375–381.

Mayman, M. (1968). Early memories and character structure. *Journal of Projective Techniques and Personality Assessment, 32*, 306–316.

Mayman, M. (1977). A multi-dimensional view of the Rorschach movement response. In M. Rickers-Ovsiankina (Ed.), *Rorschach psychology* (pp. 229–250). Huntington, NY: Krieger.

Mednick, S., & Mednick, M. (1967). *Examiner's manual: Remote Associates Test*. Boston: Houghton Mifflin.

Miale, F. (1977). Symbolic imagery in Rorschach material. In M. Rickers-Ovsiankina (Ed.), *Rorschach psychology* (pp. 421–454). Huntington, NY: Krieger.

Murray, H. (1938). *Explorations in personality*. New York: Oxford University Press.

Murray, H. (1943). *Thematic Apperception Test*. New York: International Universities Press.

Murray, J., & Russ, S. (1981). Adaptive regression and types of cognitive flexibility. *Journal of Personality Assessment, 45*, 59–65.

Myers, I. (1962). *Manual: The Myers–Briggs Type Indicator*. Palo Alto, CA: Consulting Psychologists Press.

Polkinghorne, D. (1983). *Methodology for the human sciences: Systems of inquiry*. Albany: State University of New York.

Potash, H. (1989, March). *Teaching the art of projective assessment*. Paper presented at the annual meeting of the Society for Personality Assessment, New York.

Rader, G., & Schill, T. (1973). Blind test interpretation to overcome student resistance to projective techniques courses. *Journal of Personality Assessment, 37*(3), 213–216.

Rapaport, D., Gill, M., & Schafer, R. (1968). *Diagnostic psychological testing* (2nd ed., R. Holt, Ed.). New York: International Universities Press.

Rickers-Ovsiankina, M. (Ed.). (1977). *Rorschach psychology*. Huntington, NY: Krieger.

Ritzler, B. (1993). SPA task force on training guidelines and credentialing in assessment: Recommendations for minimum standards. *SPA Exchange, 3*, 9–12.

Rothenberg, A. (1994). Studies in the creative process: An empirical investigation. In J. Masling & R. Bornstein (Eds.), *Empirical perspectives on object relations* (pp. 195–246). Washington, DC.: American Psychological Assocation.

Russ, S. (1978). Teaching personality assessment: Training issues and teaching approaches. *Journal of Personality Assessment, 42*(5), 452–456.

Russ, S. (1993). *Affect and creativity*. Hillsdale, NJ: Lawrence Erlbaum Associates.

Schachtel, E. (1959). *Metamorphosis*. New York: Basic Books.

Schachtel, E. (1966). *Experiential foundations of Rorschach's test*. New York: Basic Books.

Schachtel, E. (1967). Experiential qualities of the Rorschach blots. *Journal of Projective Techniques and Personality Assessment, 31*(4), 11–16.

Schafer, R. (1978). *Aspects of internalization.* New York: International Universities Press.

Scribner, C. (1989). *Interpreting the interpreter: Case studies of ten intuitive DAP interpreters.* Unpublished doctoral dissertation, University of Tennessee, Knoxville.

Scribner, C., & Handler, L. (1987). The interpreter's personality in Draw-A-Person interpretation: A study of interpersonal style. *Journal of Personality Assessment, 51*(1), 112–122.

Scribner, C., & Handler, L. (1993, March). *Intuitive DAP interpreters: An investigation of the lifestyles of good and poor interpreters.* Paper presented at the annual meeting of the Society for Personality Assessment, San Francisco.

Szumotalska, E. (1992). *Severity and types of depressive affect as related to perceptual style: Relationship of anaclitic and introjective depressive configuration to holistic versus analytic similarity judgments.* Unpublished doctoral dissertation, New School for Social Research, New York.

Tallent, N. (1992). *The practice of psychological assessment.* Englewood Cliffs, NJ: Prentice-Hall.

Torrance, E. (1966). *Torrance tests of creative thinking: Directions manual and scoring guide* (Verbal Test Booklet A). Princeton, NJ: Scholastic Testing Service.

Torrance, E. (1974). *Torrance tests of creative thinking: Norms-technical manual.* Princeton, NJ: Scholastic Testing Service.

Urist, J. (1977). The Rorschach test and the assessment of object relations. *Journal of Personality Assessment, 41,* 3–9

Weener, P., & Tzeng, O. (1972). The effects of subjective organization instructions and verbal creativity on the recall of random and organized lists. *Acta Psychologica Taiwonica, 14,* 38–43.

Westen, D. (1991a). Clinical assessment of object relations using the TAT. *Journal of Personality Assessment, 56,* 56–74.

Westen, D. (1991b). Social cognitions and object relations. *Psychological Bulletin, 109,* 429–455.

Williams, F. (1980). *Creativity assessment packet (CAP).* Buffalo, NY: D.O.K. Publishers.

Winnicott, D. W. (1971). *Playing and reality.* New York: Basic Books.

Yalof, J. (1996). *Training and teaching the mental health professional.* Northvale, NJ: Jason Aronson.

25

Teaching Child Assessment from a Developmental-Psychodynamic Perspective

Sandra W. Russ
Case Western Reserve University

It is a challenge today, in the age of managed care, to teach psychological assessment from a developmental-psychodynamic perspective. A series of questions arise: What do we teach? How do we teach it? On what do we focus ? What is essential? What can we eliminate? What are realistic goals for graduate students?

In preparation for writing this chapter, I reviewed my previous writings in the area of training in clinical child psychology and in assessment. To my great relief, I found that I still agree with most of it. Because the field of psychological assessment has progressed in the last 20 years, there is a larger empirical base for methods of assessment than there used to be. Therefore, in teaching assessment, we have a responsibility to integrate current research as much as possible and to generate enthusiasm about possible research questions.

WHAT DO WE TEACH?

The core ingredients that should be included in teaching child assessment to graduate students are: a developmental-psychodynamic framework, an array of psychological tests, the use of assessment in the evaluation of treatment, psychometric properties of tests, and the link between personality research and assessment.

Developmental-Psychodynamic Framework

As important as teaching the essentials of psychological testing and individual tests is the teaching of an overall framework for understanding the individual.

In the area of child psychology, the consensus in the field is that a developmental framework must be used. Various training conferences in clinical child psychology have stressed the importance of using a developmental framework in training programs (Tuma, 1985). Within the developmental framework, a variety of theoretical approaches exist, some major ones being behavioral, cognitive behavioral, psychodynamic, interpersonal, client centered, and family systems. Because my orientation is psychodynamic, I teach from a developmental-psychodynamic perspective. I try to convey that the developmental framework is essential, whereas the psychodynamic perspective is optional—it is but one approach among many. I think that this is the only responsible way to teach child assessment given our current knowledge base. There is a strong consensus in the field that developmental processes must be considered when working with children. There is not a consensus about which theoretical approach is most useful. Actually, especially in the child area, integrated treatment approaches are being developed (Knell, 1993; Wachtel, 1994). Therefore, students need to be exposed to a variety of theoretical approaches and to their theoretical rationale and empirical base, so that they can intelligently integrate theoretical approaches.

Clinical Program Context.   Basic principles of child development should permeate the clinical child program, so that the assessment sequence does not occur in isolation. Russ (1990) identified two key elements in graduate programs necessary to facilitate a developmental approach in students.

First, a developmental approach should be used in all clinical child courses. One cannot really teach child assessment, psychopathology, or intervention without using a developmental approach. Stroufe and Rutter (1984) pointed out that "perhaps the central proposition underlying a developmental perspective is that the course of development is lawful" (p. 21). Cicchetti (1984) stated that we can learn more about child pathology by studying normal functioning and more about normal functioning by studying child pathology. Serafica and Wenar (1985) stressed the importance of being familiar with the rate, emergence, and maturation of various functions. These principles of child development should permeate the clinical child program.

A second key ingredient that facilitates a developmental approach in a clinical program is research experience with children. Research experience bridges the gap between developmental theory and clinical child training (Russ, 1990). Research with children is an excellent integrator of developmental theory and clinical child issues. Because a research project usually focuses on a few specific variables intensively, the student learns about the developmental course of a process such as self-esteem, object relations, or fantasy. One must ask "What is appropriate for this age?"; "What is the developmental course?"; "How does this variable relate to other processes?"; "How do family and environmental factors affect the developmental course of this variable?"; and "How is this process affected by specific interventions?" By focusing so intensively on a few variables, the student really learns a developmental framework. Also, research experience exposes students to normal populations. For example, a student who is carrying out research on children's play in school populations of 7- to 10-years-olds learns a great deal about what normal play looks like at these ages.

Psychodynamic Framework.   The psychodynamic framework views childhood disturbance within a developmental context (Tuma & Russ, 1993). Problems arise when the developmental process has gone off track (Freud, 1965b). Anna Freud (1963/1965a, 1965b) described developmental tasks and milestones. As Tuma and Russ pointed out, a major contribution of psychoanalytic theory has been the understanding of the development of internal personality structure and functions such as object permanence and the developmental tasks that accompany psychosexual stages.

In teaching a psychodynamic framework to beginning graduate students, it is important to start with broad and essential concepts. One important concept is that of internalized conflict. The internalization of conflict that results in guilt and anxiety underlies many of the internalizing disorders of children, such as the anxiety disorders and depression. Much child psychopathology reflects the exaggerated use of defense mechanisms, compromise formations, and overt symptoms that reflect anxiety and guilt (Tuma & Russ, 1993).

A second major concept is that of object relations. The development of object relations involves the building of psychological structures necessary for adequate attachment, interpersonal relations, separation/individuation, and the resolution of developmental stages that follow (Blanck & Blanck, 1986; Mahler, 1975). Children who have inadequately developed object relations have structural deficits that impair a variety of functions, and are conceptualized as having psychotic or characterological disorders. Children with milder deficits in object relations are frequently egocentric, demonstrate an absence of shame and guilt, and have difficulty empathizing with others. When accompanied by impulse control problems, these children often act out and are antisocial. The broad syndrome of externalizing disorders describes these children, who, from a psychodynamic theoretical point of view, have major developmental problems in a number of areas.

Psychological assessment within a developmental-psychodynamic framework attempts to obtain a developmental picture of the child in specific areas of cognitive and personality functioning. Assessment determines how the child is functioning in areas of basic cognitive processes, object relations, capacity for empathy, internalized conflicts, capacity for delay of gratification, self-esteem, and coping resources. The overall profile of the child on these specific processes is then matched with a diagnostic category, such as anxiety disorder or borderline personality disorder.

The student who wants to go beyond basic psychodynamic concepts is referred to Chethik (1989), who stated that the purpose of an assessment is to understand specific problem areas and the underlying forces that have created the problems. Chethik provided an outline for carrying out a psychodynamic assessment. He listed five major categories of assessment: (a) drive assessment (libidinal and aggressive), which includes psychosexual phase development and object relations; (b) ego assessment, which includes defensive functions, quality of object relations, relation to reality, nature of thinking processes, drive regulation, central autonomous functions (intelligence, perception, language), and synthetic functions (integration experience, and ego functioning relative to age and developmental stages); (c) superego assessment, which is the extent of guilt versus fear of external authority; (d) genetic-dynamic formulation, which includes sources of conflict; and (e) treatment recommendations.

Within a psychodynamic framework, assessment should help the therapist assess the child's motivation for treatment, capacity to establish a good therapeutic alliance, and ability to use play and/or verbalization. Assessment should also identify basic conflicts, transference issues, and possible pitfalls, especially early in treatment (Tuma & Russ, 1993).

Teach an Array of Tests

The student needs to learn which tests best tap specific cognitive, affective, and personality processes. As therapy becomes more focused on specific processes (Freedheim & Russ, 1992; Shirk & Russell, 1996), the demands on the assessment process increasingly will be to identify problems in specific areas. Whether one administers a full battery of tests or administers highly specialized tests will depend on the reason for referral and the amount of other information that exists about the child and the context. Either way, the assessor must know what is available and how to evaluate what is available. I continue to think that the best way to teach this array of tests in a short period of time is to teach a few core tests in depth, with exposure to a variety of other tests for children. Teaching a standard battery in depth gives the student expertise with commonly used and respected tests and provides a model for how to learn other tests when needed. For example, a solid grounding in the Thematic Apperception Test (TAT) should generalize to the wide array of storytelling tests, such as the Children's Apperception Test (CAT), or the Roberts Apperception Test. The student should know how to apply basic principles of standardized administration and scoring, rules of interpretation, and evaluation of reliability and validity to all tests. Exposure to a variety of other tests teaches students what is available and how to find them.

Students must also be aware of which tests are most appropriate for different ethnic minority populations. Dana (1996; see also chap. 18 of this volume) has stressed the importance of developing cultural competence with multicultural populations. He stated that one must be concerned about the potential confound between culture and psychopathology. Those who work in the field of assessment need to examine the validity of various psychological tests for different ethnic minority populations and develop new culture-specific tests. Dana (1996; see also chap. 18 of this volume) discusses the TEMAS (Tell-Me-A-Story; Constantino, Malgady, & Rogler, 1988) as a picture storytelling test that has psychometric credibility and is placed within a context of cultural life experiences. The test can be used with children and consists of culture-specific sets of pictures for various ethnic groups, such as African-American and

Hispanic groups. Some norms are available for each group. It is important that students become aware of the issues involved in assessment of ethnic minority populations, that they know what tests are appropriate for these populations, and that they are motivated to develop new, more appropriate tests in the future. Jones and Herndon (1992) have discussed the general mistrust of testing by many individuals in the African-American community. Students need to be part of a serious and intense effort in the field of assessment to develop culture-specific tests as well as a new understanding of issues involved in the assessment of multicultural populations.

When one has the luxury of time, the best approach to psychological assessment is to use a battery of psychological tests combined with a play or interview session. The use of a battery of tests taps processes in a variety of areas and helps answer questions about the severity and pervasiveness of the child's problems. Because managed care has resulted in pressure to move quickly in clinical practice, one must pick and choose carefully which assessment methods to use. However, students need to have experience with standard batteries before they can intelligently decide what to select for a particular case.

The fact that most child psychologists use tests that tap different psychological processes is reflected in the results of recent surveys of child practitioners. Archer, Maruish, Imhof, and Piotrowski (1991), in a survey focusing on psychological assessment of adolescents, found that the most frequently used tests were the Wechsler Intelligence Scales, the Rorschach (ranked second overall), Bender-Gestalt, TAT, Sentence Completion, and the MMPI. Of those respondents who used a standard assessment battery (139 of 165), the most frequently used measures were the Wechsler, Rorschach, and TAT. Watkins (1991), in a review of the survey literature, concluded that a core battery of the WAIS–R/WISC–R, MMPI, Rorschach, and TAT has continued to be used over a 30-year period. This core battery is used with both adults and children.

The marketplace continues to need psychologists who have skills in psychological assessment. Weiner (1992) suggested that psychological assessment is an important function in service delivery positions. Kinder (1994) surveyed job announcements in the APA Monitor and found that 64% of job openings in the "real world" listed psychological assessment as important in the position requirements. On the other hand, in academic settings, no position listed assessment skills as a requirement. Projective tests in particular have been devalued in academic settings. Piotrowski and Zalewski (1993) found that although 85% of clinical programs still teach projective tests, 45% of training directors predicted that the teaching of projective techniques would decline in the future. Watkins (1990) made the point that when times are hard in assessment (as they are today with managed-care demands), projective tests are heavily criticized. Nevertheless, the Rorschach and TAT (and other storytelling tests) have remained heavily used and their empirical base has increased substantially (Weiner, 1996). Projective tests are especially important for assessment within a psychodynamic framework because they yield information about underlying conflicts and personality dynamics, personality structure, and object relations.

When teaching a standard battery, it helps to be clear about what kinds of processes are measured by different tests. The following description comes from Tuma and Russ (1993).

Measures of intelligence and perceptual motor functioning (such as the Bender-Gestalt) yield information about basic cognitive functioning. Even if there is not a specific question about school performance, the intelligence test is valuable because it assesses how well the child is functioning in a variety of cognitive and perceptual areas. Intelligence tests provide an anchor for a developmental assessment.

Projective tests give information about the personality structure and personality dynamics of the child. Play and interview information are useful for this purpose as well. Frequently, the Rorschach and storytelling projective technique (e.g., the TAT, the CAT, and the Roberts Apperception Test for Children) are used together.

The Rorschach is especially valuable in describing personality structure (Exner, 1986). Exner discussed how the Rorschach reveals the organizing principles that the individual uses to deal with the world. This is true of children as well as adults. The Rorschach assesses reality testing, the capacity to perceive what others commonly perceive in situations, and how affect influences cognitive functioning. It also assesses the way in which the child experiences the world in terms of availability of affect, capacity to experience negative affects, and internal representations of other people.

Projective tests that involve telling stories complement the Rorschach by assessing personality dynamics. The child's wishes, fears, conflicts, and specific areas of emotional distress can emerge. Increasingly available are projective tests containing stimuli appropriate for younger children and ethnic minorities. Drawings and fantasy play can also be used as diagnostic instruments that are especially valuable in revealing personality dynamics.

Projective tests are being rediscovered with the growing focus on the development of object relations as a key element in a child's development. Projective tests are especially suited to assessing object relations. In a recent review of the literature, Stricker and Healey (1990) defined object relations as concerning "the cognitive, affective, and emotional processes that mediate interpersonal functioning in close relationships" (p. 219). Understanding the developmental level of the child's object relations gives clues to the interpersonal world of the child and offers a framework for explaining interpersonal difficulties the child may be having. Stricker and Healey also reviewed the major Rorschach-based and TAT-based object relations scales. These scales are relatively new and are still being validated. Interpersonal content has always been part of projective tests, but these new scales and the growing theoretical literature on object relations enable us to develop a more comprehensive understanding of this area with a more systematic evaluation of this variable.

Stricker and Healey (1990) discussed two measures of object relations that are appropriate for children. One measure is Urist's Mutuality of Autonomy Scale (MOAS; Urist, 1977). The MOAS scores all responses applied to relationships manifested in Rorschach content (i.e., humans, animals, natural forces), typically but not necessarily manifested in movement responses, meas-uring the level of separation-individuation. For example, movement responses are scored for the amount of reciprocity and mutuality between figures, con-ceived as differentiation along a continuous line of development, ranging from primitive, undifferentiated fusion to the capacity for empathy and investment in others, while maintaining mutual autonomy (Lerner, 1991). The MOAS has been validated with child populations. Researchers using this measure have produced a growing body of validity studies with children that have found that it is predictive of theoretically relevant criteria, such as object representations, interpersonal behavior, dream reports (Gluckman & Tuber, 1996), and coping with severe environmental stress (Donahue & Tuber, 1993; Levine & Tuber, 1993; Tuber & Coates, 1989).

A second measure, the TAT-based Object Relations and Social Cognition Scale, developed by Westen (1991a, 1991b), assesses four dimensions of object relations: complexity and differentiation of representations of people, affect tone in relationship paradigms, capacity for emotional involvement in relation-ships and moral standards, and understanding of social causality. It has been used to investigate a number of issues concerning the object relations of children (e.g., the object relations of sexually and physically abused female children, Ornduff & Kelsey, 1996; the quality of depression in adolescents with borderline personality disorder, Wixom, Ludolph, & Westen, 1993; and the ability of the scale to distinguish female borderline adolescents from normal and other disturbed female adolescents, Block, Westen, Ludolph, Wixom, & Jackson. 1991). Students might also benefit from reading an article by Westen et al. (1991) concerning the development of object relations in children and adoles-cents.

It is important that for each test, the scores, determinants, or repetitive themes be tied to specific processes and dynamics. For example, on the Ror-schach, which processes are being measured by the different determinants should be clearly discussed. It is also important that age norms for each of these scores be considered, so that a developmental approach is utilized. Finally, placing the overall pattern of test results within a psychodynamic framework is an important step.

Assessing Children's Play. Assessing children's play is a valuable addition to a standard test battery. Although many young children cannot really engage in an interview, they can engage in play. Until recently, there were very few standardized measures of children's play available. Schaeffer, Gitlen, and San-grund (1991) have reviewed the growing number of current play measures. I developed the Affect in Play Scale (Russ, 1987, 1993) to measure fantasy and affect in children's play. This standardized measure of children's puppet play evaluates the quality of the child's fantasy and imagination, the amount and kind of affect expressed, and the modulation of the child's emotion. The fact that this validated measure of children's play, and others, are now available has implications for the area of assessment (Russ, 1995). Assessment of play prior to treatment can determine whether the child can use play in psychotherapy.

Play assessment can also be another method for assessing availability of emotion and the modulation and regulation of the emotion. Play assessment can reveal conflicts that the child is dealing with. Thematic analysis of the play can be compared with thematic analysis of the CAT or TAT. We can also learn about the child's ability to use fantasy and cognitive organization that is independent of intelligence. Finally, play assessment is well suited to a repeated measures design during the psychotherapy process. Changes in the quality of play and/or in the themes in the play should occur during therapy. Different types of changes should occur for different types of children. For example, the constricted child should express more affect in play after therapy. The acting-out child should show better modulation of affect in play after treatment.

When students watch videotapes of different kinds of players, they develop a good feel for the many different types of play. We need to develop age norms for these measures and continue to build a base for construct validity.

Use of Assessment in Evaluation of Treatment

The use of assessment methods to plan and evaluate treatment outcome should be part of the basic assessment sequence. Traditionally, assessment has been used for optimal treatment planning. In the future, assessment will and should be used for treatment evaluations as well. Kazdin (1993) stressed the need to integrate assessment and evaluation and single-case designs wherever possible in clinical practice, in spite of the fact that controlled laboratory conditions cannot be achieved. Systematic assessment and evaluation can be integrated into single-case research design. Kazdin stressed the importance of ongoing assessment and repeated measurement over time.

Maruish (1994) has pointed out that assessment skills are essential in treatment planning and outcome assessment. He stressed that psychologists should take advantage of the opportunity that the changes in health care delivery are providing. Psychological assessment is essential in problem identi-fication, treatment decision making and treatment planning, and outcome measurement. Students need to learn how to choose tests for the purpose of treatment planning and outcome assessment. They also must learn appropriate research design and statistics for these functions (Kazdin, 1993; Newman, 1994).

Ogles and Lunnen (1996) suggested a number of issues to consider when selecting among instruments. One needs to decide whether measures should be global or specific, pre-post or retrospective, self-report or rated, or individualized or standardized.

One important criterion for selecting tests for outcome assessment is that they be sensitive to change processes in psychotherapy. Shirk and Russell (1996) have presented a framework for conceptualizing interventions with children in terms of problems in specific internal processes and intervention strategies that bring about changes in them. When using this framework, the assessor must identify problems in specific cognitive, affective, and interpersonal processes, within a developmental perspective.

Weiner and Exner (1991) offered a good example of the use of the Rorschach as a measure of change in psychotherapy. They used a repeated measures design with adults and compared long-term and short-term approaches. A large number of Rorschach determinants significantly changed over time. The determinants tapped variables that were altered by psychotherapy.

Psychometric Properties

Up-to-date information on test reliability and validity should be taught along with test administration and scoring. Ideally, students will have a separate course in tests and measurements. However, even with a separate course, students should learn about evaluating a test as they are learning that test. Especially important is the validity information about treatment outcome (Weiner, 1996). The meta-analysis being carried out by Meyer and Handler for the Society for Personality Assessment on this topic should be mandatory reading in all assessment courses.

The student's exposure to current validity data frequently has the effect of creating an interest in carrying out a validity study. A standard question on my assessment exam is to design a validity study for a score on the Rorschach that would investigate a particular question.

Link Between Personality Research and Assessment

Good research in the areas of affect and personality and cognitive-affective interaction is dependent on having good measures of those processes. When students realize this link between research and assessment, then the importance of understanding psychological assessment becomes evident. Spielberger (1992) has discussed the fact that assessment is important in much personality research because constructs must be measured. Examples of how this is true should be offered. In the psychodynamic area, reviewing programmatic research in object relations while teaching the TAT is a natural integration of research and assessment.

HOW TO TEACH

Integration of Seminar and Practica

An ideal training model continues to be a seminar in assessment and field experience in a practicum setting. Our program at Case Western Reserve University has a two-semester seminar in assessment during the first year of the graduate program. Some supervised assessment of individual clinical cases occurs during this year. An assessment practicum placement occurs during the second year of the program. This placement intensively focuses on assessment, with supervision occurring in the placement. The child placements are separate from the adult placements. Student feedback has been very positive about the usefulness of a full-time practicum placement that focuses solely on assessment.

Case Presentations

An essential part of the seminar in personality assessment is the presentation of case examples. As soon as students have learned the basics of administration and scoring of projective tests, I introduce the presentation of cases into the course. Student feedback has repeatedly stressed this component as being most helpful in teaching basic concepts of test interpretation. Case presentations are helpful in a variety of ways.

Case presentations help students integrate developmental-psychodynamic theory with child assessment. They learn how to utilize a developmental perspective in approaching an individual child. Hearing the sophisticated clinician discuss what is appropriate for a 7-year-old, how normal development compares with the development of this particular 7-year-old, and why development has gone awry is helpful.

Case presentations also present the kinds of dilemmas that psychological testing can resolve. Is this child resisting school because of separation anxiety, a focused phobia, or a thought disorder? How severe is another child's depression? How capable is a child of forming a therapeutic alliance in therapy? It is especially important that students understand how assessment has helped with treatment planning in these case presentations.

Case presentations also enable the presenter to model the process of test interpretation. The process of hypothesis formation and hypothesis testing should be modeled during these presentations. Which are empirically validated indicators of dysphoric affect and which are not? How much evidence is needed before a statement goes into a psychological report? The decision-making role of the clinician can be spelled out.

When I present a case, I openly discuss how I came to a specific conclusion. For example, how have I weighed the evidence for dysphoric affect in a 9-year-old? Rules of thumb are: (a) How valid is the indicator based on the research?; (b) how many times did different indicators occur across different tests?; and (c) how far away from the data is a particular theoretical speculation? I tell students that it is good for them to have "hunches" about various possibilities when reviewing test data, but that a hunch should not go into a psychological report unless the evidence backs it up. Evidence for personality dynamics is usually less empirically based and instead typically involves levels of inference in interpretation rather than indicators of personality structure, such as reality testing. Evidence for fear of success, for example, might involve interpretation of TAT and interview themes that makes sense within a psychodynamic framework, but does not have much empirical support. The number of indicators and overall pattern of test material become important in coming to a clinical judgment about this kind of issue.

It is important to expose students to a variety of psychologists who present cases, at both advanced and beginning stages of their careers. I have increasingly had advanced graduate students give case presentations in introductory seminars because they can so easily articulate issues with which beginning students are wrestling. Advanced graduate students can also teach basics of administration and scoring and help students develop a professional attitude.

Open Discussion of Issues

Time for open discussion and debate of current issues in psychological assessment is important to build into the seminar. Most of the issues of concern to students 20 years ago are still current.

Categorizing Individuals. Many students are uncomfortable diagnosing children or making statements about them that they feel are negative. They feel uncomfortable labeling a child. Strupp (1976) made the point that the notion that assessment is harmful to individuals is "one of the great pseudoissues besetting our field– (p. 564). He pointed out that it is humanly impossible not to think and evaluate one's experience at some level. Psychotherapy itself is a continual process of hypothesis formulation and decision making about how to intervene. Assessment helps us make good decisions about intervention.

Meaningful Use of Tests. Students are concerned that tests will not be used in a meaningful fashion. Students must experience for themselves that testing makes a difference. The practica experience is crucial in the endeavor. The student must learn how treatment planning can evolve from the testing that can be used to enhance the development of the child. Students can also be exposed to new assessment approaches such as Finn's therapeutic use of assessment (Finn & Tonsager, 1992; see also chap. 20 of this volume). In addition, Handler (Handler and Hilsenroth, 1994) has devised a fantasy animal drawing and storytelling procedure that is used simultaneously as a diagnostic and a therapeutic procedure.

Appreciate Strengths and Weaknesses of Tests. Students need to strike a balance between critically evaluating tests and appreciating their usefulness. Students tend to go in one direction or the other and need help in striking a balance.

Skepticism about the Marketability of Assessment Skills. Since the advent of managed care, students are quite concerned about the future of psychological assessment. It is helpful for students to have the history of psychological assessment. The popularity of assessment has waxed and waned for various reasons, but assessment has been a fundamental skill of clinical psychologists since the beginning of the field. In order to research a question or to understand an individual, we must be able to measure in a systematic fashion.

Skepticism about Projective Tests.   Beginning students have had increasing skepticism about projective tests during the last few years. Whether this is
occurring just in our program or whether it is a national trend is hard to know,
but I would guess it is a national trend. The attacks against projective tests have
been intense and visible in the media. For example Dawes' (1994) *House of
Cards* included a widely discussed attack on the Rorschach. The empirical
support of the Rorschach (Weiner, 1996) must be presented in order to counter
these attacks. Practica experiences where projective tests are used and used well
are most helpful in altering student views.

GOALS OF TRAINING IN ASSESSMENT

In 1978, I outlined goals of graduate training in assessment (Russ, 1978). I would
make the same recommendations today, with a few additions. The original list
is as follows. On completion of graduate training, the student could:

1. Decide when testing is necessary.
2. Competently put together an assessment battery that is relevant to the
    purpose of the testing.
3. Competently administer, score, and interpret standard tests used in
    clinical settings.
4. Make appropriate basic recommendations (not necessarily refined), using
    a variety of intervention approaches.
5. Write clear, concise reports for various purposes.
6. Give feedback to client, family, and school in an effective manner.
7. Know how to evaluate test construction (reliability, standardization,
    validity).
8. Be aware of ethical issues in assessment.
9. Be able to utilize some theoretical framework in test interpretation
    (learning theory, psychodynamic, developmental, etc.). A high level of
    theoretical integration of tests results should not be expected until the
    internship year.

I would make two important additions to this list.

10. Know how to use assessment to evaluate treatment outcome.
11. Understand the issues involved in assessment of ethnic minority popula-
     tions.

Brabender (1996) has stressed the importance of developing evaluative
instruments to determine assessment competence in students. She described a
thorough oral examination at Widener University that appears to be very
comprehensive. Graduate programs need to evaluate different models for

teaching assessment and have more interaction with one another about teaching approaches.

Conclusion

The challenge in teaching child assessment from a developmental-psychodynamic perspective is to integrate the old with the new. Basics of a developmental approach and of psychodynamic theory should be taught, along with basics of administration, scoring, and interpretation of a standard battery of tests. In addition, basic principles of evaluating psychometric properties should be covered. To teach only these basics in today's health care environment is insufficient to prepare students for the changing world of psychology. We must also teach how to use tests to measure change in psychotherapy and how to design the studies, as well as how to teach students to focus and assess specific cognitive, affective, personality, and behavioral processes. Finally, we should encourage students to utilize their newfound assessment skills to investigate research questions in cognition, emotion, and personality research. This description sounds quite similar to the Boulder Model of training on which so many clinical training programs are based. The integration of research and practice is especially important in the area of psychological assessment.

REFERENCES

Archer, R., Maruish, M., Imhof, E., & Piotrowski, C. (1991). Psychological test usage with adolescent clients: 1990 survey findings. *Professional Psychology Research and Practice, 22*, 247–252.

Blanck, R., & Blanck, G. (1986). *Beyond ego psychology: Developmental object relations theory.* New York: Columbia University Press.

Block, J., Westen, D., Ludolph, P., Wixom, J., & Jackson, A. (1991). Distinguishing female borderline adolescents from normal and other disturbed female adolescents. *Psychiatry, 54*(1), 89–103.

Brabender, V. (1996, March). *Assessing student Rorschach competence in practica and internship.* Paper presented at the meeting of the Society for Personality Assessment, Denver.

Chethik, M. (1989). *Techniques of child therapy: Psychodynamic strategies.* New York: Guilford.

Cicchetti, D. (1984). The emergence of developmental psychopathology. *Child Development, 55*, 1–7.

Constantino, G., Malgady, R. G., & Rogler, L. H. (1988). *TEMAS (Tell-Me-A-Story) Manual.* Los Angeles: Western Psychological Services.

Dana, R. (1996). Culturally competent assessment practices in the United States. *Journal of Personality Assessment, 66*, 472–487.

Dawes, R. (1994). *House of cards: Psychology and psychotherapy built on myth.* New York: The Free Press.

Donahue, P., & Tuber, S. (1993). Rorschach adaptive fantasy images and coping in children under severe environmental stress. *Journal of Personality Assessment, 60*(3), 421–434.

Exner, J. (1986). *The Rorschach: A comprehensive system* (Vol. 1, 2nd ed.). New York: Wiley.

Finn, S. E., & Tonsager, M. E. (1992). Therapeutic effects of providing MMPI-2 test feedback to college students awaiting therapy. *Psychological Assessment, 4,* 278–287.

Freedheim, D.K., & Russ, S.W. (1992). Psychotherapy with children. In C. E. Walker & M. C. Roberts (Eds.), *Handbook of clinical child psychology* (2nd ed., pp. 765–780). New York:Wiley.

Freud, A. (1965a). The concept of developmental lines. In *The Writings of Anna Freud* (Vol. 6, pp. 62–87). New York: International Universities Press. (Original work published 1963).

Freud, A. (1965b). *Normality and pathology in childhood: Assessments of development.* New York: International Universities Press.

Gluckman, E., & Tuber, S. (1996). Object representations, interpersonal behavior, and their relationship to the dream reports of latency age girls. *Bulletin of the Menninger Clinic, 60*(1), 102–118.

Handler, L., & Hilsenroth, M. (1994, March). *The use of a fantasy animal drawing and story-telling technique in assessment for psychotherapy.* Paper presented at the annual meeting of the Society for Personality Assessment, Chicago.

Jones, R., & Herndon, C. (1992). The status of Black children and adolescents in the academic setting: Assessment and treatment issues. In C. Eugene Walker & M. Roberts (Eds.), *Handbook of Clinical Child Psychology* (2nd ed., pp. 901–917). New York: Wiley.

Kazdin, A. (1993). Evaluation in clinical practice: Clinically sensitive and systematic methods of treatment delivery. *Behavior Therapy, 24,* 11–45.

Kinder, B. (1994). Where the action is in personality assessment. *Journal of Personality Assessment, 62*(3), 585–588.

Knell, S. (1993). *Cognitive-Behavioral play therapy.* Northvale, NJ: Jason Aronson.

Lerner, P. (1991). *Psychoanalytic theory and the Rorschach.* Hillsdale, NJ: The Analytic Press.

Levine, L., & Tuber, S. (1993). Measures of mental representation: Clinical and theoretical considerations. *Bulletin of the Menninger Clinic, 57*(1), 69–87.

Mahler, M.S. (1975). On human symbiosis and the vicissitudes of individuation. *Journal of the American Psychoanalytic Association, 23,* 740–763.

Maruish, M.E. (1994). Introduction. In M. Maruish (Ed.), *The use of psychological testing for treatment planning and outcome assessment* (pp. 3–21). Hillsdale, NJ: Lawrence Erlbaum Associates.

Newman, F. (1994). Selection of design and statistical procedures for progress and outcome assessment. In M. Maruish (Ed.), *The use of psychological testing for treatment planning and outcome assessment* (pp. 111–136). Hillsdale, NJ: Lawrence Erlbaum Associates.

Ogles, B. M., & Lunnen, K. M. (1996, July). Outcome measurement: Research tools for clinical practice. *The Ohio Psychologist,* pp. 21–26.

Ornduff, S., & Kelsey, R. (1996). Object relations of sexually and physically abused female children. *Journal of Personality Assessment, 66*(1), 91–105.

Piotrowski, C., & Zalewski, C. (1993). Training in psychodiagnostic testing in APA-approved PsyD and PhD clinical psychology programs. *Journal of Personality Assessment, 61*, 394–405.

Russ, S. W. (1978). Teaching psychological assessment: Training issues and teaching approaches. *Journal of Personality Assessment, 42*, 452–456.

Russ, S. W. (1987). Assessment of cognitive affective interaction in children: Creativity, fantasy, and play research. In J. E. Butcher & C. Spielberger (Eds.), *Advances in personality assessment* (Vol. 6., pp. 141–155). Hillsdale, NJ: Lawrence Erlbaum Associates.

Russ, S. W. (1990) The integration of developmental perspective with clinical child training. In P. Magrab, & P. Wohlford (Eds.), *Improving psychology services for children and adolescents with severe mental disorders: Clinical training in psychology* (pp. 95–99). Washington DC: American Psychological Association.

Russ, S. W. (1993). *Affect and creativity: The role of affect and play in the creative process.* Hillsdale, NJ: Lawrence Erlbaum Associates.

Russ, S. W. (1995). Play psychotherapy research: State of the science. In T. Ollendick & R. Prinz (Eds.) *Advances in clinical child psychology* (pp. 365–391). New York: Plenum.

Schaefer, C., Gitlin, K., & Sandgrund, A. (1991). *Play diagnoses and assessment.* New York: Wiley.

Serafica, F., & Wenar, C. (1985). A developmental perspective on training clinical child psychologists: The Ohio State University Clinical Child Psychology Program. In J. Tuma (Ed.), *Proceedings: Conference on Training Clinical Child Psychologists* (pp. 116–120). Washington, DC: American Psychological Association.

Shirk, S., & Russell, R. (1996). *Change processes in child psychotherapy.* New York: Guilford.

Spielberger, C. (1992, Spring). New horizons for personality assessment. *SPA Exchange,* pp. 6–7.

Stricker, G., & Healey, B. (1990). Projective assessment of object relations: A review of the empirical literature. *Psychological Assessment: A Journal of Consulting and Clinical Psychology, 2*, 219–230.

Stroufe, L. & Rutter, M. (1984). The domain of developmental psychopathology. *Child Development, 55*, 17–29.

Strupp, H. (1976). Clinical psychology, irrationalism, and the erosion of excellence. *American Psychologist, 31*, 561–571.

Tuber, S., & Coates, S. (1989). Indices of psychopathology in the Rorschachs of boys with severe gender identity disorder: A comparison with normal control subjects. *Journal of Personality Assessment, 53*, 100–112.

Tuma, J. (1985). Recommendations: Conference on training clinical child psychologists. In J. Tuma (Ed.), *Proceedings: Conference on Training Clinical Child Psychologists* (pp. 168–169). Washington, DC: American Psychological Association.

Tuma, J., & Russ, S. W. (1993). Psychoanalytic psychotherapy with children. In T. Kratochwill & R. Morris (Eds.), *Handbook of psychotherapy with children and adolescents* (pp. 131–161). Boston: Allyn & Bacon.

Urist, J. (1977). The Rorschach test and the assessment of object relations. *Journal of Personality Assessment, 41*, 3–9.

Wachtel, E. (1994). *Treating troubled children and their families.* New York: Guilford.

Watkins, C. (1991). What have surveys taught us about the teaching and practice of psychological assessment? *Journal of Personality Assessment, 56*(3) 453–465.

Weiner, I. C. (1992). Current developments in psychodiagnosis. *The Independent Practitioner, 12*, 114–119.

Weiner, I. C. (1996). Some observations on the validity of the Rorschach Inkblot Method. *Psychological Assessment, 8*, 206–213.

Weiner, I. C. & Exner, J. (1991). Rorschach changes in long-term and short-term psychotherapy. *Journal of Personality Assessment, 56*(3), 453–465.

Westen, D. (1991a). Clinical assessment of object relations using the TAT. *Journal of Personality Assessment, 56*, 56–74.

Westen, D. (1991b). Social cognitions and object relations. *Psychological Bulletin, 109*, 429–455.

Westen, D., Klepser, J., Ruffins, S., Silverman, M., Lifton, N., & Boekamp, J. (1991). Object relations in childhood and adolescence: The development of working representations. *Journal of Consulting and Clinical Psychology, 59*(3), 400–409.

Wixom, J., Ludolph, P., & Westen, D. (1993). The quality of depression in adolescents with borderline personality disorder. *Journal of the American Academy of Child and Adolescent Psychiatry, 32*(6), 1172–1177.

VII

ASSESSMENT IN INTERNSHIP
EXPERIENCES

As we indicated in the Preface, two chapters on hospital-based internship assessment learning experiences were included because it is in this type of internship setting that assessment is used most frequently. Although both chapters in this section focus on personality assessment training in a hospital-based internship setting, they are different in some respects. Lovitt focuses primarily on supervision and the supervision process, as well as on a discussion of conceptual and theoretical issues, whereas Blais and Eby address the difficulties encountered in getting the interns started doing assessment during the first 2 weeks of the internship year. They also review issues that are important to supervision from within the context of an observational learning experience, by watching a senior staff psychologist conduct an assessment consultation. We anticipate that these two chapters will be very helpful to students who are preparing to apply to internships or to those who are just beginning their internship training.

Robert Lovitt, in his chapter titled "Teaching Assessment Skills in Internship Settings," describes general principles of hospital-based consultation. Lovitt provides a clear-cut outline of assessment skills needed in the internship setting, along with information concerning ways in which to develop these different skills. He gives valuable examples throughout. Lovitt describes general principles of hospital-based consultation, such as the need to clarify referral issues with the patient and the referral source. Students are taught to review the patient's history to determine patterns of adaptive failure that would be important to study in order to clarify the focus of the evaluation, and the patient is also encouraged to develop referral questions. Students are also encouraged to use several frames of reference and theoretical orientations to interpret test data. Several administrative and technical issues emphasized by supervisors are reviewed in this chapter. Lovitt encourages trainees to take highly active roles in processing assessment information while performing consultations in this medical setting. A model for teaching students to assume a problem-solving conceptual orientation during the assessment process is described.

Mark A. Blais and Marla D. Eby, in a chapter that is colorfully titled "Jumping Into Fire: Internship Training in Personality Assessment," review many of the same principles discussed by Lovitt, but they utilize a different format. They have the reader follow the personality assessment training process of a single case, from the point of receiving the referral issue(s), followed by helping to formulate appropriate referral questions, to the nuances of how to provide quick and concise feedback to the treatment team. They also review the outline of an assessment course taught during the assessment year that focuses on an expansion of skills learned after the students' training in their graduate programs.

26

Teaching Assessment Skills in Internship Settings

Robert Lovitt
University of Texas Southwestern Medical Center at Dallas

The internship setting is where students begin to synthesize diverse experiences acquired from the academic classroom and structured practicum placements. Dealing with health problems in a multidisciplinary setting requires that the student integrate diverse bodies of technical knowledge in a systematic and interpersonally sensitive manner. The psychology supervisor directs this process most effectively when he or she models, mentors, and structures experiences so that each student finishes the year having achieved a set of clearly articulated skills (Table 26.1).

This chapter presents a model and discusses techniques that describe ways to work toward achieving some of these goals. The insights are generated from experiences of supervising psychology interns in a captive and free-standing internship (Brabender, 1991). Administrative management of a psychology service as well as clinical supervision in a medical setting is critical for effective teaching to occur. Internship experiences described take place in a large county hospital of approximately 1,200 beds, which is the major teaching hospital for

TABLE 26.1
Terminal Internship Goals

Master fundamentals of scoring, administration, and interpretation of major psychological tests

Learn basics of data integration

Integrate data with appropriate theoretical concepts

Interpret data from a biopsychosocial perspective

Learn fundamentals of consultation

Function as problem-solving consultant

Provide therapeutic feedback

the University of Texas Southwestern Medical Center at Dallas. Psychology students interact with psychiatric residents and psychiatry faculty. They also interact with social workers, nursing trainees, psychology faculty members, and a broad range of residents from various medical services. Services in which students rotate are inpatient psychiatry, outpatient psychiatry, emergency services, and a consultation-liaison psychiatry service. Psychological assessment and consultation are actively utilized and are viewed as important services on all of these units.

An orientation of problem-solving consultation (Lovitt, 1988; Maloney & Ward, 1976; Tallent, 1992) with conceptual and empirical processing of data (Weiner, 1986) underlies diagnostic activity. Conceptualization, problem solving, and consultation while using psychological tests are the focus of this teaching. Interns are taught to use tests with several sources of data to answer clinical questions. Diagnostic and treatment questions are resolved by employing a series of skills in order to generate test data that are integrated with pertinent referral questions and appropriate theoretical and technical concepts. The supervision is dependent on interdisciplinary contact in settings that are constructed, monitored, and modified so interns can learn and practice skills in a unique medical culture (Lovitt, 1992). Selected aspects of supervision and program development in teaching interns conceptual problem solving are reviewed.

REASON FOR ASSESSMENT

Problem-solving consultation begins by articulating and clarifying problems that exist for the patient and referring professional. *Reason for assessment* typically has been referred to as the "referral problem." Teachers often attribute main responsibility for generating the referral question to the referring professional. This is a limited and unsatisfactory way to generate pertinent referral questions because it places the psychologist in the mind set of a technician. This restricted focus tends to seriously minimize and overlook critical activities that should occur at this stage and that can enhance the quality of the consultation.

Contrasting the diagnostic roles of technician (psychometrician) with those of the consultant helps to clarify this point for the trainee. A technician assumes minimal independence in generating output that impacts upon the management of patients. The technician has responsibility for administering and scoring procedures that have been *ordered*. Final clinical interpretation is conducted by the referring physician. The consultant, on the other hand, conducts an independent review of pertinent history and clinical findings. He or she then responds to the referent's concerns by selecting procedures that are defined as relevant and interprets the data (tests and history) to answer all questions the consultant believes are pertinent to referral issues. In carrying out this task the consultant has full latitude to address issues that are considered relevant. The consultant may then generate referral questions that have not been articulated by referring sources and investigate them if it is thought that they are pertinent to the patient's difficulties.

Effective consultation occurs when we understand the referral question as stemming from three sources: (a) the referring professional, (b) the patient, and (c) the psychologist. Even experienced referral sources often do not directly ask the most important referral questions (Cohen, 1980; Maloney & Ward, 1976). The most appropriate referral questions are typically discovered after extensive review of pertinent historical data by the psychologist. A "good" referral question generates information critical to patient care that referring persons previously did not possess. The psychologist should be providing new information or should be reframing old information critical to patient care.

Trainees are instructed to listen to referral sources in order to understand *multiple* levels of communication. At one level we listen to the facts of the case. We bring to the case several *frames of reference* that we use to understand behavior. Some of these frames of reference might be theoretical (psychodynamic, psychoanalytic, developmental, behavioral), others treatment focused (rehabilitation, psychotherapeutic or taxonomic *DSM–IV*). Pertinent behavior is processed using these frames of references in order to ask of oneself: Given what the referent already knows about the patient, what can we add to increase degrees of freedom regarding management? It must be determined precisely what the referring person (patient or professional) understands and does not understand about the patient's behavior. Assessment, no matter how skillful, that answers questions and provides information already known is of little value. Reports elegantly written and astute in conclusions that do not add to the existing information base cannot be justified in terms of time, effort, and money spent by consumers. It is important that the trainee be taught to differentiate between what is understood and not understood on the part of the referring person and to focus assessment efforts in the latter area.

Generating a good referral question begins with teaching trainees to review history and determine what *patterns* of adaptive failure exist that are repetitive and limiting to the patient. These failures should be initially described and understood in behavioral terms. We encourage students to track these problematic behaviors developmentally and to describe them in terms of the environmental context in which they occur. Students are taught to obtain an in-depth cross-sectional pattern of the patient's performance in several critical life areas, such as work, family, and recreation. Dysfunctional performances are noted. A judgment is then made as to whether these problems materially impair the patient's functioning in ways related to the *patient's* current difficulties. If the judgment is a positive one, the trainee is taught to think about whether these behaviors are related to a *syndrome* of psychiatric disorder and to think about the *personality processes* that may underline problematic behaviors. (Syndromes and personality processes are discussed more thoroughly later in the chapter.) After this review the trainee is encouraged to make a judgment concerning which behaviors are most problematic and need to be more thoroughly investigated (referral question) to provide a meaningful consultation. Referral questions generated by the psychologist may be ones that have never been considered by the professional or the patient. For example, a psychiatrist requests a consultation about a 45-year-old man with a history of compulsive gambling, obsessional activity, and depression. There is a long-standing relationship with the psychiatrist and it is understood that he basically asks for assistance in generating a treatment program. A review of the patient's history and discussion with the psychiatrist reveals that the psychiatrist has an excellent understanding of the psychodynamics underlying the patient's behavior and that he has a clear diagnostic sense of what is wrong with the patient. However, the patient has never had a steady job and is disheartened by this life problem. The patient and psychiatrist have not asked for specific assistance in assessing and targeting strengths, weaknesses, and reasons for the limited job history. After reviewing the history and assessing the current situation, it may be suggested to the patient that it would be productive to focus on vocational issues. The evaluation centers around assessing vocational issues because of the recommendation of the psychologist. This question had not initially been asked by anyone. The psychologist reframes dynamic, diagnostic, and treatment issues to more fully understand why the patient rarely works. Issues of cognitive style and structure are related to vocational and work issues.

PATIENT REFERRAL QUESTIONS

Several reasons exist for encouraging patients to generate questions they would like to have addressed via the psychological examination. In medical settings, large percentages of referrals are generated by physicians regarding patients who may have limited motivation to engage in personal exploration; several patients may have significant resistances to these procedures. For example, a patient who enters the hospital with a broken arm may be referred for a psychological consultation because the patient refuses to take medications due to paranoid ideation. The patient may not realize that this ideation is a problem and may see the presenting problem as a broken arm. Before the trainee can engage in an in-depth exploration with the patient, some type of alliance must be established between psychologist and patient for the patient to be motivated to engage in a psychological exploration. There is a style of rapport-building interview in which trainees are encouraged to engage to generate maximum cooperation in order to obtain maximally beneficial test data (e. g., avoiding short TAT and Rorschach records or MMPIs with high K scores).

In the rapport-building interview, we encourage the patient to generate questions that they would like to have answered during the course of assessment. We encourage the patient to develop a sense of control and investment in the evaluation. We do not want the patient to experience the testing as if something is being done to him or her. We want patients to believe the evaluation will address issues about which they are vitally concerned. We seek to minimize resistances and enhance the quality of the patient's participation in the evaluation. We have regularly found significant percentages of patients with limited motivation to participate in testing because of passive aggressive, paranoid, and other apprehensive affective and cognitive states. Most referral sources do not adequately prepare patients for psychological testing. Some referral sources communicate negative attitudes about all those questions that must be answered. To obtain maximum participation, students are instructed regarding specifics of how to conduct a facilitating interview.

The student is taught to begin the interview by encouraging the patient to share their perception of why he or she is in the hospital. Ordinarily a question like "what kinds of problems bring you into the hospital (clinic)" will initiate this process. Patients typically respond with any combination of four categories of explanations: (a) someone brought them here (police, parents, or other family members), (b) they have an illness, such as depression or cardiac difficulties, (c) they have experienced behavioral activities that restricted them in some way (e. g., the patient is not able to work or is so unhappy and upset that they are not able to take care of their children), or (d) they experienced a series of overwhelming negative feelings such as intense anger or intense feelings of lack of worth. Trainees are encouraged to accept and initially support the patient in whichever category they emphasize. The student is encouraged to work with the patient so that the patient can clearly articulate how this condition has a limiting and disturbing impact upon pertinent and important behaviors and how it produces negative feeling states. If a patient insists that the only reason that they are here is because they were forced into the hospital by the police the student can help the patient see how this condition is interfering with behaviors that the patient considers important (e. g., working or being involved in sports, and how it has generated a series of negative feelings). From this point the patient is encouraged to recognize that these behavioral limitations and feelings are unpleasant states and ones of which the patient wishes to be free. The psychological assessment is offered as an independent way of generating information that will help the patient regain control over his or her life and allow them to reconnect with the behaviors and conditions that they feel have been lost. The evaluation is presented as a series of opportunities for the psychologist to get to know the patient and to assist the patient in regaining access to those conditions in which he or she wishes to be involved. The evaluation may be offered as a means of mediating between differences of opinions expressed between the patient and the police. The psychologist is careful to present him or herself as an independent agent, not on anyone's side, but interested in the patient's welfare. The ensuing evaluation is specifically linked with efforts to provide the patient with alternatives about that which is distressful. The evaluation is set up so that the patient has specific motivation to display coping strategies, defenses, and interpersonal traits as fully as possible. This effort helps the patient and the psychologist establish an alliance in order to clarify and understand the nature of the problems that are distressing to the patient. In the final analysis patients have the right to refuse to participate in the psychological evaluation; students are encouraged to communicate in their attitude a respect for this right. Before the evaluation is begun, students are taught to explicitly ask the patient if they are ready and willing to participate in the evaluation. If the patient says "no," the student then communicates that they will return at another time to reevaluate the patient's decision. Even if a patient could be coerced into such participation, we are typically not able to generate helpful data on psychological tests from extremely defensive patients. Students are encouraged to acknowledge this right on the part of patients and seek to maximize a sense of cooperative and genuine collaboration between psychologist and patient.

In summary, the student is trained to encourage a clarification of the patient's perception of the current difficulty and to link the assessment procedures to this perceived perception. What emerges is often a different perspective and set of concerns on the part of the patient from what the referring professional or psychologist has defined as a referral issue. Those concerns that are articulated at this time serve as one of the foundations around which feedback will be offered to the patient.

FRAME OF REFERENCE

Appropriate interpretation occurs after data have been considered from several conceptual and technical frames of reference. This activity accompanies conceptual and empirical data processing. The impact of biopsychosocial variables on data must be routinely evaluated and taught to trainees performing in medical settings. One of the most important of these is the impact of biological variables, specifically the effects of disease processes on psychological functioning (Engle, 1980) and as they are reflected in psychological test data (Graham, 1993). Psychologists intending to function in a behavioral medicine setting must have an appreciation of the impact of disease on personality functioning (Green, 1993). To gain this experience students are assigned to rotations on a consultation-liaison service. In this setting they routinely evaluate patients with a broad range of disease processes in conjunction with psychiatric difficulties. There is extensive research (Green, 1993) indicating that patients who are ill have a series of routine disruptive emotional reactions as part of their adaptation. These reactions often are not pathological but are temporarily adaptive (but painful and disruptive) reactions to disease. Although not pathological they may cause transitory deviations from the norm on psychological tests (Lovitt, 1997). Trainees are sensitized to these processes and are taught to modify their expectations of what to expect on testing on the basis of these experiences. This training allows them to develop an appreciation for the profound effect that disease routinely has on the operation of personality processes and psychological test data. When interpreting personality test data, we routinely review the medical histories of patients. Students review psychological test data for large samples of such patients. They develop norms for such patients that differ from standard norms developed for major test instruments. Accurate interpretation in these populations (particularly on Scales 1,2, and 3 of the MMPI–2) occur when there is an understanding of these differences as partially secondary to disease and not always a somatization process.

In medical and psychiatric settings, it is necessary to communicate in the technical language used in organizing and directing clinical work; this begins with the language of DSM–IV. A large percentage of referral questions begin around identifying Axis I and Axis II diagnoses and their treatment implications (Sweeney, Clarkin, & Fitzgibbon, 1987). For many patients these classifications may be made by a careful review of history and clinical findings. For others the diagnostic picture is unclear and treatment is begun as an educated trial-and-error activity based on the best "guess" as to what the diagnosis is. It is important to teach psychology trainees how to establish their credibility on a service—credibility independent of their psychology supervisor. Most physicians need to be actively taught by psychologists as to how and when our consultation efforts expedite timely and effective treatment. During daily rounds the clinical status of each patient is reviewed by the treatment team. Trainees are taught to independently appraise the data being reviewed by the team in order to (a) appraise the confidence level of the physician concerning their best guess diagnosis, and (b) appraise whether our assessment efforts can appreciably refine the diagnosis. This is done most effectively by demonstrating to the student how such refinement is done. The supervisor should consistently participate in these conferences and model behavior for trainees. The rationale and consultation style of the supervisor is critically discussed with the student; the student is encouraged to increasingly take responsibility for this activity. In those cases in which we believe psychological assessment will add to the diagnosis, we make such a recommendation. In our setting this recommendation is usually responded to in a positive manner. The early identification of patients for whom a psychological consultation would be helpful is a major role for psychology staff in a medical setting. This is particularly true in managed-care environments where increased pressure exists to eliminate psychological testing. It behooves psychologists to regularly demonstrate the relevance of assessment in medical settings. There can be significant resistance or naive enthusiasm on the part of medical referring sources. A frequently encountered resistance is the genuine belief on the part of some physicians that a good history and clinical examination are all that is really needed to resolve pertinent issues in a great majority of cases. Other physicians may routinely refer inappropriate cases, such as patients who are clinically unable to participate in testing because of depression or psychosis. Psychologists must routinely deal with these attitudes from an educational and not from a confrontational perspective.

A starting point is to inform trainees of the necessity of understanding major clinical and historical criteria for Axis I and Axis II syndromes delineated in DSM–IV (American Psychiatric Association, 1994). The student is instructed and encouraged to learn how to measure and evaluate each of these criteria in the most efficient manner. Some of these criteria are measured most effectively by history (e. g., sleep loss) and others by psychological testing (e.g., thought disorder). Throughout the internship year, attention is directed to historical data and their regular integration with psychometric data in generating conclusions. Students are regularly supervised about where in the historical data they may find pertinent criteria for each Axis I and Axis II diagnosis. Knowledge of these criteria is utilized by the student in guiding their diagnostic interview and helping in the selection of appropriate tests. For example, with a schizophrenic patient knowledge of the criteria might encourage the student to carefully interview the patient for the presence of hallucinations, and if present, to determine how they are experienced and the type of understanding the patient has about these hallucinations. If issues of a thought disorder are unclear, the student could then be guided toward selecting specific tests and looking at specific test parameters to assess whether a thought disorder is present and the type of thought disorder that exists. The student is encouraged to think in this format for the differing Axis I and Axis II groups.

The appropriate use of pertinent biopsychosocial variables and concepts allows us to process data and guide the course of assessment activity. The use of theory and constructs plays several roles in this process (Lovitt, 1987). They play a crucial role in refining referral questions, guiding selection of tests, focusing attention on pertinent test parameters, and modifying and guiding test interpretation. Assessors may employ an infinitely broad array of theories to modify test interpretation; those constructs selected should be relevant to efficient and comprehensive management of referral questions typically encountered in a given work setting. Differing work settings support the use of differing theoretical constructs. Someone being trained to provide services in a rehabilitation setting would use different theoretical constructs from someone functioning in a psychoanalytic institute. The constructs that trainees are encouraged to use are ones most helpful in psychiatric and general medical settings. In these settings we find a broad range of psychiatric problems in patients who come from a broad range of socioeconomic settings, with vastly different sets of motivations and treatment needs. Supervision also focuses around the encouragement of students to identify with positive and constructive assessment attitudes. A limiting attitude is one in which theoretical orientations are explicitly or unintentionally ranked so that some theoretical orientations are seen as superior to others. Students are encouraged to view differing theories as being more or less suited to differing work settings and differing referral questions. The types of constructs used to understand patients from a psychoanalytic perspective might have limited utility with a patient from a lower socioeconomic life position with a spinal cord injury, who is in need of rehabilitation services. With several exceptions students are discouraged from routinely using the same theoretical orientation in differing rotational settings. They are encouraged instead to draw on constructs from psychodynamic, developmental, social, cognitive behavioral, and psychiatric frames of reference within which to interpret their data. There are, however, a core set of psychodynamic constructs to which students are instructed to routinely pay attention, either from history or clinical findings. These are constructs fundamental to understanding dysfunctional human behavior in any and all clinical settings. Inclusion of these constructs leads to evaluation of several processes underlying dysfunctional behavior in the most effective fashion. It is only by employing such an orientation that we can effectively intervene in the great majority of cases. A list of the constructs that we routinely utilize and assess may be found in Table 26.2.

TABLE 26.2
Constructs Routinely Assessed in Personality Assessment

Reality-testing operations	Thought processes
Defenses	Coping style range and effectiveness
Stress capacity	Interpersonal style
Self concept	Symptom picture
Intellectual level	Cognitive limitations

INTERPRETATION

One of the most difficult areas to teach is the process of data integration. Recent offerings have addressed this complex issue (Beutler & Berren, 1995; Ganellen, 1996; Lovitt, 1993; Meyer, 1997). Students at the end of the internship year are expected to have familiarized themselves with the fundamental stages of this process. These fundamental stages are dependent on the student understanding the complex multifaceted nature of behavior and that behavior varies as a function of diverse developmental, biological, environmental, and psychodynamic forces. There is no single adequate measure of behavior. The differing measures of a similar behavior (tests or history) are to be understood as measuring differing aspects of the behavior. The differing measures of behavior are to be integrated by the psychologist to capture the complexity of behavior. Students are expected to evaluate the adequacy of test data or a behavioral sample and to weigh its contribution to interpretation based on the "goodness" of the data. A Rorschach record with low R (15) and high lambda (1.5) might be given less weight in assessing the presence of a thought disorder because of limitations brief records possess in assessing thought disorder.

Students are taught to incorporate knowledge of contrasting strengths of differing tests before generating interpretations. For example, the MMPI is a more effective instrument in assessing somatization disorder then is the Rorschach and therefore should be weighted more heavily (Lovitt and Claassen, 1997).

In conceptual problem solving, we articulate diagnostic possibilities and personality processes pertinent to those behaviors that are being evaluated. Historical, clinical, and test data that evaluate syndromes and personality processes are identified. Students then incorporate reliability and validity information into their thinking so they may evaluate the sturdiness or goodness of each sample of data they are employing. For example, a patient has a 9-year-old son about whom she is concerned because of lying behavior. In order to understand and treat the behavior properly, we must first target the cause. See Table 26.3 for possible etiological causes of lying behavior. Each potential cause of "lying" must be considered. Omission of any of these possibilities excludes the possibility of its assessment. If one does not consider a hearing loss, it may never be evaluated or detected. Each potential cause of the dysfunctional behavior must be ruled out during the evaluation. Students are taught to identify the historical, clinical, and test manifestations of each of the etiologies and to evaluate them in the most appropriate manner. This focused approach to data analysis stands in contrast to the case study format (Tallent, 1983). The case study format is often used in introductory workshops, introductory courses, and practicum settings. In this format test data and other sources of information are evaluated to say everything that can be said about a patient. When using a focused approach, trainees are instructed to look for the distinctive and unique test patterns associated with syndromes and specific personality processes, in order to address specifically formulated referral questions. Students are also taught how to evaluate each of these areas in an empirical manner by drawing on validated relationships between test indices and pertinent behaviors.

ADMINISTRATION

Effective teaching can occur only when consistent attention is directed toward establishing and maintaining a psychology service in a medical setting. This presents problems unique to teaching hospitals and services within medical schools. To maintain success requires constant monitoring of several activities. Effective consultation depends on students being thoroughly familiar with the medical environment and referral and practice patterns of their team members. We place a major emphasis on trainees working collaboratively with physicians and members of the health care team. Students make daily rounds with the medical team. They become familiar with the sights and smells of the hospital. They develop familiarity with routine diagnostic and laboratory tests and with the transition from regressed personality functioning accompanying illness to the reemergence of coping abilities. Trainees play the role of behavioral and diagnostic consultant and psychotherapist in this setting. Physicians have to be dealt with so psychological services are perceived as supportive of and collaborative rather than competitive with psychiatry. Attempts to establish consulting relationships with medical services, without the support of psychiatry, may be particularly problematic. Consultation and teaching to medical students and residents is of highest priority. Those activities that facilitate rapid patient diagnosis and treatment and that draw upon technologies not routinely taught to physicians are particularly valued.

TABLE 26.3
Potential Causes of "Lying"

Psychosis	Hearing deficit
Mental retardation	Attention deficit
Anxiety disorder	Thought disorder
Family dysfunction	Cultural reasons
Personality disorder	Learning disorder

The supervisor must constantly serve as a buffer between the medical personnel and the psychology interns. Many interns have limited preparation for the protocol of hospital behavior. It takes some time for psychology students to become accustomed to such routine activities as consistent charting, 24-hour responsibility, and constant needs for coverage. The need for rapid turnaround and rapid writing of reports can be particularly problematic. The supervisor may also need to regulate the ebb and flow of referrals to make certain that psychology interns have a consistent supply of work and are not overwhelmed. The psychology service cannot "shut down" during vacation time and when students have problematic examinations. The psychology supervisor should be prepared to shoulder the clinical responsibility themselves if this is necessary and to monitor constantly the progress of work to make certain that work is received in a timely manner. There may be times that a psychology trainee may have difficulty becoming accustomed to traumatic injuries and illnesses. At these times the psychology supervisor may need to become particularly active in facilitating this process while teaching the trainee to behave in a professional and appropriate manner.

Students are expected to become knowledgeable concerning psychiatry, general medicine, nursing, social work, and occupational therapy. In psychiatric settings they are expected to become informed regarding psychopharmacology, the various psychotherapies, the impact of disease upon behavioral functioning, psychodynamics, and the impact of developmental milestones on psychological functioning. It is during patient staffings and teaching conferences that the various disciplines present their findings and the patient data from the various disciplines are integrated. The more knowledgeable the student is about the other disciplines the more adequately can the student modify their interpretation taking into account all of the relevant factors impacting upon assessment data. The students are expected to modify their interpretation of test data as they incorporate additional data from the other disciplines. For example, an interpretation of an MMPI might be significantly modified after hearing a patient's health history, or the interpretation of a Rorschach with disordered thinking might be modified on hearing intensive behavioral descriptions of the patient's performance from nursing and occupational therapy. Because all of the data pertinent to a case might not be available until the staff meeting takes place, this necessitates that a student be able to make immediate modifications or changes in test interpretation and feedback. During supervision students are regularly informed that what emerges from supervision is the best available interpretation of the data based on currently available information. If in the judgment of the psychologist other disciplines present good pertinent data that are contradictory to the current test evaluation, the student may need to modify the interpretation at the last moment. This activity dictates that students must be able to (a) identify *pertinent* new information from large amounts of novel information, (b) ask themselves whether the data impact upon the current evaluation, and (c) generate a new best explanation to fit the current data.

Presenting at case conferences has singular teaching value. Students must learn to think rapidly and be prepared to make last-minute modifications in their interpretations. Professionals from other disciplines will typically ask unexpected questions and/or present unexpected data. Using a focused problem-solving approach allows trainees the greatest flexibility in responding to the questions. Students are typically most comfortable presenting at psychiatric case conferences one test at a time; this is easier because it involves less integration. It is only with extensive practice that the student is able to shift to discussing pertinent referral issues rather than tests.

SUMMARY

The major goals of the internship year are articulated and the means to achieve these goals are described in this chapter. The internship setting has a unique role in the overall training and development of the psychology trainee. During this time students have the opportunity to integrate material learned in academic settings, and structured practicum placements with experiences in a health care setting. Psychology supervisors must actively direct and monitor this process so that students will achieve maximum learning benefits.

Students who are trained to function as problem-solving consultants are most adequately equipped to perform in this setting. Trainees are taught to use psychological tests with several sources of data to answer pertinent clinical questions. Interns are taught to become actively involved in articulating and clarifying referral questions. Referring persons are often unable to identify what the most important referral questions are and consultation proceeds most effectively when the trainee anticipates the need for an active role on their part. This allows trainees to learn how to set up a consultation so that the most satisfactory result may be generated. Trainees are instructed to listen to referral sources in order to understand multiple levels of communication. At one level they listen to the facts of the case and several frames of references are used in order to understand clinical and test data. Students are taught to review history to determine patterns of adaptive failure that may be addressed in order to clarify the focus of the evaluation. The patient is also encouraged to generate referral questions. This encourages the patient to become actively and candidly involved in the evaluation; this approach is often instrumental in generating useful information. The student is taught specific interview strategies in order to assist the patient in generating referral questions.

Students are encouraged to use several frames of reference and theoretical orientations in order to understand test data. Particular attention is directed toward allowing students to understand the impact of illness and disease upon psychological test functioning. Students are also encouraged to employ different theoretical concepts in different settings. A psychoanalytic frame of reference might be helpful to patients' ongoing insight-oriented psychotherapy, whereas a rehabilitation orientation might be more appropriate in a patient from a lower socioeconomic background, with a spinal cord injury.

A particularly difficult task is to assist students in learning to integrate various types of assessment data. Students are taught to incorporate knowledge about contrasting strengths of different tests and to evaluate the goodness of data sets before interpreting them.

The psychology supervisor consistently deals with administrative matters in running a psychology service. Effective teaching depends on students being thoroughly familiar with the medical environment and practice patterns of team members. Students need to develop familiarity with routine diagnostic and laboratory tests and their impact upon behavioral data. Supervisors serve as a buffer between medical personnel and the psychological trainee. At the beginning of the internship year, many interns have limited preparation for the realities of hospital behavior. The supervisor spends considerable time throughout the year in monitoring the progress of students and making certain that effective communication between the intern and other disciplines occurs. Of particular value are presentations at case conferences. In these settings students learn to think rapidly and to be prepared to make last-minute modifications in their interpretations.

ACKNOWLEDGMENT

The author would like to express his appreciation to Kaye Starr Woolery for her assistance in the preparation of this manuscript.

REFERENCES

American Psychiatric Association. (1994). *Diagnostic and statistical manual of mental disorders* (4th ed.) Washington, DC: Author.

Beutler, L., & Berren, M. (Eds.). (1995). *Integrative assessment of adult personality.* New York: Guilford.

Brabender, V. (1991). Training competent assessors: Administrative issues. *SPA Exchange, 5,* 2.

Cohen, L. J. (1980). The unstated problem in a psychological testing referral. *American Journal of Psychiatry, 137,* 1173–1176.

Engle, G. (1980). The clinical application of the biopsychosocial model. *American Journal of Psychiatry, 137,* 535–544.

Ganellen, R. (1996). *Interpreting the Rorschach and MMPI–2 in personality assessment.* Hillsdale, NJ: Lawrence Erlbaum Associates.

Graham, J. R. (1993). *MMPI–2: Assessing personality and psychopathology* (2nd ed.). New York: Oxford University Press.

Green, S. A. (1993). Principles of medical psychotherapy. In A. Stoudemire & B. Fogel (Eds.), *Psychiatric care of the medical patient* (pp. 3–18). New York: Oxford University Press.

Lovitt, R. (1987). A conceptual model and case study for the psychological assessment of psudoseizures with the Rorschach. *Journal of Personality Assessment, 5,* 207–219.

Lovitt, R. (1988). Current practice of psychological assessment: Response to Sweeney, Clarkin and Fitzgibbon. *Professional Psychology: Research and Practice, 19,* 516–521.

Lovitt, R. (1992) .Teaching the psychology intern assessment skills in a medical setting. *Journal of Training and Practice in Professional Psychology,* 6,27–34.

Lovitt, R. (1993). A strategy for integrating a normal MMPI–2 and dysfunctional Rorschach in a severely compromised patient. *Journal of Personality Assessment,* 60,141–147.

Lovitt, R., & Claassen, C. (1997). Rorschach assessment of personality factors in chronic fatigue syndrome. In R. Meloy, M. Acklin, C. Gacono, C. Peterson, & J. Murray (Eds.), *Contemporary Rorschach assessment.* Hillsdale, NJ: Lawrence Erlbaum Associates.

Maloney, M. & Ward, M. (1976). *Psychological assessment.* New York: Oxford University Press.

Meyer, G. (1997). On the integration of personality assessment methods: The Rorschach and MMPI. *Journal of Personality Assessment, 86,* 297–330.

Sweeney, J. A., Clarkin, J. F. & Fitzgibbon, M. L. (1987). Current practice of psychological assessment. *Professional Psychology: Research and Practice, 18,* 377–380.

Tallent, N. (1983). *Psychological report writing* (2nd ed.). Englewood Cliffs, NJ: Prentice-Hall.

Tallent, N. (1992). *The Practice of psychological assessment.* New York: Prentice-Hall.

Weiner, I. (1986). Conceptual and empirical perspectives in the Rorschach assessment of psychopathology. *Journal of Personality Assessment, 50,* 472–479.

27

Jumping Into Fire: Internship Training in Personality Assessment

Mark A. Blais
Massachusetts General Hospital/Harvard Medical School
Marla D. Eby
The Cambridge Hospital/Harvard Medical School

The internship year is the culmination of clinical training for doctoral psychology students, and it is a time when learning occurs primarily through the delivery of supervised clinical services. The primary goal of the internship year is to produce competent, entry-level clinicians, who can function professionally under minimal supervision. For the skills required in personality assessment, achieving this goal can be very challenging.

Psychology departments in Academic Medical Centers (AMCs) offer highly desirable predoctoral internship positions (Sheridan & Choca, 1991). Traditionally, AMC-based internships have placed a strong emphasis on teaching and providing psychological assessment services (Durand, Blanchard, & Mindell, 1988; Kinder, 1994; Watkins, 1994). AMC internships continue to emphasize psychological assessment despite a decrease in the preparation of doctoral psychology students to provide assessment services (Durand et al., 1988). This chapter outlines an approach to teaching and practicing psychological assessment that has helped us address the challenge of training students who are less advanced in their understanding of psychological assessment, while continuing, year round, to provide competent assessment services for our departments. In particular we have focused this chapter on the initial process of getting interns "on board" with respect to these skills, as this has become an increasingly important process. In addition to drawing upon our own teaching experience, the assessment experience of a number of recent intern graduates was obtained through an informal survey and helped to inform this chapter.

In contrast with graduate school testing experiences, which tend to develop assessment skills in a sequential fashion, internship training requires the total process of psychological assessment to be addressed right from the start of the training year. For example, we require interns to conduct complete assessment evaluations and prepare written reports within a few weeks of starting the program. Internship programs then must be designed to ensure that trainees are able to provide quality assessment services to patients year round, while also teaching, across the internship year, the knowledge and skills necessary for obtaining a minimum professional level of competence in psychological assessment. To accomplish this complex objective, we employ an approach to assessment training that features three components: observational learning (modeling), flexible time-sensitive individual and group supervision, and an advanced assessment seminar. In all these components we focus on the entirety of the assessment process throughout the training year.

All AMC professional training programs emphasize learning through doing (under supervision). The motto of "See one, do one, teach one" aptly expresses this educational philosophy. Our experience indicates that psychology students can feel out of place in such a service-oriented training program. It is important to recognize this at the outset of the internship year and to help students adjust to this new learning environment (Belar, 1991). Two resources can be helpful in this regard: Kingsbury's (1987) article outlining the differences in training between the clinical psychologist and the psychiatrist, and Fine's (1994) book, *The Wards*, a guide for medical students starting their clerkships.

OBSERVATIONAL LEARNING

Modeling or observational learning is one of the most powerful teaching vehicles available to AMC internship faculty. Modeling allows faculty to demonstrate the full range of skills required of a professional assessment consultant. Also, observing senior faculty carry out an assessment consultation helps dispel the belief that assessment is a second-rate professional activity (Retzlaff, 1992). Whereas it is common for medical students to accompany senior staff on daily patient rounds, few doctoral psychology students experience this form of learning. One of the most effective techniques for getting interns on board is to, early in the year, have them observe a staff psychologist conduct a complete assessment consultation. Observing the entire assessment process provides interns with a framework for conceptualizing their own assessment work and furnishes useful reference points for future teaching and supervision.

A successful hospital assessment consultation has three requirements: it must (a) have a short turnaround time (measured from request to completion), (b) obtain test data that inform the case, and (c) cause little disruption to ongoing patient care. This view of assessment consultation work was well outlined by Sweeney, Clarkin, and Fitzgibbon (1987), who emphasized a rapid, problem-focused framework for psychological assessment. Modeling is an ideal way to teach the complex skills necessary for conducting an assessment consultation. Also, through modeling a staff psychologist can efficiently teach a group of interns the workings of a medical floor: where the nurses' station is located, how it is set up, how to find and read a patient's chart, and how to identify the patient's physician and primary nurse. Although these skills may appear unrelated to assessment competence, such procedural knowledge must be mastered before interns can focus their attention on doing the actual psychological assessments. Furthermore, modeling is specially helpful in teaching two essential aspects of hospital assessment, developing a referral question(s) and selecting the appropriate tests to answer the referral question(s).

Many psychology students begin their internship expecting that appropriate referral questions will accompany each request for testing. Our experience indicates that this often does not occur in hospital work. Physicians typically request assessment consultations on troublesome or complex cases. In such situations referral questions are likely to be poorly developed. Often they are either too narrow (is this patient depressed?), or too broad (are there any psychological factors affecting this patient's treatment?). Psychologists, as professional consultants, must be skilled in helping colleagues refine their assessment questions (Lovitt, 1994). This refinement process starts by speaking with the referring physician. A 5-minute clinical case review will usually get the psychologist familiar with the case and the treatment dilemmas. The psychologist can then translate the case information into an appropriate referral question. This question can then be reflected back to the physician with a clear statement indicating how the psychological consultation can help with the case. The psychologist must also state what type of information he or she will provide to the physician, and when he or she will provide it.

The following case served as an observational learning experience for a new group of psychology interns, taught by the first author (MB):

A psychological assessment was requested on an 18-year-old, right-handed, single, White, male college student. He had been admitted, 3 days earlier, from the emergency room (ER) to a general hospital psychiatry unit following excessive use of pain medication. In the ER he reported that he was in a great deal of facial pain and had been taking extra medication. The ER physician found the patient to be mildly confused and disoriented, and the patient was hospitalized overnight for observation. By the next morning his mental status had cleared, but he complained of extreme facial pain and expressed vague suicidal ideation. He was admitted for a pain work-up and a psychiatric evaluation.

He was difficult to care for on the ward, and got into frequent struggles with the nursing staff over unit rules. A pain consultation was inconclusive and while on the unit his pain seemed to decrease. The psychiatry resident found him guarded about his degree of depression and suicidal ideation. Psychological testing was requested to help find out "if the patient was really suicidal or just character-disordered." The resident, feeling pressured by the attending psychiatrist, wanted the test results *immediately*. As the unit psychologist, I reflected back that the case was diagnostically unclear and the patient's behavior was frustrating staff. *A psychological assessment might provide some diagnostic clarity, along with insights into the patient's personality style, current functioning, and risk of suicidality.* However, I cautioned the psychiatric resident that the usefulness of the evaluation would depend, in part, on the patient's cooperation. Also, I promised verbal feedback by morning rounds the day after tomorrow. Last, I informed the resident that he would need to reassess the patient's suicide risk before discharge whatever the outcome of the testing, because testing could not substitute for clinical judgment at the time of discharge.

The brief interchange just outlined indicates how such a case discussion can develop a clear framework for the assessment consultation. By the conclusion of the case review, I was aware that I had been called in to help on a difficult case (a guarded, possibly suicidal patient) and that high expectations were being placed on the outcome of the consultation. I told the psychiatrist about the type of information the assessment would contain and how (verbally) and when (before morning rounds, which typically begin at 9:00 a.m.) he would be informed of the findings. Also, I informed the psychiatrist that he would have to evaluate the patient's suicide risk before discharge. Creating such an explicit framework helps to reduce misunderstandings and avoid the angry exchanges that can occur when unexpressed expectations are not met.

I met with the interns as a group and informed them that the psychiatrist was requesting a differential diagnosis focusing on Axis I versus Axis II pathology. He also needed a description of the patient's current psychological functioning, particularly regarding suicidal preoccupation and risk for self-harm. Through this discussion the interns also learned the interactive nature of structuring a consultation and developing a referral question.

The next important step in conducting an assessment consultation is to select the appropriate instruments for answering the referral questions. Graduate schools typically train students to administer full Menninger batteries (Rapaport, Gill, & Schafer, 1968), made up of a WAIS–R, Rorschach, and the TAT. Thus, interns have little training in the differential application of psychological tests (Beutler, 1995). Hospital assessment work, with its time pressures and the physical limitations of the patients (especially fatigue), requires a focused assessment strategy often employing fewer tests. Information obtained from a patient's primary nurse can be helpful in deciding the number of tests to include in the battery. In the aforementioned case, the nurse reported that the patient was physically intact, with good stamina, but was very demanding, and needed much personal attention. Also, he frequently told staff that he had the IQ of a genius. From the information I now had on the patient, I knew that physical fatigue would not be a problem, but his guardedness, as reported by the psychiatrist, could limit his ability or willingness to engage in the testing.

A review of the medical chart revealed that the patient had graduated early from high school and was currently in his second year at a prestigious university. He had developed severe facial pain at age 13. This condition had received various diagnoses and had failed to respond to multiple treatments, including medication trials. One inpatient treatment for pain rehabilitation had failed to improve his condition. Over the years he had briefly seen a few mental health professionals, again without any reported benefit. His current medications were: Valium 5 mg tid (three times a day); Elavil 100 mg, nightly; and Percocet, nightly. This chart information helped the interns and me to see his current hospitalization as part of a complex and long-standing pattern of psychological and physical difficulties.

All available information should be considered in composing a strategy for answering a referral question. The time constraints for this consultation would argue for a minimal assessment battery (the Rorschach and one self-report test), whereas the murkiness of the case and the question of suicidal ideation suggest the need for a more complete assessment. This is just the kind of clinical dilemma that students have to learn to recognize and to resolve during their internship year. Through modeling, interns can observe a staff psychologist think through these difficult problems. Furthermore, the process and reasoning underlying the resolution of these problems can be openly discussed. In this way interns are taught how to think about the issues of test selection (the risks and benefits of each test) in a real-time, real-life situation. This is the knowledge interns need to acquire in order to move from the level of technician to that of being a professional assessment consultant.

I designed the following strategy for the current assessment situation: A seven-subtest short form of the Wechsler Adult Intelligence Scale–Revised (WAIS–R–SSSF) would be given first, followed by the Rorschach Inkblot Method (RIM; Weiner, 1994), four TAT (Murray, 1943) cards (#'s 1, 3GF, 12M, and 14), and the PAI (Morey, 1991). I selected the WAIS–R–SSSF (Ward, 1990) for its brief administration time (20 to 30 minutes) and its ability to provide accurate IQ data (assessing cognitive functioning). Also, given that the patient was guarded with the psychiatrist, I thought that the WAIS–R would engage him in the testing. I chose the Rorschach as the second test in the battery because the patient's guardedness made projective test data crucial for the personality assessment. Furthermore, the novelty of the Rorschach might help maintain the patient's involvement in the assessment.

I try to teach interns to design an assessment strategy so that the minimum data necessary for answering the principal referral question are obtained first. In this case I felt that the WAIS–R–SSSF and the Rorschach would provide the least data necessary for this assessment consultation. I selected the four TAT cards to provide supplemental projective data primarily regarding the nature of the patient's object relations, core interpersonal themes, and degree of suicidal ideation. Last, I needed a self-report test of psychopathology, but it seemed likely that the patient would either not complete one or portray himself in an exceedingly favorable light. The PAI was selected for use due to its shorter length (344 items), and the ability to score a short form of the test using only the first 199 items. Also, the PAI contains several treatment-planning scales that can provide important information.

The assessment of this patient was conducted in private by me. However, I then included the interns in the protocol analysis and interpretation through a group supervision session the next morning. In this group session, copies of the scored protocol were passed out and the interns joined with me in interpreting and integrating the test data. In this way the interns continued to be part of the real-time, real-life process of completing the assessment consultation.

The goal of the group session was to identify the principal findings and interpretations from each test and integrate these data into the complex picture of the patient's current psychological functioning. I asked each intern to focus on one test protocol, and to offer her or his impressions of the data. I organized these test interpretations into the basic categories of thought quality, affect, defenses, and relationship to self and others. This provided the interns with a chance to see how inter- and intratest data can be organized and integrated. This discussion thus helped to show the interns how to think about the level and type of functioning each test reveals.

The WAIS–R–SSSF data provided a screen of the patient's cognitive functioning and assessed the quality and consistency of his functioning in highly structured situations. The WAIS–R data provided an estimate of the patient's current best possible level of functioning (Zetzer & Beutler, 1995). The patient's WAIS–R scores were as follows; Full Scale IQ 106, Verbal IQ 120, and Performance IQ 87 (all IQs were estimated). Attention and concentration (Digit Span 7 [age-adjusted scaled score]) and visual spatial skills were both weak (Block Design 8) compared with his verbal ability (Similarities 17 & Information 13). The patient's overall cognitive functioning was not as effective as one might have assumed, given his verbal abilities and level of education. The significant VIQ /PIQ split could represent a long-standing learning disability, but this seemed unlikely given his strong high-school performance. Alternatively, his cognitive disruption could be due to depression and/or anxiety and the effects of his current medications.

The Rorschach (with Exner [1986] administration and scoring) provides a view of the patient's deeper psychological functioning. It reveals the workings of the whole personality (Weiner, 1994). The test was valid (R = 20, lambda = .43). One Index was positive, suggesting possible depression (DEPI = 5) or a proneness to depressive experiences. The Suicide Constellation (S-Con) was negative at a score of 4. His psychological resources were adequate, but he had no set coping style (EB = 5:4). Situational stress was reducing his functioning (D and Adjusted D, -2 and 0). His affective experience was dominated by helplessness (Y = 4), painful internalized affect (C' = 4), and unmet dependency/nurturance needs (T = 2) (all consistent with depression due to situational factors). He displayed poor perceptual accuracy (X + % = .55, F + % = .60, X - % = .10, S - % = 1.00, Xu % = .35, and WSum6 = 4), which was mainly due to the overpersonalization of perceptions and the disruptive effect of anger. However, he was not psychotic (X - % = .10). He had an immature egocentric and narcissistic character style (3r + (2)/R = .55 and Fr + rF = 2). His defensive functioning (2AB + Art + Ay = 4 and Ma:Mp = 1:4) included excessive intellectualization, escapes into fantasy, and the use of externalizing defenses (Fr + rF = 2). In interpersonal relationships (COP = 3, AG = 1, M- = 0, H:(H)Hd(Hd) = 3:3) he views others as friendly, but he can also be oppositional (S = 4). Application of the P. Lerner and H. Lerner (1980) defense scale to the three human figure responses revealed midlevel idealization (I1) and devaluation (DV2) defenses (consistent with a narcissistic character style). These conceptually derived scores suggested that he would likely alternate between idealizing and devaluing others and their efforts to help him.

The four TAT card themes were as follows: Card 1, "The parents are pressuring the little boy." The story was quite short, possibly due to his oppositional tendencies. The main themes included external pressure to achieve, long-term passive resistance to that pressure, along with a wish to be understood by his parents (authority figures). The stories that followed were longer and richer, suggesting that he can overcome his oppositional qualities. Card 3GF, "It's a tragedy." The main theme involved a sense of tragedy due either to the death of a loved one or a personal failure. Painful emotions were experienced in isolation and the hero could not reach out for help, but wished to be comforted. Card 12M, "He has a chronic illness." The main theme was that someone was sick and someone was trying to help. The sick person wanted to be helped and had been waiting a long time for help. The ending was ambivalent, "he may or may not get better." Card 14, "This one is full of hope." "He's been in the dark for a long time; now he sees that he can do something to get out." In this story, problems are overcome without outside help. These TAT stories are consistent with a dysphoric affective state and further suggest a core interpersonal experience of feeling misunderstood, while longing for nurturance and empathic contact.

The PAI (which the patient did complete) provides a surface picture of the patient's psychological functioning and is likely to indicate how he will present himself on clinical interview. The PAI profile was valid. He reported minimal psychopathology; his mean clinical elevation of 53 (T-score) was not consistent with being an inpatient. This suggests either little overt distress or a reluctance to express emotional pain. Either way he will not appear to others, including his caregivers, to be as psychologically impaired as the rest of the assessment data reveals him to be. He reported mild clinical depression (T-score = 71) and excessive concern about his physical functioning (T-score = 85), further suggesting that on clinical interview his depressive symptoms will be overshadowed by his excessive physical complaints and concerns. This pattern could also lead to an underestimation of his true psychological distress. A grandiose sense of self, consistent with the pronounced signs of a narcissistic character style on the Rorschach, was suggested by one PAI subscale. On the treatment consideration scales he showed little interest in psychologically oriented treatments, a perception of high levels of social stress, and minimal suicidal ideation (T-score = 54).

The teaching benefit of this type of live protocol review and interpretation is substantial. In this situation, the thinking behind each interpretation can be made explicit, and the process of test data interpretation and integration can be shared with trainees. The trainees learn where, in each test, to look for particular types of information. They also learn how inter- and intratest data are combined to add depth and dimension to their understanding of the patient's psychological functioning. The staff psychologist can then show how the newly organized and integrated test data can be applied to the referral question(s).

In my teaching I emphasize the need to answer the referral question(s) directly and clearly, because this is what the physician will expect to receive from the consultation. The present referral questions were addressed as follows: *Question 1: Differential Diagnosis.* The assessment data, both projective and objective, strongly suggest the presence of a clinical depression. This depression is likely masked to some extent by both the patient's focus on his physical functioning (the facial pain) and his inability or unwillingness to express his emotional pain. As a result, his depression is likely more significant and disruptive to his functioning than he is reporting. In addition, character issues (Axis II pathology), such as narcissistic character traits, are complicating the patient's treatment and will need to be addressed. *Question 2: Current Psychological Functioning.* The patient's functioning is greatly reduced due to both his depression and situational stressors. These stressors are influencing both his emotional and intellectual functioning. His ability to organize, plan, and cope is currently limited. This is important to emphasize because his caregivers may overestimate his level of functioning due to his strong verbal skills. *Question 3: Suicidal Risk.* On testing he does not appear to be actively suicidal (either on the self-report or projective tests). However, in his current state of being emotionally overwhelmed, depressed, and having reduced coping ability, he should be considered at an increased risk for impulsive self-harm. His safety should be monitored closely.

The final step in this observational learning experience is to have the interns present when the verbal report of the test findings is given to the referring physician. Psychology students typically have little training in providing concise, well-organized oral feedback of assessment findings. I believe that an oral assessment report should cover three areas: the validity of the data and the faith the consultant has in the interpretations, how the data inform the referral question(s), and the treatment recommendations that follow from the assessment findings. In this case, with regard to the first area, all the data were valid and I had strong faith in the interpretations that were made from the data, because most of the findings were validated across multiple tests and multiple assessment methods. How the test data inform the referral questions has already been reviewed.

We feel that at the internship level of training it is important to focus significant attention and teaching on translating test data into *useful* treatment recommendations. This can ultimately be the most important result of a well-conducted assessment consultation. In order to develop useful recommendations, interns have to learn the real-world implications of the test data. Maruish's (1994) *The Use of Psychological Testing for Treatment Planning and Outcome Assessment* is an invaluable resource for helping interns understand the behavioral correlates and the treatment implications of the test data. Furthermore, the matching of test data and responses with actual behavior makes assessment come alive, and helps to integrate assessment knowledge with the interns' generally broader understanding of psychotherapy and general psychology. Again this must be a focus of learning and teaching right from the start of the intership year.

The following recommendations were developed in the case reviewed earlier. The obtained test data suggest that the patient's depression was being less than optimally treated, so a more aggressive treatment of his depression was recommended. The patient was emotionally overwhelmed and displayed reduced coping ability. From this, it was recommended that either his hospitalization should be extended or he be referred to a day treatment program for added external structure. A further implication of this finding was that the patient should not return immediately to the pressures of full-time college attendance. Given that little has changed in either his functioning or his environment, this might result in a further deterioration in his condition. The patient's treatment is complicated by his denial of psychopathology and his immature character style. It was recommended that outpatient psychotherapy initially focus on concrete external issues related to improving his functioning and increasing his social support. Later, when his condition was more stable, the therapy could explore the nature and quality of his interpersonal style, and his relationship to authority figures. Neuropsychological testing should be pursued, after his depression was more adequately treated.

I delivered these recommendations by phone, also with the intern group present. By observing this exchange of information, the interns were able to view how I handled inquiries, challenges, and questions. Also, they observed my tone, my nondefensive interactional style, and my conviction in the importance of these findings for the patient's care. I have found interns, insecure with their assessment skills, risk conveying their findings in either an overly rigid or excessively weak and watered-down manner.

Having psychology trainees observe a complete assessment consultation at the start of their internship provides a solid foundation for learning and practicing assessment throughout the year. It equips interns with a cognitive framework for understanding and guiding their early assessment assignments. It allows assessment supervisors to assume that each intern is familiar with the fundamentals of hospital consultation. It provides the supervisor and intern a common assessment experience that can be drawn upon in future discussions. In this approach to teaching personality assessment, practical learning is enhanced by observational learning, combined with sufficient and time-sensitive individual and group supervision. This should be supplemented by an advanced assessment seminar that focuses on broadening the intellectual and theoretical understanding of personality assessment.

THE ADVANCED ASSESSMENT SEMINAR

The second author (ME) has taught a testing seminar at a teaching hospital for many years, and the following remarks reflect the recent evolution of this task. Teaching a testing seminar to psychology interns in the clinical setting has always been a challenge, and is now even more so with the increased time pressures of managed care. How does one teach a subject (testing) that for many is peripheral to their main interest in psychology, with a required output (writing reports) that is anathema to many students, and get them to do it in a hurry? Furthermore, many students have the feeling that, unlike the "benign" process of psychotherapy, testing is a painful or at least unpleasant procedure for the patient, and that the tester must therefore don the mantle of the patient's persecutor to do it. This of course seems antitherapeutic, and many psychologists hate doing it and say so. Students hear this, and even more, will observe that hardly any psychologists they know actually *do* testing.

Nonetheless, it is our contention that psychological testing, when taught well, is an important cornerstone to the psychologist's way of thinking about patients, even if that psychologist later eschews testing in favor of a dynamically oriented therapy practice, for at the heart of the latter is clinical and dynamic formulation, the time-honored reason for doing psychological (and especially projective) testing in the first place.

Through this route lies the way for an alliance with almost any student around the daunting task of psychological testing. Yet, even here the way is perilous. So often the role of "persecutor" is transferred to the supervisor or teacher of psychological testing, especially when the work seems dry and tedious, and the standards for output are high. This cannot always be avoided; testing and scoring procedures are hard work, and writing well is even harder for most people. But these pains can be better endured in the company of a teacher—I should say mentor, really—whose love for the material that testing uncovers is palpable and passionate.

So when I meet for the first time with the members of my testing seminar, my goals are several. First, I want to convey a sense of enthusiasm and interest for the work. In doing this, I am aware of icing the cake, so to speak, with a slightly humorous and manic flavor. To counter this, I try to be as precise as possible in detailing why I think testing is important, and what the tester can do for a patient. This argument is woven tightly with ideas about how clinical formulation (placing the patient in a spectrum of diagnosis and severity of illness) and dynamic formulation (describing who the patient is) are both important to treatment. (For a further description of this approach to formulation, the work of Perry, Cooper, & Michels [1987] is informative.) Parenthetically, I think the latter task, of describing who the patient is, has become taboo for some psychologists who are trying to justify the "science" of their work, even though Sigmund Koch (1959) and other historians of science outline a clear descriptive role for scientists and for psychologists in particular.

By the time I face the psychology interns in a testing seminar, they have had a wide variety of experiences. Most have had some basic scoring experience in graduate seminars (usually, but not always, including Exner's [1986] scoring system for the Rorschach). However, some have seen fewer than 5 patients for psychological testing, and some have seen more than 50. Thus the final task for the initial meeting is to obtain a reading on both the experience and interests of the group. If the group is small enough, I do this by going around the room and asking each participant individually.

A second introductory meeting must focus on administration and clinical feedback to the patient, but here again the goal is to underline the alliance between the tester and the patient. It sounds simple-minded, but the first goal of testing is to get it done. Many trainees have been taught to begin the testing session with a lengthy clinical interview—sometimes as long as 45 minutes—before even one test is administered. With some patients, to begin this way can heighten anxiety about starting (or ever finishing) the tests. Indeed, sometimes it may reflect the tester's own anxiety about doing testing instead of the more familiar clinical interview. Furthermore, it gives the patient a different "set" about what the testing may be about before it even starts. After a brief introduction, testing should begin; history taking and the gleaning of further clinical information can usually be done by chart review, a discussion for the referring source, and a brief discussion with the patient at the end of the testing. At that point, the patient generally has some positive sense of having completed the work, and the tester may have a better sense of how to focus historical and clinical data gathering. This procedure is distinctly different from the assessment approach typically followed in an outpatient setting, where the interview is usually carried out in some detail, before any testing is begun (see Handler, Fowler, & Hilsenroth, chap. 24 of this volume).

A second and similar difficulty arises when the tester allows him or herself to be drawn into a lengthy discussion with the patient about the purpose of the testing. Here again, there is a danger of colluding with the patient's avoidance of the task, or, alternatively, of responding to the patient's transference feelings of omnipotence that are directed toward the tester. Such discussions can often be more profitable between the patient and the referring therapist, and, in any case, seem to lose their luster for the patient if they are deferred until the testing itself is completed. A third bind can occur when the tester arranges a feedback session to discuss the results of the testing with the patient. As one can imagine, such sessions can be filled with much anxiety for the patient, interfering with a clear comprehension of whatever is said, and usually, the patient never gets another chance to see the tester to clarify things. To some extent, this can be avoided if the feedback session is done with the patient and the referring clinician together. The session should focus on the patient's questions first, with an emphasis on strengths and capacities, and only then can a discussion emerge about how certain vulnerabilities might arise from the same matrix. Such joint feedback sessions can thus serve as a consultation to the therapist, and it provides a chance for both the patient and the referring therapist to discuss their work together.

A third introductory session *must* focus on report writing. I used to defer this task until later in the year, but this is no help to interns who have to write reports sooner. Furthermore, this session can focus the intern on what testing is about, and it makes the final product seem less intimidating. Finally, it sets the tone for the course. By submitting a number of my own sample reports for general discussion, I have the opportunity to model presentation of casework in class.

The content of the testing report could well serve as a chapter by itself, and numerous formats are used by different clinicians. I always present a prototypical format in outline form, so that interns have a general guideline for their work. In general, this includes a section on cognitive functioning, in which a pattern analysis of the cognitive tests helps identify possible organic factors, psychiatric illness, and cognitive style. A subsequent section on personality functioning outlines the patient's experience of the world, areas of conflict, defensive style, object relations, and the risks and diagnostic compromises that result. A summary section and treatment recommendations then follow.

However, I seldom organize an assessment report in exactly the same way twice; I prefer to use the material more freely, based on what most needs saying about a given patient. Thus, one report might emphasize the high risk of self-harm and the factors driving it, whereas another might begin with the extreme sense of isolation felt by the patient and how it colors their world experience. Although the nature of referral questions is important in organizing the report, sometimes it is the question that no one thought to ask that may be most important in defining the experience of a patient.

After these three introductory sessions, I then embark on the body of the work for the seminar, which consists of weekly sessions (of 1 hour and 20 minutes duration) for 9 months. My goals for this period are twofold: to introduce new scoring techniques and perspectives on the material, and to provide solid examples of a wide variety of cases. In doing this, I have a given terrain that I want to cover, including certain scoring systems, and examples of certain prototypical diagnoses and problems. After some years of fiddling with a workable format, in which I tried teaching the scoring methods and cases separately, I have found that a dynamic interplay between theoretical/scoring methods and relevant case illustrations seems to work best. This approach makes clinical sense because each theoretical contribution and scoring supplement has been developed primarily to solve certain clinical problems. A further advantage of this approach is that it tends to integrate the inexperienced testers in the class with the more experienced testers from the start. Everyone can enter a case discussion, and the more experienced participants can comfortably serve as the class "experts" for the theoretical and scoring points for the cases, whereas others have equally important insights about the material itself.

The course that I teach is highly focused on the use of the WAIS–R (sometimes the WISC–III), the Rorschach, and the TAT, though the course approach discussed here has also worked for discussion of measures such as the MMPI and other personality inventories. I thus begin with the WAIS–R, and emphasize the use of pattern analysis, both for organic dysfunction as well as for various psychiatric diagnoses. This approach is highlighted by a focus on alcoholism and dementia, where I present case prototypes of three patients in each category, each in a different stage of the illness, to illustrate how patterns might change over time. We then turn to testing cases from seminar members where alcoholism or Alzheimer's disease may be important factors in the differential diagnosis. These intern cases are invariably less clear-cut, and spirited analysis then ensues about both the WAIS–R as well as the projective material. Almost inevitably, the differential between dementia and depression comes to the fore.

The focus then shifts to the projective tests, and a brief review of Exner's (1986) scoring system is in order. Again, pattern analysis is emphasized, with particular stress on Exner's Suicide Constellation and the Depression Index. We review journal articles around evaluating depression and suicide, and I present the testing protocol of a clear-cut prototypically depressed and suicidal patient. Following this, we then take up the more complex case where an intern is struggling with the assessment of depression and the risk of self-harm.

As we thus enter the world of the deeply disturbed patient, the question of differential diagnosis among types of psychoses becomes an important one. A helpful adjunct here is Johnston and Holzman's (1979) Thought Disorder Index; however, its very complexity causes many clinicians to avoid it. I have found that providing a well-organized summary of the system, with relevant scoring examples throughout, enables most students to use its main principles effectively. We then apply it both to a more typical schizophrenic example provided by me, and a student example where differential diagnosis (often between bipolar illness vs. schizophrenia) is a key issue.

Because we work in a multicultural setting, at this juncture questions about diagnosing serious mental disorders in patients from other cultures emerge. For the past 2 years, this section of the course has included an intern-provided testing protocol of a Haitian patient, and we invite a psychologist from the Haitian clinic to analyze the material with us. This session has been a favorite with students who enjoy discussing the complexities of cultural background against the material provided by the testing.

By this point, interns are eager to learn more about the content of the testing material to further understand the dynamics of individual patients. This task can be both deepened and disciplined by the introduction of scoring systems, such as Westen's (1991) scoring of the TAT, and Holt's (1978) scoring of the Rorschach, where content is scored precisely and methodically. Holt's system is sufficiently complex to warrant some simplification, and I have chosen to focus on his libidinal and aggressive primary process scores. We use these scores to draw a dynamic "map" of the patient, and note how the interplay between Holt content and Exner perceptual reality testing and special scores further informs our picture of a patient's strengths and vulnerabilities. Again, we use an intern's protocol and score it with this system as an adjuct to the Exner scoring already done.

After developing this notion of the content of certain conflicts, it makes sense to discuss defense analysis. Here there are numerous systems to choose from, and a whole semester could easily be spent on this topic alone. It is especially interesting at this juncture, however, to focus on borderline defenses (especially idealization and projective identification), and these are particularly well developed in a scoring system developed by Cooper and Arnow (1988). Here again, I provide concise summary scoring sheets with clear-cut examples, and we then proceed to use these to score an intern's testing protocol of a patient where personality disorder is part of the differential diagnosis.

Personality diagnoses are closely linked to posttraumatic stress disorder, and we then review Saunders' (1991) guidelines for differentiating borderline patients without a history of sexual abuse to those with such a history. We then proceed to use these guidelines for evaluating intern testing protocols where sexual abuse is suspected.

At the end of the course, special topics are taken up according to the interest of the participants, such as drawing and psychotic art, and neuropsychological findings in AIDS patients. To all of these we try to use theoretical and research findings to illustrate further what might be happening with a given case. The purpose behind the general method described here, where prototypical cases and more complex cases are constantly juxtaposed against new scoring systems and new ways of looking at data, is to create a twofold ability in the student: to think openly and creatively, but also to think with discipline and an eye for both converging lines of evidence, and for best evidence.

The method I have outlined here has emerged from a number of years of teaching psychological testing in a hospital setting; I try to alter the material each year and use student protocols to keep the course and my experience of it fresh. I have found several principles to be helpful. First, I do as much work as possible ahead of time to make the material understandable to interns. This includes numerous handouts of articles, summaries of articles, and summaries of scoring systems. Second, I have found that I can sometimes do more with less, and so distilling a part of an adjunctive (non-Exner) scoring system with a particular purpose in mind will serve better than trying to convey the enormity of each detailed system.

CONCLUSION

The teaching strategies presented in this chapter require considerable invest-ment of internship faculty time and energy. However, their application can result in many rewards for trainees and staff. Psychology trainees are introduced to a sophisticated approach to personality assessment. They learn to function as valued consultants in a medical setting, a skill that can serve them throughout their careers.

The relevance of assessment findings to the treatment of patients is clearly demonstrated and learned. Perhaps the most important benefit is that all the interns surveyed indicated that this approach to assessment training resulted in them becoming better clinicians and psychotherapists. Particularly, they felt that this experience caused them to conceptualize their patients with greater complexity and sophistication. We feel that this is the ultimate goal of all internship training.

REFERENCES

Belar, C. (1991). Professionalism in medical settings. In J. Sweet, R. Rozensky, & S. Tovian (Eds.), *Handbook of clinical psychology in medical settings* (pp. 81–92). New York: Plenum.

Beutler, L. (1995). Issues in selecting an assessment battery. In L. Beutler & M. Berren (Eds.), *Integrative assessment of adult personality* (pp. 65–93). New York: Guilford.

Cooper, S., & Arnow, D. (1988). An object relations view of the borderline defenses: A Rorschach analysis. In M. Kissen (Ed.), *Assessing object relations phenomena* (pp.143–171). New York: International Universities Press.

Durand, V., Blanchard, E., & Mindell, J. (1988). Training in projective tests: Survey of clinical training directors and internship directors. *Professional Psychology: Research and Practice, 19, 236–238.*

Exner, J. (1986). *The Rorschach: A comprehensive system.* (Vol. 1, 2nd ed.). New York: Wiley.

Fine, P. (1994). *The wards: An Introduction to clinical clerkship.* Boston: Little, Brown & Company.

Holt, R. (1978). *Methods in clinical psychology.* Vol. 1. New York: Plenum.

Johnston, M., & Holzman, P. (1979). *Assessing schizophrenic thinking.* San Francisco: Jossey-Bass.

Kinder, B. (1994). Where the action is in personality assessment. *Journal of Personality Assessment, 62, 585–588.*

Kingsbury, S. (1987). Cognitive differences between clinical psychologist and psychiatrist. *American Psychologist, 42, 152–156.*

Koch, S. (Ed.). (1959). *Psychology: A study of a science.* New York: McGraw-Hill.

Lerner, P., & Lerner, H. (1980). Rorschach assessment of primitive defenses in borderline personality structure. In J. Kwawer, H. Lerner, P. Lerner, & A. Sugarman (Eds), *Borderline phenomena and the Rorschach test* (pp. 257–274). New York: International Universities Press.

Lovitt, R. (1994). From testing to assessment. *Society for Personality Assessment Exchange, 4(1), 7–8.*

Maruish, M. (1994). *The use of psychological testing for treatment planning and outcome assessment.* Hillsdale, NJ: Lawrence Erlbaum Associates.

Morey, L. (1991). *Personality assessment inventory.* Odessa, FL: Psychological Assessment Resources.

Murray, H. (1943). *Thematic Apperception Test.* Cambridge, MA: Harvard University Press.

Perry, S., Cooper, A., & Michels, R. (1987). The psychodynamic formulation: Its purpose, structure and clinical application. *American Journal of Psychiatry, 144 (5),* 543–550.

Rapaport, D., Gill, M., & Schafer, R. (1968). *Diagnostic psychological testing,* (Rev. ed., R. Holt, Ed.) New York: International Universities Press.

Retzlaff, P. (1992). Professional training in psychological assessment: New teachers and new tests. *Journal of Training and Practice in Professional Psychology, 6, 45–50.*

Saunders, E. (1991). Rorschach indicators of chronic childhood sexual abuse in female borderline inpatients. *Bulletin of the Menninger Clinic, 55(1), 48–71.*

Sheridan, E., & Choca, J. (1991). Educational preparation and clinical training within a medical setting. In J. Sweet, R. Rozensky, & S. Tovian (Eds.), *Handbook of clinical psychology in medical settings* (pp.45–58). New York: Plenum.

Sweeney, J., Clarkin, J., & Fitzgibbon, M. (1987). Current practice of psychological assessment. *Professional Psychology: Research and Practice, 18, 377–380.*

Ward, L. (1990). Prediction of Verbal, Performance and Full Scale IQs from short forms of the WAIS–R. *Journal of Clinical Psychology*, 46, 436–440.

Watkins, C. E. (1994). Do projective techniques get a "bum rap" from clinical psychology training directors? *Journal of Personality Assessment*, 63, 387–389.

Weiner, I. (1994). The Rorschach Inkblot Method (RIM) is not a test: Implications for theory and practice. *Journal of Personality Assessment*, 62, 498–504.

Westen, D. (1991). Clinical assessment of object relations using the TAT. *Journal of Personality Assessment*, 56, 56–74.

Zetzer, H., & Beutler, L. (1995). The assessment of cognitive functioning and the WAIS–R. In L. Beutler & M. Berren (Eds.), *Integrative assessment of adult personality.* (pp. 121–186). New York: Guilford.

Author Index

A

Achenbach, T. M., 9, 10, *27*
Acklin, M. W., 37, *41*, 221, 227, 231,
    379, 390
Acosta-Belen, E., 334, *342*
Adair, H. E., 375, 378, *389*
Affleck, D., 300, *317*
Ainsworth, M., 18, *29*, 62, 68, 217, *232*,
    311, *317*, 439, *450*
Akbar, N., 331, *342*
Alarcon, R., 418, *426*
Albee, G., 271, *292*
Aleksandrowitz, D., 395, *408*
Alexander, C. M., 339, *345*
Alexander, I. E.,. 250, *264*
Alexie, S., 336, *342*
Allen, I. M., 331, *342*
Allen, J., 329, *342*
Allen, R., 154, *163*
Allison, J., 297, 303, *316*
Allport, G. W., 167, *188*
Alterman, A. I., 204, *213*
Altman, H. F., 156, *163*
American Psychiatric Association, 417,
    425, 477, *483*
American Psychological Association,
    238, *246*
Anderson, J.,
Anderson, J. R., 405, *408*, 392, *411*
Anderson, W., 156, *162*
Andrews, A. A., 13, 21, *29*
Andronikof-Sanglade, A., 21, *28*
Angelo, T. A., 92, *101*
Applebaum, S., 17, *27*
Archer, R. P., 8, *27*, 227, *231*, 418, *426*,
    457, *465*
Arkes, H. E., 92, 99, 100, *101*

Arlow, J., 53, *58*, 395, *408*
Arnold, B., 329, 332, 333, *343*
Arnow, D., 51, *58*, 64, 65, 67, 130, *132*,
    227, *232*, 497, *499*
Aronow, E., 37, *44*, 216, *231*
Atkinson, J. W., 258, 259, *264, 265*
Atkinson, L., 305, *316*

B

Baba, R., 217, *231*
Baker, B., 303, *316*
Baker, L., 92, *101*
Baldwin, J. A., 330, *342*
Ballim, A., 392, *408*
Bandura, A., 209, *214*
Banerji, R., 392, *410*
Barbour, C. G., 130, *133*
Barlow, J. M., 395, *410*
Barnden, J., 392, *408*
Barrick, M. R., 23, *27*
Barron, F., 255, *264*
Bass, B. A., 330, *346*
Baughman, E. E., 124, *132*
Beck, A. T., 243, *246*
Beck, N., 305, *316*
Beck, S. J., 216, *231*
Belar, C., 486, *498*
Bell, Y. R., 330, *342*
Bellak, L., 296, 297, *316*
Bem, S. L., 263, *264*
Ben-Porath, Y. S., 151, 154, 155, 157,
    162, 163, 418, *426*
Bennett, M. J., 326, *342*
Bensley, A. D., 93, *101*
Berg, M., 37, *41*
Bergan, J., 18, *27*
Bergman, A., 109, 115, *117*

501

Berman, S., 291, 294
Berman, W., 47, 58
Berndt, D. J., 237, 246
Bernstein, D. A., 90, 101
Berren, M., 479, 483
Berryhill-Papke, E., 328, 329, 342
Beutler, L. E., 18, 27, 296, 297, 309,
        313, 315, 320, 479, 483, 488,
        490, 499, 500
Bihlar, B., 18, 27
Billson, J. M., 333, 342
Black, J. D., 23, 28
Blades, J., 72, 81
Blaha, J., 306, 316
Blanchard, E., 485, 499
Blanck, G., 270, 292, 455, 465
Blanck, R., 455, 465
Blatt, S., 13, 21, 27, 47, 48, 50, 58, 129,
        132, 217, 232, 283, 291, 292,
        294, 297, 303, 316, 396, 400,
        408, 432, 433, 435, 449
Block, J., 260, 264, 459, 465
Blondheim, S. H., 129, 134
Bloom-Feshbach, J., 110, 117
Bloom-Feshbach, S., 110, 117
Blum, G. S., 129, 132
Boekamp, J., 459, 468
Bond, M., 263, 264, 337, 342, 344
Bondy, E., 92, 101
Bonnett, M., 392, 408
Bontempo, R., 337, 346
Boone, D., 298, 316
Bootzin, R. R., 130, 132
Bornstein, R. F., 129, 132
Borodovsky, L. G., 331, 345
Borum, R., 202, 214
Bouchard, M., 440, 450
Bower, G. H., 130, 132
Bowlby, J., 115, 117
Boyer, L. B., 328, 336, 344
Boyle, G. J., 204, 214
Brabender, V., 394, 408, 464, 465, 471,
        483
Brack, C. J., 83, 102
Brack, G., 83, 102
Braff, D., 226, 233
Bransford, J., 85, 88, 101
Brenneis, C. B., 129, 132
Brickman, A., 52, 58
Brodie, S., 71, 80
Brooks, R., 399, 408

Brown, A., 92, 101
Brown, L. S., 204, 213
Brown, R. C., 154, 163
Browning, D., 301, 316
Bruhn, A., 396, 398, 408
Bruner, J., 251, 264
Buck, J., 282, 292
Buckley, J., 23, 30
Burke, W. F., 130, 132
Burley, T., 269, 271, 292, 406, 408, 435,
        436, 450
Burns, R., 282, 291, 292, 403, 408
Butcher, J. N., 4, 17, 27, 149, 152, 154,
        155, 156, 162, 163, 418, 426

C

Cable, G. W., 392, 411
Campbell, D. T., 8, 27, 174, 186, 188
Canino, I. A., 334, 342
Capra, F., 32, 41
Carbonell, J. G., 392, 408
Carlson, L., 259, 265
Carlsson, A., 18, 27
Carroll, J., 305, 317
Carter, F., 336, 342
Carter, R. T., 331, 339, 342
Cartwright, D. S., 21, 27
Casas, J. M., 329, 339, 342
Cashel, M. L., 206, 214
Cattell, R. B., 174, 188
Cervantes, R. C., 341, 342
Chapman, J., 100, 101, 121, 132
Chapman, L., 100, 101, 121, 132
Chasseguet-Smirgel, J., 114, 117
Chethik, M., 455, 465
Choca, J. P., 188, 189, 485, 499
Choney, S. K., 328, 329, 336, 342
Church, S., 23, 27
Cicchetti, D., 418, 426, 454, 465
Claassen, C., 479, 484
Clark, C. X., 337, 344
Clark, R. A., 259, 265
Clarkin, J. F., 227, 232, 477, 484, 486,
        499
Cleveland, S. E., 124, 128, 129, 132, 134
Clinton, D., 18, 27
Coates, S., 459, 467
Cohen, C., 109, 117
Cohen, J., 306, 309, 317
Cohen, L. J., 473, 483

Constantino, G., 456, 465
Coonerty, S., 130, 132
Cooper, A., 494, 499
Cooper, J. L., 89, 90, 101
Cooper, S. H., 51, 58, 64, 65, 66, 67,
		130, 132, 227, 232, 497, 499
Corrigan, B., 197, 214
Costa, P. T., Jr., 8, 27
Covey, S. R., 90, 101
Coyne, J., 418, 426
Craig, R. J., 188, 189
Cramer, P., 130, 132, 251, 253, 254, 256,
		260, 261, 263, 264
Cressen, R., 283, 292
Crocker, J., 130, 132
Cronbach, L. J., 127, 132, 193, 214
Cross, W. E., Jr., 330, 342
Cuéllar, I., 329, 332, 333, 339, 343
Cullen, C., 331, 343
Cummins, J., 305, 317
Curtis, J., 336, 346
Curtiss, G., 299, 319
Cyr, J., 305, 316

D

Dahlstrom, L. E., 156, 162
Dahlstrom, W. G., 4, 27, 149, 154, 156,
		162
Daldrup, R. J., 18, 27
Damarin, R., 418, 426
Dana, R. H., 26, 28, 327, 329, 332, 333,
		337, 338, 339, 341, 343, 359,
		373, 456, 465
Dansereau, D. F., 90, 95, 101
Das, J., 305, 317
Davis, R. D., 165, 167, 171, 175, 183,
		189
Dawes, R. M., 10, 28, 99, 101, 197, 214,
		464, 465
Deabler, H. L., 271, 293
DeCato, C. M., 240, 241, 246
Dees, S. M., 95, 101
del Rosario, P., 418, 426
DeLaCruz, D., 154, 163
Demorest, A. P., 250, 264
Denmark, R., 438, 450
Dennis, W., 291, 292
Derry, S., 91, 102
DeWolfe, A., 305, 319
Diaz-Guerrero, R., 338, 343
Diaz-Loving, R., 338, 343

Dicken, C. F., 23, 27
Dickstein, L., 301, 317
Die, A., 301, 318
Dinoff, M., 125, 132
Dirkes, M., 438, 450
Dirks, J. F., 18, 28
Domino, G., 437, 450
Donahue, D., 123, 132, 459, 466
Draguns, J. G., 339, 345
Dreyfus, H., 405, 408
Dreyfus, S., 405, 408
Dubro, A., 418, 427
Duckworth, J. C., 156, 162
Duit, R., 391, 392, 408
Duker, J., 156, 163
Durand, V., 485, 499
Dworkin, R., 301, 318
Dyer, F. J., 188, 189
Dyk, R., 308, 320

E

Earley, B. F., 334, 342
Eber, H. W., 174, 188
Edelson, J., 394, 409
Edwards, D. W., 154, 162, 163
Ekstein, R., 395, 409
Elizur, A., 128, 129, 132
Ellenberger, H. F., 216, 232
Ellison, R., 330, 343
Elwood, R., 418, 426
Engle, D., 18, 27
Engle, G., 476, 483
Epstein, S., 186, 189
Erickson, J., 418, 426
Erikson, E., 112, 117
Erlenmeyer-Kimling, L., 301, 318
Ernst, G. W., 392, 410
Evans, G. E., 392, 409
Evans, R., 301, 392, 409
Exner, D. E., 217, 232
Exner, J., 4, 8, 13, 21, 28, 30, 46, 58, 62,
		66, 67, 74, 75, 80, 81, 96, 102,
		129, 132, 215, 216, 217, 219,
		220, 221, 222, 223, 225, 226,
		232, 233, 239, 241, 242, 244,
		246, 348, 358, 363, 373, 375,
		378, 379, 380, 390, 408, 417,
		418, 419, 421, 423, 426, 427,
		433, 442, 450, 458, 461, 466,
		468, 490, 494, 496, 499

F

Farris, M., 396, *410*
Faterson, H., 308, *320*
Faust, D., 10, *28*, 99, *102*
Fechner-Bates, S., 418, *426*
Feinberg, J., 308, *317*
Festinger, L., 67, 68
Fine, H. J., 395, *410*
Fine, P., 486, *499*
Finley, J., 435, 438, *450*
Finn, S. E., 6, 10, 18, *28*, 157, *163*, 313, *317*, 348, 358, 359, 360, 361, 363, 365, 366, *373*, 414, 419, *426*, 463, 466
Fischer, C. T., 6, *28*, 313, *317*, 348, 351, 357, *358*, 359, *373*, 431, *450*
Fischoff, B., 123, *132*
Fisher, S., 128, 129, *132*
Fiske, D. W., 8, 21, *27*, 123, *133*, 174, 186, *188*
Fithian, M., 291, *293*
Fitts, P., 405, *409*
Fitzgibbon, M. L., 477, 484, 486, *499*
Flavell, J., 83, 92, *102*
Fleming, M., 298, 299, *318*
Flores, J., 204, *214*
Ford, R., 13, 21, *27*, 283, 291, 292, 294, 435, *449*
Fowler, C., 10, 19, 24, *28*, 269, 378, *390*, 400, 401, *409*, 444, *450*
Frank, G., 120, *132*
Frank, L. K., 217, *232*, 393, *409*
Frank, R., 305, *316*
Frank, S. J., 97, *102*
Frankiel, R., 109, *117*
Freedheim, D. K., 456, *466*
Freeman, F., 309, *317*
French, C., 329, *342*
Freud, A., 455, *466*
Freud, S., 32, 41, 47, *58*, 108, 110, 111, *117*, 395, *409*, 455, *466*
Fried, R., 228, *232*
Friedman, A. F., 156, *163*
Friedman, G., 130, *132*
Friedman, H., 128, *132*
Furth, H., 302, *317*

G

Gacono, C. B., 226, *232*

Ganellen, R. J., 8, 10, *28*, 227, *232*, 418, *426*, 479, *483*
Garb, H. N., 11, 12, *28*, 123, *133*
Gardner, H., 295, *317*
Garfield, S., 300, *317*
Gediman, H., 296, 297, *316*
Gentner, D., 392, *409*
Giambelluca, F. C., 217, *232*
Gibby, R. G., 124, *133*
Gilberstadt, H., 156, *163*
Gill, M., 8, *30*, 62, 68, 70, *81*, 217, 227, 233, 297, 298, 299, *318*, 375, 379, 380, 390, 393, *410*, 431, 433, *451*, 488, *499*
Gilligan, C., 173, *189*
Gitlin, K., 459, *467*
Gittinger, J., 306, *319*
Glasser, A., 283, *293*
Gleser, G. C., 263, *264*
Glick, M., 129, *132*
Gluckman, E., 459, *466*
Gold, L., 130, *135*
Goldfried, M. R., 128, 129, *133*
Goldstein, E. B., 130, *133*
Goldstein, M., 417, *426*
Goleman, D., 295, *317*
González, G., 333, 339, *343*
Goodenough, D., 308, *320*
Gordon, R., 418, *426*
Gorlitz, P., 130, *132*
Gough, H. G., 127, *133*, 263, *264*
Graham, J. R., 4, *27*, 149, 150, 152, 154, 155, 156, *162*, *163*, 418, 421, *426*, 476, *483*
Gray-Little, B., 338, *343*
Green, S. A., 476, *483*
Greene, R. L., 8, *28*, 72, 150, *81*, 152, 153, 154, 156, 157, 158, *163*, 433, *450*
Greeno, J. G., 88, *102*
Greenson, R., 114, *117*, 290, *292*
Greenway, P., 359, *373*
Grolnick, S., 268, 271, *292*
Gross, L., 125, *133*
Grover, K. P., 338, *344*
Grubb, H. J., 329, *343*
Guérette, L., 440, *450*
Guilford, J., 406, *409*
Guinan, J. F., 269, *292*
Gynther, M. D., 156, *163*

H

Haan, N., 263, 264
Habenicht, D., 282, 291, 293, 433, 450
Haddad, F., 305, 317
Hall, E., 130, 132
Haller, D. L., 156, 163
Halonen, J. S., 86, 97, 102
Halpern, D. F., 83, 84, 85, 95, 97, 102, 103
Hamlin, R., 271, 292
Hammer, E., 282, 293
Handler, L., 10, 13, 14, 18, 19, 22, 23, 24, 27, 28, 29, 30, 37, 41, 70, 137, 146, 217, 227, 232, 235, 239, 244, 246, 267, 268, 269, 270, 271, 273, 282, 286, 288, 291, 292, 293, 294, 313, 317, 394, 397, 399, 400, 401, 406, 408, 409, 432, 433, 435, 436, 438, 440, 444, 450, 452, 463, 466
Harris, S., 124, 133, 134
Harris, R. E., 175, 189
Hartmann, H., 115, 117
Hartman, W., 291, 293
Harty, M., 45, 59
Hathaway, S. R., 149, 163
Hayles, V. R., Jr., 331, 343
Haynes, C., 93, 101
Healey, B. J., 129, 135, 458, 467
Heise, M. R., 389, 390
Helms, J. E., 329, 330, 343
Henry, W., 212, 214
Herndon, C., 457, 466
Herrigal, S., 405, 409
Hesselbrock, M., 418, 426
Hesselbrock, V., 418, 426
Hillix, W. A., 123, 135
Hilsenroth, M. J., 10, 13, 19, 23, 24, 27, 28, 29, 37, 41, 227, 232, 235, 244, 246, 269, 293, 378, 390, 400, 401, 409, 432, 450, 463, 466
Hobbs, J. R., 392, 409
Hoffmann, T., 333, 343
Hogan, L., 336, 343
Hogan, R., 435, 450
Holland, D., 338, 344
Holsopple, J. Q., 144, 146

Holt, R. R., 11, 18, 29, 62, 68, 99, 102, 128, 130, 133, 217, 232, 311, 317, 439, 450, 497, 499
Holzman, P. S., 380, 390, 497, 499
Home, H., 48, 51
Hornby, R., 333, 343
Horwitz, B., 305, 316
Horwitz, E., 305, 316
Houtz, J., 438, 450
Howard, K. I., 21, 29
Howell, C. T., 9, 10, 27
Hsu, F. L. K., 335, 343
Hui, C. H., 327, 337, 343, 346
Hunt, M., 99, 102
Hurley, J. R., 269, 292
Hurt, S. W., 227, 232
Hurvich, M., 296, 297, 316
Hutton, H., 72, 81
Huxley, T., 172, 175, 189
Hwang, C. H., 334, 344
Hyman, R., 438, 450

I

Ihilevich, D., 263, 264
Imhof, E., 457, 465
Irwin, M., 333, 344
Iwamasa, G., 326, 345

J

Jackson, A., 459, 465
Jackson, D. N., 23, 30, 174, 189, 193, 214, 263, 264
Jackson, J. S., 334, 344, 345
Jacobson, E., 48, 51
Jaffe, L., 393, 409
Jaimes, M. A., 335, 344
James, W., 111, 117
Jenkins, A. H., 334, 344
Jensen, J. R., 327, 344
Jensen, L. C., 327, 344
Johnson, C. A., 336, 344
Johnson, D. L., 336, 344
Johnson, D. W., 90, 102
Johnson, M., 391, 392, 406, 409, 410
Johnson, M. J., 338, 344
Johnson, R. T., 90, 102
Johnston, M. H., 380, 390, 497, 499
Jones, R., 334, 344, 457, 466
Judd, L., 417, 426

Juliano, J., 305, *317*
Jung, C. G., 396, 402, *409*

K

Kaden, S., 128, *134*
Kadera, S. W., 13, 21, *29*
Kaemmer, B., 4, *27*, 149, *162*
Kahn, M., 301, *319*
Kahn, R., 418, *427*
Kain, C. D., 338, *344*
Kalter, N., 303, *318*
Kamphaus, R., 301, *317*
Kanel, K., 338, *344*
Kaplan, E. J., 83, 98, *102*
Karp, S., 308, *320*
Karson, M., 305, 315, *317*
Kaufman, A., 297, 305, 309, *317, 318*
Kaufman, S., 282, 291, 292, 403, 408
Kazaoka, K., 418, *426*
Kazdin, A., 460, *466*
Keefe, S. E., 334, *344*
Keller, J. W., 130, *134*
Kelly, E. L., 123, *133*
Kelsey, R., 459, *467*
Keniston, K., 255, *264*
Kerber, K., 130, *135*, 393, *411*
Kernberg, O., 64, *68*, 108, *117*, 402, *409*
Kies, D. A., 83, 98, *102*
Kinder, B. N., 23, *30*, 131, *133*, 457, 466, 485, 499
King, A., 98, *102*
Kingsbury, S., 486, *499*
Kinsman, R. A., 18, *28*
Kirby, K., 99, *102*
Kirtner, W. L., 21, *27*
Kissen, M., 291, *293*
Kitayama, S., 327, 328, *344*
Klein, G., 48, *51*
Klein, R. E., 333, *344*
Kleinmuntz, B., 11, *29*
Klepser, J., 459, *468*
Klingler, D., 306, *317*
Klonoff, E. A., 329, 330, 331, 339, *344*
Klopfer, B., 17, *29*, 62, *68*, 217, *232*, 311, *317*, 328, 336, *344*, 439, *450*
Klopfer, W., 17, *29*, 62, *68*, 217, *232*, 311, *317*, 439, *450*
Knell, S., 454, *466*
Koch, S., 494, *499*

Kochman, T., 334, *344*
Koestner, R., 8, 10, *29*, 263, *265*
Kohut, H., 47, *58*, 113, *117*, 270, 273, *293*, 436, *450, 451*
Koppitz, E., 267, 282, 291, *293*
Kopta, S. M., 21, *29*
Koss, M. P., 155, *163*
Koss-Chioino, J., 334, *344*
Kot, J., 269, *293*
Krakowski, A., 23, *29*
Krause, M. S., 21, *29*
Krauskopf, C., 306, *318*
Kris, E., 273, *293*, 399, 406, *409*, 436, *451*
Krishnamurthy, R., 9, *27*, 227, *231*
Krohn, A., 129, *133*
Kurpius, D. J., 83, *102*
Kwawer, J., 63, *68*

L

Lachar, D., 155, 156, *163*
Lake, R., 305, *316*
Lakoff, G., 392, 406, *410*
Lambert, M. J., 13, 21, *29*
Landrine, H., 329, 330, 331, 339, *344*
Lanfeld, E., 303, *318*
Langer, S., 391, 392, *410*
Langfeldt, V., 72, *81*
Langs, R., 396, *410*
Leary, T., 210, *214*
Leckliter, I., 305, *318*
Leech, S., 359, *373*
Leichtman, M., 75, 76, *81*, 217, *232*
Lennon, T. J., 204, *214*
Lepper, M. R., 100, *102*
Lerner, H., 45, 47, 48, 52, *58*, 59, 64, *68*, 109, *117*, 129, 130, *133*, 433, 449, 490, *499*
Lerner, P., 37, 40, *41*, 46, 47, *51*, 52, *58*, 59, 64, *68*, 76, *81*, 109, *117*, 129, *133*, 217, *232*, 393, 394, 397, *410*, 431, 433, *451*, 459, 466, 490, *499*
Lesley, C. , 336, *344*
Lester, D., 243, *246*
Leung, K., 337, *346*
Levenberg, S., 271, *293*
Levin, J. R., 91, *102*
Levine, L., 459, *466*
Levine, M., 302, *318*

Levinger, L., 434, *451*
Levitt, R., 298, *318*
Lew, S., 329, *345*
Lewak, R., 156, *163*, 414, 419, *426*
Lewinsohn, P., 283, *293*
Libb, J., 418, *426*
Lichtenberg, J., 64, *68*
Lichtenstein, S., 123, *132*
Lichty, W., 305, *316*
Lifton, N., 459, *468*
Lin, M. M., 204, *213*
Lindfors, O., 18, *29*
Lindner, R. M., 217, *232*
Lingoes, J. C., 175, *189*
Lipsitz, J., 301, *318*
Lobitz, W., 418, *427*
Lochhead, J., 99, *103*
Loevinger, J., 174, *189*, 193, *214*
Loewald, H., 109, 110, *117*
Lohr, N., 130, *135*, 297, *319*, 393, *411*
Lonner, W. G., 339, *345*
López, S. R., 338, *344*
Lord, C. G., 100, *102*
Lord, E., 124, *133*
Lovitt, R., 235, *246*, 472, 476, 478, 479, 483, 484, 487, *499*
Lowell, E. L., 258, 259, *265*
Lucio, G., 72, *81*
Ludolph, P., 459, 465, *468*
Lunazzi de Jubany, H., 217, *232*
Lunnen, K. M., 460, *466*
Lutz, K. A., 392, *411*
Lykes, M. B., 327, *344*
Lyles, W. K., 124, *133*
Lyons, J., 432, *451*

M

MacEvitt, M., 301, *317*
Machover, K., 282, 291, *293*
MacKinnon-Slaney, F., 93, *102*
Magnussen, N. G., 125, *133*
Mahler, M., 109, 115, *117*, 455, *466*
Malcolm, J., 127, *134*
Maldonado, R., 329, 332, *343*
Malenka, D. J., 90, *103*
Malgady, R. G., 334, *344*, 456, *465*
Maloney, M., 283, *293*, 472, 473, *484*
Manis, M., 8, 10, *30*
Marchese, M. C., 127, *134*
Marín, G., 334, *344*

Marks, P. A., 156, *163*
Markus, H. R., 327, 328, *344*
Marlow, D., 418, *426, 427*
Marsden, G., 303, *318*
Martin, H., 365, *373*
Martin-Cannici, C., 206, *214*
Martindale, C., 437, *451*
Maruish, M. E., 20, 21, *29*, 457, 460, 465, 466, 492, *499*
Masling, J. M., 123, 124, 127, 129, *133, 134*
Matarazzo, J., 297, 305, *318*
May, R. R., 259, 260, 263, *265*
Mayer, J., 295, *318*
Mayman, M., 8, 10, *30*, 48, 51, 59, 114, *117*, 129, *133*, 396, 400, *410*, 431, *451*
McAdams, D. P., 258, 259, 263, *265*
McBurney, D. H., 95, *102*
McCann, J. T., 188, *189*, 418, *426*
McClelland, D. C., 8, 10, *29*, 258, 259, 262, 263, *264, 265*
McConaughy, S. H., 9, 10, *27*
McCormick, A., 305, *319*
McCrae, R. R., 8, *27*
McDade, S. A., 94, *102*
McDermott, P. A., 204, *213*
McDowell, C., 379, *390*
McGee, D. P., 337, *344*
McGhie, A. P., 327, *344*
McGowan, J., 271, *294*
McIlvried, E., 308, *317*
McKeachie, W., 89, 95, *102*
McKinley, J. C., 149, *163*
McWilliams, N., 71, *81*
Medicine, B., 335, *346*
Mednick, M., 302, *318*, 435, 436, *451*
Mednick, S., 302, *318*, 435, 436, *451*
Meehl, P. E., 11, *28*, 99, 100, *102*, 127, 128, *134*, 193, 207, 211, *214*
Mellins, C. A., 338, *344*
Meloy, J. R., 220, 226, *232, 233*
Mendoza, R. H., 332, *344*
Meredith, K., 18, *27*
Merritt, F., 305, *316*
Merry, W., 18, *27*
Meuhlman, T., 301, *319*
Meyer, G. J., 8, 9, 10, 14, 18, *29*, 479, 484
Meyer, M. L., 124, *134*
Meyer, R., 418, *426*

Meyers, C., 83, 86, 91, 98, *102*
Meyers, J., 414, 419, *426*
Mezzich, J., 418, *426*
Miale, F. R., 144, *146*, 397, *410*, 448, *451*
Michels, R., 494, *499*
Milgram, N., 302, *317*
Miller, D. R., 124, *133, 134*
Miller, S. B., 10, *29*
Milliones, J., 330, *345*
Millon, C., 165, 175, *189*
Millon, T., 8, *29*, 165, 167, 169, 171, 175, 177, 183, *189*
Min, P. G., 334, *345*
Mindell, J., 485, *499*
Miner, M., 72, *81*
Mintz, E., 406, *410*
Mio, J. S., 326, *345*
Mittenberg, W., 298, *318*
Mohr, D., 18, *27*
Momaday, N. S., 336, *345*
Moore-West, M., 90, *103*
Moreland, K. L., 37, *41*, 216, *231*
Morey, L. C., 8, *29*, 190, 191, 194, 201, 204, 205, 206, 208, 209, 212, 213, *214*, 489, *499*
Morgan, C. D., 250, *265*
Morran, D. K., 83, *102*
Morris, C. G., 130, *134*
Morrison, T. L., 154, *162, 163*
Mortimer, R. L., 17, *29*
Mount, M. K., 23, *27*
Mowat, F., 336, *345*
Muhlenkamp, A., 23, *29*
Murray, D. C., 271, *293*
Murray, H. A., 250, 254, 262, *265*, 399, *403, 410*, 435, 437, *450*, 489, *499*
Murray, J., 418, *426*, 437, *450*
Murstein, B. I., 145, *146*
Myers, I., 435, *450*

N

Nagata, D. K., 334, *345*
Naglieri, J., 305, *318*
Nalesnik, D., 240, *246*
Navarra, J., 418, *426*
Neher, L. A., 123, *135*
Neighbors, H. W., 334, *345*
Nelson, L., 418, *426*
Newman, F., 20, *30*, 460, *466*
Newman, M., 359, *373*

Nichols, D. S., 152, 156, *163*
Nicola, G., 392, *410*
Nist, S. L., 99, *102*
Nobo, J., 301, *318*
Nummedal, S. G., 84, *103*
Nygren, M., 18, *27*

O

OConnell, M., 65, 66, *67*
Odbert, H. S., 167, *188*
Ogdon, D., 282, *293*
Ogles, B. M., 460, *466*
Okazaki, S., 331, *345*
Orlinsky, D. E., 21, *29*
Ornduff, S. R., 206, *214*, 459, *467*
O'Grady, K., 305, *318*

P

Padawer, J., 21, *30*
Padilla, A. M., 334, 341, 342, 344, *345*
Paolo, A., 298, *319*
Parisi, S., 217, *232*
Parker, J., 305, *316*
Parker, K., 305, *318*
Parker, T., 305, *316*
Parsons, J., 23, *29*
Partipilo, M., 124, *134*
Patten, M., 305, *319*
Payne, M., 23, *30*
Pedersen, P. B., 339, *345*
Perry, J. C., 10, *30*, 64, 65, 66, 67, 130, *132, 134*, 227, *232*
Perry, S., 494, *499*
Perry, W., 226, *233*
Pes, P., 217, *232*
Phillips, L., 128, *134*, 399, *410*
Piaget, J., 115, 116, *117*
Piedmont, R., 298, 299, *318*
Piersma, H., 418, *427*
Pine, F., 47, *59*, 109, 115, *117*
Piotrowski, C., 130, 131, *134*, 149, *163*, 227, *233*, 457, 465, *467*
Piotrowski, Z. A., 396, 400, 402, *410*
Polkinghorne, D., 431, *451*
Pollio, H. R., 395, *410*
Pollio, M. R., 395, *410*
Ponterotto, J. G., 329, 331, 333, 339, *345*
Posner, M., 405, *409*
Post, R., 418, *427*

Potash, H. M., 138, 142, 146, 431, 451
Powell, G. J., 330, 346
Preston, E., 100, 102
Pruyser, P. W., 359, 373
Pytluk, S. D., 329, 342

Q

Quinlan, D., 301, 316

R

Rabie, L., 129, 134
Rader, G., 444, 451
Ramirez, M., III, 332, 335, 341, 345
Ramos, M., 301, 318
Ramseur, H. P., 331, 345
Rapaport, D., 8, 30, 62, 68, 70, 74, 81,
    115, 117, 217, 227, 233, 297,
    298, 299, 318, 375, 379, 380,
    390, 393, 410, 431, 433, 451,
    488, 499
Rassenfosse, M., 23, 30
Reed, S. K., 392, 410
Reider, N., 395, 411
Reik, T., 126, 127, 134
Reilly, B., 90, 103
Retzlaff, P., 486, 499
Reyes-Lagunes, I., 72, 81
Reyher, J., 267, 282, 288, 293
Reynolds, C., 305, 318
Rezler, A., 23, 30
Reznikoff, M., 37, 41, 216, 227, 231, 232
Rhyne, M. C., 338, 344
Rickard-Figueroa, K., 329, 345
Rickers-Ovsiankina, M., 433, 451
Rico, G., 93, 103
Rieser, J., 85, 88, 101
Riethmiller, R., 14, 30, 268, 270, 282,
    294
Rigney, J. W., 392, 411
Rinn, R .C., 388, 390
Ritz, S., 235, 246
Ritzler, B., 37, 41, 50, 58, 129, 134, 240,
    246, 394, 411, 432, 451
Robbins, M., 64, 68
Robbins, R. R., 328, 329, 336, 342
Robertson, I. T., 23, 30
Robins, C., 283, 294
Robinson, J. L., 334, 345
Rockwell, G., 303, 319

Rodnick, E., 417, 426
Rodriguez, O., 334, 344
Rogers, R., 204, 206, 214
Rogler, L. H., 334, 342, 456, 465
Rorschach, H., 70, 81, 215, 216, 221,
    233
Rosen, A., 207, 211, 214
Rosenberg, S., 305, 319
Rosenblatt, B., 48, 59
Rosenthal, R., 124, 135
Ross, J. M., 90, 103
Rothenberg, A., 437, 451
Rothstein, M., 23, 30
Routh, D. K., 70, 81
Royer, J. M., 392, 411
Ruffins, S., 459, 468
Rushton, J. P., 173, 189
Russ, S. W., 130, 135, 406, 411, 437,
    440, 443, 444, 451, 454, 455,
    456, 458, 459, 464, 467
Russell, R., 456, 460, 467
Russell, S., 392, 411
Rutherford, M. J., 204, 213
Rutter, M., 454, 467
Ryan, J., 298, 305, 318, 319

S

Sabaroche, H., 23, 30
Sabnani, H. B., 331, 333, 345
Salgado de Snyder, N., 341, 342
Salovey, P., 295, 318, 319
Sampson, E. E., 327, 345
Sanders, R., 124, 134
Sandgrund, A., 459, 467
Sandler, J., 48, 59
Sanford, N., 258, 265
Santostefano, S., 391, 403, 411
Sarbin, T. R., 251, 265
Sarrel, L., 291, 294
Sarrel, P., 291, 294
Sattler, J. M., 123, 132, 135
Saunders, D., 303, 306, 317, 318, 319
Saunders, E., 497, 499
Sawyer, J., 127, 128, 135
Schachtel, E. G., 121, 135, 217, 233,
    243, 246, 349, 358, 431, 432,
    436, 451, 452
Schaefer, C., 459, 467
Schafer, R., 7, 8, 30, 32, 37, 41, 49, 51,
    59, 62, 68, 70, 75, 76, 81, 121,

123, 127, 131, *135*, 217, 224, 227, *233*, 251, 265, 297, 298, 299, *318, 319*, 375, 379, 380, 390, 393, 399, *410, 411*, 431, 432, 433, *451, 452*, 488, *499*
Schauble, L., 91, *102*
Schill, T., 301, *319*, 444, *451*
Schimek, J. G., 129, *132*
Schinka, J. A., 202, 204, *214*, 299, *319*
Schlesinger, H. J., 37, *41*
Schmidt, L., 271, *294*
Schramke, C. J., 11, *28*
Schroeder, D. G., 366, *373*
Schustack, M., 392, *411*
Schutz, W., 263, *265*
Schwaber, P., 110, *117*
Schwartz, J., 298, *318*
Schwarz, W., 216, *233*
Schwenk, T., 418, *426*
Sciara, A., 220, *233*
Scott, R., 72, *81*
Scribner, C., 270, 271, *294*, 435, 436, *452*
Seeman, W., 156, *163*
Segal, H., 297, *319*
Seidenberg. M., 305, *316*
Seligman, M. E., 21, *30*
Serafica, F., 454, *467*
Sewell, K. W., 204, 206, *214*
Shapiro, D., 71, 73, *81*
Sharpe, E., 395, *411*
Shaw, D., 309, *319*
Shectman, F., 45, *59*
Shedler, J., 8, 10, *30*
Shengold, L., 395, *411*
Sheridan, E., 485, *499*
Sherwood, N. E., 151, 155, 157, *162*
Sherwood, R., 85, 88, *101*
Sherwood, V., 109, *117*
Shipley, T., 258, *265*
Shirk, S., 456, 460, *467*
Shneidman, E. S., 255, *265*
Siddiqui, N., 204, *213*
Siegel, M., 71, *80*
Siegert, R., 305, *319*
Silk, K., 130, *135*, 297, *319*, 393, *411*
Silverman, M., 459, *468*
Silverstein, A., 305, *318, 319*
Silverstein, M. L., 150, *164*, 235, *246*
Simkins, L., 125, *135*
Simon, H., 406, *411*

Simpson, D. D., 95, *101*
Singer, M., 22, *30*
Sjostrom, B. R., 334, *342*
Skinner, H., 174, *189*
Slap, J., 64, 68
Sletten, I. W., 156, *163*
Sloane, K., 418, *426*
Slovic, P., 123, *132*
Smith, A., 298, *319*
Smith, B. L., 70, 74, 75, *81*, 217, *233*, 393, *411*
Smith, C. P., 258, 259, *265*
Smith, K. A., 90, *102*
Smith, W. H., 17, *29*
Society for Personality Assessment, 414, *427*
Sokolove, R., 298, 299, *318*
Soskin, W. F., 120, *135*
Spence, D. P., 251, *265*
Spencer, H., 172, *190*
Spengler, P. M., 100, *103*
Spielberger, C., 461, *467*
Sprandel, H., 309, *319*
Stark, K., 268, 269, *294*
Steele, R. S., 48, *59*, 262, *265*
Steele, S., 334, *345*
Stewart, A. J., 259, *265*
Stone, L., 115, *118*
Storms, L., 414, 419, *426*
Stout, C. J., 93, 94, 97, *103*
Strauman, T., 418, *427*
Stricker, G., 128, 129, *133, 135*, 458, *467*
Strohmer, D. C., 100, *103*
Stroufe, L., 454, *467*
Strupp, H., 463, *467*
Sue, S., 331, *345*
Sugarman, A., 37, *41*, 47, *59*, 130, *133*, 393, 399, *411*
Suinn, R. M., 329, *345*
Suzuki, L. A., 339, *345*
Suzuki, S., 405, *411*
Sweeney, J. A., 477, 484, 486, *499*
Szumotalska, E., 435, *452*

T

Tallent, N., 92, 432, 435, *452*, 472, 480, *484*
Tatsuoka, M. M., 174, *188*
Taylor, A., 305, *319*
Tellegen, A. M., 4, *27*, 149, *162*

Tennen, H., 418, 426
Tett, R. P., 21, 23, 30
Tharinger, D., 268, 269, 294
Thomas, C. S., 330, 346
Thomas, S., 305, 316
Thompson, A. E., 130, 135
Thompson, G., 298, 318
Thurstin, H., 418, 426
Timbrook, R. E., 154, 163
Tipton, R. M., 235, 246
Toman, K., 21, 30, 269, 293
Tonsager, M. E., 6, 18, 28, 313, 317,
        359, 360, 361, 363, 365, 366,
        373, 463, 466
Topper, M. D., 336, 346
Torrance, E., 437, 452
Townsend, J. W., 333, 344
Trenerry, M. R., 238, 246
Trexler, L., 243, 246
Triandis, H. C., 327, 337, 346
Trimble, J. E., 334, 335, 339, 345, 346
Tuber, S., 459, 466, 467
Tucker, D., 305, 316
Tuma, J., 454, 455, 456, 458, 467
Tzeng, O., 438, 452

                    U

Uba, L., 334, 346
Urist, J., 22, 30, 64, 68, 129, 135, 227,
        233, 433, 452, 458, 468
Ustad, K., 204, 206, 214

                    V

Van Denburg, E., 188, 189
Vanderploeg, R., 299, 319
VanOss Marín, B., 334, 344
Veroff, J., 258, 265
Vigil, S., 329, 345
Viglione, D., 130, 134, 226, 233
Voth, H., 395, 411
Vye, N., 85, 88, 101
Vygotsky, L. S., 85, 86, 103

                    W

Wachtel, E., 454, 468
Wade, C., 93, 103

Wagner, C. F., 378, 390
Wagner, E. E., 375, 376, 377, 378, 380,
        388, 389, 390
Waite, R., 315, 319
Waldman, I., 305, 319
Waldman, M., 128, 134
Walker, E. L., 124, 133
Wallbrown, F., 306, 316
Waller, N., 305, 319
Walter, J. M., 90, 103
Ward, L., 489, 500
Ward, M., 472, 473, 484
Watkins, C. E., 131, 135, 235, 246, 457,
        468, 485, 500
Watts, F. N., 97, 103
Webb, J. T., 156, 163
Webb, N. M., 90, 103
Wechsler, D., 4, 30, 295, 297, 319, 320
Weener, P., 438, 452
Weibel-Orlando, J., 335, 346
Weinberger, J., 8, 10, 29, 263, 265
Weiner, I. B., 13, 21, 30, 74, 81, 128,
        129, 133, 215, 218, 220, 222,
        225, 227, 231, 233, 237, 242,
        246, 348, 363, 417, 418, 427,
        457, 461, 464, 468, 472, 484,
        489, 490, 500
Weiss, J., 303, 316
Weissman, A., 243, 246
Weissman, H. N., 154, 162, 163
Welch, J., 335, 336, 346
Welsh, G. S., 156, 162
Wenar, C., 454, 467
Werner, H., 115, 118
Westen, D., 4, 22, 30, 130, 135, 261,
        263, 265, 297, 319, 393, 411,
        433, 452, 459, 465, 468, 497,
        500
Wetzler, S., 418, 427
Wheeler, W. M., 128, 129, 135
Whimbey, A., 99, 103
White, J. L., 334, 346
Whitehead, A. N., 84, 103
Wickes, T. A., 125, 135
Wiener, G., 302, 320
Wiggins, J. S., 155, 164
Wilks, Y., 392, 408
Williams, C. L., 152, 155, 156, 162
Williams, F., 437, 452
Williams, P. S., 392, 411
Willock, B., 393, 411

Wilson, E. O., 172, 173, *190*
Winget, B. M., 123, *135*
Winnicott, D., 75, *81*, 116, *118*, 268,
    294, 298, *320*, 404, 406, *411*,
    437, *452*
Winter, D. G., 258, 259, *265*
Witkin, H., 308, *320*
Wixom, J., 459, 465, 468
Woods, D. R., 97, *103*
Workman, K., 418, *426*
Wright, K., 395, *411*
Wrobel, T. A., 155, *163*
Wyatt, G. E., 330, *346*

Y

Yalof, J., 240, *246*, 443, 447, *452*
Yama, M., 283, *294*

Z

Zaballero, A. R., 204, *213*
Zalewski, C., 131, *134*, 149, *163*, 457,
    467
Zetzer, H., 296, 297, 309, 313, 315, *320*,
    490, *500*
Zimet, C., 297, *316*
Zimmerman M., 10, *30*

Subject Index

A

Academic medical centers, 25, 485
Acculturation Rating Scale for Mexican-Americans, 329
African-American Acculturation Scale, 329
Assessing the social subject, 137
Assessment, 3, 417, *see also* Assessment training; Child assessment; Personality
  academic programs, 131
  accuracy, 126
  advanced class, 431–432
  Austen-Riggs, Center, 45, 70
  case illustration, 49
  and the Comprehensive System, 69, 74
  conceptual approach, 46
  conflict free ego sphere, 74
  cookbook interpretations, 72, 433
  cultural sensitivity, 339
  and diagnosis, 418
  and difficulty, 13, 434
  and ego psychology, 115, 432
  empathic understanding, 45
  empirical approach, 46
  examiner's role, 121–124
    gender, 124
    patient conditioning, 125
    statistical vs. clinical, 127
  examiner–patient relationship, 48, 52, 122
  experience-distant perspective, 48
  experience-near interpretations, 48, 432
  experiential aspects, 45, 431
  feedback, 126
  human science approach in, 431
  in internship settings, 471, 486, *see also* Consultation
  advanced seminar in, 486, 493
  inpatient assessment, 495
  modeling, 486
  observational learning in, 486
  outpatient assessment, 495
  report writing, 493
  supervision, 486
  interpretation errors, 120
  invalid profiles, 52
  jargon in, 48
  and learner's personality, 435–436
  manifest behavior, 48
  and Menninger Foundation, 70
  and middle-level language, 49
  and MMPI–2, 72
  patient's experience, 51
  person centered vs test centered, 71–72
  prediction in, 417–418
  and projective identification, 51
  and psychometric data, 433, 472
  referral questions, 417
  resistance in, 434
  role model, 56
  Rorschach, 433
  self–object transference, 51
  sign approach, 71
  subjective world, 48
  supervision, 53, 56
  and symbolic activity, 48
  technician, 472
  test report, 77–79
  and theory, 43–44, 47, 50, 69–70, 115, 432
  transference, 51, 53
  and Wechsler scales, 73
Assessment Training, 3, 107
  and analytic neutrality, 113
  frame, 114
  and humanistic attitude, 108, 112
    and test reports, 113

513

and identity, 107
and internalization, 107, 111
and Piaget's theory, 109

C

Child Assessment
    developmental approach, 453
    diagnosis in, 463
    managed care in, 463
    projective tests in, 458
    psychodynamic approach, 453–455
    Rorschach in, 458–461
    training goals in, 464
Children's Apperception Test, 456
Consultation, 471–472, 475, 477, 485,
            489, see also Internship
    and biopsychosocial variables, 478
    case study, 487
    cognitive functions, 490
    communication in, 473
    constructs in, 479
    and DSM–IV, 477
        axis I diagnosis, 477
        axis II diagnosis, 477
    focused assessment strategy in, 489
    frames of reference, 473
    interpretation in, 479
    to medical residents, 480
    to medical students, 480
    multiple levels, 473
    PAI in, 489–491
    and patient referral questions,
            473–474, 489
    pattern of adaptive failure, 473
    Rorschach in, 490
    selecting instruments, 488
    WAIS–R in, 489
Critical thinking, 85
Cultural assessment
    culture specific disorders, 341
    and MMPI–2, 341
    and Rorschach, 341
Cultural identity, 329
    and acculturation measures, 332

D

Disease model, 170
Dissemination
    and class exercise, 421
    computer aids in, 420
    hypothesis formulation, 419
    integration of information, 420–421
    to lay person, 424

to patient, 424
practice in, 425
and Rorschach, 421
and verbal consultations, 424

F

Figure drawings
    advantages of, 291
    artistic ability, 283
    control for, 288
    body image disturbances, 283
    developmental skill, 291
    effects of culture, 291
    effects of therapy, 283, 285–287
    hospitalized patients, 284
    interpretation, 268
        affiliativeness in, 269
        case illustrations, 274, 288
        classroom holding environment,
            271
        empathy in, 269
        experiential, 268
        flexibility in, 269
        generalized other, 272
        intuition in, 269
        loss of distance, 272
        objective, 268
        and psychoanalytic listening, 273
        and regression in the service of
            the ego, 273
        sign approach in, 269
    stylistic factors, 282
    symbolic factors, 282
    unique contribution, 290
Functional personality domains, 168

I

Individualism–Collectivism Scale, 327
Internalization
    and boundaries, 110
    and good-enough parent, 110
    and professional identity, 111
        and ethical standards, 112
        and theoretical orientation, 112
    and values, 111
Internship training, 485, see also Consult-
            ation
Interpersonal skills, 137
Interpretations
    and cognitive flexibility, 435
    and convergent thinking, 435
    and creativity, 435, 437

and divergent thinking, 435
and empathy, 435
encouragement in, 446
group process in, 439
and homospatial process, 437
interpersonal statements in, 449
and intuition, 435
and janusian process, 437
and loss of distance, 436
and object relations, 437
resistance in, 440, 444
and Rorschach, 439, 442
sequential interpretation in, 448
Socratic method in, 445
teacher facilitation, 444, 448

K

Kinetic Family Drawings, 433

L

Learning assessment, 138
Barnum statements, 35
case study strategies, 94
and classroom culture, 97
concept mapping, 97
conflict in, 34
and countertransferance, 140
and critical thinking, 83–84, 88
and difficulty, 31
and divergent thinking, 90
and ego building, 138
and expert voice, 34
fear of overpathologizing, 35
and generalized other, 140
and impression formation, 144
and integration of data, 34, 39, 55
managing insecurities, 35
and personal boundaries, 32
and personal responsibility, 33
problem solving procedures, 89, 92, 94
and reconciling divergent views, 90
regression in the service of the ego, 38
resistance in, 31, 35, 54
role modeling, 97, 119
role of instructor, 38–39
and self doubt, 34
simulation strategies, 91
subject–examiner interaction, 141
tabula rasa phhilosophy, 138
and talk aloud strategies, 99
and teaching methods, 84
theory in, 38

training, 55
and transference, 142
use of self, 37
visualization strategies, 95
writing strategies, 93
zone of proximal development, 85
Learning collaborative assessment, see
    Learning therapeutic assess-
    ment
Learning Therapeutic Assessment, 360
anxiety in, 360
challenging stereotyped roles, 360
course rating in, 361
performance feedback in, 361
responsibility of instructor, 361
specifying referral questions, 361
students as collaborators, 361

M

Metaphor
and Bruhn's precis system, 398
and cognitive psychology, 405–406
and creativity, 405, 407
and dreams, 396, 402
and early memories, 396
examples, 399, 401, 404
and experiencing, 392, 403, 407
history of use, 394
and interpretive framework, 397, 448
and loss of distance, 399
and object relations, 396, 400
and psychotherapy, 400, 406
and Rorschach, 396, 402–403
and self, 395–397, 399
and symbolism, 400
and transference, 395
Miale-Holsopple Sentence Completion
    Test, 144
Millon Clinical Multiaxial Inventory
    (MCMI–III), 165
avoidant domain, 184
and base rates, 176
case study, 178–179, 183
and comorbidity, 181
and configurational scale interpreta-
    tion, 180
and contextual scale interpretation,
    180
and dimensional scale intrepetation,
    180
functional characteristics, 182
and multiaxial model, 169
and multiple item assignments, 175

and personality disorders, 171
and severe axis II pathology, 181
structural characteristics, 182
table of comparisons in, 184
and weighting system, 175
MMPI–2
  2-7/7-2 code type, 153
  Caldwell report, 161
  and canned statements, 150
  case example, 159
  code type vs content interpretation, 152, 155
  content scales, 157
  faking bad, 157
  faking good, 157
  first factor scales, 151
  interpretation, 151
    scale 4, 151
    scale 8, 151
    scale elevation, 150
  low point clinical scales, 160
  Minnesota report, 161
  and MMPI comparison, 154
  prototypic code type, 153
  response styles, 152
  simulated profile, 158
  Structural Summary, 156
  test taking attitudes, 158
  therapeutic assessment, 157
  True Response Inconsistency Scale (TRIN), 158
  Wiggins Content scales, 155
Modes of adaptation, 173
Mutuality of Automony Scale, 458

O

Object Relations and Social Cognition Scale, 459

P

Personality assessment, 3
  and acculturation, 329
  Asian Americans and extended self, 328
  base rates, 11
  case examples, 3, 19, 24, 334
  and cost reduction, 20
  cultural influences, 325, 327
  and the cultural self, 326
    building awareness, 331
  culturally competent practice, 338
  depression, 9
  and Developmental Inventory of Black Consciousness, 330
  emic contexts, 325, 332–333
  errors in, 11
  etic contexts, 325, 337
  and experiential process, 15
  forensic issues, 25
  goals and purposes, 6, 12
  Hispanic Americans and extended selves, 328
  identification of strengths, 14
  identification of weaknesses, 14
  ideographic vs nomothetic, 8
  illumination of underlying conditions, 16
  method variance in, 8
  Native Americans and permeable boundaries, 328
  and nigrescence stages, 330
  older views, 7
  permeability of boundaries, 328
  quality control, 20
  and racial identity, 329–330
  and relational problems, 22
  research, 26
  vs. testing, 4, 50
  as therapy, 18
  in treatment planning, 17
  in work settings, 23
Personality Assessment Inventory (PAI), 191
  age influences, 203
  assultive potential, see Harm to others
  conceptual rationale, 192
  configural interpretations, 192
  Defensiveness Index, 206
  and diagnosis, 208
  environmental perception, 211
  gender influences, 203
  and harm to others, 211
  item interpretation, 196
  individual scales, 192, 204
  interpersonal style, 210
  interpretative guide, 191
  and LOGIT analysis, 208
  Malingering Index, 206
  norms, 192, 201
  profile configuration, 207
  racial influences, 203
  reliability, 192, 201
  response sets, 205
  scale discrimination, 197
  self concept, 209
  self harm, 211
  standardization, 201
  subscale discrimination, 198
  suicide potential, see Self harm

test bias in, 195
  validity, 192–194, 196, 201, 206
Polarity model of personality, 172
Primary process, 437
Projective testing
  actuarial dimensions, 119
  attitudes towards, 130
  interpersonal dimensions, 119
  predictions, 123
Projective tests
  and diagnosis, 393
  learning difficulty, 392
  theory, 394

R

Remote Associates Test, 302, 437
  and cognitive flexibility, 302
  and convergent thinking, 302
Replicatory strategies, 173
Report writing
  language use in, 422
Roberts Apperception Test, 456
Rorschach, *see also* Rorschach autism;
        Rorschach Comprehensive System
  administration, 63, 239–240
  and Apache shaman, 328
  body image, 128
  boundary disturbance in, 63
  defensive operations in, 64, 227
  determinants as greeting cards, 348
  devaluation, 65
  and developmental level, 128
  elaborations, 62, 66
  ethical issues, 237
  FABCOM, 377
  and graduate training, 227
  and homosexualality, 128
  inquiry, 239
  integration, 238
    and history data, 238
  interpretation, 62–63, 242
  and life world, 347
  and MMPI, 227
  and Mutuality of Autonomy scale
      (MAO), 227
  and neurosis, 128
  object relations in, 63, 129
  and oral dependency, 129
  and primary process, 130
  professional issues, 237
  research, 244
  and schizophrenia, 128

scoring, 128, 219, 240
  lecture, 241
  practice, 241
  and space responses, 76, 230
  as standardized situation, 63
  and suicide potential, 128
  teaching, 242
    collaboration, 353–354, 357
    determinants, 348
    evaluation of preformance, 244
    experiential approach, 357
    individualized approach, 356
    locations, 348
    personal meanings, 356
    referral questions, 355
    report writing, 355
    Rorschachese descriptions, 351
    structural summary, 350
  teaching surveys, 235
    Hilsenroth and Handler, 235
    Tipton et al, 235
  testing of limits, 239
  theory, 61
    and structure, 61
  validity, 65
Rorschach autisms, 375
  as absurdities, 375
  and diagnosis, 378
  example, 380–386
  hyperattentional (HYPER), 377
  hypoattentional (HYPO), 377
  and Rapaport, 379
  relationship (RELER), 378
  Tripartate Classification(TRAUT),
      377, 385
Rorschach Comprehensive System, 215,
      230
  AdjD, 228
  affect, 223
  aggressive past (AgPast), 226
  aggressive potential (AgPot), 226
  and Beck, 216
  composite indices, 222
  conceptual foundations, 220
  and content scores, 228–229
  and cooperative movement, 230
  Coping Deficit Index (CDI), 225
  coping style, 228
  database, 219
  decision making, 221
  Depression Index (DEPI), 225
  EB style, 228
  empirical foundations, 220
  and Exner, 217
  Hypervigilance Index (HVI), 225
  ideation, 223

ideographic perspectives, 218
incongruous combination (INCOM),
    230
information processing, 221, 223
and Klopfer, 217
norms, 219
Populars, 228
reflections, 228
and Hermann Rorschach, 216
Schizophrenia Index (SCZI), 225
self perception, 223
sequential search strategy, 224
and step down hypothesis, 230
Suicide Index, 243
workbook, 241
WSUM6, 375

S

Society for Personality Assessment, 414
    training standards, 414
Structural personality domains, 168

T

Teaching
    child assessment, 453, *see also* Child
            assessment
        case presentations, 462
        developmental approach, 452
        framework, 453
        play assessment in, 459
        research experience, 454
        seminars, 461
        single case research design, 460
        tests, 456
        treatment planning, 460
    demonstration of assessment task,
            363
    feedback to instructors, 363, 366
    feedback to students, 364
    MMPI–2, 149
        and blind interpretation, 159
        and teacher experience, 149
    role playing, 364
Therapeutic assessment, 359, *see also*
            Learning therapeutic assess-
            ment; MMPI–2; Rorschach
    case example, 366
    power differential, 371
    preparation of written report, 366
    principals of, 360
    report to faculty, 366
Tell-Me-A-Story, 456
Test construction, 174

Test results, 413
    dissemination, 414
        client preparation in, 419
        and communication skills, 415
        goals of, 416
        modeling of, 414
        purpose, 426
        steps in, 416
        verbal, 413
    report writing, 413, 423
    and role playing, 413
    and structural feedback, 413
Thematic Apperception Test (TAT), 247
    and autobiography, 255
        student conferences, 256
    biases, 248
    case studies, 250, 252, 254–255
    defense mechanisms in, 260
    history, 247
    interpretation, 250, 257
        card pull, 145, 253
        content, 253
        impression formation, 145
        listening, 257
        multiple perspectives in, 251
        narrative theory and, 251
        repression, 145
    learning, 248
        resistance in, 248
    levels of personality, 263
    life history themes, 250
    reliability, 262
    research, 258
        achievement motivation, 258
        experience sampling method, 259
        gender identity assessment, 259
        physiological need, 258
        predicting behavior, 259
    self study, 255
    workshops, 262

W

Wechsler Intelligence Scales
    and content analysis, 313
    and ego functions, 296
    emotional intelligence, 295
    examiner assistance, 312
    and factor analysis, 305
    and hysteroid approach, 307
    and inquiry phase in, 309
    interpersonal intelligence, 295
    and interpersonal stress, 308
    and interpretation, 307
    intertest scatter, 298
    intrapersonal intelligence, 295

intratest scatter, 298
loss of distance, 306
missing easy items, 307
and object relations, 297
patient–examiner interaction, 308
and perceptual style, 308
as personality instruments, 295
and psychological differentiation, 308
Rapaport's approach, 297–299
and sign approach, 301
and stylistic clues, 307, 313
subtests

Arithmetic, 310
Block Design, 303
Comprehension, 301
Digit Symbol, 301, 304
Information, 307
Object Assembly, 303
Picture Arrangement, 297
Picture Completion, 301
Similarities, 301, 307
and testing of the limits phase, 311
verbal-performance dichotomy, 308